Brilliant

Microsoft®

Office 2010

Steve Johnson

Perspection, Inc.

Prentice Hall
is an imprint of

Harlow, England • London • New York • Boston • San Francisco • Toronto
Sydney • Tokyo • Singapore • Hong Kong • Seoul • Taipei • New Delhi
Cape Town • Madrid • Mexico City • Amsterdam • Munich • Paris • Milan

Pearson Education Limited
Edinburgh Gate
Harlow
Essex CM20 2JE
England

and Associated Companies throughout the world

Visit us on the World Wide Web at:
www.pearsoned.co.uk

Original edition, entitled MICROSOFT® OFFICE 2010 ON DEMAND, 1st edition, 0789742780 by
JOHNSON, STEVE; PERSPECTION, INC., published by Pearson Education, Inc., publishing as Que/Sams,
Copyright © 2010 Perspection, Inc.

This UK edition published by PEARSON EDUCATION LTD, Copyright © 2010

This edition is manufactured in the USA and available for sale only in the United Kingdom, Europe, the
Middle East and Africa.

The right of Steve Johnson to be identified as the author of this work has been asserted by him in
accordance with the Copyright, Designs and Patents Act 1988.

ISBN: 978-0-273-73608-0

British Library Cataloguing-in-Publication Data
A catalogue record for this book is available from the British Library

10 9 8 7 6 5 4 3 2
14 13 12

Printed and bound in the United States of America

Brilliant Guides

What you need to know and how to do it

When you're working on your computer and come up against a problem that you're unsure how to solve, or want to accomplish something in an application that you aren't sure how to do, where do you look?? Manuals and traditional training guides are usually too big and unwieldy and are intended to be used as an end-to-end training resource, making it hard to get to the info you need right away without having to wade through pages of background information that you just don't need at that moment – and helplines are rarely that helpful!

Brilliant guides have been developed to allow you to find the info you need easily and without fuss and guide you through the task using a highly visual, step-by-step approach – providing exactly what you need to know when you need it!!

Brilliant guides provide the quick easy-to-access information that you need, using a detailed index and troubleshooting guide to help you find exactly what you need to know, and then presenting each task on one or two pages. Numbered steps then guide you through each task or problem, using numerous screenshots to illustrate each step. Added features include "See Also…" boxes that point you to related tasks and information in the book, whilst "Did you know?…" sections alert you to relevant expert tips, tricks and advice to further expand your skills and knowledge.

In addition to covering all major office applications, and related computing subjects, the *Brilliant* series also contains titles that will help you in every aspect of your working life, such as writing the perfect CV, answering the toughest interview questions and moving on in your career.

Brilliant guides are the light at the end of the tunnel when you are faced with any minor or major task!

Acknowledgements

Perspection, Inc.

Brilliant Microsoft Office 2010 has been created by the professional trainers and writers at Perspection, Inc. to the standards you've come to expect from Que publishing. Together, we are pleased to present this training book.

Perspection, Inc. is a software training company committed to providing information and training to help people use software more effectively in order to communicate, make decisions, and solve problems. Perspection writes and produces software training books, and develops multimedia and Web-based training. Since 1991, we have written more than 100 computer books, with several bestsellers to our credit, and sold over 5 million books.

This book incorporates Perspection's training expertise to ensure that you'll receive the maximum return on your time. You'll focus on the tasks and skills that increase productivity while working at your own pace and convenience.

We invite you to visit the Perspection web site at:

www.perspection.com

Acknowledgements

The task of creating any book requires the talents of many hard-working people pulling together to meet impossible deadlines and untold stresses. We'd like to thank the outstanding team responsible for making this book possible: the writer, Steve Johnson; the editor, Adrian Hyde; the production editors, James Teyler and Beth Teyler; proofreader, Adrian Hyde; and the indexer, Katherine Stimson.

At Que publishing, we'd like to thank Greg Wiegand and Laura Norman for the opportunity to undertake this project, Cindy Teeters for administrative support, and Sandra Schroeder for your production expertise and support.

Perspection

About The Author

Steve Johnson has written more than 50 books on a variety of computer software, including Adobe Photoshop CS4, Adobe Flash CS4, Adobe Dreamweaver CS4, Adobe InDesign CS4, Adobe Illustrator CS4, Microsoft Windows 7, Microsoft Office 2007, Microsoft Office 2008 for the Macintosh, and Apple Mac OS X Snow Leopard. In 1991, after working for Apple Computer and Microsoft, Steve founded Perspection, Inc., which writes and produces software training. When he is not staying up late writing, he enjoys playing golf, gardening, and spending time with his wife, Holly, and three children, JP, Brett, and Hannah. Steve and his family live in Pleasanton, California, but can also be found visiting family all over the western United States.

a

Contents

C

Introduction

Welcome to *Brilliant Microsoft Office 2010*, a visual quick reference book that shows you how to work efficiently with Microsoft Office. This book provides complete coverage of basic to advanced Office skills.

How This Book Works

You don't have to read this book in any particular order. We've designed the book so that you can jump in, get the information you need, and jump out. However, the book does follow a logical progression from simple tasks to more complex ones. Each task is presented on no more than two facing pages, which lets you focus on a single task without having to turn the page. To find the information that you need, just look up the task in the table of contents or index, and turn to the page listed. Read the task introduction, follow the step-by-step instructions in the left column along with screen illustrations in the right column, and you're done.

What's New

If you're searching for what's new in Office 2010, just look for the icon: **New!**. The new icon appears in the table of contents and throughout this book so you can quickly and easily identify a new or improved feature in Office 2010. A complete description of each new feature appears in the New Features guide in the back of this book.

Keyboard Shortcuts

Most menu commands have a keyboard equivalent, such as Ctrl+P, as a quicker alternative to using the mouse. A complete list of keyboard shortcuts is available on the Web at *www.perspection.com*.

How You'll Learn

How This Book Works

What's New

Keyboard Shortcuts

Step-by-Step Instructions

Real World Examples

Workshops

Microsoft Certified Applications Specialist

Get More on the Web

Step-by-Step Instructions

This book provides concise step-by-step instructions that show you "how" to accomplish a task. Each set of instructions includes illustrations that directly correspond to the easy-to-read steps. Also included in the text are time-savers, tables, and sidebars to help you work more efficiently or to teach you more in-depth information. A "Did You Know?" provides tips and techniques to help you work smarter, while a "See Also" leads you to other parts of the book containing related information about the task.

Real World Examples

This book uses real world examples files to give you a context in which to use the task. By using the example files, you won't waste time looking for or creating sample files. You get a start file and a result file, so you can compare your work. Not every topic needs an example file, such as changing options, so we provide a complete list of the example files used through out the book. The example files that you need for project tasks along with a complete file list are available on the Web at *www.perspection.com.*

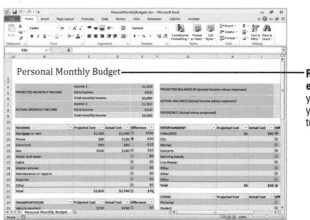

Easy-to-follow introductions focus on a single concept.

Illustrations match the numbered steps.

Numbered steps guide you through each task.

See Also points you to related information in the book.

Did You Know? alerts you to tips, techniques and related information.

Real world examples help you apply what you've learned to other tasks.

Workshops

This book shows you how to put together the individual step-by-step tasks into in-depth projects with the Workshop. You start each project with a sample file, work through the steps, and then compare your results with a project results file at the end. The Workshop projects and associated files are available on the Web at *www.perspection.com*.

Workshops

Introduction

The Workshop is all about being creative and thinking outside of the box. These workshops will help your right-brain soar, while making your left-brain happy, by explaining why things work the way they do. Exploring possibilities is great fun; however, always stay grounded with knowledge of how things work.

Getting and Using the Project Files

Each project in The Workshop includes a start file to help you get started with the project, and a final file to provide you with the results of the project so you can see how well you accomplished the task.

Before you can use the project files, you need to download them from the Web. You can access the files at *www.perspection.com* in the software downloads area. After you download the files from the Web, uncompress the files into a folder on your hard drive to which you have easy access from your Microsoft Office program.

Project 1: Creating a Drop-Down List

Skills and Tools: Create a drop-down list

Entering data in a worksheet can be tedious and repetitive. To make the job easier and get consistent accurate data, you can create a drop-down list of entries you define. To create a drop-down list, you create a list of valid entries in a single column or row without blanks, define a name, and then use the List option in the Data Validation dialog box. To enter data using a drop-down list, click the cell with the defined drop-down list, click the list arrow, and then click the entry you want.

The Project

In this project, you'll learn how to create a drop-down list from a named range of cells for use in conditional formatting.

The Process

1. Open Excel 2010, open DropDown_start.xlsm, and then save it as DropDown.xlsm.
2. Click the Numbers tab.

The **Workshops** walks you through in-depth projects to help you put Microsoft Office to work.

Microsoft Certified Applications Specialist

This book prepares you for the Microsoft Certified Applications Specialist (MCAS) exam for Microsoft Office 2010 programs. Each MCAS certification exam has a set of objectives, which are organized into broader skill sets. To prepare for the certification exam, you should review and perform each task identified with a MCAS objective to confirm that you can meet the requirements for the exam. Information about the MCAS program is available in the back of this book. The MCAS objectives and the specific pages that cover them are available on the Web at *www.perspection.com*.

Microsoft Certified Applications Specialist

About the MCAS Program

The Microsoft Certified Applications Specialist (MCAS) certification is the globally recognized standard for validating expertise with the Microsoft Office suite of business productivity programs. Earning an MCAS certificate acknowledges you have the expertise to work with Microsoft Office programs. To earn the MCAS certification, you must pass a certification exam for the Microsoft Office desktop applications of Microsoft Office Word, Microsoft Office Excel, Microsoft Office PowerPoint, Microsoft Office Outlook, or Microsoft Office Access. (The availability of Microsoft Certified Applications Specialist certification exams varies by program, program version, and language. Visit *www.microsoft.com* and search on *Microsoft Certified Applications Specialist* for exam availability and more information about the program.) The Microsoft Certified Applications Specialist program is the only Microsoft-approved program in the world for certifying proficiency with Microsoft Office programs.

What Does This Logo Mean?

It means this book has been approved by the Microsoft Certified Applications Specialist program to be certified courseware for learning Microsoft Office Word 2010, Excel 2010, PowerPoint 2010 and Outlook 2010, and preparing for the certification exam. This book will prepare you for the Microsoft Certified Applications Specialist exam for Microsoft Office Excel 2010. Each certification level has a set of objectives, which are organized into broader skill sets. The Microsoft Certified Applications Specialist objectives and the specific pages throughout this book that cover the objectives are available on the Web at *www.perspection.com*.

EX10S4.1
PP10S-2.2

Get More on the Web

In addition to the information in this book, you can also get more information on the Web to help you get up to speed faster with Office 2010. Some of the information includes:

Transition Helpers

◆ **Only New Features.** Download and print the new feature tasks as a quick and easy guide.

Productivity Tools

◆ **Keyboard Shortcuts.** Download a list of keyboard shortcuts to learn faster ways to get the job done.

More Content

◆ **Photographs.** Download photographs and other graphics to use in your Office documents.

◆ **More Content.** Download new content developed after publication. For example, you can download a complete chapter on Office SharePoint Server.

You can access these additional resources on the Web at *www.queondemand.com* or *www.perspection.com*.

Working Together on Office SharePoint Documents

S

Introduction

Microsoft Windows SharePoint Services is a collection of products and services which provide the ability for people to engage in communication, document and file sharing, calendar events, sending alerts, tasks planning, and collaborative discussions in a single community solution.

Office SharePoint Server 2010 is a product that uses Windows SharePoint Services technology to work effectively with Microsoft Office 2010 programs. You can create a slide library on a Office SharePoint site in PowerPoint 2010, use Office SharePoint list data to create reports in Access 2010, create a meeting workspace and synchronize calendar and contacts in Outlook 2010, design browser form templates in InfoPath 2010, and save worksheets on an Office SharePoint site in Excel 2010. In many of the Office 2010 programs, you can update properties for a server document in a Document Information Panel, and participate in workflows, which is the automated movement of documents or items through a sequence of actions or tasks, such as document approval.

Office 2010 programs use the Document Management task pane to access many Office SharePoint Server 2010 features. The Document Management task pane allows you to see the list of team members collaborating on the current project, find out who is online, send an e-mail message, and review tasks and other resources. You can also use the Document Management task pane to create document workspaces where you can collect, organize, modify, share, and discuss Office documents.

Before you can use Office SharePoint Server 2010, the software needs to be set up and configured on a Windows 2003 Server or later by your network administrator. You can view Office SharePoint Server sites using a Web browser or a mobile device while you're on the road.

What You'll Do

View and Navigate Office SharePoint Sites

Create a Document Workspace Site

Create a Document Library Site

Add and Upload Documents to a Site

Add Pages to a Site

Publish Slides to a Library

Saving a File to a Document Management Server

View Versions of Documents

Check Documents In and Out to Edit

Work with Shared Workspace

View Team Members

Create Lists

Create Events

Hold Web Discussions

Set Up Alerts

Customize Quick Launch or Top Link Bar

1

Additional content is available on the Web. You can download a chapter on SharePoint.

Getting Started with Office

Introduction

As you manage your business and personal worlds, you continually need to accomplish more, and do it better and faster. Microsoft Office 2010 provides you with the tools to do all this and more. Each of its programs—Word, Excel, Power-Point, Access, Outlook, Publisher, OneNote, and InfoPath (Designer and Filler)—has a special function, yet they all work together.

Office **Word 2010** is a word processing program you can use to create documents, such as letters, manuals, and reports. Office **Excel 2010** is a spreadsheet program you can use to organize, analyze, and present data, such as a budget or expense report. Office **PowerPoint 2010** is a presentation program you can use to create and deliver professional presentations. Office **Access 2010** is a database program you can use to store and manage large collections of related information, such as addresses. Office **Outlook 2010** is a communication and information management program you can use to manage e-mail messages, appointments, contacts, tasks, and notes. Office **Publisher 2010** is a publishing program you can use to create newsletters, catalogs, and invitations. Office **OneNote 2010** is a digital notebook program you can use to gather, manage, and share notes and information. Office **InfoPath 2010** (Designer and Filler) are information gathering programs you can use to design, collect, share, and reuse data in dynamic forms.

Each Office program uses a similar structure of windows, ribbons, toolbars, and dialog boxes, so you can focus on creating the best document in the least amount of time. You can perform your most basic actions the same way in every program. For example, in each Office program, you open, save, and close documents with the same buttons or commands. When you have a question, the identical help feature is available throughout the Office programs.

What You'll Do

Start an Office Program

View an Office Program Window

Use the Ribbon and Choose Commands

Work with the Ribbon and Toolbars

Choose Dialog Box Options

Use the Status Bar

Create a Blank Office Document

Create a Document Using a Template

Open or Convert an Existing Office Document

Use Task and Window Panes

Arrange Windows

Switch Views

Document Properties

Get Help While You Work

Save an Office Document with Different Formats

Check Compatibility

Recover an Office Document

Maintain and Repair Office

Get Office Updates on the Web

Close a Document and Exit Office

Starting an Office Program

The two quickest ways to start a Microsoft Office program are to select it on the Start menu or double-click a shortcut icon on the desktop. By providing different ways to start a program, Office lets you work the way you like and start programs with a click of a button. When you start an Office program, a program window opens, displaying a blank document, where you can begin working immediately.

Start an Office Program

1. Click the **Start** button on the taskbar.

2. Point to **All Programs**.

3. Click **Microsoft Office**.

4. Click the Office 2010 program you want to open.

   If Microsoft Office asks you to activate the program, follow the instructions to complete the process.

   TIMESAVER *To change the product key later, click the File tab, click Help, click the Change Product Key link, enter the product key, and then click Continue.*

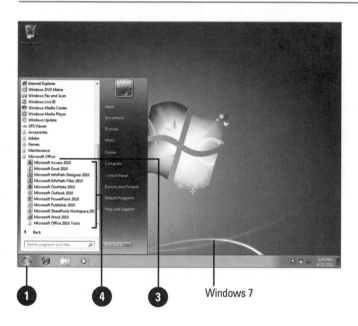

Windows 7

Did You Know?

You can create a program shortcut from the Start menu to the desktop. Click the Start menu, point to All Programs, click Microsoft Office, right-click a Microsoft Office 2010 program, point to Send To, and then click Desktop (Create Shortcut).

You can start an Office program and open an Office file from Windows Explorer. Double-clicking any Office file icon in Windows Explorer opens that file and the Office program.

For Power Users

Need More Office 2010 Computing Power

If you're a power user or analyst that needs to create bigger, more complex Office documents, you should use the 64-bit version of a Microsoft Office 2010 program (**New!**). The 64-bit version of an Office program is built specifically for 64-bit computers. For example, in the 64-bit version of Excel, you can break through the physical memory (RAM) limitation of 2 GB that exists with the 32-bit version, and crunch numbers with ease. If you're using the 32-bit version, Office 2010 programs significantly boosts performance levels (**New!**) over previous versions for importing, filtering, sorting, copying, and pasting large amounts of data, as well as opening and saving large files.

Viewing an Office Program Window

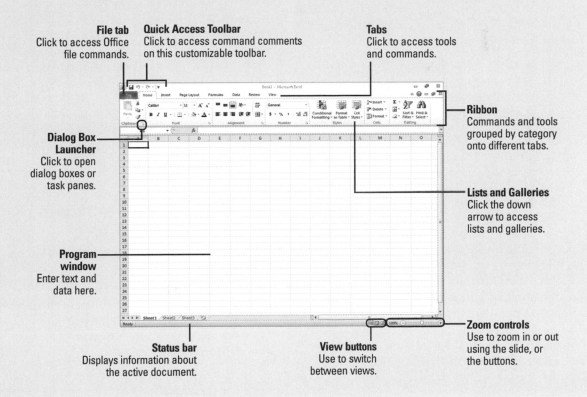

File tab
Click to access Office file commands.

Quick Access Toolbar
Click to access command comments on this customizable toolbar.

Tabs
Click to access tools and commands.

Ribbon
Commands and tools grouped by category onto different tabs.

Dialog Box Launcher
Click to open dialog boxes or task panes.

Lists and Galleries
Click the down arrow to access lists and galleries.

Program window
Enter text and data here.

Status bar
Displays information about the active document.

View buttons
Use to switch between views.

Zoom controls
Use to zoom in or out using the slide, or the buttons.

Using the Ribbon

The **Ribbon** has a new look for Office 2010. The Office button in Office 2007 has been replaced by the File tab (**New!**). The Ribbon is located at the top of the document window and is comprised of **tabs** that are organized by task or objects. The controls on each tab are organized into **groups**, or subtasks. The controls, or **command buttons**, in each group execute a command, or display a menu of commands or a drop-down gallery. Controls in each group provide a visual way to quickly make document changes.

> **TIMESAVER** *To minimize the Ribbon, click the Minimize the Ribbon button (Ctrl+F1)* (**New!**) *or double-click the current tab. Click a tab to auto display it (Ribbon remains minimized). Click the Expand the Ribbon button (Ctrl+F1) or double-click a tab to maximize it.*

If you prefer using the keyboard instead of the mouse to access commands on the Ribbon, Microsoft Office provides easy to use shortcuts. Simply press and release the Alt or F10 key to display **KeyTips** over each feature in the current view, and then continue to press the letter shown in the KeyTip until you press the one that you want to use. To cancel an action and hide the KeyTips, press and release the Alt or F10 key again. If you prefer using the keyboard shortcuts found in previous versions of Microsoft Office, such as

Ctrl+P (for Print), all the keyboard shortcuts and keyboard accelerators work exactly the same in Microsoft Office 2010. Office 2010 includes a legacy mode that you can turn on to use familiar Office 2003 keyboard accelerators.

Tabs

Office provides three types of tabs on the Ribbon. The first type is called a **standard** tab—such as File, Home, Insert, Review, View, and Add-Ins—that you see whenever you start Office. The second type is called a **contextual** tab—such as Picture Tools, Drawing, or Table—that appears only when they are needed based on the type of task you are doing. Office recognizes what you're doing and provides the right set of tabs and tools to use when you need them. The third type is called a **program** tab—such as Print Preview—that replaces the standard set of tabs when you switch to certain views or modes.

Live Preview

When you point to a gallery option, such as WordArt, on the Ribbon, Office displays a **live preview** of the option change so that you can see exactly what your change will look like before committing to it.

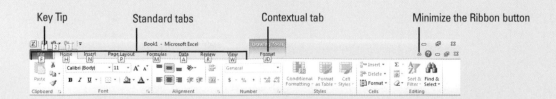

Key Tip   Standard tabs   Contextual tab   Minimize the Ribbon button

Choosing Commands

Office commands are organized in groups on the Ribbon, Quick Access Toolbar, and Mini-Toolbar. Commands are available as buttons or options on the Ribbon, or as menus on button or option arrows or the File tab (**New!**). The Quick Access Toolbar and Mini-Toolbar display frequently used buttons that you may be already familiar with from Office 2003 and 2007, while the File tab on the Ribbon displays file related menu commands. In addition to the File tab, you can also open a **shortcut menu** with a group of related commands by right-clicking a program element.

Choose a Menu Command Using the File Tab

1 Click the **File** tab on the Ribbon.

2 Click the command you want.

TIMESAVER *You can use a shortcut key to choose a command. Press and hold down the first key and then press the second key. For example, press and hold the Ctrl key and then press S (or Ctrl+S) to select the Save command.*

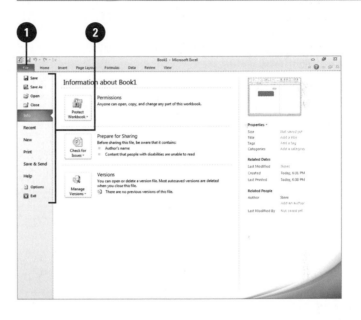

Choose a Menu Command from a Shortcut Menu

1 Right-click an object (a cell or graphic element).

TIMESAVER *Press Shift+F10 to display the shortcut menu for a selected command.*

2 Click a command on the shortcut menu. If the command is followed by an arrow, point to the command to see a list of related options, and then click the option you want.

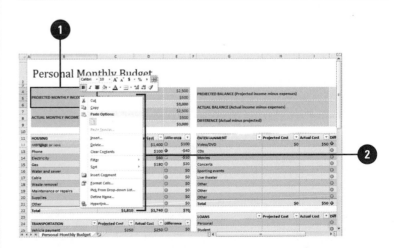

Working with the Ribbon and Toolbars

Office includes its most common commands, such as Save and Undo, on the **Quick Access Toolbar**. Click a toolbar button to choose a command. If you are not sure what a toolbar button does, point to it to display a ScreenTip. When an Office program starts, the Quick Access Toolbar appears at the top of the window, unless you've changed your settings. You can customize the Quick Access Toolbar or Ribbon (**New!**) by adding command buttons or groups to it. You can also move the toolbar below or above the Ribbon so it's right where you need it. In addition to the Quick Access Toolbar, Office also displays the Mini-Toolbar when you point to selected text. The **Mini-Toolbar** appears above the selected text and provides quick access to formatting tools.

Choose a Command Using a Toolbar or Ribbon

◆ **Get command help**. If you're not sure what a button does, point to it to display a ScreenTip. If the ScreenTip includes *Press F1 for more help*, press F1.

◆ **Choose a command**. Click the button, or button arrow, and then click a command or option.

ScreenTip

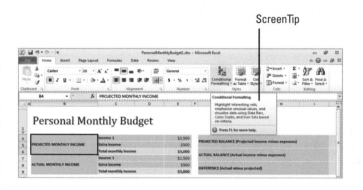

Add or Remove Items from the Quick Access Toolbar

◆ **Add or remove a common button**. Click the Customize Quick Access Toolbar list arrow, and then click a button name (checked item appears on the toolbar).

◆ **Add a Ribbon button or group**. Right-click the button or group name on the Ribbon, and then click Add to Quick Access Toolbar.

◆ **Remove a button or group**. Right-click the button or group name on the Quick Access Toolbar, and then click Remove from Quick Access Toolbar.

Customize Quick Access Toolbar list arrow

Click to add or remove frequently used buttons

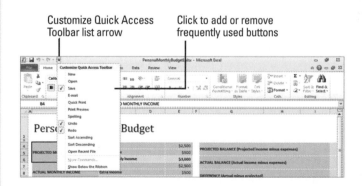

Right-click to add a button or group

Customize the Ribbon or Quick Access Toolbar

1. Click the **File** tab, and then click **Options**.

2. Click the **Customize Ribbon** (**New!**) or **Quick Access Toolbar**.

3. Click the **Choose commands from** list arrow, and then click **All Commands** or a specific Ribbon.

4. Click the list arrow (right column), and then select the tabs or toolbar you want to change.

5. For the Ribbon, click **New Tab** to create a new tab, or click **New Group** to create a new group on the selected tab (right column).

6. To import or export a customized Ribbon or Quick Access Toolbar, click the **Import/Export** list arrow, select a command, and then select an import file or create an export file.

7. Click the command you want to add (left column) or remove (right column), and then click **Add** or **Remove**.

   ◆ To insert a separator line between buttons in the Quick Access Toolbar, click **<Separator>**, and then click **Add**.

8. Click the **Move Up** and **Move Down** arrow buttons to arrange the order.

9. To reset the Ribbon or Quick Access Toolbar, click the **Reset** list arrow, and then select a reset option.

10. Click **OK**.

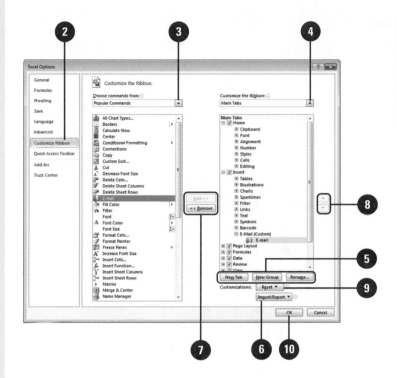

For Your Information

Moving Toolbars and the Ribbon

You can move the Quick Access Toolbar to another location. Click the Customize Quick Access Toolbar list arrow, and then click Show Below The Ribbon or Show Above The Ribbon. You can minimize the Ribbon (**New!**). Click the Minimize The Ribbon (Ctrl+F1) button on the right side of the Ribbon (to the left of the Help button). Click the Expand The Ribbon button to maximize it. When the Ribbon is minimized, you can click a tab to auto maximize it. When you click an option or in the document, the Ribbon minimizes again. Just like an auto-hide option.

Changing ScreenTips

You can turn off or change ScreenTips. Click the File tab, click Options, click General, click the ScreenTip Style list arrow, click Don't Show Feature Descriptions In ScreenTips or Don't Show ScreenTips, and then click OK.

Choosing Dialog Box Options

A **dialog box** is a window that opens when you click a Dialog Box Launcher or a link. **Dialog Box Launchers** are small icons that appear at the bottom corner of some groups. When you point to a Dialog Box Launcher, a ScreenTip with a thumbnail of the dialog box appears to show you which dialog box opens. A dialog box allows you to supply more information before the program carries out the command you selected. After you enter information or make selections in a dialog box, click the OK button to complete the command. Click the Cancel button to close the dialog box without issuing the command. In many dialog boxes, you can also click an Apply button to apply your changes without closing the dialog box.

Choose Dialog Box Options

All dialog boxes contain the same types of options, including the following:

- **Tabs**. Each tab groups a related set of options. Click a tab to display its options.

- **Option buttons**. Click an option button to select it. You can usually select only one.

- **Up and down arrows**. Click the up or down arrow to increase or decrease the number, or type a number in the box.

- **Check box**. Click the box to turn on or off the option. A checked box means the option is selected; a cleared box means it's not.

- **List box**. Click the list arrow to display a list of options, and then click the option you want.

- **Text box**. Click in the box and type the requested information.

- **Button**. Click a button to perform a specific action or command. A button name followed by an ellipsis (...) opens another dialog box.

- **Preview box**. Many dialog boxes show an image that reflects the options you select.

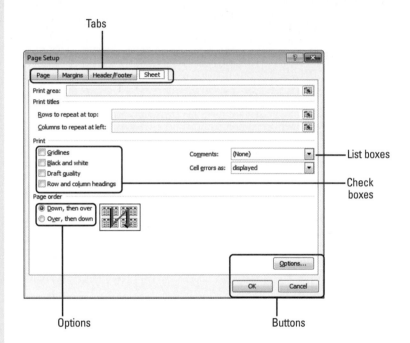

Tabs

List boxes

Check boxes

Options

Buttons

For Your Information

Navigating a Dialog Box

Rather than clicking to move around a dialog box, you can press the Tab key to move from one box or button to the next. You can also use Shift+Tab to move backward, or Ctrl+Tab and Ctrl+Shift+Tab to move between dialog box tabs.

Using the Status Bar

The **Status bar** appears across the bottom of your screen and displays document information—such as cell mode, Office theme name, and current display zoom percentage—and some Office program controls, such as view shortcut buttons, zoom slider, and Fit To Window button. With the click of the mouse, you can quickly customize exactly what you see on the Status bar. In addition to displaying information, the Status bar also allows you to check the on/off status of certain features, such as Signatures, Permissions, Selection Mode, Page Number, Caps Lock, Num Lock, Macro Recording and Playback, and much more.

Add or Remove Items from the Status Bar

◆ **Add Item**. Right-click the Status bar, and then click an unchecked item.

◆ **Remove Item**. Right-click the Status bar, and then click a checked item.

See Also

See "Adding a Signature Line" on page 586 or "Recording a Macro" on page 657 for information on changing the status of items on the Status bar.

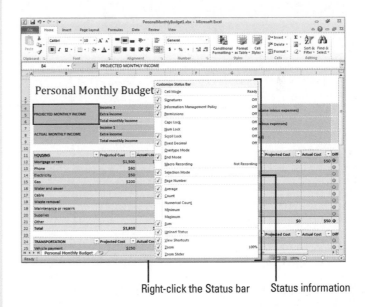

Right-click the Status bar   Status information

Creating a Blank Office Document

When you start an Office program, the program window opens with a new Office document—a presentation, workbook, document, database, publication, etc.—so that you can begin working in it. You can also start as many new Office documents as you want whenever an Office program is running. Each new document displays a default name—such as Presentation1 or Book1—numbered according to how many new documents you have started during the work session until you save it with a more meaningful name. The document name appears on the title bar and taskbar buttons.

Start a Blank Office Document

① Click the **File** tab, and then click **New**.

> **TIMESAVER** *To create a blank Office document without a dialog box, press Ctrl+N.*

The New screen appears.

② Click **Blank <Document>**.

③ Click **Create**.

A new blank document appears in the Office program window.

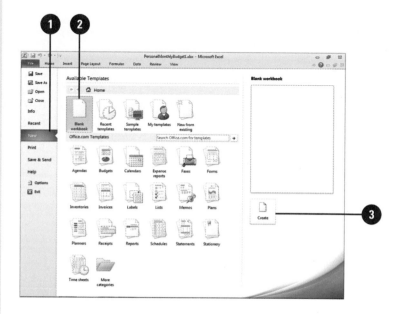

Blank workbook

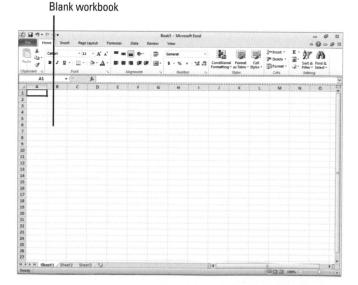

Creating a Document Using a Template

Office provides a collection of professionally designed templates that you can use to help you create documents. Start with a template when you have a good idea of your content but want to take advantage of a template's professional look. A **template** is an Office program file that provides you with a unified document design, which includes themes, so you only need to add text and graphics. In the New screen, you can choose a template from those already installed with Office or from the Microsoft Office Online Web site, an online content library. You can choose an Office.com template from one of the listed categories.

Create an Office Document with a Template

1. Click the **File** tab, and then click **New**.

2. Choose one of the following:
   - Click the **Recent templates** category, and then click a recently used template.
   - Click the **Sample templates** category, and then click a template.
   - Click the **My templates** category to open a dialog box.
   - Click the **New from existing** category to open a dialog box to select a template file.
   - Double-click an Office.com Templates folder (if needed), and then click a template.

3. To navigate, click the **Home**, **Next**, or **Previous** button.

4. Click **Create** or **Download**.

5. If necessary, click the template you want, and then click **OK**.

Did You Know?

You can download template packs on the Web. Go to *www.microsoft.com*, click the Office link, and then search for Office Templates.

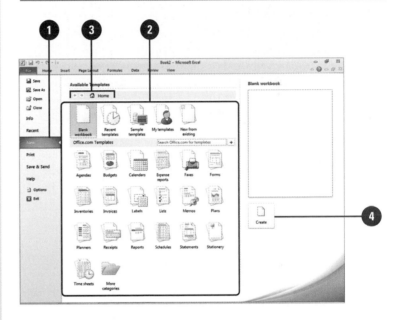

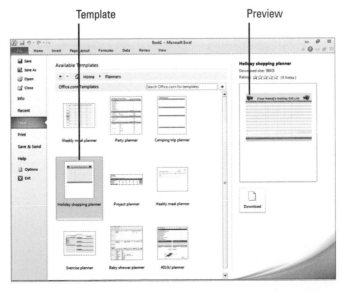

Template   Preview

Opening an Existing Office Document

You can open an Office document and start Office simultaneously, or you can open an Office document or file created in another program after you start an Office program. You can open an existing Office document by using the File tab (**New!**). On the File tab, you can choose the Open command to locate and select the document you want or choose a recently used document from the Recent documents list. Similar to the Windows Start menu, the Recent Documents list allows you to pin documents to the list that you want to remain accessible regardless of recent use. The Pin icon to the right of the file name on the File tab makes it easy to pin or unpin as needed.

Open an Office Document from the Program Window

1. Click the **File** tab, and then click **Open**.

2. If you want to open a specific file type, click the **Files of type** list arrow, and then click a file type.

3. If the file is located in another folder, click the **Look In** list arrow, and then navigate to the file.

4. Click the Office file you want, and then click **Open**, or click the **Open** button arrow, and then click one of the following options:

   ◆ **Open Read-Only** to open the selected file with protection.

   ◆ **Open as Copy** to open a copy of the selected file.

   ◆ **Open in Browser** to open the selected Web file in a browser.

   ◆ **Open in Protected View** to open the selected file in protected view (**New!**).

   ◆ **Open and Repair** to open the damaged file.

   ◆ **Show previous versions** to show previous versions of Office documents.

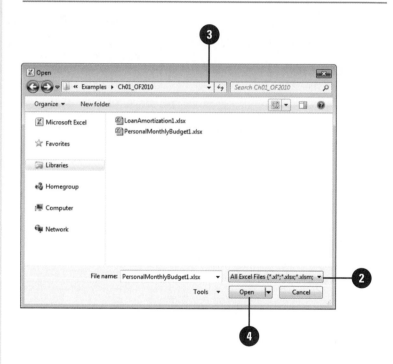

For Your Information

Using the Office Program Viewer

An Office program Viewer—PowerPoint, Word, and Excel—is a program used to open and view Office documents on computers that don't have Microsoft Office installed. The Office program Viewer is available for download from the Microsoft Office Online Web site in the downloads section. Check the Microsoft Web site for software requirements.

Open a Recently Opened Documents or Places

1. Click the **File** tab, and then click **Recent**.

2. Click the Office document you want to open.

   ◆ **Pin a document/folder.** Click the Pin icon (right-side) to display a green pin (document is pinned) on the Recent Documents or Recent Places list (**New!**).

   ◆ **Unpin a document/folder.** Click the Pin icon (right-side) to display a grey pin on the Recent Documents or Recent Places list (**New!**).

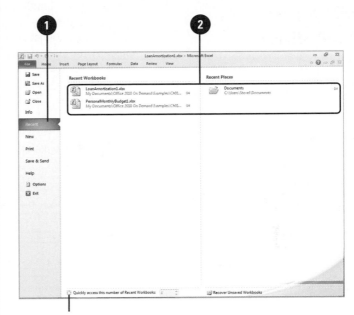

Select to add recent documents to the File tab

Did You Know?

You can add recently used documents to the File tab. (**New!**) Click the File tab, click Recent, select the Quickly Access This Number Of Recent <documents> check box, and then specify the number of documents you want to display.

You can change the number of recently opened files that appear on the File tab. Click the File tab, click Options, click Advanced, change the Show This Number Of Recent Documents list, and then click OK.

You can change the default file location of the Open dialog box. Click the File tab, click Options, click Save, enter a new location in the Default File Location box, and then click OK.

For Your Information

Managing Files in the Open or Save Dialog

When you open the Open or Save As dialog box, you can manage files directly in the dialog box. You can delete or rename a file in a dialog box. In the Open or Save As dialog box, click the file, click the Tools list arrow (XP) or the Organize button (7 or Vista), and then click Delete or Rename. You can also quickly move or copy a file in a dialog box. In the Open or Save As dialog box, right-click the file you want to move or copy, click Cut or Copy, open the folder where you want to paste the file, right-click a blank area, and then click Paste.

Converting an Existing Office Document

When you open an Office document from 97-2003, Office 2010 goes into compatibility mode—indicated on the title bar—where it disables new features that cannot be displayed or converted well by previous versions. When you save an Office document, Office 2010 programs save 97-2003 files in their older format using compatibility mode. The document stays in compatibility mode until you convert it to the 2010 file format.

Convert an Office Document 97-2003 to Office 2010

1. Open the Office Document 97-2003 you want to convert to the Office 2010 file format.

   The Office Document 97-2003 document opens in compatibility mode.

2. Click the **File** tab, and then click **Info**.

3. Click **Convert**.

4. Click **OK** to convert the file to new Office Document 2010 format.

   Office exits compatibility mode, which is only turned on when a previous version is in use.

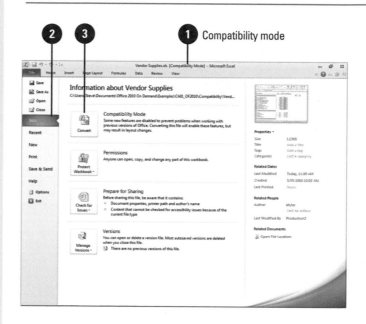

Compatibility mode

Using Task and Window Panes

Task panes are separate windows that appear when you need them, such as Document Recovery, or when you click a Dialog Box Launcher icon, such as Office Clipboard and Clip Art. A task pane displays various options that relate to the current task. **Window panes** are sections of a window, such as a split window. If you need a larger work area, you can use the Close button in the upper-right corner of the pane to close a task or window pane, or move a border edge (for task panes) or **splitter** (for window panes) to resize it.

Work with Task and Window Panes

◆ **Open a Task Pane**. It appears when you need it or when you click a Dialog Box Launcher icon.

◆ **Close a Task or Window Pane**. Click the Close button in upper-right corner of the pane.

◆ **Resize a Task Pane**. Point to the Task Pane border edge until the pointer changes to double arrows, then drag the edge to resize it.

◆ **Resize a Window Pane**. Point to the window pane border bar until the pointer changes to a double bar with arrows, then drag the edge to resize it.

Did You Know?

You can insert window panes. Click the View tab, and then click the Split button in the Window group.

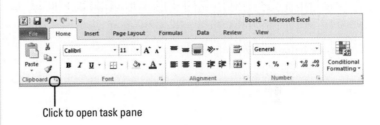

Click to open task pane

Task pane options

Close

Arranging Windows

Every Office program and document opens inside a **window**, which contains a title bar, Ribbon, and work area. This is where you create and edit your data. Most often, you'll probably fill the entire screen with one window. But when you want to move or copy information between programs or documents, it's easier to display several windows at once. You can arrange two or more windows from one program or from different programs on the screen at the same time. However, you must make the window active to work in it. You can also click the document buttons on the taskbar to switch between open documents.

Resize and Move a Window

◆ **Maximize button**. Click to make a window fill the entire screen.

◆ **Restore Down button**. Click to reduce a maximized window to a reduced size.

◆ **Minimize button**. Click to shrink a window to a taskbar button. To restore the window to its previous size, click the taskbar button.

◆ **Close button**. Click to shut a window.

Restore Down button

Minimize button

Close button

Maximize button

Resize and Move a Window Using a Mouse

1 If the window is maximized, click the **Restore Down** button.

2 Use the following methods:

◆ **Move**. Move the mouse over the title bar.

◆ **Resize**. Move the mouse over one of the borders of the window until the mouse pointer changes into a two-headed arrow. The directions of the arrowheads show you the directions in which you can resize the window.

3 Drag to move or resize the window.

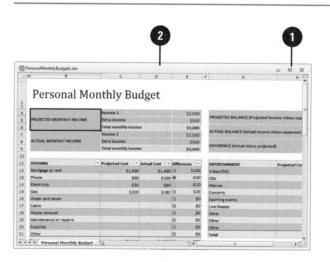

Arrange or Switch Between Windows

1 Open the documents you want to arrange or switch between.

2 Click the **View** tab.

3 In the Window group, perform any of the following:

- ◆ Click **Switch Windows**, and then click the document name you want.

- ◆ Click **Arrange All**, click an arrange window option (Tiled, Horizontal, Vertical, or Cascade), and then click OK.

- ◆ Click **New Window** to open a new window containing a view of the current document.

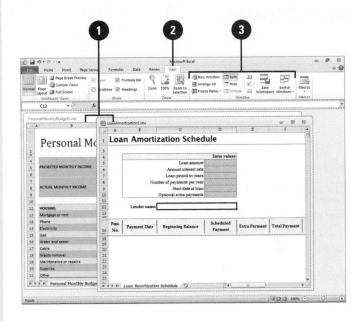

Compare Windows Side By Side

1 In Word and Excel, open the documents you want to arrange or switch between.

2 Click the **View** tab.

3 In the Window group, perform any of the following:

- ◆ Click **View Side By Side** to compare two worksheets vertically.

- ◆ Click **Synchronous Scrolling** to synchronize the scrolling of two documents so that they scroll together. To enable this feature turn on View Side By Side.

- ◆ Click **Reset Window** to reset the window position of the documents being compared side-by-side so that they share the screen equally. To enable this feature turn on View Side By Side.

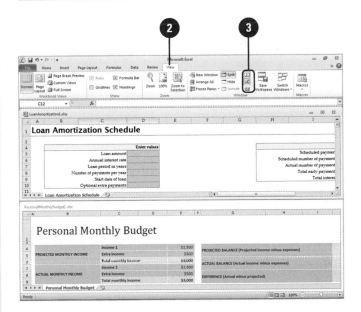

Switching Views

Each Office program provides different views to help you work with and display information. To quickly switch between views—such as Normal, Page Layout, and Print Layout—you can use buttons on the view selector in the lower-right corner of the Program window. **Normal view** is the main view in PowerPoint and Excel. It lets you focus on entering, modifying, and managing your data. **Page Layout view** and **Print Layout view** are the printout-related views in Excel and Word respectively. They let you focus on how your document is going to look when you print it. In addition to the view selector, you can also use view buttons on the View tab to switch between views.

Switch Between Views

◆ **Use the View Selector.** On the right-side of the Status bar, click any of the view buttons.

  ◆ **Word.** Print Layout, Full Screen Reading, Web Layout, Outline, and Draft.

  ◆ **Excel.** Normal, Page Layout, and Page Break Preview.

  ◆ **PowerPoint.** Normal, Slide Sorter, and Slide Show.

  ◆ **Access.** Form, Datasheet, Layout, Design, PivotTable, and PivotTable; varies depending on the Access object.

◆ **Use the View tab.** Click the View tab, and then click any of the view buttons.

  ◆ **Word.** Print Layout, Full Screen Reading, Web Layout, Outline, and Draft.

  ◆ **Excel.** Normal, Page Layout, Page Break Preview, and Full Screen.

  ◆ **PowerPoint.** Normal, Slide Sorter, Notes Pages, and Slide Show.

View tab buttons

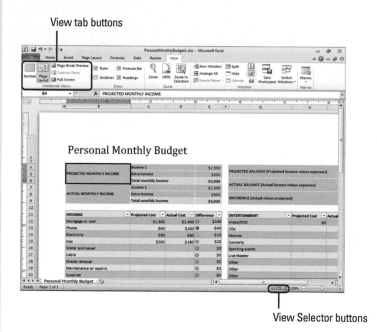

View Selector buttons

Documenting Properties

Office automatically documents properties while you work—such as file size, save dates, and various statistics—and allows you to document other properties, such as title, author, subject, keywords, category, and status. You can view or edit standard document properties or create advanced custom properties by using the **Document Information Panel**, which is an XML-based Microsoft InfoPath 2010 form hosted in the Office program. You can use document properties—also known as **metadata**—to help you manage and track files; search tools can use the metadata to find a document based on your search criteria. If you associate a document property to an item in the document, the document property updates when you change the item.

View and Edit Document Properties

1. Click the **File** tab, and then click **Info**.

2. To display other properties, click the **Properties** button, and then select an option:

   ◆ **Show Document Panel.** Shows Document panel in the document.

   ◆ **Advanced Properties.** Displays the Properties dialog box.

   ◆ **Show All Properties.** Displays more options in Info screen.

3. Enter the standard properties, such as author, title, subject, keywords, category, status, and comments.

Did You Know?

You can view or change document properties when you open or save a file. In the Open or Save As dialog box, select the document you want, click the arrow next to the Views, and then click Details to view file size and last changed date, or click Properties to view all information. If you want to insert or change author names or keywords, click the Authors box or Tags box, and then type what you want.

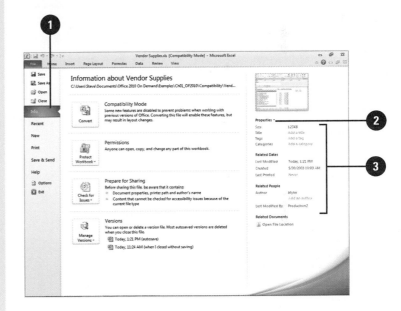

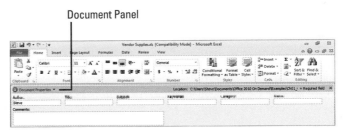

Document Panel

Getting Help While You Work

At some time, everyone has a question or two about the program they are using. The Office Help Viewer provides the answers and resources you need, including feature help, articles, tips, templates, training, and downloads. By connecting to Office.com on the Microsoft Web site, you not only have access to standard product help information, but you also have access to updated information over the Web without leaving the Help Viewer. The Web browser-like Help Viewer allows you to browse an extensive catalog of topics using a table of contents to locate information, or ask a question or enter phrases to search for specific information. When you use any of these help options, a list of possible answers is shown to you with the most likely answer or most frequently-used at the top of the list.

Use the Help Viewer to Get Answers

1. Click the **Help** button on the Ribbon.

   TIMESAVER *Press F1.*

2. Locate the Help topic you want.

   ◆ Click a Help category on the home page, and then click a topic (? icon).

   ◆ Click the **Show/Hide Table of Contents** button on the toolbar, click a help category (book icon) and then click a topic (? icon).

3. Read the topic, and then click any links to get Help information.

4. Click the **Back**, **Forward**, **Stop**, **Refresh**, and **Home** buttons on the toolbar to move around in the Help Viewer.

5. If you want to print the topic, click the **Print** button on the toolbar.

6. To keep the Help Viewer window (not maximized) on top or behind, click to toggle the **Keep On Top** button (pin pushed in) and **Not On Top** button (pin not pushed in) on the toolbar.

7. When you're done, click the **Close** button.

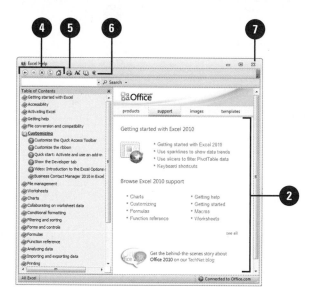

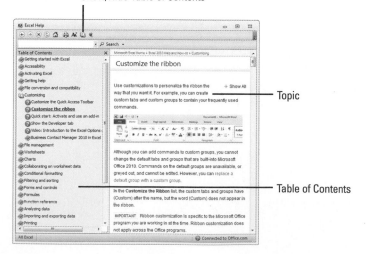

Show/Hide Table of Contents

Topic

Table of Contents

Search for Help

1 Click the **Help** button on the Ribbon.

2 Click the **Search button** list arrow below the toolbar, and then select the location and type of information you want.

3 Type one or more keywords in the Search For box, and then click the **Search** button.

4 Click a topic.

5 Read the topic, and then click any links to get information on related topics or definitions.

6 When you're done, click the **Close** button.

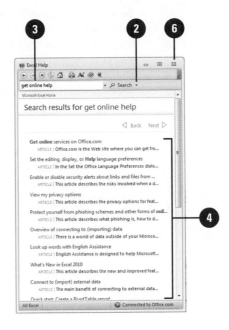

Check Help Connection Status

1 Click the **Help** button on the Ribbon.

2 Click the Connection Status at the bottom of the Help Viewer.

3 Click the connection option where you want to get help information:

◆ **Show content from Office.com** to get help from this computer and the internet (online).

◆ **Show content only from this computer** to get help from this computer only (offline).

This setting is maintained for all Office 2010 program Help Viewers.

4 When you're done, click the **Close** button.

Saving an Office Document

When you create an Office document, save it as a file on your computer so you can work with it later. When you save a document for the first time or if you want to save a copy of a file, use the Save As command. When you want to save an open document, use the Save button on the Quick Access Toolbar. When you save a document, Office 2010 saves 97-2003 files in an older format using compatibility mode and new 2010 files in an XML (Extensible Markup Language) based file format. The XML format significantly reduces file sizes, provides enhanced file recovery, and allows for increased compatibility, sharing, reuse, and transportability. An Office 97-2003 document stays in compatibility mode—indicated on the title bar—until you convert it to the new 2010 file format. Compatibility mode disables new features that cannot be displayed or converted well by previous versions.

Save a Document for Office 2010

1. Click the **File** tab, and then click **Save As**.

2. Click the **Save in** list arrow, and then click the drive or folder where you want to save the file.

3. Type a document file name.

4. Click the **Save as type** list arrow, and then click **<Program> <Document>**, such as Word Document, or Excel Workbook.

5. To enter Document properties, click the **Authors** or **Tags** box, and then enter the text you want.

6. Click **Save**.

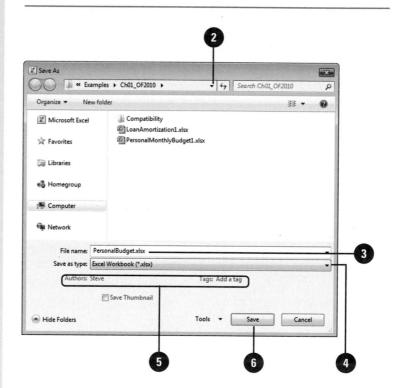

Did You Know?

You can access options from the Save dialog box. In the Save dialog box, click Tools, and then click the command option you want, either General, Web, or Compress Pictures.

Save an Office 97-2003 Document

1. Open the Office 97-2003 document you want to continue to save in the 97-2003 format.

   The 97-2003 document opens in compatibility mode.

2. Click the **Save** button on the Quick Access Toolbar, or click the **File** tab, and then click **Save**.

   The Office program stays in compatibility mode.

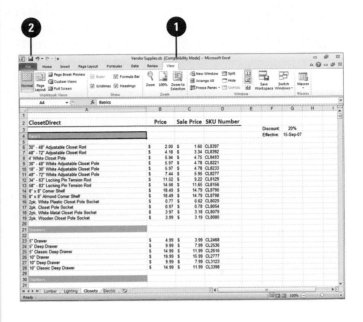

Set Save Options

1. Click the **File** tab, and then click **Options**.

2. In the left pane, click **Save**.

3. Set the save options you want:

   ◆ **Default Save Format.** Click the **Save files in this format** list arrow, and then click the default format you want.

   ◆ **Default File Location.** Specify the complete path to the folder location where you want to save your document.

4. Click **OK**.

Saving an Office Document with Different Formats

Office 2010 is a versatile suite of programs that allow you to save your documents in a variety of different formats—see the table on the following page for a complete list and description. For example, you might want to save your document as a Web page that you can view in a Web browser. Or you can save a document in an earlier 97-2003 version in case the people you work with have not upgraded to Office 2010. If you save a document to 97-2003, some new features and formatting are converted to uneditable pictures or not retained. The new format is compatible with Office 2003, Office XP, and Office 2000 with a software patch. However, for best results, if you're creating a document for someone with Word 97 to Word 2003, it's better to save it with the .doc file format. In addition to the new XML-based file format, Excel also allows you to save a workbook in a binary file format (or BIFF12), which is based on the segmented compressed file format. This file format is most useful for large or complex workbooks, and optimized for performance and backward compatibility.

Save an Office Document with Another Format

1. Click the **File** tab, and then click **Save & send**.

2. Click **Change File Type**.

3. Click the file type you want.

4. Click the **Save As** button.

   The Save As dialog box opens with the selected file type.

   ◆ You can also click the **File** tab, click **Save As**, and then select a file format.

5. Click the **Save in** list arrow, and then select the location where you want to save the file.

6. Type a file name.

7. Click **Save**.

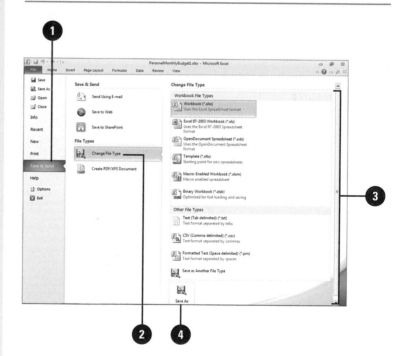

See Also

See "Creating a PDF Document" on page 618 or "Creating an XPS Document" on page 619 for information on using and saving a file with different formats.

Office 2010 Save File Formats

Save As file type	Extension	Used to save
Word Document	.docx	Word 2007-2010 document
Word Macro-Enabled Document	.docm	Word 2007-2010 document that contains Visual Basic for Applications (VBA) code
Excel Workbook	.xlsx	Excel 2007-2010 workbook
Excel Macro-Enabled Workbook	.xlsm	Excel 2007-2010 workbook that contains Visual Basic for Applications (VBA) code
Excel Binary Workbook	.xlsb	Excel 2007-2010 workbook with a binary compressed format for large or complex workbooks
Excel 97-2003 Workbook	.xls	Excel 97 to Excel 2003 workbook
Excel Template	.xltx	Excel 2007-2010 template
Excel Macro-Enabled Template	.xltm	Excel 2007-2010 template that includes macros
Excel 97-2003 Template	.xlt	Excel 97-2003 template
PowerPoint Presentation	.pptx	PowerPoint 2007-2010 presentation
PowerPoint Macro-Enabled Presentation	.pptm	PowerPoint 2007-2010 presentation that contains Visual Basic for Applications (VBA) code
PowerPoint 97-2003	.ppt	PowerPoint 97 to PowerPoint 2003 presentation
PowerPoint Template	.potx	PowerPoint 2007-2010 template
PowerPoint Macro-Enabled Template	.potm	PowerPoint 2007-2010 template that includes macros
PowerPoint 97-2003 Template	.pot	PowerPoint 97 to PowerPoint 2003 template
PowerPoint Show	.pps; .ppsx	PowerPoint 2007-2010 presentation that opens in Slide Show view
PowerPoint Macro-Enabled Show	.ppsm	PowerPoint 2007-2010 show that includes macros
PowerPoint 97-2003 Show	.ppt	PowerPoint 97-2003 presentation that opens in Slide Show view
Access 2002-2003 Database	.mdb	Access 2002 to Access 2003 database
Access 2010 Database	.accdb	Access 2007-2010 database
Access Projects	.adp	Access project file
Publisher publication	.pub	Publisher file
PDF	.pdf	Fixed-layout electronic file format that preserves document formatting developed by Adobe
XPS Document Format	.xps	Fixed-layout electronic file format that preserves document formatting developed by Microsoft
Single File Web Page	.mht; .mhtml	Web page as a single file with an .htm file
Web Page	.htm; .html	Web page as a folder with an .htm file

Checking Compatibility

The Compatibility Checker identifies the potential loss of functionality when you save an Office 2010 document in the Office 97-2003 document file format. The Compatibility Checker generates a report that provides a summary of the potential losses and the number of occurrences in the document. Use the report information to determine what caused each message and for suggestions on how to change it. If the loss is due to a new feature in Office 2010, you might be able to simply remove the effect or feature. In other cases, you might not be able to do anything about it. To maintain a visual appearance, SmartArt graphics and other objects with new effects are converted to bitmaps to preserve their overall look and cannot be edited.

Check Compatibility

1. Click the **File** tab, and then click **Info**.

2. Click the **Check For Issues** button, and then click **Check Compatibility**.

   Office checks compatibility of the document for non supported features in earlier versions of the Office program.

3. View the compatibility summary information, so you can make changes, as necessary.

4. To have the compatibility checker review the Office document when the Office program saves the file, select the **Check compatibility when saving this <Document>** check box.

5. Click **OK**.

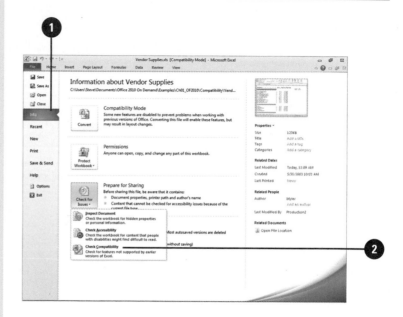

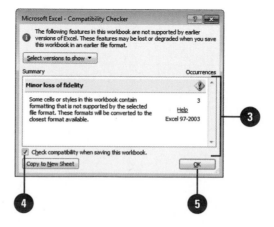

Checking Accessibility

The Accessibility Checker (**New!**) identifies potential difficulties that people with disabilities might have reading or interactive with an Office document. The Accessibility Checker generates a list of errors and warning and possible fixes in the Accessibility Checker panel. Use the information to determine what caused each issue and for suggestions on how to fix it. In addition to the Accessibility Checker, you can also add alternative text (also known as alt text) (**New!**) to objects and other items to provide information for people with visual impairments who may be unable to easily or fully see it. Alternative text also helps people with screen readers understand the content in a document. You can create alternative text for shapes, pictures, charts, tables, SmartArt graphics, or other objects. When you point to an object with alternative text in a screen reader or DAISY (digital Accessible Information System) or in most browsers, the alternative text appears.

Check Accessibility and Add Alternative Text

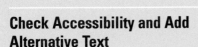

1. Click the **File** tab, and then click **Info**.

2. Click the **Check For Issues** button, and then click **Check Accessibility**.

   Office checks compatibility for content that people with disabilities might find difficult to read.

3. View the compatibility summary information of errors and warnings in the Accessibility Checker panel.

4. Select an issue under Inspection Results to find out how to fix it under Additional Information.

5. To add alternative text, right-click the object or item, point to a command (varies depending on the object or item), such as Format, click **Alternative Text** or **Alt Text**, enter a title and description, and then click **OK**.

6. When you're done with the Accessibility Checker panel, click the **Close** button on the panel.

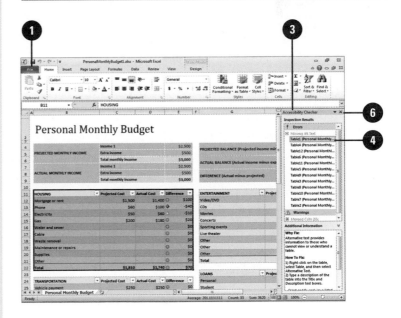

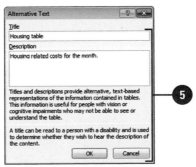

Recovering an Office Document

If an Office program encounters a problem and stops responding, the program automatically tries to recover the file. The recovered files are stored and managed by Office. You can use the Manage Versions button (**New!**) on the Info screen under the File tab to open any available recovered unsaved files. If you have a lot of recovered files, you can also delete all file versions to save disk space. To use the AutoRecover option, you need to enable it in the Save category of the Options dialog box. You can set AutoRecover options to periodically save a temporary copy of your current file, which ensures proper recovery of the file and allows you to revert to an earlier version of a file. In addition, if you didn't save your changes when you closed a document, you can select an AutoRecover option to save your work as a safe guard (**New!**).

Recover or Revert an Office Document Version

1. Click the **File** tab, and then click **Info**.

2. To open a recovered or previous version, click a file from the available list.

3. Click the **Manage Versions** button, and then click **Recover Unsaved <Documents>**.

   TIMESAVER *Click the File tab, click Recent, and then click Recover Unsaved <Documents> folder icon.*

4. Select the file version you want to recover.

5. Click **Open**.

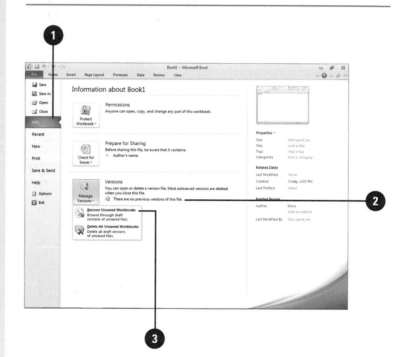

Did You Know?

You can delete all draft versions of unsaved files. Click the File tab, click Info, click the Manage Versions button, click Delete All Unsaved <Document>, and then click Yes to confirm the deletions.

Use AutoRecover

1. Click the **File** tab, and then click **Options**.

2. In the left pane, click **Save**.

3. Select the **Save AutoRecover information every** *x* **minutes** check box.

4. Enter the number of minutes, or click the **Up** and **Down** arrows to adjust the minutes.

5. Select the **Keep the last Auto Recovered file if I close without saving** check box as a safe guard to save your work if you don't save it (**New!**).

6. Specify the complete path to the folder location where you want to save your AutoRecover file.

7. To disable AutoRecover for a specific document, perform the following:

    ◆ Click the **File** list arrow, select the document you want to disable.

    ◆ Select the **Disable AutoRecover for this <Document> only** check box.

8. Click **OK**.

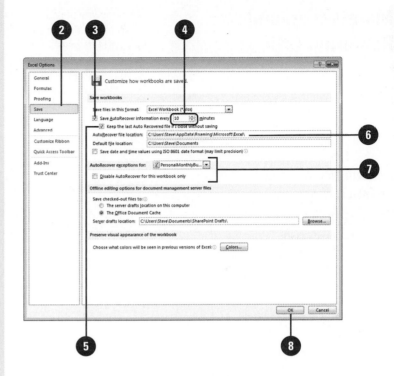

Maintaining and Repairing Office

At times you may determine that an Office program is not working as efficiently as it once did. This sometimes happens when you install new software or move files into new folders. Office does the work for you with the Repair option, which locates, diagnoses, and fixes any errors in the program itself. Note that this feature does not repair personal files like documents, presentations, or workbooks. If the Repair option does not fix the problem, you might have to reinstall Office. If you need to add or remove features, reinstall Office, or remove it entirely, you can use Office Setup's maintenance feature.

Perform Maintenance on Office Programs

1. Insert the Office disc in your drive or navigate to the folder with the setup program.

2. In Windows Explorer, double-click the Setup icon.

3. Click one of the following maintenance buttons.

   ◆ **Add or Remove Features** to change which features are installed or remove specific features.

   ◆ **Remove** to uninstall Microsoft Office 2010 from this computer.

   ◆ **Repair** to repair Microsoft Office 2010 to its original state.

   ◆ **Enter a Product Key** to type the product registration key (located in the product packaging) for Office 2010.

4. Click **Continue**, and then follow the wizard instructions to complete the maintenance.

> **See Also**
>
> *See "Working with Office Safe Modes" on page 602 for information on fixing problems with a Microsoft Office 2010 program.*

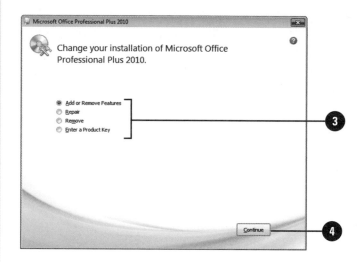

Add or Remove Features

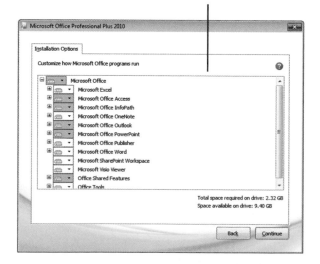

Getting Updates on the Web

Office offers a quick and easy way to update an Office program with any new software downloads that improve the stability and security of the program. From the Help screen on the File tab, simply click the Check for Updates button to connect to the Microsoft Update Web site to have your computer scanned for necessary updates, and then choose which Office updates you want to download and install.

Get Office Updates on the Web

① Click the **File** tab, and then click **Help**.

② Click **Check for Updates** to open the Microsoft Update Web site.

③ Click one of the update buttons to find out if you need updates, and then choose the updates you want to download and install.

Did You Know?

You can contact Microsoft for help. You can get support over the phone, chat, or e-mail messages. To get online help, click the File tab, click Help, and then click Contact Us.

You can get better help information. At the bottom of a help topic, click Yes, No, or I Don't Know to give Microsoft feedback on the usefulness of a topic.

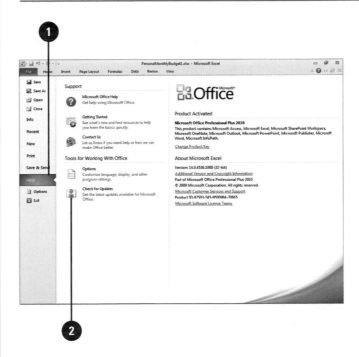

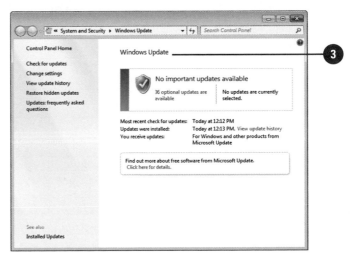

Closing a Document and Exiting Office

After you finish working on a document, you can close it. Closing a document makes more computer memory available for other activities. Closing a document is different from exiting, or quitting, a program; after you close a document, the program is still running. When you're finished using the program, you should exit it. To protect your files, always save your documents and exit before turning off the computer.

Close an Office Document

1. Click the **Close** button on the Document window, or click the **File** tab, and then click **Close**.

   TIMESAVER Press Ctrl+W.

2. If you have made changes to any open files since last saving them, a dialog box opens, asking if you want to save changes. Click **Yes** to save any changes, or click **No** to ignore your changes.

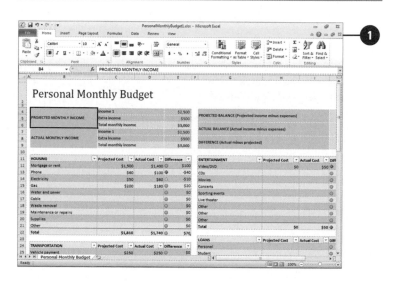

Exit an Office Program

1. Click the **Close** button on the Program window, or click the **File** tab, and then click **Exit**.

2. If you have made changes to any open files since last saving them, a dialog box opens asking if you want to save changes. Click **Yes** to save any changes, or click **No** to ignore your changes.

Program window Close button

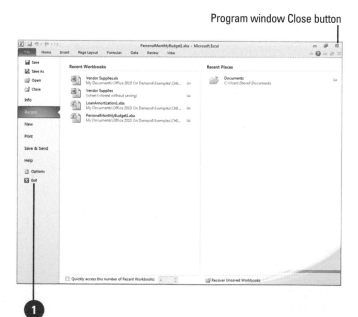

Using Shared Office Tools

Introduction

The Microsoft Office 2010 programs are designed to work together so you can focus on what you need to do, rather than how to do it. In fact, the Office programs share tools and features for your most common tasks so you can work uninterrupted and move seamlessly from one program to another. All the Office programs work with text and objects in the same way. As a result, once you learn how to move, find, correct, and comment on text in one program, you can perform these tasks in every program. If you know how to perform a task in Word, you already know (for the most part) how to perform the same task in Excel, Access, Outlook, PowerPoint, Publisher, InfoPath (Designer and Filler), and OneNote.

In addition, Office offers a Find and Replace feature that allows you to look for labels and values and make changes as necessary. When you need to spell check your document, Office can check and suggest spelling corrections. You can even customize the spelling dictionary by adding company specific words into AutoCorrect so that the spell checker doesn't think it's a misspelled word. The Actions feature works with other Microsoft Office programs to enhance your documents. Contact information can be pulled from your address book in Outlook, to your Office document. Stock symbols can trigger a Smart Tag choice to import data on a publicly traded company. Additional research and language tools area available to build up the content of your documents.

If you accidentally make a change to a cell, you can use the Undo feature to remove, or "undo," your last change. The Office program remembers your recent changes, and gives you the opportunity to undo them. If you decide to Redo the Undo, you can erase the previous change. This is useful when moving, copying, inserting and deleting information.

What You'll Do

Edit Text

Copy and Move Text

Find and Replace Text

Correct Text Automatically

Insert Information the Smart Way

Check Spelling

Change Proofing Options

Use Custom Dictionaries

Insert Symbols

Find the Right Words

Insert Research Material

Translate Text to Another Language

Use Multiple Languages

Undo and Redo an Action

Zoom the View In and Out

Preview a Document

Print a Document

Create a Template

Editing Text

Before you can edit text, you need to highlight, or select, the text you want to modify. Then you can delete, replace, move (cut), or copy text within one document or between documents even if they're from different programs. In either case, the steps are the same. Text you cut or copy is temporarily stored in the Office Clipboard. When you paste the text, the Paste Options button appears below it. When you click the button, a menu appears with options to specify how Office pastes the information in the document. To copy or move data without using the Clipboard, you can use a technique called **drag-and-drop**. Drag-and-drop makes it easy to copy or move text short distances.

Select and Edit Text

1. Move the I-beam pointer to the left or right of the text you want to select.

2. Drag the pointer to highlight the text, or click in the document to place the insertion point where you want to make a change.

   TIMESAVER *Double-click a word to select it; triple-click a paragraph to select it.*

3. Perform one of the following editing commands:

   ◆ To replace text, type your text.

   ◆ To delete text, press the Backspace key or the Delete key.

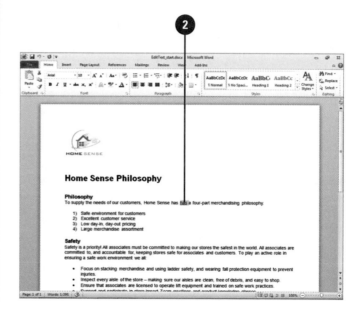

Insert and Delete Text

1 Click in the document to place the insertion point where you want to make the change.

◆ To insert text, type your text.

◆ To delete text, press the Backspace key or the Delete key.

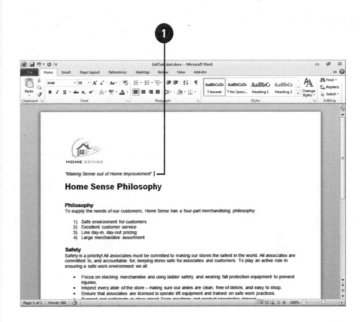

Copy or Move Text Using Drag-and-Drop

1 If you want to drag text between programs or documents, display both windows.

2 Select the text you want to move or copy.

TIMESAVER *You can also select objects and other elements.*

3 Point to the selected text, and then click and hold the mouse button.

If you want to copy the text, also press and hold Ctrl. A plus sign (+) appears in the pointer box, indicating that you are dragging a copy of the selected text.

4 Drag the selection to the new location, and then release the mouse button and keyboard.

5 Click anywhere in the document to deselect the text.

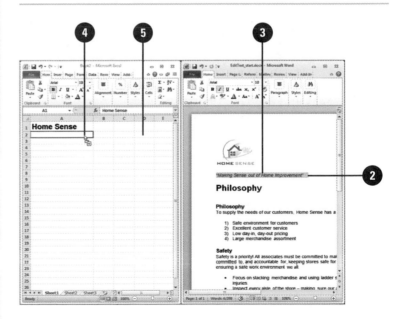

Copying and Moving Text

You can **copy** and **move** text or data from one location to another on any Office document. When you copy data, a duplicate of the selected information is placed on the Clipboard. When you move text, the selected information is removed and placed on the Clipboard. To complete the copy or move, you must **paste** the data stored on the Clipboard in another location. The live preview (**New!**) allows you to view your paste results before you actually paste it. With Microsoft Office, you can use the Office Clipboard to store multiple pieces of information from several different sources in one storage area shared by all Office programs. You can paste these pieces of information into any Office program, either individually or all at once. With Paste Special, you can control what you want to paste and even perform mathematical operations in Excel.

Copy or Move Using the Clipboard

1. Select the cell or range that contains the data you want to copy.

2. Click the **Home** tab.

3. Click the **Copy** or **Cut** button.

4. Click the location where you want to paste the data.

5. Click the **Paste** button or click the **Paste** button arrow, point to an option to display a live preview (**New!**) of the paste, and then click to paste the item.

    When you point to a paste option for the live preview, use the ScreenTip to determine the option.

    The data remains on the Clipboard, available for further pasting, until you replace it with another selection.

    If you don't want to paste this selection anywhere else, press Esc to remove the marquee.

6. If you want to change the way the data pastes into the document, click the **Paste Options** button, point to an option for the live preview (**New!**), and then select the option you want.

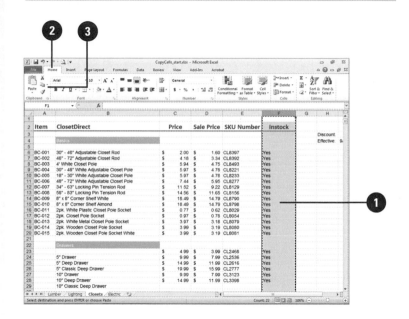

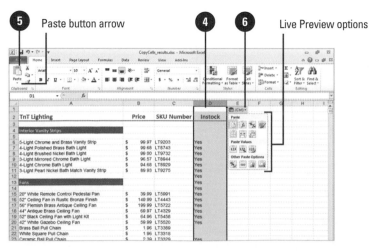

Paste button arrow · Live Preview options

Copy and Paste Data to the Office Clipboard

1. Click the **Home** tab.

2. Click the **Clipboard Dialog Box Launcher**.

3. Select the data you want to copy.

4. Click the **Copy** button.

   The text or data is copied into the Clipboard task pane.

5. Click the location where you want to paste data.

6. Click the Office Clipboard item you want to paste, or point to the item, click the list arrow, and then click **Paste**.

   ◆ To change Office Clipboard options, click the **Options** button on the pane.

7. Click the **Close** button in the task pane.

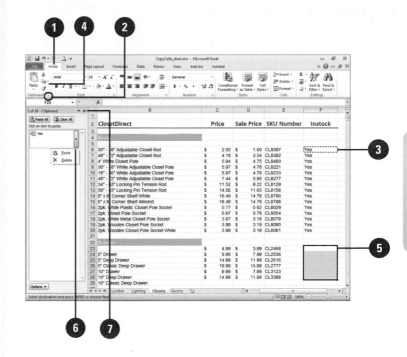

Paste Data with Special Results

1. Select the text or data that you want to copy.

2. Click the **Home** tab.

3. Click the **Copy** button.

4. Click the location where you want to paste the text or data.

5. Click the **Paste** button, and then click **Paste Special**.

6. Click the option buttons with the paste results you want.

7. Click **OK**.

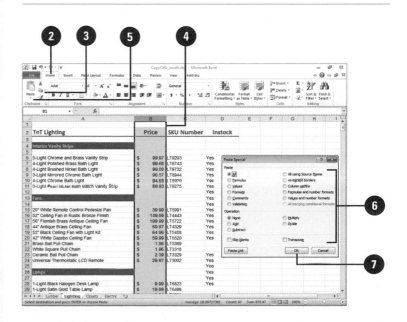

Finding and Replacing Text

The Find and Replace commands make it easy to locate or replace specific text or formulas in a document. For example, you might want to find each figure reference in a long report to verify that the proper graphic appears. Or you might want to replace all references to cell A3 in your Excel formulas with cell G3. The Find and Replace dialog boxes vary slightly from one Office program to the next, but the commands work essentially in the same way.

Find Text

① Click at the beginning of the Office document.

② Click the **Home** tab.

③ Click the **Find** button or **Find & Select** button, and then click **Find**.

④ Type the text you want to find.

⑤ Click **Find Next** until the text you want to locate is highlighted.

You can click **Find Next** repeatedly to locate each instance of the cell content.

⑥ To find all cells with the contents you want, click **Find All**.

⑦ If a message box opens when you reach the end of the document, click **OK**.

⑧ Click **Close**.

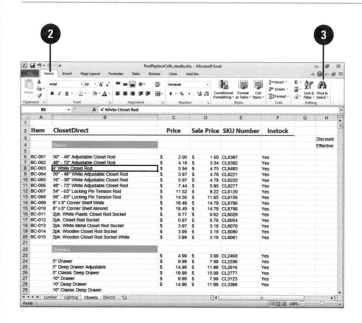

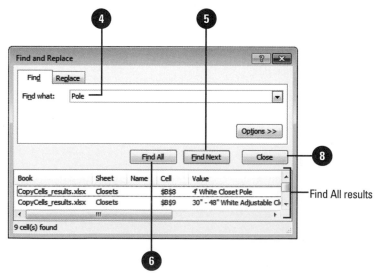

Find All results

Did You Know?

You can go to different locations in Word. Click the Home tab, click the Find button arrow, click Go To, select the Go To What option you want, specify a location, and then click Next or Previous. When you're done, click Close.

Replace Text

1. Click at the beginning of the Office document.

2. Click the **Home** tab.

3. Click the **Replace** button or **Find & Select** button, and then click **Replace**.

4. Type the text you want to search for.

5. Type the text you want to substitute.

6. Click **Find Next** to begin the search, and then select the next instance of the search text.

7. Click **Replace** to substitute the replacement text, or click **Replace All** to substitute text throughout the entire document.

   You can click **Find Next** to locate the next instance of the cell content without making a replacement.

8. If a message box appears when you reach the end of the document, click **OK**.

9. Click **Close**.

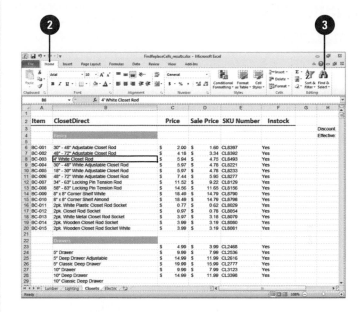

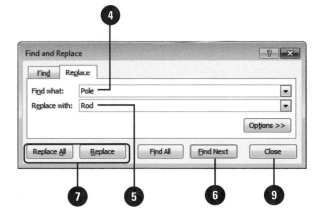

Correcting Text Automatically

Office's **AutoCorrect** feature automatically corrects common capitalization and spelling errors as you type. AutoCorrect comes with hundreds of text and symbol entries you can edit or remove. You can add words and phrases to the AutoCorrect dictionary that you misspell, or add often-typed words and save time by just typing their initials. You can use AutoCorrect to quickly insert symbols. For example, you can type (c) to insert ©. Use the AutoCorrect Exceptions dialog box to control how Office handles capital letters. If you use math symbols in your work, you can use Math AutoCorrect to make it easier to insert them. It works just like AutoCorrect (**New!**). When you point to a word that AutoCorrect changed, a small blue box appears under the first letter. When you point to the small blue box, the AutoCorrect Options button appears, which gives you control over whether you want the text to be corrected. You can also display the AutoCorrect dialog box and change AutoCorrect settings.

Turn On AutoCorrect

1. Click the **File** tab, and then click **Options**.

2. Click **Proofing**, and then click **AutoCorrect Options**.

3. Click the **AutoCorrect** tab.

4. Select the **Show AutoCorrect Options buttons** check box to display the button to change AutoCorrect options when corrections arise.

5. Select the **Replace Text As You Type** check box.

6. Select the capitalization related check boxes you want AutoCorrect to change for you.

7. To change AutoCorrect exceptions, click **Exceptions**, click the **First Letter** or **INitial CAps** tab, make the changes you want, and then click **OK**.

8. To use Math AutoCorrect, click the **Math AutoCorrect** tab, and then select the **Use Math AutoCorrect rules outside of math regions** check box.

9. Click **OK**, and then click **OK** again.

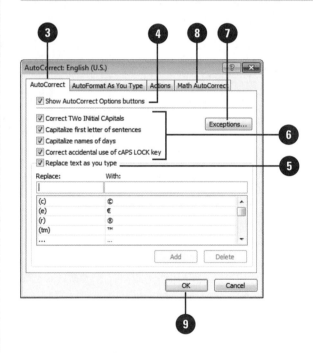

Add or Edit an AutoCorrect Entry

1. Click the **File** tab, and then click **Options**.

2. Click **Proofing**, and then click **AutoCorrect Options**.

3. Click the **AutoCorrect** tab.

4. Do one of the following:

    ◆ **Add.** Type a misspelled word or an abbreviation.

    ◆ **Edit.** Select the one you want to change.

5. Type the replacement entry.

6. Click **Add** or **Replace**. If necessary, click **Yes** to redefine entry.

7. Click **OK**, and then click **OK** again.

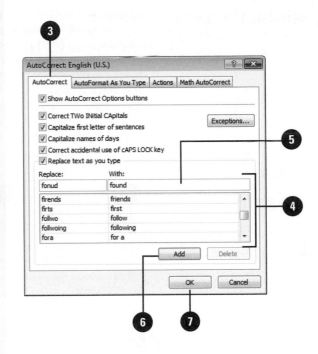

Replace Text as You Type

◆ To correct capitalization or spelling errors automatically, continue typing until AutoCorrect makes the required correction.

Point to the small blue box under the corrected text, and then click the AutoCorrect Options button list arrow to view your options. Click an option, or click a blank area of the document to deselect the AutoCorrect Options menu.

◆ To create a bulleted or numbered list, type 1. or * (for a bullet), press Tab or Spacebar, type any text, and then press Enter. AutoCorrect inserts the next number or bullet. To end the list, press Backspace to erase the extra number or bullet.

Examples of AutoCorrect Changes

Type of Correction	If You Type	AutoCorrect Inserts
Capitalization	cAP LOCK	Cap Lock
Capitalization	TWo INitial CAps	Two Initial Caps
Capitalization	thursday	Thursday
Common typos	can;t	can't
Common typos	windoes	windows
Superscript ordinals	2nd	2nd
Stacked fractions	1/2	½
Smart quotes	" "	" "
Em dashes	Madison--a small city in Wisconsin--is a nice place to live.	Madison—a small city in Wisconsin—is a nice place to live.
Symbols	(c)	©
Symbols	(r)	®

Inserting Information the Smart Way

Change Options for Actions

1. Click the **File** tab, and then click **Options**.

2. In the left pane, click **Proofing**, and then click **AutoCorrect Options**.

3. Click the **Actions** tab.

4. Select the **Enable additional actions in the right-click menu** check box.

5. Select the check boxes with the actions you want.

6. To add more actions, click **More Actions**, and then follow the online instructions.

7. Click **OK**.

8. Click **OK** again.

Actions, a replacement for smart tags, help you integrate actions typically performed in other programs directly in an Office program. For example, you can insert a financial symbol to get a stock quote, add a person's name and address in a document to the contacts list in Microsoft Outlook, or copy and paste information with added control. The Office program analyzes what you type and recognizes certain types that it marks with actions. The types of actions you can take depend on the type of data in the cell with the action. To use an action, you right-click an item to view any custom actions associated with it

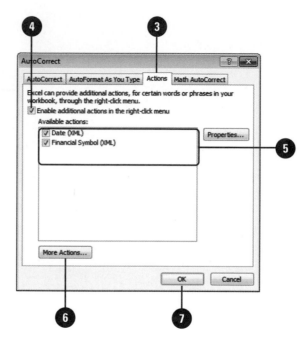

Insert Information Using an Action

1. Click an item, such as a cell, where you want to insert an action.

2. Type the information needed for the action, such as the date, a recognized financial symbol in capital letters, or a person's name from you contacts list, and then press Spacebar.

3. Right-click the item, and then point to **Additional Options** (name varies depending on item).

4. Click the action option you want; options vary depending on the action. For example, click Insert Refreshable Stock Price to insert a stock quote.

5. In Excel, click the **On a new sheet** option or the **Starting at cell** option, and then click **OK**.

Did You Know?

You can remove an action from text or item. Select text or item, and then press Delete to remove it.

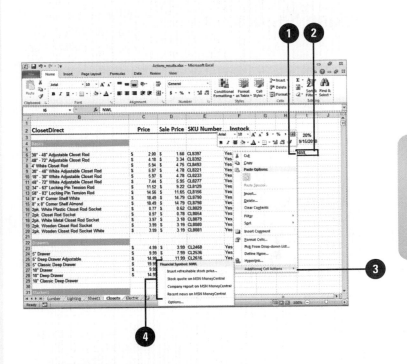

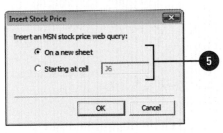

Stock information page

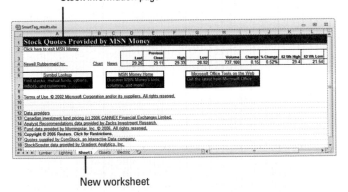

New worksheet

Checking Spelling

A document's textual inaccuracies can distract the reader, so it's important that your text be error-free. Each Office program provides a spelling checker—common for all Office 2010 programs—so that you can check the spelling in an entire document for words not listed in the dictionary (such as misspellings, names, technical terms, or acronyms) or duplicate words (such as *the the*). You can correct these errors as they arise or after you finish the entire document. You can use the Spelling button on the Review tab to check the entire document using the Spelling dialog box, or you can avoid spelling errors on a document by enabling the AutoCorrect feature to automatically correct words as you type.

Check Spelling All at Once

1. Click the **Review** tab.

   ◆ In Access, click the **Home** tab; in Outlook, click the **Review** tab in a Message window.

2. Click the **Spelling** or **Spelling & Grammar** button.

3. If the Spelling dialog box opens, choose an option:

   ◆ Click **Ignore Once** to skip the word, or click **Ignore All** to skip every instance of the word.

   ◆ Click **Add to Dictionary** to add a word to your dictionary, so it doesn't show up as a misspelled word in the future.

   ◆ Click a suggestion, and then click **Change** or **Change All**.

   ◆ Select the correct word, and then click **AutoCorrect** to add it to the AutoCorrect list.

   ◆ If no suggestion is appropriate, click in the document and edit the text yourself. Click **Resume** to continue.

4. The Office program will prompt you when the spelling check is complete, or you can click **Close** to end the spelling check.

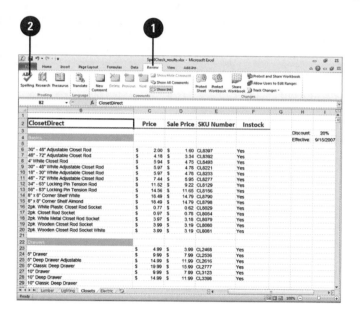

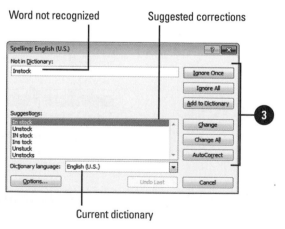

Word not recognized

Suggested corrections

Current dictionary

Changing Proofing Options

You can customize the way Microsoft Office spell checks a document by selecting proofing settings in Options. Some spelling options apply to specific Office programs, such as Check spelling as you type, while other options apply to all Microsoft Office programs, such as Ignore Internet and file addresses, and Flag repeated words. If you have ever mistakenly used their instead of *there*, you can use contextual spelling to fix it. While you work in a document, you can can set options to have the spelling checker search for mistakes in the background.

Change Spelling Options

① Click the **File** tab, and then click **Options**.

② In the left pane, click **Proofing**.

③ Select or clear the Microsoft Office spelling options you want.

- ◆ **Ignore words in UPPERCASE.**

- ◆ **Ignore words that contain numbers.**

- ◆ **Ignore Internet and file addresses.**

- ◆ **Flag repeated words.**

- ◆ **Enforce accented uppercase in French.**

- ◆ **Suggest from main dictionary only.** Select to exclude your custom dictionary.

④ Click **OK**.

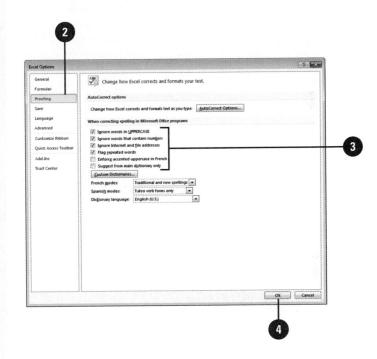

Using Custom Dictionaries

Before you can use a custom dictionary, you need to enable it first. You can enable and manage custom dictionaries by using the Custom Dictionaries dialog box. In the dialog box, you can change the language associated with a custom dictionary, create a new custom dictionary, or add or remove an existing custom dictionary. If you need to manage dictionary content, you can also change the default custom dictionary to which the spelling checker adds words, as well as add, delete, or edit words. All the modifications you make to your custom dictionaries are shared with all your Microsoft Office programs, so you only need to make changes once. If you mistakenly type an obscene or embarrassing word, such as *ass* instead of *ask*, the spelling checker will not catch it because both words are spelled correctly. You can avoid this problem by using an exclusion dictionary. When you use a language for the first time, Office automatically creates an exclusion dictionary. This dictionary forces the spelling checker to flag words you don't want to use.

Use a Custom Dictionary

1. Click the **File** tab, and then click **Options**.

2. In the left pane, click **Proofing**.

3. Click **Custom Dictionaries**.

4. Select the check box next to **CUSTOM.DIC (Default)**.

5. Click the **Dictionary language** list arrow, and then select a language for a dictionary.

6. Click the options you want:

   ◆ Click **Edit Word List** to add, delete, or edit words.

   ◆ Click **Change Default** to select a new default dictionary.

   ◆ Click **New** to create a new dictionary.

   ◆ Click **Add** to insert an existing dictionary.

   ◆ Click **Remove** to delete a dictionary.

7. Click **OK** to close the Custom Dictionaries dialog box.

8. Click **OK**.

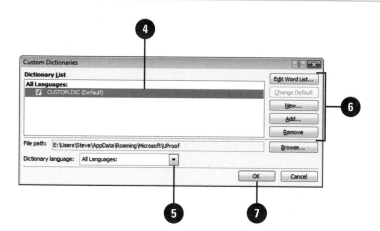

Inserting Symbols

Office programs come with a host of symbols for every need. Insert just the right one to keep from compromising a document's professional appearance with a missing accent or mathematical symbol (å). In the Symbol dialog box, you use the Recently used symbols list to quickly insert a symbol that you want to insert again. If you don't see the symbol you want, use the Font list to look at the available symbols for other fonts installed on your computer.

Insert Symbols and Special Characters

1. Click the document where you want to insert a symbol or character.

2. Click the **Insert** tab, and then click the **Symbol** button.

3. To see other symbols, click the **Font** list arrow, and then click a new font.

4. Click a symbol or character.

   You can use the Recently used symbols list to use a symbol you've already used.

5. Click **Insert**.

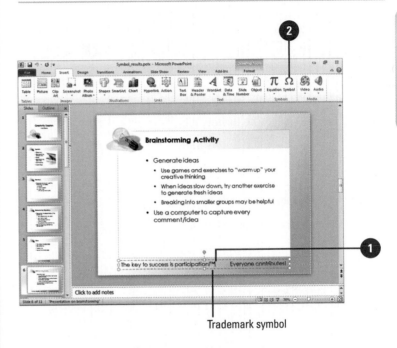

Trademark symbol

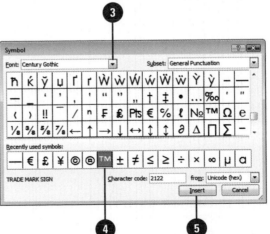

Did You Know?

You can insert a symbol using a character code. When the From box displays ASCII (decimal), you can use the number shown in the Character Code box to insert a character or symbol. Place your insertion point where you want the character on the slide, make sure Num Lock is on, hold down the Alt key, and then use the numeric keypad to type 0 (zero) followed by the character code. Then release the Alt key. The code applies to the current code page only, so some characters may not be available this way.

Finding the Right Words

Repeating the same word in a document can reduce a message's effectiveness. Instead, replace some words with synonyms or find antonyms. If you need help finding exactly the right words, use the shortcut menu to look up synonyms quickly or search a Thesaurus for more options. This feature can save you time and improve the quality and readability of your document. You can also install a Thesaurus for another language. Foreign language thesauruses can be accessed under Research Options on the Research task pane.

Use the Thesaurus

1. Select the text you want to translate.

2. Click the **Review** tab.

   ◆ In Outlook, click the **Review** tab in a Message window.

3. Click the **Thesaurus** button.

4. Click the list arrow, and then select a **Thesaurus**, if necessary.

5. Point to the word in the Research task pane.

6. Click the list arrow, and then click one of the following:

   ◆ **Insert** to replace the word you looked up with the new word.

   ◆ **Copy** to copy the new word and then paste it within the document.

   ◆ **Look Up** to look up the word for other options.

7. When you're done, click the **Close** button on the task pane.

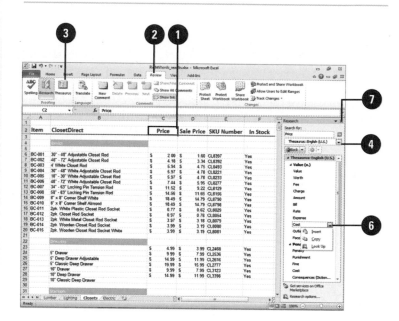

Inserting Research Material

With the Research task pane, you can access data sources and insert research material right into your text without leaving your Office program. The Research task pane can help you access electronic dictionaries, thesauruses, research sites, and proprietary company information. You can select one reference source or search in all reference books. This research pane allows you to find information and quickly and easily incorporate it into your work.

Research a topic

1. Click the **Review** tab.

   ◆ In Outlook, click the **Review** tab in a Message window.

2. Click the **Research** button.

3. Type the topic you would like to research.

4. Click the list arrow, and then select a reference source, or click **All Reference Books**.

5. To customize which resources are used for translation, click **Research options**, select the reference books and research sites you want, and then click **OK**.

6. Click the **Start Searching** button (green arrow).

7. Select the information in the task pane that you want to copy.

   To search for more information, click one of the words in the list or click a link to an online site.

8. Select the information you want, and then copy it.

   In the Research task pane, you can point to the item you want, click the list arrow, and then click **Copy**.

9. Paste the information into your document.

10. When you're done, click the **Close** button on the task pane.

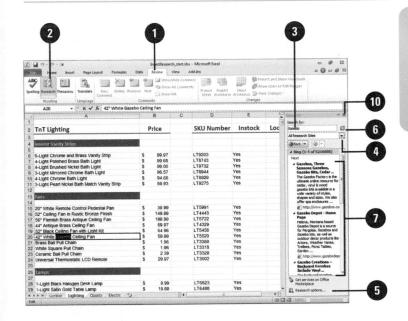

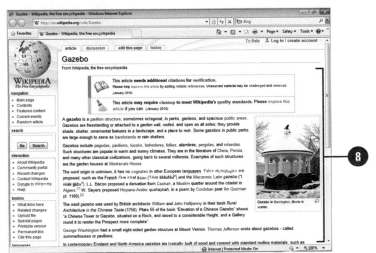

Translating Text to Another Language

With the Research task pane, you can translate single words or short phrases into different languages by using bilingual dictionaries. The Research task pane provides you with different translations and allows you to incorporate it into your work. If you need to translate an entire document for basic subject matter understanding, Web-based machine translation services are available. A machine translation is helpful for general meaning, but may not preserve the full meaning of the content.

Translate Text

1. Select the text you want to translate.

2. Click the **Review** tab.

   ◆ In Outlook, click the **Review** tab in a Message window.

3. Click the **Translate** button.

4. If necessary, click **Translate Selected Text**.

   ◆ To show a machine translation in a Web browser, click the **Translate** button, and then click **Translate Document**.

5. Click the **From** list arrow, and then select the language of the selected text.

6. Click the **To** list arrow, and then select the language you want to translate into.

7. To customize which resources are used for translation, click **Translation options**, select the look-up options you want, and then click **OK**.

8. Right-click the translated text in the Research task pane that you want to copy, and then click **Copy**.

9. Paste the information into your document.

10. When you're done, click the **Close** button on the task pane.

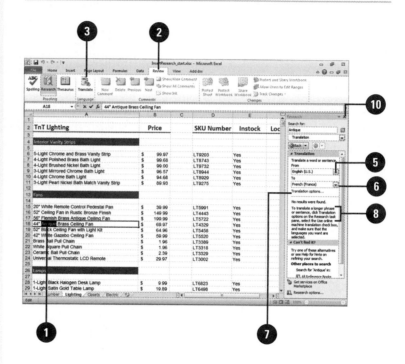

For Your Information

Using the Mini Translator

In Word, Outlook, PowerPoint, or OneNote, you can enable the Mini Translator (**New!**) that translates words or phrases in a small window when you point to them. To choose a Mini Translator language, click the Review tab, click the Translation button, click Mini Translator, select the language you want the word translated to, and then click OK. Point to a word or selected phrase to display the Mini Translator. In the Mini Translator, click the Expand button to open the Research pane; click the Play button to hear a pronunciation of the translated text; or click the Copy button to use the translated text in another document.

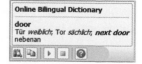

Using Multiple Languages

International Microsoft Office users can change the language that appears on their screens by changing the default language settings. Users around the world can enter, display, and edit text in all supported languages—including European languages, Japanese, Chinese, Korean, Hebrew, and Arabic—to name a few. You'll probably be able to use Office programs in your native language. If the text in your document is written in more than one language, you can automatically detect languages or designate the language of selected text so the spelling checker uses the right dictionary. You can set preferences for editing, display, ScreenTip, and Help languages (**New!**). If you don't have the keyboard layout or related software installed, you can click links to add or enable them (**New!**).

Add a Language to Office Programs

1. Click the **File** tab, click **Options**, and then click **Language**.

   ◆ You can also click **Start** on the taskbar, point to **All Programs**, click **Microsoft Office**, click **Microsoft Office Tools**, and then click **Microsoft Office 2010 Language Preferences**.

2. Click the **Language** list arrow, and then select the language you want to enable.

3. Click **Add**.

4. To enable the correct keyboard layout for the installed language, click the **Not enabled** link to open the Text Services and Input Language dialog box, where you can select a keyboard layout, and then click **OK**.

5. Set the language priority order for the buttons, tabs, and Help for the Display and Help languages.

6. Set your ScreenTip language to Match Display Language or a specific language.

7. Click **OK**, and then click **Yes** (if necessary) to quit and restart Office.

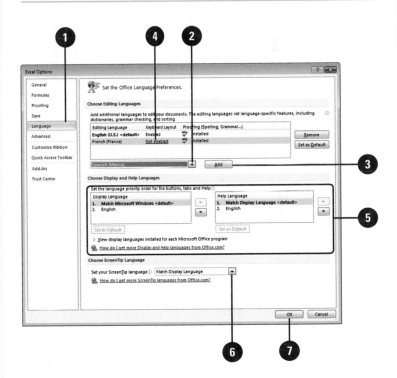

Undoing and Redoing an Action

You may realize you've made a mistake shortly after completing an action or a task. The Undo feature lets you "take back" one or more previous actions, including data you entered, edits you made, or commands you selected. For example, if you were to enter a number in a cell, and then decide the number was incorrect, you could undo the entry instead of selecting the data and deleting it. A few moments later, if you decide the number you deleted was correct after all, you could use the Redo feature to restore it to the cell.

Undo an Action

1. Click the **Undo** button on the Quick Access Toolbar to undo the last action you completed.

2. Click the **Undo** button arrow on the Quick Access Toolbar to see recent actions that can be undone.

3. Click an action. Office reverses the selected action and all actions above it.

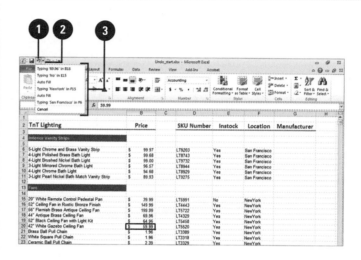

Redo an Action

1. Click the **Redo** button on the Quick Access Toolbar to restore your last undone action.

   TROUBLE? *If the Redo button is not available on the Quick Access Toolbar, click the Customize Quick Access Toolbar list arrow, and then click Redo.*

2. Click the **Redo** button arrow on the Quick Access Toolbar to see actions that can be restored.

3. Click the action you want to restore. All actions above it will be restored as well.

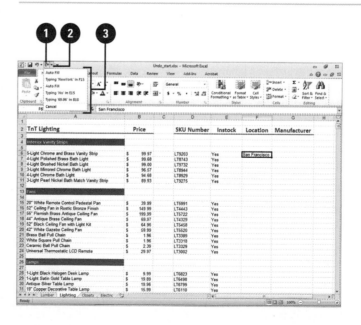

Zooming the View In and Out

Working with the Zoom tools gives you one more way to control exactly what you see in an Office document. The Zoom tools are located in the bottom-right corner of the window. Large documents, presentations, or worksheets can be difficult to work with and difficult to view. Many Office documents, when viewed at 100%, are larger than the maximized size of the window. When this happens, viewing the entire document requires reducing the zoom.

Change the View

1 Use any of the following zoom options available on the Status bar:

- ◆ **Zoom Out**. Click to zoom out (percentage gets smaller).

- ◆ **Zoom In**. Click to zoom in (percentage gets larger).

- ◆ **Slider**. Drag to zoom out or in to the percentage you want.

- ◆ **Zoom Level**. Click to display the Zoom dialog box, where you can select the magnification you want.

2 For additional zoom options, click the **View** tab, and then use any of the following options:

- ◆ **Zoom**. Click to display the Zoom dialog box, where you can select the magnification you want.

  This is the same as Zoom Level above.

- ◆ **100%**. Click to display the view at 100%.

- ◆ **Zoom to Selection**. Click to zoom the current selection in view.

Zoom dialog box
in Excel

Previewing a Document

Before printing, you should verify that the page looks the way you want. You save time, money, and paper by avoiding duplicate printing. Print Preview shows you the exact placement of your data on each printed page. You can view all or part of your document as it will appear when you print it. Print Preview shows you the pages based on the properties of the selected printer. For example, if the selected printer is setup to print color, Print Preview displays in color. The Print screen (**New!**) on the File tab makes it easy to zoom in and out to view data more comfortably, set margins and other page options, preview page breaks, and print. The options vary slightly in the different Office programs.

Preview a Document

1. Click the **File** tab, and then click **Print**.

2. Click the **Zoom to Page** button to toggle the zoom in and out to the page.

3. If you want, do either of the following:

   ◆ To adjust the zoom in Word and PowerPoint, drag the **Zoom** slider or click the **Zoom In** or **Zoom Out** buttons.

   ◆ To adjust margins visually in Excel, click the **Show Margins** button, and then drag the margin lines where you want.

4. To switch pages, click the **Next Page** or **Previous Page** button, or enter a specific page in the Current Page box.

5. If you want to print, click the **Print** button.

Print Preview in Excel

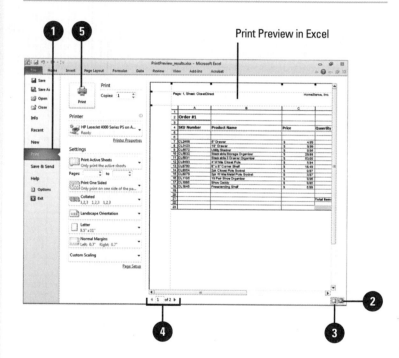

Printing a Document

When you're ready to print your Office document, you can choose several printing options on the Print screen (**New!**) on the File tab, such as choosing a new printer, selecting the number of pages in the document you want printed and the number of copies, specifying the page size, margins, and orientation, and selecting any scaling or pages to fit on a printed page. You can also use the Page Setup dialog box to control the appearance of pages (options vary depending on the Office program), such as whether gridlines are displayed, whether column letters and row numbers are displayed, and whether to include print titles. You can quickly print a copy of your document without using the Print screen by clicking the Quick Print button on the Quick Access Toolbar.

Print All or Part of a Document

1. Click the **File** tab, and then click **Print**.

   TIMESAVER *To print without the Print screen, press Ctrl+P, or click the Quick Print button on the Quick Access Toolbar.*

2. Click the **Printer** list arrow, and then click the printer you want to use.

3. To change printer properties, click the **Printer Properties** link, select the options you want, and then click **OK**.

4. Select whether you want to print the entire document or only the pages you specify.

5. Select what you want to print; the options available vary depending on the Office program.

6. To change page options, click the **Page Setup** link, select the options you want, and then click **OK**.

7. Click **Print**.

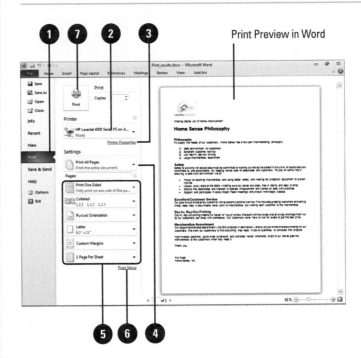

Print Preview in Word

Creating a Template

You can create your own template as easily as you create a document. Like those that come with Office, custom templates can save you time. Perhaps each month you create an inventory document in which you enter repetitive information; all that changes is the actual data. By creating your own template, you can have a custom form that is ready for completion each time you take inventory. A template file saves all the customization you made to reuse in other Office documents. Although you can store your template anywhere you want, you may find it handy to store it in the Templates folder that Microsoft Office uses to store its templates. If you store your design templates in the Templates folder, those templates appear as options when you choose the New command on the File tab, and then click My templates.

Create a Template

1. Enter all the necessary information in a new document—including formulas, labels, graphics, and formatting.

2. Click the **File** tab, and then click **Save As**.

3. Click the **Save as type** list arrow, and then select a template format.

   - **<Program> Template**. Creates a template for Office 2010.

   - **<Program> Macro-Enabled Template**. Creates a template for Office 2010 with macros.

   - **<Program> 97-2003 Template**. Creates a template for Office 97-2003.

   Microsoft Office templates are typically stored in the following location:

   Windows 7 or Vista. C:/Users /*your name*/AppData/Roaming /Microsoft/Templates

   Windows XP. C:/Documents and Settings/*your name*/Application Data/Microsoft/Templates

4. Type a name for your template.

5. Click **Save**.

Templates folder

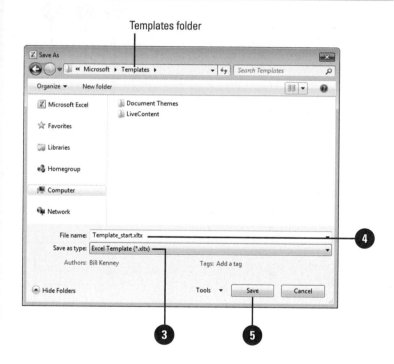

Adding Art to Office Documents

Introduction

Although well-illustrated documents can't make up for a lack of content, you can capture your audiences' attention if your documents are vibrant and visually interesting. Microsoft Office comes with a vast array of clip art, and there are endless amounts available through other software packages or on the Web. When going online to look at clips, you can categorize them so that it's easier to find the best choice for your Office document. You can use the Microsoft Online Web site (Office.com) to search for and download additional clip art.

You can easily enhance an Office document by adding a picture—one of your own or one of the hundreds that come with Microsoft Office. If you need to modify your pictures, you can resize them, compress them for storage, change their brightness or contrast, recolor them, or crop them.

WordArt is another feature that adds detail to your document. Available in other Office programs, WordArt can bring together your documents—you can change its color, shape, shadow, or size. Because WordArt comes with so many style choices, time spent customizing your documents is minimal.

In Office programs, you can insert SmartArt graphics to create diagrams that convey processes or relationships. Office provides a wide-variety of built-in SmartArt graphic types from which to choose, including graphical lists, process, cycle, hierarchy, relationship, matrix, and pyramid. Using built-in SmartArt graphics makes it easy to create and modify charts without having to create them from scratch.

Instead of adding a table of dry numbers, insert a chart. Charts add visual interest and useful information represented by lines, bars, pie slices, or other markers. Office uses Microsoft Excel to embed and display the information in a chart.

What You'll Do

Locate and Insert Clip Art

Insert a Picture

Insert a Picture Screen Shot

Add an Artistic Style to a Picture

Add a Quick Style to a Picture

Apply a Shape and Border to a Picture

Apply Picture Effects

Modify Picture Size

Compress a Picture

Correct and Recolor a Picture

Crop, Rotate and Recolor a Picture

Remove a Picture Background

Create and Format WordArt Text

Apply and Modify WordArt Text Effects

Create and Format SmartArt Graphics

Modify a SmartArt Graphic

Add Pictures to a SmartArt Graphic

Create an Organization Chart

Insert and Create a Chart

Change a Chart Layout and Style

Change Chart Labels

Format Line and Bar Charts

Edit Chart Data

Save a Chart Template

Locating and Inserting Clip Art

To add a clip art image to a document, you can click the Insert Clip Art button on the Insert tab to open the Clip Art task pane. The Clip Art task pane helps you search for clip art and access the clip art available in the Clip Organizer and on Office.com, a clip gallery that Microsoft maintains on its Web site. You can limit search results to a specific collection of clip art or a specific type of media file. After you find the clip art you want, you can click it to insert it, or point to it to display a list arrow. Then click an available command, such as Insert, Make Available Offline, Edit Keywords, and Delete from Clip Organizer.

Locate and Insert Clip Art

1 Click the **Insert** tab.

2 Click the **Clip Art** button.

3 Type the keyword(s) associated with the clip you are looking for.

To narrow your search, do one of the following:

◆ To limit search results to a specific collection of clip art, click the **Search For** list arrow, and then select the collections you want to search.

◆ To limit search results to a specific type of media file, click the **Results Should Be** list arrow, and then select the check box next to the types of clips you want to find.

◆ To display Office.com content, select the **Include Office.com** content check box (**New!**).

◆ To access clip art on Office.com, click the link at the bottom of the Clip Art task pane. Search and download images from the Office.com.

4 Click **Go**.

Clips matching the keywords appear in the Results list.

5 Click the clip you want, and then resize it, if necessary.

6 Click the **Close** button on the task pane.

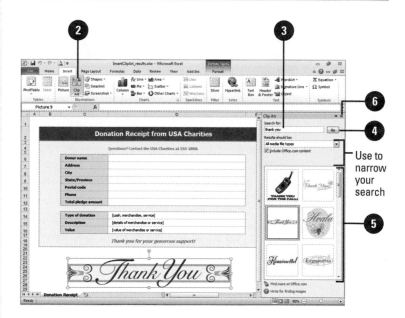

Use to narrow your search

For Your Information

Understanding Clip Art Objects

Clip art objects (pictures and animated pictures) are images made up of geometric shapes, such as lines, curves, circles, squares, and so on. These images, known as vector images, are mathematically defined, which makes them easy to resize and manipulate. A picture in the Microsoft Windows Metafile (.wmf) file format is an example of a vector image. Clip Gallery also includes sounds or motion clips, which you can insert into a document. A **motion clip** is an animated picture—also known as an animated GIF—frequently used in Web pages. When you insert a sound, a small icon appears representing the sound file.

Inserting a Picture

Office makes it possible for you to insert pictures, graphics, scanned photographs, art, photos, or artwork from a CD-ROM or other program into a document. When you use the Picture button on the Insert tab, you specify the source of the picture. When you insert pictures from files on your hard disk drive, scanner, digital camera, or Web camera, Office allows you to select multiple pictures, view thumbnails of them, and insert them all at once, which speeds up the process.

Insert a Picture from a File

1. Click the **Insert** tab.

2. Click the **Picture** button.

3. Click the **Look in** list arrow, and then select the drive and folder that contain the file you want to insert.

4. Click the file you want to insert.

5. Click **Insert**.

   ◆ To link a picture file, click the **Insert** button arrow, and then click **Link to File**.

   ◆ To insert and link a picture file, click the **Insert** button arrow, and then click **Insert and Link**.

   TROUBLE? *If you see a red "x" instead of a picture or motion clip in your document, then you don't have a graphics filter installed on your computer for that clip.*

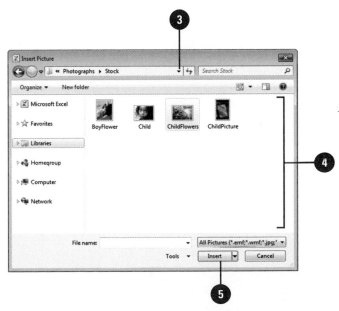

Did You Know?

You can change a picture. Select the picture, click the Change Picture button on the Format tab, select a picture, and then click Insert.

You can add graphic formats. If the graphic format you want to insert is not in the list, you can use Office Setup's Add or Remove Features option to install additional graphic formats.

Inserting a Picture Screen Shot

If you're working on a training manual, presentation, or document that requires a picture of your computer screen, then the Screenshot button (**New!**) on the Insert tab just made your life a lot easier. You use the Screen Clipping tool to drag a selection around the screen area that you want to capture, and then select the picture from the Screenshot gallery. The Screenshot gallery holds multiple screen shots, so you can capture several screens before you insert them into your document. After you insert the screen shot into a document, you can use the tools on the Picture Tools tab to edit and improve it.

Insert a Picture Screen Shot

1 Click the **Insert** tab.

2 Click the **Screenshot** button.

3 Click **Screen Clipping**.

4 Display the screen you want to capture, and then drag the large plus cursor to select the screen area to capture.

5 Click the **Screenshot** button, and then click the thumbnail of the screen shot you want to insert.

6 Use the tools on the Picture Tools tab to edit and improve the screen shot.

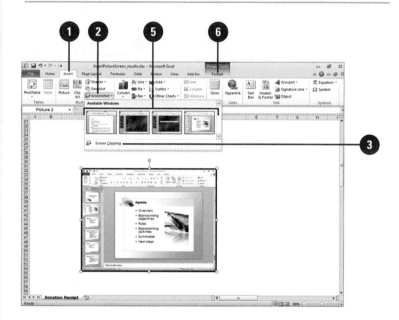

Did You Know?

You can copy the window or screen contents. To make a copy of the active window, press Alt+Print Scrn. To copy the entire screen as it appears on your monitor, press Print Scrn.

Adding an Artistic Style to a Picture

With the Artistic Quick Style gallery (**New!**), you can transform a picture into a piece of artwork. The Artistic Quick Style gallery makes it easy to change the look of a picture to a sketch, drawing, or painting. The Picture Quick Style gallery provides a variety of different formatting options—such as Pencil Sketch, LIne Drawing, Watercolor Sponge, Mosaic Bubble, Glass, Pastels Smooth, Plastic Wrap, Photocopy, and Paint Strokes—to create a professional look. To quickly see if you like an Artistic Quick Style, point to a thumbnail in the gallery to display a live preview of it in the selected shape. If you like it, you can apply it.

Add an Artistic Style to a Picture

1. Click the picture you want to change.

2. Click the **Format** tab under Picture Tools.

3. Click the **Artistic Effects** button.

   The current style appears highlighted in the gallery.

4. Point to a style.

   A live preview of the style appears in the picture.

5. Click the style you want from the gallery to apply it to the selected picture.

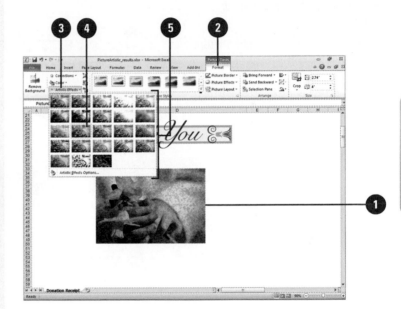

Adding a Quick Style to a Picture

Instead of changing individual attributes of a picture—such as shape, border, and effects—you can quickly add them all at once with the Picture Quick Style gallery. The Picture Quick Style gallery provides a variety of different formatting combinations to create a professional look. To quickly see if you like a Picture Quick Style, point to a thumbnail in the gallery to display a live preview of it in the selected shape. If you like it, you can apply it.

Add a Quick Style to a Picture

1. Click the picture you want to change.

2. Click the **Format** tab under Picture Tools.

3. Click the scroll up or down arrow, or click the **More** list arrow in the Picture Styles group to see additional styles.

   The current style appears highlighted in the gallery.

4. Point to a style.

   A live preview of the style appears in the current shape.

5. Click the style you want from the gallery to apply it to the selected picture.

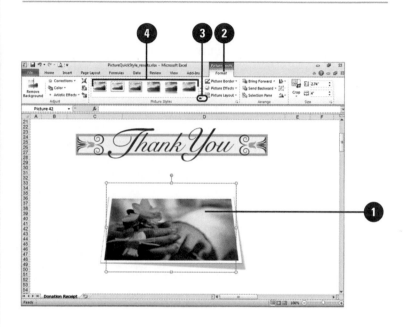

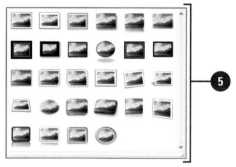

Did You Know?

You can save a shape as a picture in the PNG format. Right-click the shape, click Save As Picture, type a name, and then click Save.

Applying a Shape to a Picture

After you insert a picture into your document, you can select it and apply one of Office's shapes to it. The picture appears in the shape just like it has been cropped. The Crop to Shape gallery (**New!**) makes it easy to choose the shape you want to use. Live preview is not available with the Crop to Shape gallery. You can try different shapes to find the one you want. If you don't find the one you want, you can use the Reset Picture button to return the picture back to its original state.

Apply a Shape to a Picture

1. Click the picture you want to change.

2. Click the **Format** tab under Picture Tools.

3. Click the **Crop** button arrow, and then point to **Crop to Shape**.

4. Select the shape you want to apply to the selected picture.

Did You Know?

You can quickly return a picture back to its original form. Select the picture, click the Format tab, and then click the Reset Picture button.

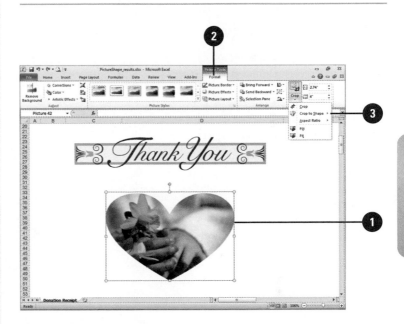

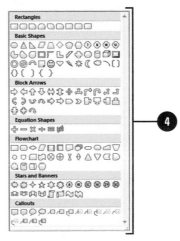

Applying a Border to a Picture

After you insert a picture, you can add and modify the picture border by changing individual outline formatting using the Picture Border button on the Format tab under Picture Tools. The Picture Border button works just like the Shape Outline button and provides similar options to add a border, select a border color, and change border width and style. You can try different border combinations to find the one you want. If you don't find one that works for you, you can use the No Outline command on the Picture Border gallery to remove it.

Apply a Border to a Picture

1. Click the picture you want to change.

2. Click the **Format** tab under Picture Tools.

3. Click the **Picture Border** button.

4. Click a color, or point to **Weight**, or **Dashes**, and then select a style, or click **More Lines** to select multiple options.

5. Drag a sizing handle to change the size or angle of the line or arrow.

Did You Know?

You can remove a border. Select the picture, click the Format tab, click the Picture Border button, and then click No Outline.

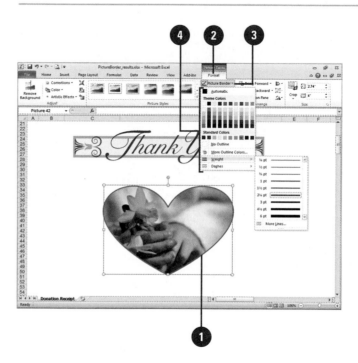

Applying Picture Effects

You can change the look of a picture by applying effects, such as shadows, reflections, glow, soft edges, and 3-D rotations. You can also apply effects to a shape by using the Picture Effects gallery for quick results, or by using the Format Shape dialog box for custom results. From the Picture Effects gallery, you can apply a built-in combination of 3-D effects or individual effects to a picture. To quickly see if you like a picture effect, point to a thumbnail in the Picture Effects gallery to display a live preview of it. If you like it, you can apply it. If you no longer want to apply a picture effect to an object, you can remove it. Simply select the picture, point to the effect type on the Picture Effects gallery, and then select the No effect type option.

Add an Effect to a Picture

1. Click the picture you want to change.

2. Click the **Format** tab under Picture Tools.

3. Click the **Picture Effects** button, and then point to one of the following:

   ◆ **Preset** to select No 3-D, one of the preset types, or More 3-D Settings.

   ◆ **Shadow** to select No Shadow, one of the shadow types, or More Shadows.

   ◆ **Reflection** to select No Reflection or one of the Reflection Variations.

   ◆ **Glow** to select No Glow, one of the Glow Variations, or More Glow Colors.

   ◆ **Soft Edges** to select No Soft Edges or a point size to determine the soft edge amount.

   ◆ **3-D Rotation** to select No Rotation, one of the rotation types, or More 3-D Settings.

   When you point to an effect, a live preview of the style appears in the current shape.

4. Click the effect you want from the gallery to apply it to the selected shape.

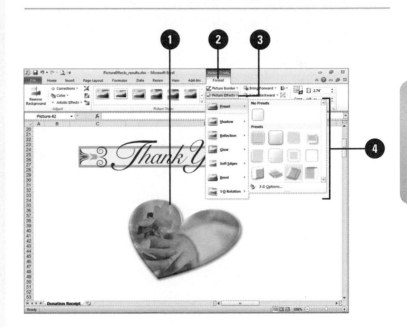

Modifying Picture Size

Once you have inserted a picture, clip art and other objects into your document, you can adapt them to meet your needs. Like any object, you can resize a picture. You can use the sizing handles to quickly resize a picture or use height and width options in the Size group on the Format tab to resize a picture more precisely. If you want to set unique or multiple options at the same time, you can use the Size and Position dialog box. These options allow you to make sure your pictures keep the same relative proportions as the original and lock size proportions.

Resize a Picture

1. Click the object you want to resize.

2. Drag one of the sizing handles to increase or decrease the object's size.

   ◆ Drag a middle handle to resize the object up, down, left, or right.

   ◆ Drag a corner handle to resize the object proportionally.

Resize a Picture Precisely

1. Click the object you want to resize.

2. Click the **Format** tab under Picture Tools.

3. Click the up and down arrows or enter a number (in inches) in the Height and Width boxes on the Ribbon and press Enter.

   If the **Lock aspect ratio** check box is selected in the Size and Position dialog box, height or width automatically changes when you change one of them. Click the **Size Dialog Box Launcher** to change the option.

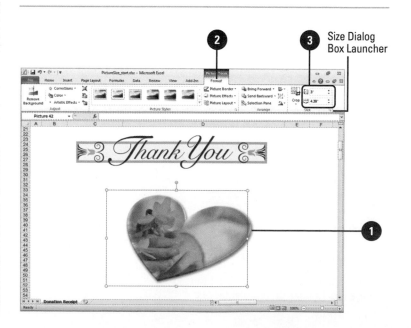

Size Dialog Box Launcher

Precisely Scale a Picture

① Click the object you want to resize.

② Click the **Format** tab under Picture Tools.

③ Click the **Size Dialog Box Launcher**.

④ To keep the picture proportional, select the **Lock aspect ratio** check box.

⑤ To keep the picture the same relative size, select the **Relative to original picture size** check box.

⑥ Click the up and down arrows or enter a number in the Height and Width boxes in one of the following:

   ◆ **Size.** Enter a height and width size in inches.

   ◆ **Scale.** Enter a percentage size.

   If the Lock aspect ratio check box is selected, height or width automatically changes when you change one of them.

⑦ If you want to remove your changes, click **Reset**.

⑧ Click **Close**.

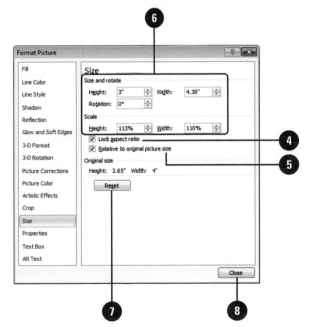

Did You Know?

Resizing bitmaps can cause distortion. Bitmap images are made up of dots, and do not lend themselves as easily to resizing because the dots can't expand and contract, which can lead to distortion. To avoid distortion, resize bitmaps proportionally and try to resize smaller instead of larger.

Compressing a Picture

Office allows you to compress pictures in order to minimize the file size of the image. In doing so, however, you may lose some visual quality, depending on the compression setting (**New!**). You can pick the resolution that you want for the pictures in a document based on where or how they'll be viewed (for example, on the Web or printed). You can also set other options, such as Delete cropped areas of picture, to get the best balance between picture quality and file size or automatically compress pictures when you save your document.

Compress a Picture

1. Click to select the pictures you want to compress.

2. Click the **Format** tab under Picture Tools.

3. Click the **Compress Pictures** button.

4. Select the **Apply only to this picture** check box to apply compression setting to only the selected picture. Otherwise, clear the check box to compress all pictures in your document.

5. Select or clear the **Delete cropped areas of pictures** check box to reduce file.

6. Click the **Print**, **Screen**, **E-mail**, or **Document** (**New!**) option to specify a target output.

7. Click **OK**.

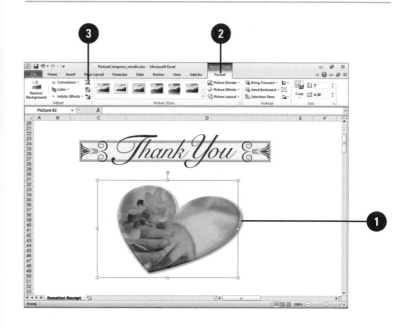

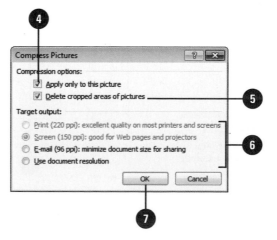

Correcting a Picture

Once you have inserted a picture, you can control the image's colors, brightness, and contrast using Picture tools. The brightness and contrast controls let you make simple adjustments to the tonal range of a picture. The brightness and contrast controls change a picture by an overall lightening or darkening of the image pixels. In addition, you can sharpen and soften pictures by a specified percentage (**New!**). You can experiment with the settings to get the look you want. If you don't like the look, you can use the Reset Picture button to return the picture back to its original starting point.

Change Brightness and Contrast or Sharpen and Soften

1. Click the picture you want to change.

2. Click the **Format** tab under Picture Tools.

3. Click the **Corrections** button, and then do one of the following:

   ◆ **Brightness and Contrast.** Click a brightness and contrast option.

   A positive brightness lightens the object colors by adding more white, while a negative brightness darkens the object colors by adding more black. A positive contrast increases intensity, resulting in less gray, while a negative contrast to decrease intensity, resulting in more gray.

   ◆ **Sharpen and Soften.** Click a sharpen and soften option.

4. To set custom correction percentages, click the **Corrections** button, click **Picture Corrections Options**, specify the options you want, and then click **Close**.

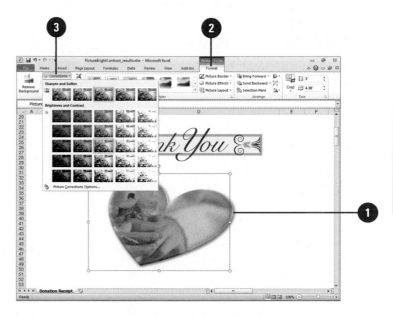

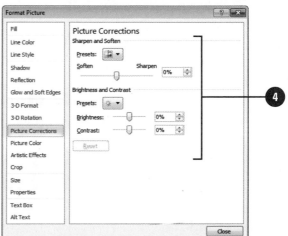

Recoloring a Picture

You can recolor clip art and other objects to match the color scheme of your document. For example, if you use a flower clip art as your business logo, you can change shades of pink in the spring to shades of orange in the autumn. The Color Picture Quick Style gallery (**New!**) provides a variety of different recolor formatting combinations. To quickly see if you like a Color Picture Quick Style, point to a thumbnail in the gallery to display a live preview of it in the selected shape. If you like it, you can apply it. You can also use a transparent background in your picture to avoid conflict between its background color and your document's background. With a transparent background, the picture takes on the same background as your document.

Recolor a Picture

① Click the picture whose color you want to change.

② Click the **Format** tab under Picture Tools.

③ Click the **Color** button.

④ Click one of the Color options.

 ◆ **Recolor.** Click an option to apply a color type:

 No Recolor. Click this option to remove a previous recolor.

 Grayscale. Converts colors into whites, blacks and shades of gray between black and white.

 Sepia. Converts colors into very light gold and yellow colors like a picture from the old west.

 Washout. Converts colors into whites and very light colors.

 Black and White. Converts colors into only white and black.

 ◆ **Color Saturation** or **Color Tone.** Click an option to apply a color saturation or tone based on the recolor selection.

 ◆ **More Variations.** Point to this option to select a specific color.

 ◆ **Picture Color Options.** Click this option to set custom recolor options by percentage.

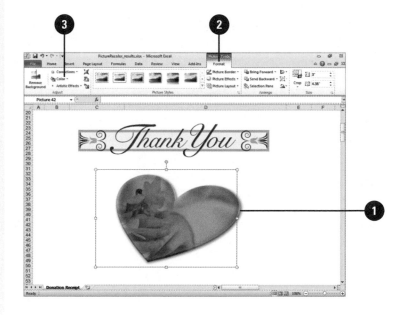

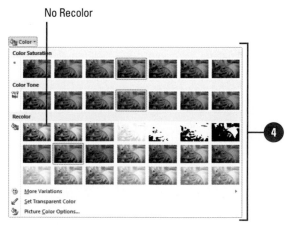

No Recolor

Set a Transparent Background

1. Click the picture you want to change.

2. Click the **Format** tab under Picture Tools.

3. Click the **Color** button, and then click **Set Transparent Color**.

4. Move the pointer over the object until the pointer changes shape.

5. Click the color you want to set as transparent.

6. Move the pointer over the picture where you want to apply the transparent color, and then click to apply it.

7. When you're done, click outside the image.

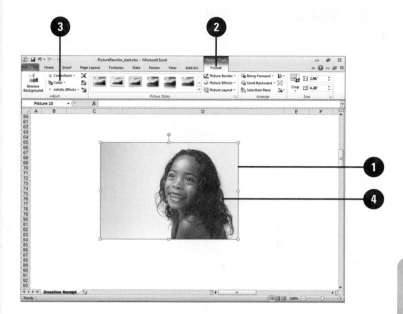

Did You Know?

Why is the Set Transparent Color command dimmed? Setting a color as transparent works only with bitmaps. If you are working with an object that is not a bitmap, you will not be able to use this feature.

You can't modify some pictures in Office. If the picture is a bitmap (.BMP, .JPG, .GIF, or .PNG), you need to edit its colors in an image editing program, such as Adobe Photoshop, Microsoft Paint, or Paint Shop Pro.

You can reset a picture back to its original state. Click the picture you want to reset, click the Format tab under Picture Tools, and then click the Reset Picture button.

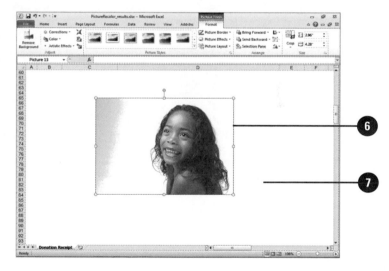

Cropping and Rotating a Picture

You can crop clip art to isolate just one portion of the picture. Because clip art uses vector image technology, you can crop even the smallest part of it and then enlarge it, and the clip art will still be recognizable. You can also crop bitmapped pictures, but if you enlarge the area you cropped, you lose picture detail. Use the Crop button to crop an image by hand. In addition, you can crop a picture while maintaining a selected resize aspect ratio (**New!**) or crop a picture based on a fill or fit (**New!**). You can also rotate a picture by increments or freehand.

Crop a Picture Quickly

1. Click the picture you want to crop.

2. Click the **Format** tab under Picture Tools.

3. Click the **Crop** button.

4. Drag the sizing handles until the borders surround the area you want to crop.

5. Click outside the image when you are finished.

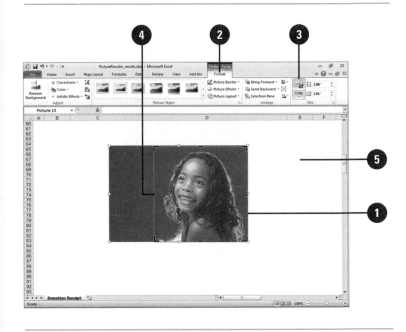

Crop a Picture with an Aspect Ratio

1. Click the picture you want to crop.

2. Click the **Format** tab under Picture Tools.

3. Click the **Crop** button arrow, point to **Aspect Ratio**, and then select an aspect ratio.

4. Drag the sizing handles until the borders surround the area you want to crop.

5. Click outside the image when you are finished.

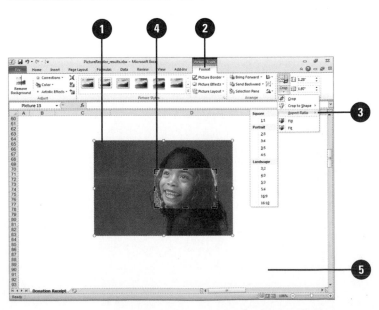

Crop a Picture with a Fill or Fit

① Click the picture you want to crop.

② Click the **Format** tab under Picture Tools.

③ Click the **Crop** button arrow, and then select an option:

◆ **Fill.** Resizes the picture so the entire picture area is filled while maintaining the aspect ratio. Any area outside of the picture area is cropped.

◆ **Fit.** Resizes the picture so the entire picture displays inside the picture area while maintaining the aspect ratio.

④ Drag the sizing handles until the borders surround the area you want to crop.

⑤ Click outside the image when you are finished.

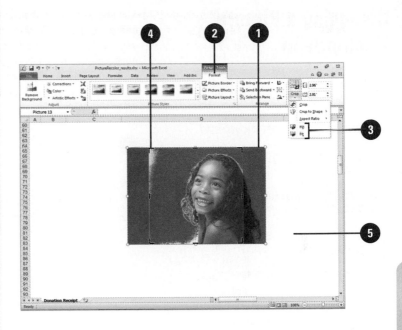

Rotate a Picture

① Click the object you want to rotate.

② Position the pointer (which changes to the Free Rotate pointer) over the green rotate lever at the top of the object, and then drag to rotate the object.

③ Click outside the object to set the rotation.

Did You Know?

You can rotate or flip a picture. Select the picture, click the Format tab, click the Rotate button, and then click Rotate Right 90, Rotate Left 90, Flip Vertical, Flip Horizontal, or click More Rotation Options.

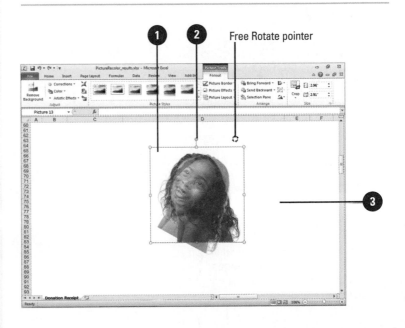

Free Rotate pointer

Removing a Picture Background

Sometimes you want to use an element from a picture instead of the entire picture. With the Remove Background command (**New!**), you can specify the element you want in a picture, and then remove the background. You can use automatic background removal or you can manually draw lines to specify which parts of the picture background you want to keep and which to remove.

Remove a Picture Background

1. Click the picture you want to change.

2. Click the **Format** tab under Picture Tools.

3. Click the **Remove Background** button.

4. Drag the handles on the marquee lines to specify the part of the picture you want to keep. The area outside the marquee gets removed.

5. To manually specify which areas to keep and which areas to remove, do the following:

    ◆ **Mark Areas to Keep.** Click the button, and then draw lines to specify which parts of the picture you do not want automatically removed.

    ◆ **Mark Areas to Remove.** Click the button, and then draw lines to specify which parts of the picture you do want removed in addition to those automatically marked.

    ◆ **Delete Mark.** Click the button, and then click marked lines to remove them.

6. Click the **Keep Changes** button to close and keep the removal or click the **Discard All Changes** button to close and cancel the automatic removal.

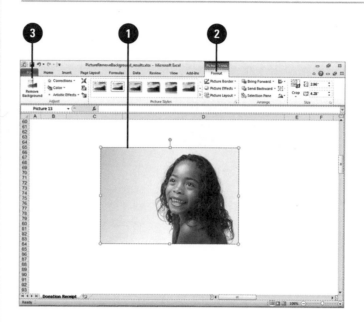

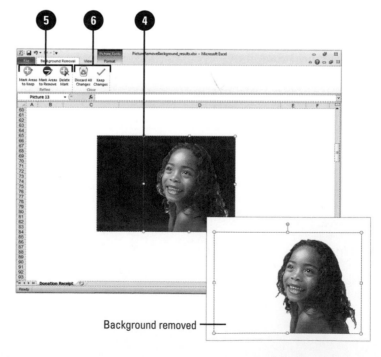

Background removed

Creating WordArt Text

The WordArt feature lets you create stylized text to draw attention to your most important words. Most users apply WordArt to a word or a short phrase, such as *Big Smiles*. You should apply WordArt to a document sparingly. Its visual appeal and unique look requires uncluttered space. When you use WordArt, you can choose from a variety of text styles that come with the WordArt Quick Style gallery, or you can create your own using tools in the WordArt Styles group. To quickly see if you like a WordArt Quick Style, point to a thumbnail in the gallery to display a live preview of it in the selected text. If you like it, you can apply it. You can also use the free angle handle (pink diamond) inside the selected text box to adjust your WordArt text angle.

Insert WordArt Text

1. Click the **Insert** tab.

2. Click the **WordArt** button, and then click one of the WordArt styles.

   A WordArt text box appears on the document with selected placeholder text.

3. Type the text you want WordArt to use.

   ◆ Drag a resize handle as needed to increase or decrease the size of the WordArt text box.

4. If applicable, use the Font and Paragraph options on the Home tab to modify the text you entered.

5. To edit WordArt text, click to place the insertion point where you want to edit, and then edit the text.

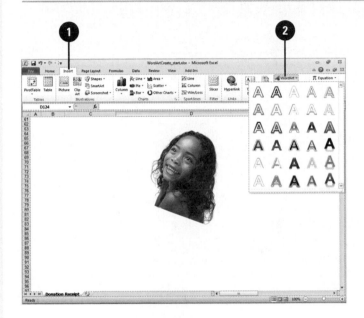

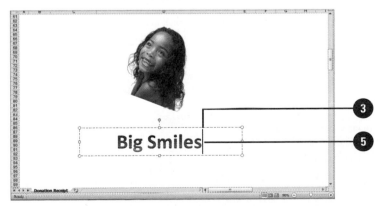

Did You Know?

You can convert text in a text box to WordArt. Select the text box, click the Format tab under Drawing Tools, and then click the WordArt text style you want from the Ribbon.

You can remove WordArt text. Select the WordArt text you want to remove, click the Format tab, click the Quick Styles button, and then click Clear WordArt.

Formatting WordArt Text

In addition to applying one of the preformatted WordArt styles, you can also create your own style by shaping your text into a variety of shapes, curves, styles, and color patterns. The WordArt Styles group gives you tools for changing the fill and outline of your WordArt text. To quickly see if you like a WordArt Style, point to a thumbnail in the gallery to display a live preview of it in the selected text. If you like it, you can apply it.

Apply a Different WordArt Style to Existing WordArt Text

1. Click the WordArt object whose style you want to change.

2. Click the **Format** tab under Drawing or WordArt Tools.

3. Click the scroll up or down arrow, or click the **More** list arrow in the WordArt Styles group to see additional styles.

   The current style appears highlighted in the gallery.

4. Point to a style.

   A live preview of the style appears in the current shape text.

5. Click the style you want from the gallery to apply it to the selected shape.

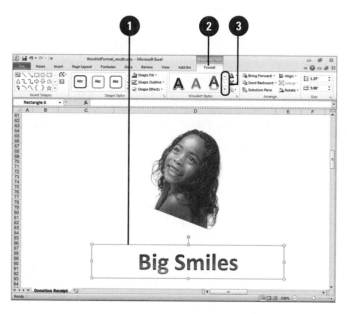

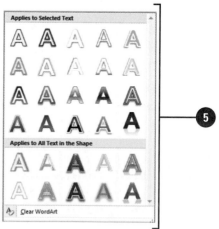

Did You Know?

You can add more formatting to WordArt text. Select the WordArt object, click the Home tab, and then use the formatting button in the Font and Paragraph groups.

You can change the WordArt fill color to match the background. Click the WordArt object, right-click the object, click Format Shape, click the Background option, and then click Close.

Apply a Fill to WordArt Text

1. Click the WordArt object you want to change.

2. Click the **Format** tab under Drawing or WordArt Tools.

3. Click the **Text Fill** or **Shape Fill** button arrow, and then click or point to one of the following:

   ◆ **Color** to select a theme or standard color.

   ◆ **No Fill** to remove a fill color.

   ◆ **Picture** to select a picture file.

   ◆ **Gradient** to select No Gradient, one of the shadow types, or More Gradients.

   ◆ **Texture** to select one of the texture types, or More Textures.

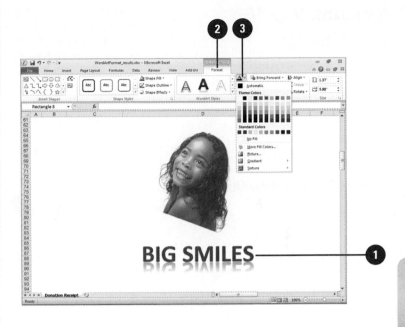

Apply an Outline to WordArt Text

1. Click the WordArt object you want to change.

2. Click the **Format** tab under Drawing or WordArt Tools.

3. Click the **Text Outline** or **Shape Outline** button arrow.

4. Click a color, or point to **Weight** or **Dashes**, and then select a style.

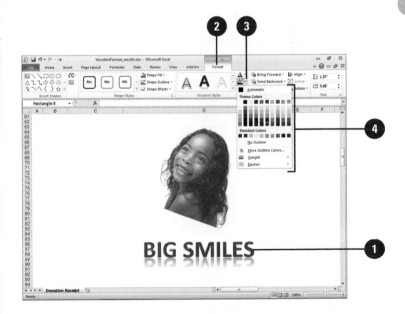

Applying WordArt Text Effects

You can change the look of WordArt text by applying effects, such as shadows, reflections, glow, soft edges, 3-D rotations, and transformations. You can apply effects to a shape by using the Text Effects gallery for quick results. From the Text Effects gallery you can apply a built-in combination of 3-D effects or individual effects to WordArt text. To quickly see if you like the effect, point to a thumbnail in the Text Effects gallery to display a live preview of it. If you like it, you can apply it. If you no longer want to apply the effect, you can remove it. Simply, select the WordArt text, point to the effect type on the Text Effects gallery, and then select the No effect type option.

Apply an Effect to WordArt Text

1. Click the WordArt object you want to change.

2. Click the **Format** tab under Drawing or WordArt Tools.

3. Click the **Text Effects** button.

   ◆ For Word, use the Shadow Effects and 3D Effects buttons.

4. Point to one of the following:

   ◆ **Shadow** to select No Shadow, one of the shadow types (Outer or Inner), or More Shadows.

   ◆ **Reflection** to select No Reflection or one of the Reflection Variations.

   ◆ **Glow** to select No Glow, one of the Glow Variations, or More Glow Colors.

   ◆ **Bevel** to select No Bevel, one of the bevel variations, or More 3-D Settings.

   ◆ **3-D Rotation** to select No Rotation, one of the rotation types (Parallel, Perspective, or Oblique), or More 3-D Settings.

   ◆ **Transform** to select No Transform, or one of the transform types (Follow Path or Warp).

5. Click the effect you want to apply to the selected shape.

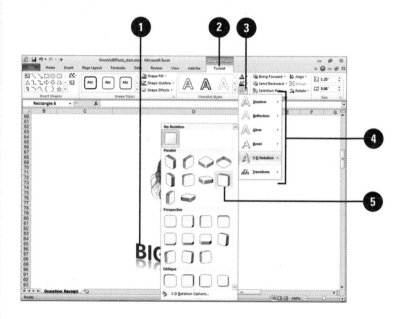

WordArt text effect

Modifying WordArt Text Position

You can apply a number of text effects to your WordArt objects that determine alignment and direction. The effects of some of the adjustments you make are more pronounced for certain WordArt styles than others. Some of these effects make the text unreadable for certain styles, so apply these effects carefully. You can apply effects to a shape by using the Format Shape dialog box for custom results. You can also use the free rotate handle (green circle) at the top of the selected text box to rotate your WordArt text.

Change WordArt Text Direction

1. Right-click the WordArt object you want to change, and then click **Format Shape** or **Format WordArt**.

2. If necessary, click **Text Box** in the left pane.

3. Click the **Vertical alignment** or **Horizontal alignment** list arrow, and then select an option: Top, Middle, Bottom, Top Center, Middle Center, or Bottom Center.

4. Click the **Text Direction** list arrow, and then select an option: **Horizontal, Rotate all text 90°, Rotate all text 270°,** or **Stacked**.

5. Click **Close**.

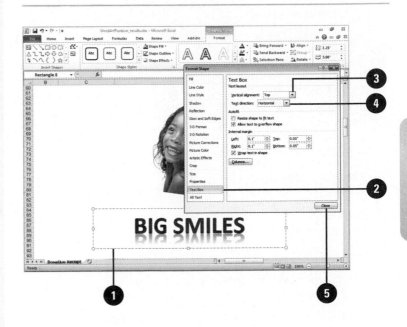

Rotate WordArt Text

1. Click the WordArt object you want to change.

2. Drag the free rotate handle (green circle) to rotate the object in any direction you want.

3. When you're done, release the mouse button.

4. Click outside the object to deselect it.

Creating SmartArt Graphics

SmartArt graphics allow you to create diagrams that convey processes or relationships. Office provides a wide variety of built-in SmartArt graphic types, including graphical lists, process, cycle, hierarchy, relationship, matrix, pyramid, picture (**New!**), and Office.com (**New!**). Using built-in SmartArt graphics makes it easy to create and modify charts without having to create them from scratch. To quickly see if you like a SmartArt graphic layout, point to a thumbnail in the gallery to display a live preview of it in the selected shape. If you like it, you can apply it.

Create a SmartArt Graphic

1. Click the **Insert** tab.

2. Click the **SmartArt** button.

   TIMESAVER *In a PowerPoint content placeholder, you can click the SmartArt icon to start.*

3. In the left pane, click a category, such as All, List, Process, Cycle, Hierarchy, Relationship, Matrix, or Pyramid.

4. In the middle pane, click a SmartArt graphic style type.

5. Click **OK**.

   The SmartArt graphic appears in the document.

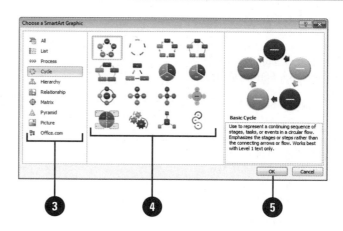

Did You Know?

You can change a SmartArt diagram type. Select the SmartArt graphic, click the Design tab under SmartArt Tools, click the More list arrow for Layouts, click More Layout, select a diagram type, and then click OK.

You cannot drag text into the Text pane. Although you can't drag text into the Text pane, you can copy and paste text.

You can create a blank SmartArt graphic. In the Text pane, press Ctrl+A to select all the placeholder text, and then press Delete.

SmartArt Graphic Purposes

Type	Purpose
List	Show non-sequential information
Process	Show steps in a process or timeline
Cycle	Show a continual process
Hierarchy	Show a decision tree or create an organization chart
Relationship	Illustrate connections
Matrix	Show how parts relate to a whole
Pyramid	Show proportional relationships up and down
Picture	Convert a picture to a SmartArt graphic (**New!**)
Office.com	Show SmartArt graphics from Office.com (**New!**)

6 Click the **Text Pane** button, or click the control with two arrows along the left side of the selection to show the Text pane.

7 Label the shapes by doing one of the following:

◆ Type text in the [Text] box.

You can use the arrow keys to move around the Text pane, or use the Promote or Demote buttons to indent.

◆ At the end of a line, press Enter to insert a line (shape), or select line text, and then press Delete to remove a line (shape).

◆ Click a shape, and then type text directly into the shape.

8 When you're done, click outside of the SmartArt graphic.

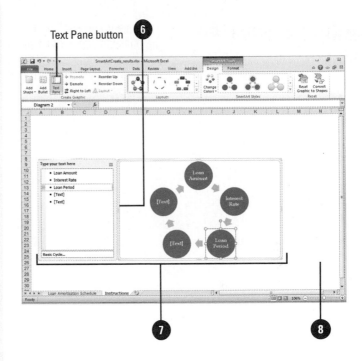
Text Pane button

Convert Text to a SmartArt Graphic

1 In PowerPoint, select the text box with the text you want to convert to a SmartArt graphic.

2 Click the **Home** tab.

3 Click the **Convert to SmartArt Graphic** button.

The gallery displays layouts designed for bulleted lists.

4 To view the entire list of layout, click **More SmartArt Graphics**.

5 Point to a layout.

A live preview of the style appears in the current shape.

6 Click the layout for the SmartArt graphic you want from the gallery to apply it to the selected shape.

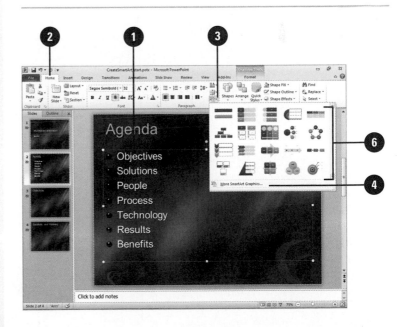

Formatting a SmartArt Graphic

If your current SmartArt graphics don't quite convey the message or look you want, use live preview to quickly preview layouts in the Quick Styles and Layout Styles groups and select the one you want. If you only want to change the color, you can choose different color schemes using theme colors by using the Change Color button. If the flow of a SmartArt graphic is not the direction you want, you can change the orientation.

Apply a Quick Style to a SmartArt Graphic

1. Click the SmartArt graphic you want to modify.

2. Click the **Design** tab under SmartArt Tools.

3. Click the scroll up or down arrow, or click the **More** list arrow in the Quick Styles group to see additional styles.

4. Point to a style.

   A live preview of the style appears in the current shape.

5. Click the layout for the SmartArt graphic you want from the gallery.

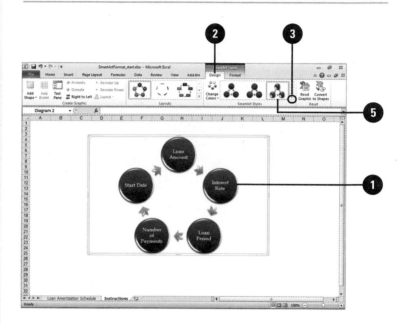

Change a Smart Graphic Orientation

1. Click the SmartArt graphic you want to modify.

2. Click the **Design** tab under SmartArt Tools.

3. Click the **Right to Left** button.

   The button toggles, so you can click it again to switch back.

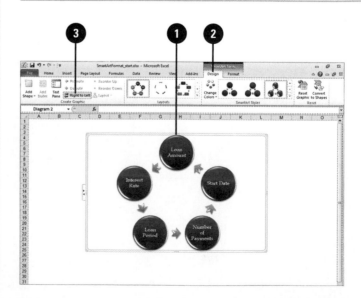

Change a SmartArt Graphic Layout

① Click the SmartArt graphic you want to modify.

② Click the **Design** tab under SmartArt Tools.

③ Click the scroll up or down arrow, or click the **More** list arrow in the Layout Styles group to see additional styles.

The gallery displays layouts designed for bulleted lists.

④ To view the entire list of diagram layouts, click **More Layouts**.

⑤ Point to a layout.

A live preview of the style appears in the current shape.

⑥ Click the layout for the SmartArt graphic you want from the gallery.

⑦ If you opened the entire list of layouts, click **OK**.

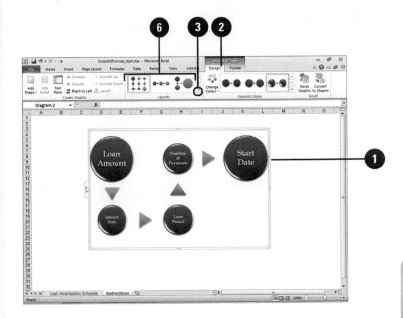

Change a SmartArt Graphic Colors

① Click the SmartArt graphic you want to modify.

② Click the **Design** tab under SmartArt Tools.

③ Click the **Change Colors** button.

The gallery displays the current layout with different theme colors.

④ Point to a style.

A live preview of the style appears in the current shape.

⑤ Click the layout for the SmartArt graphic you want from the gallery.

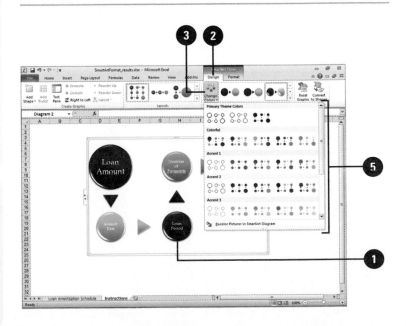

Modifying a SmartArt Graphic

After you create a SmartArt graphic, you can add, remove, change, or rearrange shapes to create a custom look. For shapes within a SmartArt graphic, you can change the shape from the Shape gallery or use familiar commands, such as Bring to Front, Send to Back, Align, Group, and Rotate, to create your own custom SmartArt graphic. If you no longer want a shape you've added, simply select it, and then press Delete to remove it.

Add a Shape to a SmartArt Graphic

1. Select the shape in the SmartArt graphic you want to modify.

2. Click the **Design** tab under SmartArt Tools.

3. Click the **Add Shape** button to insert a shape at the end, or click the **Add Shape** button arrow, and then select the position where you want to insert a shape.

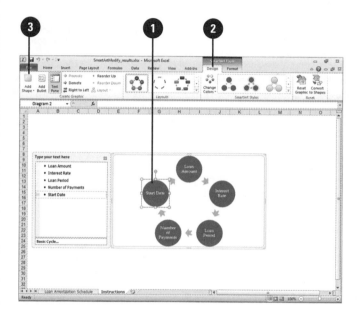

Change Shapes in a SmartArt Graphic

1. Select the shapes in the SmartArt graphic you want to modify.

2. Click the **Format** tab under SmartArt Tools.

3. Click the **Change Shape** button, and then click a shape.

Did You Know?

You can reset a SmartArt graphic back to its original state. Select the SmartArt graphic, click the Design tab under SmartArt Tools, and then click the Reset Graphic button.

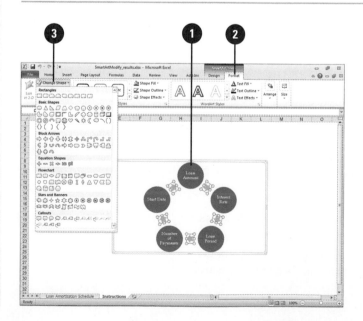

Adding Pictures to a SmartArt Graphic

With SmartArt graphic layouts (**New!**), you can insert pictures in the SmartArt shapes. In addition to the pictures, you can also add descriptive text using the Text pane or shape itself. The process is very simple. Insert a SmartArt picture layout, insert pictures, and then add descriptive text. If you already have pictures in your document, you can convert them to a SmartArt graphic.

Add a SmartArt Graphic to a Picture

1. Use either of the following to add pictures to a SmartArt graphic:

   ◆ **Create New.** Click the **Insert** tab, click the **SmartArt** button, click **Picture**, click a layout, and then click **OK**.

   ◆ **Convert Picture.** Select a picture, click the **Format** tab under Picture Tools, click the **Picture Layout** button, and then select a layout.

2. To add a shape, click the **Design** tab under SmartArt Tools, click the **Add Shape** button arrow, and then select the type of shape you want to add.

3. To add a picture, double-click a graphic placeholder, select a picture file, and then click **Insert**.

4. Label the shapes by doing one of the following:

   ◆ Type text in the [Text] box.

   ◆ Click a shape, and then type text directly into the shape.

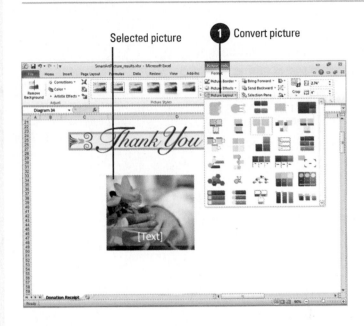

Selected picture

Convert picture

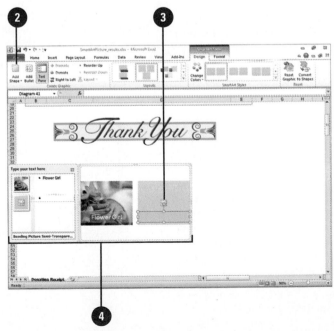

Creating an Organization Chart

An organization chart shows the reporting relationships between individuals in an organization. For example, you can show the relationship between a manager and employees within a company. You can create an organization chart using a SmartArt graphic or using Microsoft Organization Chart. A SmartArt graphic organization chart makes it easy to add shapes using the graphic portion or the Text pane. Like any SmartArt graphic, you can add special effects—such as soft edges, glows, or 3-D effects, and animation—to an organization chart.

Create an Organization Chart Using a SmartArt Graphic

1. Click the **Insert** tab.

2. Click the **SmartArt** button.

3. In the left pane, click **Hierarchy**.

4. Click an organization chart type.

5. Click **OK**.

6. Label the shapes by doing one of the following:

   ◆ Type text in the [Text] box.

   ◆ Click a shape, and then type text directly into the shape.

7. To add shapes from the Text pane, place the insertion point at the beginning of the text where you want to add a shape, type the text you want, press Enter, and then to indent the new shape, press Tab or to promote, press Shift+Tab.

   You can also click the Add Shape button arrow on the Design tab under SmartArt Tools, and then select the type of shape you want to add.

8. To change the layout or style, click the **Design** tab under SmartArt Tools, click the scroll up or down arrow, or click the **More** list arrow in the Layouts group or Quick Styles group, and then select a layout or style.

9. When you're done, click outside of the SmartArt graphic.

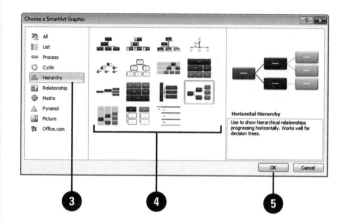

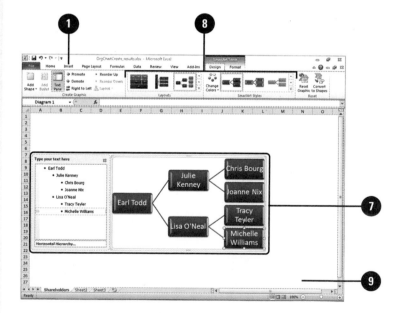

Inserting and Creating a Chart

A **chart** provides a visual, graphical representation of numerical data. Charts add visual interest and useful information represented by lines, bars, pie slices, or other markers. A group of data values from a worksheet row or column of data makes up a **data series**. Each data series has a unique color or pattern on the chart. Titles on the chart, horizontal (x-axis), and vertical (y-axis) identify the data. Gridlines are horizontal and vertical lines to help the reader determine data values in a chart. When you choose to place the chart on an existing sheet, rather than on a new sheet, the chart is called an **embedded object**. You can then resize or move it just as you would any graphic object. Start by choosing the chart type that is best suited for presenting your data. There are a wide variety of chart types, 2-D and 3-D formats, from which to choose.

Insert and Create a Chart

1. Select the data you want to use to create a chart.

2. Click the **Insert** tab.

3. Use one of the following methods:

    ◆ **Basic Chart Types.** Click a chart button (Column, Line, Pie, Bar, Area, Scatter, Other Charts) in the Charts group, and then click the chart type you want.

    ◆ **All Chart Types.** Click the **Charts Dialog Box Launcher**, click a category in the left pane, click a chart, and then click **OK**.

4. To change the chart type, click the **Change Chart Type** button on the Design tab under Chart Tools.

Did You Know?

Office uses Excel to embed a chart. Office programs now use Microsoft Excel to embed and display a chart.

You can reset chart formatting. Click the chart you want to reset, click the Format tab under Chart Tools, and then click the Reset to Match Style button.

You can delete a chart. Click the chart object, and then press Delete.

Charts Dialog Box Launcher

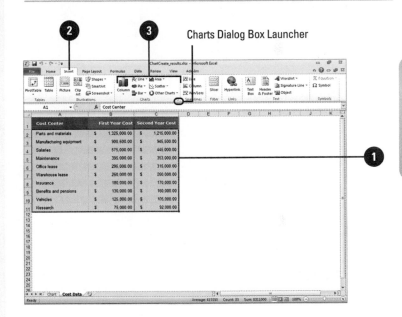

Select a Chart Category

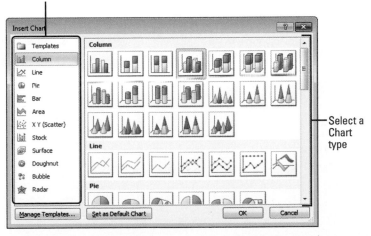

Select a Chart type

Changing a Chart Layout and Style

Office's pre-built chart layouts and styles can make your chart more appealing and visually informative. Start by choosing the chart type that is best suited for presenting your data. There are a wide variety chart types, available in 2-D and 3-D formats, from which to choose. For each chart type, you can select a predefined chart layout and style to apply the formatting you want. If you want to format your chart beyond the provided formats, you can customize a chart. Save your customized settings so that you can apply that chart formatting to any chart you create.

Change a Chart Layout or Style

1. Select the chart you want to change.

2. Click the **Design** tab under Chart Tools.

3. To change the chart layout, click the scroll up or down arrow, or click the **More** list arrow in the Chart Layouts group, and then click the layout you want.

4. To change the chart style, click the scroll up or down arrow, or click the **More** list arrow in the Chart Styles group, and then click the chart style you want.

Did You Know?

You can quickly access chart formatting options. Double-click a chart element to open a formatting dialog box (**New!**).

You can record macros with chart elements. When you use the macro recorder with charts, it now records formatting changes to charts and other objects (**New!**).

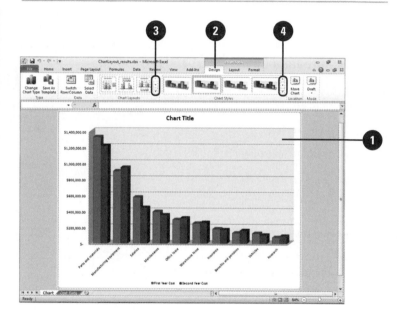

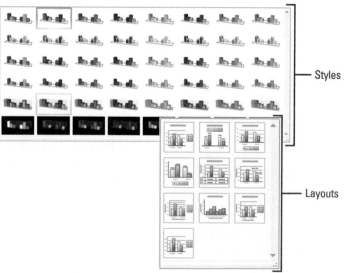

Styles

Layouts

Changing Chart Labels

The layout of a chart typically comes with a chart title, axis titles, and a legend. However, you can also include other elements, such as data labels, and a data table. A **legend** is a set of text labels that helps the reader connect the colors and patterns in a chart with the data they represent. Legend text is derived from the data series plotted within a chart. You can rename an item within a legend by changing the text in the data series. If the legend chart location doesn't work with the chart type, you can reposition the legend at the right, left, top or bottom of the chart or overlay the legend on top of the chart on the right or left side. **Data labels** show data values in the chart to make it easier for the reader to see, while a Data table shows the data values in an associated table next to the chart. If you want a customized look, you can set individual options using the Format dialog box.

Change the Chart Labels

① Select the chart you want to modify.

② Click the **Layout** tab under Chart Tools.

③ Click any of the following in the Labels section of the Ribbon:

- ◆ **Chart Tile** to display or position the main chart title. Double-click the text box to modify text.

- ◆ **Axis Titles** to display the horizontal and vertical axis titles.

- ◆ **Legend** to display or position the chart legend.

- ◆ **Data Labels** to show or hide data labels.

- ◆ **Data Table** to show or hide a data table along with the chart.

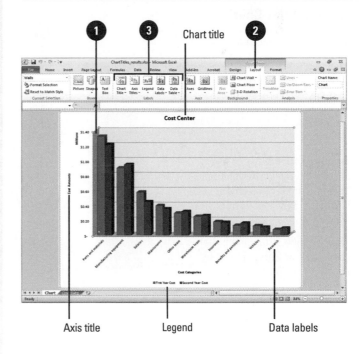

Chart title

Axis title   Legend   Data labels

Did You Know?

You can link a chart or axis title to a worksheet cell. On the chart, click the chart or axis title you want to link, click in the formula bar, type equal sign (=), select the worksheet cell that contains the data or text you want to display in the chart, and then press Enter.

Formatting Line and Bar Charts

If you're using a line or bar chart, you can add trendlines, series lines, drop lines, high-low lines, up/down bars, or error bars with different options to make the chart easier to read. **Trendlines** are graphical representations of trends in data that you can use to analyze problems of prediction. For example, you can add a trendline to forecast a trend toward rising revenue. **Series lines** connect data series in 2-D stacked bar and column charts. **Drop lines** extend a data point to a category in a line or area chart, which makes it easy to see where data markers begin and end. **High-low lines** display the highest to the lowest value in each category in 2-D charts. Stock charts are examples of high-low lines and up/down bars. **Error bars** show potential error amounts graphically relative to each data marker in a data series. Error bars are usually used in statistical or scientific data.

Format Line and Bar Charts

1. Select the line or bar chart you want to modify.

2. Click the **Layout** tab under Chart Tools.

3. In the Analysis group, click any of the following:

   ◆ **Trendline** to remove or add different types of trendlines: Linear, Exponential, Linear Forecast, and Two Period Moving Average.

   ◆ **Lines** to hide Drop Lines, High-Low Lines or Series Lines, or show series lines on a 2-D stacked Bar/Column Pie or Pie or Bar of Pie chart.

   ◆ **Up/Down Bars** to hide Up/Down Bars, or show Up/Down Bars on a line chart.

   ◆ **Error Bars** to hide error bars or show error bars with using Standard Error, Percentage, or Standard Deviation.

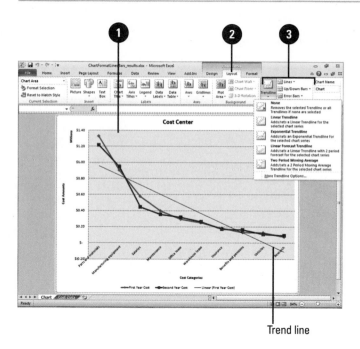

Trend line

Editing Chart Data

You can edit chart data in a worksheet one cell at a time, or you can manipulate a range of data. If you're not sure what data to change to get the results you want, use the Edit Data Source dialog box to help you. In previous versions, you were limited to 32,000 data points in a data series for 2-D charts. Now you can have as much as your memory to store (**New!**). You can work with data ranges by series, either Legend or Horizontal. The Legend series is the data range displayed on the axis with the legend, while the Horizontal series is the data range displayed on the other axis. Use the Collapse Dialog button to temporarily minimize the dialog to select the data range you want. After you select your data, click the Expand Dialog button to return back to the dialog box.

Edit the Data Source

① Click the chart you want to modify.

② Click the **Design** tab under Chart Tools.

③ Click the **Select Data** button on the Design tab under Chart Tools.

④ In the Select Data Source dialog box, use any of the following:

◆ **Chart data range.** Displays the data range of the plotted chart.

◆ **Switch Row/Column.** Click to switch plotting the data series from rows or columns.

◆ **Add.** Click to add a new Legend data series to the chart.

◆ **Edit.** Click to make changes to a Legend or Horizontal series.

◆ **Remove.** Click to remove the selected Legend data series.

◆ **Move Up and Move Down.** Click to move a Legend data series up or down in the list.

◆ **Hidden and Empty Cells.** Click to plot hidden data and determine what to do with empty cells.

⑤ Click **OK**.

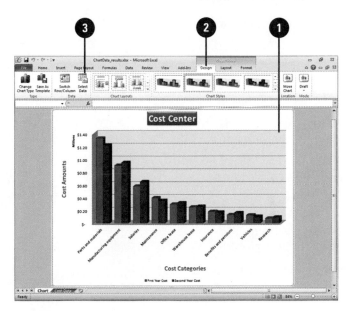

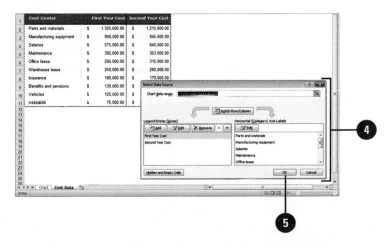

Saving a Chart Template

A chart template file (.crtx) saves all the customization you made to a chart for use in other documents. You can save any chart in a document as a chart template file and use it to form the basis of your next document chart, which is useful for standard company financial reporting. Although you can store your template anywhere you want, you may find it handy to store it in the Templates/Charts folder that Microsoft Office uses to store its templates. If you store your design templates in the Templates/Charts folder, those templates appear as options when you insert or change a chart type using My Templates. When you create a new chart or want to change the chart type of an existing chart, you can apply a chart template instead of re-creating it.

Create a Custom Chart Template

1. Click the chart you want to save as a template.

2. Click the **Design** tab under Chart Tools.

3. Click the **Save As Template** button.

4. Make sure the Charts folder appears in the Save in box.

   Microsoft Office templates are typically stored in the following location:

   Windows 7 or Vista. C:/Users/*your name*/AppData/Microsoft/Roaming/Templates/Charts

   Windows XP. C:/Documents and Settings/*your name*/Application Data/Microsoft/Templates/Charts

5. Type a name for the chart template.

6. Click **Save**.

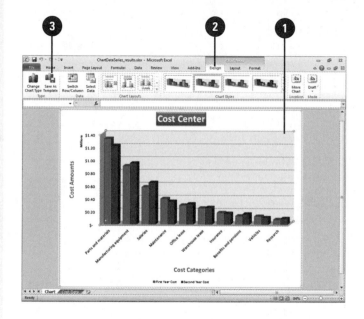

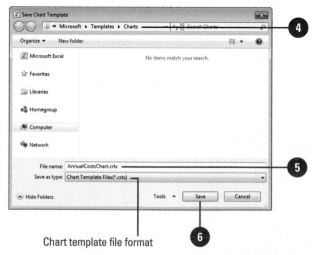

Chart template file format

Adding Shapes to Office Documents

Introduction

When you want to add objects to a document, you can use Microsoft Office as a drawing package. Office provides a wide range of predesigned shapes, line options or freeform tools that allow you to draw, size, and format your own shapes and forms.

You can add several types of drawing objects to your Office documents—shapes, text boxes, lines, and freeforms. **Shapes** are preset objects, such as stars, circles, or ovals. **Text boxes** are objects with text, a shape without a border. **Lines** are simply the straight or curved lines (arcs) that can connect two points or are used as arrows. **Freeforms** are irregular curves or polygons that you can create as a free-hand drawing.

Once you create a drawing object, you can move, resize, nudge, copy or delete it on your documents. You can also change its style by adding color, creating a fill pattern, rotating it, and applying a shadow or 3-D effect. Take a simple shape and by the time you are done adding various effects, it could become an attractive piece of graphic art for your document. If you'd like to use it later, you can save it to the Clip Organizer.

Object placement on your documents is a key factor to successfully communicating your message. To save time and effort, multiple objects should be grouped if they are to be considered one larger object. Grouping helps you make changes later on, or copy your objects to another document. Office has the ability to line up your objects with precision—rulers and guides are part of the alignment process to help you. By grouping and aligning, you are assured that your drawing objects will be accurately placed.

What You'll Do

Draw and Resize Shapes

Add Text to a Shape

Create and Edit Freeforms

Add a Quick Style to a Shape and Shape Text

Apply Fill Colors and Shape Effects

Apply Picture, Texture and Gradient Fills

Distribute Objects and Align to Grids and Guides

Change Stacking Order

Rotate and Flip Objects

Group and Ungroup Objects

Select Objects Using the Selection Pane

Drawing and Resizing Shapes

Office supplies ready-made shapes, ranging from hearts to lightning bolts to stars. The ready-made shapes are available directly on the Shapes gallery on the Insert and Format tabs. Once you have placed a shape on a document, you can resize it using the sizing handles. Many shapes have an **adjustment handle**, a small yellow or pink diamond located near a resize handle that you can drag to alter the shape. For precision when resizing, use the Size Dialog Box Launcher to specify the new size of the shape.

Draw a Shape

1. Click the **Insert** tab.

2. Click the **Shapes** button.

3. Click the shape you want to draw.

4. Drag the pointer on the document where you want to place the shape until the drawing object is the shape and size that you want.

   The shape you draw uses the line and fill color defined by the document's theme.

   TIMESAVER *To draw a proportional shape, hold down Shift as you drag the pointer.*

Did You Know?

You can quickly delete a shape. Click the shape to select it, and then press Delete.

You can draw a perfect circle or square. To draw a perfect circle or square, click the Oval or Rectangle button on the Shapes gallery, and then press and hold Shift as you drag.

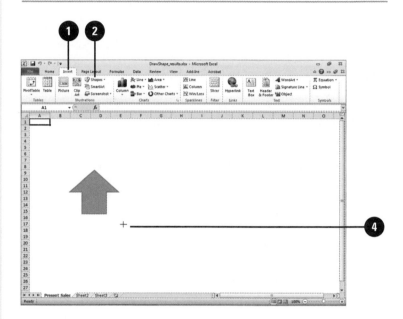

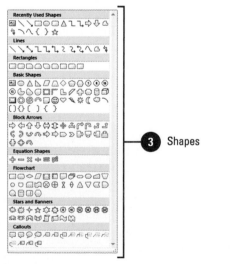

3 Shapes

Resize a Shape

1. Select the shape you want to resize.

2. Drag one of the sizing handles.

   ◆ To resize the object in the vertical or horizontal direction, drag a sizing handle on the side of the selection box.

   ◆ To resize the object in both the vertical and horizontal directions, drag a sizing handle on the corner of the selection box.

   ◆ To resize the object with precise measurements, click the **Format** tab under Drawing Tools, and then specify exact height and width settings in the Size group.

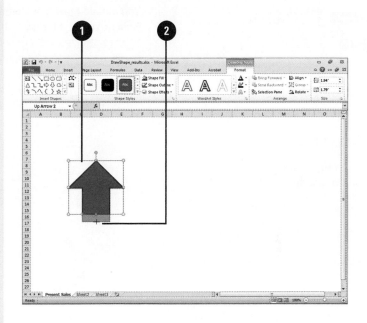

Adjust a Shape

1. Select the shape you want to adjust.

2. Click one of the adjustment handles (small yellow diamonds), and then drag the handle to alter the form of the shape.

Did You Know?

You can replace a shape. Replace one shape with another, while retaining the size, color, and orientation of the shape. Click the shape you want to replace, click the Format tab, click the Edit Shape button, point to Change Shape, and then click the new shape you want.

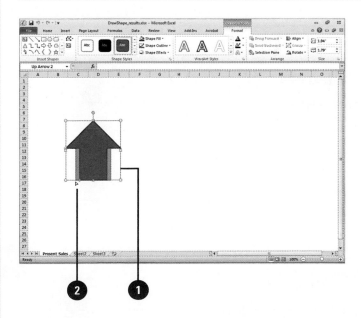

Adding Text to a Shape

You can add text to a shape in the same way you add text to a text box. Simply, select the shape object, and then start typing. Shapes range from rectangles and circles to arrows and stars. When you place text in a shape, the text becomes part of the object. If you rotate or flip the shape, the text rotates or flips too. You can use tools, such as an alignment button or Font Style, on the Mini-Toolbar and Home tab to format the text in a shape like the text in a text box.

Add Text to a Shape

1. Select the shape in which you want to add text.

2. Type the text you want.

3. To edit the text in a shape, click the text to place the insertion point, and then edit the text.

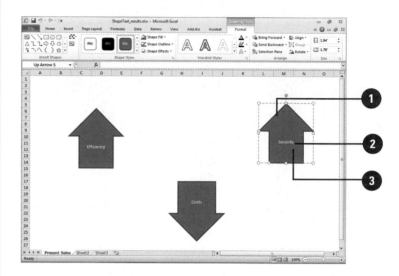

Create a Text Box

1. Click the **Insert** tab.

2. Click the **Text Box** button.

3. Perform one of the following:

   ◆ To add text that wraps, drag to create a box, and then start typing.

   ◆ To add text that doesn't wrap, click and then start typing.

4. To delete a text box, select it, and then press Delete.

5. Click outside the selection box to deselect the text box.

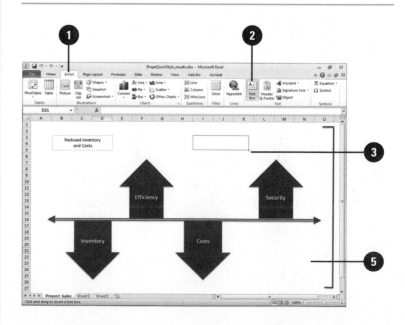

Creating and Editing Freeforms

When you need to create a customized shape, use the Office freeform tools. Choose a freeform tool from the Lines category in the list of shapes. Freeforms are like the drawings you make with a pen and paper, except that you use a mouse for your pen and a document for your paper. A freeform shape can either be an open curve or a closed curve. You can edit a freeform by using the Edit Points command to alter the vertices that create the shape.

Draw a Freeform Polygon

1. Click the **Insert** tab.

2. Click the **Shapes** button and then click **Freeform** in the Shapes gallery under Lines.

3. Click the document where you want to place the first vertex of the polygon.

4. Move the pointer, and then click to place the second point of the polygon. A line joins the two points.

   ◆ To draw a line with curves, drag a line instead of clicking in steps 3 and 4.

5. Continue moving the mouse pointer and clicking to create additional sides of your polygon.

6. Finish the polygon. For a closed polygon, click near the starting point. For an open polygon, double-click the last point in the polygon.

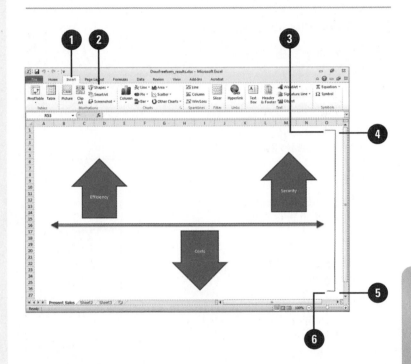

Did You Know?

You can convert a shape to a freeform. Select the shape, click the Edit Shape button, and then click Convert To Freeform.

You can switch between a closed curve and an open curve. Right-click the freeform drawing, and then click Close Path or Open Path.

For Your Information

Modifying a Freeform

Each vertex indicated by a black dot (a corner in an irregular polygon and a bend in a curve) has two attributes: its position, and the angle at which the curve enters and leaves it. You can move the position of each vertex and control the corner or bend angles. You can also add or delete vertices as you like. When you delete a vertex, Office recalculates the freeform and smooths it among the remaining points. Similarly, if you add a new vertex, Office adds a corner or bend in your freeform. To edit a freeform, click the freeform object, click the Format tab under Drawing Tools, click the Edit Shape button, click Edit Points, modify any of the points (move or delete), and then click outside to set the new shape.

Adding a Quick Style to a Shape

Instead of changing individual attributes of a shape—such as shape fill, shape outline, and shape effects—you can quickly add them all at once with the Shape Quick Style gallery. The Shape Quick Style gallery provides a variety of different formatting combinations. To quickly see if you like a Shape Quick Style, point to a thumbnail in the gallery to display a live preview of it in the selected shape. If you like it, you can apply it.

Add a Quick Style to a Shape

1. Select the shapes you want to modify.

2. Click the **Format** tab under Drawing Tools.

3. Click the scroll up or down arrow, or click the **More** list arrow in the Shapes Styles group to see additional styles.

   The current style appears highlighted in the gallery.

4. Point to a style.

   A live preview of the style appears in the current shape.

5. Click the style you want from the gallery to apply it to the selected shape.

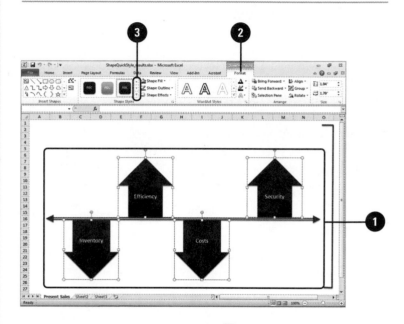

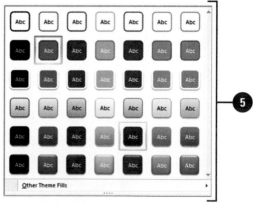

Did You Know?

You can add a Quick Style to a text box. A shape is a text box without a fill and outline (border), so you can apply a Quick Style to a text box using the same steps.

Adding a Quick Style to Shape Text

Instead of changing individual attributes of text in a shape, such as text fill, text outline, and text effects, you can quickly add them all at once with the WordArt Quick Style gallery. The WordArt Quick Style gallery provides a variety of different formatting combinations. To quickly see if you like a WordArt Quick Style, point to a thumbnail in the gallery to display a live preview of it in the selected shape. If you like it, you can apply it.

Add a Quick Style to Shape Text

1. Select the shapes with the text you want to modify.

2. Click the **Format** tab under Drawing Tools.

3. Click the scroll up or down arrow, or click the **More** list arrow in the WordArt Styles group to see additional styles.

   The current style appears highlighted in the gallery.

4. Point to a style.

   A live preview of the style appears in the current shape text.

5. Click the style you want from the gallery to apply it to the selected shape.

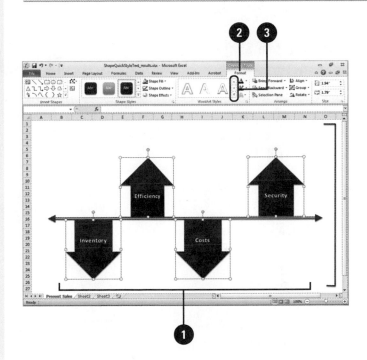

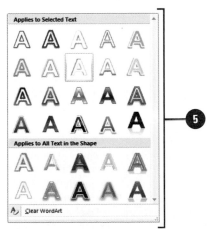

Did You Know?

You can arrange shapes in a SmartArt graphic. Select the shape in the SmartArt graphic, click the Format tab under SmartArt Tools, click the Arrange button, and then use any of the arrange button options: Bring To Front, Send To Back, Align, Group, or Rotate.

You can edit a SmartArt graphic shape in 2-D. Select the SmartArt graphic with the 3-D style, click the Format tab under SmartArt Tools, and then click the Edit In 2-D button.

Applying Color Fills

When you create a closed drawing object such as a square, it applies the Shape Fill color to the inside of the shape, and the Shape Outline color to the edge of the shape. A line drawing object uses the Shape Outline color. You can set the Shape Fill to be a solid, gradient, texture or picture, and the Shape Outline can be a solid or gradient. If you want to make multiple changes to a shape at the same time, the Format Shape dialog box allows you to do everything in one place. If the solid color appears too dark, you can make the color fill more transparent. If you no longer want to apply a shape fill to an object, you can remove it.

Apply a Color Fill to a Shape

1. Select the shape you want to modify.

2. Click the **Format** tab under Drawing Tools.

3. Click the **Shape Fill** button.

4. Select the fill color option you want.

5. To remove a color fill, click the **Shape Fill** button, and then click **No Fill**.

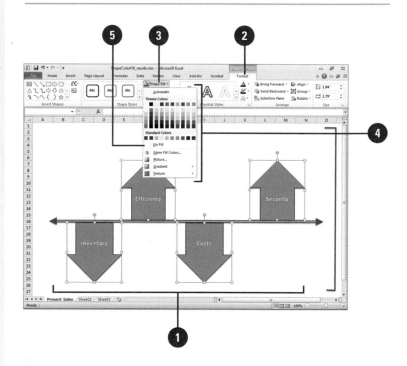

Did You Know?

You can set the color and line style for an object as the default. Right-click the object, and then click Set As Default Shape. Any new objects you create will use the same styles.

You can use the document background as the fill for a shape. Right-click the object, click Format Shape, click Fill in the left pane, click the Background option, and then click Close.

You can undo changes made in the Format Shape dialog box. Since changes made in the Shape Format dialog box are instantly applied, it's not possible to Cancel the dialog box. To remove changes, click the Undo button on the Quick Access Toolbar.

For Your Information

Formatting a SmartArt Shape

In the same way you can apply shape fills, outlines, and effects to a shape, you can also apply them to shapes in a SmartArt graphic. You can modify all or part of the SmartArt graphic by using the Shape Fill, Shape Outline, and Shape Effects buttons. Shape Fill can be set to be a solid, gradient, texture or picture, or set the Shape Outline to be a solid or gradient. In addition, you can change the look of a SmartArt graphic by applying effects, such as glow and soft edges. If a shape in a SmartArt graphic contains text, you can use WordArt style galleries to modify shape text.

Apply a Shape Color Fill with a Transparency

① Right-click the shape you want to modify, and then click **Format Shape** or **Format AutoShape**.

② In the left pane, click **Fill**.

③ Click the **Solid fill** option.

④ Click the **Color** button, and then select the fill color you want.

⑤ Drag the **Transparency** slider or enter a number from 0 (fully opaque) to 100 (fully transparent).

All your changes are instantly applied to the shape.

⑥ Click **Close**.

TROUBLE? *To cancel changes, click the Undo button on the Quick Access Toolbar.*

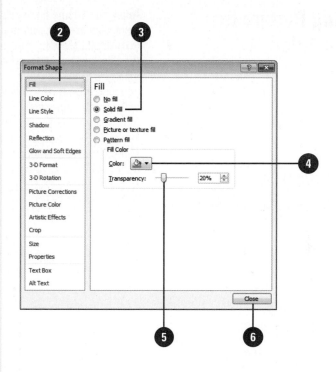

Apply a Color Outline to a Shape

① Select the shape you want to modify.

② Click the **Format** tab under Drawing Tools.

③ Click the **Shape Outline** button.

④ Select the outline color you want.

⑤ To remove an outline color, click the **Shape Outline** button, and then click **No Outline**.

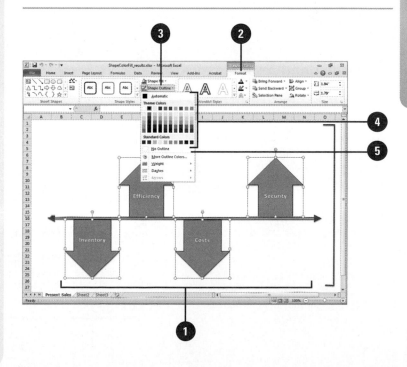

Applying Picture or Texture Fills

Applying a shape fill to a drawing object can add emphasis or create a point of interest in your document. You can insert a picture or clip art or texture into a shape. You can insert a picture from a file or clip art from the Clip Art task pane, or paste one in from the Office Clipboard. Stretch a picture or texture to fit across the selected shape or repeatedly tile it horizontally and vertically to fill the shape. When you stretch a image, you can also set offsets, which determine how much to scale a image to fit a shape relative to the edges. A positive offset number moves the image edge toward the center of the shape, while a negative offset number moves the image edge away from the shape. If the image appears too dark, you can make the picture more transparent.

Apply a Picture or Texture Fill to a Shape

1. Select the shape you want to modify.

2. Click the **Format** tab under Drawing Tools.

3. Click the **Shape Fill** button.

   ◆ Click **Picture**, locate and select a picture file you want, and then click **Insert**.

   ◆ Point to **Texture**, and then select a texture.

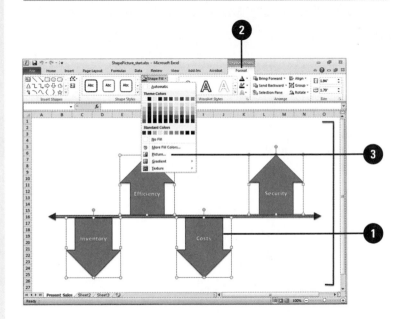

Did You Know?

You can apply a custom picture fill.
Right-click the object you want to modify, click Format Shape, click Fill, click the Picture Or Texture Fill option, click File, Clipboard, or Clip Art to select a picture, select the tile, stretch, and transparency options you want, and then click Close.

You can apply a custom texture fill.
Right-click the object you want to modify, click Format Shape, click Fill, click the Picture Or Texture Fill option, click the Texture button, select a texture, select the offset, scale, alignment, mirror and transparency options you want, and then click Close.

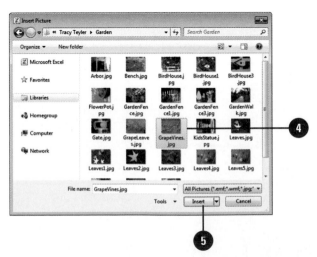

Applying Gradient Fills

Gradients are made up of two or more colors that gradually fade into each other. They can be used to give depth to a shape or create realistic shadows. Apply a gradient fill to a shape—now including lines—by using a gallery or presets for quick results, or by using the Format Shape dialog box for custom results. A gradient is made up of several gradient stops, which are used to create non-linear gradients. If you want to create a gradient that starts blue and goes to green, add two gradient stops, one for each color. Gradient stops consist of a position, a color, and a transparency percentage.

Apply a Gradient Fill to a Shape

1. Select the shape you want to modify.

2. Click the **Format** tab under Drawing Tools.

3. Click the **Shape Fill** button.

4. Point to **Gradient**, and then select a gradient from the gallery.

   Four gradient modes are available: linear (parallel bands), radial (radiate from center), rectangle (radiate from corners), and path (radiate along path).

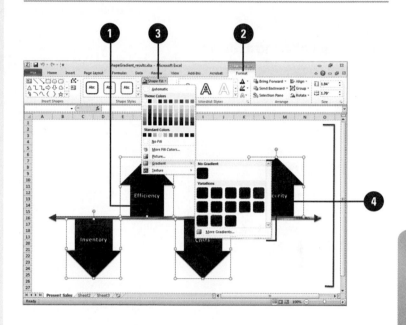

Apply a Gradient Fill with Presets

1. Right-click the shape you want to modify, and then click **Format Shape** or **Format AutoFormat**.

2. In the left pane, click **Fill**.

3. Click the **Gradient fill** option.

4. Click the **Preset colors** button arrow, and then select the built-in gradient fill you want.

   All your changes are instantly applied to the shape.

5. Click **Close**.

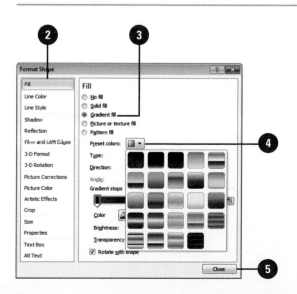

Applying Shape Effects

You can change the look of a shape by applying effects, like shadows, reflections, glow, soft edges, bevels, and 3-D rotations. Apply effects to a shape by using the Shape Effects gallery for quick results, or by using the Format Shape dialog box for custom results. From the Shape Effects gallery you can apply a built-in combination of 3-D effects or individual effects to a shape. To quickly see if you like a shape effect, point to a thumbnail in the Shape Effects gallery to display a live preview of it in the selected shape. If you like it, you can apply it. If you no longer want to apply a shape effect to an object, you can remove it. Simply select the shape, point to the effect type in the Shape Effects gallery, and then select the No effect type option.

Add a Preset Effect to a Shape

1. Select the shape you want to modify.

2. Click the **Format** tab under Drawing Tools.

3. Click the **Shape Effects** button, and then point to **Preset**.

   ◆ For Word, use the Shadow Effects and 3D Effects buttons.

   The current effect appears highlighted in the gallery.

4. Point to an effect.

   A live preview of the style appears in the current shape.

5. Click the effect you want from the gallery to apply it to the selected shape.

6. To remove the preset effect, click the **Shape Effects** button, point to **Preset**, and then click **No Presets**.

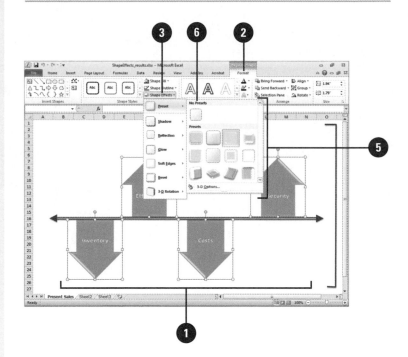

Did You Know?

3-D effects take precedence. If you add a 3-D effect, such as a bevel or 3-D rotation, to a shape and then add soft edges, the soft edge effect doesn't appear in the shape until you delete the 3-D effect.

Add Individual Effects to a Shape

1. Select the shape you want to modify.

2. Click the **Format** tab under Drawing Tools.

   ◆ For Word, use the Shadow Effects and 3D Effects buttons.

3. Click the **Shape Effects** button, and then point to one of the following:

   ◆ **Shadow** to select No Shadow, one of the shadow types (Outer, Inner, or Perspective), or More Shadows.

   ◆ **Reflection** to select No Reflection or one of the Reflection Variations.

   ◆ **Glow** to select No Glow, one of the Glow Variations, or More Glow Colors.

   ◆ **Soft Edges** to select No Soft Edges, or a point size to determine the soft edge amount.

   ◆ **Bevel** to select No Bevel, one of the bevel variations, or More 3-D Settings.

   ◆ **3-D Rotation** to select No Rotation, one of the rotation types (Parallel, Perspective, or Oblique), or More 3-D Settings.

   When you point to an effect, a live preview of the style appears in the current shape.

4. Click the effect you want from the gallery to apply it to the selected shape.

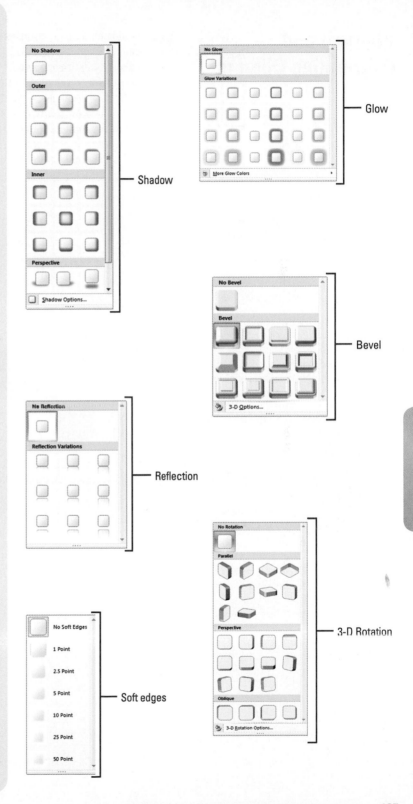

Shadow

Glow

Reflection

Bevel

Soft edges

3-D Rotation

Aligning and Distributing Objects

In addition to using grids and guides to align objects to a specific point, you can align a group of objects to each other. The Align commands make it easy to align two or more objects relative to each other vertically to the left, center, or right, or horizontally from the top, middle, or bottom. To evenly align several objects to each other across the document, either horizontally or vertically, select them and then choose a distribution option. Before you select an align command, specify how you want Office to align the objects. You can align the objects in relation to the document or to the selected objects.

Distribute Objects

1. Select the objects you want to distribute.

2. Click the **Format** tab under Drawing Tools.

3. Click the **Align** button.

4. On the Align menu, click the alignment method you want.

   ◆ Click **Snap to Grid** if you want the objects to align relative to the document grid.

   ◆ Click **Snap to Shape** if you want the objects to align relative to each other.

5. On the Align submenu, click the distribution command you want.

   ◆ Click **Distribute Horizontally** to evenly distribute the objects horizontally.

   ◆ Click **Distribute Vertically** to evenly distribute the objects vertically.

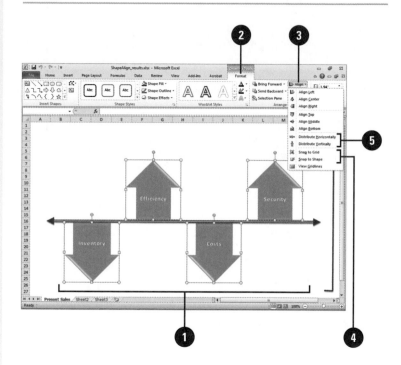

Align Objects with Other Objects

1. Select the objects you want to align.

2. Click the **Format** tab under Drawing Tools.

3. Click the **Align** button.

4. On the Align menu, click the alignment method you want.

   ◆ Click **Snap to Grid** if you want the objects to align relative to the document grid.

   ◆ Click **Snap to Shape** if you want the objects to align relative to each other.

5. On the Align menu, click the alignment command you want.

   ◆ Click **Align Left** to line up the objects with the left edge of the selection or document.

   ◆ Click **Align Center** to line up the objects with the center of the selection or document.

   ◆ Click **Align Right** to line up the objects with the right edge of the selection or document.

   ◆ Click **Align Top** to line up the objects with the top edge of the selection or document.

   ◆ Click **Align Middle** to line up the objects vertically with the middle of the selection or document.

   ◆ Click **Align Bottom** to line up the objects with the bottom of the selection or document.

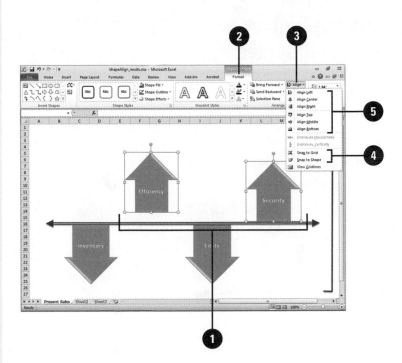

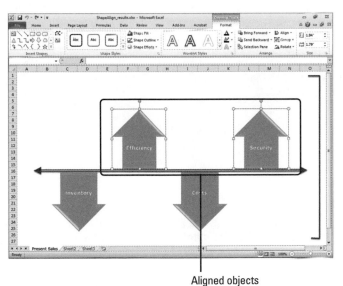

Aligned objects

Aligning Objects to Grids and Guides

PowerPoint guides can align an individual object or a group of objects to a vertical or horizontal guide. Turning on the visible grid or visible guides option makes it easier to create, modify, and align a shape. Within the Grid and Guides dialog box, you can select from a variety of options, such as snapping objects to the grid or to other objects and displaying drawing and smart guides (**New!**) on-screen. To align several objects to a guide, you first turn the guides on. Then you adjust the guides and drag the objects to align them to the guide.

Turn On or Turn Off the Visible Grid or Guides

1. In PowerPoint, click the **Home** tab.

2. Click the **Arrange** button, point to **Align**, and then click **Grid Settings**.

   TIMESAVER *To open the dialog box, right-click a blank slide area, and then click Grid and Guides.*

3. Select or clear the **Display grid on screen** check box.

4. Select or clear the **Display drawing guides on screen** check box.

5. Select or clear the **Display smart guides when shapes are aligned** check box (**New!**).

6. Click **OK**.

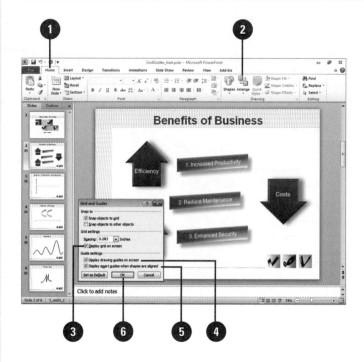

Set Objects to Snap into Place

1. In PowerPoint, click the **Home** tab.

2. Click the **Arrange** button, point to **Align**, and then click **Grid Settings**.

   TIMESAVER *To open the Grid and Guides dialog box, right-click a blank area of the slide, and then click Grid and Guides.*

3. Select the **Snap objects to grid** check box or select the **Snap objects to other objects** check box.

4. Click **OK**.

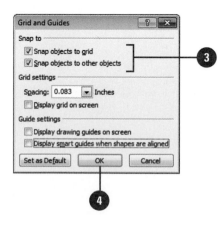

Add, Move, or Remove a Guide

◆ To move a guide, drag it.

◆ To add a new guide, press and hold the Ctrl key, and then drag the line to the new location. You can place a guide anywhere on the slide.

◆ To remove a guide, drag the guide off the slide. You cannot remove the original guides, they must be turned off.

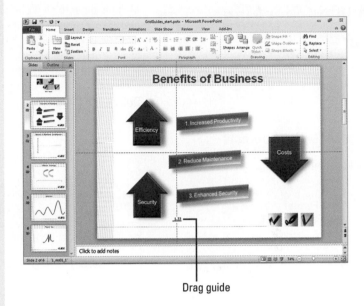

Drag guide

Align an Object to a Guide

① If necessary, display guides on the screen (horizontal and vertical).

② Drag the object's center or edge near the guide. PowerPoint aligns the center or edge to the guide.

Did You Know?

You can use the keyboard to override grid settings. To temporarily override settings for the grids and guides, press and hold the Alt key as you drag an object.

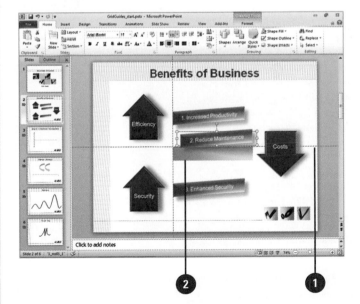

Changing Stacking Order

Multiple objects on a document appear in a stacking order, like layers of transparencies. Stacking is the placement of objects one on top of another. In other words, the first object that you draw is on the bottom and the last object that you draw is on top. You can change the order of this stack of objects by using Bring to Front, Send to Back, Bring Forward, and Send Backward commands on the Format tab under Drawing or Picture Tools.

Arrange a Stack of Objects

1. Select the objects you want to arrange.

2. Click the **Format** tab under Drawing or Picture Tools.

3. Click the stacking option you want.

   ◆ Click the **Bring to Front** button arrow, and then click **Bring to Front** or **Bring Forward** to move a drawing to the top of the stack or up one location in the stack.

   ◆ Click the **Send to Back** button arrow, and then click **Send to Back** or **Send Backward** to move a drawing to the bottom of the stack or back one location in the stack.

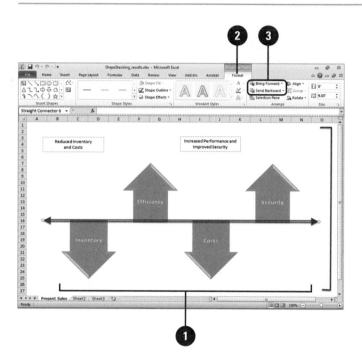

Did You Know?

You can view a hidden object in a stack. Press the Tab key or Shift+Tab to cycle forward or backward through the objects until you select the object you want.

You can connect two shapes. Click the Insert tab, click the Shapes button or list arrow, click a connector (located in the Lines category), position the pointer over an object handle (turns red), drag the connector to the object handle (turns red) on another object. An attached connector point appears as red circles, while an unattached connector point appears as light blue.

Rotating and Flipping Objects

After you create an object, you can change its orientation on the document by rotating or flipping it. Rotating turns an object 90 degrees to the right or left; flipping turns an object 180 degrees horizontally or vertically. For a more freeform rotation, which you cannot achieve in 90 or 180 degree increments, drag the green rotate lever at the top of an object. You can also rotate and flip any type of picture—including bitmaps—in a document. This is useful when you want to change the orientation of an image, such as changing the direction of an arrow.

Rotate an Object to any Angle

1. Select the object you want to rotate.

2. Position the pointer (which changes to the Free Rotate pointer) over the green rotate lever at the top of the object, and then drag to rotate the object.

3. Click outside the object to set the rotation.

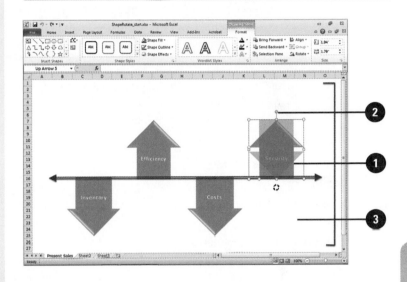

Rotate or Flip an Object Using Preset Increments

1. Select the object you want to rotate or flip.

2. Click the **Format** tab under Drawing or Picture Tools.

3. Click the **Rotate** button, and then click the option you want.

   ◆ **Rotate.** Click Rotate Right 90° or Rotate Left 90°.

   ◆ **Flip.** Click Flip Vertical or Flip Horizontal.

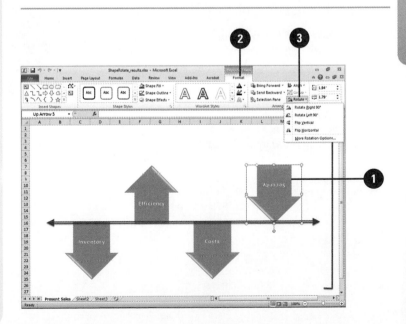

Grouping and Ungrouping Objects

Objects can be grouped, ungrouped, and regrouped to make editing and moving them easier. Rather than moving several objects one at a time, you can group the objects and move them all together. Grouped objects appear as one object, but each object in the group maintains its individual attributes. You can change an individual object within a group without ungrouping. This is useful when you need to make only a small change to a group, such as changing the color of a single shape in the group. You can also format specific shapes, drawings, or pictures within a group without ungrouping. Simply select the object within the group, change the object or edit text within the object, and then deselect the object. However, if you need to move an object in a group, you need to first ungroup the objects, move it, and then group the objects together again. After you ungroup a set of objects, Office remembers each object in the group and regroups those objects in one step when you use the Regroup command. Before you regroup a set of objects, make sure that at least one of the grouped objects is selected.

Group Objects Together

1. Select the shapes you want to group together.

2. Click the **Format** tab under Drawing or Picture Tools.

3. Click the **Group** button, and then click **Group**.

Did You Know?

You can use the Tab key to select objects in order. Move between the drawing objects on your document (even those hidden behind other objects) by pressing the Tab key.

You can use the shortcut menu to select Group related commands. Right-click the objects you want to group, point to Group, and then make your selections.

You can no longer ungroup tables. Due to the increased table size and theme functionality, tables can no longer be ungrouped.

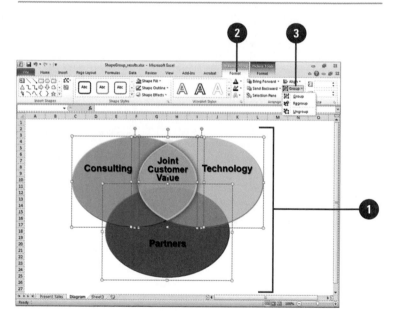

Ungroup Objects

1. Select the grouped object you want to ungroup.

2. Click the **Format** tab under Drawing or Picture Tools.

3. Click the **Group** button, and then click **Ungroup**.

See Also

See "Selecting Objects Using the Selection Pane" on page 114 for information on selecting "hard-to-select" objects.

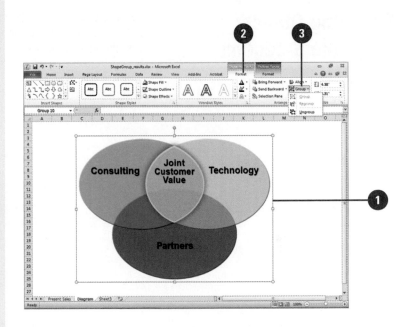

Regroup Objects

1. Select one of the objects in the group of objects you want to regroup.

2. Click the **Format** tab under Drawing or Picture Tools.

3. Click the **Group** button, and then click **Regroup**.

Did You Know?

You can troubleshoot the arrangement of objects. If you have trouble selecting an object because another object is in the way, you can use the Selection pane to help you select it.

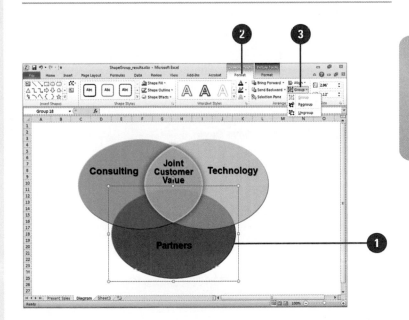

Selecting Objects Using the Selection Pane

Sometimes it's hard to select an object when it is behind another one. With the Selection task pane, you can now select individual objects and change their order and visibility. When you open the Selection task pane, Office lists each shape on the current document by name (in terms of object type). You can click a shape title to select a "hard-to-select" object on the document, use the Re-order buttons to change the stacking order on the document, or click the eye icon next to a shape title to show or hide "hard-to-see" individual objects.

Select Objects Using the Selection Pane

1. Display the documents with the objects you want to select.

2. Click the **Format** tab under Drawing or Picture Tools.

3. Click the **Selection Pane** button.

   Titles for all the shapes on the current document appear in the task pane.

4. To select an object, click the title in the task pane.

   To select more than one object, hold down the Ctrl key while you click object titles.

5. To change the order of the objects, select an object, and then click the Re-order **Move Up** or **Move Down** buttons in the task pane.

6. To show or hide individual objects, click the eye icon in the task pane.

7. When you're done, click the **Close** button on the task pane.

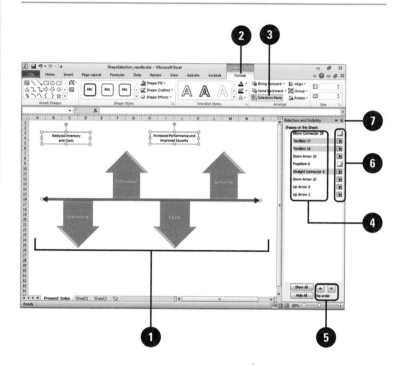

Formatting Office Documents

Introduction

Microsoft Office provides several tools for making your documents look more attractive and professional. Without formatting, a document can look like a sea of meaningless information. To highlight important information, you can change the appearance of selected text by applying attributes, such as boldface, italics, and underline. Once you've set up your documents, additional changes are available to customize your document's look. You can change the default font and font size, or maybe you'd like to adjust the alignment of text or data.

Not everyone has an eye for color, and pulling it all together can be daunting, so Office provides you with professionally designed themes, which you can apply to any document. A **theme** is a set of unified design elements that provides a consistent look for a document by using color themes, fonts, and effects, such as shadows, shading, and animations.

What You'll Do

Format Text

Change Alignment

Use the Format Painter

Add Custom Colors

Understand Themes

View and Apply a Theme

Create Theme Colors

Choose Theme Fonts

Choose Theme Effects

Create a Custom Theme

Choose a Custom Theme

Formatting Text

A **font** is a collection of alphanumeric characters that share the same typeface, or design, and have similar characteristics. You can format text and numbers with font attributes—such as bolding, italics, or underlining—to enhance data to catch the reader's attention. The basic formats you apply to text are available on the Home tab in the Font group or in the Font dialog box. Some of the formats available in the Font dialog box include strikethrough, and single or double normal and accounting underline. When you point to selected text, Office displays the Mini-Toolbar above it. The **Mini-Toolbar** provides easy access to common formatting buttons, such as font, font size, increase and decrease font size, bold, italic, font color, and increase and decrease list level. If you don't want to display the Mini-Toolbar, you can use Options to turn it off.

Format Text Quickly

1. Select the text you want to format.

2. Click the **Home** tab.

3. To change fonts, click the **Font** list arrow on the Ribbon or Mini-Toolbar, and then point for a live preview, or click the font you want, either a theme font or any available fonts.

   The font name appears in the font style.

   To change the font size, click one or more of the font size buttons on the Ribbon or Mini-Toolbar:

   ◆ Click the **Font Size** list arrow, and then click the font size you want.

   ◆ Click the **Increase Font Size** button or **Decrease Font Size** button.

   To apply other formatting, click one or more of the formatting buttons on the Ribbon or Mini-Toolbar: **Bold**, **Italic**, **Underline**, **Shadow**, **Strikethrough**, or **Font Color**.

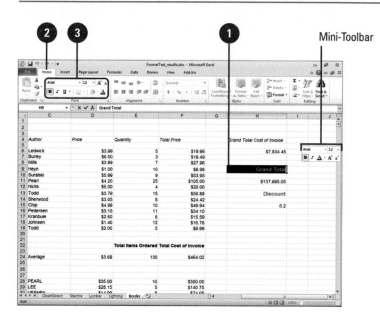

Mini-Toolbar

Format Text Using the Format Cells Dialog Box

1 Select the text you want to format.

2 Click the **Home** tab.

3 Click the **Font Dialog Box Launcher**.

The dialog box opens, displaying the Font tab.

4 Select the font, font style, and font size you want.

5 Select or clear the effects you want or don't want: **Strikethrough**, **Superscript**, and **Subscript**.

6 If you want, click the **Font Color** list arrow, and then click a color.

7 If you want, click the **Underline** list arrow, and then click a style.

8 Click **OK**.

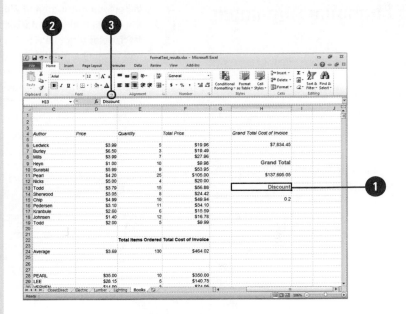

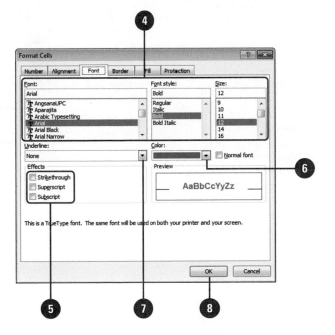

Did You Know?

You can tell the difference between a TrueType and printer font. A TrueType (outline) font is a font that uses special software capabilities to print exactly what is seen on the screen. A printer (screen) font is a font that comes only in specified sizes. If you are creating a document for publication, you need to use printer fonts.

What is a point? The size of each font character is measured in points (a point is approximately 1/72 of an inch). You can use any font that is installed on your computer on a document, but the default is 10-point Arial.

Each computer has different fonts installed. Users with whom you share files may not have all the fonts you've used in a document installed on their computers.

Changing Alignment

When you enter data in a cell, Office aligns labels on the left edge of the cell and aligns values and formulas on the right edge of the cell. **Horizontal alignment** is the way in which Office aligns the contents of a cell relative to the left or right edge of the cell; **vertical alignment** is the way in which Office aligns cell contents relative to the top and bottom of the cell. Office also provides an option for changing the flow and angle of characters within a cell. The **orientation** of the contents of a cell is expressed in degrees. The default orientation is 0 degrees, in which characters are horizontally aligned within a cell.

Change Alignment Using the Ribbon

① Select a cell or range containing the data to be realigned.

② Click the **Home** tab.

③ Click any of the alignment buttons on the Ribbon:

◆ Click **Align Left**, **Center**, or **Align Right** to align cell contents left to right.

◆ Click **Top Align**, **Middle Align**, or **Bottom Align** to align cell contents from top to bottom.

◆ Click **Decrease Indent** or **Increase Indent** to shift cell contents to the left or right.

◆ Click **Orientation**, and then click **Angle Counterclockwise**, **Angle Clockwise**, **Vertical Text**, **Rotate Text Up**, or **Rotate Text Down** to rotate cell contents.

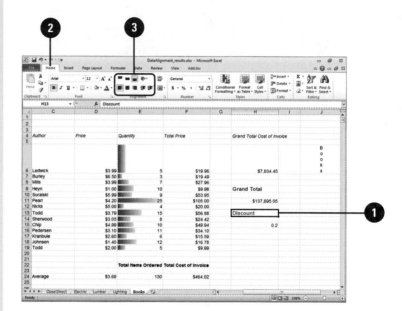

Change Alignment Using the Format Dialog Box

1 Select a cell or range containing the data to be realigned.

2 Click the **Home** tab.

3 Click the **Alignment** or **Paragraph Dialog Box Launcher**.

The Format Cells dialog box opens, displaying the Alignment tab.

4 Click the **Horizontal** list arrow or the **Vertical** list arrow, and then select an alignment.

5 Select an orientation. Click a point on the map, or click the **Degrees** up or down arrow.

6 If you want, select one or more of the Text control check boxes.

7 Click the **Text Direction** list arrow, and then select a direction: **Context**, **Left-to-Right**, or **Right-to-Left**.

8 Click **OK**.

Did You Know?

You can use the Format Cells dialog box to select other alignment options. Many more alignment options are available from the Format Cells dialog box, but for centering across columns and simple left, right, and center alignment, it's easier to use the Home or Format tab buttons.

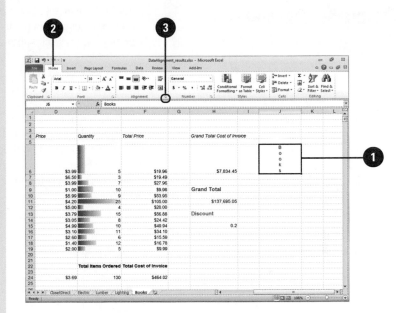

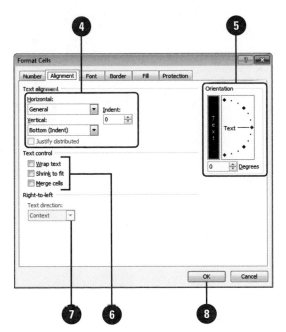

Using the Format Painter

After formatting a cell on a document, you might want to apply those same formatting changes to other cells on the document. For example, you might want each subtotal on your document to be formatted in italic, bold, 12-point Times New Roman, with a dollar sign, commas, and two decimal places. Rather than selecting each subtotal and applying the individual formatting to each cell, you can **paint** (that is, copy) the formatting from one cell to others. The Format Painter lets you "pick up" the style of one section and apply, or "paint," it to another. To apply a format style to more than one item, double-click the Format Painter button on the Home tab instead of a single-click. The double-click keeps the Format Painter active until you want to press Esc to disable it, so you can apply formatting styles to any text or object you want in your document.

Apply a Format Style Using the Format Painter

1 Select a cell or range containing the formatting you want to copy.

2 Click the **Home** tab.

3 Click the **Format Painter** button.

   If you want to apply the format to more than one item, double-click the Format Painter button.

4 Drag to select the text or click the object to which you want to apply the format.

5 If you double-clicked the Format Painter button, drag to select the text or click the object to which you want to apply the format, and then press Esc when you're done.

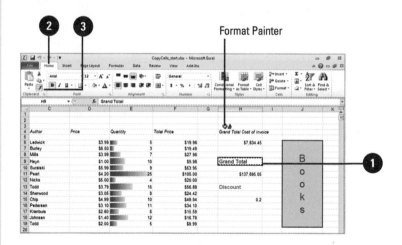

Format Painter

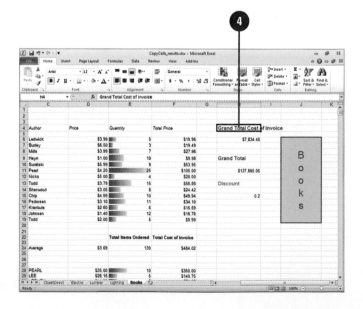

Did You Know?

You can use the Esc key to cancel format painting. If you change your mind about painting a format, cancel the marquee by pressing Esc.

Adding Custom Colors

In addition to the standard and theme colors, Office allows you to add more colors to your document. These additional colors are available on each color button palette on the Ribbon or in a dialog box, such as the Fill Color or Font Color button. These colors are useful when you want to use a specific color, but the document color theme does not have that color. Colors that you add to a document appear in all color palettes and remain in the palette even if the color theme changes.

Add a Color to the Menus

1. Click the **Font Color** button on the Home tab, and then click **More Colors**.

    This is one method. You can also use other color menus to access the Colors dialog box.

2. Click the **Custom** tab.

3. Click the **Color model** list arrow, and then click **RGB** or **HSL**.

4. Select a custom color using one of the following methods:

    ◆ If you know the color values, enter them, either Hue, Sat, Lum, or Red, Green, and Blue.

    ◆ Drag across the palette until the pointer is over the color you want. Drag the black arrow to adjust the amount of black and white in the color.

    The new color appears above the current color at the bottom right.

5. Click **OK**.

    The current selection is changed to the new color, plus the new color is added to the Recent Colors section of all document color menus.

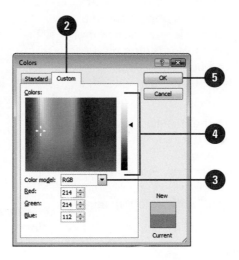

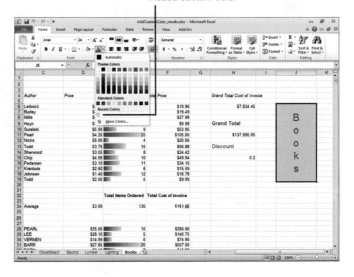

Added custom color

Understanding Themes

A theme helps you create professional-looking documents that use an appropriate balance of color for your document content. You can use a default color theme or create a custom one.

Themes in Office are made up of a palette of twelve colors. These colors appear on color palettes when you click a color-related button, such as Fill Color or Font Color button on the Home tab or in a dialog box. These twelve colors correspond to the following elements in a document:

Four Text and Background. The two background colors (light and dark combinations) are the canvas, or drawing area, color of the document. The two text colors (light and dark combinations) are for typing text and drawing lines, and contrast with the background colors.

Six Accent. These colors are designed to work as a complementary color palette for objects, such as shadows and fills. These

colors contrast with both the background and text colors.

One hyperlink. This color is designed to work as a complementary color for objects and hyperlinks.

One followed hyperlink. This color is designed to work as a complementary color for objects and visited hyperlinks.

The first four colors in the Theme Colors list represent the document text and background colors (light and dark for each). The remaining colors represent the six accent and two hyperlink colors for the theme. When you apply another theme or change any of these colors to create a new theme, the colors shown in the Theme Colors dialog box and color palettes change to match the current colors.

Accent 5   Accent 4   Accent 6   Accent 1   Accent 3

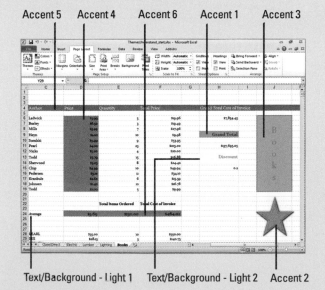

Text/Background - Light 1   Text/Background - Light 2   Accent 2

Twelve theme colors

Sample color themes: Dark and Light

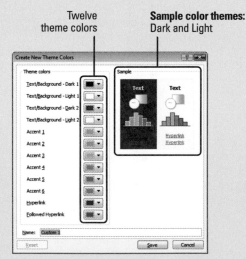

Viewing and Applying a Theme

A document theme consists of theme colors, fonts, and effects. You can quickly format an entire document with a professional look by applying a theme. Office comes with more themes and styles (**New!**). To quickly see if you like a theme, point to one on the themes gallery to display a ScreenTip with name and information about it, and a live preview of it on the current document. If you like the theme, you can apply it. When you apply a theme, the background, text, graphics, charts, and tables all change to reflect the theme. You can choose from one or more standard themes. When you add new content, the document elements change to match the theme ensuring all of your material will look consistent. You can even use the same theme in other Microsoft Office programs, such as Word and PowerPoint, so all your work matches. Can't find a theme you like? Search Microsoft Office.com on the Web.

View and Apply a Theme

1. Open the document you want to apply a theme.

2. Click the **Page Layout** or **Design** tab.

3. Click the **Themes** button or **More** list arrow to display the themes gallery.

4. Point to a theme.

   A live preview of the theme appears in the document, along with a ScreenTip.

5. Click the theme you want to apply to the active document.

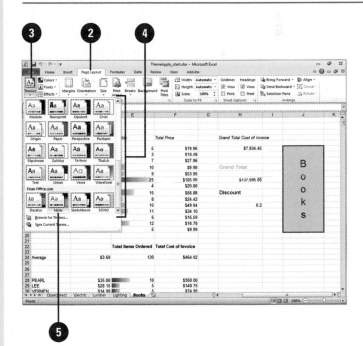

Did You Know?

You can apply themes from Office.com. Click the Page Layout or Design tab, click the Themes button, scroll to the bottom of the list, and then select an available Office.com theme. Go to Office.com to download and use other online themes.

You can create a new presentation based on a theme. In PowerPoint, click the File tab, click New, click Installed Themes in the left pane, click a theme, and then click Create.

Creating Theme Colors

You may like a certain color theme except for one or two colors. You can change an existing color theme and apply your changes to the entire document. You can add other custom colors to your theme by using RGB (Red, Green, and Blue) or HSL (Hues, Saturation, and Luminosity) color modes. The RGB color mode is probably the most widely used of all the color modes. You can accomplish this by using sliders, dragging on a color-space, or entering a numeric value that corresponds to a specific color. Once you create this new color theme, you can add it to your collection of color themes so that you can make it available to any document.

Apply or Create Theme Colors

1. Open the document you want to apply a color theme.

2. Click the **Page Layout** or **Design** tab.

3. To apply theme colors to a document, click the **Theme Colors** button, and then click a color theme.

   ◆ To apply individual theme colors, click an element, click a color button, such as Font Color, and then click a theme color.

4. To create theme colors, click the **Theme Colors** button, and then click **Create New Theme Colors**.

5. Click the Theme Colors buttons (Text/Background, Accent, or Hyperlink, etc.) for the colors you want to change.

6. Click a new color, or click **More Colors** to select a color from the **Standard** or **Custom** tab, and then click **OK**.

7. If you don't like your color choices, click the **Reset** button to return all color changes to their original colors.

8. Type a new name for the color theme.

9. Click **Save**.

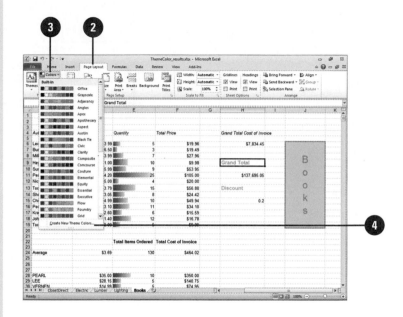

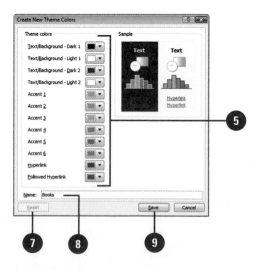

Select Custom Colors

1. Select a cell or range you want to apply a custom color.

2. Click the **Font Color** button on the Home tab, and then click **More Colors**.

   This is one method. You can also use other color menus to access the Colors dialog box.

3. Click the **Custom** tab.

4. Click the **Color model** list arrow, and then click **RGB** or **HSL**.

5. Select a custom color using one of the following methods:

   ◆ If you know the color values, enter them, either Hue, Sat, Lum, or Red, Green, and Blue.

   ◆ Drag across the palette until the pointer is over the color you want. Drag the black arrow to adjust the amount of black and white in the color.

   The new color appears above the current color at the bottom right.

6. Click **OK**.

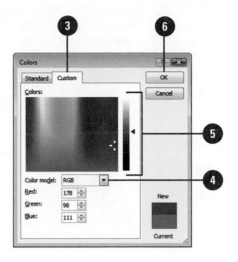

The Properties of Color

Characteristic	Description
Hue	The color itself; every color is identified by a number, determined by the number of colors available on your monitor.
Saturation	The intensity of the color. The higher the number, the more vivid the color.
Luminosity	The brightness of the color, or how close the color is to black or white. The larger the number, the lighter the color.
Red, Green, Blue	Primary colors of the visible light spectrum. RGB generates color using three 8-bit channels: 1 red, 1 green, and 1 blue. RGB is an additive color system, which means that color is added to a black background. The additive process mixes various amounts of red, green and blue light to produce other colors.

Choosing Theme Fonts

A document theme consists of theme colors, fonts, and effects. Theme fonts include heading and body text fonts. Each document uses a set of theme fonts. When you click the Theme Fonts button on the Page Layout tab, the name of the current heading and body text font appear highlighted in the gallery menu. To quickly see if you like a theme font, point to one on the menu, and a live preview of it appears on the current document. If you want to apply the theme, click it on the menu. You can apply a set of theme fonts to another theme or create your own set of theme fonts.

Apply and Choose Theme Fonts

1. Open the document you want to apply theme fonts.

2. Click the **Home** tab.

3. Select the cell or range you want to change, click the **Font** list arrow, and then click the theme font you want.

   TIMESAVER *To select the entire document, press Ctrl+A.*

4. Click the **Page Layout** or **Design** tab.

5. Click the **Theme Fonts** button.

   The current theme fonts appear highlighted on the menu.

   TIMESAVER *Point to the Fonts button to display a ScreenTip with the current theme fonts.*

6. Click the theme fonts you want from the gallery menu.

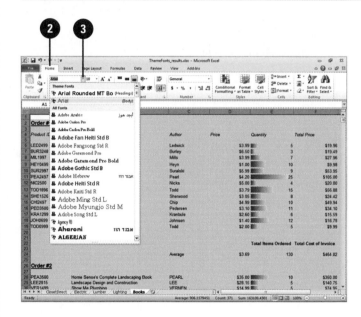

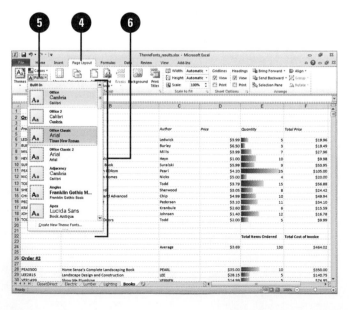

Create Theme Fonts

1. Click the **Page Layout** or **Design** tab.

2. Click the **Theme Fonts** button, and then click **Create New Theme Fonts**.

3. Click the **Heading font** list arrow, and then select a font.

4. Click the **Body font** list arrow, and then select a font.

5. Type a name for the custom theme fonts.

6. Click **Save**.

Did You Know?

The Font Color button on the Ribbon displays the last font color you used. To apply this color to another selection, simply click the button, not the list arrow.

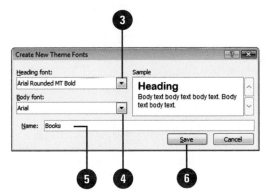

Choosing Theme Effects

Theme effects are sets of lines, fills, and special effects styles for shapes, graphics, charts, SmartArt, and other design elements. By combining the lines, fills, and special effects styles with different formatting levels (subtle, moderate, and intense), Office provides a variety of visual theme effects. Each document uses a set of theme effects. Some are more basic while others are more elaborate. When you click the Theme Effects button on the Page Layout tab, the name of the current theme effects appears highlighted in the gallery menu. While you can apply a set of theme effects to another theme, you cannot create your own set of theme effects at this time.

View and Apply Theme Effects

1. Open the document you want to apply a theme effect.

2. Click the **Page Layout** or **Design** tab.

3. Click the **Theme Effects** button.

    The current theme effects appear highlighted on the menu.

    TIMESAVER *Point to the Effects button to display a ScreenTip with the current theme effects name.*

4. Click the theme effects you want from the menu.

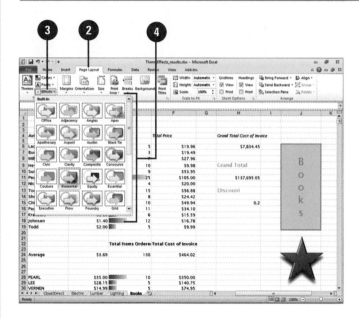

Did You Know?

You can delete a custom theme effects or fonts. On the Page Layout or Design tab, click the Theme Effects or Theme Fonts button, right-click the theme you want to edit, click Edit, click Delete, and then click Yes.

See Also

See "Viewing and Applying a Theme" on page 123 for information on applying a theme from the Themes gallery.

Creating a Custom Theme

If you have special needs for specific colors, fonts, and effects, such as a company sales or marketing document, you can create your own theme by customizing theme colors, theme fonts, and theme effects, and saving them as a theme file (.thmx), which you can reuse. You can apply the saved theme to other documents. When you save a custom theme, the file is automatically saved in the Document Themes folder and added to the list of custom themes used by Office 2007/2010 and other Office programs. When you no longer need a custom theme, you can delete it.

Create a Custom Theme

1. Click the **Page Layout** or **Design** tab, and then create a theme by customizing theme colors, theme fonts, and theme effects.

2. Click the **Themes** button, and then click **Save Current Theme**.

3. Type a name for the theme file.

4. Click **Save**.

Did You Know?

You can remove a custom theme from the gallery menu. Simply move or delete the theme file from the Document Themes folder into another folder.

Custom theme

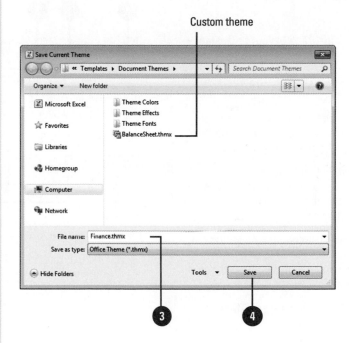

Choosing a Custom Theme

When you can create your own theme by customizing theme colors, theme fonts, and theme effects, and saving them as a theme file (.thmx), you can apply the saved theme to other documents. When you save a custom theme file in the Document Themes folder, you can choose the custom theme from the Themes gallery. If you save a custom theme file in another folder location, you can use the Browse for Themes command to locate and select the custom theme file you want to reuse.

Choose and Apply a Custom Theme

1. Click the **Page Layout** or **Design** tab.

2. Click the **Themes** button to see additional themes.

3. Point to the gallery you want to display the theme name, and then click the one you want.

4. To select and apply a custom theme from a file, click the **Themes** button, and then click **Browse for Themes**.

5. If you want to open a specific file type, click the **Files of type** list arrow, and then select an Office Theme file type:

   ◆ Office Themes and Themed Documents.

   ◆ Office Themes.

   ◆ Office Themes and <Program> Templates.

6. If the file is located in another folder, click the **Look in** list arrow, and then navigate to the file.

7. Click the theme file you want.

8. Click **Open**.

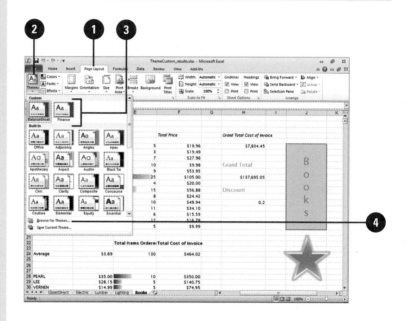

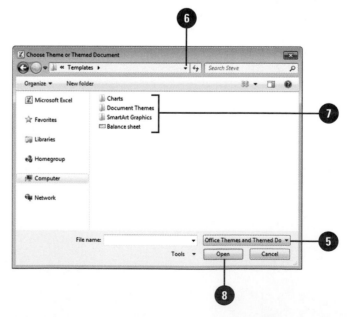

Creating a Document with Word

Introduction

Whether you're typing a carefully worded letter, creating a professional resume, or producing a can't-miss promotional newsletter for your business or neighborhood group, Microsoft Office Word 2010 is the program for you. Word contains all the tools and features you need to produce interesting documents that say exactly what you mean and that have the look to match.

Microsoft Word is designed especially for working with text, so it's a snap to create and edit letters, reports, mailing lists, tables, or any other word-based communication. What makes Word perfect for your documents is its editing capabilities combined with its variety of views. For example, you can jot down your ideas in Outline view. Then switch to Normal view to expand your thoughts into complete sentences and revise them without retyping the entire page. When you're done revising the document, switch to Reading view to read and proof your work. Tools such as the Spelling and Grammar Checker help you present your thoughts accurately, clearly, and effectively. Finally, in Print Layout view you can quickly add formatting elements, such as bold type and special fonts, to make your documents look professional.

With Word, you can create and publish blog postings and manage multiple blog accounts. A blog—short for Web log—is a Web site that provides journal style information on a particular subject, such as news or personal diaries. A blog combines text, images, and links to other blogs, Web pages, and related topics.

What You'll Do

View the Word Window

Move Around in a Document

Change Document Views

Read a Document

Navigate a Document

Set Up the Page

Set Up the Page Margins

Create an Outline

Select Text

Check Spelling and Grammar

Insert New Pages and Sections

Add Headers and Footers

Insert Page Numbers and the Date and Time

Create a Blog Posting on the Web

Viewing the Word Window

File tab
Click to access Office Word file commands.

Quick Access Toolbar
Click to access command comments on this customizable toolbar.

Tabs
Click to access tools and commands.

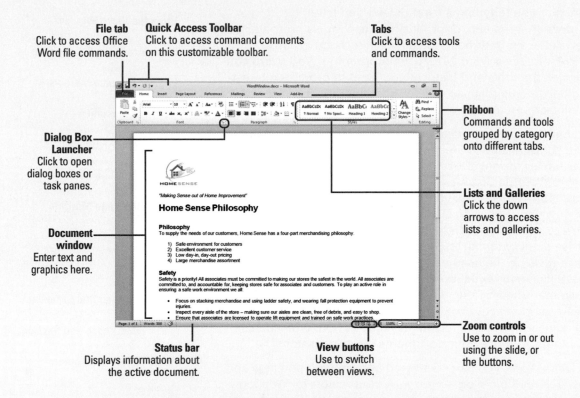

Dialog Box Launcher
Click to open dialog boxes or task panes.

Document window
Enter text and graphics here.

Ribbon
Commands and tools grouped by category onto different tabs.

Lists and Galleries
Click the down arrows to access lists and galleries.

Zoom controls
Use to zoom in or out using the slide, or the buttons.

Status bar
Displays information about the active document.

View buttons
Use to switch between views.

Moving Around in a Document

As your document gets longer, some of your work shifts out of sight. You can easily move any part of a document back into view. **Scrolling** moves the document line by line. **Paging** moves the document page by page. **Browsing** moves you through your document by the item you specify, such as to the next word, comment, picture, table, or heading. The tools described here move you around a document no matter which document view you are in.

Scroll, Page, and Browse Through a Document

◆ To scroll through a document one line at a time, click the up or down scroll arrow on the vertical scroll bar.

◆ To quickly scroll through a document, click and hold the up or down scroll arrow on the vertical scroll bar.

◆ To scroll to a specific page or heading in a document, drag the scroll box on the vertical scroll bar until the page number or heading you want appears in the yellow box.

◆ To page through the document one screen at a time, press Page Up or Page Down on the keyboard.

◆ To browse a document by page, edits, headings, or other items, click the Select Browse Object button, and then click that item. If a dialog box opens, enter the name or number of the item you want to find, and then click the Previous or Next button to move from one item to the next.

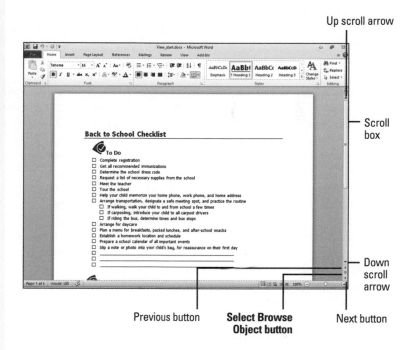

Up scroll arrow

Scroll box

Down scroll arrow

Previous button

Select Browse Object button

Next button

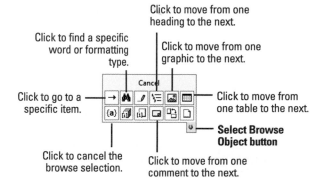

Click to move from one heading to the next.

Click to find a specific word or formatting type.

Click to move from one graphic to the next.

Click to go to a specific item.

Click to move from one table to the next.

Select Browse Object button

Click to cancel the browse selection.

Click to move from one comment to the next.

Changing Document Views

Word displays the contents of a document in different ways to help you work efficiently with your content. The available views include Print Layout, Full Screen Reading, Web Layout, Outline, and Draft. You can change the window view from the View tab, or you can click a Document view button at the bottom right corner of the Word window.

Print Layout view displays a gray gap between each page to clearly delineate where each actual page break occurs. Word displays each new document in Print Layout view by default. This view is best for previewing your work before printing, and it works well with the Zoom feature on the View tab to increase and decrease the page view size and display multiple pages of the same document simultaneously onscreen.

Full Screen Reading view displays the full screen and removes distracting screen elements to provide a more comfortable view to read your documents. You can also display the Thumbnail pane or the Document Map to

quickly jump to different parts of your document. When you're done, you can use the Close button.

Web Layout view displays the document as it will appear on the Web. You can save documents as HTML code to make Web content creation easy.

Outline view displays the document as an outline with headings and subheadings. When you shift to Outline view, each heading has a clickable plus or minus sign next to it to expand or collapse the content under the heading. You can drag a plus, or minus sign to move the heading and all of its associated text.

Draft view displays the document as a single, long piece of "paper," divided into pages by perforation marks. This view is fine for composition but inadequate for editing or previewing your work prior to printing or other publication.

Print Layout view

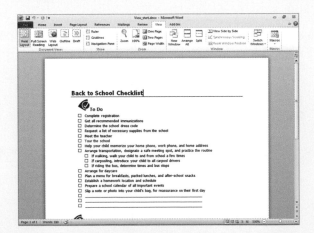

Full Screen Reading view

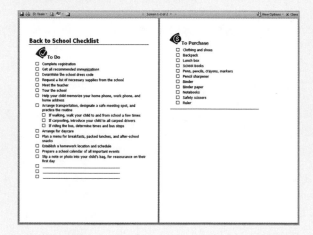

Web Layout view

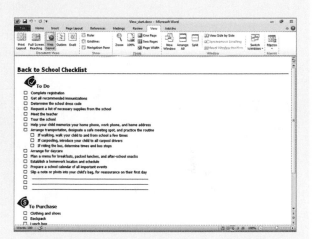

Outline view

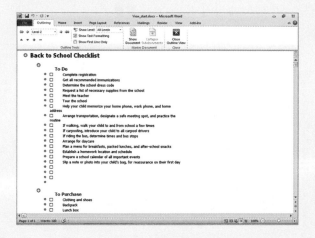

Draft view

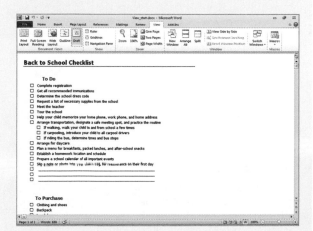

Reading a Document

You can avoid eye strain when you want to read a document with the Full Screen Reading view. The Full Screen Reading view is designed with tools optimized for reading a document. Word changes the screen size and removes distracting screen elements to provide a more comfortable view for reading your documents. In the Full Screen Reading view, you can display the Navigation pane (**New!**) with the Browse Heading or Browse Pages tab to quickly jump to different parts of your document. You can also save, print, access tools, highlight text, and insert comments. If you have a Tablet PC, you can write comments and changes directly on the page using the tablet's stylus.

Read a Document

1. Click the **Full Screen Reading View** button.

   ◆ The Full Screen Reading View button is also available on the View tab.

2. To display the text in a larger or smaller size, click the **View Options** button, and then click **Increase Text Size** or **Decrease Text Size**.

3. To display two pages at once or a single page, click the **View Options** button, and then click **Show One Page** or **Show Two Pages**.

   TIMESAVER *Press Esc to deselect the document, type a number, and then press Enter to go to a page.*

4. When you're done, click the **Close** button.

Did You Know?

You can disable open e-mail attachments in Full Screen Reading view. Click the File tab, click Options, click General, clear the Open E-mail Attachments In Full Screen Reading View check box, and then click OK.

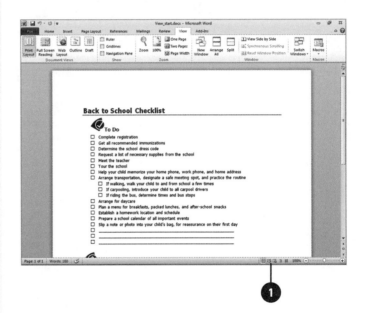

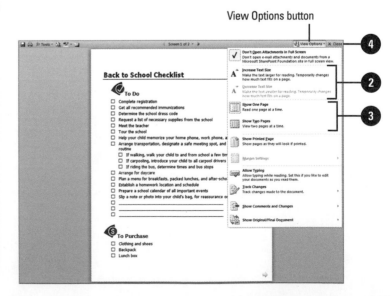

View Options button

Display Headings or Page View

1. Click the **Full Screen Reading View** button.

2. Click the **Navigation** button, and then click **Navigation Pane**.

3. Click the **Browse Headings** or **Browse Pages** tab.

4. Click a heading name or thumbnail of a page to display it.

5. To close the Navigation pane, click the **Close** button on the pane.

6. When you're done, click the **Close** button.

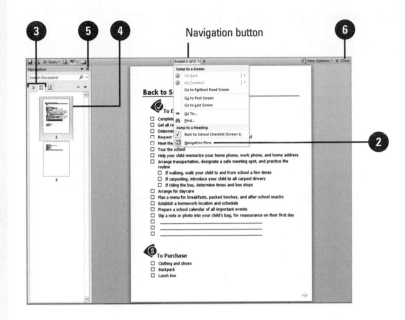

Change Full Screen Reading View Options

1. Click the **Full Screen Reading View** button.

2. Click the **View Options** buttons.

3. Click the view you want to display.

   ◆ **Don't Open Attachments in Full Screen**.

   ◆ **Show Printed Page**.

   ◆ **Margin Settings**.

   ◆ **Allow Typing**.

   ◆ **Track Changes**.

   ◆ **Show Comments and Changes**.

   ◆ **Show Original/Final Document**.

4. When you're done, click the **Close** button.

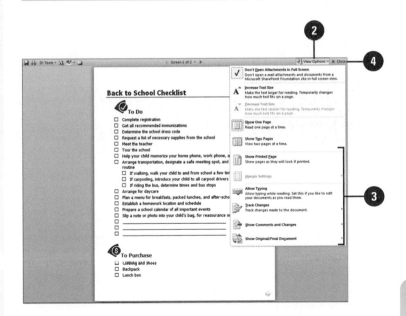

Navigating a Document

If you have a long document with headings or you're searching for keywords, you can use the Navigation pane (**New!**) to find your way around it. In the Navigation pane, you can view thumbnails for all pages, search for key phrases, quickly move between headings, promote or demote headings, insert new headings, browse headings from a co-author, rearrange heading content, and collapse/ expand heading levels of an outline. You can perform any of these tasks in the Navigation panel by using the following tabs: Browse Headings, Browse Pages, and Browse Search Results.

Navigate a Document

1. Click the **View** tab.

2. Click the **Navigation Pane** check box.

3. To work with headings, click the **Browse Headings** tab, and then do any of the following:

   ◆ **Display a Heading.** Click the heading name, or click the **Previous Heading** or **Next Heading** button.

   ◆ **Collapse/Expand a Heading.** Click the arrow next to the heading name.

   ◆ **Move a Heading.** Drag the heading name to another location in the pane. The heading and its content move together.

   ◆ **Create a Heading.** Right-click a heading name, and then click **New Heading Before** or **New Heading After**.

   ◆ **Promote or Demote a Heading.** Right-click a heading name, and then click **Promote** or **Demote**.

4. To view page thumbnails, click the **Browse Pages** tab.

5. To perform and view search results, click in the Search box, type keywords, press enter, and then click the **Browse Search Results** tab.

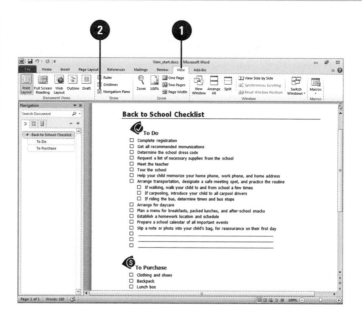

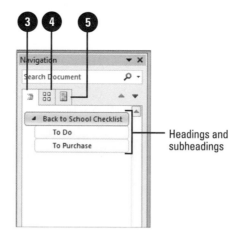

Headings and subheadings

Setting Up the Page

Every document you produce and print might need a different page setup. You can achieve the look you want by printing on a standard paper size (such as letter, legal, or envelope), international standard paper sizes, or any custom size that your printer accepts. The default setting is 8.5 x 11 inches, the most common letter and copy size. You can also print several pages on one sheet. You can also select the page orientation (portrait or landscape) that best fits the entire document or any section. **Portrait** orients the page vertically (taller than it is wide) and **landscape** orients the page horizontally (wider than it is tall).

Set the Page Orientation and Size Quickly

1. Click the **Page Layout** tab.

2. To quickly change the page orientation, click the **Orientation** button, and then click **Landscape** or **Portrait**.

3. To quickly change the page size, click the **Size** button, and then click the size you want.

4. To set a custom page size, click the **Size** button, click **More Paper Sizes**, select the options you want, and then click **OK**.

   ◆ **Paper Size.** Select a paper size or specify the height and width.

   ◆ **Paper Source.** Select the paper source for the first page and other pages.

   ◆ **Apply To.** Click This Section, This Point Forward, or Whole Document.

   ◆ **Default.** Changes the default settings for all new documents. Click Default, and then click Yes.

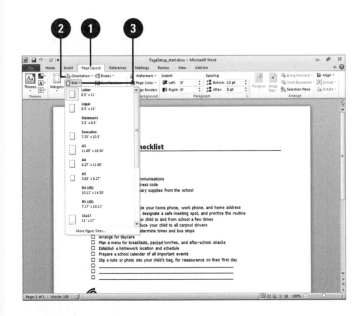

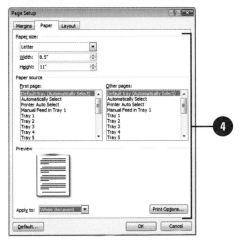

Setting Up the Page Margins

Margins are the blank space between the edge of a page and the text. The default setting for Word documents is 1.25 inches on the left and right, and 1 inch on the top and bottom. You can use the mouse pointer to adjust margins visually for the entire document, or you can use the Page Setup dialog box to set precise measurements for an entire document or a specific section. When you shift between portrait and landscape page orientation, the margin settings automatically change. If you need additional margin space for binding pages into a book or binder, you can adjust the left or right gutter settings. Gutters allow for additional margin space so that all of the document text remains visible after binding. Unless this is your purpose, leave the default settings in place.

Adjust Margins Visually

① Click the **Page Layout** tab.

② If necessary, click the **View Ruler** button to display it.

◆ You can also select the **Ruler** check box on the View tab.

③ Position the pointer over a margin boundary on the horizontal or vertical ruler.

④ Press and hold Alt, and then click a margin boundary to display the measurements of the text and margin areas as you adjust the margins.

⑤ Drag the left, right, top, or bottom margin boundary to a new position.

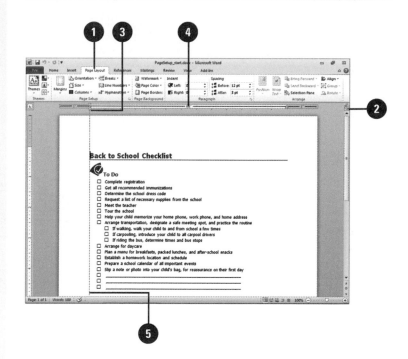

Select Standard Margins Quickly

1. Click the **Print Layout** tab.

2. Click the **Margins** button, and then click the margin setting you want:

   - ◆ **Normal**.
   - ◆ **Narrow**.
   - ◆ **Moderate**.
   - ◆ **Wide**.
   - ◆ **Mirrored**.
   - ◆ **Office 2003 Default**.

Create Custom Margins Using Page Setup

1. Click the **Print Layout** tab.

2. Click the **Margins** button, and then click **Custom Margins**.

   The Page Setup dialog box opens, displaying the Margins tab.

3. Type new margin measurements (in inches) in the Top, Bottom, Left, or Right boxes, and Gutter boxes.

4. Click the page orientation you want.

5. Click the **Apply to** list arrow, and then click **Selected Text**, **This Point Forward**, or **Whole Document**.

6. To make the new margin settings the default for all new Word documents, click **Default**, and then click **Yes**.

7. Click **OK**.

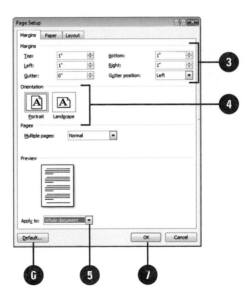

Creating an Outline

Outlines are useful for organizing information, such as topics in an essay. An outline typically consists of main headings and subheadings. You can create an outline from scratch in Outline view or change a bulleted or numbered list into an outline using the bullets and numbering commands on the Home tab. In Outline view, you can use buttons in the Outlining Tools group or drag the mouse pointer to move headings and subheadings to different locations or levels.

Create an Outline from Scratch

1. In a new document, click the **Outline View** button.

2. Type a heading, and then press Enter.

3. To assign a heading to a different level and apply the corresponding heading style, place the insertion point in the heading, and then click the **Promote** or **Demote** button until the heading is at the level you want, or click **Promote to Heading** or **Promote to Body** button.

   To move a heading to a different location, place the insertion point in the heading, and then click the **Move Up** or **Move Down** button until the heading is moved where you want it to go.

   The subordinate text under the heading moves with the heading.

4. To show text formatting or the first line only, select the **Show Text Formatting** or **Show First Line Only** check boxes.

   To show a specific level, click the **Show Level** list arrow, and then select the level you want.

5. When you're done, click the **Close Outline View** button.

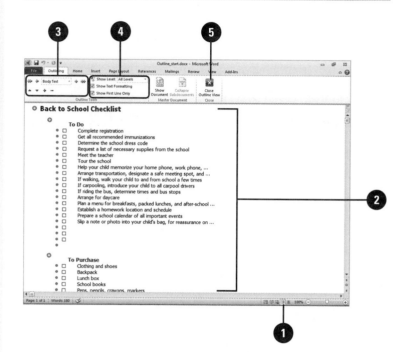

Selecting Text

The first step in working with text is to highlight, or **select**, the text you want. Once you've selected it, you can copy, move, format, and delete words, sentences, and paragraphs. When you finish with or decide not to use a selection, you can click anywhere in the document to **deselect** the text.

Select Text

1. Position the pointer in the word, paragraph, line, or part of the document you want to select.

2. Choose the method that accomplishes the selection you want to complete in the easiest way.

   Refer to the table for methods to select text.

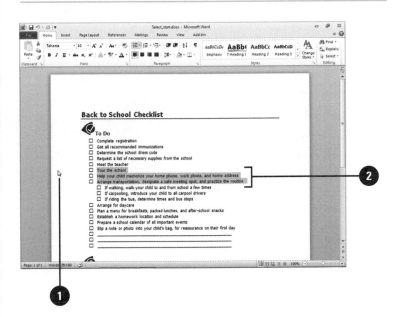

Did You Know?

AutoComplete finishes your words.
As you enter common text, such as your name, months, today's date, and common salutations and closings, Word provides the rest of the text in a ScreenTip. Press Enter to have Word complete your words.

Selecting Text	
To select	**Do this**
A single word	Double-click the word.
A single paragraph	Triple-click a word within the paragraph.
A single line	Click in the left margin next to the line.
Any part of a document	Click at the beginning of the text you want to highlight, and then drag to the end of the section you want to highlight.
A large selection	Click at the beginning of the text you want to highlight, and then press and hold Shift while you click at the end of the text that you want to highlight.
The entire document	Triple-click in the left margin.
An outline heading or subheading in Outline view	Click the bullet, plus sign, or minus sign.

Checking Spelling and Grammar

As you type, a red wavy line appears under words not listed in Word's dictionary (such as misspellings or names) or duplicated words (such as *the the*). A green wavy underline appears under words or phrases with grammatical errors. You can correct these errors as they arise or after you finish the entire document. Before you print your final document, use the Spelling and Grammar checker to ensure that your document is error-free.

Correct Spelling and Grammar as You Type

1 Right-click a word with a red or green wavy underline.

2 Click a substitution, or click Ignore All (or Grammar) to skip any other instances of the word.

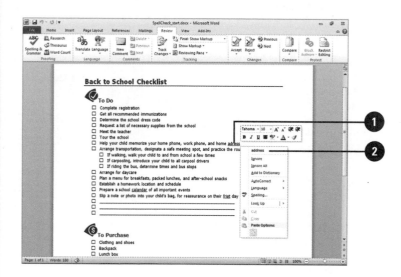

Change Spelling and Grammar Options in Word

1 Click the **File** tab, and then click **Options**.

2 In the left pane, click **Proofing**.

3 Select or clear the spelling and grammar option check boxes you want.

4 To hide spelling or grammar errors in a document, click the **Exceptions for** list arrow, select the document, and then select or clear check boxes.

5 Click **OK**.

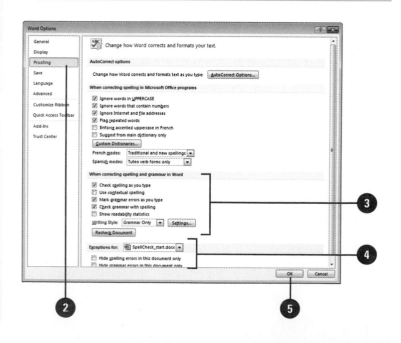

Correct Spelling and Grammar

1. Click at the beginning of the document or select the text you want to correct.

2. Click the **Review** tab.

3. Click the **Spelling & Grammar** button.

   As it checks each sentence in the document, Word provides alternatives for misspelled words or problematic sentences.

4. To check spelling only, clear the **Check grammar** check box.

5. Choose an option:

   ◆ Click **Ignore Once** to skip the word or rule, or click **Ignore All** or **Ignore Rule** to skip every instance of the word or rule.

   ◆ Click **Add to Dictionary** to add a word to your dictionary, so it doesn't show up as a misspelled word in the future.

   ◆ Click a suggestion, and then click **Change** to make a substitution.

   ◆ If no suggestion is appropriate, click in the document and edit the text yourself. Click **Resume** to continue.

6. Click **OK** to return to the document.

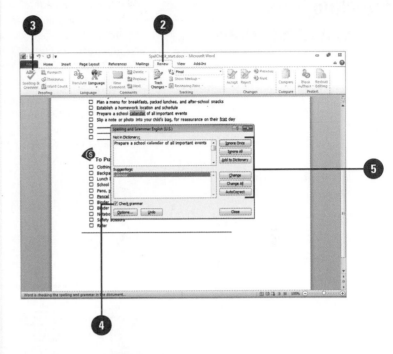

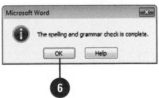

Did You Know?

You can add a familiar word to your dictionary. Right-click the wavy line under the word in question, and then click Add To Dictionary.

You can hyphenate words. Click the Page Layout tab, click the Hyphenation button, and then click an option.

Inserting New Pages and Sections

When you fill a page, Word inserts a page break and starts a new page. As you add or delete text, this **soft page break** moves. A soft page break appears as a dotted gray line in Normal view. To start a new page before the current one is filled, insert a **hard page break** that doesn't shift as you edit text. A hard page break appears as a dotted gray line with the text page break centered in Normal view. A **section** is a mini-document within a document that stores margin settings, page orientation, page numbering, and so on. In Page Layout view, you can show or hide the white space on the top and bottom of each page and the gray space between pages.

Insert and Delete a Hard Page Break

1. Click where you want to insert a hard page break.

2. Use one of the following:

   ◆ **Page Break.** Click the **Insert** tab, and then click the **Page Break** button.

   ◆ **Blank Page.** Click the **Insert** tab, and then click the **Blank Page** button.

   ◆ **Page or Section Break.** Click the **Page Layout** button, click **Page Break**, and then click the page break option you want.

   TIMESAVER *Press Ctrl+Enter to insert a page break.*

3. To delete a page break, click the page break in Print Layout view, and then press the Delete key. To move a page break, drag it to a new location.

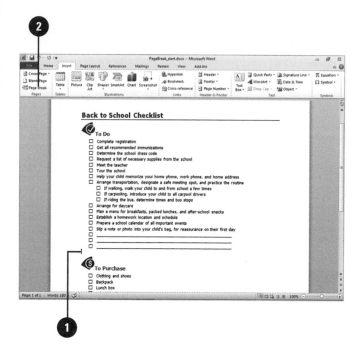

Did You Know?

You can opt to start a new line, but not a new paragraph. Insert a text wrapping break to force text to the next line in the same paragraph—the perfect tool to make a phrase fall on one line. Press Shift+Enter where you want to insert a text wrapping break.

Insert and Delete a Section Break

1. Click where you want to insert a section break.

2. Click the **Page Layout** tab.

3. Click the **Page Break** button, and then select the type of section break you want.

   ◆ **Next Page**. Starts the section on a new page.

   ◆ **Continuous**. Starts the section wherever the point is located.

   ◆ **Even Page**. Starts the section on the next even-numbered page.

   ◆ **Odd Page**. Starts the section on the next odd-numbered page.

4. To delete a section break, click the section break in Print Layout view, and then press Delete.

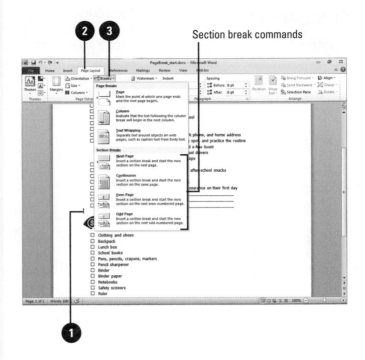

Section break commands

Show or Hide White Space Between Pages

1. Click the **Print Layout View** button.

2. Scroll to the bottom of a page, and then point to the gap between two pages. (The Hide White Space cursor or Show White Space cursor appears.)

3. Click the gap between the pages to show or hide the white space.

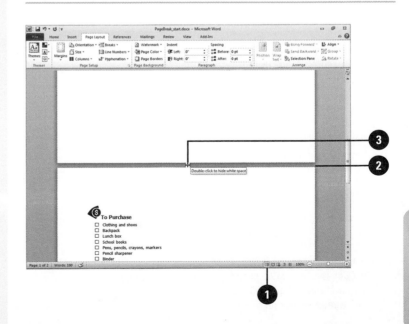

Adding Headers and Footers

Most books, including this one, use headers and footers to help you keep track of where you are. A **header** is text printed in the top margin of every page within a document. **Footer** text is printed in the bottom margin. Commonly used headers and footers contain your name, the document title, the filename, the print date, and page numbers. If you divide your document into sections, you can create different headers and footers for each section.

Create and Edit Headers and Footers

1. Click the **Insert** tab.

2. Click the **Header** or **Footer** button.

3. Click a built-in header or footer, or click **Edit Header** or **Edit Footer** to modify an existing one.

   TIMESAVER *Double-click a header or footer to edit it.*

   The Design tab under Header & Footer Tools displays on the Ribbon.

4. If necessary, click the **Go to Header** or **Go to Footer** button to display the header or footer text area.

5. Click the header or footer box, and then type the text you want. Edit and format header or footer text as usual.

6. To insert common items in a header or footer, click a button (**Date & Time**, **Quick Parts**, **Picture**, or **Clip Art**) in the Insert group.

7. When you're done, click the **Close Header and Footer** button.

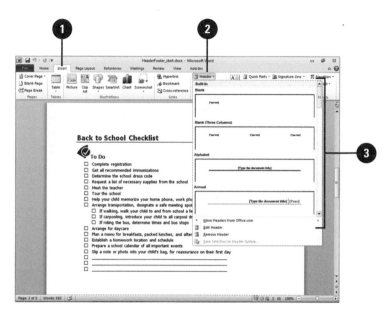

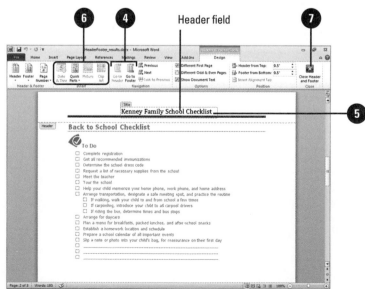

Header field

Did You Know?

You can quickly remove a header or footer. Click the Insert tab, click the Header or Footer button, and then click Remove Header or Remove Footer.

Create Different Headers and Footers for Different Pages

1. Click the **Insert** tab.

2. Click the **Header** or **Footer** button.

3. Click a built-in header or footer, or click **Edit Header** or **Edit Footer** to modify an existing one.

   The Design tab under Header & Footer Tools displays on the Ribbon.

4. To create different headers or footers for odd and even pages, click to select the **Different Odd & Even Pages** check box.

   To create a unique header or footer for the document's first page, click to select the **Different First Page** check box.

   To show document text, select the **Show Document Text** check box.

5. When you're done, click the **Close Header and Footer** button.

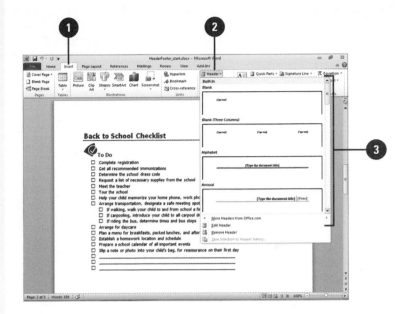

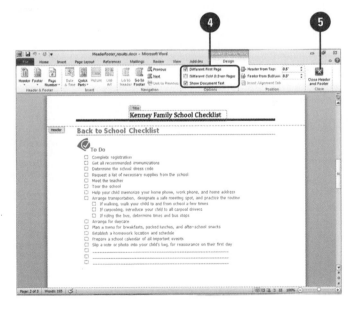

Did You Know?

You can change header and footer position. Double-click the header or footer you want to change, and then adjust the Header from Top or Footers from Bottom settings on the Ribbon.

There are default tab stops used to align header and footer text. Typically, headers and footers have two default tab stops. The first, in the middle, centers text. The second, on the far right, aligns text on the right margin. To left align text, don't press Tab. You can add and move the tab stops as needed. In addition, you can use the alignment buttons on the Home tab.

Inserting Page Numbers and the Date and Time

Page numbers help you keep your document in order or find a topic from the table of contents. Number the entire document consecutively or each section independently; pick a numbering scheme, such as roman numerals or letters. When you insert page numbers, you can select the position and alignment of the numbers on the page. The date and time field ensures you know which printout is the latest. Word uses your computer's internal calendar and clock as its source. You can insert the date and time for any installed language. Add page numbers and the date in a footer to conveniently keep track of your work.

Insert and Format Page Numbers

1. Click the **Insert** tab.

2. Click the **Page Number** button.

3. Point to the position you want (**Top of Page**, **Bottom of Page**, **Page Margins**, or **Current Position**), and then select a position.

4. Click the **Page Number** button, and then click **Format Page Numbers**.

5. Click the **Number format** list arrow, and then select a numbering scheme.

6. Select the starting number.

7. Click **OK**.

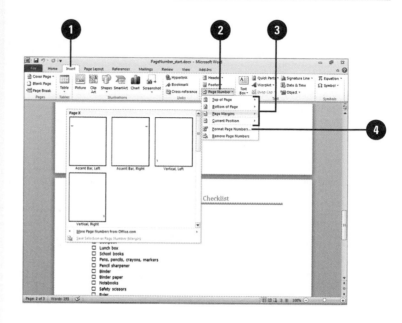

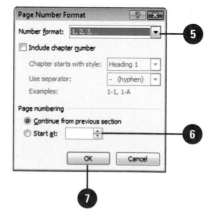

Did You Know?

You can quickly remove page numbers. Click the Insert tab, click the Page Number button, and then click Remove Page Numbers.

Insert the Date or Time

1. To insert the date or time on a single page, display the page, and then click the **Insert** tab.

   ◆ To place the date or time on every page, display or insert a header or footer.

   The Design tab under Header & Footer Tools displays on the Ribbon.

2. Click to place the insertion point where you want to insert the date or time.

3. Click the **Date & Time** button.

4. If necessary, click the **Language** list arrow, and then select a language.

5. To have the date or time automatically update, select the **Update automatically** check box.

6. Click the date and time format you want.

7. To set the current date and time (based on your computer clock) as the default, click **Set As Default**, and then click **Yes**.

8. Click **OK**.

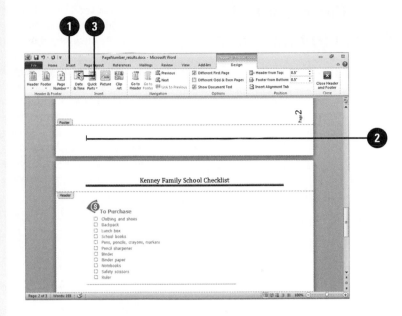

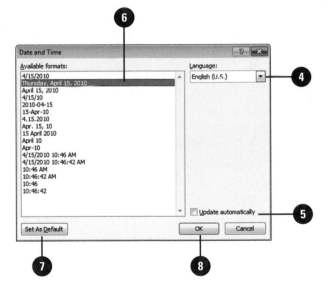

Creating a Blog Posting on the Web

A **blog** is a Web site that provides journal style information on a particular subject, such as news or a diary. Blog is short for Web log. However, you may have heard of other types: vlog (video) or podcasting (audio). A blog combines text, images, and links to other blogs, Web pages, and related topics. In Word, you can create and publish blog postings. Before you can publish a posting, you need to setup an account with a blog service provider and then register it with Word, where you can manage them. Service providers include Windows Live Spaces, Blogger, and Microsoft Windows SharePoint Services with more coming online all the time. Most services are free, so everyone can create an account. Visit Windows Live Space at *http://spaces.live.com* or Blogger at *http://www.blogger.com* and follow the online instructions.

Create a Blog Posting

1. Click the **File** tab, and then click **New**.

2. Click **Blog post**.

3. Click **Create**.

4. If you have not registered a blog account with Word, click **Register Now** or click **Register Later**.

5. To open your blog on the Web, click the **Home Page** button.

6. To open an existing blog posting, click the **Open Existing** button, select the blog, and then click **OK**.

7. To create a new blog posting, select the placeholder title, type a new title, and then type the blog message you want below it.

   ◆ To insert a blog category, click the **Insert Category** button, and then select a category.

   ◆ To insert visuals, click the **Insert** tab, and then use the buttons to insert other content.

8. To post the blog, click the **Publish** button arrow, and then click **Publish** or **Publish as Draft**.

9. When you're done, close and save the posting as a Word document.

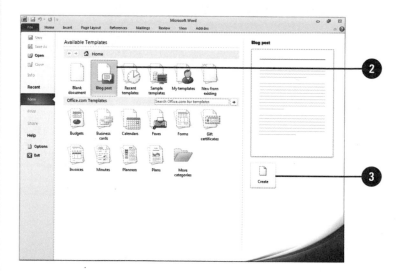

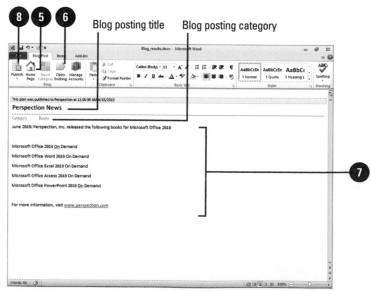

Blog posting title   Blog posting category

Formatting a Document with Word

Introduction

The text of your document is complete, but now you want others to think your document is fun, professional, interesting, dynamic, and extraordinary. Try Microsoft Office Word 2010 to use extensive formatting features in order to lay out the information in your documents and create the exact look and mood you want.

Word documents are based on templates, which are pre-designed and preformatted files that serve as the foundation of the documents. Each template is made up of styles that have common design elements, such as coordinated fonts, sizes, and colors, as well as, page layout designs. Start with a Word template for memos, reports, fax cover pages, Web pages, and so on. Apply the existing styles for headings, titles, body text, and so forth. Then modify the template's styles, or create your own to better suit your needs. Make sure you get the look you want by adding emphasis using italics, boldface, and underline, changing text alignment, adjusting line and paragraph spacing, setting tabs and indents, and creating bulleted and numbered lists. When you're done, your document is sure to demand attention and convey your message in its appearance.

What You'll Do

Format Text for Emphasis

Find and Replace Formatting

Change Paragraph Alignment

Change Line Spacing

Display Rulers

Set Paragraph Tabs

Set Paragraph Indents

Change Character Spacing

Apply a Quick Style

Change a Style Set

Create and Modify Styles

Create Bulleted and Numbered Lists

Hide Text

Formatting Text for Emphasis

You'll often want to format, or change the style of, certain words or phrases to add emphasis to parts of a document. In addition to the standard formatting options—**Bold**, *Italic*, <u>Underline</u>, etc.—Word provides additional formatting effects to text, including Shadow (**New!**), Outline (**New!**), Reflection (**New!**), Glow (**New!**), 3-D (**New!**), Highlight, Strikethrough, Double Strikethrough, Superscript, Subscript, Emboss, Engrave, Small Caps, All Caps, and Hidden. To help you format sentences correctly and change capitalization, you can change text case.

Apply Formatting Text Effects

1. Select the text you want to format.

2. Click the **Home** tab.

3. Click the formatting (**Font, Font Style, Size, Bold, Italic, Underline** (select a style and color), **Strikethrough, Superscript, Subscript,** and **Font Color**) you want.

4. To add a visual effect to text, click the **Text Effect** button, and then click the option you want:

   ◆ A combination text effect.

   ◆ Outline

   ◆ Shadow

   ◆ Reflection

   ◆ Glow

   ◆ **Clear Text Effects.** Removes effect.

5. To change text case, click the **Case** button, and then click the option you want:

   ◆ Sentence case.

   ◆ lowercase

   ◆ UPPERCASE

   ◆ Capitalize Each Word

   ◆ tOGGLEcASE

6. To highlight text, click the **Highlight** button arrow, and then click the color you want.

   ◆ **Add highlight.** Click a color.

   ◆ **Remove highlight.** Click **No Color**.

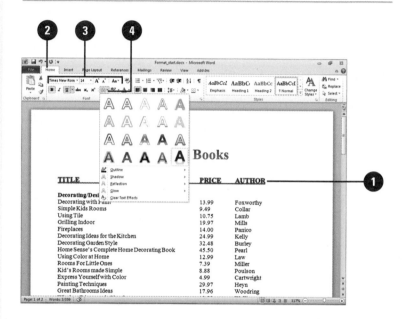

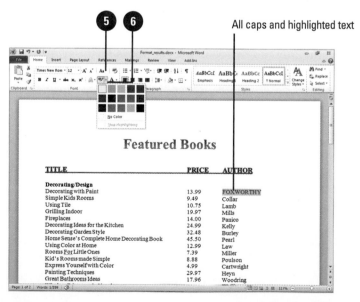

All caps and highlighted text

Apply Other Formatting Effects to Text

1. Select the text you want to format.

2. Click the **Home** tab.

3. Click the **Font Dialog Box Launcher**.

4. Click the formatting (**Font**, **Font Style**, **Size**, **Font color**, **Underline style**, and **Underline color**) you want.

5. Click to select the effects (**Strikethrough**, **Double strikethrough**, **Superscript**, **Subscript**, **Small caps**, **All caps**, and **Hidden**) you want.

6. To custom text effects, such as a text fill or outline with a solid or gradient, shadow, reflection, glow and soft edges, or 3-D format, click **Text Effects**, specify the options you want, and then click **Close** (**New!**).

7. Check the results in the Preview box.

8. To make the new formatting options the default for all new Word documents, click **Set As Default**, and then click **Yes**.

9. Click **OK**.

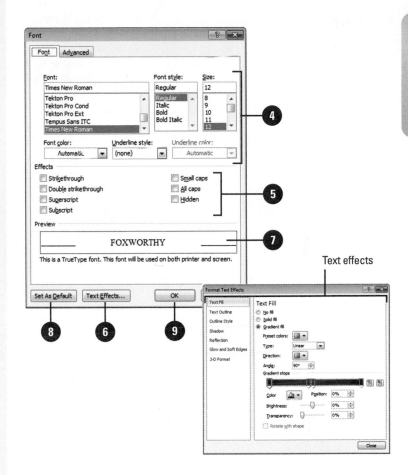

Text effects

Did You Know?

You can quickly clear formatting. Select the text to which you want to clear formatting, click the Home tab, and then click the Clear Formatting button.

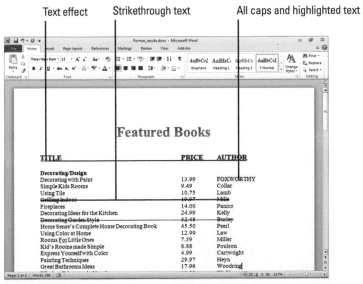

Text effect   Strikethrough text   All caps and highlighted text

Finding and Replacing Formatting

Suddenly you realize all the bold text in your report would be easier to read in italics. Do you spend time making these changes one by one? No. The Find and Replace feature locates the formatting and instantly substitutes new formatting. If your search for a formatting change is an easy one, click Less in the Find and Replace dialog box to decrease the size of the dialog box. If your search is a more complex one, click More to display additional options. With the Match Case option, you can specify exact capitalization. The Reading Highlight button highlights items found to make them easier to read. The Go To tab quickly moves you to a place or item in your document.

Find Formatting

1 Click the **Home** tab.

2 Click the **Find** button.

3 To clear any previous settings, click **No Formatting**.

4 If you want to locate formatted text, type the word or words.

5 Click **More**, click **Format**, and then click the formatting you want to find.

6 To highlight located items, click **Reading Highlight**, and then click **Highlight All**.

7 Click **Find Next** to select the next instance of the formatted text.

8 Click **OK** to confirm Word finished the search.

9 Click **Close** or **Cancel**.

Current find settings

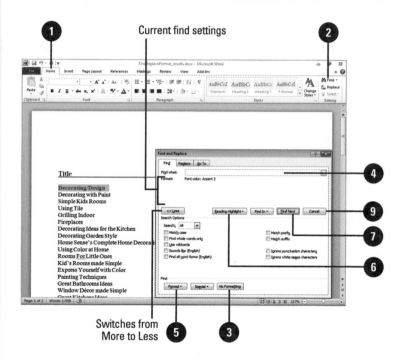

Switches from
More to Less

Did You Know?

You can find an item or location.
In Word, you can search for an item, such as bookmark or comment, or location, such as a page or section. Click the Home tab, click the Find button arrow, click Go To, click an item to find, enter an item number or name, click Next, Previous, or Go To to locate the item, and then click Close.

Replace Formatting

① Click the **Home** tab.

② Click the **Replace** button.

③ If you want to locate formatted text, type the word or words.

④ Click the **More** button, click **Format**, and then click the formatting you want to find. When you're done, click **OK**.

⑤ Press Tab, and then type any text you want to substitute.

⑥ Click **Format**, and then click the formatting you want to substitute. When you're done, click **OK**.

⑦ To substitute every instance of the formatting, click **Replace All**.

To substitute the formatting one instance at a time, click **Find Next**, and then click **Replace**.

If you want to cancel the replace, click **Cancel**.

⑧ If necessary, click **Yes** to search from the beginning of the document.

⑨ Click **OK** to confirm Word finished searching.

⑩ Click **Close** or **Cancel**.

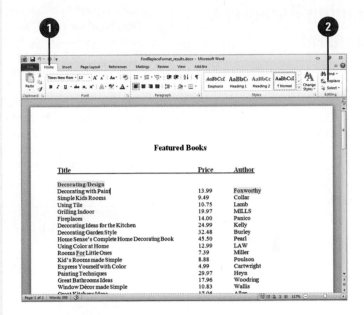

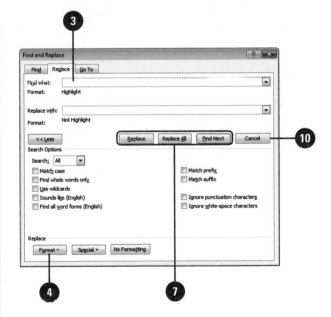

Did You Know?

You can find and replace special characters and document elements.
In Word, you can search for and replace special characters (for example, an em dash) and document elements (for example, a tab character). Click More in the Find and Replace dialog box, click Special, and then click the item you want from the menu.

Changing Paragraph Alignment

Text starts out positioned evenly along the left margin, and uneven, or **ragged**, at the right margin. Left-aligned text works well for body paragraphs in most cases, but other alignments vary the look of a document and help lead the reader through the text. **Right-aligned text**, which is even along the right margin and ragged at the left margin, is good for adding a date to a letter. **Justified text** spreads text evenly between the margins, creating a clean, professional look, often used in newspapers and magazines. **Centered text** is best for titles and headings. You can use Click-And-Type to quickly center titles or set different text alignment on the same line, or you can use the alignment buttons on the Home tab to set alignment on one or more lines.

Align New Text with Click-And-Type

◆ Position the I-beam at the left, right, or center of the line where you want to insert new text.

When the I-beam shows the appropriate alignment, double-click to place the insertion point, and then type your text.

Click-And-Type Text Pointers

Pointer	Purpose
	Left-aligns text
	Right-aligns text
	Centers text
	Creates a new line in the same paragraph
	Creates a text around a picture

Align Existing Text

1. Position the I-beam, or select at least one line in each paragraph to align.

2. Click the appropriate button on the Home tab.

   ◆ **Align Left** button

   ◆ **Center** button

   ◆ **Align Right** button

   ◆ **Justify** button

Changing Line Spacing

The lines in all Word documents are single-spaced by default, which is appropriate for letters and most documents. But you can easily change your document line spacing to double or 1.5 lines to allow extra space between every line. This is useful when you want to make notes on a printed document. Sometimes, you'll want to add space above and below certain paragraphs, for headlines, or indented quotations to help set off the text.

Change Line Spacing

1. Select the text you want to change.

2. Click the **Home** tab.

3. Click the **Line Spacing** button arrow, and then click a spacing option.

   ◆ To apply a new setting, click the number you want.

   ◆ To apply the setting you last used, click the **Line Spacing** button.

   ◆ To enter precise parameters, click **Line Spacing Options**, specify the line or paragraph settings you want, and then click **OK**.

   ◆ To apply the setting you last used, click **Add Space Before Paragraph** or **Add Space After Paragraph**.

   TIMESAVER *Press Ctrl+1 for single-spacing, Ctrl+5 for 1.5 spacing, or Ctrl+2 for double-spacing.*

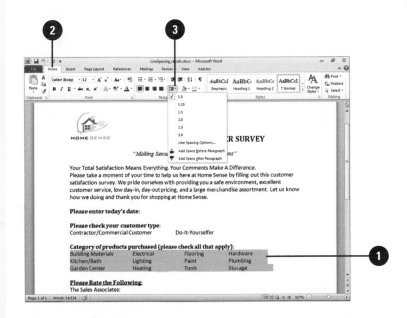

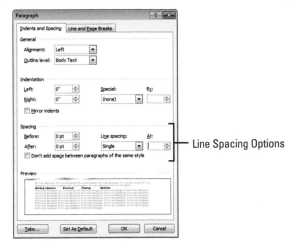

Line Spacing Options

Displaying Rulers

Word rulers do more than measure. The **horizontal ruler** above the document shows the length of the typing line and lets you quickly adjust left and right margins and indents, set tabs, and change column widths. The **vertical ruler** along the left edge of the document lets you adjust top and bottom margins and change table row heights. You can hide the rulers to get more room for your document. As you work with long documents, use the document map to jump to any heading in your document. Headings are in the left pane and documents in the right.

Show and Hide the Rulers

1 Click the **View** tab.

2 Select or clear the **Ruler** check box.

> **TIMESAVER** *Click the View Ruler button at the top of the vertical scroll bar.*

◆ To view the horizontal ruler, click the **Web Layout View** or **Draft View** button.

◆ To view the horizontal and vertical rulers, click the **Print Layout View** button.

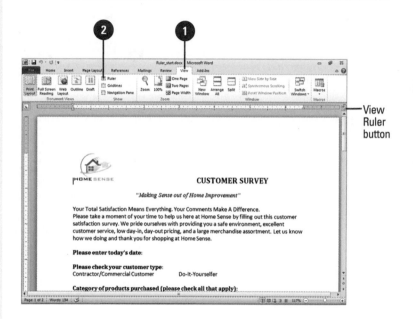

View Ruler button

Did You Know?

You can change the ruler measurements. Change the ruler to show inches, centimeters, millimeters, points, or picas. Click the File tab, click Options, click Advanced, click the Show Measurement In Units list arrow, select the measurement you want, and then click OK.

You can set your text to be hyphenated. Hyphenation prevents ugly gaps and short lines in text. Click the Page Layout tab, click the Hyphenation button, and then click None, Automatic, or Manual, or Hyphenation Options. Click Hyphenation Options to set the hyphenation zone and limit the number of consecutive hyphens (usually two), and then click OK.

Setting Paragraph Tabs

In your document, **tabs** set how text or numerical data aligns in relation to the document margins. A **tab stop** is a predefined stopping point along the document's typing line. Default tab stops are set every half-inch, but you can set multiple tabs per paragraph at any location. Choose from four text tab stops: left, right, center, and decimal (for numerical data). The bar tab inserts a vertical bar at the tab stop. You can use the Tab button on the horizontal ruler to switch between the available tabs.

Create and Clear a Tab Stop

1. Select one or more paragraphs in which you want to set a tab stop.

2. Click the **Tab** button on the horizontal ruler until it shows the type of tab stop you want.

3. Click the ruler where you want to set the tab stop.

4. If necessary, drag the tab stop to position it where you want.

   To display a numerical measurement in the ruler where the tab is placed, press and hold Alt as you drag.

5. To clear a tab stop, drag it off the ruler.

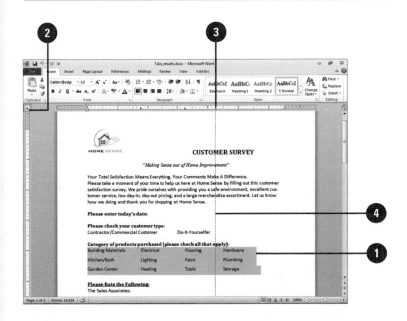

Did You Know?

You can view formatting marks.
Sometimes it's hard to see the number of spaces or tabs between words. You can change the view to display formatting marks, a period for space and an arrow for tabs. Click the Home tab, and then click Show/Hide ¶ button to toggle on and off. Click the File tab, click Options, click Display, select the formatting mark check boxes you want to view, and then click OK.

Tab Stops

Tab Stop	Purpose
L	Aligns text to the left of the tab stop
⅃	Aligns text to the right of the tab stop
⊥	Centers text on the tab stop
⊥·	Aligns numbers on the decimal point
I	Inserts a vertical bar at the tab stop

Setting Paragraph Indents

Quickly indent lines of text to precise locations from the left or right margin with the horizontal ruler. Indent the first line of a paragraph (called a **first-line indent**) as books do to distinguish paragraphs. Indent the second and subsequent lines of a paragraph from the left margin (called a **hanging indent**) to create a properly formatted bibliography. Indent the entire paragraph any amount from the left and right margins (called **left indents** and **right indents**) to separate quoted passages.

Indent Paragraph Lines Precisely

1. Click the **View Ruler** button to display the Ruler.

2. Click the paragraph or select multiple paragraphs to indent:

   ◆ To change the left indent of the first line, drag the First-line Indent marker.

   ◆ To change the indent of the second and subsequent lines, drag the Hanging Indent marker.

   ◆ To change the left indent for all lines, drag the Left Indent marker.

   ◆ To change the right indent for all lines, drag the Right Indent marker.

   As you drag a marker, the dotted guideline helps you accurately position the indent. You can also press and hold Alt to see a measurement in the ruler.

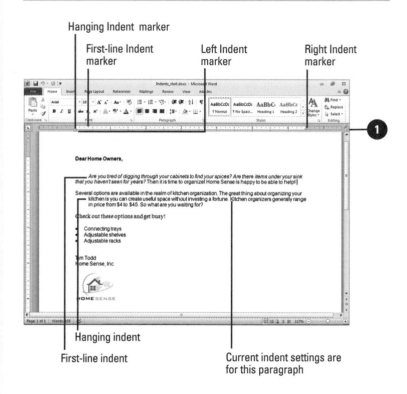

Hanging Indent marker

First-line Indent marker

Left Indent marker

Right Indent marker

Hanging indent

First-line indent

Current indent settings are for this paragraph

Did You Know?

You can indent using the Tab key. You can indent the first line of a paragraph by clicking at the beginning of the paragraph, and then pressing Tab. You can indent the entire paragraph by selecting it, and then pressing Tab.

Indent a Paragraph

1. Click the paragraph, or select multiple paragraphs to indent.

2. Click the **Home** tab.

3. Click the **Increase Indent** button or **Decrease Indent** button to move the paragraph right or left one-half inch.

Did You Know?

You can add line numbers to a document or page. Click the Page Layout tab, click the Line Numbers button, and then click Continuous, Restart Each Page, Restart Each Section, Suppress for Current Paragraph, or Line Numbering Options.

Set Indentation Using the Tab Key

1. Click the **File** tab, and then click **Options**.

2. In the left pane, click **Proofing**, and then click **AutoCorrect Options**.

3. Click the **AutoFormat As You Type** tab.

4. Select the **Set left- and first-indent with tabs and backspaces** check box.

5. Click **OK**.

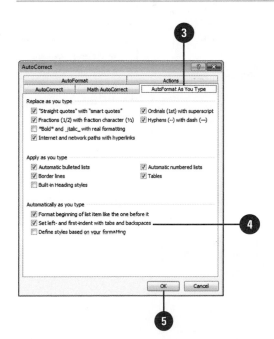

Changing Character Spacing

Kerning is the amount of space between each individual character that you type. Sometimes the space between two characters is larger than others, which makes the word look uneven. You can use the Font dialog box to change the kerning setting for selected characters. Kerning works only with OpenType/TrueType or Adobe Type Manager fonts. You can expand or condense character spacing to create a special effect for a title, or re-align the position of characters to the bottom edge of the text—this is helpful for positioning the copyright or trademark symbols. In addition, you can set text formatting for OpenType/TrueType fonts (**New!**) that include a range of ligature settings (where two or three letters combine into a single character), number spacing and forms, and stylistic sets (added font sets in a given font). Many of these options are based on specifications from font designers.

Change Character Spacing

1. Select the text you want to format.

2. Click the **Home** tab.

3. Click the **Font Dialog Box Launcher**.

4. Click the **Advanced** tab.

5. Click the **Spacing** list arrow, click an option, and then specify a point size to expand or condense spacing by the amount specified.

6. Click the **Position** list arrow, click an option, and then specify a point size to raise or lower the text in relation to the baseline (bottom of the text).

7. Select the **Kerning for fonts** check box, and then specify a point size.

8. Check the results in the Preview box.

9. To make the new formatting options the default for all new Word documents, click **Set As Default**, and then click **Yes**.

10. Click **OK**.

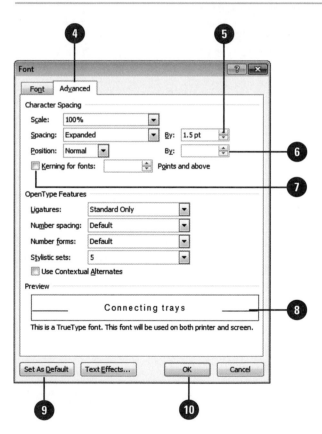

Change OpenType Features

① Select the text you want to format.

② Click the **Home** tab.

③ Click the **Font Dialog Box Launcher**.

④ Click the **Advanced** tab.

⑤ Click any of the follow list arrows, and then select an option:

◆ **Ligatures.** Select **Standard Only** (current standard), **Standard and Contextual** (current standard plus font specific additions), **Historical and Discretionary** (old standard), or **All** (**New!**).

◆ **Number Spacing.** Select **Default** (specified by font designer), **Proportional** (varying width spacing), or **Tabular** (same width spacing) (**New!**).

◆ **Number Forms.** Select **Default** (specified by font designer), **Lining** (same height, not below base-line, or **Old-Style** (flow above or below the line of text) (**New!**).

◆ **Stylistic Sets.** Select **Default** (specified by font designer) or a specific set number (**New!**).

⑥ Select the **Use Contextual Alternates** check box to provide fine-tuning of letters or letter combinations based on the surrounding characters (**New!**).

⑦ Check the results in the Preview box.

⑧ To make the new formatting options the default for all new Word documents, click **Set As Default**, and then click **Yes**.

⑨ Click **OK**.

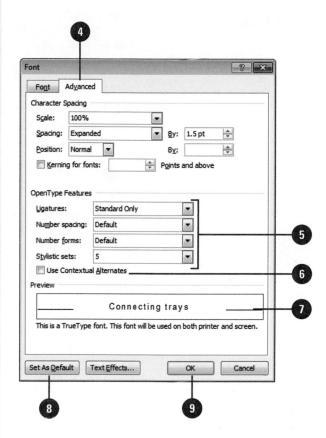

Applying a Quick Style

A **style** is a collection of formatting settings saved with a name in a document or template that you can apply to text at any time. Word provides different style sets to make it easy to format text. Each style set consists of a variety of different formatting style combinations, which you can view using the Quick Style gallery. To quickly see if you like a Quick Style, point to a thumbnail in the gallery to display a live preview of it in the selected text. If you like it, click the thumbnail to apply it.

Apply a Style

1. Select the text to which you want to apply a style.

2. Click the **Home** tab.

3. Click the scroll up or down arrow, or click the **More** list arrow in the Styles group to see additional styles.

4. Click the style you want to apply from the gallery.

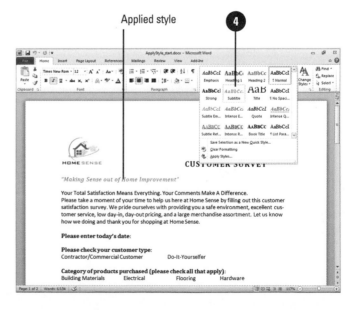

Applied style

Did You Know?

You can clear style formatting. Select the text you want to clear, click the Home tab, and then click the Clear Formatting button.

You can reset the document back to document Quick Styles. Click the Home tab, click the Change Styles button, point to Style Set, and then click Reset Document Quick Steps.

You can reset the document back to document Quick Styles from a template. Click the Home tab, click the Change Styles button, point to Style Set, and then click Reset To Quick Steps From Template, locate and select the template, and then click OK.

Changing a Style Set

Word provides predefined style sets—such as Classic, Elegant, Simple, Modern, Formal, Fancy, and Distinctive—to make it easy to format an entire document. Each style set consists of a variety of different formatting style combinations, which you can view using the Quick Style gallery.

Change a Style Set

1. Click the **Home** tab.

2. Click the **Change Styles** button.

3. Point to **Style Set**, and then click the style set you want.

> ### Did You Know?
>
> *You can set the default style set.* Click the Home tab, click the Change Styles button, point to Style Set, and then click the style set you want to use as the default. Click the Change Styles button, and then click Set As Default.

Create a Style Set

1. Format a document with the style that you want to save.

2. Click the **Home** tab.

3. Click the **Change Styles** button.

4. Point to **Style Set**.

5. Click **Save as Quick Style Set**.

6. Type a file name.

7. If necessary, click the **Save as type** list arrow, and then click **Word Templates**.

8. Click **Save**.

Applied style

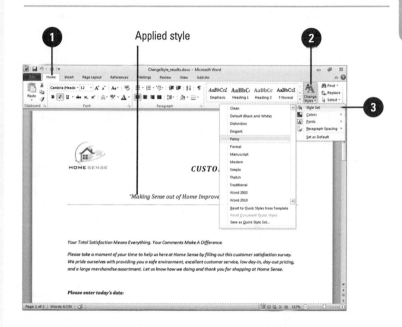

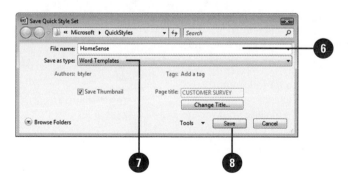

Creating and Modifying Styles

Word provides a variety of styles to choose from. But sometimes you need to create a new style or modify an existing one to get the exact look you want. When you create a new style, specify if it applies to paragraphs or characters, and give the style a short, descriptive name that describes its purpose so you and others recall when to use that style. A **paragraph style** is a group of format settings that can be applied only to all of the text within a paragraph (even if it is a one-line paragraph), while a **character style** is a group of format settings that is applied to any block of text at the user's discretion. To modify a style, adjust the formatting settings of an existing style.

Create a New Style

1. Select the text whose formatting you want to save as a style.

2. Click the **Home** tab.

3. Click the scroll up or down arrow, or click the **More** list arrow in the Styles group, and then click **Save Selection as a New Quick Style**.

4. Type a short, descriptive name.

5. Click **Modify**.

6. Click the **Style type** list arrow, and then click **Paragraph** to include the selected text's line spacing and margins in the style, or click **Character** to include only formatting, such as font, size, and bold, in the style.

7. Click the **Style for following paragraph** list arrow, and then click the name of style you want to be applied after a paragraph with the new style.

8. Select the formatting options you want.

9. To add the style to the Quick style gallery, select the **Add to Quick Style list** check box.

10. Click **OK**.

11. Click **OK**.

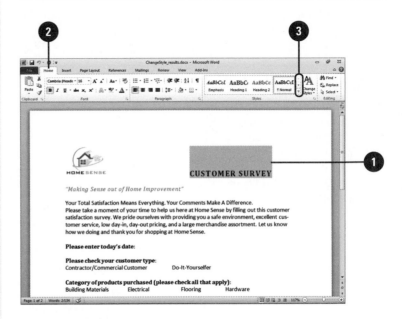

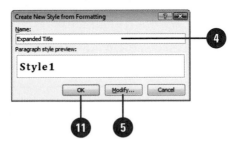

Modify a Style

1. Click the **Home** tab.

2. Click the scroll up or down arrow, or click the **More** list arrow in the Styles group.

3. Right-click the style you want to modify, and then click **Modify**.

4. Specify any style changes (Style based on or Style for following paragraphs) you want.

5. Click **Format**, and then click the type of formatting you want to modify:

   ◆ To change character formatting, such as font type and boldface, click **Font**.

   ◆ To change line spacing and indents, click **Paragraph**.

6. Select the formatting options you want.

7. Check the Preview box, and review the style description. Make any formatting changes as needed.

8. To add the style to the Quick style gallery, select the **Add to Quick Style list** check box.

9. Click **OK**.

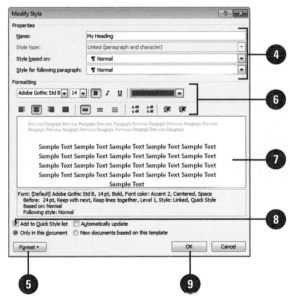

Did You Know?

You can view the list of styles. Click the Home tab, click the More list arrow in the Styles group, click Apply Style, and then click the Styles button to display the Styles list. From the Styles list pane, you can create a new style, inspect styles, manage styles, and change style options.

Creating Bulleted and Numbered Lists

The best way to draw attention to a list is to format the items with bullets or numbers. You can even create multi-level lists. For different emphasis, change any bullet or number style to one of Word's many pre-defined formats. For example, switch round bullets to check boxes or Roman numerals to lowercase letters. You can also insert a picture as a bullet or customize the numbering list style—including fixed-digits, such as 001, 002, etc. (**New!**). If you move, insert, or delete items in a numbered list, Word sequentially renumbers the list for you.

Create a Bulleted List

1. Click where you want to create a bulleted list.

2. Click the **Home** tab.

3. Click the **Bullets** button arrow, and then select a bullet style.

4. Type the first item in your list, and then press Enter.

5. Type the next item in your list, and then press Enter.

6. Click the **Bullets** button, or press Enter again to end the list.

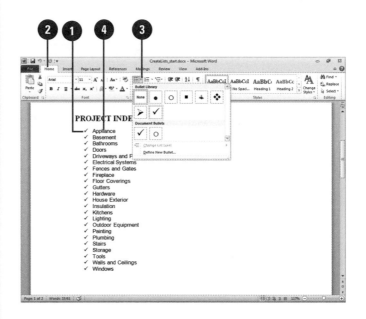

Create a Numbered List

1. Click where you want to create a numbered list.

2. Click the **Home** tab.

3. Click the **Numbering** button arrow, and then select a numbering style.

4. Type the first item in your list, and then press Enter.

5. Type the next item in your list, and then press Enter.

6. Click the **Numbering** button, or press Enter again to end the list.

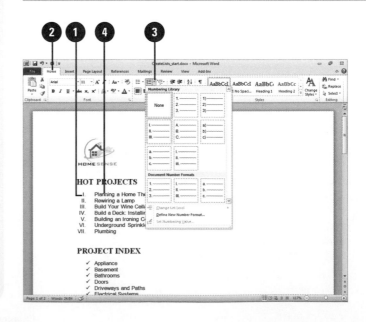

Change Bullet or Number Styles

1. Select the list, and then click the Home tab.

2. Click the **Bullets** or **Numbering** button arrow.

3. Click a predefined format, or click **Define New Bullet** or **Define New Number Format**.

4. Select the appropriate options:

   ◆ **Bullet.** Click **Symbol**, **Picture**, or **Font**, and then select the picture you want.

   ◆ **Number.** Select a numbering style (**New!**), font, and format.

5. Specify the alignment and any other formatting you want.

6. Click **OK**.

Create a Multi-Level Bulleted or Numbered List

1. Start the list as usual.

2. Press Tab to indent a line to the next level bullet or number, type the item, and then press Enter to insert the next bullet or number.

3. Press Shift+Tab to return to the previous level bullet or number.

4. To format the multi-level list, select the list, click the **Multi-Level List** button on the Home tab, and then select a format.

Did You Know?

You can quickly create a numbered list. Click to place the insertion point at the beginning of a line, type 1., press the Spacebar, type the first item, and then press Enter. Press Enter or Backspace to end the list.

Bullet styles

Number styles

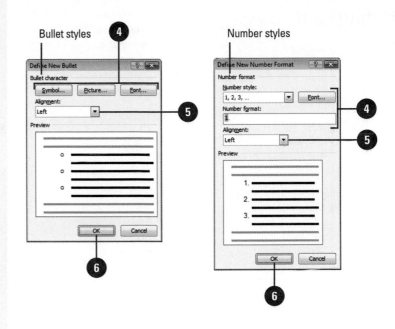

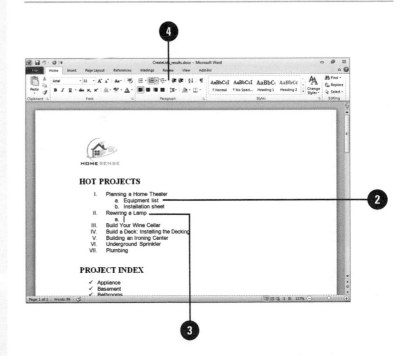

Hiding Text

If you have confidential information in a document or text that you don't want others to see, you can hide the text. When you hide text, you can't view or print the text unless you select the Hidden Text option in the Options dialog box. When you display or print hidden text, the characters appear with a dotted lined underneath. Hiding text does not protect your text from being seen, but it does conceal it from others.

Hide or Unhide Text

1. Select the text you want to hide or the hidden text.

2. Click the **Home** tab, and then click the **Font Dialog Box Launcher**.

3. Click the **Font** tab.

4. Select or clear the **Hidden** check box.

5. Click **OK**.

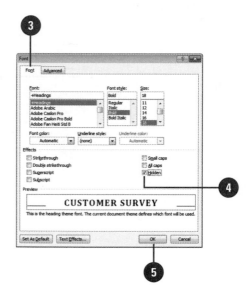

Display or Print Hidden Text

1. Click the **File** tab, and then click **Options**.

2. In the left pane, click **Display**.

3. Select the **Hidden text** check box.

4. Select the **Print hidden text** check box.

5. Click **OK**.

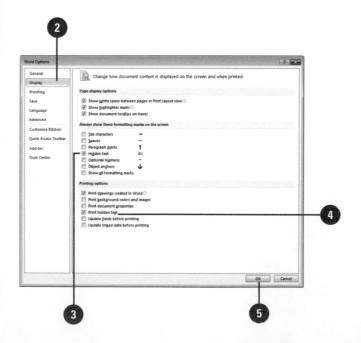

Enhancing a Document with Word

Introduction

Once you've mastered the basics, Microsoft Office Word 2010 has plenty of advanced features to enhance your documents. Whether it's a single-page flyer or a twenty-page report, you can arrange the text and add enhancements that make your document appealing and easy to read.

After you create your basic document, consider how you can improve its appearance and communicate its message more effectively. For example, if your document is a brochure or newsletter, arrange the text in columns and add an enlarged capital letter to the first word in each paragraph to add style and grab the readers attention. Or organize information in a table to draw attention to important data or clarify the details of a complicated paragraph.

Another way to impress clients, business associates, social groups, or even family members is to create personalized form letters for any occasion—an upcoming meeting, a holiday greeting, or a family announcement. Create a formatted document and enter text that doesn't change. Any data that changes from person to person (such as names) goes into another file, which you merge with the form letter. In a snap, you've got personalized letters that show you care.

What You'll Do

Add Desktop Publishing Effects

Add a Watermark

Add Page Backgrounds

Arrange Text in Columns

Wrap Text Around an Object

Work with Text Boxes

Insert Building Blocks

Create and Modify a Table

Enter Text in a Table and Adjust Cells

Format a Table and Calculate a Value

Address Envelopes and Labels

Create a Form Letter and Labels

Insert a Table of Contents

Create an Index and Captions

Create a Table of Figures

Create Footnotes or Endnotes

Create a Bookmark

Insert Cross References

Compare and Merge Documents

Use Track Changes

Add a Cover Page

Adding Desktop Publishing Effects

A few simple elements—drop caps, borders, and shading—make your newsletters and brochures look like a professional produced them. A **drop cap** is the enlarged first letter of a paragraph that provides instant style to a document. Instead of using a desktop publishing program to create a drop cap effect, you can quickly achieve the same thing in Word. You can change the drop cap position, font, and height, and then enter the distance between the drop cap and paragraph.

Add a Drop Cap

1 Click the **Print Layout View** button.

2 Click the **Insert** tab.

3 Click the paragraph where you want the drop cap.

4 Click the **Drop Cap** button, and then select the drop cap style you want.

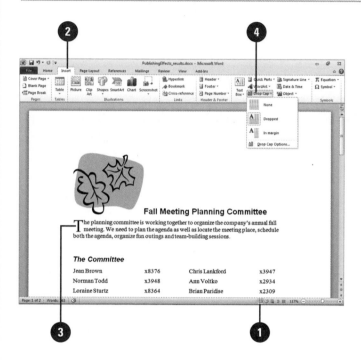

Customize a Drop Cap

1 Click the **Print Layout View** button.

2 Click the **Insert** tab.

3 Click the paragraph with the drop cap.

4 Click the **Drop Cap** button, and then click **Drop Cap Options**.

5 Click a drop cap position.

6 Change the drop cap font and height, and then enter the distance between the drop cap and text.

7 Click **OK**.

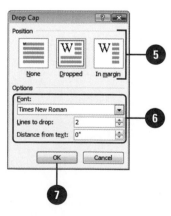

Adding a Watermark

A **watermark** is a background effect—some text or a graphic, that prints in a light shade behind your text on your document. You can use a washed out version of your company logo, or you can add text such as SAMPLE, DRAFT, PROPOSAL, or CONFIDENTIAL. If you can't find the watermark you need, check out Office.com (**New!**). If you decide to change your watermark, it's as easy as typing in some new text.

Add or Remove a Watermark

1. Click the **Print Layout View** button.

2. Click the **Page Layout** tab.

3. Click the **Watermark** button.

4. Do one of the following:

   ◆ **Add.** Click the border you want to add.

   ◆ **Add from Office.com.** Click **More Watermarks from Office.com (New!)**.

   ◆ **Remove.** Click **Remove Page Border**.

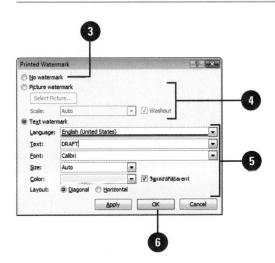

Customize a Watermark

1. Click the **Print Layout View** button, and then click the **Page Layout** tab.

2. Click the **Watermark** button, and then click **Custom Watermark**.

3. To remove a watermark, click the **No watermark** option.

4. To insert a picture as a watermark, click the **Picture watermark** option, click **Select Picture**, select a picture, and then click **OK**.

5. To customize watermark text, click the **Text watermark** option, and then select the settings you want.

6. Click **OK**.

Adding Page
Backgrounds

Borders are lines or graphics that appear around a page, paragraph, selected text, or table cells. With borders, you can change the line style, width, and colors, and you can add shadows and 3D effects. In addition to a page border, you can also change the page color. If you apply a theme color as the page color, it changes if you change the document theme. **Shading** is a color that fills the background of selected text, paragraphs, or table cells. For more attractive pages, add clips or columns.

Add Borders and Shading

1. Select the text you want to have a border.

2. Click the **Page Layout** tab.

3. Click the **Page Borders** button.

4. Click the **Borders** tab.

5. Do one of the following:

   ◆ Click a box setting to modify all border edges.

   ◆ Click the edge in the diagram to modify individual border edges.

6. Click a border style, color, and width.

7. Click the **Shading** tab.

8. Click the **Fill** list arrow, and then click a fill color.

9. Click **OK**.

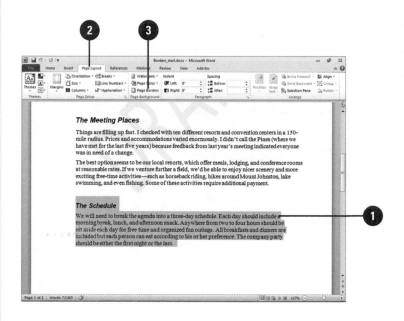

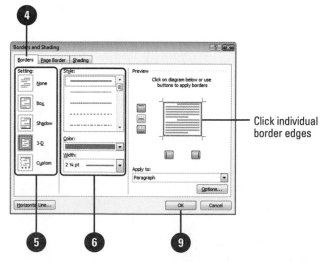

Click individual border edges

Add or Remove a Page Border

1. Click the page you want to have a border.

2. Click the **Page Layout** tab.

3. Click the **Page Borders** button.

4. Click the **Page Border** tab.

5. Click a box setting.

6. Click a line style, or click the Art list arrow, and then select a line or art style.

7. Click a **Width** list arrow, and then select a width.

8. Click the **Apply to** list arrow, and then select the pages you want to have borders.

9. Click **OK**.

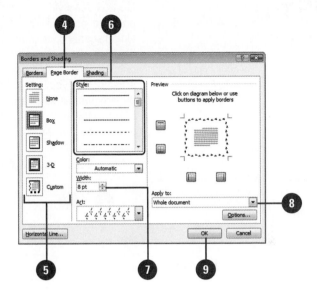

Add Page Color

1. Click the page you want to add a page color.

2. Click the **Page Layout** tab.

3. Click the **Page Color** button.

4. Do one of the following:

   ◆ **Add.** Click the color you want to add.

   ◆ **Remove.** Click **No Color**.

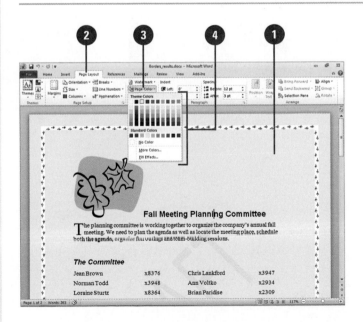

Arranging Text in Columns

Newspaper-style columns can give newsletters and brochures a more polished look. You can format an entire document, selected text, or individual sections into columns. You can create one, two, or three columns of equal size. You can also create two columns and have one column wider than the other. Word fills one column with text before the other, unless you insert a column break. **Column breaks** are used in two-column layouts to move the text after the insertion point to the top of the following column. You can also display a vertical line between the columns. To view the columns side by side, switch to print layout view.

Create Columns

1. Click the **Page Layout** tab.

2. Select the text you want to arrange in columns.

3. Click the **Columns** button.

4. Select the number of columns you want.

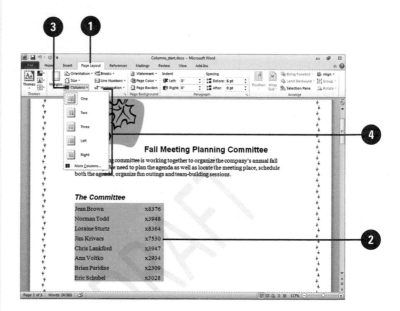

Did You Know?

You can remove columns quickly. Select the columns, click the Columns button on the Page Layout tab, and then click the first column.

You can align text in a column. Click the Align Left, Center, Align Right, or Justify button on the Home tab to align paragraphs in columns.

Modify Columns

1. Click the **Page Layout** tab, and then click in the columns you want to modify.

2. Click the **Columns** button, and then click **More Columns**.

3. Click a column preset format.

4. If necessary, enter the number of columns you want.

5. Enter the width and spacing you want for each column.

6. To place a vertical line between columns, select the **Line between** check box.

7. Click **OK**.

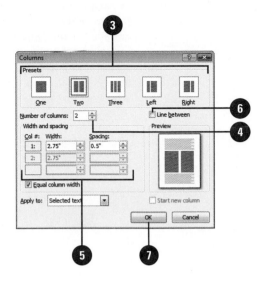

Insert a Column Break

1. Click where you want to insert a column break.

2. Click the **Page Layout** tab.

3. Click the **Break** button, and then click **Column**.

4. To delete a column break, click the column break dotted line in Draft view or select lines above and below the break, and then press the Delete key.

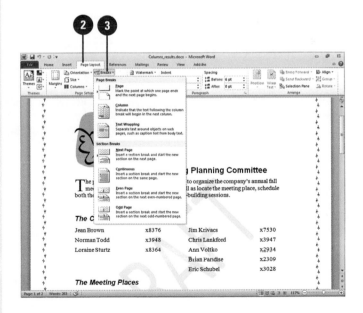

Wrapping Text Around an Object

When integrating pictures, charts, tables, or other graphics with your text, you need to wrap the text around the object regardless of where it is placed on the page. Rather than having to constantly reset margins and make other tedious adjustments, Word simplifies this task with the text wrapping feature. Unless your object or table is large enough to span the entire page, your layout will look more professional if you wrap your text around it instead of leaving excessive white space.

Change the Text Position Around an Object or Picture

1. Select the picture or object.

2. Click the **Page Layout** tab.

3. Click the **Position** button, and then click the text wrapping option you want.

4. To customize text position, click the **Position** button, click **More Layout Options**, specify the options you want, and then click **OK**.

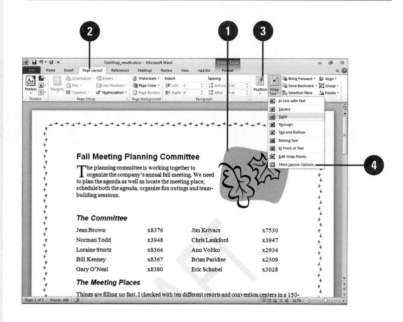

Text wrapping options

Wrap Text Around an Object or Picture

1. Select the picture or object.

2. Click the **Page Layout** tab.

3. To change text position, click the **Position** button, select a position or click **More Layout Options**, specify the options you want, and then click **OK**.

4. Click the **Wrap Text** button, and then click the text wrapping option you want.

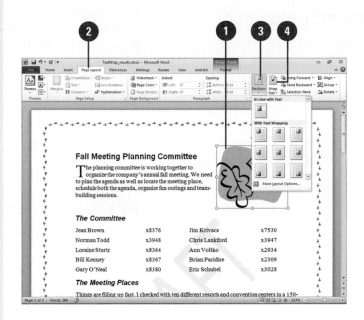

Wrap Text Tightly Around an Object or Picture

1. Select the picture or object.

2. Click the **Page Layout** tab.

3. To change text position, click the **Position** button, select a position or click **More Layout Options**, specify the options you want, and then click **OK**.

4. Click the **Wrap Text** button, and then click **Tight**.

5. Click the **Wrap Text** button, and then click **Edit Wrap Points**.

6. Drag edit points around the object or picture to tighten text around it.

7. Click a blank area of the document to deselect the object or picture.

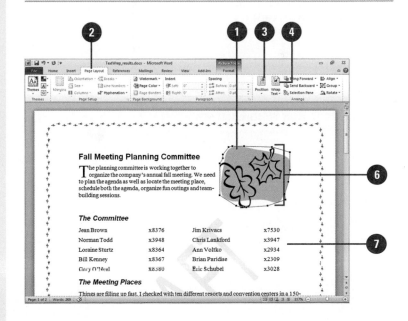

Working with Text Boxes

In addition to normal text on a page, you can also create independent text boxes to hold other types of information—such as titles, heading, pull quotes, and side bars—similar to those found on a desktop publishing page. You can insert a text box with predefined information or you can create a blank text box. If you can't find the predefined text box you need, check out Office.com (**New!**). You can even link two or more text boxes together to have text flow to different parts of a document. If you no longer need the text boxes to link, you can quickly break the link.

Insert a Text Box Pull Quote or Side Bar

1. Click where you want to insert a text box.

2. Click the **Insert** tab.

3. Click the **Text Box** button.

4. Click the predefined text box you want to insert.

   ◆ **Add from Office.com.** Click **More Text Boxes from Office.com (New!)**.

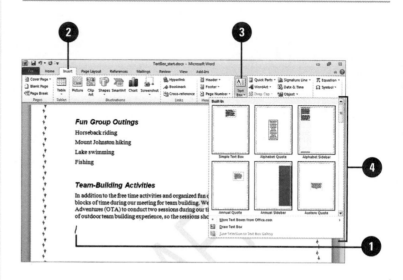

Create a Text Box from Existing Text

1. Select the text you want to place in a text box.

2. Click the **Insert** tab.

3. Click the **Text Box** button.

4. Click **Draw Text Box**.

Did You Know?

You can change text direction in a text box. Select the text box you want to modify, click the Text Direction button on the Format tab under Drawing Tools.

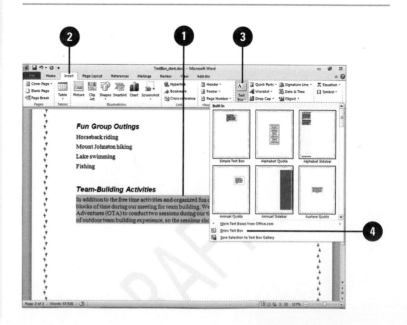

Create a Text Box

1. Click the **Insert** tab.

2. Click the **Text Box** button.

3. Point to where you want to place the text box, and then drag to create a text box the size you want.

4. If necessary, click the text box to select it.

5. Type the text you want.

6. To resize the text box, drag a size handle.

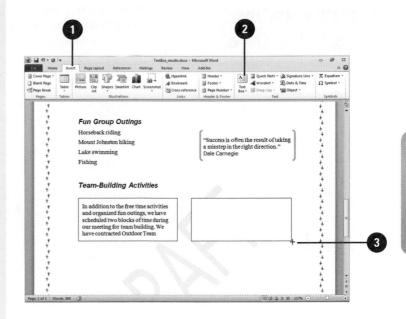

Link Text Boxes

1. Select the source text box.

2. Click the **Format** tab under Drawing Tools.

3. Click the **Create Link** button.

4. Point to the destination text box (the pointer changes to a pitcher), and then click to link the text boxes.

Did You Know?

You can break a link. Select the text box with the link you want to break, click the Break Link button on the Format tab under Drawing Tools, and then click the destination text box to break the link.

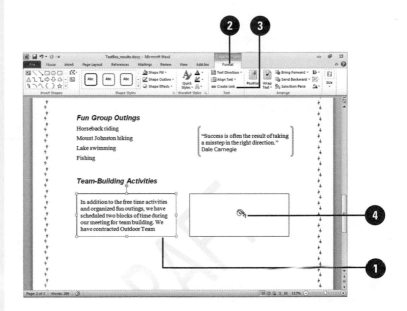

Inserting Building Blocks Using Quick Parts

A **Quick Part** is a defined field or set of fields that contains information you can use throughout a document. Word calls these building blocks. Instead of typing the company name, address and phone number every time you need it in a document, you can insert a text box field with the information. Word provides a variety of defined Quick Parts—including Author, Company, Company Address, Company E-mail, Manager and Status—you can quickly insert in a document. The Quick Part fields insert information you provide in Document Properties or a placeholder, which you can fill in the first time. If a predefined field doesn't meet your needs, you can create your own or get more on Office.com. If you need to modify a Quick Part, you can use the building block organizer, which stores your custom Quick Parts and those provided by Word. Word uses Quick Parts as part of the program to build page covers, headers and footers, pull quotes, and side bar to name a few.

Insert a Quick Part Building Block

1. Click where you want to insert a text box.

2. Click the **Insert** tab.

3. Click the **Quick Parts** button.

4. Point to **Document Property**, and then click the predefined Quick Part you want to insert.

5. Modify the predefined Quick Part; click the list arrow (if available) to define it.

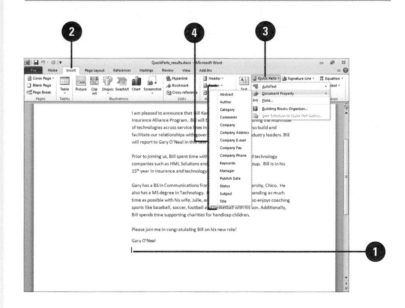

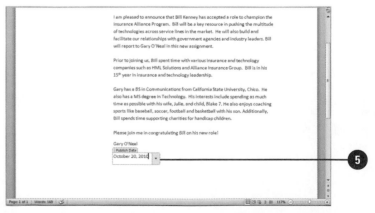

Create a Quick Part Field

1. Click the **Insert** tab.

2. Click the **Quick Parts** button, and then click **Field**.

3. Click the **Categories** list arrow, and then click a category to narrow down the field names.

4. Click the field name you want to use.

5. Specify field property information.

6. Click the format you want to apply.

7. Click **OK**.

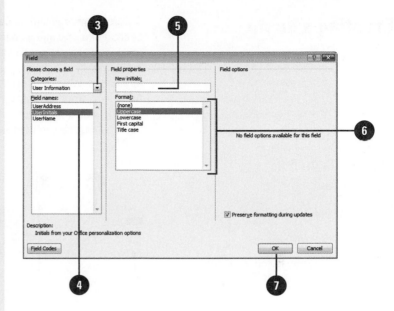

Work with Building Blocks

1. Click the **Insert** tab.

2. Click the **Quick Parts** button, and then click **Building Blocks Organizer**.

3. Select the Quick Part building block you want to modify.

4. Click **Edit Properties**.

5. Specify the properties you want to change, including Name, Gallery, Category, Description, Save in, and Options.

6. Click **OK**.

7. To insert or delete a building block, select it, and then click **Insert** or **Delete**.

8. Click **Close**.

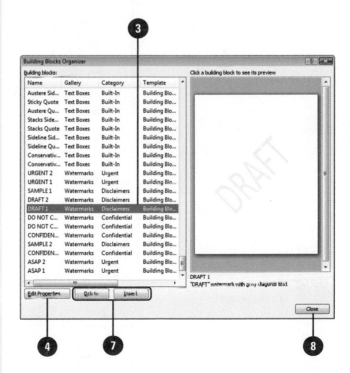

Creating a Table

A **table** organizes information neatly into rows and columns. The inter-section of a row and a column is called a **cell**. You can draw a custom table with various sized cells and then enter text, or you can create a table from existing text separated by paragraphs, tabs, or commas. In addition, now you can create **nested tables** (a table created within a table cell), **floating tables** (tables with text wrapped around them), or **side-by-side tables** (separate but adjacent tables). If you decide not to use a table, you can convert it to text.

Create a Table from Existing Text

1. Select the text for the table.

2. Click the **Insert** tab.

3. Click the **Table** button, and then click **Convert Text to Table**.

4. Enter the number of columns.

5. Select an AutoFit column width option.

6. Click a symbol to separate text into cells.

7. Click **OK**.

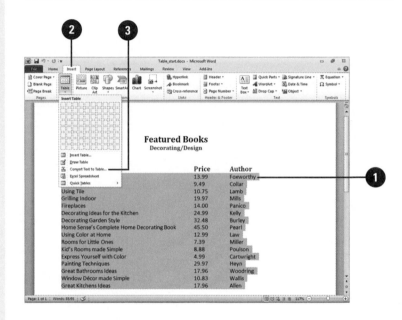

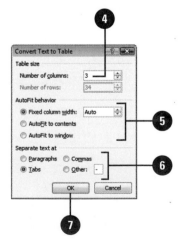

Did You Know?

You can convert a table back to text. Select the table, click the Layout tab under Table Tools, click the Convert To Text button, select the Separate Text With option, typically Tabs, and then click OK.

Entering Text in a Table

Once you create your table, you enter text into cells just as you would in a paragraph, except pressing Tab moves you from cell to cell. As you type in a cell, text wraps to the next line, and the height of a row expands as you enter text that extends beyond the column width. The first row in the table is good for column headings, whereas the left-most column is good for row labels. Before you can modify a table, you need to know how to select the rows and columns of a table.

Enter Text and Move Around a Table

1 The insertion point shows where text that you type will appear in a table. After you type text in a cell:

- ◆ Press Enter to start a new paragraph within that cell.

- ◆ Press Tab to move the insertion point to the next cell to the right (or to the first cell in the next row).

- ◆ Press the arrow keys or click in a cell to move the insertion point to a new location.

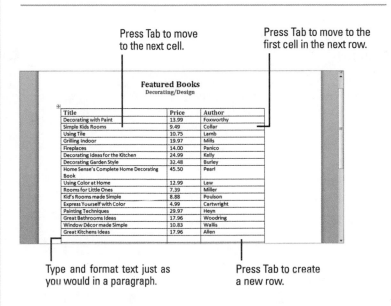

Press Tab to move to the next cell.

Press Tab to move to the first cell in the next row.

Type and format text just as you would in a paragraph.

Press Tab to create a new row.

Select Table Elements

Refer to this table for methods of selecting table elements, including:

- ◆ The entire table
- ◆ One or more rows and columns
- ◆ One or more cells

Did You Know?

You can delete contents within a cell. Select the cells whose contents you want to delete, and then press Backspace or Delete.

Selecting Table Elements

To Select	Do This
The entire table	Click ⊞ next to the table, or click anywhere in the table, click the Layout tab, click the Select button, and then click Select Table.
One or more rows	Click in the left margin next to the first row you want to select, and then drag to select the rows you want.
One or more columns	Click just above the first column you want to select, and then drag with ↓ to select the columns you want.
The column or row with the insertion point	Click the Layout tab, click the Select button, and then click Select Column or Select Row.
A single cell	Drag a cell or click the cell with ➴
More than one cell	Drag with ➴ to select a group of cells.

Modifying a Table

As you begin to work on a table, you might need to modify its structure by adding more rows, columns, or cells to accommodate new text, graphics, or other tables. The table realigns as needed to accommodate the new structure. When you insert rows, columns, or cells, the existing rows shift down, the existing columns shift right, and you choose what direction the existing cells shift. Similarly, when you delete unneeded rows, columns, or cells from a table, the table realigns itself.

Insert Additional Rows or Columns

1. Select the row above which you want the new rows to appear, or select the column to the left of which you want the new columns to appear.

2. Drag to select the number of rows or columns you want to insert.

3. Click the **Layout** tab under Table Tools.

4. Click the Row & Column buttons you want:

   ◆ **Insert Above**.

   ◆ **Insert Below**.

   ◆ **Insert Left**.

   ◆ **Insert Right**.

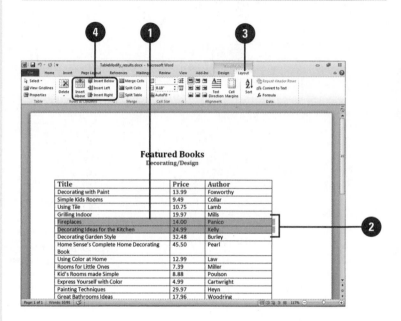

Delete Table, Rows, Columns, or Cells

1. Select the rows, columns, or cells you want to delete.

2. Click the **Layout** tab under Table Tools.

3. Click the **Delete** button, and then click the delete option you want:

   - **Delete Cells**. Select the direction in which you want the remaining cells to shift to fill the space, and then click OK.

   - **Delete Columns**.

   - **Delete Rows**.

   - **Delete Table**.

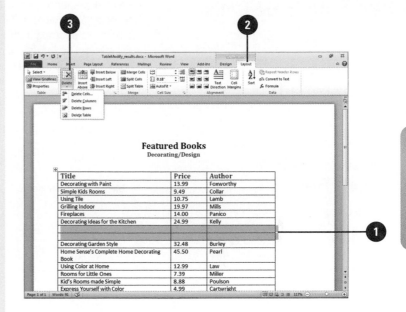

Did You Know?

You can set column widths to fit text. Word can set the column widths to fit the cells' contents or to fill the space between the document's margins. Click in the table, click the Layout tab under Table Tools, click the AutoFit button in the Cell Size group, and then click AutoFit To Contents or AutoFit To Window.

You can evenly distribute columns and rows. Select the columns or rows you want to distribute evenly in a table, click the Layout tab under Table Tools, and then click the Distribute Vertically or Distribute Horizontally button in the Cells Size group.

Adjusting Table Cells

Often there is more to modifying a table than adding or deleting rows or columns; you need to make cells just the right size to accommodate the text you are entering in the table. For example, a title in the first row of a table might be longer than the first cell in that row. To spread the title across the top of the table, you can merge (combine) the cells to form one long cell. Sometimes, to indicate a division in a topic, you need to split (or divide) a cell into two. You can also split one table into two at any row. Moreover, you can modify the width of any column and height of any row to better present your data.

Merge and Split Table Cells and Tables

◆ To merge two or more cells into a single cell, select the cells you want to merge, click the **Layout** tab under Table Tools, and then click the **Merge Cells** button.

◆ To split a cell into multiple cells, click the cell you want to split, click the **Layout** tab under Table Tools, and then click the **Split Cells** button. Enter the number of rows or columns (or both) you want to split the selected cell into, clear the **Merge cells before split** check box, and then click **OK**.

◆ To split a table into two tables separated by a paragraph, click in the row that you want as the top row in the second table, click the **Layout** tab under Table Tools, and then click the **Split Table** button.

◆ To merge two tables into one, delete the paragraph between them.

Did You Know?

You can quickly adjust columns and rows. Position the pointer over the boundary of the column or row you want to adjust until it becomes a resize pointer. Drag the boundary to a new location.

Merge and Split buttons

The three cells in this row will merge into one.

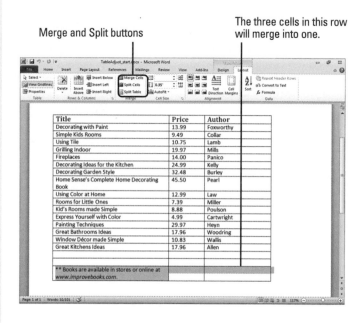

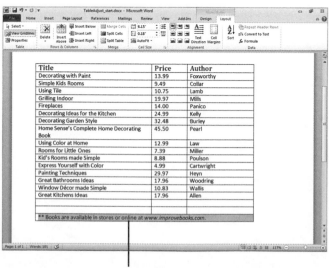

Merged cells

Adjust Column Widths and Row Heights

1 Select the columns or rows you want to change.

2 Click the **Layout** tab under Table Tools.

3 Point to the column or width (cursor changes to a double-arrow), and then drag to adjust it or manually change the Height and Width boxes in the Cell Size group:

◆ **Height.** To change the row height, enter a height in the Height box and then press Enter, or use the Up and Down arrows.

◆ **Width.** To change the column width, enter a width in the Width box and then press Enter, or use the Up and Down arrows.

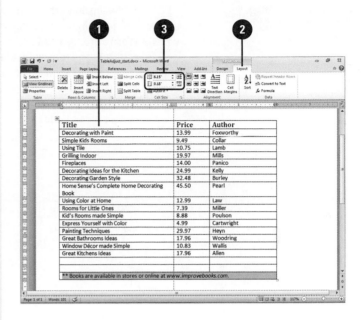

Change Table Properties

1 Click in the table you want to change.

2 Click the **Layout** tab under Table Tools.

3 Click the **Properties** button.

4 Click an alignment option, and then specify an indent from the left (when you select the Left alignment option).

5 Click a text wrapping option.

6 Click **OK**.

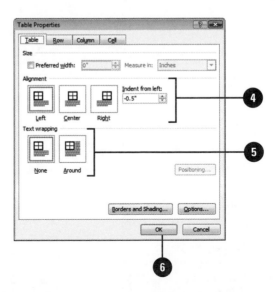

Formatting a Table

Tables distinguish text from paragraphs. In turn, formatting, alignment, and text direction distinguish text in table cells. Start by applying one of Word's predesigned table formats using Quick Styles. Then customize your table by realigning the cells' contents both horizontally and vertically, changing the direction of text within selected cells, such as the column headings, and resizing the entire table. You can modify borders and shading using the Design and Layout tabs under Table Tools to make printed tables easier to read and more attractive.

Change Text Direction Within Cells

1. Select the cells you want to change.

2. Click the **Layout** tab under Table Tools.

3. Click the **Text Direction** button until the text is the direction you want.

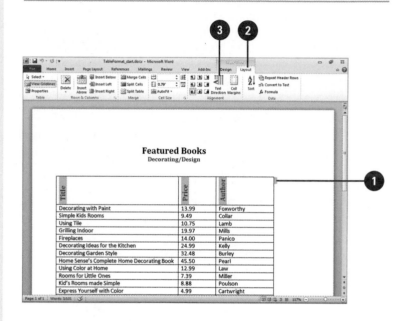

Align Text Within Cells

1. Select the cells, rows, or columns you want to align.

2. Click the **Layout** tab under Table Tools.

3. Click one of the alignment buttons.

Did You Know?

You can create nested tables. Select the table or cells, click the Home tab, click the Cut or Copy button, right-click the table cell, and then click Paste As Nested Table.

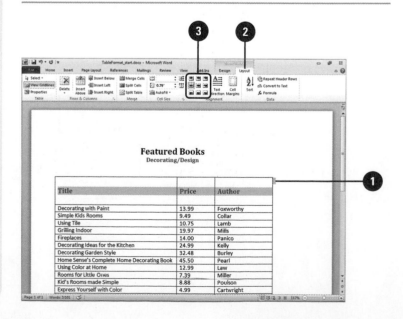

Sort the Contents of a Table

1. Click in the table or select the columns or rows you want to sort.

2. Click the **Layout** tab under Table Tools.

3. Click the **Sort** button.

4. Click the **Sort by** list arrow, and then select how you want to sort the data.

5. Specify the type of data, how the table is using the data, and the direction of the sort.

6. To sort by multiple columns or rows, select Then by options.

7. Click **OK**.

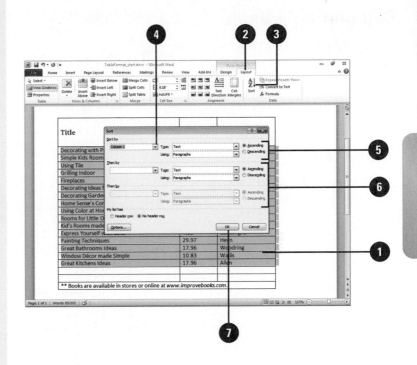

Format a Table Using Quick Styles

1. Click in the table you want to format.

2. Click the **Design** tab under Table Tools.

3. Click the scroll up or down arrow, or click the **More** list arrow in the Table Styles group.

4. Click the style you want to apply from the gallery.

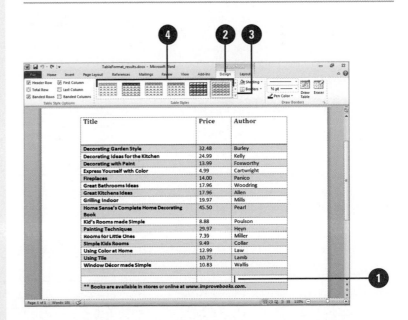

Calculating a Value in a Table

Sometimes the simple equations proposed by Word do not adequately cover what you are trying to calculate in the table. When that is the case, you need to create a custom equation to do the work. The Formula dialog box give you a choice of 18 paste functions to help you create your formula. Should you need help, you can activate Help to see examples of how to use each paste function, or for more complex formulas, try Microsoft's Online Community to look for advice from other users.

Calculate a Value

1. Click the cell in which you want the result to appear.

2. Click the **Layout** tab under Table Tools.

3. Click the **Formula** button. If Word proposes a formula that you do not want to use, delete it from the Formula box.

4. Click the **Paste Function** list arrow, and then select a function.

5. To reference the contents of a table cell, type the cell references in the parentheses in the formula. For instance, to average the values in cells a1 through a4, the formula would read =Average(a1,a4). If you are doing the average of a row in the last column of the row, simplify this to =Average(left).

6. In the Number format box, enter a format for the numbers. For example, to display the numbers as a decimal percentage, click 0.00%. For now, enter 0 to display the average as the nearest whole number. To display a true average, enter 0.00 in the Number Format box.

7. Click **OK**.

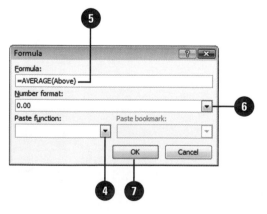

Addressing Envelopes and Labels

When you write a letter, you can use Word to print an address on an envelope or mailing label. Word scans your document to find a delivery address. You can use the one Word finds, enter another one, or select one from your Address Book. You can specify a return address, or you can omit it. Addresses can contain text, graphics, and bar codes. The POSTNET bar code is a machine-readable depiction of a U.S. zip code and delivery address; the FIM-A code identifies the front of a courtesy reply envelope. You can print a single label or multiple labels.

Address and Print Envelopes

1. Click the **Mailings** tab, click the **Envelopes** button, and then click the **Envelopes** tab, if necessary.

2. Type the recipients name and address, or click the **Insert Address** button to search for it.

3. Type your name and address.

4. Click **Options**, select a size, placement, bar code, font, and then click **OK**.

5. Insert an envelope in your printer, and then click **Print**.

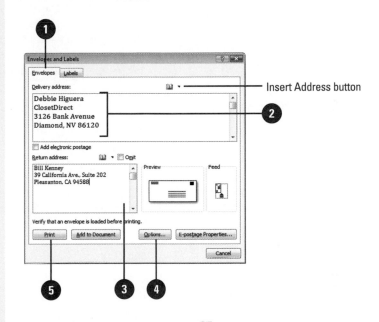

Insert Address button

Address and Print Mailing Labels

1. Click the **Mailings** tab, click the **Labels** button, and then click the **Labels** tab.

2. Type the recipients name and address, or click the **Insert Address** button to search for it.

3. Select which labels to print.

4. Click **Options**, select a type or size, and then click **OK**.

5. Insert labels in your printer, and then click **Print**.

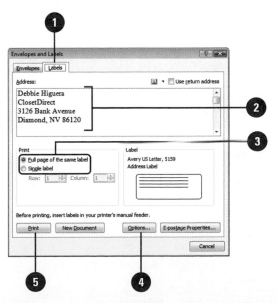

Creating a Form Letter

Did you ever send the same letter to several people and spend a lot of time changing personal information, such as names and addresses? If so, form letters will save you time. **Mail merge** is the process of combining names and addresses stored in a data file with a main document (usually a form letter) to produce customized documents. There are four main steps to merging. First, select the document you want to use. Second, create a data file with the variable information. Third, create the main document with the boilerplate (unchanging information) and merge fields. Each merge field corresponds to a piece of information in the data source and appears in the main document with the greater than and less than characters around it. For example, the <<Address Block>> merge field corresponds to name and address information in the data source. Finally, merge the main document with the data source to create a new document with all the merged information.

Create a Form Letter Using Mail Merge

1. Click the **Mailings** tab.

2. Click the **Start Mail Merge** button, and then click **Step by Step Mail Merge Wizard**. The Mail Merge task pane opens. Step 1 of 6 appears on the task pane.

3. Click a document type option (such as Letters), and then click **Next** at the bottom of the task pane. Step 2 of 6 appears on the task pane.

4. Click a starting document option (such as Use The Current Document), and then click **Next** at the bottom of the task pane. Step 3 of 6 appears on the task pane.

5. Click a recipient option (such as Use An Existing List or Type A New List), click **Browse**, double-click a data document, click **OK** to select the mail recipients, and then click **Next** at the bottom of the task pane. Step 4 of 6 appears on the task pane.

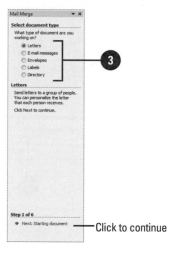

Click to continue

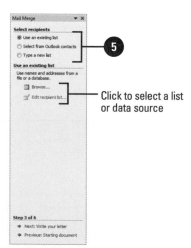

Click to select a list or data source

6 Type your letter, click a location in the document, and then click one of the field items on the task pane (such as Address Block or Greeting Line), select the options you want, click **OK**, and then click **Next** at the bottom of the task pane. Step 5 of 6 appears on the task pane.

7 Preview the data in the letter and make any changes, and then click **Next** at the bottom of the task pane. Step 6 of 6 appears on the task pane.

8 Click **Edit individual letters**.

9 Click the **All** option, and then click **OK**.

10 When you're done, click the **Close** button on the task pane, and then save the form letter.

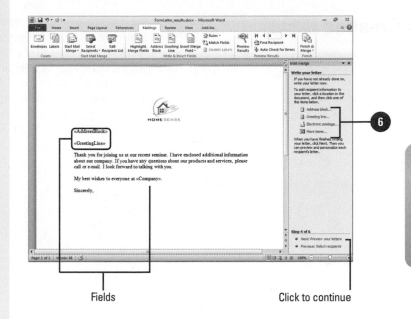

Fields   Click to continue

Did You Know?

You can have common words used as field names. Information in a data file is stored in merge fields, labeled with one-word names, such as FirstName, LastName, City, and so on. You insert merge field names in the main document as blanks, or placeholders, for variable information. When you merge the data file and main document, Word fills in the blanks with the correct information.

You should beware of those extra spaces. Don't press the Spacebar after entering data in a field. Extra spaces will appear in the document between the data and the next word or punctuation, leaving ugly gaps or floating punctuation. Add spaces and punctuation to your main document instead.

Creating Labels

You can use a data document to create more than one kind of merge document. For example, you can use a data document to print mailing labels or envelopes to use with your mailing. The process for creating mailing labels is similar to the mail merge process for form letters, except that you insert the merge field into a main document that contains a table with cells in a specific size for labels. During the process for creating mailing labels, you can select brand-name labels in a specific size, such as Avery Standard 1529. After you merge the data into the main document with the labels, you can print the labels on a printer.

Create Labels Using Mail Merge

1. Click the **Mailings** tab.

2. Click the **Start Mail Merge** button, and then click **Step by Step Mail Merge Wizard**. The Mail Merge task pane opens. Step 1 of 6 appears on the task pane.

3. Click the **Labels** option, and then click **Next** at the bottom of the task pane. Step 2 of 6 appears on the task pane.

4. Click a starting document option button (such as Change Document Layout), and then click **Label Options**.

5. Select the label options you want, click **OK**, and then click **Next** at the bottom of the task pane. Step 3 of 6 appears on the task pane.

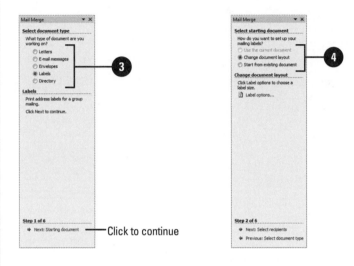

Click to continue

6 Click a recipient option button (such as Use An Existing List or Type A New List), click **Browse**, double-click a data document, select a data source and click **OK**, select the recipients you want and click **OK**, and then click **Next** at the bottom of the task pane. Step 4 of 6 appears on the task pane.

7 Click in the first label of the document, and then click one of the field items on the task pane (such as Address Block or Greeting Line), select the options you want, and then click **OK**.

8 Click **Update all labels**, and then click **Next** at the bottom of the task pane. Step 5 of 6 appears on the task pane.

9 Preview the data in the letter and make any changes, and then click **Next** at the bottom of the task pane. Step 6 of 6 appears on the task pane.

10 Click **Print**.

11 Click a Print Records option and then click **OK**.

12 When you're done, click the **Close** button on the task pane, and then save the labels.

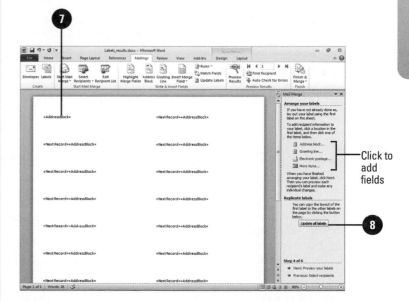

Click to add fields

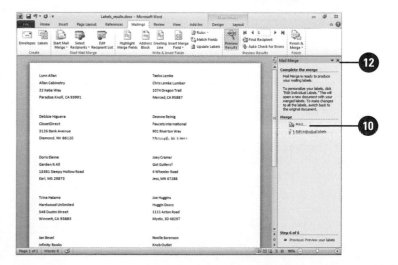

Inserting a Table of Contents

A **table of contents** provides an outline of main topics and page locations. Word builds a table of contents based on the styles in a document that you choose. By default, Heading 1 is the first-level entry, Heading 2 the second level, and so on. In a printed table of contents, a **leader**, a line whose style you select, connects an entry to its page number. In Web documents, entries become hyperlinks. Hide nonprinting characters before creating a table of contents so text doesn't shift to other pages as you print.

Insert a Table of Contents

1. Position the insertion point where you want the table of contents.

2. Click the **References** tab.

3. Click the **Table of Contents** button.

4. Do one of the following:

   ◆ **Add.** Click a Table of Contents style from the gallery.

   ◆ **Remove.** Click **Remove Table of Contents**.

   ◆ **Customize.** Click **Insert Table of Contents**, click the **Table of Contents** tab, select the format, levels, and options you want, and then click **OK**.

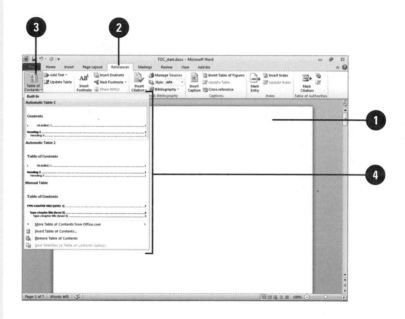

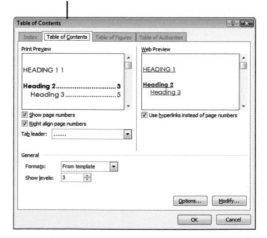

Use to customize a Table of Contents

Did You Know?

You can update the table of contents. As you continue to add information to a document, you can quickly update the table of contents. Click the References tab, and then click the Update Table button in Table of Contents group.

You can add a specific paragraph to the table of content. Select the paragraph you want to add, click the References tab, and then click the Add Text button in the Table of Contents group.

Creating an Index

An index appears at the end of a document and alphabetically lists the main topics, names, and items used in a long document. Each index listing is called an entry. You can create an index entry for a word, phrase, or symbol for a topic. In an index, a cross-reference indicates another index entry that is related to the current entry. There are several ways to create an index. Begin by marking index entries. Some index entries will refer to blocks of text that span multiple pages within a document.

Create an Index

1. Click the **References** tab.

2. To use existing text as an index entry, select the text. To enter your text as an index entry, click at the point where you want the index entry inserted.

3. Click the **Mark Entry** button or press Alt+Shift+X.

4. Type or edit the entry. The entry can be customized by creating a sub-entry or a cross-reference to another entry.

5. To format the text for the index, right-click it in the Main Entry or Sub-entry box, click **Font**, select your formatting options, and then click **OK**.

6. To select a format for the page numbers that will appear in the index, select the **Bold** or **Italic** check boxes.

7. To mark the index entry, click **Mark** or **Mark All** for all similar text.

   Repeat steps 2-7 for additional index entries, and then click **Close**.

8. Go to the page where you want to display your Index.

9. Click the **Insert Index** button.

10. Click the **Index** tab, and then select any options you want.

11. Click **OK**.

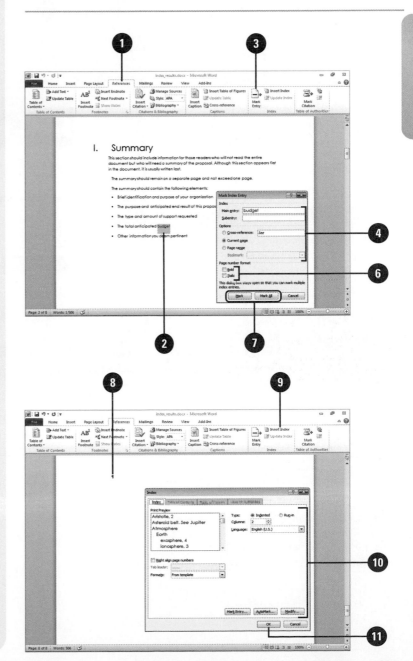

Creating Captions

Captions are helpful not only to associate images with the text that refers to them, but also to provide the reader with amplifying information about the figure, table, chart, or other illustration displayed. You can use preset captions provided, such as Figure, or you can create your own custom caption for your document.

Insert a Caption

1. Select the image that you want to caption.

2. Click the **References** tab.

3. Click the **Insert Caption** button.

4. If you want to use a Label other than the default setting of Figure, which is appropriate for most art, click the **Label** list arrow, and then click **Equation** or **Table**.

5. If you want to use a numbering sequence other than the default setting of 1,2,3…, click **Numbering**, make your selections, and then click **OK**.

6. Click **OK**.

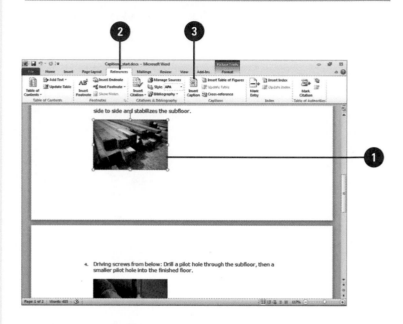

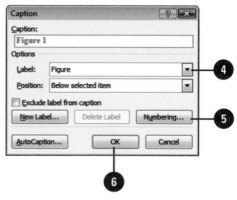

Did You Know?

You can have Word automatically add a caption field. Whenever you insert a particular type of file, such as a bitmapped image, click AutoCaption. In the Add Caption When Inserting list, click the check boxes to select the instances where you want the feature to apply, select the Label, Positioning and Numbering options you want, and then click OK.

You can add custom labels for captions. Click New Label, type the name of the New Label, and then click OK.

Creating a Table of Figures

If you are creating a document in which there are many illustrations (art, photographs, charts, diagrams etc.), it is often helpful to the reader of your document to provide a Table of Figures. A **Table of Figures** is like a Table of Contents except that it deals only with the graphic content of a document, not the written content. To create the Table of Figures, Word looks for text with the Style code that you specify (Figure, Table, etc). You can also add a **tab leader** to make the table easier to read.

Create a Table of Figures

1. Position the insertion point where you want the Table of Figures to appear.

2. Click the **References** tab.

3. Click the **Insert Table of Figures** button.

4. Click the **Table of Figures** tab.

5. Click the **Tab leader** list arrow, and then select the tab leader you want to use.

6. Click the **Formats** list arrow, and then select the format you want to use for the Table of Figures.

7. If you want to create a Table of Figures from something other than the default Figure style, or the Table style, click **Options**.

8. Click the **Style** list arrow, select the text formatting that you want Word to search for when building the Table of Figures, and then click **Close**. All figure callouts of the selected style are tagged for inclusion in the Table of Figures.

9. Click **OK**.

10. Click **OK**.

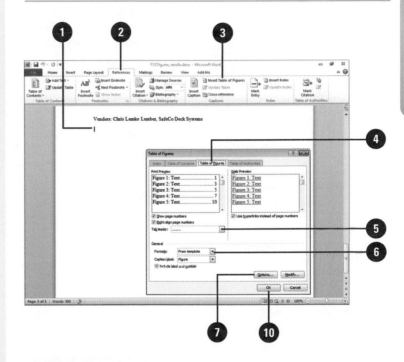

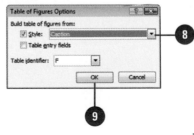

Table of Figures

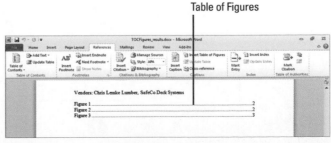

Creating Footnotes or Endnotes

Footnotes are used to provide additional information that is inappropriate for the body of the text, and to document your references for information or quotes presented in the body of the document. Footnotes are appropriate for academic, scientific, and, occasionally, business purposes. Footnotes appear at the bottom of the page on which the information is cited, and Word automatically inserts a reference mark at the insertion point to associate the information presented with the note at the bottom of the page. Creating and manipulating endnotes is identical to performing the same functions for footnotes. Endnotes differ from footnotes in that they appear at the end of the document or section (in the case of longer documents), not the bottom of the page on which the reference mark appears.

Create a Footnote or Endnote

1. Position the insertion point where you want to insert a footnote.

2. Click the **References** tab.

3. To quickly create a footnote or endnote, click the **Insert Footnote** or **Insert Endnote** button, and then enter footnote or endnote text.

4. To create or customize the footnote or endnote, click the **Footnotes Dialog Box Launcher**.

5. Click the **Footnotes** or **Endnotes** option, click the list arrow next to the option, and then select the location where you want to place the footnote or endnote.

6. Verify that the Number Format option of 1,2,3... is selected.

7. Click **Insert** to insert a reference mark in the text. Word moves the insertion point to the bottom of the page corresponding to the number of the reference mark.

8. Type the text of your footnote or endnote.

9. Click the **Show Notes** button and the **Next Footnote** button to show/hide notes and locate them.

10. Click in the document to continue with your work.

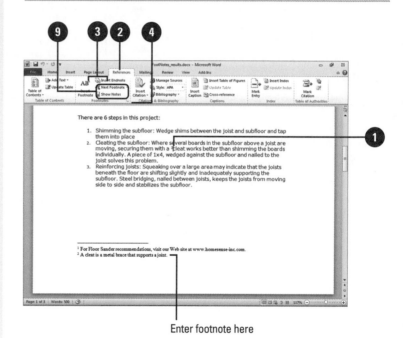

Enter footnote here

Creating a Bookmark

Instead of scrolling through a long document to find a specific word, phrase or section you can use bookmarks. **Bookmarks** are used to mark text so that you, or your reader, can quickly return to it. Using bookmarks as a destination make it easy to navigate through a long document. You can also navigate through documents with bookmarks by selecting a bookmark as a destination in the Go To dialog box.

Create a Bookmark

1. Click in your document where you want to insert a Bookmark.

2. Click the **Insert** tab.

3. Click the **Bookmark** button.

4. Type a one word descriptive name for your Bookmark.

5. Click **Add**.

Did You Know?

You can go to different locations in Word. Click the Home tab, click the Find button arrow, click Go To, select the Go To What option you want, specify a location, and then click Next or Previous. When you're done, click Close.

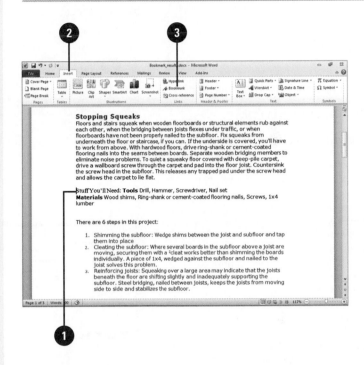

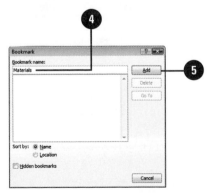

Inserting Cross References

Cross references direct the reader to related information located elsewhere in the document. Cross references can refer to figures or illustrations, sidebars, section headings, even individually marked paragraphs. Without distracting the reader of the document, cross references can be an easy tool to help navigate through a larger document. You can cross-reference only items in the same document. To cross-reference an item in another document, you need to first combine the documents into a master document.

Create a Cross Reference

1. Select the text that starts the cross reference in the document.

2. Click the **References** tab.

3. Click the **Cross-Reference** button.

4. Click the **Reference type** list arrow, and then select the type of item to which you will refer (heading, footnote, bookmark, etc.).

5. Click the **Insert reference to** list arrow, and then select the type of data (page, paragraph number, etc.) that you will be referencing.

6. Click the specific item, by number, to which you want to refer.

7. To let users move to the referenced item, select the **Insert as hyperlink** check box.

8. If the **Include above/below** check box is selected, click it to include data regarding the relative position of the referenced item.

9. Click **Insert**.

10. Repeat the steps for each additional cross reference that you want to insert into the document, and then click either **Close** or **Cancel**.

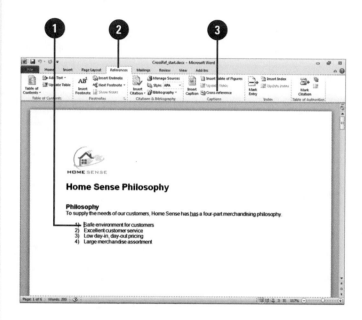

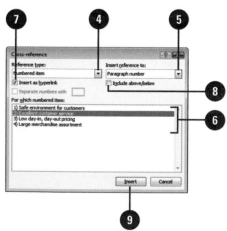

Comparing and Merging Documents

If you want to compare an earlier version of a document with the current version, or if you receive multiple edited versions of the original document back from the recipients, you can compare the documents and merge the changes into one document. The changes can be merged into one document or viewed for comparison. When you compare or merge documents, the text that differs between the two versions will be highlighted in a different color or with track reviewing marks.

Compare and Merge Documents

1. Click the **Review** tab.

2. Click the **Compare** button, and then click **Compare**.

   To merge documents, click the **Compare** button, and then click **Merge**.

3. Click the **Original document** list arrow, and then select the original document you want to use, or click the **Browse** button and double-click it.

4. Click the **Revised document** list arrow, and then select the revised document you want to use, or click the **Browse** button and double-click it.

   If necessary, click **More**.

5. Select and clear the comparison settings you want and don't want.

6. Click the Show changes at option you want (**Character level** or **Word level**).

7. Click the Show changes in option you want (**Original document**, **Revised document**, or **New document**).

8. Click **OK**.

9. If necessary, select a keep formatting option, and then click **OK**.

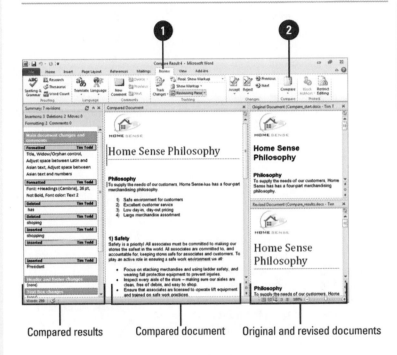

Compared results   Compared document   Original and revised documents

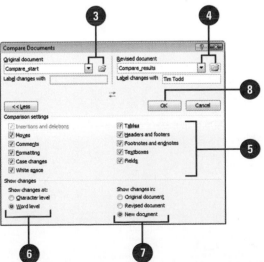

Using Track Changes

Tracking changes in a document allows you to make revisions to a document without losing the original text. Word shows changed text in a different color from the original text and uses revision marks, such as underlines, to distinguish the revised text from the original. You can review changes by using the Review tab, which contains buttons that let you accept and reject changes and comments. If you compare and merge two documents, you can review the changes and accept or reject the results.

Track Changes as You Work

1. Open the document you want to edit.

2. Click the **Review** tab.

3. Click the **Track Changes** button, and then click **Track Changes**.

    TIMESAVER *Click Track Changes on the Status bar or press Ctrl+Shift+E to turn tracking on or off.*

4. Make changes to your document. The changes are reflected using alternate color characters, along with comments in balloons at the side of the screen (if you are in Print Layout view) or displayed in a separate window at the bottom of the screen (if you are in Draft view).

5. Click the **Track Changes** button to turn off track changes.

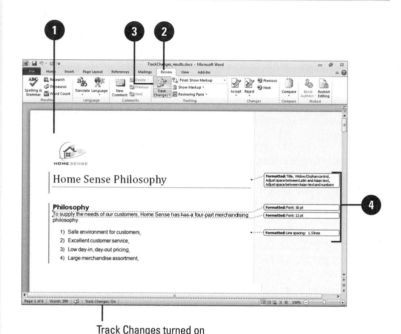

Track Changes turned on

Did You Know?

You can show or hide balloons. Click the Review tab, click the Balloons button, and then select Show Revisions In Balloons, Show Revisions Inline, or Show Only Comments And Formatting In Balloons.

Review Changes

1. Open the document you want to review.

2. Click the **Review** tab.

3. Use the buttons on the Review tab to review changes:

   ◆ Click the **Next** button or the **Previous** button to view changes one at a time.

   ◆ Click the **Accept** button or the **Reject** button to respond to the revisions.

   ◆ Click the **Accept** button arrow, and then click **Accept All Changes in Document** to accept all changes at once.

   ◆ Click the **Reject** button arrow, and then click **Reject All Changes in Document** to reject all changes at once.

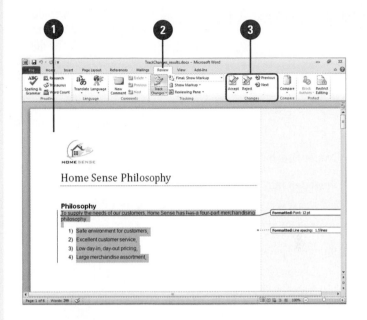

Did You Know?

You can display different versions of reviewing marks. Click the Review tab, click the Display For Review list arrow, and then select an option (Final Showing Markup, Final, Original Showing Markup, or Original).

You can show or hide individual reviewers. Click the Review tab, click the Show Markup button, point to Reviewers, and then click the reviewer you want to show or hide.

You can show or hide the Reviewing pane. The Reviewing pane shows a list of changes in a pane. Click the Review tab, click the Reviewing Pane button, and then click the option you want.

For Your Information

Adding and Removing Comments

Comments are useful when someone who is editing the document has questions pertaining to the document. When you insert a comment in Print Layout view, it opens a balloon where you want to enter a comment. To insert a comment, click the Review tab, place the insertion point where you want the comment, click the New Comment button, and then type a comment. To edit a comment, click in the comment balloon and edit normally. To remove a comment, right-click it, and then click Delete or use the Delete button on the Review tab. Each comment includes the name and initials of the person who made the comment, which you can change in the Options dialog box. Click the File tab, click Options, click General, make any changes to the username and initials, and then click OK.

Adding a Cover Page

A cover page provides an introduction to a report, or an important memo you want to circulate to others. Word makes it easy to add a cover page to any document. You can quickly select one from a gallery of styles that fit your document. If you can't find the cover page you need, check out Office.com (**New!**). Each cover page includes text boxes sample text, which you can change, and defined fields, such as a title and author's name, that automatically get filled in with information from document properties.

Insert a Cover Page

1. Click the **Insert** tab.

2. Click the **Cover Page** button to display a gallery of cover pages.

3. Click the cover page you want.

   ◆ **Add from Office.com.** Click **More Cover Pages from Office.com (New!)**.

   Word inserts a cover at the beginning of your document.

4. To remove a cover page, click the **Cover Page** button, and then click **Remove Current Cover Page**.

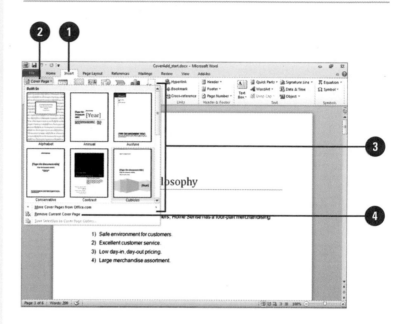

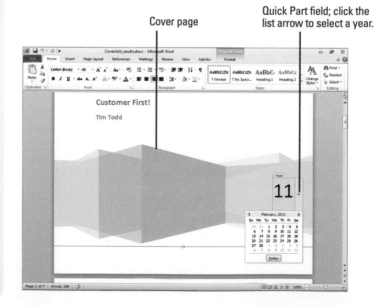

Cover page

Quick Part field; click the list arrow to select a year.

Creating a Worksheet with Excel

Introduction

At times, you'll need to reorganize a workbook by adding additional worksheets, moving their appearance order within the workbook, or even deleting an unused or outdated worksheet. You can rename worksheets to better show the theme of your workbook. When using your workbook, there may be times when you'll want to hide certain worksheets due to sensitive or confidential information. You can also freeze the column and row headings to ease viewing a long list of data.

On any worksheet, you can insert and delete cells, rows, and columns. You can adjust column width and row height so that you can structure the worksheet exactly the way you want. It's easy to make changes because Microsoft Office Excel updates cell references in existing formulas as necessary whenever you modify a worksheet and automatically recalculates formulas to ensure that the results are always up-to-date.

Perhaps each month you create an inventory worksheet in which you enter repetitive information; all that changes is the actual data. By creating your own template, you can have a custom form that is ready for completion each time you take inventory. Formatting, formulas and other settings are already set up, so that you can begin working on the task at hand. A template file saves all the customization you made to reuse in other workbooks. Microsoft Excel comes with a variety of pre-made templates that you can use for your own business and personal needs.

What You'll Do

View the Excel Window

Select Cells

Move Around the Workbook

Enter Labels and Values on a Worksheet

Enter Values Quickly with AutoFill

Edit and Clear Cell Contents

Insert and Delete Cell Contents

Select Rows, Columns, and Special Ranges

Select and Name a Worksheet

Insert and Delete a Worksheet

Move and Copy a Worksheet

Hide and Unhide Worksheets and Workbooks

Hide and Unhide a Column or Row

Insert and Delete a Column or Row

Adjust Column Width and Row Height

Split a Worksheet into Panes

Freeze and Unfreeze a Column or Row

Show and Hide Workbook Elements

Viewing the Excel Window

File tab
Click to access Office
Excel file commands.

Quick Access Toolbar
Click to access command comments
on this customizable toolbar.

Tabs
Click to access tools
and commands.

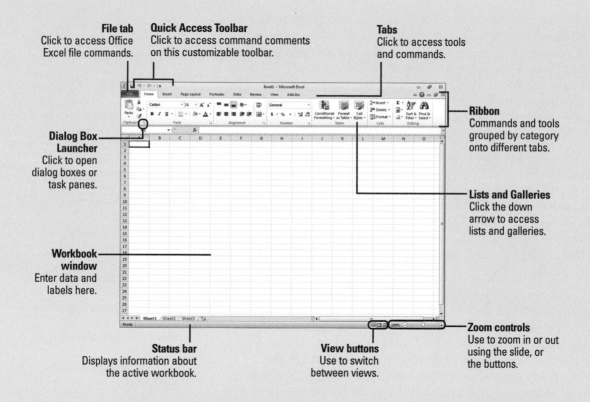

Dialog Box Launcher
Click to open
dialog boxes or
task panes.

Ribbon
Commands and tools
grouped by category
onto different tabs.

Lists and Galleries
Click the down
arrow to access
lists and galleries.

Workbook window
Enter data and
labels here.

Status bar
Displays information about
the active workbook.

View buttons
Use to switch
between views.

Zoom controls
Use to zoom in or out
using the slide, or
the buttons.

Selecting Cells

In order to work with a cell—to enter data in it, edit or move it, or perform an action—you **select** the cell so it becomes the active cell. When you want to work with more than one cell at a time—to move or copy them, use them in a **formula**, or perform any group action—you must first select the cells as a **range**. A range can be **contiguous** (where selected cells are adjacent to each other) or **non-contiguous** (where the cells may be in different parts of the worksheet and are not adjacent to each other). As you select a range, you can see the range reference in the Name box. A **range reference** contains the cell address of the top-left cell in the range, a colon (:), and the cell address of the bottom-right cell in the range.

Select a Contiguous Range

1. Click the first cell that you want to include in the range.

2. Drag the mouse to the last cell you want to include in the range.

   TIMESAVER *Instead of dragging, hold down the Shift key, and then click the lower-right cell in the range.*

   When a range is selected, the top-left cell is surrounded by the cell pointer, while the additional cells are selected.

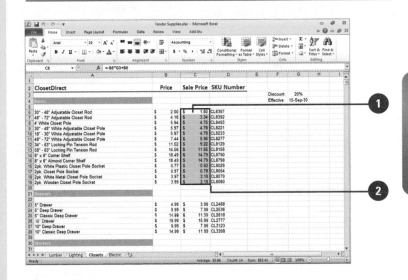

Select a Non-contiguous Range

1. Click the first cell you want to include in the range.

2. Drag the mouse to the last contiguous cell, and then release the mouse button.

3. Press and hold Ctrl, and then click the next cell or drag the pointer over the next group of cells you want in the range.

   To select more, repeat step 3 until all non-contiguous ranges are selected.

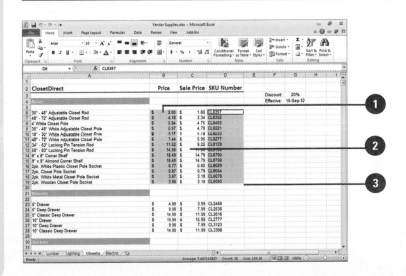

Moving Around the Workbook

You can move around a worksheet using your mouse or the keyboard. You might find that using your mouse to move from cell to cell is most convenient, while using various keyboard combinations is easier for quickly covering large areas of a worksheet. Or, you might find that entering numbers on the keypad and pressing Enter is a better method. Certain keys on the keyboard—Home, End, and Delete to name a few—are best used as shortcuts to navigate in the worksheet. However, there is no right way; whichever method feels the most comfortable is the one you should use.

Use the Mouse to Navigate

Using the mouse, you can navigate to:

◆ Another cell

◆ Another part of the worksheet

◆ Another worksheet

To move from one cell to another, point to the cell you what to move to, and then click.

When you click the wheel button on the IntelliMouse, the pointer changes shape. Drag the pointer in any direction to move to a new location quickly.

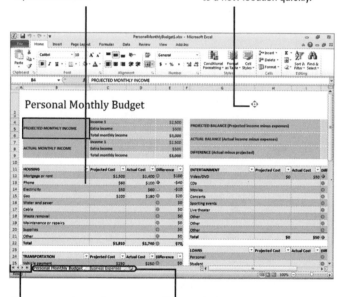

To see more sheet tabs without changing the location of the active cell, click a sheet scroll button.

To move from one worksheet to another, click the tab of the sheet you want to move to.

For Your Information

Storing More Data in Excel

Office Excel takes advantage of new technology to help you store more data and increase performance. Excel now supports over 1 million rows and 16 thousand columns in each worksheet, dual-processors and multi-threaded chips, memory management up to 2 GB, and up to 16 million colors.

Use the Keyboard to Navigate

Using the keyboard, you can navigate in a worksheet to:

- Another cell
- Another part of the worksheet

  Refer to the table for keyboard shortcuts for navigating around a worksheet.

Did You Know?

You can change or move cell selections after pressing Enter. When you press Enter, the active cell moves down one cell. To change the direction, click the File tab, click Options, click Advanced, select the After Pressing Enter, Move Selection check box, click the Direction list arrow, select a direction, and then click OK.

Go To a Specific Location

1. Click the **Home** tab.

2. Click the **Find & Select** button, and then click **Go To**.

3. Select a location or type a cell address to where you want to go.

4. To go to other locations (such as comments, blanks, last cell, objects, formulas, etc.), click **Special**, select an option, and then click **OK**.

   TIMESAVER *To open the Special dialog box directly, click the Find & Select button, and then click Go To Special.*

5. Click **OK**.

Keys For Navigating in a Worksheet

Press This Key	To Move
Left arrow	One cell to the left
Right arrow	One cell to the right
Up arrow	One cell up
Down arrow	One cell down
Enter	One cell down
Tab	One cell to the right
Shift+Tab	One cell to the left
Page Up	One screen up
Page Down	One screen down
End+arrow key	In the direction of the arrow key to the next cell containing data or to the last empty cell in current row or column
Home	To column A in the current row
Ctrl+Home	To cell A1
Ctrl+End	To the last cell in the worksheet containing data

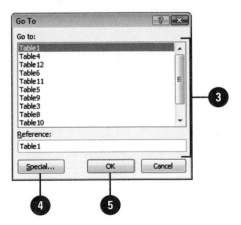

Entering Labels on a Worksheet

Labels turn a worksheet full of numbers into a meaningful report by identifying the different types of information it contains. You use labels to describe the data in worksheet cells, columns, and rows. You can enter a number as a label (for example, the year 2010), so that Excel does not use the number in its calculations. To help keep your labels consistent, you can use Excel's **AutoComplete** feature, which automatically completes your entries (excluding numbers, dates, or times) based on previously entered labels.

Enter a Text Label

1. Click the cell where you want to enter a label.

2. Type a label. A label can include uppercase and lowercase letters, spaces, punctuation, and numbers.

3. Press Enter, or click the **Enter** button on the formula bar.

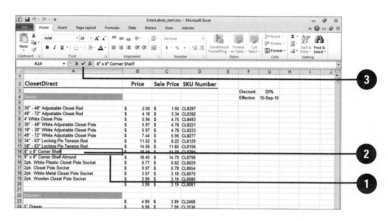

Enter a Number as a Label

1. Click the cell where you want to enter a number as a label.

2. Type ' (an apostrophe). The apostrophe is a label prefix and does not appear on the worksheet.

3. Type a number value.

4. Press Enter, or click the **Enter** button on the formula bar.

If a green triangle appears, it indicates a smart tag. Select the cell to display the Error Smart Tag button, where you can select options related to the label.

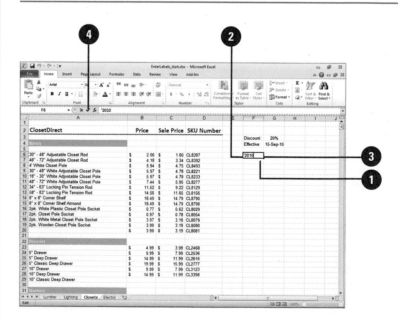

Enter a Label Using AutoComplete

1. Type the first few characters of a label.

   If Excel recognizes the entry, AutoComplete completes it.

2. To accept the suggested entry, press Enter or click the **Enter** button on the formula bar.

3. To reject the suggested completion, simply continue typing.

Did You Know?

Excel doesn't recognize the entry. The AutoComplete option may not be turned on. To turn on the feature, click the File tab, click Options, click Advanced, select the Enable AutoComplete For Cell Values check box, and then click OK.

Long labels might appear truncated. When you enter a label that is wider than the cell it occupies, the excess text appears to spill into the next cell to the right—unless there is data in the adjacent cell. If that cell contains data, the label will appear truncated—you'll only see the portion of the label that fits in the cell's current width. Click the cell to see its entire contents displayed on the formula bar.

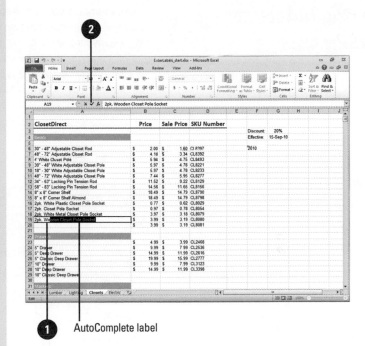

AutoComplete label

Entering Values on a Worksheet

You can enter values as whole numbers, decimals, percentages, or dates using the numbers on the top row of your keyboard, or by pressing your Num Lock key, the numeric keypad on the right. When you enter a date or the time of day, Excel automatically recognizes these entries (if entered in an acceptable format) as numeric values and changes the cell's format to a default date or time format. You can also change the way values, dates or times of day are shown.

Enter a Value

1. Click the cell where you want to enter a value.

2. Type a value.

3. Press Enter, or click the **Enter** button on the formula bar.

Did You Know?

You can use the numeric keypad to enter numbers. Make sure NUM appears in the lower-right corner of the status bar before you begin using the numbers.

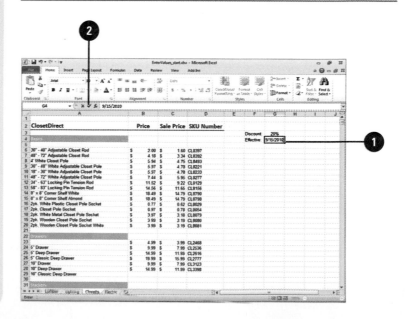

Enter a Date or Time

1. To enter a date, type the date using a slash (/) or a hyphen (-) between the month, day, and year in a cell or on the formula bar.

   To enter a time, type the hour based on a 12-hour clock, followed by a colon (:), followed by the minute, followed by a space, and ending with an "a" or a "p" to denote A.M. or P.M.

2. Press Enter, or click the **Enter** button on the formula bar.

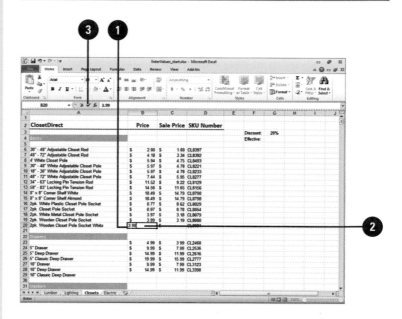

Entering Values Quickly with AutoFill

AutoFill is a feature that automatically fills in data based on the data in adjacent cells. Using the **fill handle**, you can enter data in a series, or you can copy values or formulas to adjacent cells. A single cell entry can result in a repeating value or label, or the results can be a more complex series. You can enter your value or label, and then complete entries such as days of the week, weeks of the year, months of the year, or consecutive numbering.

Enter Repeating Data or Series Using AutoFill

1. Select the first cell in the range you want to fill.

2. Enter the starting value to be repeated, or in a series.

3. Position the pointer on the lower-right corner of the selected cell. The pointer changes to the fill handle (a black plus sign).

4. Drag the fill handle over the range you want the value repeated.

5. To choose how to fill the selection, click the **AutoFill Options** button, and then click the option you want.

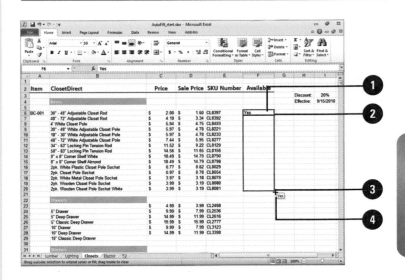

Create a Custom Fill

1. If you want to use an existing list, select the list of items.

2. Click the **File** tab, and then click **Options**.

3. In the left pane, click **Advanced**.

4. Click **Edit Custom Lists**.

5. Click the option you want.

   ◆ **New list.** Click **NEW LIST**, type the entries you want, press Enter after each. Click **Add**.

   ◆ **Existing list.** Verify the cell reference of the selected list that appears in the Import list, and then click **Import**.

6. Click **OK**, and then click **OK** again.

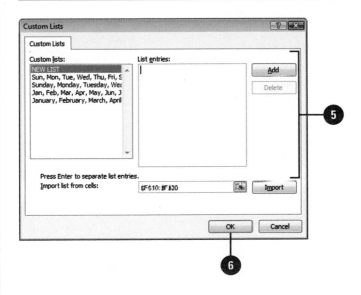

Editing Cell Contents

Even if you plan ahead, you can count on having to make changes on a worksheet. Sometimes it's because you want to correct an error. Other times it's because you want to see how your worksheet results would be affected by different conditions, such as higher sales, fewer units produced, or other variables. You can edit data just as easily as you enter it, using the formula bar or directly editing the active cell.

Edit Cell Contents

1 Double-click the cell you want to edit. The insertion point appears in the cell.

The Status bar now displays Edit instead of Ready.

2 If necessary, use the Home, End, and arrow keys to position the insertion point within the cell contents.

3 Use any combination of the Backspace and Delete keys to erase unwanted characters, and then type new characters as needed.

4 Click the **Enter** button on the formula bar or press Enter to accept the edit, or click the Esc button to cancel the edit.

The Status bar now displays Ready instead of Edit.

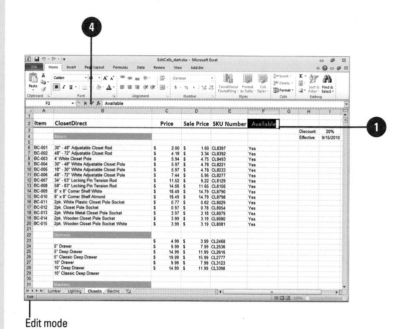

Edit mode

Did You Know?

You can change editing options. Click the File tab, click Options, click Advanced, change the editing options you want, and then click OK.

You can edit cell contents using the formula bar. Click the cell you want to edit, click to place the insertion point on the formula bar, and then edit the cell contents.

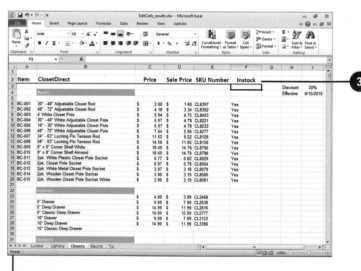

Ready mode

Clearing Cell Contents

You can clear a cell to remove its contents. Clearing a cell does not remove the cell from the worksheet; it just removes from the cell whatever elements you specify: data, comments (also called **cell notes**), or formatting instructions. When clearing a cell, you must specify whether to remove one, two, or all three of these elements from the selected cell or range.

Clear Cell Contents, Formatting, and Comments

1. Select the cell or range you want to clear.

2. Click the **Home** tab.

3. Click the **Clear** button, and then click any of the following options:

   ◆ **Clear All.** Clears contents and formatting.

   ◆ **Clear Formats.** Clears formatting and leaves contents.

   ◆ **Clear Contents.** Clears contents and leaves formatting.

   ◆ **Clear Comments.** Clears comments; removes purple triangle indicator.

   TIMESAVER *To quickly clear contents, select the cell or range you want to clear, right-click the cell or range, and then click Clear Contents, or press Delete.*

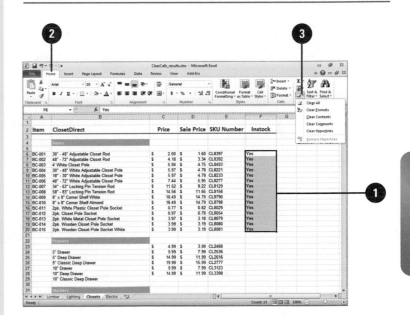

Did You Know?

You can find or replace cell contents. Click the cell or cells containing content you want to replace. Click the Home tab, click the Find & Select button, and then click Find. You can click the Replace tab for additional options.

Inserting and Deleting Cell Contents

You can **insert** new, blank cells anywhere on the worksheet in order to enter new data or data you forgot to enter earlier. Inserting cells moves the remaining cells in the column or row in the direction of your choice, and Excel adjusts any formulas so they refer to the correct cells. You can also **delete** cells if you find you don't need them; deleting cells shifts the remaining cells to the left or up—just the opposite of inserting cells. When you delete a cell, Excel removes the actual cell from the worksheet.

Insert a Cell

1 Select the cell or cells where you want to insert the new cell(s).

2 Click the **Home** tab.

3 Click the **Insert Cells** button arrow, and then click **Insert Cells**.

> **TIMESAVER** *Click the Insert Cells button to quickly insert cells and shift to the right.*

4 Click the option you want:

- ◆ **Shift Cells Right** to move cells to the right one column.

- ◆ **Shift Cells Down** to move cells down one row.

- ◆ **Entire Row** to move the entire row down one row.

- ◆ **Entire Column** to move entire column over one column.

5 Click **OK**.

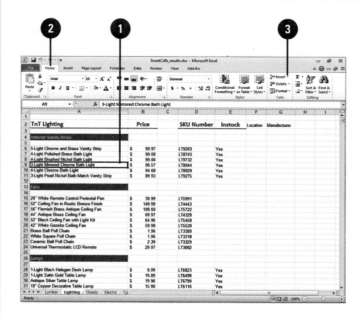

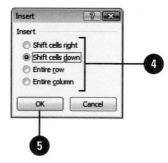

Delete a Cell

1. Select the cell or range you want to delete.

2. Click the **Home** tab.

3. Click the **Delete Cells** button arrow, and then click **Delete Cells**.

   TIMESAVER *Click the Delete Cells button to quickly delete cells and shift to the left.*

4. Click the option you want.

   ◆ **Shift Cells Left** to move the remaining cells to the left.

   ◆ **Shift Cells Up** to move the remaining cells up.

   ◆ **Entire Row** to delete the entire row.

   ◆ **Entire Column** to delete the entire column.

5. Click **OK**.

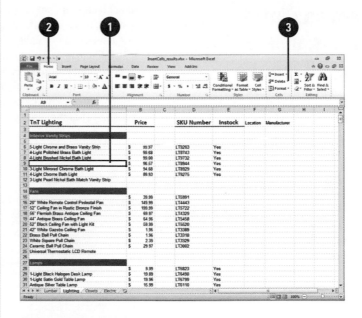

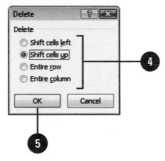

Did You Know?

There is a difference between deleting a cell and clearing a cell. Deleting a cell is different from clearing a cell: deleting removes the cells from the worksheet; clearing removes only the cell contents, or format, or both.

Selecting Rows, Columns, and Special Ranges

In addition to selecting a range of contiguous and non-contiguous cells in a single worksheet, you may need to select entire rows and columns, or even a range of cells across multiple worksheets. Cells can contain many different types of data, such as comments, constants, formulas, or conditional formats. Excel provides an easy way to locate these and many other special types of cells with the Go To Special dialog box. For example, you can select the Row Differences or Column Differences option to select cells that are different from other cells in a row or column, or select the Dependents option to select cells with formulas that refer to the active cell.

Select Entire Rows or Columns

◆ To select a single row or column, click in the row or column heading, or select any cell in the row or column, and press Shift+spacebar.

◆ To select multiple adjacent rows or columns, drag in the row or column headings.

◆ To select multiple nonadjacent rows or columns, press Ctrl while you click the borders for the rows or columns you want to include.

Did You Know?

You can select the entire worksheet quickly. Click the Select All button located above the row number 1 and the left of column A.

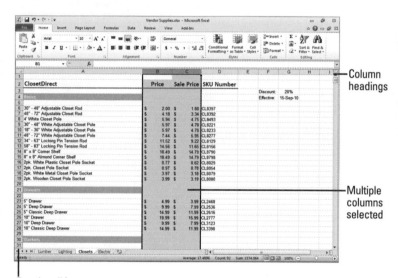

Column headings

Multiple columns selected

Row headings

Select Multisheet Ranges

1 Select the range in one sheet.

2 Select the worksheets to include in the range.

To select contiguous worksheets, press Shift and click the last sheet tab you want to include. To select non-contiguous worksheets, press Ctrl and click the sheets you want.

When you make a worksheet selection, Excel enters Group mode.

3 To exit Group mode, click any sheet tab.

Make Special Range Selections

1 If you want to make a selection from within a range, select the range you want.

2 Click the **Home** tab.

3 Click the **Find & Select** button, and then click **Go To Special**.

TIMESAVER *Press F5 to open the Go To Special dialog box.*

4 Click the option in which you want to make a selection. When you click the Formulas option, select or clear the formula related check boxes.

5 Click **OK**.

If no cells are found, Excel displays a message.

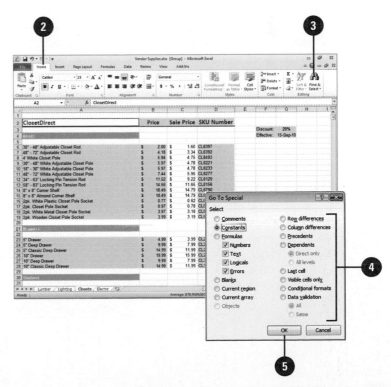

Group selection

Selecting and Naming a Worksheet

Each new workbook opens with three worksheets (or sheets), in which you store and analyze values. You can work in the active, or selected, worksheet. The default worksheet names are Sheet1, Sheet2, and Sheet3, which appear on the sheet tab, like file folder labels. As you create a worksheet, give it a meaningful name to help you remember its contents. The sheet tab size adjusts to fit the name's length, so using short names means more sheet tabs will be visible. If you work on a project that requires more than three worksheets, add additional sheets to the workbook so all related information is stored in one file.

Select a Worksheet

1. If necessary, click a sheet tab scroll button to display other tabs.

2. Click a sheet tab to make it the active worksheet.

3. To select multiple worksheets, press and hold Ctrl as you click other sheet tabs. When multiple worksheets are selected, [Group] appears in the title bar.

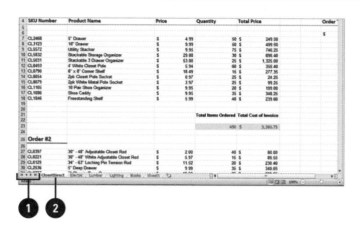

Name or Rename a Worksheet

1. Double-click the sheet tab you want to name.

   ◆ You can also click the **Home** tab, click the **Format** button, and then click **Rename**.

2. Type a new name.

3. Press Enter.

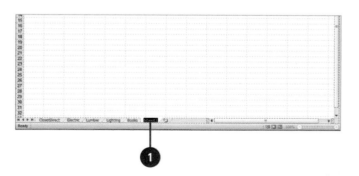

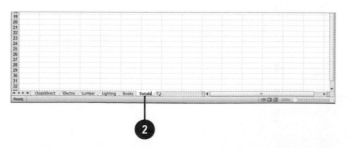

Inserting and Deleting a Worksheet

You can add or delete sheets in a workbook. If, for example, you are working on a project that requires more than three worksheets, you can insert additional sheets in one workbook rather than open multiple workbooks. You can insert as many sheets in a workbook as you want. On the other hand, if you are using only one or two sheets in a workbook, you can delete the unused sheets to save disk space. Before you delete a sheet from a workbook, make sure you don't need the data. You cannot undo the deletion.

Insert a Worksheet

1. Click the sheet tab to the right of where you want to insert the new sheet.

2. Click the **Insert Worksheet** icon at the end of the sheet tabs.

   TIMESAVER *Press Shift+F11.*

   ◆ You can also click the **Home** tab, click the **Insert Cells** button, and then click **Insert Sheet**.

   A new worksheet is inserted to the left of the selected worksheet.

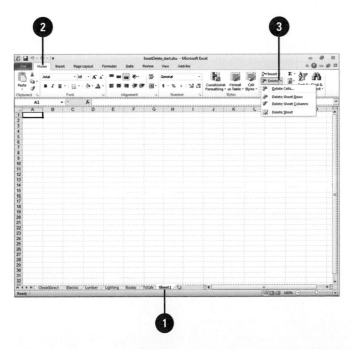

New sheet

Delete a Worksheet

1. Click the sheet tab of the worksheet you want to delete.

2. Click the **Home** tab.

3. Click the **Delete** button arrow, and then click **Delete Sheet**.

4. Click **Delete** to confirm the deletion.

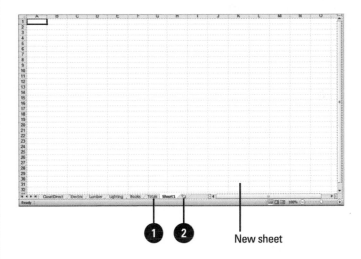

Moving and Copying a Worksheet

After adding several sheets to a workbook, you might want to reorganize them. You can arrange sheets in chronological order or in order of importance. You can easily move or copy a sheet within a workbook or to a different open workbook. Copying a worksheet is easier and often more convenient then re-entering similar information on a new sheet. If you are moving or copying a worksheet a short distance, you should use the mouse. For longer distances, you should use the Move or Copy command.

Move a Worksheet Within a Workbook

1 Click the sheet tab of the worksheet you want to move, and then hold down the mouse button.

2 When the mouse pointer changes to a sheet of paper, drag it to the right of the sheet tab where you want to move the worksheet.

3 Release the mouse button.

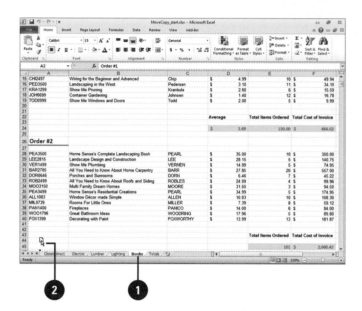

Did You Know?

You can give your worksheet a different background. Click the tab of the sheet on which you want to insert a background, click the Page Layout tab, and then click the Background button. Select the picture you want to use as a background, and then click Open.

You can use groups to affect multiple worksheets. Click a sheet tab, press and hold Shift, and click another sheet tab to group worksheets. Right-click a grouped sheet tab, and then click Ungroup Sheet on the shortcut menu.

Copy a Worksheet

1. Click the sheet tab of the worksheet you want to copy.

   TIMESAVER *Press and hold the Ctrl key while you drag a sheet name to copy a worksheet.*

2. Click the **Home** tab.

3. Click the **Format** button arrow, and then click **Move or Copy Sheet**.

4. If you want to copy the sheet to another open workbook, click the **To book** list arrow, and then select the name of that workbook. The sheets of the selected workbook appear in the Before Sheet list.

   TROUBLE? *If the workbook you want to copy to does not show up in the To Book drop-down list, you must first open the workbook.*

5. Click a sheet name in the Before Sheet list. Excel inserts the copy to the left of this sheet.

6. Select the **Create a copy** check box.

7. Click **OK**.

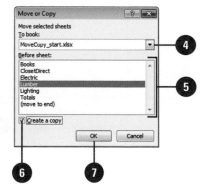

Did You Know?

You can copy or move a sheet to a different workbook. You must first open the other workbook, and then switch back to the workbook of the sheet you want to copy or move.

You can use the Create A Copy check box to move a worksheet. Clear the Create A Copy check box in the Move or Copy dialog box to move a worksheet rather than copy it.

Hiding and Unhiding Worksheets and Workbooks

Not all worksheets and workbooks should be available to everyone. You can keep sensitive information private without deleting it by hiding selected worksheets or workbooks. For example, if you want to share a workbook with others, but it includes confidential employee salaries, you can simply hide a worksheet. Hiding worksheets does not affect calculations in the other worksheets; all data in hidden worksheets is still referenced by formulas as necessary. Hidden worksheets do not appear in a printout either. When you need the data, you can unhide the sensitive information.

Hide or Unhide a Worksheet

1. Click the sheet tab you want to hide.

2. Click the **Home** tab.

3. Click the **Format** button, point to **Hide & Unhide**, and then click the command you want.

   ◆ **Hide Sheet**.

   ◆ **UnHide Sheet**, select the worksheet you want to unhide, and then click **OK**.

   TIMESAVER *Right-click the sheet you want to hide, and then click Hide.*

Hide or Unhide a Workbook

1. Open the workbook you want to hide.

2. Click the **View** tab.

3. Click the command you want.

   ◆ **Hide**.

   ◆ **Unhide**, select the workbook you want to unhide, and then click **OK**.

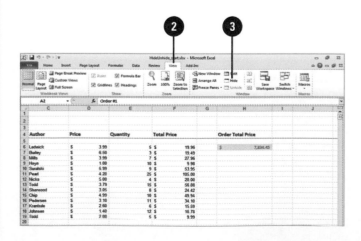

Hiding and Unhiding a Column or Row

Not all the data on a worksheet should be available to everyone. You can hide sensitive information without deleting it by hiding selected columns or rows. For example, if you want to share a worksheet with others, but it includes confidential employee salaries, you can simply hide the salary column. Hiding columns and rows does not affect calculations in a worksheet; all data in hidden columns and rows is still referenced by formulas as necessary. Hidden columns and rows do not appear in a printout either. When you need the data, you can unhide the sensitive information.

Hide a Column or Row

1. Click the column or row header button of the column or row you want to hide. (Drag to select multiple header buttons to hide more than one column or row.)

2. Click the **Home** tab.

3. Click the **Format** button, point to **Hide & Unhide**, and then click **Hide Columns** or **Hide Rows**.

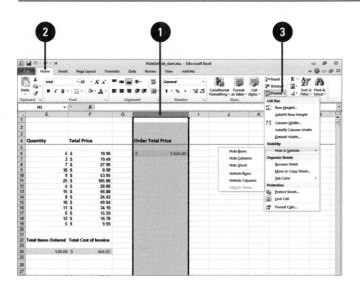

Unhide a Column or Row

1. Drag to select the column or row header buttons on either side of the hidden column or row.

2. Click the **Home** tab.

3. Click the **Format** button, point to **Hide & Unhide**, and then click **Unhide Columns** or **Unhide Rows**.

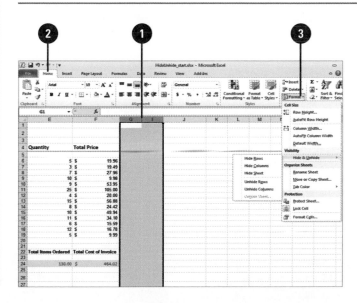

Inserting a Column or Row

You can insert blank columns and rows between existing data, without disturbing your worksheet. Excel repositions existing cells to accommodate the new columns and rows and adjusts any existing formulas so that they refer to the correct cells. Formulas containing absolute cell references will need to be adjusted to the new columns or rows. When you insert one or more columns, they insert to the left. When you add one or more rows, they are inserted above the selected row.

Insert a Column or Row

1. Click to the right of the location of the new column you want to insert.

   To insert a row, click the row immediately below the location of the row you want to insert.

2. Click the **Home** tab.

3. Click the **Insert** button arrow, and then click **Insert Sheet Columns** or **Insert Sheet Rows**.

4. To adjust formatting, click the **Insert Options** button, and then click a formatting option.

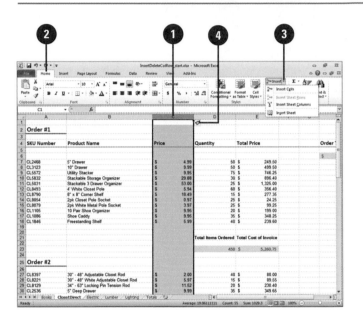

Insert Multiple Columns or Rows

1. Drag to select the column header buttons for the number of columns you want to insert.

   To insert multiple rows, drag to select the row header buttons for the number of rows you want to insert.

2. Click the **Home** tab.

3. Click the **Insert** button arrow, and then click **Insert Sheet Columns** or **Insert Sheet Rows**.

4. To adjust formatting, click the **Insert Options** button, and then click a formatting option.

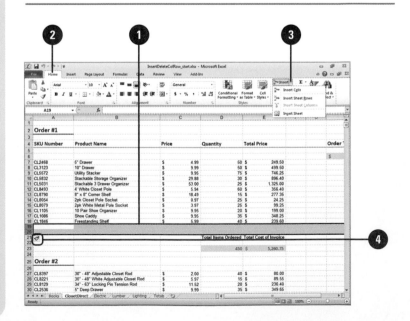

Deleting a Column or Row

At some point in time, you may want to remove an entire column or row of data from a worksheet rather than deleting or editing individual cells. You can delete columns and rows just as easily as you insert them. Formulas will need to be checked in your worksheet prior to deleting a row or column, especially when referencing absolute cell addresses. Remaining columns and rows move to the left or up to join the other remaining data.

Delete a Column or Row

1. Select the column header button or row header button that you want to delete.

2. Click the **Home** tab.

3. Click the **Delete** button arrow, and then click **Delete Sheet Columns** or **Delete Sheet Rows**.

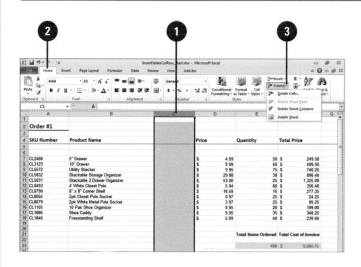

Delete Multiple Columns or Rows

1. Select the columns header buttons or rows header buttons that you want to delete.

2. Click the **Home** tab.

3. Click the **Delete** button arrow, and then click **Delete Sheet Columns** or **Delete Sheet Rows**.

Did You Know?

You can re-check your formulas. When deleting columns or rows that are referenced in a formula, it is important to adjust your formula for recalculations.

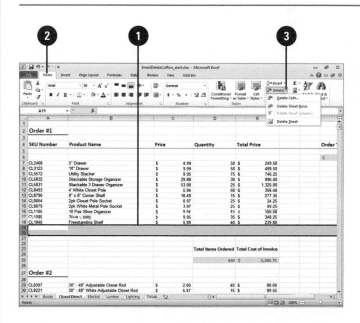

Adjusting Column Width and Row Height

You've entered labels and values, constructed formulas, and even formatted the cells, but now some of your data isn't visible; the value displays as #### in the cell. Also, some larger-sized labels are cut off. You can narrow or widen each column width to fit its contents and adjust your row heights as needed. As you build your worksheet, you can change the default width of some columns or the default height of some rows to accommodate long strings of data or larger font sizes. You can manually adjust column or row size to fit data you have entered, or you can use AutoFit to resize a column or row to the width or height of its largest entry.

Adjust Column Width or Row Height

1. Click the column or row header button for the first column or row you want to adjust.

2. If you want, drag to select more columns or rows.

3. Click the **Home** tab.

4. Click the **Format** button, and then click **Column Width** or **Row Height**.

   TIMESAVER *Right-click the selected column(s) or row(s), and then click Column Width or Row Height.*

5. Type a new column width or row height in points.

6. Click **OK**.

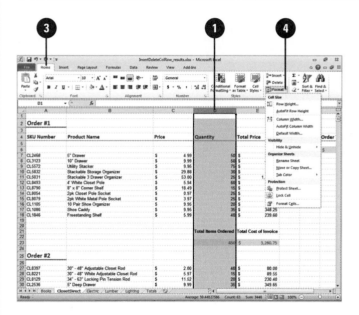

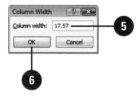

Did You Know?

What is a point? A point is a measurement unit used to size text and space on a worksheet. One inch equals 72 points.

You can change the default column width. Click the Home tab, click the Format button, click Default Width, type a column width in points, and then click OK.

Adjust Column Width or Row Height Using the Mouse

1 Position the mouse pointer on the right edge of the column header button or the bottom edge of the row header button for the column or row you want to change.

2 When the mouse pointer changes to a double-headed arrow, click and drag the pointer to a new width or height.

Change Column Width or Row Height Using AutoFit

1 Position the mouse pointer on the right edge of the column header button or the bottom edge of the row header button for the column or row you want to change.

2 When the mouse pointer changes to a double-headed arrow, double-click the mouse.

◆ You can also click the **Home** tab, click the **Format** button, and then click **AutoFit Column Width** or **AutoFit Row Height**.

Splitting a Worksheet into Panes

If you are working on a large worksheet, it can be time consuming and tiring to scroll back and forth between two parts of the worksheet. You can split the worksheet into four panes and two scrollable windows that you can view simultaneously but edit and scroll independently using the Split button. As you work in two parts of the same worksheet, you can resize the window panes to fit your task. Drag the split bar between the panes to resize the windows. No matter how you display worksheets, Excel's commands and buttons work the same as usual.

Split a Worksheet into Panes

1. Select the row, column, or cell location where you want to split a worksheet into panes.

   A column or row selection creates two panes, while a cell selection creates four panes.

2. Click the **View** tab.

3. Click the **Split** button.

   The button appears highlighted.

4. To remove the split, click the **Split** button again.

   The button doesn't appear highlighted.

Worksheet split into four panes

Scroll panes separately

Did You Know?

You can search for a value or data in a cell, and then replace it with different content. Click the cell or cells containing content you want to replace. Click the Home tab, click the Find & Select button, click Replace, specify the values or data you want to find and replace, and then click the appropriate Find or Replace buttons.

Freezing and Unfreezing a Column or Row

Large worksheets can be difficult to work with, especially on low-resolution or small screens. If you scroll down to see the bottom of the list, you can no longer see the column names at the top of the list. Instead of repeatedly scrolling up and down, you can temporarily set, or **freeze**, those column or row headings so that you can see them no matter where you scroll in the list. When you freeze a row or column, you are actually splitting the screen into one or more panes (window sections) and freezing one of the panes. You can split the screen into up to four panes and can freeze up to two of these panes. You can edit the data in a frozen pane just as you do any Excel data, but the cells remain stationary even when you use the scroll bars; only the unfrozen part of the screen scrolls. When you freeze a pane, it has no effect on how a worksheet looks when printed.

Freeze and Unfreeze a Column or Row

1 Select the column to the right of the columns you want to freeze, or select the row below the rows you want to freeze.

To freeze both, click the cell to the right and below of the column and row you want to freeze.

2 Click the **View** tab.

3 Click the **Freeze Panes** button, and then click the option you want.

◆ **Freeze Panes.** Keeps rows and columns visible based on the current selection.

◆ **Freeze Top Row.** Keeps top row visible.

◆ **Freeze First Column.** Keeps first column visible.

When you freeze a pane horizontally, all the rows **above** the active cell freeze. When you freeze a pane vertically, all the columns to the **left** of the active cell freeze.

4 To unfreeze a column or row, click the **Freeze Panes** button, and then click **Unfreeze Panes**.

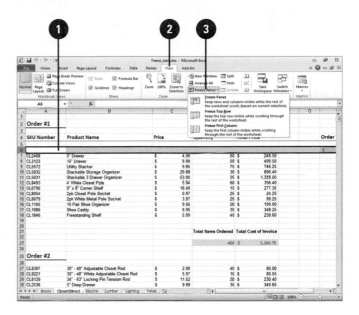

Showing and Hiding Workbook Elements

When you open a new or existing workbook, Excel displays a standard set of elements, such as the Formula Bar, Headings (columns and rows), Gridlines, and Ruler, which is available in Page Layout view. If you need a little more display room to see your data or you want to see how your data looks without the gridlines, you can quickly select or clear view settings on the Data tab in Excel to show or hide these elements.

Show or Hide Workbook Elements

1. Click the **View** tab.

2. Select or clear the check box for the element you want to show or hide.

   ◆ **Ruler**. In Page Layout view, the horizontal and vertical rulers.

   ◆ **Gridlines**. The gray outline around cells.

   ◆ **Formula Bar**. The bar below the Ribbon.

   ◆ **Headings**. The column (letters) and row (numbers) headings.

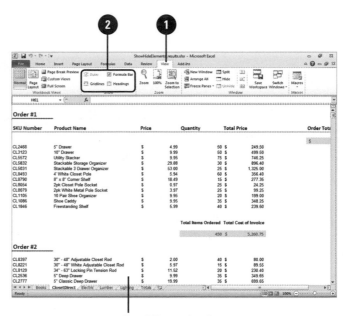

No gridlines or headings

Building a Worksheet with Excel

Introduction

Once you enter data in a worksheet, you'll want to add formulas to perform calculations. Microsoft Office Excel can help you get the results you need. Formulas can be very basic entries to more complex ones. The difficulty of the formula depends on the complexity of the result you want from your data. For instance, if you are simply looking to total this months sales, then the formula would add your sales number and provide the result. However, if you were looking to show this months sales, greater than $100.00 with repeat customers, you would take a bit more time to design the formula.

Because Microsoft Excel automatically recalculates formulas, your worksheets remain accurate and up-to-date no matter how often you change the data. Using absolute cell references anchors formulas to a specific cell. Excel provides numerous built-in functions to add to your worksheet calculations. Functions, such as AVERAGE or SUM, allow you to perform a quick formula calculation.

Another way to make your formulas easier to understand is by using name ranges in them. Name ranges—a group of selected cells named as a range—can help you understand your more complicated formulas. It is a lot easier to read a formula that uses name ranges, then to look at the formula and try to decipher it. Excel offers a tool to audit your worksheet. Looking at the "flow" of your formula greatly reduces errors in the calculation. You can see how your formula is built, one level at a time through a series of arrows that point out where the formula is pulling data from. As you develop your formula, you can make corrections to it.

What You'll Do

Understand Formulas and Referencing

Create and Edit Formulas

Name Cells and Ranges

Enter and Manage Names

Simplify a Formula with Ranges

Calculate Totals with AutoSum

Correct Formulas

Create Functions and Nested Functions

Use Nested and Text Functions

Use Lookup and Reference Functions

Summarize Data using Subtotals and Functions

Convert Text to Columns

Create and Format a Table

Create Calculations in a Table

Remove Table Rows and Columns

Sort Data in a Table

Display Parts of a Table with AutoFilter

Create Groups and Outlines

Add Data Validation to a Worksheet

Create a Drop-Down List

Understanding Formulas

Introduction

A formula calculates values to return a result. On an Excel worksheet, you can create a formula using constant values (such as 147 or $10.00), operators (shown in the table), references, and functions. An Excel formula always begins with the equal sign (=).

A **constant** is a number or text value that is not calculated, such as the number 147, the text "Total Profits", and the date 7/22/2008. On the other hand, an **expression** is a value that is not a constant. Constants remain the same until you or the system change them. An **operator** performs a calculation, such as + (plus sign) or - (minus sign). A cell **reference** is a cell address that returns the value in a cell. For example, A1 (column A and row 1) returns the value in cell A1 (see table below).

Cell Reference Examples

Reference	Meaning
A1	Cell in column A and row 1
A1:A10	Range of cells in column A and rows 1 through 10
A1:F1	Range of cells in row 1 and columns A through F
1:1	All cells in row 1
1:5	All cells in rows 5 through 10
A:A	All cells in column A
A:F	All cells in columns A through F
Profits!A1:A10	Range of cells in column A and rows 1 through 10 in worksheet named Profits

A **function** performs predefined calculations using specific values, called arguments. For example, the function SUM(B1:B10) returns the sum of cells B1 through B10. An argument can be numbers, text, logical values such as TRUE or FALSE, arrays, error values such as #NA, or cell references. Arguments can also be constants, formulas, or other functions, known as **nested functions**. A function starts with the equal sign (=), followed by the function name, an opening parenthesis, the arguments for the function separated by commas, and a closing parenthesis. For example, the function, AVERAGE(A1:A10, B1:B10), returns a number with the average for the contents of cells A1 through A10 and B1 through B10. As you type a function, a ToolTip appears with the structure and arguments needed to complete the function. You can also use the Insert Function dialog box to help you add a function to a formula.

Perform Calculations

By default, every time you make a change to a value, formula, or name, Excel performs a calculation. To change the way Excel performs calculations, click the Formulas tab, click the Calculation Options button, and then click the option you want: Automatic, Automatic Except Data Tables, or Manual. To manually recalculate all open workbooks, click the Calculate Now button (or press F9). To recalculate the active worksheet, click the Calculate Sheet button (or press Shift+F9).

Precedence Order

Formulas perform calculations from left to right, according to a specific order for each operator. Formulas containing more than one operator follow precedence order: exponentiation, multiplication and division, and then addition and subtraction. So, in the formula 2 + 5 * 7, Excel performs multiplication first and addition next for a result of 37. Excel calculates operations within parentheses first. The result of the formula (2 + 5) * 7 is 49.

Understanding Cell Referencing

Each cell, the intersection of a column and row on a worksheet, has a unique address, or **cell reference**, based on its column letter and row number. For example, the cell reference for the intersection of column D and row 4 is D4.

Cell References in Formulas

The simplest formula refers to a cell. If you want one cell to contain the same value as another cell, type an equal sign followed by the cell reference, such as =D4. The cell that contains the formula is known as a **dependent cell** because its value depends on the value in another cell. Whenever the cell that the formula refers to changes, the cell that contains the formula also changes.

Depending on your task, you can use **relative cell references**, which are references to cells relative to the position of the formula, **absolute cell references**, which are cell references that always refer to cells in a specific location, or **mixed cell references**, which use a combination of relative and absolute column and row references. If you use macros, the R1C1 cell references make it easy to compute row and column positions.

Relative Cell References

When you copy and paste or move a formula that uses relative references, the references in the formula change to reflect cells that are in the same relative position to the formula. The formula is the same, but it uses the new cells in its calculation. Relative addressing eliminates the tedium of creating new formulas for each row or column in a worksheet filled with repetitive information.

Absolute Cell References

If you don't want a cell reference to change when you copy a formula, make it an absolute reference by typing a dollar sign ($) before each part of the reference that you don't want to change. For example, A1 always refers to cell A1. If you copy or fill the formula down columns or across rows, the absolute reference doesn't change. You can add a $ before the column letter and the row number. To ensure accuracy and simplify updates, enter constant values (such as tax rates, hourly rates, and so on) in a cell, and then use absolute references to them in formulas.

Mixed Cell References

A mixed reference is either an absolute row and relative column or absolute column and relative row. You add the $ before the column letter to create an absolute column or before the row number to create an absolute row. For example, $A1 is absolute for column A and relative for row 1, and A$1 is absolute for row 1 and relative for column A. If you copy or fill the formula across rows or down columns, the relative references adjust, and the absolute ones don't adjust.

3-D References

3-D references allow you to analyze data in the same cell or range of cells on multiple worksheets within a workbook. A 3-D reference includes the cell or range reference, preceded by a range of worksheet names. For example, =AVERAGE(Sheet1:Sheet4!A1) returns the average for all the values contained in cell A1 on all the worksheets between and including Sheet 1 and Sheet 4.

Creating a Simple Formula

A **formula** calculates values to return a result. On an Excel worksheet, you can create a formula using values (such as 147 or $10.00), arithmetic operators (shown in the table), and cell references. An Excel formula always begins with the equal sign (=). The equal sign, when entered, automatically formats the cell as a formula entry. The best way to start a formula is to have an argument. An **argument** is the cell references or values in a formula that contribute to the result. Each function uses function-specific arguments, which may include numeric values, text values, cell references, ranges of cells, and so on. To accommodate long, complex formulas, you can resize the formula bar to prevent formulas from covering other data in your worksheet. By default, only formula results are displayed in a cell, but you can change the view of the worksheet to display formulas instead of results.

Enter a Formula

① Click the cell where you want to enter a formula.

② Type = (an equal sign). If you do not begin with an equal sign, Excel will display, not calculate, the information you type.

③ Enter the first argument. An argument can be a number or a cell reference.

TIMESAVER *To avoid typing mistakes, click a cell to insert its cell reference in a formula rather than typing its address.*

④ Enter an arithmetic operator.

⑤ Enter the next argument.

⑥ Repeat steps 4 and 5 as needed to complete the formula.

⑦ Click the **Enter** button on the formula bar, or press Enter.

Notice that the result of the formula appears in the cell (if you select the cell, the formula itself appears on the formula bar).

TIMESAVER *To wrap text in a cell, press Alt+Enter, which manually inserts a line break.*

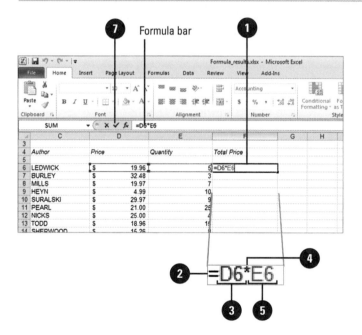

For Your Information

Understanding Order of Precedence

Formulas containing more than one operator follow the order of precedence: exponentiation, multiplication and division, and then addition and subtraction. So, in the formula 5 + 2 * 3, Excel performs multiplication first and addition next for a result of 11. Excel calculates operations within parentheses first. The result of the formula (5 + 2) * 3 is 21.

Resize the Formula Bar

◆ To switch between expanding the formula box to three or more lines or collapsing it to one line, click the double-down arrow at the end of the formula bar. You can also press Ctrl+Shift+U.

◆ To precisely adjust the height of the formula box, point to the bottom of the formula box until the pointer changes to a vertical double arrow, and then drag up or down, and then click the vertical double arrow or press Enter.

◆ To automatically fit the formula box to the number of lines of text in the active cell, point to the formula box until the pointer changes to a vertical double arrow, and then double-click the vertical arrow.

Double-down arrow

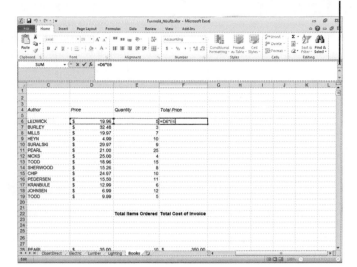

Display Formulas in Cells

① Click the **Formulas** tab.

② Click the **Show Formulas** button.

TIMESAVER *Press Ctrl+'.*

③ To turn off formula display, click the **Show Formulas** button again.

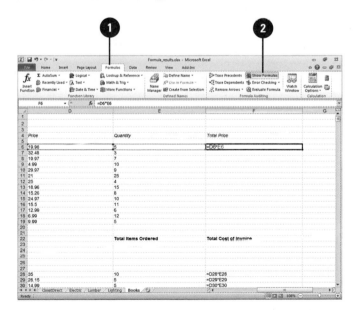

Did You Know?

Pointing to cells reduces errors. When building formulas, pointing to a cell rather than typing its address ensures that the correct cell is referenced.

You can print formulas. Click the Formulas tab, click the Show Formulas button to show formulas, click the File tab, click Print, and then click Print.

Creating a Formula Using Formula AutoComplete

To minimize typing and syntax errors, you can create and edit formulas with Formula AutoComplete. After you type an = (equal sign) and begin typing to start a formula, Excel displays a dynamic drop-down list of valid functions, arguments, defined names, table names, special item specifiers—including [(open bracket), , (comma), : (colon)—and text string that match the letters you type. An argument is the cell references or values in a formula that contribute to the result. Each function uses function-specific arguments, which may include numeric values, text values, cell references, ranges of cells, and so on.

Enter Items in a Formula Using Formula AutoComplete

① Click the cell where you want to enter a formula.

② Type = (an equal sign), and beginning letters or a display trigger to start Formula AutoComplete.

For example, type *su* to display all value items, such as SUBTOTAL and SUM.

The text before the insertion point is used to display the values in the drop-down list.

③ As you type, a drop-down scrollable list of valid items is displayed.

Icons represent the type of entry, such as a function or table reference, and a ScreenTip appears next to a selected item.

④ To insert the selected item in the drop-down list into the formula, press Tab or double-click the item.

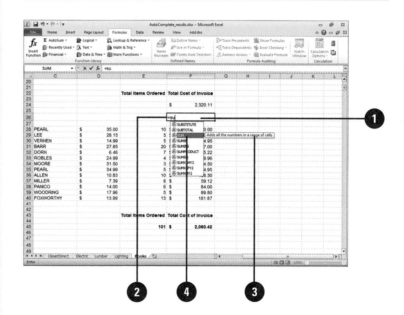

Editing a Formula

You can edit formulas just as you do other cell contents, using the formula bar or working in the cell. You can select, cut, copy, paste, delete, and format cells containing formulas just as you do cells containing labels or values. Using **AutoFill**, you can quickly copy formulas to adjacent cells. If you need to copy formulas to different parts of a worksheet, use the Office Clipboard.

Edit a Formula Using the Formula Bar

1. Select the cell that contains the formula you want to edit.

2. Press F2 to change to Edit mode.

3. If necessary, use the Home, End, and arrow keys to position the insertion point within the cell contents.

4. Use any combination of Backspace and Delete to erase unwanted characters, and then type new characters as needed.

5. Click the **Enter** button on the formula bar, or press Enter.

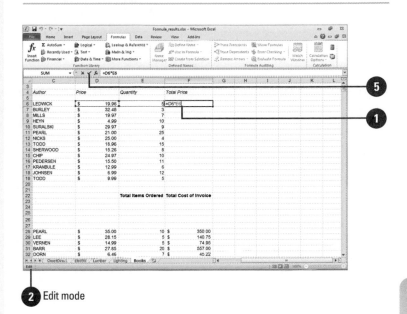

Edit mode

Copy a Formula Using AutoFill

1. Select the cell that contains the formula you want to copy.

2. Position the pointer (fill handle) on the lower-right corner of the selected cell.

3. Drag the mouse down until the adjacent cells where you want the formula pasted are selected, and then release the mouse button.

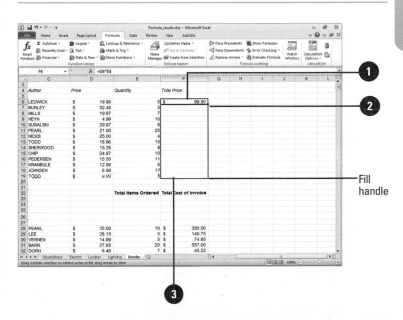

Fill handle

Naming Cells and Ranges

To make working with ranges easier, Excel allows you to name them. The name BookTitle, for example, is easier to remember than the range reference B6:B21. Named ranges can be used to navigate large worksheets. Named ranges can also be used in formulas instead of typing or pointing to specific cells. When you name a cell or range, Excel uses an absolute reference for the name by default, which is almost always what you want. You can see the absolute reference in the Refers to box in the New Name dialog box. There are two types of names you can create and use: defined name and table name. A **defined name** represents a cell, a range of cells, formula or constant, while a **table name** represents an Excel table, which is a collection of data stored in records (rows) and fields (columns). You can define a name for use in a worksheet or an entire workbook, also known as **scope**. To accommodate long names, you can resize the name box in the formula bar. The worksheet and formula bar work together to avoid overlapping content.

Name a Cell or Range Using the Name Box

1. Select the cell or range, or nonadjacent selections you want to name.

2. Click the Name box on the formula bar.

3. Type a name for the range.

   A range name can include up to 255 characters, uppercase or lowercase letters (not case sensitive), numbers, and punctuation, but no spaces or cell references.

   By default, names use absolute cell references.

4. To adjust the width of the Name box, point between the Name box and the Formula box until the pointer changes to a horizontal double arrow, and then drag left or right.

5. Press Enter. The range name will appear in the Name box whenever you select the range in the workbook.

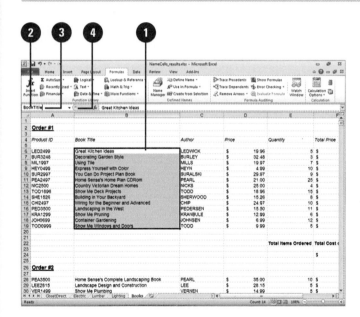

Let Excel Name a Cell or Range

① Select the cells, including the column or row header, you want to name.

② Click the **Formulas** tab.

③ Click the **Create from Selection** button.

④ Select the check box with the position of the labels in relation to the cells.

Excel automatically tries to determine the position of the labels, so you might not have to change any options.

⑤ Click **OK**.

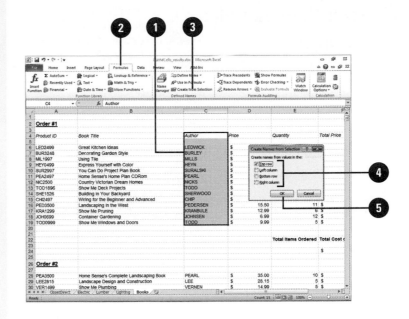

Name a Cell or Range Using the New Name Dialog Box

① Select the cell or range, or nonadjacent selections you want to name.

② Click the **Formulas** tab.

③ Click the **Define Name** button.

④ Type a name for the reference.

⑤ Click the **Scope** list arrow, and then click **Workbook** or a specific worksheet.

⑥ If you want, type a description of the name.

The current selection appears in the Refer to box.

⑦ Click the **Collapse Dialog** button, select different cells and click the **Expand Dialog** button, or type = (equal sign) followed by a constant value or a formula.

⑧ Click **OK**.

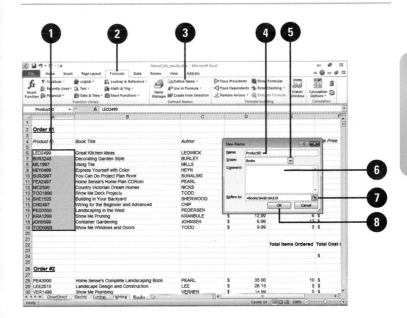

Entering Named Cells and Ranges

After you define a named cell or range, you can enter a name by typing, using the Name box, using Formula AutoComplete, or selecting from the Use in Formula command. As you begin to type a name in a formula, Formula AutoComplete displays valid matches in a drop-down list, which you can select and insert into a formula. You can also select a name from a list of available from the Use in Formula command. If you have already entered a cell or range address in a formula or function, you can apply a name to the address instead of re-creating it.

Enter a Named Cell or Range Using the Name Box

① Click the **Name box** list arrow on the formula bar.

② Click the name of the cell or range you want to use.

The range name appears in the Name box, and all cells included in the range are highlighted on the worksheet.

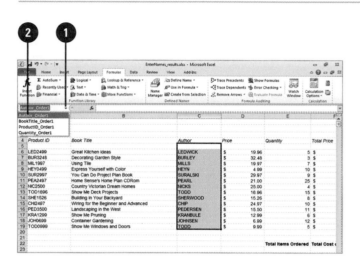

Enter a Named Cell or Range Using Formula AutoComplete

① Type = (equal sign) to start a formula, and then type the first letter of the name.

② To insert a name, type the first letter of the name to display it in the Formula AutoComplete drop-down list.

③ Scroll down the list, if necessary, to select the name you want, and then press Tab or double-click the name to insert it.

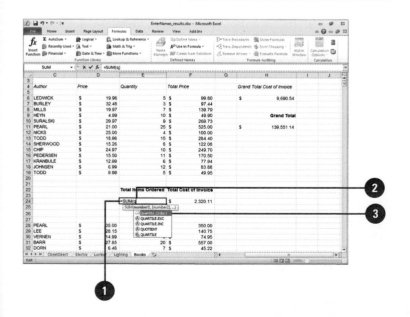

Enter a Named Cell or Range from the Use in Formula Command

1. Type = (equal sign) to start a formula.

2. Click the **Formulas** tab.

3. When you want to insert a name, click the **Use in Formula** button.

4. Use one of the following menu options:

   ◆ Click the name you want to use.

   ◆ Click **Paste Names**, select a name, and then click **OK**.

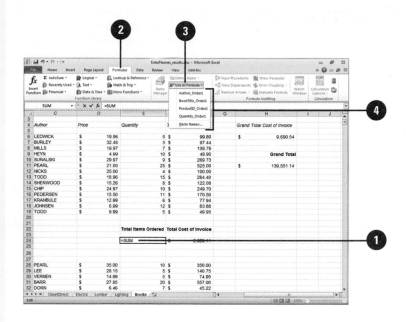

Apply a Name to a Cell or Range Address

1. Select the cells in which you want to apply a name.

2. Click the **Formulas** tab.

3. Click the **Define Name** button arrow, and then click **Apply Names**.

4. Click the name you want to apply.

5. Click **OK**.

Did You Know?

Should I select the Use row and column names option? When you select this option, Excel uses the range row and column headings to refer to the range you've selected (if a cell does not have its own name, but is part of a named range).

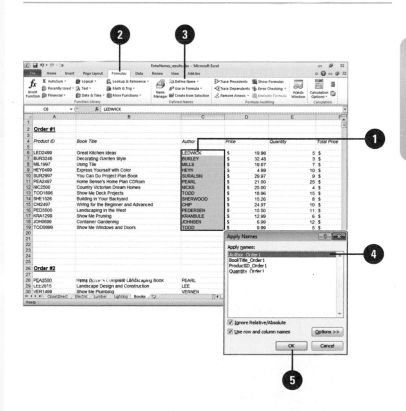

Managing Names

The Name Manager makes it easy to work with all the defined names and table names in a workbook from one location. You can display the value and reference of a name, specify the scope—either worksheet or workbook level—of a name, find names with errors, and view or edit name descriptions. In addition, you can add, change, or delete names, and sort and filter the names list. You can also use table column header names in formulas instead of cell references.

Organize and View Names

1. Click the **Formulas** tab.

2. Click the **Name Manager** button.

   TROUBLE? *You cannot use the Name Manager dialog box while you're editing a cell. The Name Manager doesn't display names defined in VBA or hidden names.*

3. Use one of the following menu options:

   ◆ **Resize columns.** Double-click the right side of the column header to automatically size the column to fit the largest value in that column.

   ◆ **Sort names.** Click the column header to sort the list of names in ascending or descending order.

   ◆ **Filter names.** Click the Filter button, and then select the filter command you want. See table for filter option details.

4. Click **Close**.

Column header

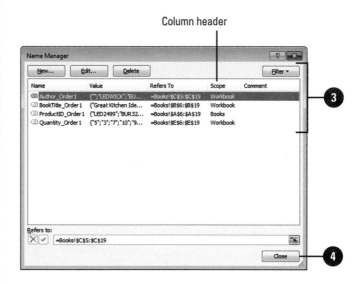

Did You Know?

What happens when you zoom in on a name range? When you zoom the view of the worksheet to 39 percent or less, Excel adds a blue border around the labels you have created. The blue border does not print.

Name Manager Filter Options

Option	Result
Names Scoped to Worksheet	Displays names local to a worksheet
Names Scoped to Workbook	Displays names global to a workbook
Names with Errors	Displays names with values that contain errors (such as #NAME, #VALUE, etc.)
Names without Errors	Displays names without errors
Defined Names	Displays names defined by you or by Excel
Table Names	Displays table names

Change a Name

① Click the **Formulas** tab.

② Click the **Names Manager** button.

③ Click the name you want to change.

④ Click **Edit**.

⑤ Type a new name for the reference in the Name box.

⑥ Change the reference. Enter a range or use the **Collapse** button to select one.

⑦ Click **OK**.

⑧ In the Refers to area, make any changes you want to the cell, formula, or constant represented by the name.

To cancel unwanted changes, click the **Cancel** button or press Esc, or to save changes, click the **Commit** button or press Enter.

⑨ Click **Close**.

Did You Know?

You can delete a name range. Click the Formulas tab, click the Name Manager button, select the names you want to delete, click Delete or press Delete, click OK to confirm, and then click Close.

What happens when you change a label reference? If you change the name of a reference label, Excel automatically makes the change to every formula in which the name is used.

You can label names that are relative. When you use a label name in a formula or function, Excel sees it as a relative reference. You can copy the formula to other cells, or use AutoFill to copy it and the reference changes.

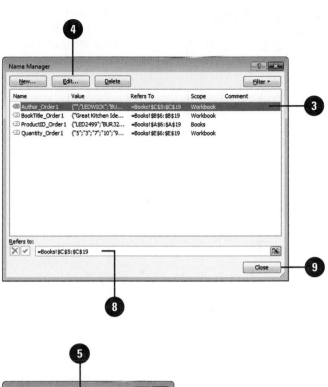

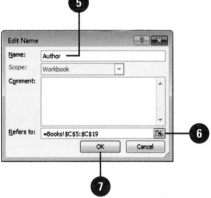

Simplifying a Formula with Ranges

You can simplify formulas by using ranges and range names. For example, if 12 cells on your worksheet contain monthly budget amounts, and you want to multiply each amount by 10%, you can insert one range address in a formula instead of inserting 12 different cell addresses, or you can insert a range name. Using a range name in a formula helps to identify what the formula does; the formula =TotalOrder*0.10, for example, is more meaningful than =SUM(F6:F19)*0.10.

Use a Range in a Formula

1. Put your cursor where you would like the formula. Type an equal sign (=) followed by the start of a formula, such as *=SUM(*.

2. Click the first cell of the range, and then drag to select the last cell in the range. Excel enters the range address for you.

3. Complete the formula by entering a close parentheses, or another function, and then click the **Enter** button.

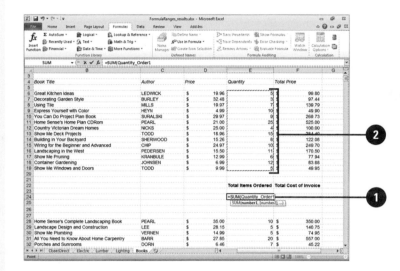

Use a Range Name in a Formula

1. Put your cursor where you would like the formula. Type an equal sign (=) followed by the start of a formula, such as *=SUM(*.

2. Press F3 to display a list of named ranges.

   ◆ You can also click the **Use in Formula** button on the Formulas tab, and then click **Paste**.

3. Click the name of the range you want to insert.

4. Click **OK**.

5. Complete the formula by entering a close parentheses, or another function, and then click the **Enter** button.

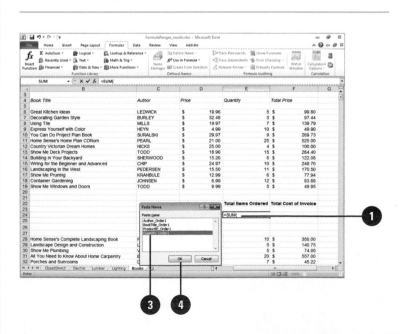

Calculating Totals with AutoSum

A range of cells can easily be added using the **AutoSum** button on the Formulas tab. AutoSum suggests the range to sum, although this range can be changed if it's incorrect. AutoSum looks at all of the data that is consecutively entered, and when it sees an empty cell, that is where the AutoSum stops. You can also use AutoSum to perform other calculations, such as AVERAGE, COUNT, MAX, and MIN. Subtotals can be calculated for data ranges using the Subtotals dialog box. This dialog box lets you select where the subtotals occur, as well as the function type.

Calculate Totals with AutoSum

1. Click the cell where you want to display the calculation.

   ◆ To sum with a range of numbers, select the range of cells you want.

   ◆ To sum with only some of the numbers in a range, select the cells or range you want using the Ctrl key. Excel inserts the sum in the first empty cell below the selected range.

   ◆ To sum both across and down a table of number, select the range of cells with an additional column to the right and a row at the bottom.

2. Click the **Formulas** tab.

3. Click the **AutoSum** button.

   TIMESAVER *Press Alt+= to access the AutoSum command.*

4. Click the **Enter** button on the formula bar, or press Enter.

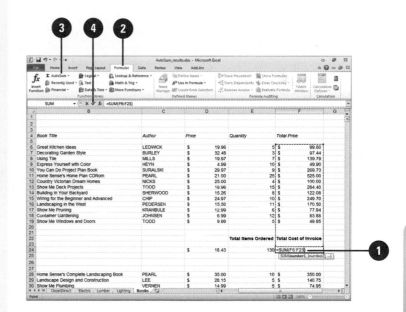

Did You Know?

You can select additional AutoFill commands. Click the Home tab, and then click the Fill button to select additional commands such as Up, Down, Left, Right, Series, or Justify.

Correcting Formulas

Excel has several tools to help you find and correct problems with formulas. One tool is the **Watch window** and another is the **Error checker**. The Watch window keeps track of cells and their formulas as you make changes to a worksheet. Excel uses an error checker in the same way Microsoft Word uses a grammar checker. The Error checker uses certain rules, such as using the wrong argument type, a number stored as text or an empty cell reference, to check for problems in formulas.

Watch Cells and Formulas

1. Select the cells you want to watch.

2. Click the **Formulas** tab.

3. Click the **Watch Window** button.

4. Click the **Add Watch** button on the Watch Window dialog box.

5. Click **Add**.

6. Click **Close**.

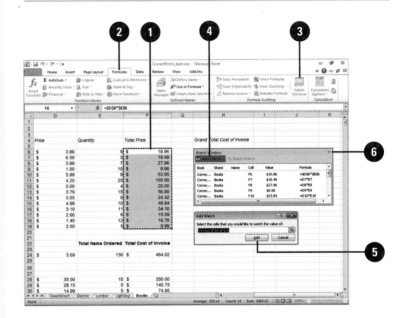

Remove Cells from the Watch Window

1. Click the **Formulas** tab.

2. Click the **Watch Window** button.

3. Select the cells you want to delete. Use the Ctrl key to select multiple cells.

4. Click **Delete Watch**.

5. Click **Close**.

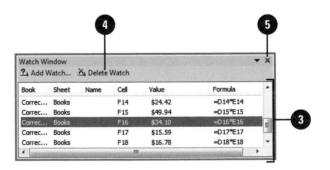

Set Error Checking Options

① Click the **File** tab, and then click **Options**.

② In the left pane, click **Formulas**.

③ Select the **Enable background error checking** check box.

④ Point to the help icons at the end of the error checking rule options to display a ScreenTip describing the rule.

⑤ Select the error checking rules check boxes you want to use.

⑥ Click **OK**.

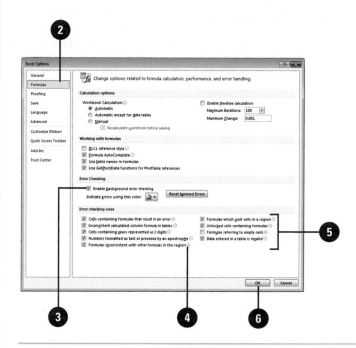

Correct Errors

① Open the worksheet where you want to check for errors.

② Click the **Formulas** tab.

③ Click the **Error Checking** button.

The error checker scans the worksheet for errors, generating the Error Checking dialog box every time it encounters an error.

④ If necessary, click **Resume**.

⑤ Choose a button to correct or ignore the problem.

◆ **Help on this error.**

◆ **Show Calculation Steps.** Click Evaluate to see results.

◆ **Ignore Error.**

◆ **Edit in Formula Bar.**

◆ **Previous** or **Next**.

⑥ If necessary, click **Close**.

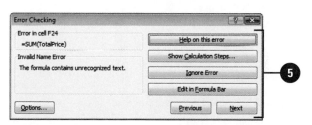

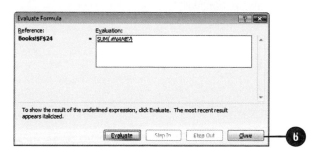

Auditing a Worksheet

In a complex worksheet, it can be difficult to understand the relationships between cells and formulas. Auditing tools enable you to clearly determine these relationships. When the **Auditing** feature is turned on, it uses a series of arrows to show you which cells are part of which formulas. When you use the auditing tools, **tracer arrows** point out cells that provide data to formulas and the cells that contain formulas that refer to the cells. A box is drawn around the range of cells that provide data to formulas.

Trace Worksheet Relationships

① Click the **Formulas** tab.

② Use any of the following options:

◆ Click the **Trace Precedents** button to find cells that provide data to a formula.

◆ Click the **Trace Dependents** button to find out which formulas refer to a cell.

◆ Click the **Error Checking** button arrow, and then click **Trace Error** to locate the problem if a formula displays an error value, such as #DIV/0!.

◆ Click the **Remove Arrows** button arrow, and then click **Remove Precedent Arrows**, **Remove Dependent Arrows**, or **Remove All Arrows** to remove precedent and dependent arrows.

③ If necessary, click **OK** to locate the problem.

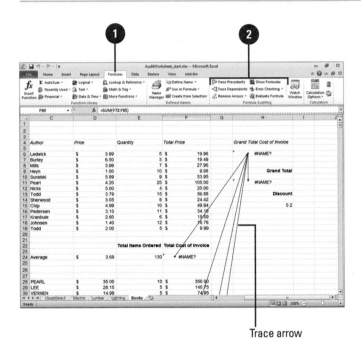

Trace arrow

Creating Functions

Functions are predesigned formulas that save you the time and trouble of creating commonly used or complex equations. Trying to write a formula that calculates various pieces of data, such as calculating payments for an investment over a period of time at a certain rate, can be difficult and time-consuming. The **Insert Function** feature simplifies the process by organizing Excel's built-in formulas, called functions, into categories so they are easy to find and use. A function defines all the necessary components (also called arguments) you need to produce a specific result; all you have to do is supply the values, cell references, and other variables. You can even combine one or more functions.

Enter a Function Using Insert Function

1. Click the cell where you want to enter the function.

2. Click the **Insert Function** button on the Formula bar or click the **Function Wizard** button on the Formulas tab.

3. Type a brief description that describes what you want to do in the Search for a function box, and then click **Go**.

4. If necessary, click a function category you want to use.

5. Click the function you want to use.

6. Click **OK**.

7. Enter the cell addresses in the text boxes. Type them or click the **Collapse Dialog** button to the right of the text box, select the cell or range using your mouse, and then click the **Expand Dialog** button.

8. Click **OK**.

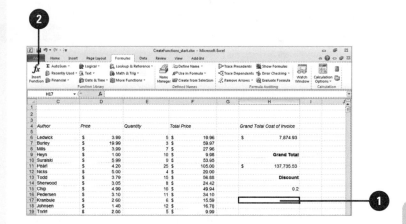

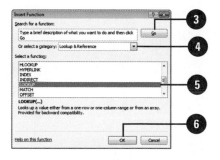

Creating Functions Using the Library

To make it easier to find the function you need for a specific use, Excel has organized functions into categories—such as Financial, Logical, Text, Date & Time, Lookup & Reference, Math & Trig, and other functions—on the Formulas tab. Functions—such as beta and chi-squared distributions—for the academic, engineering, and scientific community have been improved for more accuracy (**New!**). Some statistical functions have been renamed for consistency with the real world (**New!**). After you use a function, Excel places it on the recently used list. When you insert a function from the Function Library, Excel inserts the function in the formula bar and opens a Function Argument dialog box, where you can enter or select the cells you want to use in the function.

Enter a Function Using the Function Library

1. Click the cell where you want to enter the function.

2. Click the **Formulas** tab.

3. Type = (an equal sign).

4. Click the button (**Financial, Logical, Text, Date & Time, Lookup & Reference, Math & Trig, More Functions**, or **Recently Used**) from the Function Library with the type of function you want to use, click a submenu if necessary, and then click the function you want to insert into a formula.

   Excel inserts the function you selected into the formula bar with a set of parenthesis, and opens the Function Arguments dialog box.

5. Type the argument or select the cell or range you want to insert in the function.

   You can click the Collapse Dialog button to the right of the text box, select the cell or range using your mouse, and then click the Expand Dialog button.

6. Click **OK**.

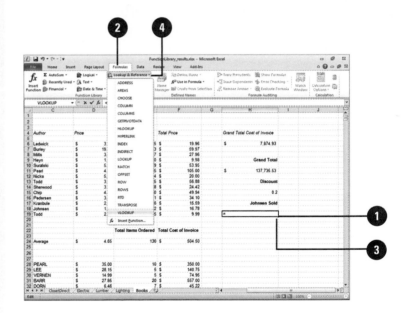

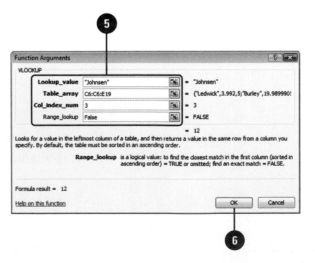

Calculating Multiple Results

An array formula can perform multiple calculations and then return either a single or multiple result. For example, when you want to count the number of distinct entries in a range, you can use an array formula, such as {=SUM(1/COUNTIF(range,range))}. You can also use an array formula to perform a two column lookup using the LOOKUP function. An array formula works on two or more sets of values, known as **array arguments**. Each argument must have the same number of rows and columns. You can create array formulas in the same way that you create other formulas, except you press Ctrl+Shift+Enter to enter the formula. When you enter an array formula, Excel inserts the formula between { } (brackets).

Create an Array Formula

1. Click the cell where you want to enter the array formula.

2. Click the **Formulas** tab.

3. Type = (an equal sign).

4. Use any of the following methods to enter the formula you want.

   ◆ Type the function.

   ◆ Type and use Formula AutoComplete.

   ◆ Use the Function Wizard.

   ◆ Use button in the Function Library.

5. Press Ctrl+Shift+Enter.

   { } (brackets) appear around the function to indicate it's an array formula.

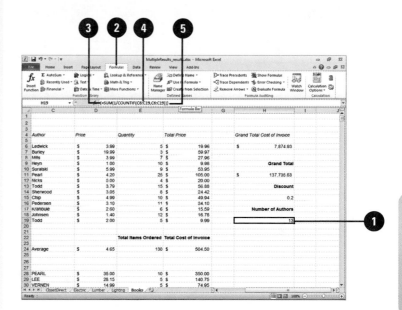

Using Nested Functions

A nested function uses a function as one of the arguments. Excel allows you to nest up to 64 levels of functions. Users typically create nested functions as part of a conditional formula. For example, IF(AVERAGE(B2:B10)>100,SUM(C2:G10),0). The AVERAGE and SUM functions are nested within the IF function. The structure of the IF function is IF(condition_test, if_true, if_false). You can use the AND, OR, NOT, and IF functions to create conditional formulas. When you create a nested formula, it can be difficult to understand how Excel performs the calculations. You can use the Evaluate Formula dialog box to help you evaluate parts of a nested formula one step at a time.

Create a Conditional Formula Using a Nested Function

1. Click the cell where you want to enter the function.

2. Click the **Formulas** tab.

3. Type = (an equal sign).

4. Click a button from the Function Library with the type of function you want to use, click a submenu if necessary, and then click the function you want to insert into a formula.

   For example, click the Logical & Reference button, and then click COUNTIF.

   Excel inserts the function you selected into the formula bar with a set of parenthesis, and opens the Function Arguments dialog box.

5. Type a function as an argument to create a nested function, or a regular argument.

   For example, =COUNTIF(E6:E19), ">"&AVERAGE(E6:E19)).

6. Click **OK**.

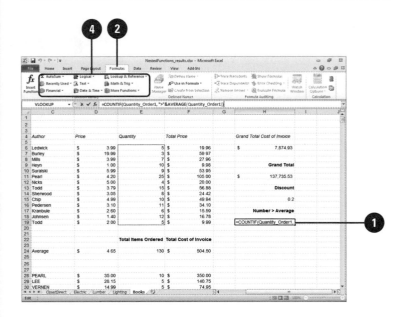

Conditional Formula Examples

Formula	Result
=AND(A2>A3, A2<A4)	If A2 is greater than A3 and less than A4, then return TRUE, otherwise return FALSE
=OR(A2>A3, A2<A4)	If A2 is greater than A3 or A2 is less than A4, then return TRUE, otherwise return FALSE
=NOT(A2+A3=24)	If A2 plus A3 is not equal to 24, then return TRUE, otherwise return FALSE
IF(A2<>15, "OK", "Not OK")	If the value in cell A2 is not equal to 15, then return "OK", otherwise return "Not OK"

Using Text Functions

You can use text functions to help you work with text in a workbook. If you need to count the number of characters in a cell or the number of occurrences of a specific text string in a cell, you can use the LEN and SUBSTITUTE functions. If you want to narrow the count to only upper or lower case text, you can use the UPPER and LOWER functions. If you need to capitalize a list of names or titles, you can use the PROPER function. The function capitalizes the first letter in a text string and converts all other letters to lowercase.

Use Text Functions

1. Create a data range in which the left-most column contains a unique value in each row.

2. Click the cell where you want to place the function.

3. Type = (equal sign), type a text function, specify the argument for the selected function, and then press Enter.

Some examples include:

- =LEFT(A4,FIND(" ",A4)-1)

- =RIGHT(A4,LEN(A4-FIND("*",SUBSTITUTE(A4," ","*",LEN(A4)-LEN(SUBSTITUTE(A4," ",""))))))

- =UPPER(A4)

- =LOWER(A4)

- =PROPER(A4)

Or click the **Formulas** tab, click the **Text** button, click text function, specify the function arguments, and then click **OK**.

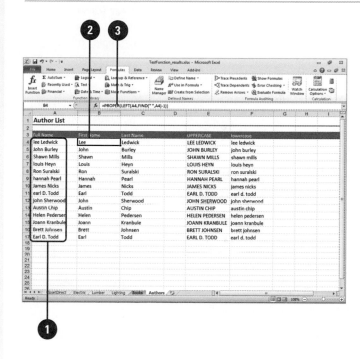

Using Lookup and Reference Functions

You can use lookup and reference functions in Excel to easily retrieve information from a data list. The lookup functions (VLOOKUP and HLOOKUP) allow you to search for and insert a value in a cell that is stored in another place in the worksheet. The HLOOKUP function looks in rows (a horizontal lookup) and the VLOOKUP function looks in columns (a vertical lookup). Each function uses four arguments (pieces of data) as shown in the following definition: =VLOOKUP (lookup_value, table_array, col_index_num, range_lookup). The VLOOKUP function finds a value in the left-most column of a named range and returns the value from the specified cell to the right of the cell with the found value, while the HLOOKUP function does the same to rows. In the example, =VLOOKUP(12,Salary,2,TRUE), the function looks for the value 12 in the named range Salary and finds the closest (next lower) value, and returns the value in column 2 of the same row and places the value in the active cell. In the example, =HLOOKUP ("Years",Salary,4,FALSE), the function looks for the value "Years" in the named range Salary and finds the exact text string value, and then returns the value in row 4 of the column.

Use the VLOOKUP Function

① Create a data range in which the left-most column contains a unique value in each row.

② Click the cell where you want to place the function.

③ Type **=VLOOKUP(**value, named range, column, **TRUE** or **FALSE**)**, and then press Enter.

Or click the **Formulas** tab, click the **Look & Reference** button, click **VLOOKUP**, specify the function arguments, and then click **OK**.

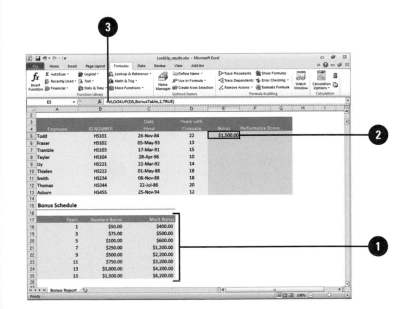

Did You Know?

You can use Paste Special to copy only formulas. Select the cells containing the formulas you want to copy, click the Copy button on the Home tab, click where you want to paste the data, click the Paste button arrow, click Paste Special, click the Formulas button, and then click OK.

Use the HLOOKUP Function

① Create a data range in which the uppermost row contains a unique value in each row.

② Click the cell where you want to place the function.

③ Type **=HLOOKUP(***value, named range, row,* **TRUE** *or* **FALSE)**, and then press Enter.

Or click the **Formulas** tab, click the **Look & Reference** button, click **HLOOKUP**, specify the function arguments, and then click **OK**.

Did You Know?

You can also use the Lookup Wizard add-in. Excel also includes a Lookup Wizard to help you lookup information step-by-step. Use the Add-In pane in Excel Options to load the Lookup Wizard add-in, click the Formulas tab, click the LookUp button, and then follow the wizard instructions.

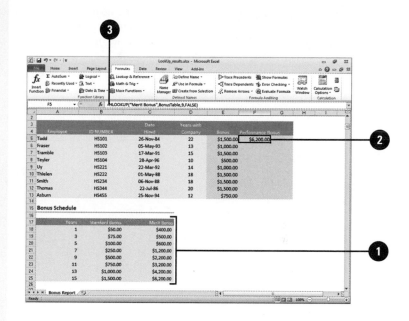

Lookup Function Arguments

Argument	Description
lookup_value	The value found in the row or the column of the named range. You can use a value, cell reference or a text string (enclosed in quotation marks).
table_array	The named range of information in which Excel looks up data.
col_index_num	The numeric position of the column in the named range (counting from the left) for the value to be returned (use only for VLOOKUP).
row_index_num	The numeric position of the row in the named range (counting from the top) for the value to be returned (use only for HLOOKUP).
range_lookup	The value returned when the function is to find the nearest value (TRUE) or an exact match (FALSE) for the lookup_value. The default value is TRUE.

Summarizing Data Using Subtotals

If you have a column list with similar facts and no blanks, you can automatically calculate subtotals and grand totals in a list. Subtotals are calculated with a summary function, such as SUM, COUNT, or AVERAGE, while Grand totals are created from detailed data instead of subtotal values. **Detailed data** is typically adjacent to and either above or below or to the left of the summary data. When you summarize data using subtotals, the data list is also outlined to display and hide the detailed rows for each subtotal.

Subtotal Data in a List

① Organize data in a hierarchical fashion—place summary rows below detail rows and summary columns to the right of detail columns.

② Select the data that you want to subtotal.

③ Click the **Data** tab.

④ Use sort buttons to sort the column.

⑤ Click the **Subtotal** button.

⑥ Click the column to subtotal.

⑦ Click the summary function you want to use to calculate the subtotals.

⑧ Select the check box for each column that contains values you want to subtotal.

⑨ To set automatic page breaks following each subtotal, select the **Page break between groups** check box.

⑩ To show or hide a summary row above the detail row, select or clear the **Summary below data** check box.

⑪ To remove subtotals, click **Remove All**.

⑫ Click **OK**.

⑬ To add more subtotals, use the **Subtotal** button again.

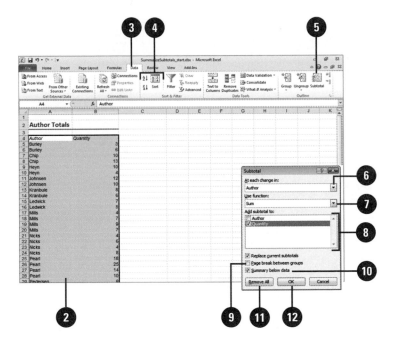

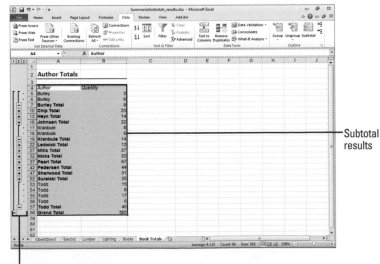

Subtotal results

Use +/- button to expand/collapse subtotals.

Summarizing Data Using Functions

You can use conditional functions, such as SUMIF, COUNTIF, and AVERAGEIF to summarize data in a workbook. These functions allow you to calculate a total, count the number of items, and average a set of numbers based on a specific criteria. You can use the SUMIF function to add up interest payment for accounts over $100, or use the COUNTIF function to find the number of people who live in CA from an address list. If you need to perform these functions based on multiple criteria, you can use the SUMIFS, COUNTIFS, and AVERAGEIFS functions. If you need to find the minimum or maximum in a range, you can use the summarizing functions MIN and MAX.

Use Summarize Data Functions

1. Click the cell where you want to place the function.

2. Type = (equal sign), type a text function, specify the argument for the selected function, and then press Enter.

   Some examples include:

   ◆ =AVERAGE(D6:D19)

   ◆ ={=SUM(1/COUNTIF(C6:C19, C6:19))}

   ◆ =SUMIF(C6:C19,"Todd", Quantity_Order1)

   ◆ =SUM(Quantity_Order1)

   Or click the **Formulas** tab, click the **More Functions** button, point to **Statistical**, click a data function, specify the function arguments, and then click **OK**.

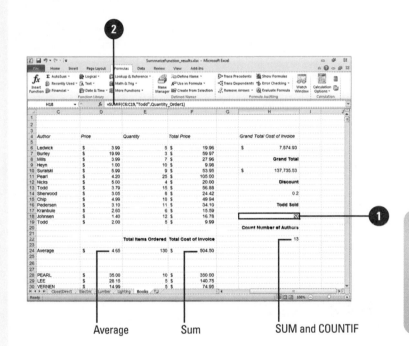

Average   Sum   SUM and COUNTIF

Did You Know?

You can use several functions to count items in a range. The COUNT function counts the number of cells that contain numbers within the list of arguments, while the COUNTA function counts the number of cells that are not empty and the values within the list of arguments.

Converting Text to Columns

The Convert to Columns Wizard helps you separate simple cell contents into different columns. For example, if a cell contains first and last names, you can use the Convert to Columns Wizard to separate first and last name into different columns. The wizard uses the delimiter—such as a tab, semicolon, comma, space, or custom—to determine where to separate the cell contents into different columns; the wizard options vary depending on the delimiter type. For example, the cell contents *Julie, Kenney* uses the comma delimiter.

Convert Text to Columns

1. Select the range you want to covert to columns.

2. Click the **Data** tab.

3. Click the **Text to Columns** button.

4. In Step 1, click **Delimited**.

5. Click **Next**.

6. In Step 2, select the delimiter type you want to use, and then clear the other check boxes.

   The wizard options vary depending on the selected delimiter.

7. Click **Next**.

8. In Step 3, click a column in the Data preview box, click the **Text** option, and then repeat this for each column you want.

9. Click the **Collapse Dialog** button, select a new destination for the separated data, and then click the **Expand Dialog** button.

10. Click **Finish**.

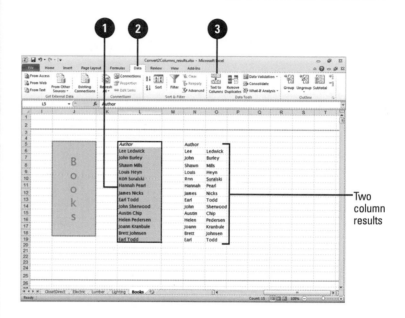

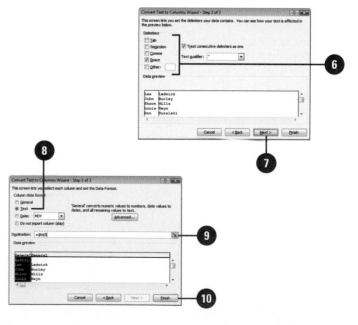

Creating a Table

To create a table in Excel, you can enter data on worksheet cells, just as you do on any other worksheet data, but the placement of the field names and range must follow these rules: (1) Enter field names in a single row that is the first row in the list (2) Enter each record in a single row (3) Do not include any blank rows within the range (4) Do not use more than one worksheet for a single range. You can enter data directly in the table. Don't worry about entering records in any particular order; Excel tools can organize an existing list alphabetically, by date, or in almost any order you can imagine.

Create a Table

1. Open a blank worksheet, or use a worksheet that has enough empty columns and rows for your table.

2. Enter a label for each field in adjacent columns across the first row of the table.

3. Enter field information for each record in its own row; start with the row directly below the field names.

4. Select the range of cells for the table, including labels.

5. Do any of the following:

   ◆ Click the **Insert** tab, and then click the **Table** button.

   ◆ Click the **Home** tab, click the **Format as Table** button, and then select a table style.

6. If necessary, adjust the table size, and select the **My table has headers** check box.

7. Click **OK**.

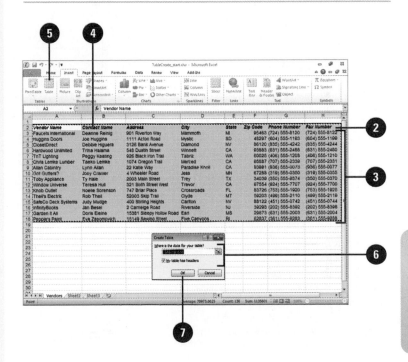

Table

Did You Know?

You can delete or clear a data table. Select the table, and then press Delete to delete the entire table. Select the table, click the Home tab, click the Clear button, and then click Clear Contents.

Formatting a Table

Formatting worksheet table data can be quick and easy with Table Quick Styles. To make formatting data more efficient, Excel has a gallery of table styles based on the current theme. A table style includes preset combinations of fill colors and patterns, font attributes, borders, and font colors that are professionally designed to enhance your worksheets. You can apply a Table Quick Style using the Home or Design tab under Table Tools.

Apply a Quick Style to a Table

1 Select a cell or range in the table to which you want to apply a Quick Style.

2 Do any of the following:

◆ Click the **Design** tab under Table Tools, click the **More** arrow under Table Styles, and then select a table style.

◆ Click the **Home** tab, click the **Format as Table** button, and then select a table style.

Table styles

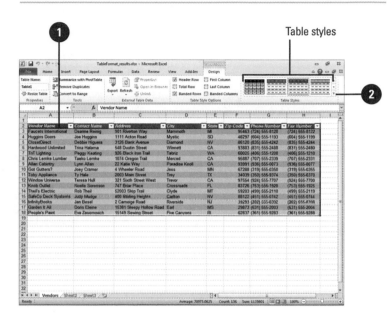

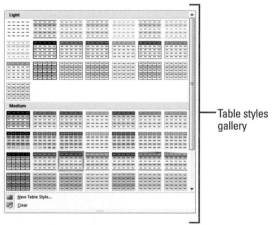

Table styles gallery

Did You Know?

You can copy cell formats with Format Painter. Select the cell or range whose formatting you want to copy, double-click the Format Painter button on the Home tab, select the cells you want to format, and then click the Format Painter button.

You can remove or clear a table style. Click a cell in the table, click the Design tab under Table Tools, click the More arrow under Table Styles, and then click Clear.

You can print an Excel table. Click a cell within the table, click the File tab, click Print, click the Table option, and then click OK.

Formatting Table Elements

When you create a table in a worksheet, Excel displays a standard set of elements, including headings, columns, and rows. You can select options on the Design tab under Table Tools to quickly format a table. These options allow you to format the header row, and first and last column as special. You can also format even columns or rows differently than odd columns or rows. If you want to total numbers in a column, you can format the bottom row of a table for column totals. If you no longer want these formatting elements, you can hide them. If you hide the header row, the table header AutoFilters and any applied filters are removed from the table.

Show or Hide Table Formatting Elements

1. Select a cell or range in the table you want to modify.

2. Click the **Design** tab under Table Tools.

3. Select or clear the check box for the element you want to show or hide:

   ◆ **Header Row** to format the top row of the table as special.

   ◆ **Totals Row** to format the bottom row of the table for column totals.

   ◆ **First Column** to format the first column of the table as special.

   ◆ **Last Column** to format the last column of the table as special.

   ◆ **Banded Column** to format even columns differently than odd columns.

   ◆ **Banded Rows** to format even rows differently than odd rows.

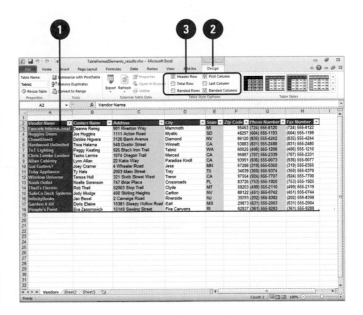

Creating Calculations in a Table

You can quickly total data in a table using the Total Row option. When you display a total row at the end of the table, a drop-down list appears for each total cell along with the word *Total* in the leftmost cell. The drop-down list allows you to select a function to perform a calculation. If the function you want is not available in the drop-down list, you can enter any formula you want in a total row cell. If you're not using a total function, you can delete the word *Total*.

Total the Data in a Table

1 Click a cell in a table.

2 Click the **Design** tab under Table Tools.

3 Select the **Total Row** check box.

The total row appears as the last row in the table and displays the word *Total* in the leftmost cell.

4 Click the cell in the column for which you want to calculate a total, and then click the drop-down list arrow.

5 From the drop-down list, select the function you want to use to calculate the total.

TIMESAVER *Enter a formula in the row directly below a table without a total row to create a total row without the word Total.*

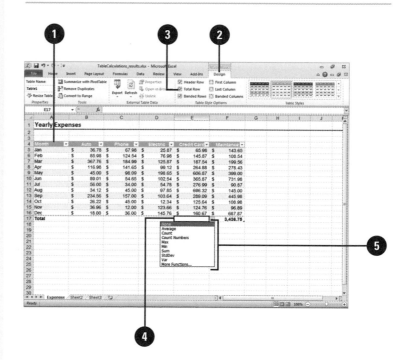

Did You Know?

You can create a calculated column.
A calculated column uses a single formula that adjusts for each row in a table. To create a calculated column, click a cell in a blank table column, and then type a formula. The formula is automatically filled into all cells of the column. Not every cell in a calculated column needs to be the same. You can enter a different formula or data to create an exception.

Removing Table Rows and Columns

If you no longer need a row or column in a table, you can quickly remove it using Delete commands on the Home tab. You delete rows and columns in a table the same way you delete rows and columns in a worksheet. As you enter data in a table, sometimes you accidentally enter the same data more than once. Instead of searching for duplicates manually, Excel can search for duplicates and then remove them for you.

Delete Rows or Columns from a Table

1. Click a cell in the table where you want to delete a row or column.

2. Click the **Home** tab.

3. Click the **Delete** button arrow, and then click **Delete Table Rows** or **Delete Table Columns**.

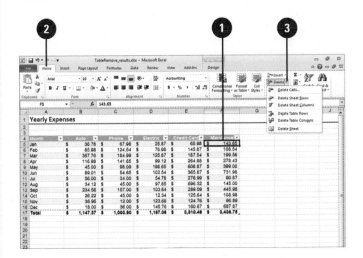

Remove Duplicate Rows from a Table

1. Click a cell in the table.

2. Click the **Design** tab under Table Tools.

3. Click the **Remove Duplicates** button.

4. Select the columns with duplicates you want to remove. You can click **Select All** or **Unselect All**.

5. Click **OK**.

6. Click **OK** to remove duplicates.

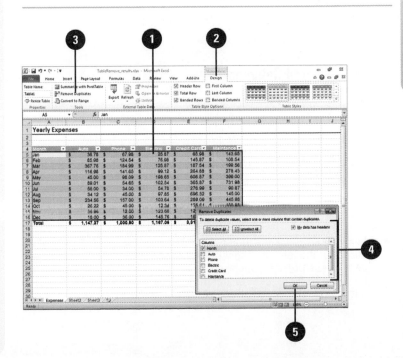

Working with Tables

After you create a table, you can sort the entries, add new entries, and display totals. You can insert rows anywhere in a table or add rows at the bottom of the table. To add a blank row at the end of the table, select any cell in the last row of the table, and then press Enter, or press Tab in the last cell of the last row. If you no longer need the data in table form, you can convert the list back to normal Excel data. Selecting table rows and columns is different than selecting worksheet rows and columns. Selecting cells is the same.

Insert a Row or Column

1. Click a cell in the table where you want to insert a row or column. To insert multiple rows or columns, select more than one row or column.

2. Click the **Home** tab.

3. Click the **Insert** button arrow, and then do one of the following:

   ◆ **Rows.** Click **Insert Table Rows Above** or **Insert Table Rows Below**.

   ◆ **Columns.** Click **Insert Table Columns to the Left** or **Insert Table Columns to the Right**.

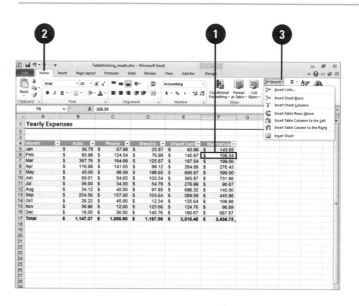

Select Rows and Columns

◆ **Column.** Click the top edge of the column header or the column in the table to select column data (press Ctrl+Spacebar). Double-click the top edge to select the entire column (press Ctrl+Spacebar twice).

◆ **Row.** Click the left border of the row.

◆ **Entire Table.** Click the upper-left corner of the table to select table data (press Ctrl+A). Double-click the upper-left corner to select the entire table (press Ctrl+A twice).

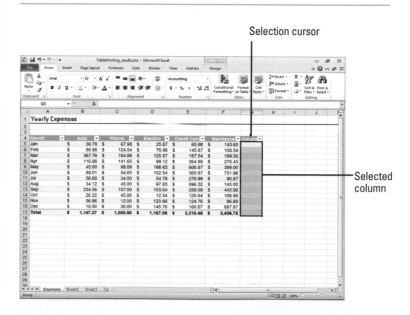

Selection cursor

Selected column

Resize a Table

① Click a cell in the table.

② Click the **Design** tab under Table Tools.

③ Click the **Resize Table** button.

④ Type the range you want to use for the table.

You can click the **Collapse Dialog** button, select the range you want, and then click the **Expand Dialog** button.

TIMESAVER *To resize the table using the mouse, drag the triangular resize handle at the lower-right corner of the table to select the range you want.*

⑤ Click **OK**.

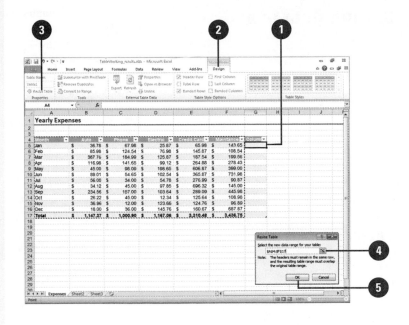

Convert a Table to a Range

① Click a cell in the table.

② Click the **Design** tab under Table Tools.

③ Click the **Convert to Range** button.

④ Click **Yes** to confirm the change.

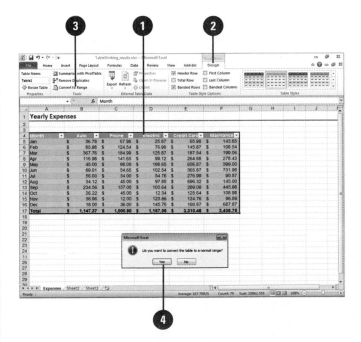

Sorting Data in a Table

After you enter records in a list, you can reorganize the information by sorting the records. For example, you might want to sort records in a client list alphabetically by last name or numerically by their last invoice date. **Ascending order** lists records from A to Z, earliest to latest, or lowest to highest. **Descending order** lists records from Z to A, latest to earliest, or highest to lowest. You can sort the entire list or use AutoFilter to select the part of the list you want to display in the column. You can also sort a list based on one or more **sort fields**—fields you select to sort the list. A sort, for example, might be the telephone directory numerically by area code and then alphabetically by last name. If you have manually or conditionally formatted a range or table column by cell or font color or by an icon set, you can sort by these cell attributes using the Sort button.

Sort Data Quickly

1. Click the table cell with the field name by which you want to sort.

    ◆ You can also click a column header list arrow, and then click **Sort A to Z** or **Sort Z to A**.

2. Click the **Data** tab.

3. Click the **Sort Ascending** or the **Sort Descending** button.

    The list arrow displays an icon indicating the field is sorted.

4. To clear or reapply a data sort, do the following:

    ◆ To clear all filters in a worksheet and redisplay all rows, click the **Clear** button.

    ◆ To reapply a filter, click the **Reapply** button.

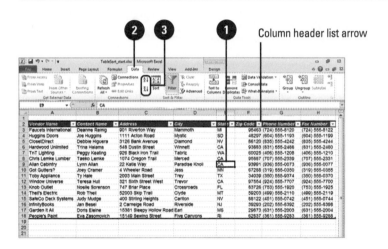

Column header list arrow

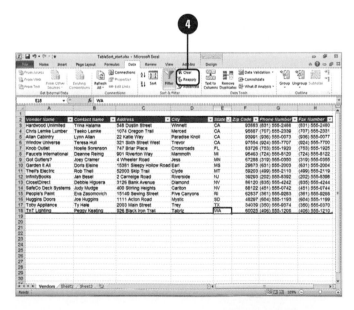

Did You Know?

You can sort data in rows. If the data you want to sort is listed across a row instead of down a column, click the table cell you want to sort by, click the Data tab, click the Sort button, click the Sort Left To Right option, and then click OK.

Sort a Table Using Multiple Fields and Attributes

1. Click anywhere within the table range.

2. Click the **Data** tab.

3. Click the **Sort** button.

4. Click the **Column** list arrow, and then select a sort field.

5. Click the **Sort on** list arrow, and then select a sort field: **Values**, **Cell Color**, **Font Color**, or **Cell Icon**.

   ◆ You can also click a column header list arrow, point to **Sort by Color**, click **Custom Sort**, and then use **Font Color** or **Cell Color** option for Sort On.

6. Click the **Order list** list arrow, and then select a sort field: **A to Z**, **Z to A**, or **Custom List**.

7. To add another level of sorting, click **Add Level**, and then repeat steps 4 through 6.

8. To change the sort order, select a sort, and then click the **Move Up** or **Move Down** buttons.

9. To delete or copy a sort level, select a sort, and then click the **Delete Level** or **Copy Level**.

10. Click **OK**.

    The list arrow displays an icon indicating the field is sorted.

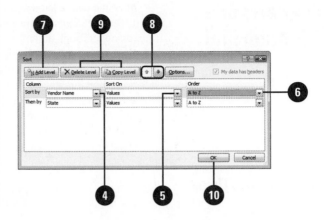

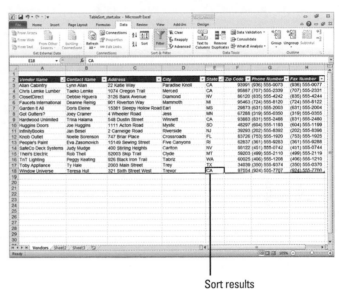

Sort results

Did You Know?

You can sort data with the case sensitive option. Click the table cell you want to sort by, click the Data tab, click the Sort button, click Options, and then select the Case Sensitive check box, and then click OK.

Displaying Parts of a Table with AutoFilter

Working with a list that contains numerous records can be difficult—unless you can narrow your view of the list. For example, rather than looking through an entire inventory list, you might want to see records that come from one distributor. The **AutoFilter** feature creates a list of the items found in each field, which is useful in tables and PivotTables. You select the items that you want to display in the column field by using the column header list arrow and AutoFilter menu. The column headers in a table now remain visible in long lists for ease of use (**New!**). In the AutoFilter menu, you can use the Search box to quickly find what you want in a long list (**New!**). Then you can work with the filtered list.

Display Specific Records Using AutoFilter

1. Click anywhere within the table.

2. Click the **Data** tab.

3. If necessary, click the **Filter** button to highlight and turn it on.

4. Click the column header list arrow where you want to set filter criteria.

5. Select the filter criteria you want:

   ◆ **Select Items.** Select the items that records must match to be included in the table.

   ◆ **Search.** Enter search criteria, and then press Enter (**New!**).

   ◆ **Built-in Filters.** Point to **<Column Name> Filters**, and then select a filter option.

6. Repeat steps 4 and 5 to filter out more records using other fields.

   The list arrow displays an icon indicating the field is filtered.

7. To clear a filter, click the list arrow of the field, and then click **Clear Filter From <Column Name>**.

   ◆ To clear all filters and redisplay all rows, click the **Clear** button.

   ◆ To reapply a filter, click the **Reapply** button.

8. To turn off AutoFilter, click the **Filter** button to deselect it.

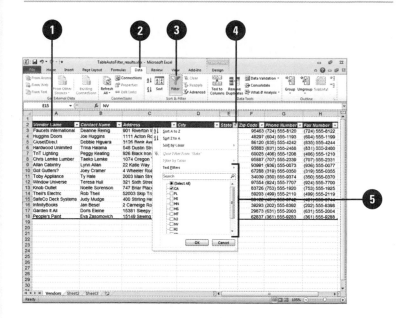

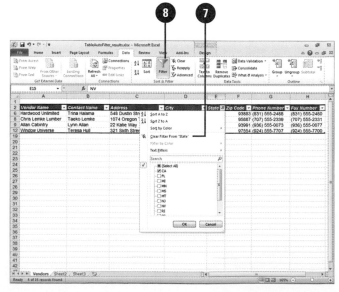

Creating Custom Searches

There are many times you'll want to search for records that meet multiple criteria. For example, you might want to see out-of-stock records of those orders purchased from a particular distributor. Using the AutoFilter feature and the Custom command, you can create complex searches. You can use **logical operators** to measure whether an item in a record qualifies as a match with the selected criteria. You can also use the **logical conditions** AND and OR to join multiple criteria within a single search. The result of any search is either true or false; if a field matches the criteria, the result is true. The OR condition requires that only one criterion be true in order for a record to qualify. The AND condition, on the other hand, requires that both criteria in the statement be true in order for the record to qualify.

Create a Custom Search Using AutoFilter

1. Click anywhere within the table range.

2. Click the **Data** tab.

3. Click the list arrow next to the first field you want to include in the search.

4. Point to **<type> Filter**, and then click **Custom Filter** to enable the command (a check mark appears).

5. Click the **Field** list arrow (on the left), and then select a logical operator.

6. Click the list arrow (on the right), and then select a field choice.

7. If you want, click the **And** or **Or** option.

8. If you want, click the list arrow (on the left), and then select a logical operator.

9. If you want, click the list arrow (on the right), and then select a field choice.

10. Click **OK**.

The list arrow displays an icon indicating the field is filtered.

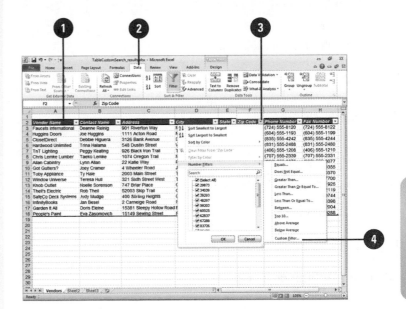

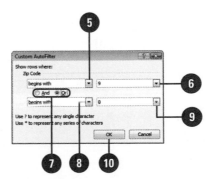

Creating Groups and Outlines

A sales report that displays daily, weekly, and monthly totals in a hierarchical format, such as an outline, helps your reader to sift through and interpret the pertinent information. In outline format, a single item can have several topics or levels of information within it. An outline in Excel indicates multiple layers of content by displaying a plus sign (+) on its left side. A minus sign (-) indicates that the item has no contents, is fully expanded, or both.

Create an Outline or Group

① Organize data in a hierarchical fashion—place summary rows below detail rows and summary columns to the right of detail columns.

② Select the data that you want to outline.

③ To create an outline, click the **Data** tab, click the **Group** button arrow, and then click **Auto Outline**.

④ To create a group, click the **Data** tab, click the **Group** button arrow, and then click **Group**. Click the **Rows** or **Columns** option, and then click **OK**.

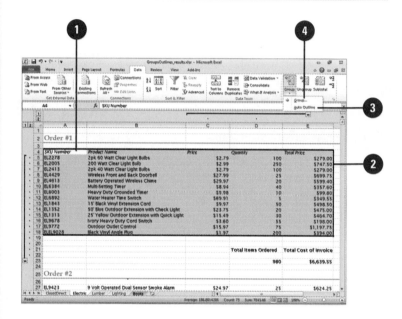

Work an Outline or Group

◆ Click a plus sign (+) to expand an outline level; click a minus sign (-) to collapse an outline level.

Did You Know?

You can ungroup outline data. Select the data group, click the Data tab, click the Ungroup button arrow, and then click Ungroup, click the Rows or Columns option, and then click OK.

You can clear an outline. Select the outline, click the Data tab, click the Group button arrow, and then click Clear Outline.

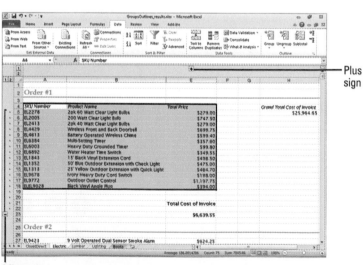

Adding Data Validation to a Worksheet

Worksheet cells can be adjusted so that only certain values can be entered. Controlling how data is entered decreases errors and makes a worksheet more reliable. You might, for example, want it to be possible to enter only specific dates in a range of cells. You can use **logical operators** (such as equal to, not equal to, less than, or greater than) to set validation rules. When invalid entries are made, a message—developed and written by you—appears indicating that the entry is in violation of the validation rules. The rule set will not allow data to flow into the cell.

Create Validation Rules

1 Select the range you want covered in the validation rules.

2 Click the **Data** tab.

3 Click the **Data Validation** button.

4 Click the **Settings** tab.

5 Click the **Allow** list arrow, and then select a value type.

Options vary depending on the Allow value type you select.

6 Click the **Data** list arrow, and then select a logical operator.

7 Enter values or use the **Collapse Dialog** button to select a range for the minimum and maximum criteria.

8 Click the **Input Message** tab, and then type a title and the input message that should be displayed when invalid entries are made.

9 Click the **Error Alert** tab, and then select an alert style, type a title, and error message.

10 Click **OK**.

11 To view invalid data, click the **Data Validation** button arrow, and then click **Circle Invalid Data**. To clear the circles, click the **Data Validation** button arrow, and then click **Clear Validation Circles**.

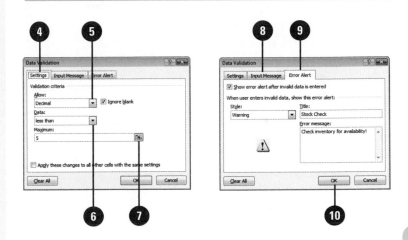

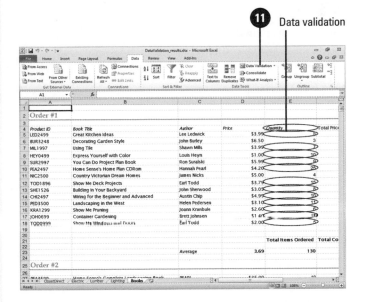

Data validation

Creating a Drop-Down List

Entering data in a table can be tedious and repetitive. To make the job easier, you can create a drop-down list of entries you define. This way you get consistent, accurate data. To create a drop-down list, create a list of valid entries in a single column or row without blanks, define a name, and then use the List option in the Data Validation dialog box. To enter data using a drop-down list, click the cell with the defined drop-down list, click the list arrow, and then click the entry you want.

Create a Drop-Down List

1. Type entries in a single column or row without blanks in the order you want.

2. Select the cell range, click the **Name** box, type a name, and then press Enter.

3. Select the cell where you want the drop-down list.

4. Click the **Data** tab.

5. Click the **Data Validation** button.

6. Click the **Settings** tab.

7. Click the **Allow** list arrow, and then click **List**.

8. Enter values or use the **Collapse Dialog** button to select a range of valid entries.

9. Click the **Input Message** tab, and then type a title and the input message that should be displayed when invalid entries are made.

10. Click the **Error Alert** tab, and then select an alert style, type a title, and error message.

11. Click **OK**.

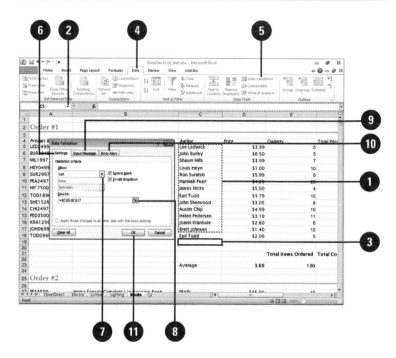

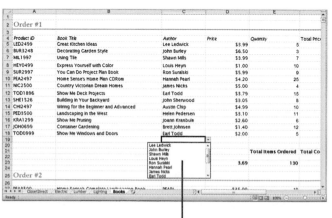

Drop-Down list

Designing a Worksheet with Excel

Introduction

Microsoft Office Excel offers several tools for making your worksheets look more attractive and professional. Without formatting, a worksheet can look like a sea of meaningless data. To highlight important information, you can change the appearance of selected numbers and text by adding dollar signs, commas, and other numerical formats. If you want to format a range of cells in a worksheet you can quickly apply a cell style. A cell style is a defined collection of formats—font, font size, attributes, numeric formats, and so on—that you can store as a set and later apply to other cells. You can use one of Excel's built-in cell styles, or create one of your own.

When your Microsoft Office Excel worksheet is completed, you can preview and print its contents. You can insert page breaks to control what you print on each page. You can change the orientation of the page from the default of portrait (vertical) to landscape (horizontal). This is helpful when you have wide or multiple columns that would look better on one page. You can also adjust your margins to better fit the worksheet on the page. After you make layout adjustments you can add headers and footers on the page in Page Layout view, which lets you focus on how your worksheet is going to look when you print it. Headers are typically a descriptive title about your worksheet or workbook. Footers can include date printed, page numbers, or other company related information. Excel provides options to set the print area and customize what you want to print. For example, you might want to print a different range in a worksheet for different people. After you set the print area, you can choose to print your worksheet. The Print screen allows you to customize all the options and more, and then you can send your worksheet or entire workbook to the printer.

Formatting Numbers

You can change the appearance of the data in the cells of a worksheet without changing the actual value in the cell. You can apply **numeric formats** to numbers to better reflect the type of information they represent—dollar amounts, dates, decimals, and so on. For example, you can format a number to display up to 15 decimal places or none at all. If you don't see the number format you need, you can create a custom one.

Format Numbers Quickly

1. Select a cell or range that contains the number(s) you want to format.

2. Click the **Home** tab.

3. Click the **Number Format** list arrow, and then click any of the following formats:

   ◆ **General.** No specific format.

   ◆ **Number.** 0.75

   ◆ **Currency.** $0.75

   ◆ **Accounting.** $ 0.75

   ◆ **Short Date.** 3/17/2008

   ◆ **Long Date.** Wednesday, March 17, 2008

   ◆ **Time.** 6:00:00 PM

   ◆ **Percentage.** 75.00%

   ◆ **Fraction.** 3/4

   ◆ **Scientific.** 7.50E-01

4. To fine-tune the format, click any of the following format buttons:

   ◆ **Currency Style.** Click the button arrow to select a currency symbol.

   ◆ **Percent Style.**

   ◆ **Comma Style.**

   ◆ **Increase Decimal.**

   ◆ **Decrease Decimal.**

   You can apply multiple attributes to the range.

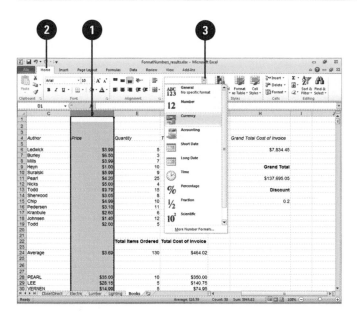

Format a Number Using the Format Cells Dialog Box

① Select a cell or range that contains the number(s) you want to format.

② Click the **Home** tab.

③ Click the **Number Dialog Box Launcher**.

The dialog box opens, displaying the Number tab.

④ Click to select a category.

⑤ Select the options you want to apply.

To create a custom format, click Custom, type the number format code, and then use one of the existing codes as a starting point.

⑥ Preview your selections in the Sample box.

⑦ Click **OK**.

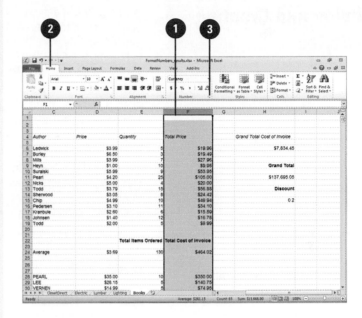

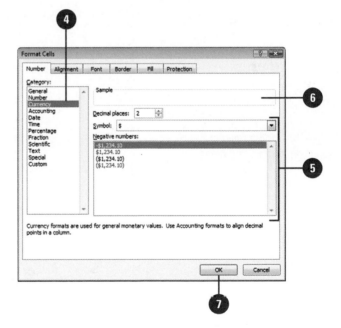

Did You Know?

You can format numbers in international currencies. In the Format Cells dialog box, click the Number tab, click Currency in the Category list, click the Symbol list arrow, and then click an international currency symbol.

You can quickly remove a numeric format or font attribute. The buttons on the Home tab Ribbon and the Mini-Toolbar are toggle buttons, which means you simply click to turn them on and off. To add or remove a numeric format or a font attribute, select the cell, range, or text, and then click the appropriate button on the Home tab or the Mini-Toolbar to turn the format or attribute off.

Applying and Creating Cell Styles

A **cell style** is a defined collection of formats—font, font size, attributes, numeric formats, and so on—that you can store as a set and later apply to other cells. For example if you always want subtotals to display in blue 14-point Times New Roman, bold, italic, with two decimal places and commas, you can create a style that includes all these formats. A cell style can help you quickly create a consistent look for your workbook. If you plan to enter repetitive information, such as a list of dollar amounts in a row or column, it's often easier to apply the desired style to the range before you enter the data. That way you can simply enter each number, and Excel formats it as soon as you press Enter. You can use one of Excel's built-in cell styles, or create one of your own. Once you create a style, it is available to you in every workbook. If you need to prevent users from making changes to specific cells, you can use a cell style that locks cells.

Apply a Cell Style

1. Select a cell or range you want to apply cell shading.

2. Click the **Home** tab.

3. Click the **Cell Styles** button, and then click the cell style you want to apply.

> **See Also**
>
> See "Applying and Creating Cell Styles" on page 284 for information on merging a style from another workbook.

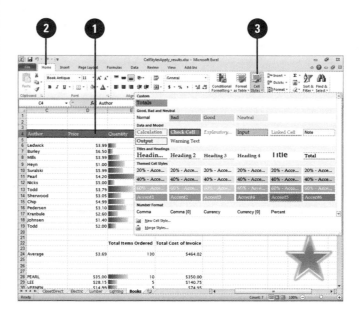

Create or Modify a Custom Cell Style

1. Select a cell or range you want to apply cell shading.

2. Click the **Home** tab.

3. Click the **Cell Styles** button, and then click **New Cell Style**, or right-click a cell style, and then click **Modify**.

4. Type a name for the cell style.

5. Click **Format**.

   The Format Cells dialog box opens.

6. Select the formatting you want on the Number, Alignment, Font, Border, Fill, and Protection tabs, and then click **OK**.

7. Clear the check boxes for any formatting you don't want to use: **Number**, **Alignment**, **Font**, **Border**, **Fill**, or **Protection**.

8. Click **OK**.

   The new cell style is available on the Cell Styles gallery.

Did You Know?

You can remove a custom cell style from a cell. Select the cell or range with the custom style you want to remove, click the Home tab, click the Cell Styles button, and then click Normal.

You can delete a cell style. To delete the cell style and remove it from all cells using it, right-click the cell style, and then click Delete.

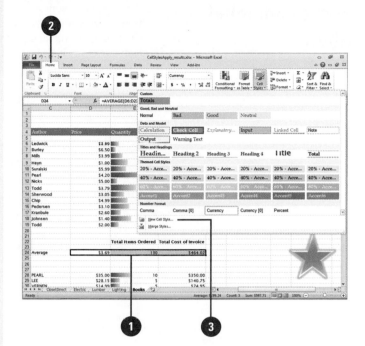

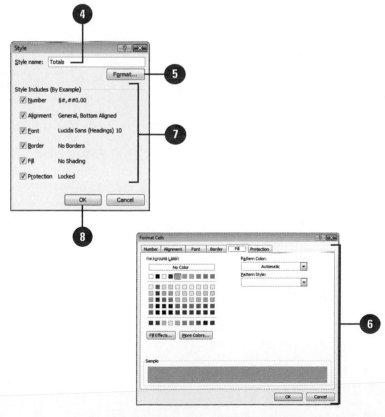

Applying Conditional Formatting

You can make your worksheets more powerful by setting up **conditional formatting**, which lets the value of a cell determine its formatting. For example, you might want this year's sales total to be displayed in red and italics if it's less than last year's total, but in green and bold if it's more. The formatting is applied to the cell values only if the values meet the condition that you specify. Otherwise, no conditional formatting is applied to the cell values. With Excel, you can apply conditional formatting only to cells that contain text, number, or date or time values. You can quickly format only top or bottom ranked values, values above or below average, unique or duplicate values, or use a formula to determine which cells to format. You can also apply multiple formatting to the same data in order to achieve the results you want (**New!**). In addition, you can refer to values in other worksheets (**New!**).

Format Cell Contents Based on Comparison

1. Select a cell or range you want to conditionally format.

2. Click the **Home** tab.

3. Click the **Conditional Formatting** button, and then point to **Highlight Cell Rules**.

4. Click the comparison rule you want to apply to conditionally format the selected data.

   ◆ **Greater Than.**

   ◆ **Less Than.**

   ◆ **Between.**

   ◆ **Equal To.**

   ◆ **Text that Contains.**

   ◆ **A Date Occurring.**

   ◆ **Duplicate Values.**

5. Specify the criteria you want. Each rule supplies different criteria.

6. Click **OK**.

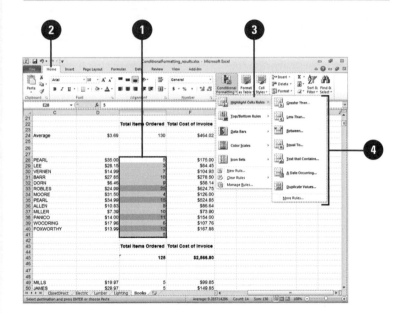

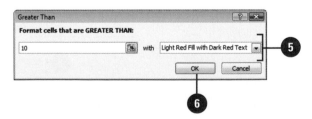

Format Cell Contents Based on Ranking and Average

1 Select a cell or range you want to conditionally format.

2 Click the **Home** tab.

3 Click the **Conditional Formatting** button, and then point to **Top/Bottom Rules**.

4 Click the comparison rule you want to apply to conditionally format the selected data.

- ◆ **Top 10 Items.**
- ◆ **Top 10 %.**
- ◆ **Bottom 10 Items.**
- ◆ **Bottom 10 %.**
- ◆ **Above Average.**
- ◆ **Below Average.**

5 Specify the criteria you want. Each rule supplies different criteria.

6 Click **OK**.

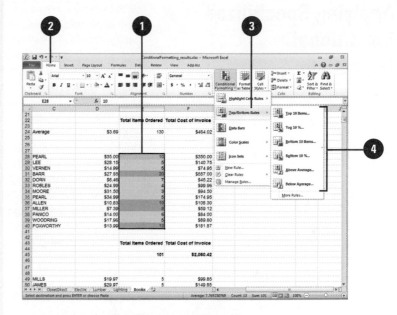

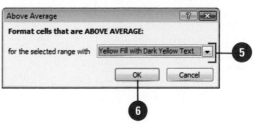

Did You Know?

You can clear conditional formatting.
Select the cell or range with the conditional formatting rules you want to clear, click the Home tab, click the Conditional Formatting button, point to Clear Rules, and then click the clear rule option you want: Clear Rules From Selected Cells, Clear Rules From Entire Sheet, Clear Rules From This Table, or Clear Rules From This PivotTable.

Applying Specialized Conditional Formatting

With Excel, you can apply specialized conditional formatting by using data bars, color scales, and icon sets. A colored **data bar** helps you see the value of a cell relative to other cells. The length of the data bar represents the value in the cell. A longer bar represents a higher value. A negative value displays a bar on the opposite side of an axis from positive values (**New!**). A **color scale** is a visual guide that helps you represent data distribution and variation using two or three color gradients. The color shade represents the value in the cell. A two-color scale represents higher and lower values, while a three-color scale represents higher, middle, and lower values. An **icon set** helps you annotate and classify data into three to five categories separated by a threshold value. Each icon represents a value in the cell. With an expand set of icons, you have even more choices (**New!**). You can apply multiple formatting to the same data in order to display the results you want (**New!**). In addition, you can refer to values in other worksheets (**New!**).

Format Using Data Bars

① Select a cell or range you want to conditionally format.

② Click the **Home** tab.

③ Click the **Conditional Formatting** button, and then point to **Data Bars**.

④ Click the colored data bar you want, either gradient or solid fills.

⑤ To create a custom data bar, click **More Rules**, specify the description you want (including bar direction), and then click **OK**.

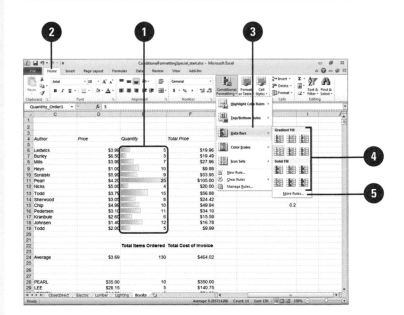

Did You Know?

You can find cells with conditional formatting. Select any cell without a conditional format, click the Home tab, click the Find & Select button arrow, and then click Conditional Formatting. To find cells with the same conditional format, click the Home tab, click the Find & Select button arrow, click Go To Special, click the Conditional Formats option, click the Same option, and then click OK.

Format Using Color Scales

1. Select a cell or range you want to conditionally format.

2. Click the **Home** tab.

3. Click the **Conditional Formatting** button, and then point to **Color Scales**.

4. Click the two or three colored scale you want.

   The top color represents higher values, the center color represents middle values (for three-color), and the bottom color represents lower values.

5. To create a custom color scale, click **More Rules**, specify the description you want, and then click **OK**.

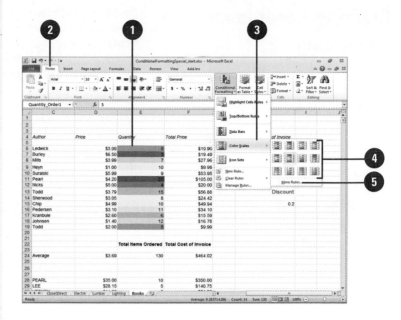

Format Using Icon Sets

1. Select a cell or range you want to conditionally format.

2. Click the **Home** tab.

3. Click the **Conditional Formatting** button, and then point to **Icon Sets**.

4. Click the colored icon sets you want.

5. To create a custom icon sets, click **More Rules**, specify the description you want, and then click **OK**.

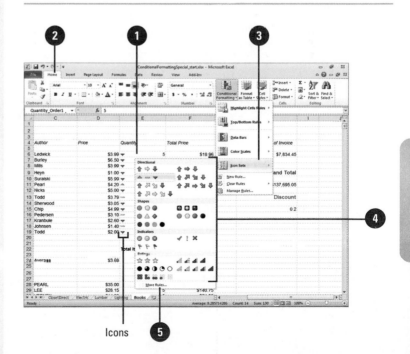

Icons

Creating Conditional Formatting

Instead of using one of the built-in conditional formatting rules, you can create your own rules. The New Formatting Rule dialog box allows you to create rules based on different rule types, such as format all cells based on their values, or use a formula to determine which cells to format. After you select a rule type, you specify the rule criteria to trigger conditional formatting. Many of the rule types include the Format button, which opens the familiar Format Cells dialog box. You can specify number, font, border, and fill formatting options. For icon sets, you can mix and match icons for a custom look as well as hide them based on your criteria (**New!**). For data bars, you can set the bar direction, and specify custom formatting for negative values (**New!**).

Create Conditional Formatting Rules

1. Click the **Home** tab.

2. Click the **Conditional Formatting** button, and then click **New Rules**.

3. Click the rule type you want.

   ◆ Format all cells based on their values.

   ◆ Format only cells that contain.

   ◆ Format only top or bottom ranked values.

   ◆ Format only values that are above or below average.

   ◆ Format only unique or duplicate values.

   ◆ Use a formula to determine which cells to format.

4. Specify the rule criteria you want to create a conditional format. Each rule type provides a different set of options you can set.

   If available, click **Format** to specify number, font, border, and fill formatting options in the Format Cells dialog box.

5. Click **OK**.

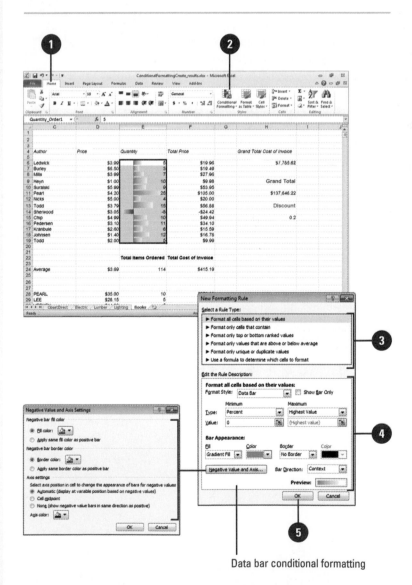

Data bar conditional formatting

Managing Conditional Formatting

When you apply conditional formatting to a cell or range of cells, Excel stores the rules associated with the conditional formatting in the Conditional Formatting Rules Manager. You can use the Conditional Formatting Rules Manager to create, edit, delete, and view all conditional formatting rules in a workbook. When two or more conditional formatting rules apply to the same cells (that conflict or not), the rules are evaluated in order of precedence as they appear in the dialog box. You can move a rule up or down in the precedence list. Conditional formatting takes precedence over a manual format, which doesn't appear in the Conditional Formatting Rules Manager.

Edit Conditional Formatting Rule Precedence

1. If you want, select the cell or range with the conditional formatting rules you want to edit.

2. Click the **Home** tab.

3. Click the **Conditional Formatting** button, and then click **Manage Rules**.

4. Click the **Show formatting rulers for** list arrow, and then select an option to show the rules you want.

5. Select the rule you want to change.

6. To move the selected rule up or down in precedence, click **Move Up** or **Move Down**.

7. To stop rule evaluation at a specific rule, select the **Stop If True** check box.

   Select this option for backwards compatibility with previous versions of Excel that don't support multiple conditional formatting rules.

8. To delete a rule, click **Delete Rule**.

9. To edit a rule, click **Edit Rule**, make the changes you want, and then click **OK**.

10. Click **OK**.

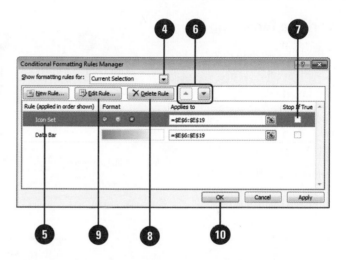

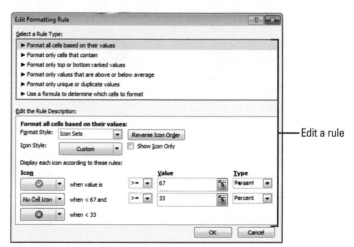

Edit a rule

Creating Sparkline Formatting

A sparkline (**New!**) is a tiny chart in the background of a cell that provides a visual representation of a data range. Sparklines are useful for showing trends in a series of data, which you can print in a worksheet. You can display line, column, and win/loss charts. After you create a sparkline chart, you can format it using the Design tab under Sparkline Tools. You can quickly select a Quick Style layout or set individual options, such as chart type, sparkline color, marker color, axis display, and control points (high, low, first, last, or any negative values). If you have several sparkline cells, you can group them together. If you no longer want to use a sparkline, you can clear it. Since a sparkline is embedded in the background, you can still enter text in the cell.

Create Sparkline Formatting

① Select the cell you want to insert a sparkline formatting chart.

② Click the **Insert** tab.

③ Click the button (**Line, Column, or Win/Loss**) with the type of sparkline you want to insert.

④ Click the **Collapse Dialog** button, select the data range for the sparkline, and then click the **Expand Dialog** button.

⑤ Click **OK**.

⑥ Click the **Design** tab under Sparkline Tools.

⑦ To edit the data or handle empty cells or zero values, click the **Edit Data** button arrow, and then click **Edit Group Location & Data**, **Edit Single Sparkline's Data**, or **Hidden & Empty Cells**.

⑧ To format a sparkline, select options on the Design tab in the Type, Show, Style, and Group sections.

⑨ To clear a sparkline, click the **Clear** button arrow, and then click **Clear Selected Sparklines**, or **Clear Selected Sparkline Groups**.

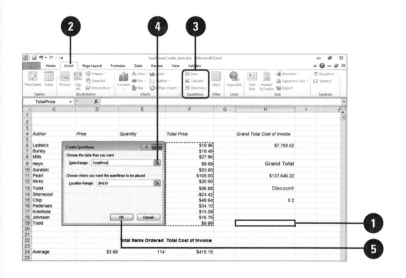

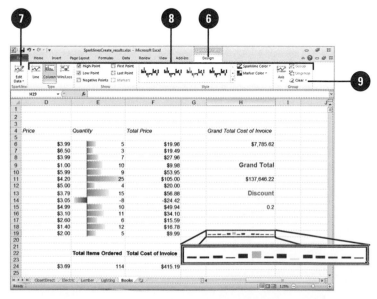

Controlling Text Flow

The length of a label might not always fit within the width you've chosen for a column. If the cell to the right is empty, text spills over into it, but if that cell contains data, the text will be truncated (that is, cut off). A cell can be formatted so its text automatically wraps to multiple lines or cell contents can also be shrinked to fit within the available space; that way, you don't have to widen the column to achieve an attractive effect. If the cell to the right is empty, cell contents can be combined, or merged, with the contents of other cells.

Control the Flow of Text in a Cell

1 Select a cell or range whose text flow you want to change.

2 Click the **Home** tab.

3 To center cell contents across selected columns, click the **Merge & Center** button arrow, and then click one of the options:

- ◆ **Merge & Center.**
- ◆ **Merge Across.**
- ◆ **Merge Cells.**
- ◆ **Unmerge Cells.**

4 To wrap text in a cell, click the **Wrap Text** button.

5 To set multiple alignment options at the same time or shrink text to fit in a cell, click the **Alignment Dialog Box Launcher**.

The Format Cells dialog box opens, displaying the Alignment tab.

6 Select one or more Text Control check boxes.

- ◆ **Wrap text** moves the text to multiple lines within a cell.
- ◆ **Shrink to fit** reduces character size to fit within a cell.
- ◆ **Merge cells** combines selected cells into a single cell.

7 Click **OK**.

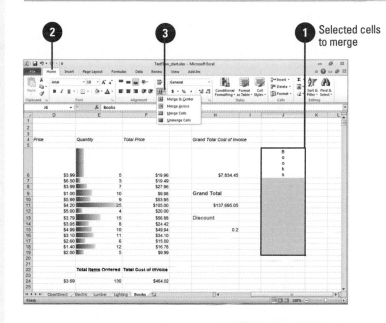

Selected cells to merge

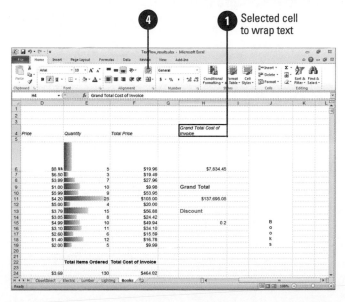

Selected cell to wrap text

Formatting Tabs and Background

Depending on your screen size, the sheet tabs at the bottom of your workbook can be hard to view. You can add color to the sheet tabs to make them more distinguishable. If you want to add artistic style to your workbook or you are creating a Web page from your workbook, you can add a background picture. When you add a background to a worksheet, the background does not print, and it's not included when you save an individual worksheet as a Web page. You need to publish the entire workbook as a Web page to include the background.

Add or Remove Color to Worksheet Tabs

① Click the sheet tab you want to color.

② Click the **Home** tab.

③ Click the **Format** button, point to **Tab Color**, and then do any of the following:

◆ **Add.** Click a color.

◆ **Remove.** Click **No Color**.

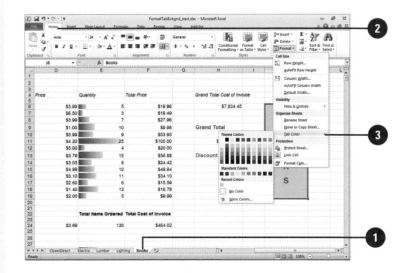

Add or Remove a Background

① Click the sheet tab to which you want to add a background.

② Click the **Page Layout** tab.

③ Click the **Background** button.

④ Select the folder with the graphic file you want to use.

⑤ Select the graphic you want.

⑥ Click **Insert**.

The Background button changes to the Delete Background button.

⑦ To remove the background, click **Delete Background** on the Page Layout tab.

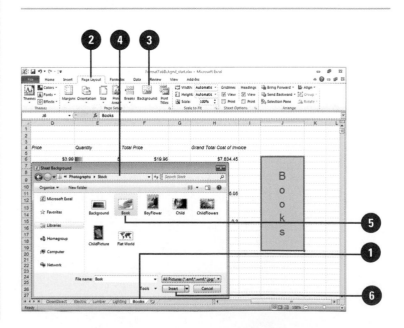

Adding Borders to Cells

The light gray grid that appears on the worksheet helps your eyes move from cell to cell. Although you can print these gridlines, sometimes a different grid pattern better emphasizes your data. For example, you might put a decorative line border around the title or a double-line bottom border below cells with totals. You can add borders of varying colors and widths to any or all sides of a single cell or range. If you prefer, you can draw a border outline or grid directly on a worksheet.

Apply or Remove a Border Using the Ribbon

① Select a cell or range to which you want to apply a border.

② Click the **Home** tab.

③ Click the **Borders** button arrow.

TIMESAVER *To apply the most recently selected border, click the Borders button.*

④ Select a border from the menu.

⑤ To remove cell borders, click **No Border**.

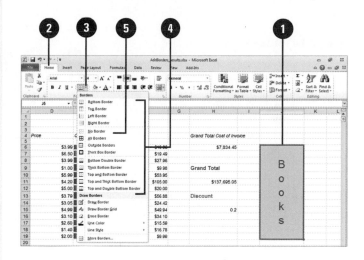

Draw a Border

① Click the **Home** tab.

② Click the **Borders** button arrow.

③ Select a draw borders option from the menu.

♦ Point to **Line Color**, and then click the color you want.

♦ Point to **Line Style**, and then click the style you want.

♦ Click **Draw Border**, and then drag a border.

♦ Click **Draw Border Grid**, and then drag a border.

♦ Click **Erase Border**, and then drag a border.

④ Press Esc to exit.

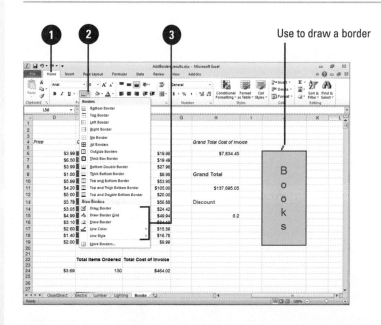

Use to draw a border

Setting Up the Page

You can set up the worksheet page to print just the way you want. In Page Layout view, you can choose **page orientation**, which determines whether Excel prints the worksheet data portrait (vertically) or landscape (horizontally), and paper size (to match the size of paper in your printer). With the Page Setup dialog box, you can also adjust the **print scaling** (to reduce or enlarge the size of printed characters). Changes made in the Page Setup dialog box are not reflected in the worksheet window. You can see them only when you preview or print the worksheet.

Change Page Orientation

① Click the **Page Layout** tab.

② Click the **Orientation** button.

The current orientation is highlighted on the menu.

③ Click **Portrait** or **Landscape** from the menu.

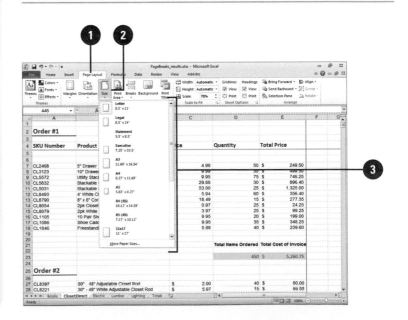

Change the Page Size

① Click the **Page Layout** tab.

② Click the **Size** button from the menu.

The current margin setting is highlighted on the menu.

③ Click **Letter** (8.5 x 11), **Letter Small** (8.5 x 11), **Tabloid** (11 x 17), **Ledger** (17 x 11, **Legal** (8.5 x 14), **Statement** (5.5 x 8.5), **Executive** (7.25 x 10.5), **A3** (11.69 x 16.54), **A4** (8.27 x 11.69), **A4 Small** (8.27 x 11.69) from the menu.

Inserting Page Breaks

If you want to print a worksheet that is larger than one page, Excel divides it into pages by inserting **automatic page breaks**. These page breaks are based on paper size, margin settings, and scaling options you set. You can change which rows or columns are printed on the page by inserting **horizontal** or **vertical page breaks**. In page break preview, you can view the page breaks and move them by dragging them to a different location on the worksheet.

Insert and Remove a Page Break

1. Select a page break location:

   ◆ **Horizontal.** Click the row to insert a page break.

   ◆ **Vertical.** Click the column to insert a page break.

   ◆ **Cell.** Click the cell below and to the right from where you want to insert a page break.

2. Click the **Page Layout** tab.

3. Click the **Breaks** button, and then click **Insert Page Break**.

4. To remove a page break, select the column or row with the page break, click the **Breaks** button, and then click **Remove Page Break**.

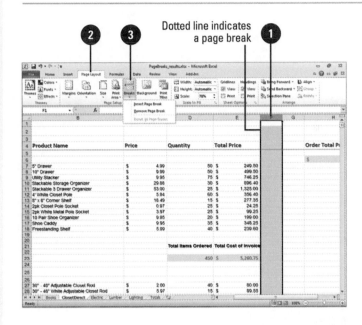

Dotted line indicates a page break

Preview and Move a Page Break

1. Click the **View** tab.

2. Click the **Page Break Preview** button.

   If the Welcome to Page Break Preview dialog box appears, select the **Do not show this dialog box again** check box, and then click **OK**.

3. Drag a page break (a thick solid or dashed blue line) to move it.

4. To exit, click the **Normal View** button.

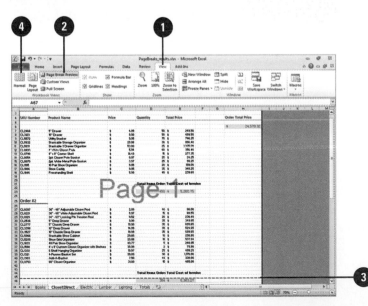

Adjusting Page Margins

A page margin is the blank areas along each edge of the paper. You can set up page margins to print your worksheets just the way you want. If you need to quickly set margins, you can use the Margins button on the Page Layout tab. Otherwise, you can use the mouse pointer to adjust margins visually for the entire document in Page Layout view, or you can use the Page Setup dialog box to set precise measurements for an entire document or a specific section. You can resize or realign the left, right, top, and bottom margins (the blank areas along each edge of the paper). Changes made in the Page Setup dialog box are not reflected in the worksheet window. You can see them only when you preview or print the worksheet.

Change the Margin Settings

1. Click the **Page Layout** tab.

2. Click the **Margins** button.

   The current margin setting is highlighted on the menu.

3. Click the option you want from the menu.

   - **Last Custom Setting.** Only available if you previously changed margin settings.

   - **Normal.**

   - **Wide.**

   - **Narrow.**

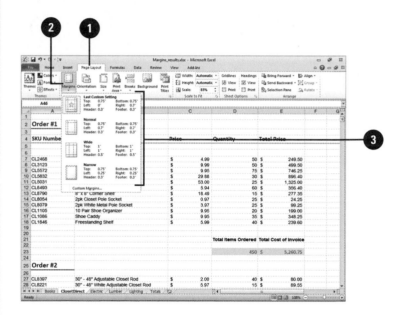

Did You Know?

You can print comments. Display the comments you want to print. Click the Page Layout tab, click the Page Setup Dialog Box Launcher, click the Sheet tab, click the Comments list arrow, click the As Displayed On Sheet or At End Of Sheet option, and then click Print.

Change the Margin Using the Mouse in Page Layout View

1. Click the **View** tab.

2. Click the **Page Layout View** button.

3. Select the **Ruler** check box.

4. Position the cursor over the left, right, top, or bottom edge of the ruler until the cursor changes to a double arrow.

   A ScreenTip appears indicating the margin name and current position.

5. Drag to change the margin.

6. To exit Page Layout view, click the **Normal** button.

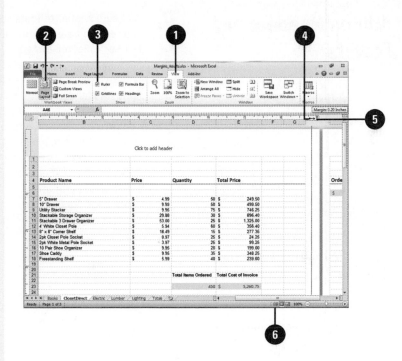

Customize Margin Settings

1. Click the **Page Layout** tab.

2. Click the **Margins** button, and then click **Custom Margins**.

   The Page Setup dialog box opens, displaying the Margins tab.

3. Click the **Top**, **Bottom**, **Left**, and **Right** up or down arrows to adjust the margins.

4. To automatically center your data, select the **Horizontally** and **Vertically** check boxes under Center on page.

5. Click **OK**.

   ◆ Or click **Print Preview** to see how the margin changes look.

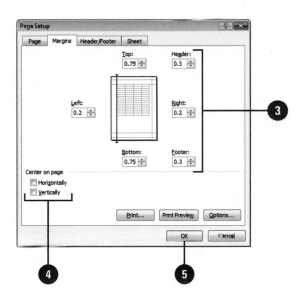

Adding Headers and Footers

Adding a header or footer to a workbook is a convenient way to make your printout easier for readers to follow. Using the Design tab under Header & Footer Tools, you can add predefined header or footer information—such as a page number and worksheet title—at the top and bottom of each page or section of a worksheet or workbook. If a predefined header or footer doesn't work, you can insert individual elements such as your computer system's date and time, the name of the workbook and sheet, a picture, or other custom information. When you insert elements in a header or footer, Excel inserts an ampersand followed by brackets with the name of the element, such as &[Page] for Page Number. Excel changes the code to the actual element when you exit headers or footers. Instead of having the same header or footer on every page, you can select options on the Design tab to create a different first page, or different odd and even pages.

Add a Predefined Header or Footer in Page Layout View

1 Click the **Insert** tab.

2 Click the **Header & Footer** button.

The worksheet appears in Page Layout view.

3 To insert predefined header and footer information, click the **Header** or **Footer** button, and then click the information you want.

A sample of the information appears on the menu. After you make a selection, Excel exits the Design tab.

4 To add more header or footer text, click the left, center, or right header or footer boxes at the top or at the bottom of the worksheet page where you want to add text to place the insertion point.

To change a header or footer, select the current text.

5 Type the text you want.

To start a new line in a header or footer text box, press Enter.

6 To close the headers or footers, click anywhere in the worksheet, or press Esc.

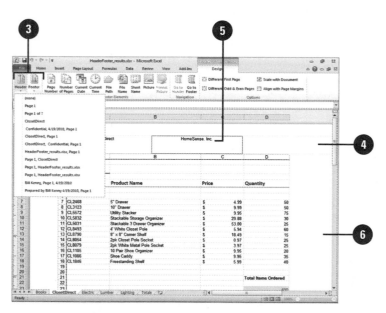

Insert Elements in a Header or Footer in Page Layout View

1. Click the **Insert** tab.

2. Click the **Header & Footer** button.

    The worksheet appears in Page Layout view.

3. Click the left, center, or right header or footer text at the top or at the bottom of the worksheet page where you want to insert an element.

4. Click the **Design** tab under Header & Footer Tools.

5. To insert individual elements, click the button in the Header & Footer Elements group you want.

6. Select or clear the options you want:

    ◆ **Different First Page.** Removes headers and footer from the first page.

    ◆ **Different Odd & Even Pages.** Different header or footer for odd and even pages.

    ◆ **Scale with Document.** Use the same font size and scaling as the worksheet.

    ◆ **Align with Page Margins.** Align header or footer margin with page margins.

7. To close the headers or footers, click anywhere in the worksheet, or press Esc.

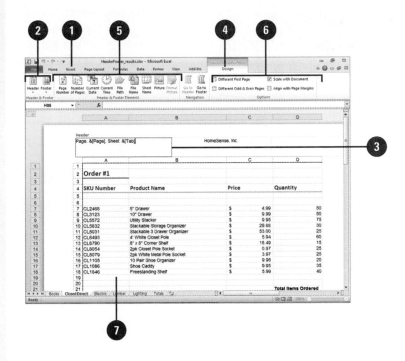

For Your Information

Inserting a Watermark

The watermark feature is not available in Excel. However, you can still perform the same function by inserting a picture in a header or footer. The picture appears behind the text and on every printed page. Click the Insert tab, click the Header & Footer button, click in the header or footer box where you want to insert a picture, click the Picture button, and then double-click the picture you want. To resize or scale the picture, click Format Picture, select the options you want on the Size tab, and then click OK. To add space above or below the picture, use the Enter key. To replace a picture, select &[Picture], click the Picture button, and then click Replace. You might need to adjust the margins so the picture and any text fit on the page the way you want.

Customizing Worksheet Printing

At some point you'll want to print your worksheet so you can distribute it to others or use it for other purposes. You can print all or part of any worksheet, and you can control the appearance of many features, such as whether gridlines are displayed, whether column letters and row numbers are displayed, or whether to include print titles, columns and rows that are repeated on each page. If you have already set a print area, it will appear in the Print Area box on the Sheet tab of the Page Setup dialog box. You don't need to re-select it.

Print Part of a Worksheet

1. Click the **Page Layout** tab.

2. Click the **Page Setup Dialog Box Launcher.**

3. Click the **Sheet** tab.

4. Type the range you want to print. Or click the **Collapse Dialog** button, select the cells you want to print, and then click the **Expand Dialog** button to restore the dialog box.

5. Click **OK**.

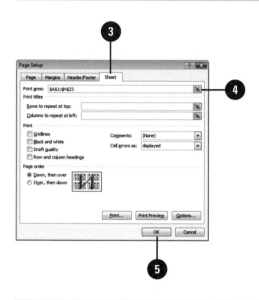

Print Row and Column Titles on Each Page

1. Click the **Page Layout** tab.

2. Click the **Print Titles** button.

The Page Setup dialog box opens, display the Sheet tab.

3. Enter the number of the row or the letter of the column that contains the titles. Or click the **Collapse Dialog** button, select the row or column with the mouse, and then click the **Expand Dialog** button to restore the dialog box.

4. Click **OK**.

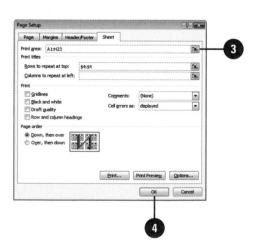

Print Gridlines, Column Letters, and Row Numbers

1. Click the **Page Layout** tab.

2. Select the **Print** check box under Gridlines.

3. Select the **Print** check box under Headings.

◆ You can also click the **Sheet Options Dialog Box Launcher** to select these print options.

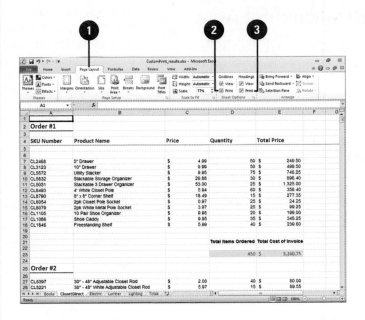

Fit a Worksheet on a Specific Number of Pages

1. Click the **Page Layout** tab.

2. Select a scaling option.

◆ Click the **Height** list arrow and the **Width** list arrow, then select the number of pages you want to force a worksheet to print.

◆ Click the **Scale** up and down arrows to scale the worksheet using a percentage.

◆ You can also click the **Scale to Fit Dialog Box Launcher** to select these options.

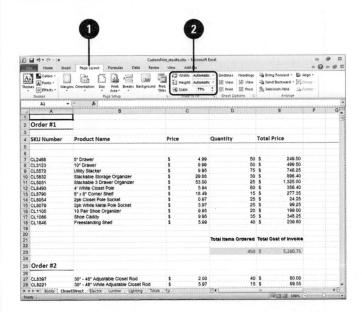

Setting the Print Area

When you're ready to print your worksheet, you can choose several printing options. The **print area** is the section of your worksheet that Excel prints. You can set the print area when you customize worksheet printing or any time when you are working on a worksheet. For example, you might want to print a different range in a worksheet for different people. In order to use headers and footers, you must first establish, or set, the print area. You can set a single cell or a contiguous or non-contiguous range.

Set the Print Area

1. Select the range of cells you want to print.

2. Click the **Page Layout** tab.

3. Click the **Print Area** button, and then click **Set Print Area**.

Did You Know?

You can add to a print area. Click the cell where you want to extend the print area, click the Page Layout tab, click the Print Area button, and then click Add To Print Area.

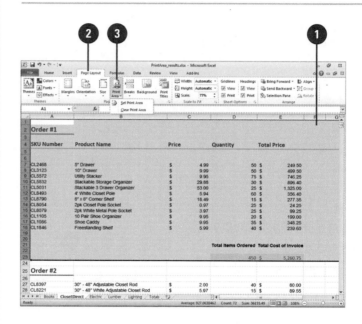

Clear the Print Area

1. Click the **Page Layout** tab.

2. Click the **Print Area** button, and then click **Clear Print Area**.

Did You Know?

You can avoid repeating rows and columns. For best results when printing a multipage worksheet, you'll want to coordinate the print area with specified print titles so that columns or rows are not repeated on a single page.

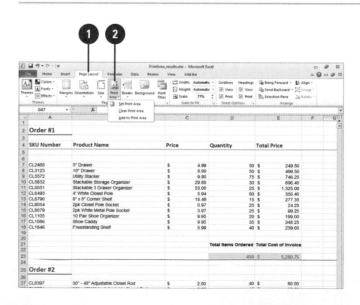

Creating a Presentation with PowerPoint

12

Introduction

When creating a new presentation, there are things to consider as you develop your content. Microsoft Office PowerPoint 2010 can help you with this process. There are various elements to a presentation that make good looking slides: bulleted lists, clip art, charts and diagrams, organization charts and tables, and media clips or pictures. All of these items are considered graphic objects, and are separate from the text objects that you enter. Objects can be moved from one part of a presentation to another. You can also resize, move, and delete them.

As you develop your presentation, there are a few things to keep in mind—keep the text easy to read and straight to the point, make sure it isn't too wordy, and have a balance of text and graphics. Too much text can lose your audience while too many graphics can distract their focus.

PowerPoint offers many tools to help develop your text. Using the AutoCorrect feature, text is corrected as you type. A built-in Thesaurus is always a few keystrokes away, as is a research option that allows you to look for information is available in PowerPoint or has links to the Web.

Once you've begun to enter your text, you can adjust the spacing, change the alignment, set tabs, and change indents. You can also format your text by changing the font style or its attributes such as adding color to your text. If you decide to enter text in outline form, PowerPoint offers you the Outline pane to jot down your thoughts and notes. If bulleted or numbered lists are your preference, you can enter your ideas in this format. Should you need to rearrange your slides, you can do this in various PowerPoint views.

What You'll Do

View the PowerPoint Window

Browse a Presentation

Understand PowerPoint Views

Create New and Consistent Slides

Enter and Edit Text

Resize Text While Typing

Change Text Spacing

Insert and Develop an Outline

Move and Indent Text

Modify a Bulleted and Numbered List

Create Text Columns

Organize Slides into Sections

Rearrange Slides

Use Slides from Other Presentations

Make Your Presentation Look Consistent

Control Slide Appearance, Layout and Background with Masters

Modify Placeholders

Add a Background Style

Insert, Modify and Format a Table

Create a Text Box

305

Viewing the PowerPoint Window

File tab
Click to access Office
PowerPoint file commands.

Quick Access Toolbar
Click to access command comments
on this customizable toolbar.

Tabs
Click to access tools
and commands.

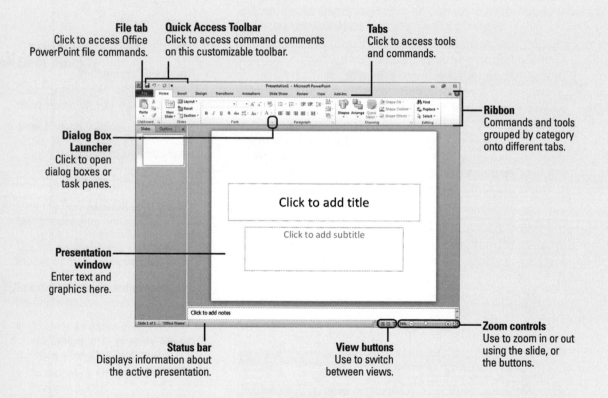

Ribbon
Commands and tools
grouped by category
onto different tabs.

Dialog Box Launcher
Click to open
dialog boxes or
task panes.

Presentation window
Enter text and
graphics here.

Status bar
Displays information about
the active presentation.

View buttons
Use to switch
between views.

Zoom controls
Use to zoom in or out
using the slide, or
the buttons.

Browsing a Presentation

You might want to browse through a completed presentation to view the contents and design of each slide and to evaluate the types of slides in a presentation in several ways. When a slide doesn't fit the screen, you can change the presentation view size, or click the scroll arrows to scroll line by line or click above or below the scroll box to scroll window by window and move to another slide. To move immediately to a specific slide, you can drag the scroll box. In Slides pane, you can click the Next Slide and Previous Slide buttons, which are located at the bottom of the vertical scroll bar, to switch between slides in a presentation.

Browse Through a Presentation

◆ Click the **Up** scroll arrow or **Down** scroll arrow to scroll line by line.

When you scroll to the top or bottom of a slide, you automatically move to the previous or next page.

◆ Click above or below the **Scroll** box to scroll window by window.

◆ Drag the **Scroll** box to move immediately to a specific slide.

As you drag, a slide indicator box appears, telling you the slide number and title.

◆ Click the **Previous Slide** or **Next Slide** button.

Did You Know?

You can use the keyboard to browse slides. Press the Page Up or Page Down key to switch between slides. If you use these keys, the slides in the Slides pane will change also.

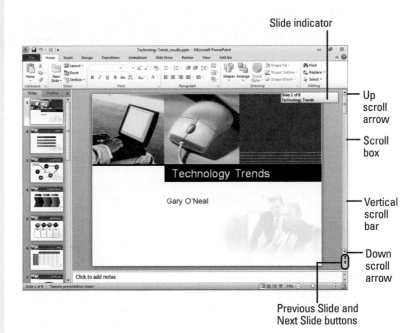

Slide indicator

Up scroll arrow

Scroll box

Vertical scroll bar

Down scroll arrow

Previous Slide and Next Slide buttons

Understanding PowerPoint Views

To help you during all phases of developing a presentation, PowerPoint provides three different views: Normal, Slide Sorter, Reading (**New!**) and Slide Show. You can switch from one view to another by clicking a view button located on the Status bar or by using the buttons in the Presentation Views group on the View tab. In any view, you can use the Zoom feature on the Status bar to increase and decrease the page view size and display the slide to fit the screen.

Normal view

Use the Normal view to work with the three underlying elements of a presentation—the outline, slide, and notes—each in its own pane. These panes provide an overview of your presentation and let you work on all of its parts. You can adjust the size of the panes by dragging the pane borders. You can use the Outline pane to develop and organize your presentation's content. Use the Slides

pane to add text, graphics, movies, sounds, and hyperlinks to individual slides, and the Notes pane to add speaker notes or notes you want to share with your audience.

Outline pane

Use the Outline pane in Normal view to develop your presentation's content. Individual slides are numbered and a slide icon appears for each slide.

Slides pane

Use the Slides pane in Normal view to preview each slide. Click the slide you want to view. You can also move through your slides using the scroll bars or the Previous Slide and Next Slide buttons. When you drag the scroll box up or down on the vertical scroll bar, a label appears that indicates which slide will be displayed if you release the mouse button.

Reading view

Reading view (**New!**) presents your slides in a slide show one at a time in a separate window. Use this view when you're ready to rehearse your presentation. This view is especially useful when you want to show two presentations in a slide show in separate windows at the same time.

Slide Sorter view

Use the Slide Sorter view to organize your slides, add actions between slides—called slide transitions—and apply other effects to your slide show. The Transitions tab helps you add slide transitions and control your presentation. When you add a slide transition, you see an icon that indicates an action will take place as one slide replaces another during a show. If you hide a slide, you see an icon that indicates the slide will not be shown during the presentation.

Slide Show view

Slide Show view presents your slides one at a time. Use this view when you're ready to rehearse or give your presentation. To move through the slides, click the screen, or press Enter to move through the show.

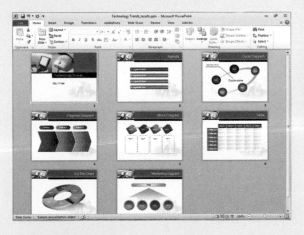

Creating New and Consistent Slides

Creating consistent looking slides makes it easier for your audience to follow and understand your presentation. PowerPoint provides a gallery of slide layouts to help you position and format slides in a consistent manner. A slide layout contains **placeholders**, such as text, chart, table, or SmartArt graphic, where you can enter text or insert elements. When you create a new slide, you can apply a standard layout or a custom layout of your own design. You can also apply a layout to an existing slide at any time. When you change a slide's layout, PowerPoint keeps the existing information and applies the new look.

Insert a New Slide

1. Click the **Home** tab.

2. Click the **New Slide** button arrow.

   TIMESAVER *To insert a slide quickly without using the gallery, click the Add Slide button (icon).*

3. In the Slide Layout gallery, click the slide layout you want to use.

Apply an Layout to an Existing Slide

1. In Normal view, display the slide you want to change.

2. Click the **Home** tab.

3. Click the **Layout** button, and then click the slide layout you want.

See Also

See "Using Slides from Other Presentations" on page 328 for information on adding slides from other presentations.

Slide layouts

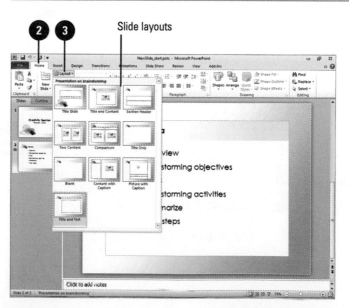

Enter Information in a Placeholder

◆ For text placeholders, click the placeholder, and then type the text.

◆ For other objects, click the icon in the placeholder, and then work with the accessory that PowerPoint starts.

Layout Placeholder

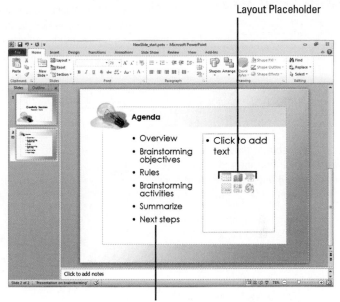

A placeholder is a border that defines the size and location of an object.

Slide Layout Placeholders

Placeholder	Description
Title	Enter title text
Bulleted	Enter bulleted list
Table	Inserts a table
Chart	Inserts a chart
Clip Art	Inserts a picture from the Clip Organizer
Picture	Inserts a picture from a file
SmartArt	Inserts a diagram, chart, or other graphics
Movie	Inserts a movie or video clip

Working with Objects

Once you create a slide, you can modify any of its objects, even those added by a slide layout. To manipulate objects, use Normal view. To perform any action on an object, you first need to select it. When you select an object, such as text or graphic, the object is surrounded by a solid-lined rectangle, called a **selection box**, with sizing handles (small white circles at the corners and small white squares on the sides) around it. You can resize, move, delete, and format selected objects.

Select and Deselect an Object

◆ To select an object, move the pointer (which changes to a four-headed arrow) over the object or edge, and then click to select.

◆ To select multiple objects, press and hold Shift as you click each object or drag to enclose the objects you want to select in the selection box. Press Ctrl+A to select all objects on a slide.

◆ To deselect an object, click outside its border.

◆ To deselect one of a group of objects, press and hold Shift, and then click the object.

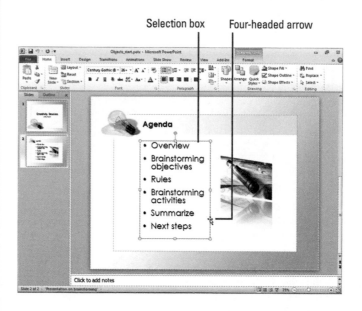

Selection box   Four-headed arrow

Resize an Object

1 Move the pointer over a sizing handle.

2 Drag the sizing handle until the object is the size you want.

TIMESAVER *Use the Shift and Ctrl keys while you drag. The Shift key constrains an edge; the Ctrl key maintains a proportional edge; and the Shift and Ctrl keys together maintains a proportional object.*

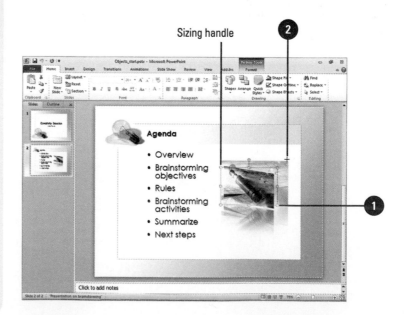

Sizing handle

Move or Copy an Object

◆ **Using the mouse**. To copy, press and hold Ctrl while you drag. Move the pointer (which changes to a four-headed arrow) over the object, and then drag it to the new location. For unfilled objects, drag the border. You can move or copy an object in a straight line by pressing Shift as you drag the object.

◆ **Using the keyboard**. To move, click the object, and then press the arrow keys to move the object in the direction you want.

◆ **Using the keyboard shortcuts**. To cut an object from a slide, select the object and then press Ctrl+X. To copy an object, select the object, and then press Ctrl+C. To paste an object on a slide, press Ctrl+V.

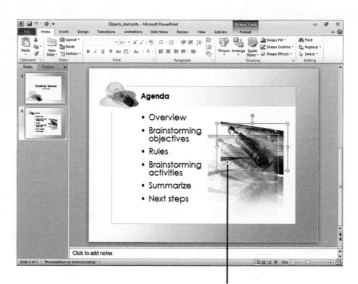

Use the four-headed arrow to drag the object to a new location.

Delete an Object

1 Click the object you want to delete.

2 Press Delete or click the **Cut** button on the Home tab.

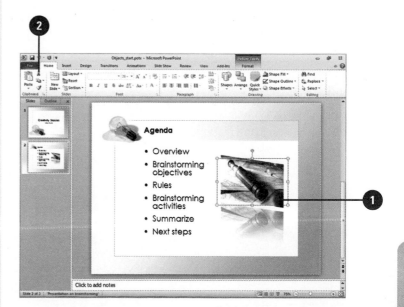

Did You Know?

You can use the Tab key to select hard-to-click objects. If you are having trouble selecting an object that is close to other objects, click a different object and then press Tab until you select the object you want. See "Selecting Objects Using the Selection Pane" on page 114 for more information on selecting hard-to-click objects.

Entering and Editing Text

In Normal view, you can type text directly into the text placeholders. A **text placeholder** is an empty text box. The insertion point (the blinking vertical line) indicates where text will appear when you type. To place the insertion point into your text, move the pointer over the text. The pointer changes to an I-beam to indicate that you can click and then type. When a selection box of dashed lines appears, your changes affect only the selected text. When a solid-lined selection box appears, changes apply to the entire text object. You can move, copy, or delete existing text; replace it with new text; and undo any changes you just made.

Enter Text into a Placeholder

1. In Normal view, click the text placeholder if it isn't already selected.

2. Type the text you want to enter.

3. Click outside the text object to deselect it.

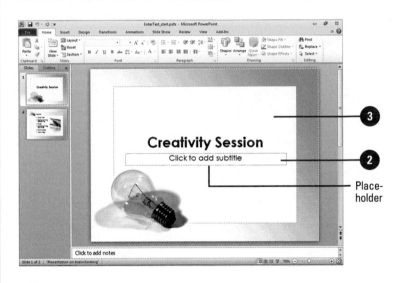

Placeholder

Insert Text

1. Click to place the insertion point where you want to insert the text.

2. Type the text.

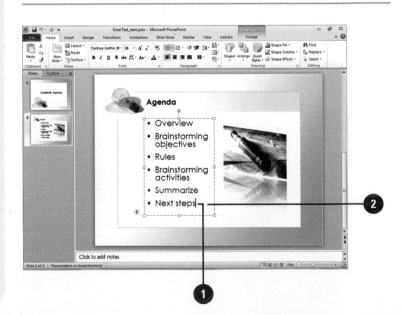

Enter Text in a Bulleted or Numbered List

1. In Normal view, click the bulleted text placeholder.

2. To switch to a numbered list, click the **Home** tab, if necessary, and then click the **Numbering** button.

3. Type the first item.

4. Press Enter.

   ◆ To increase the list level, press Tab or click the **Increase List Level** button on the Home tab.

   ◆ To decrease the list level, press Shift+Tab, or click the **Decrease List Level** button on the Home tab.

5. Type the next item.

6. Repeat steps 4 and 5 until you complete the list.

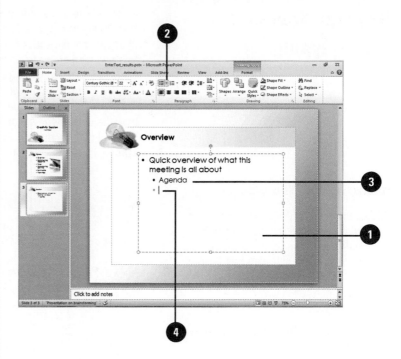

Select and Modify Text

1. Position the mouse pointer to the left of the text you want to highlight.

2. Drag the pointer over the text—just a few words, a few lines, or entire paragraphs, and then release the mouse button.

3. To select discontinuous text, press Ctrl, and then drag the pointer over text.

4. Modify the text the way you want.

   ◆ To delete text, press Delete.

   ◆ To replace text, type your new text.

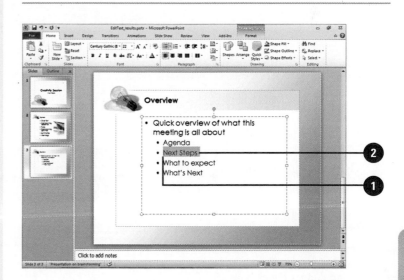

Resizing Text While Typing

If you type text in a placeholder, PowerPoint uses AutoFit to resize the text, if necessary, to fit into the placeholder. The AutoFit Text feature changes the line spacing—or paragraph spacing—between lines of text and then changes the font size to make the text fit. The AutoFit Options button, which appears near your text the first time that it is resized, gives you control over whether you want the text to be resized. The AutoFit Options button displays a menu with options for controlling how the option works. You can also display the AutoCorrect dialog box and change the AutoFit settings so that text doesn't resize automatically.

Resize Text as You Type

1 If the AutoFit Options box appears while you type, click the **AutoFit Options** button to select an option, or continue typing and PowerPoint will automatically adjust your text to fit.

2 If you click the AutoFit Options button, click the option you want to fit the text on the slide.

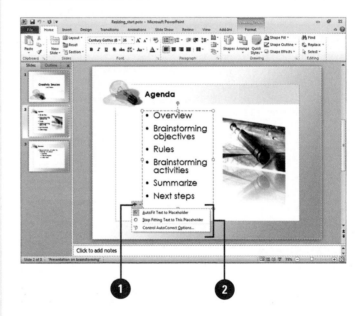

Turn Off AutoFit

1 Click the **File** tab, and then click **Options**.

2 In the left pane, click **Proofing**, and then click **AutoCorrect Options**.

3 Click the **AutoFormat As You Type** tab.

4 Clear the **AutoFit title text to placeholder** and **AutoFit body text to placeholder** check boxes.

5 Click **OK**.

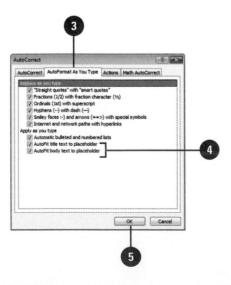

Changing Text Spacing

PowerPoint enables you to control the way text lines up on the slide. You can align text horizontally to the left or right, to the center, or to both left and right (justify) in a text object. You can also align text vertically to the top, middle, or bottom within a text object. In addition to vertical text alignment in a text object, you can also adjust the vertical space between selected lines and the space before and after paragraphs. You set specific line spacing settings before and after paragraphs in points. A **point** is equal to about 1/72 of an inch (or .0138 inches) and is used to measure the height of characters. Points are typically used in graphics and desktop publishing programs.

Adjust Line Spacing Quickly

1. Select the text box.

2. Click the **Home** tab.

3. Click the **Line Spacing** button, and then click **1.0 - 3.0**.

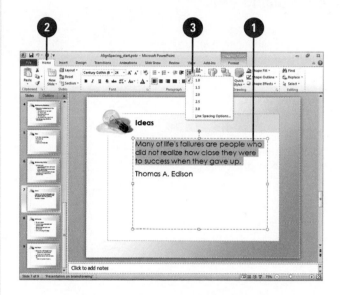

Adjust Line Spacing Exactly

1. Select the text box.

2. Click the **Home** tab.

3. Click the **Line Spacing** button, and then click **Line Spacing Options**.

4. Click the **Before Spacing** or **After Spacing** up or down arrows to specify a setting.

5. Click the **Line Spacing** list arrow, and then select a setting.

   If you select Exactly or Multiple, specify at what spacing you want.

6. Click **OK**.

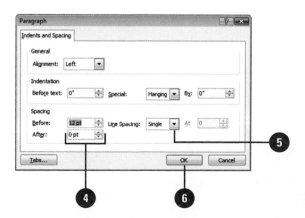

Inserting and Developing an Outline

Outlining your content is a great way to create a presentation. You can outline and organize your thoughts right in PowerPoint or insert an outline you created in another program, such as Microsoft Word. If you prefer to develop your own outline, you can create a blank presentation, and then type your outline in the Outline pane of Normal view. As you develop an outline, you can add new slides or duplicate existing ones. If you have an outline, make sure the document containing the outline is set up using outline heading styles. When you insert the outline, it creates slide titles, subtitles, and bulleted lists based on those styles.

Enter Text in the Outline Pane

1 In the Outline pane of Normal view, click to place the insertion point where you want the text to appear.

2 Type the title text you want, pressing Enter after each line.

To indent right a level for bullet text, press Tab before you type. Press Shift+Tab to indent left a level.

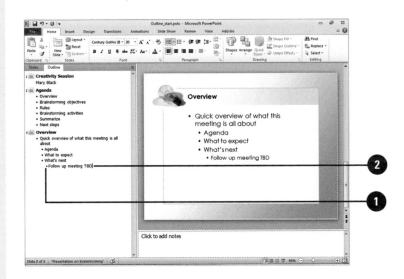

Add a Slide in the Outline Pane

1 In the Outline pane of Normal view, click at the end of the slide text where you want to insert a new slide.

2 Press Ctrl+Return, or click the **Home** tab, click the **New Slide** button arrow, and then click a layout.

Did You Know?

You can delete a slide. In the Outline or Slides pane or in Slide Sorter view, select the slide you want to delete. Press Delete, or click the Delete button in the Slides group on the Home tab.

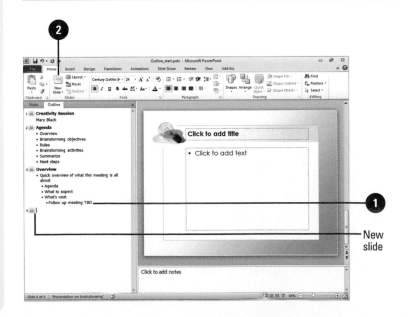

New slide

Duplicate a Slide

1. In the Outline pane of Normal view, click the slide you want to duplicate.

   TIMESAVER *To select slides in a sequence, click the first slide, hold down the Shift key, and then click the last slide. To select multiple slides, use the Ctrl key.*

2. Click the **Home** tab.

3. Click the **New Slide** button arrow.

4. Click **Duplicate Selected Slides**.

   The new slide appears directly after the slide duplicated.

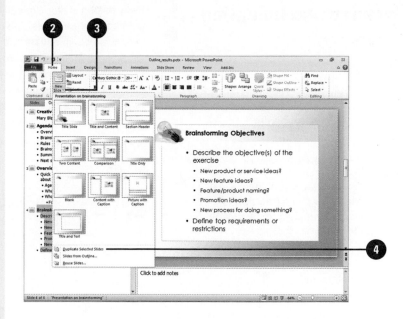

Insert an Outline from Another Program

1. In the Outline pane of Normal view, click the slide after which you want to insert an outline.

2. Click the **Home** tab.

3. Click the **New Slide** button arrow, and then click **Slides from Outline**.

4. Locate and select the file containing the outline you want to insert.

5. Click **Insert**.

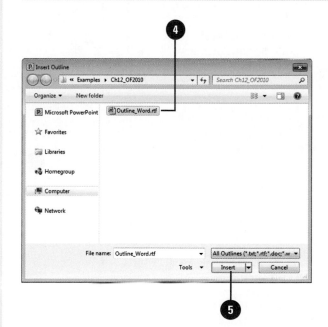

Did You Know?

You can open an outline from another program in PowerPoint. Click the File tab, click Open, click the Files Of Type list arrow, click All Outlines, and then double-click the outline file you want to open.

Moving and Indenting Text

Body text on a slide typically contains bulleted text, which you can indent to create levels. You can indent paragraphs of body text up to five levels. In an outline, these tools let you demote text from a title, for example, to bulleted text. You can view and change the locations of the indent markers within an object with text using the ruler. You can set different indent markers for each paragraph in an object. The ruler includes default tab stops at every inch; when you press the Tab key, the text moves to the next tab stop, which you can change.

Change the Indent Level

① In Normal view (Outline pane or slide), click the paragraph text or select the lines of text you want to indent.

② Click the **Home** tab.

③ Click the indent level option you want:

◆ Click the **Increase List Level** button to move the line up one level (to the left).

◆ Click the **Decrease List Level** button to move the line down one level (to the right).

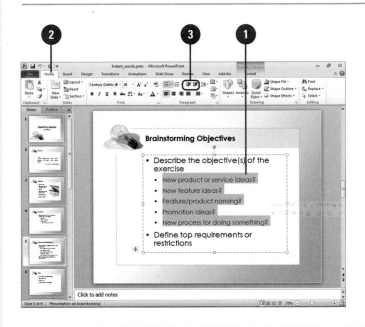

Display or Hide the Ruler

① In Normal view, click the **View** tab.

② Select the **Ruler** check box to display it, or clear the **Ruler** check box to hide it.

Did You Know?

You can use the Ruler with shape text. When you select a text object and then view the ruler, the ruler runs the length of just that text object, and the origin (zero point) of the ruler is at the box borders, starting with the upper left.

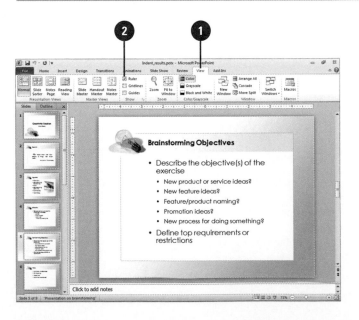

Change the Indent

1. Display the ruler.

2. Select the text for which you want to change the indentation.

3. Change the indent level the way you want.

   ◆ To change the indent for the first line of a paragraph, drag the first-line indent marker.

   ◆ To change the indent for the rest of the paragraph, drag the left indent marker.

   ◆ To change the distance between the indents and the left margin, but maintain the relative distance between the first-line and left indent markers, drag the rectangle below the left indent marker.

Set a Tab

1. Click the paragraph or select the paragraphs whose tabs you want to modify. You can also select a text object to change the tabs for all paragraphs in that object.

2. If necessary, click the **View** tab, and then select the **Ruler** check box to display the ruler.

3. Click the **Tab** button at the left of the horizontal ruler until you see the type of tab you want.

4. Click the ruler where you want to set the tab.

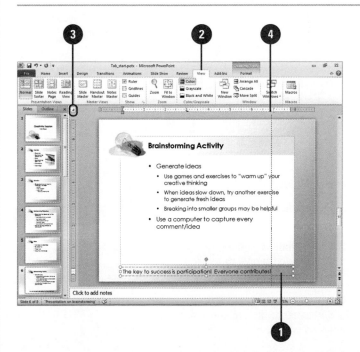

Modifying a Bulleted and Numbered List

When you create a new slide, you can choose the bulleted list slide layout to include a bulleted list placeholder. You can customize the appearance of your bulleted list in several ways, including symbols or numbering. You also have control over the appearance of your bullets, including size and color. You can change the bullets to numbers or pictures. You can also adjust the distance between a bullet and its text using the PowerPoint ruler.

Add and Remove Bullets or Numbering from Text

1 Select the text in the paragraphs in which you want to add a bullet.

2 Click the **Bullets** or **Numbering** button arrow on the Home tab, and then select the style you want.

> **TIMESAVER** *Click the Bullets or Numbering button (not the arrow) on the Home tab to turn it on with the default setting.*

3 To remove the bullet or numbering, select the text, and then click the **Bullets** or **Numbering** button on the Home tab.

Change the Distance Between Bullets and Text

1 Select the text you want to indent.

2 If the ruler isn't visible, click the **View** tab, and then select the Ruler check box.

3 Drag the indent markers on the ruler.

◆ **First-line Indent.** The top upside down triangle marker indents the first line.

◆ **Hanging Indent.** The middle triangle marker indent second line and later.

◆ **Left Indent.** The bottom square marker indent entire line.

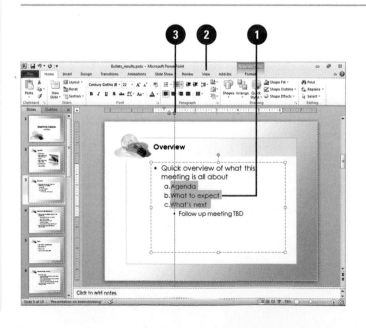

Change the Bullet or Number Character

1. Select the text or text object whose bullet character you want to change.

2. Click the **Bullets** or **Numbering** button arrow on the Home tab, and then click **Bullets and Numbering**.

3. Click the **Bulleted** or **Numbered** tab.

4. Click one of the predefined styles or do one of the following:

   ◆ Click **Picture**, and then click the picture you want to use for your bullet character.

   ◆ Click **Customize**, and then click the character you want to use for your bullet character.

5. To change the bullet or number's color, click the **Color** arrow, and then select the color you want.

6. To change the bullet or number's size, enter a percentage in the Size box.

7. Click **OK**.

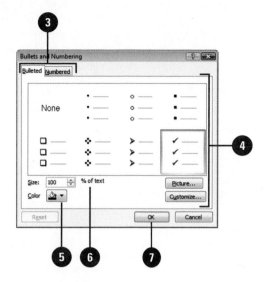

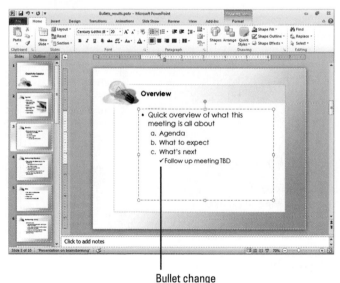

Bullet change

Did You Know?

You can select bulleted or numbered text. Position the mouse pointer over the bullet or number next to the text you want to select; when the pointer changes to the four-headed arrow, click the bullet.

You can use the mouse to increase or decrease list level text. Move the mouse pointer over the bullet you want to increase or decrease, and then when it changes to a four-headed arrow, drag the text to the left or right.

Creating Text Columns

Like Microsoft Word, PowerPoint can now create text columns within a text box. You can quickly transform a long list of text into a two, three, or more columns. After you create text columns, you can change the spacing between them to create the exact look you want. If you want to return columns back to a single column, simply change a text box to one column.

Create Text Columns

1. Select the text box.

2. Click the **Home** tab.

3. Click the **Columns** button, and then click one of the following:

   ◆ **One**, **Two**, or **Three** to quickly create text columns.

   ◆ **More Columns** to create larger text columns and change columns spacing.

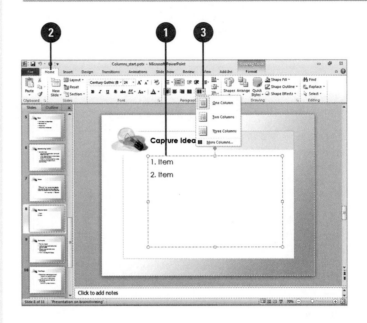

Adjust Column Spacing

1. Select the text box with the columns you want to adjust.

2. Click the **Home** tab.

3. Click the **Columns** button, and then click **More Columns**.

4. Click the Spacing **up** and **down** arrows, or enter a specific size.

5. Click **OK**.

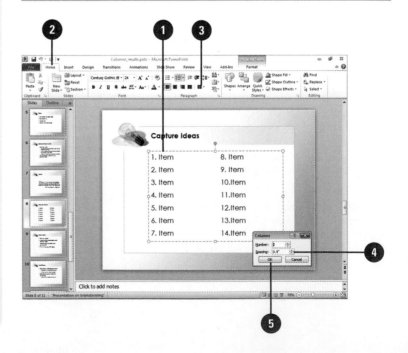

Organizing Slides into Sections

When you're working on large presentations or collaborating on a presentation with others, organizing slides into sections (**New!**) can make the workflow process easier. After you create a section of slides in a presentation, you can rename the untitled section. When you rename a section, you can include a name assignment to make it easier for others working the presentation to know which slides to modify. When you no longer need a section, you can remove individual sections, or quickly remove them all.

Organize Slides into Sections

1 Click the **Home** tab.

2 Click **Slides** pane in Normal view or click the **Slide Sorter View** button.

3 Click to place the insertion point where you want to insert a new selection or select the slide(s) you want to place into a section.

4 Click the **Section** button, and then click **Add Section**.

5 To rename a section, click the section name to select it, click the **Section** button, click **Rename Section**, type a name, and then click **OK**.

◆ To assign a name to a section, type it in when you rename a section.

6 To collapse or expand a section, click the **Collapse** or **Expand** arrow in the section name.

7 To rename a section, click the section name to select it, click the **Section** button, click **Remove Section** or **Remove All Sections**.

Did You Know?

You can print sections. Click the File tab, click Print, click the Print Range list arrow, select the section name, and then click Print.

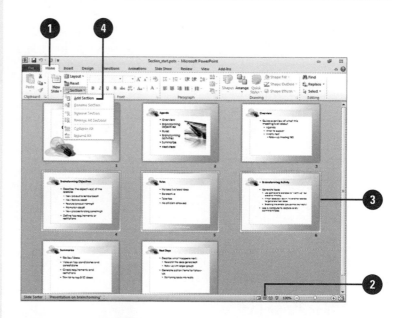

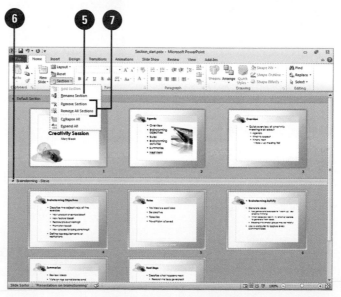

Rearranging Slides

You can instantly rearrange slides in Outline or Slides pane in Normal view or in Slide Sorter view. You can use the drag-and-drop method or the Cut and Paste buttons to move slides to a new location. In the Outline pane, you can also collapse the outline to its major points (titles) so you can more easily see its structure and rearrange slides, and then expand it back.

Rearrange a Slide in Slides Pane or Slide Sorter View

1. Click **Slides** pane in Normal view or click the **Slide Sorter View** button.

2. Select the slide(s) you want to move.

3. Drag the selected slide to a new location.

   A vertical bar appears where the slide(s) will be moved when you release the mouse button.

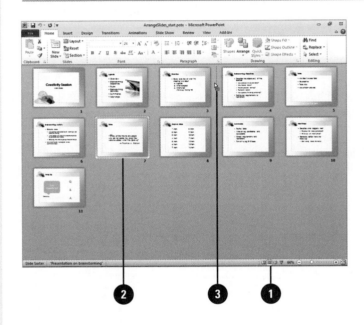

Move a Slide Using Cut and Paste

1. In the Outline or Slides pane or in Slide Sorter view, select the slide(s) you want to move.

2. Click the **Cut** button on the Home tab.

   The Clipboard task pane might open, displaying items you have cut or copied.

3. Click the new location.

4. Click the **Paste** button on the Home tab.

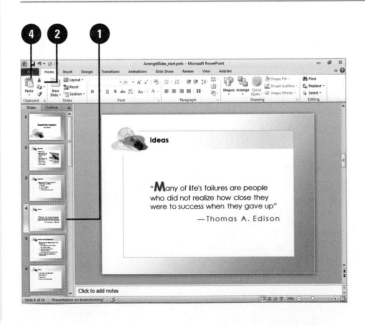

Rearrange a Slide in the Outline Pane

1. In the Outline pane in Normal view, select the slide(s) icons you want to move.

   TIMESAVER *To select slides in a sequence, click the first slide, hold down the Shift key, and then click the last slide. To select multiple slides, use the Ctrl key.*

2. Drag the selected slide up or down to move it in Outline pane to a new location.

   A vertical bar appears where the slide(s) will be moved when you release the mouse button.

Collapse and Expand Slides in the Outline Pane

1. In the Outline pane in Normal view, select the slide text you want to work with, and then:

   ◆ To collapse selected or all slides, right-click the slides, point to **Collapse**, and then click **Collapse**, or **Collapse All**.

   A horizontal line appears below a collapsed slide in Outline view.

   ◆ To expand selected or all slides, right-click the slides, point to **Expand**, and then click **Expand**, or **Expand All**.

   TIMESAVER *Double-click a slide icon in the Outline pane to collapse or expand it.*

Using Slides from Other Presentations

To insert slides from other presentations, you can open the presentation and copy and paste the slides you want, or you can use the Reuse Slides task pane. With the Reuse Slides task pane, you don't have to open the presentation first; instead, you can view a miniature of each slide in a presentation and then insert only the ones you select. If you only want to reuse the theme from another presentation, the Reuse Slides task pane can do that too.

Insert Slides from Another Presentation

1. Click the **Home** tab.

2. Click the **New Slide** button arrow, and then click **Reuse Slides**.

3. Click **Browse**, click **Browse File**, locate and select the file you want, and then click **Open**.

4. Select the slides you want to use.

   ◆ To display a larger preview, point to the slide.

   ◆ To insert a slide, click the slide.

   ◆ To insert all slides, right-click a slide, and then click **Insert All Slides**.

   ◆ To insert only the theme for all slides, right-click a slide, and then click **Apply Theme to All Slides**.

   ◆ To insert only the theme for the selected slides, right-click a slide, and then click **Apply Theme to Selected Slides**.

5. When you're done, click the **Close** button on the task pane.

Did You Know?

You can drag slides between presentations. Open the presentations, which appear in separate PowerPoint windows (**New!**), click the View tab, use the commands in the Window group to display the presentation slides, drag them between, and then use the Paste Options button to apply the theme.

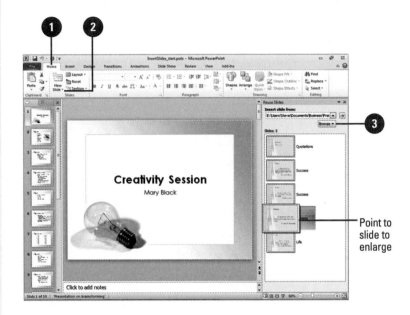

Point to slide to enlarge

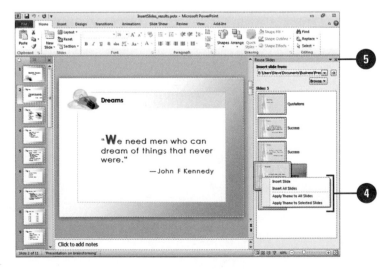

Making Your Presentation Look Consistent

Each PowerPoint presentation comes with a set of **masters**: slide, notes, and handout. A master controls the properties of each corresponding slide or page in a presentation. For example, when you make a change on a slide master, the change affects every slide. If you place your company logo, other artwork, the date and time, or slide number on the slide master, the element will appear on every slide.

Each master contains placeholders and a theme to help you create a consistent looking presentation. A placeholder provides a consistent place on a slide or page to store text and information. A theme provides a consistent look, which incorporates a color theme, effects, fonts, and slide background style. Placeholders appear on the layouts associated with the master. The notes and handout masters use one layout while the slide master uses multiple layouts. Each master includes a different set of placeholders, which you can show or hide at any time. For example, the slide master includes master title and text placeholders, which control the text format for every slide in a presentation, while the handout master includes header, footer, date, page number, and body placeholders. You can modify and arrange placeholders on all of the master views to include the information and design you want.

You can also view and make changes to a master—either slide, notes, or handout—in one of the master views, which you can access using the View tab. When you view a master, the Ribbon adds a Program tab that correspond to the master. For example, when you switch to Slide Master view, the Slide Master tab appears. The Ribbon on each master view also includes a Close Master View button, which returns you to the view you were in before you opened the master.

Slide Master view

Slide master

Slide Title layout

Slide layouts

Controlling Slide Appearance with Masters

If you want an object, such as a company logo or clip art, to appear on every slide in your presentation, place it on the **Slide Master**. All of the characteristics of the Slide Master (background color, text color, font, and font size) appear on every slide. However, if you want an object to appear on a certain slide type, place it on a slide layout in Slide Master view. The Slide Master tab contains several buttons to insert, delete, rename, duplicate, and preserve masters. You can create unique slides that don't follow the format of the masters. When you preserve a master, you protect (lock) it from being deleted. You can also arrange the placeholders the way you want them.

Include an Object on Every Slide or Only Specific Slides

1. Click the **View** tab, and then click the **Slide Master** button.

2. Add the objects you want to a slide master or slide layout, and then modify its size and placement.

    ◆ **Slide master.** Includes object on every slide.

      Slide master is the top slide miniature in the left column.

    ◆ **Slide layout.** Includes object only on the specific layout.

3. Click the **Close Master View** button on the Ribbon.

Did You Know?

You can delete a slide master. Click the View tab, click the Slide Master button, select the slide master you want to delete in the left pane, click the Delete button in the Edit Master group, and then click the Close Master View button.

You can rename a slide master. Click the View tab, click the Slide Master button, select the slide master you want to rename, click the Rename button in the Edit Master group, type a new name, click Rename, and then click the Close Master View button.

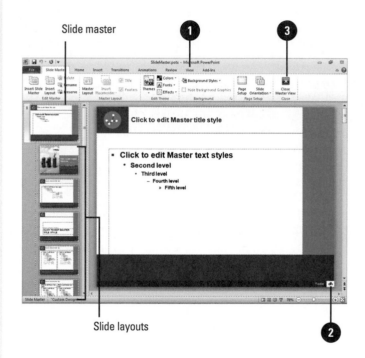

Slide master

Slide layouts

Insert a New Slide Master

1. Click the **View** tab, and then click the **Slide Master** button.

2. Click the **Insert Slide Master** button.

   The new slide master appears at the bottom of the left pane with a push pin indicating the new master is preserved.

3. Click the **Close Master View** button on the Ribbon.

   The new slide master and associated layouts appears in the Add Slide and Layout galleries at the bottom (scroll down if necessary).

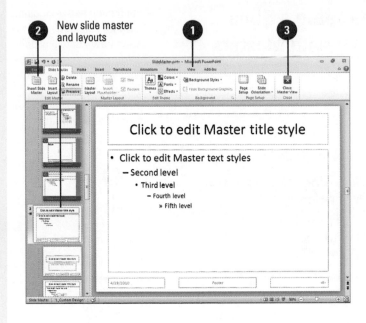

New slide master and layouts

Preserve or Not Preserve a Slide Master

1. Click the **View** tab, and then click the **Slide Master** button.

2. Click the master that you want to preserve or not preserve.

   A push pin appears under the slide master number to indicate the master is currently preserved.

3. Click the **Preserve** button to toggle it on (highlighted) and off (not highlighted).

   ◆ **Preserve.** Click the Preserve button to lock the master (highlighted).

   ◆ **Nut preserve.** Click the Preserve button to unlock the master (not highlighted), and then click Yes or No to delete the master (if not used).

4. Click the **Close Master View** button on the Ribbon.

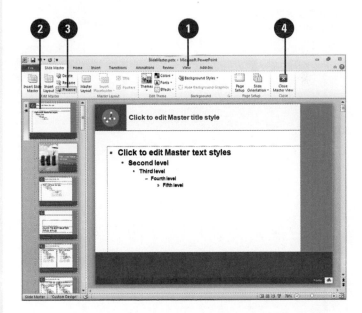

Controlling a Slide Layout with Masters

Each slide master includes a standard set of slide layouts. If the standard layouts don't meet your specific needs, you can modify one to create a new custom slide layout, or insert and create a new custom slide layout from scratch. You can use the Ribbon in Slide Master view to help you create a custom slide layout. In the Master Layout group, you can show and hide available placeholders or insert different types of placeholders, such as Content, Text, Picture, Chart, Table, Diagram, Media, and Clip Art.

Insert a New Slide Layout

1. Click the **View** tab, and then click the **Slide Master** button.

2. Select the slide master in the left pane in which you want to associate a new layout.

3. Click the **Insert Slide Layout** button.

   The new slide layout appears at the end of the current slide layouts for the slide master.

4. Click the **Close Master View** button on the Ribbon.

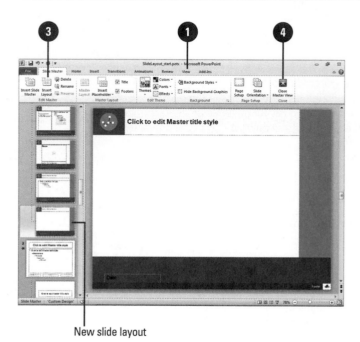

New slide layout

Create a New Slide Layout from an Existing One

1 Click the **View** tab, and then click the **Slide Master** button.

2 Right-click the slide layout you want to use, and then click **Duplicate Layout**.

The duplicate layout appears below the original one.

3 Click the **Rename** button.

4 Type a new layout name.

5 Click **Rename**.

6 Click the **Close Master View** button on the Ribbon.

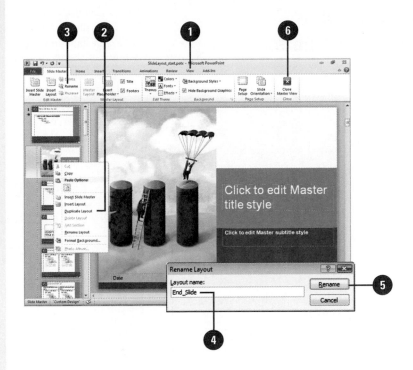

Insert a Placeholder

1 Click the **View** tab, and then click the **Slide Master** button.

2 Select the slide layout to which you want to insert a placeholder.

3 Click the **Insert Placeholder** button arrow, and then click the placeholder you want to insert.

TIMESAVER *Click the Insert Placeholder button to insert a placeholder used to hold any kind of content.*

4 On the slide, drag to create a placeholder the size you want on the slide layout.

5 Click the **Close Master View** button on the Ribbon.

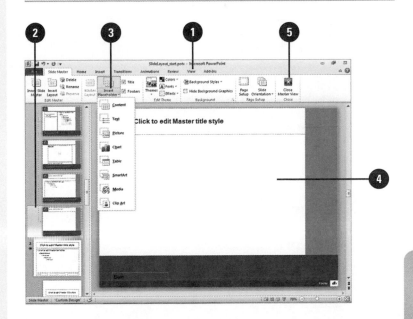

Modifying Placeholders

Each PowerPoint master comes with a different set of standard placeholders. The slide master comes with Title and Footer placeholder, while the handouts master comes with Header, Footer, Date, and Page Number placeholders. If a master doesn't contain the information you need, you can modify it by showing or hiding placeholders. After you display the placeholders you want, you can insert content—such as header or footer text—and format it like any other text box with the look you want. For example, you can format placeholder text using WordArt styles and Font and Paragraphs tools on the Home tab.

Show or Hide a Placeholder

1. Click the **View** tab, and then click the master view (**Slide Master**, **Handout Master**, or **Notes Master**) button with the master you want to change.

2. If you're in Slide Master view, select the slide master or slide layout you want to change.

3. Select or clear the check box for the placeholder you want to show or hide. Options vary depending on the master view.

   ◆ **Slide Master.** Select or clear the Title or Footers check boxes.

   ◆ **Handout Master.** Select or clear the Header, Footer, Date, or Page Number check boxes.

   ◆ **Notes Master.** Select or clear the Header, Slide Image, Footer, Date, Body, or Page Number check boxes.

4. Click the **Close Master View** button on the Ribbon.

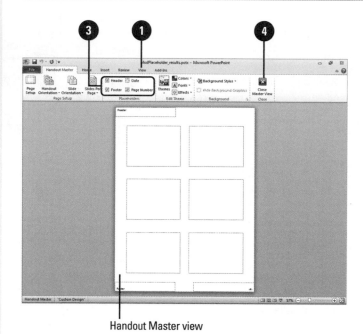

Handout Master view

Modify and Format Placeholders

1. Click the **View** tab, and then click the master view (**Slide Master**, **Handout Master**, or **Notes Master**) button with the master you want to change.

2. If you're in Slide Master view, select the slide master or slide layout you want to change.

3. Select the placeholder you want to change.

4. To add information to a place-holder, such as a header or footer, click the text box to insert the I-beam, and then type the text you want.

5. To format the placeholder, click the **Home** and **Format** (under Drawing Tools) tabs, and then use the formatting tools on the Ribbon.

   ◆ Use the WordArt Styles to apply Quick Styles from the Style gallery.

   ◆ Use tools in the Font and Paragraph groups to modify the placeholder.

6. To delete the placeholder, press the Delete key.

7. Click the **Close Master View** button on the Ribbon.

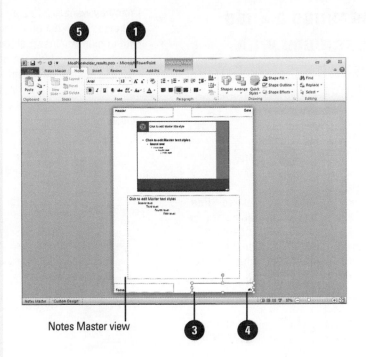

Notes Master view

Did You Know?

You can change the slide master lay-out. If you delete an item from the slide master, you can reshow it again. Select the slide master in Slide Master view, click the Slide Layout button, select the placeholder check boxes you want, and then click OK.

Controlling a Slide Background with Masters

You may want to place an object onto most slides, but not every slide. Placing the object on the slide master saves you time. Use the Insert tab to help you insert objects. Once an object is placed on the slide master, you can hide the object in any slide you want. You can even choose to hide the object on every slide or only on specific ones. If you select the slide master in Slide Master view, you can hide background graphics on all slides. If you select a slide layout, you can hide them on the selected layout.

Hide Master Background Objects on a Slide

1. Click the **View** tab, click the **Slide Master** button, and then select the slide master (for all slides) or slide layout (for specific slides) you want to hide background objects.

2. Select the **Hide Background Graphics** check box.

   ◆ To hide a background object on a single slide, display the slide in Normal view, click the Design tab, and then select the Hide Background Graphics check box.

3. Click the **Close Master View** button on the Ribbon.

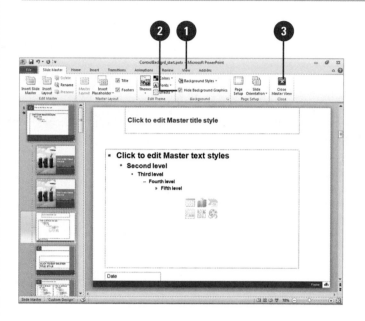

Add Background Graphics

1. Click the **View** tab, and then click the master view (**Slide Master**, **Handout Master**, or **Notes Master**) button with the master you want to change.

2. Click the **Insert** tab, click the **Insert Picture** button, locate and select the picture you want, and then click **Insert**.

3. Click the **Close Master View** button on the Ribbon.

Inserted graphic

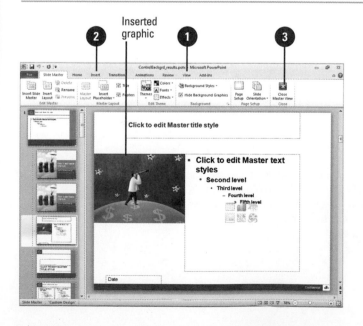

Adding a Background Style

In PowerPoint, you can add a background style to your presentation. A **background style** is a background fill made up of different combinations of theme colors. When you change a presentation theme, the background styles change to reflect the new theme colors and backgrounds. To quickly see if you like a background style, you can point to one in the Background Styles gallery to display a live preview of it with the current slide. If you like it, you can apply it.

Add a Background Style

1. Click the **Design** tab to change the background of the selected slide, or click the **View** tab, and then click the **Slide Master View** tab to change the background of the selected slide master or slide layout.

2. Click the **Background Styles** button.

    The current style appears highlighted in the gallery.

3. Point to a style to display a live preview of the style.

4. Click the style you want from the gallery to apply it to the selected slide, slide master (and all its slides), or slide layout.

    ◆ To apply the style to matching slides, all slides, selected slides, or slide master, right-click the style from the gallery, and then click an option.

5. To add a picture, texture, gradient, or artistic effect (**New!**), click the **Background Styles** button, and then click **Format Background**.

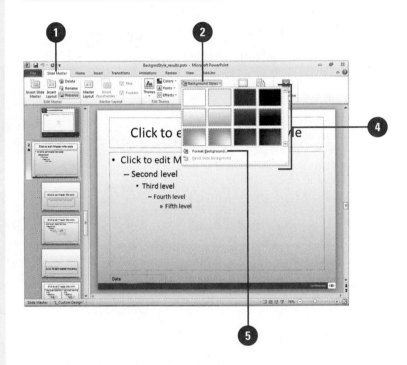

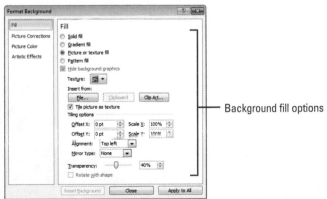

Background fill options

Did You Know?

You can reset the slide background. Click the Design tab, click the Background Styles button, and then click Reset Slide Background.

Inserting a Table

A **table** neatly organizes information into rows and columns, now up to a maximum of 75x75. The intersection of a column and row is called a **cell**. Enter text into cells just as you would anywhere else in PowerPoint, except that pressing the Tab key moves you from one cell to the next. PowerPoint tables behave much like tables in Word. You can insert tables by specifying a size, or drawing rows and columns to create a custom table. If you like to use Microsoft Excel worksheets, you can also insert and create an Excel table in your presentation.

Insert a Table Quickly

1. In Normal view, display the slide to which you want to add a table.

2. Click the **Insert** tab.

3. Click the **Table** button, and then drag to select the number of rows and columns you want, or click **Insert Table**, enter the number of columns and rows you want, and then click **OK**.

4. Release the mouse button to insert a blank grid in the document.

5. When you're done, click outside of the table.

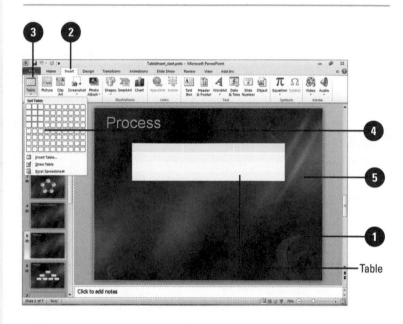

Draw a Table

1. In Normal view, display the slide to which you want to add a table.

2. Click the **Insert** tab.

3. Click the **Table** button, and then click **Draw Table**.

4. Drag the table size you want.

5. Drag horizontal lines to create rows and vertical lines to create columns.

6. When you're done, click outside of the table.

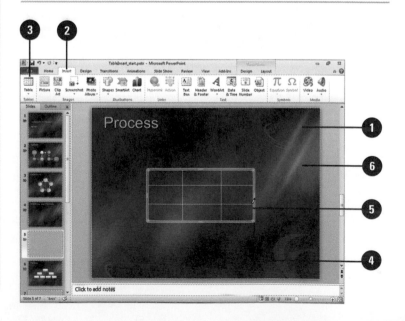

Modifying a Table

After you create a table or begin to enter text in one, you might want to add more rows or columns to accommodate the text you are entering in the table. PowerPoint makes it easy for you to format your table. You can change the alignment of the text in the cells (by default, text is aligned on the left of a cell). You can also modify the appearance and size of the cells and the table.

Insert and Delete Columns and Rows

1. Click in a table cell next to where you want the new column or row to appear.

2. Click the **Layout** tab under Table Tools.

3. To insert columns and rows, click the **Insert Above**, **Insert Below**, **Insert Left**, or **Insert Right** buttons.

4. To delete columns and rows, click the **Delete** button, and then click **Delete Columns** or **Delete Rows**.

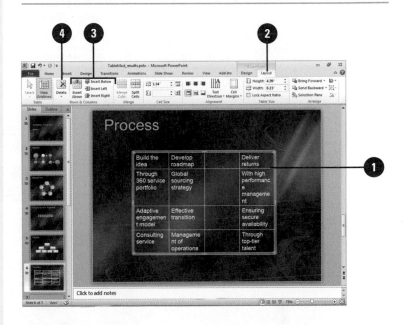

Change Cells Margins and Table Sizes

1. Select the text you want to align in the cells, rows, or columns.

2. Click the **Layout** tab under Table Tools.

3. To resize the table manually, drag a corner or middle resize handle.

   To set a specific size for the table, click the **Table Size** button, and then specify a height and width. To keep the size proportional, select the **Lock Aspect Ratio** check box.

4. To change margins, click the **Cell Margins** button, and then click a cell size margin option: Normal, None, Narrow, Wide, or Custom Margins.

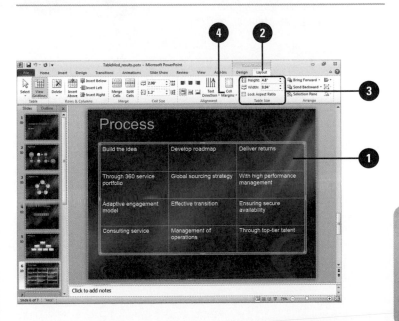

Adding a Quick Style to a Table

Instead of changing individual attributes of a table, such as shape, border, and effects, you can quickly add them all at once with the Table Quick Style gallery. The Table Quick Style gallery provides a variety of different formatting combinations. To quickly see if you like a Table Quick Style, point to a thumbnail in the gallery to display a live preview of it in the selected shape. If you like it, you can apply it. In addition to applying one of the preformatted tables from the Table Quick Style gallery, you can also create your own style by shaping your text into a variety of shapes, curves, styles, and color patterns.

Add a Quick Style to a Table

1. Click the table you want to change, or select the cells you want to modify.

2. Click the **Design** tab under Table Tools.

3. Click the scroll up or down arrow, or click the **More** list arrow in the Table Styles group to see additional styles.

   The current style appears highlighted in the gallery.

   TIMESAVER *Click the gallery title bar arrow to narrow down the list of styles: All, Document Matching, Light, Medium, or Dark.*

4. Point to a style.

   A live preview of the style appears in the current shape.

5. Click the style you want from the gallery to apply it to the selected table.

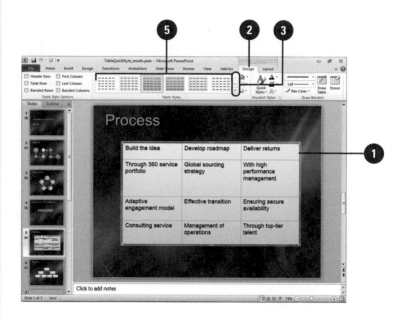

Did You Know?

You can clear table formatting. Select the table you want to change, click the Design tab under Table Tools, click the More list arrow in the Table Styles group, and then click Clear Table.

Formatting a Table

When you create a table, you typically include a header row or first column to create horizontal or vertical headings for your table information. You can use Quick Style options, such as a header or total row, first or last column, or banded rows and columns, to show or hide a special row and column formatting. The Total Row option displays a row at the end of the table for column totals. The Banded Row or Banded Column option formats even rows or columns differently from odd rows or columns to make a table easier to view. You can also insert a picture into a table to create a more polished look.

Format Table Columns

1. Click the table you want to change.

2. Click the **Design** tab under Table Tools.

3. Select any of the following row and column check box options:

   ◆ **First Column** to format the first column of the table as special.

   ◆ **Last Column** to format the last column of the table as special.

   ◆ **Banded Column** to format even columns differently than odd columns.

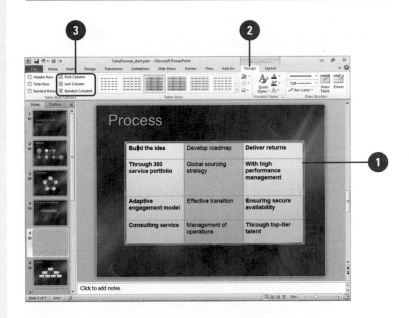

Format Table Rows

1. Click the table you want to change.

2. Click the **Design** tab under Table Tools.

3. Select any of the following row and column check box options:

   ◆ **Header Row** to format the top row of the table as special.

   ◆ **Total Row** to format the bottom row of the table for column totals.

   ◆ **Banded Rows** to format even rows differently than odd rows.

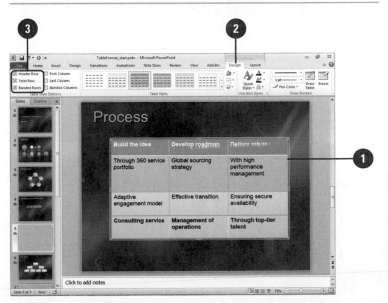

Creating a Text Box

Usually you use the title and bulleted list placeholders to place text on a slide. However, when you want to add text outside one of the standard placeholders, such as for an annotation or shape text, you can create a text box. Text boxes appear in all views and panes. In Outline pane, PowerPoint labels slides with multiple text boxes in numbered order. When you place text in a shape, the text becomes part of an object. You can format and change the object using Font options, as well as Shape and WordArt styles. You can also adjust the margins, rotate, or stack characters within a text box or a shape to create the look you want.

Create a Text Box

1. In Normal view, click the **Insert** tab.

2. Click the **Text Box** button.

3. Perform one of the following:

   ♦ To add text that wraps, drag to create a box, and then start typing.

   ♦ To add text that doesn't wrap, click and then start typing.

4. To delete a text box, select it, and the press Delete.

5. Click outside the selection box to deselect the text box.

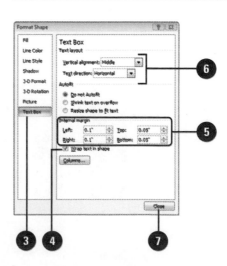

Rotated text

Adjust Text in a Text Box

1. Select an object with text.

2. Click the **Home** tab, and then click the **Drawing Dialog Box Launcher**.

3. In the left pane, click **Text Box**.

4. Select the **Wrap text in shape** check box.

5. Use the Internal margin **up** and **down** arrows to change the left, right, top, and bottom sides.

6. To change text, select a vertical alignment or text direction option.

7. Click **Close**.

Delivering a Presentation with PowerPoint

13

Introduction

When you're done preparing your slide show, it's time to consider how to show it to your audience. Microsoft Office PowerPoint 2010 gives you several ways to give and share your presentations. When you are presenting the show in person, you can use PowerPoint's slide navigation tools to move around your presentation. You can move forward and backward or move to a specific slide by using various navigation keys on the keyboard and on-screen Slide Show tools.

As you're presenting your slide show, you can highlight key ideas by using the mouse as a pointer or pen/highlighter. By annotating your slide show, you can give extra emphasis on a topic or goal for your audience. Annotations can be saved as enhancements to your presentation for later. If you are presenting a slide show using a second monitor or projection screen, PowerPoint includes the tools you need to properly navigate the display equipment.

If you are taking your presentation to another site, you might not need the entire PowerPoint package. Rather than installing PowerPoint on the sites' computer, you can pack your presentation into one compressed file, storing it on a CD. Once you reach your destination, you can expand the compressed file onto your client's computer and play it, regardless of whether that computer has PowerPoint installed. If you have the PowerPoint Viewer, you can save your presentation as a PowerPoint Show, which automatically opens in Slide Show view. If you need a video of your presentation, you can save it as a Windows Media Video.

Changing Page Setup Options

Before you print a presentation, you can use the Page Setup dialog box to set the proportions of your presentation slides—standard and wide screen—and their orientation on the page. You can also control slide numbering in the Number Slides From box. For a new presentation, PowerPoint opens with default slide page settings: on-screen slide show, landscape orientation, and slides starting at number one. Notes, handouts, and outlines are printed in portrait orientation.

Control Slide Size

1 Click the **Design** tab.

2 Click the **Page Setup** button.

3 Click the **Slides sized for** list arrow.

4 Click the size you want.

◆ **On-Screen Show** for slides that fit computer monitor with ratios of 4:3 (standard), 16:9 (wide screen HDTV's), or 16:10 (wide screen laptops).

◆ **Letter Paper** for slides that fit on 8.5-by-11-inch paper.

◆ **Ledger Paper** for slides that fit on 11-by-17-inch paper.

◆ **A3 Paper, A4 Paper, B4 (ISO) Paper,** or **B5 (ISO) Paper** for slides that fit on international paper.

◆ **35mm Slides** for 11.25-by-7.5-inch slides.

◆ **Overhead** for 10-by-7.5-inch slides that fit transparencies.

◆ **Banner** for 8-by-1-inch slides that are typically used as advertisements on a Web page.

◆ **Custom** to enter the measurements you want in the width and height boxes.

5 To orient your slides, notes, handouts, and outline, click the **Portrait** or **Landscape** option.

6 Click **OK**.

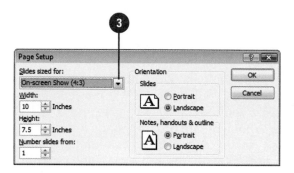

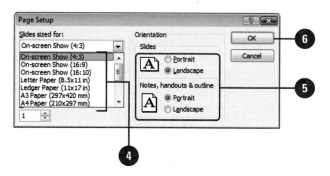

For Your Information

Using Portrait and Landscape Together

In PowerPoint, you can have only one slide orientation in a presentation. However, if you want to use portrait and landscape slide orientation in the same presentation, you can do it by creating a link between two presentations. For best results, place both presentations in the same folder on your computer. First, you create a link from the first presentation to the second presentation, and then create a link from the second presentation back. See "Creating a Hyperlink" on page 560 for instructions on creating a link to another presentation.

Adding Animation

You can use animation to introduce objects onto a slide one at a time or with special animation effects. For example, a bulleted list can appear one bulleted item at a time, or a picture or chart can fade in gradually. There are four types of animations (**New!**): Entrance, Exit, Emphasis and Motion Path (animations along a line). You can apply one or more animations to the same object. To quickly see if you like an animation, point to a name in the Animation list to display a live preview of it. If you like it, you can apply it. You can also design your own customized animations, including those with your own effects and sound elements. After you create an animation, you can use the Animation Painter (**New!**) to quickly copy it to another object, just like the Format Painter.

Apply and Preview a Animation Effect to Text or an Object

1 Select the text or object you want to animate.

2 Click the **Animations** tab.

3 Click the **Animation** list arrow, and then point to an animation.

A live preview of the style appears in the current shape.

4 Click the animation you want.

5 To add multiple animations, click the **Add Animation** button, and then click the animation you want.

6 To copy animation to another object, click the object you want to copy from, click the **Animation Painter** button, and then click the object you want to paste to.

◆ To apply the animation to multiple objects, double-click the Animation Painter button; press Esc to exit.

7 To preview an animation, click the **Preview** button.

◆ To stop an animation, click the **Preview** button again.

◆ To automatically preview an animation after adding or changing one, click the **Preview** button arrow, and then click **AutoPreview** to select it.

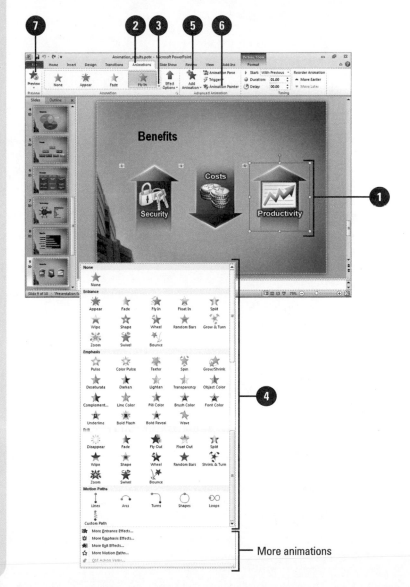

More animations

Using Specialized Animations

Using specialized animations, you can quickly apply animations specific to certain objects using the Animations tab (**New!**). For example, for a text object, you can introduce the text on your slide all at once or by word or letter. Similarly, you can introduce bulleted lists one bullet item at a time and apply different effects to older items, such as graying the items out as they are replaced by new ones. You can animate charts by introducing chart series or chart categories one at a time.

Animate Text or Bulleted Lists

1. In Normal view, select the text object you want to animate.

2. Click the **Animations** tab.

3. Click the **Animation** list arrow, and then click an animation (Entrance, Emphasis, Exit, or Motion Paths).

   ◆ For some motion paths, click points to create a path.

4. Click the **Effect Options** button, and then specify any of the following:

   ◆ **Direction.** Select a direction for the animation: **Down**, **Left**, **Right**, or **Up**.

   ◆ **Sequence.** Select a grouping for the animation: **As One Object**, **All At Once**, or **By Paragraph**.

   ◆ **Origin.** Select **Locked** or **Unlocked**.

   ◆ **Path.** Select **Edit Points** to change the animation path, or **Reverse Path Direction**.

5. To dim text after the animation, click the **Animation Dialog Box Launcher**, click the **After Animation** list arrow, click the dim text color or option you want, and then click **OK**.

6. To see the animation effect, click the **Preview** button.

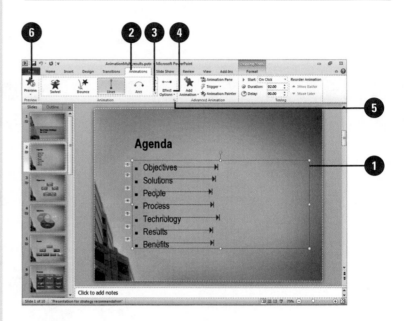

Other animation options

Dim text after the animation

Animate Shape Elements

1. In Normal view, select the shape you want to animate.

2. Click the **Animations** tab.

3. Click the **Animation** list arrow, and then click an animation (Entrance, Emphasis, Exit, or Motion Paths).

   ◆ For some motion paths, click points to create a path.

4. Click the **Effect Options** button, and then select a direction.

5. To see the animation effect, click the **Preview** button.

Did You Know?

You can view a slide's animation quickly in Slide Sorter view. In Slide Sorter view, click a slide's animation icon to view the animation.

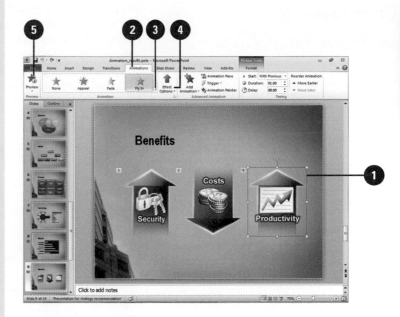

Animate Chart Elements

1. In Normal view, select the chart you want to animate.

2. Click the **Animations** tab.

3. Click the **Animation** list arrow, and then click an animation (Entrance, Emphasis, Exit, or Motion Paths).

   ◆ For some motion paths, click points to create a path.

4. Click the **Effect Options** button, and then select a grouping sequence (**As One Object**, **By Series**, **By Category**, **By Element in Series**, or **By Element in Category**).

5. To see the animation effect, click the **Preview** button.

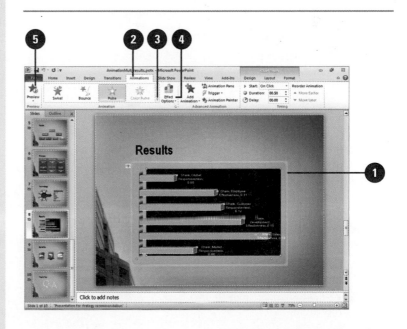

Coordinating Multiple Animations

The Animation task pane helps you keep track of your animations by listing all animated objects in a single location. Use these lists if your slides contain more than one animation, because they help you determine how the animations will work together. You can control the animation of each object, the order each object appears, the time between animation effects, when an animation takes place—on click or video bookmark trigger (**New!**)—and remove unwanted animations.

Work with Multiple Animations

1. In Normal view, select the slide objects you want to change.

2. Click the **Animations** tab.

3. Click the **Animation Pane** button.

4. Click an animated object in the Animation pane to select it.

5. To select animation options, click the list arrow, and then select an option. To remove an animation, click **Remove**.

6. To play the animations and display a timing line, click the **Play** button.

   ◆ To zoom the pane in or out, click the **Seconds** button, and then click **Zoom In** or **Zoom Out**.

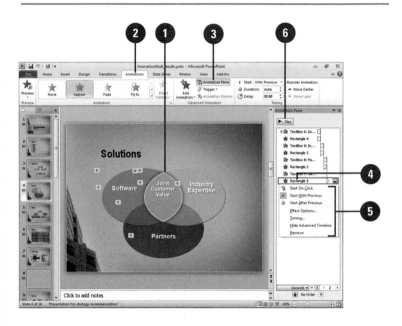

Modify the Animation Order

1. In Normal view, select the slide object you want to re-order.

   Animation sequence numbers appear next to animated objects indicating the animation order.

2. Click the **Animations** tab.

3. Click the **Move Earlier** or **Move Later** button.

   ◆ In the Animation pane, you can select an animation, and then click the **Re-Order Up** or **Down** arrow button.

4. To see the animation effect, click the **Preview** button.

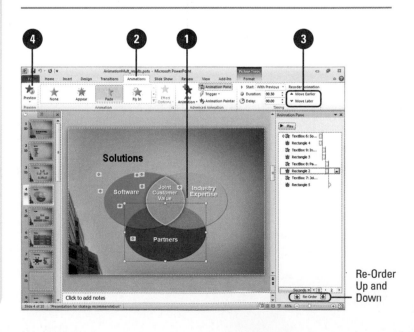

Re-Order Up and Down

Set Time Between Animations

1. In Normal view, select the slide object you want to animate.

2. Click the **Animations** tab.

3. Click the **Start** list arrow, and then click **After Previous**, **With Previous**, or **On Click**.

4. Use the **Duration** arrows to select the number of seconds to play this animation.

5. Use the **Delay** arrows to select the number of seconds to wait before playing this animation.

6. To see the animation effect, click the **Preview** button.

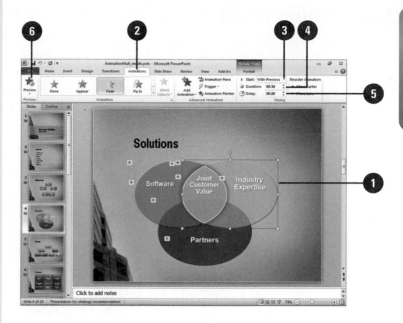

Trigger an Animation

1. In Normal view, select the slide object you want to animate.

2. Click the **Animations** tab.

3. Click the **Trigger** button, and then point to:

   ◆ **On Click of.** Select the object you want to trigger the animation.

   ◆ **On Bookmark.** Select the video bookmark you want to trigger the animation.

4. To see the animation effect, click the **Slide Show** button, and then click the object to trigger it

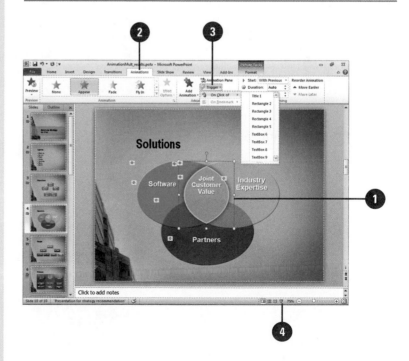

Did You Know?

You can quickly remove animations from objects. Select the objects, click the Animations tab, click the Animation list arrow, and then click None.

Adding Slide Timings

Use slide timing features to make sure that your presentation is not too long or too fast. You can specify the amount of time given to each slide or use Rehearse Timings. By rehearsing timings, you can vary the amount of time each slide appears on the screen. If you want the timings to take effect, make sure the show is set to use timings in the Set Up Show dialog box. In Slide Show View, a mouse click always advances a slide, even if the set timing has not elapsed, and holding down the mouse button prevents a timed transition until you release it.

Set or Edit Timings Between Slides

1. Click the slide(s) to which you want to set or change slide timings.

2. Click the **Transitions** tab.

3. Select the **After** check box.

4. Enter the time (in seconds) before the presentation automatically advances to the next slide after displaying the entire slide.

5. To apply the settings to all slides, click the **Apply To All** button.

Create Timings Through Rehearsal

1. Click the **Slide Show** tab.

2. Click the **Rehearse Timings** button.

3. As the slide show runs, rehearse your presentation by clicking or pressing Enter to go to the next transition or slide.

4. When you're done, click **Yes** to accept the timings.

5. To test timings, start the slide show and note when the slides advance too quickly or too slowly.

6. Review and edit individual timings in Slide Sorter view.

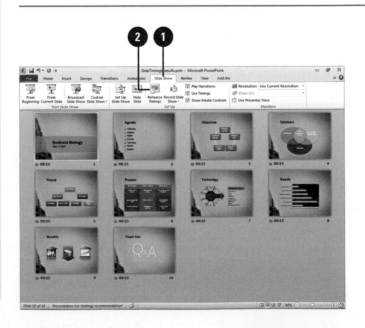

Creating Slide Transitions

If you want to give your presentation more visual interest, you can add transitions between slides. For example, you can create a fading out effect so that one slide fades out as it is replaced by a new slide, or you can have one slide appear to push another slide out of the way. If you like a more excite or dynamic effect, you can use transitions with 3-D motion effects, such as 3D rotation or orbit (**New!**). You can also add sound effects to your transitions, though you need a sound card and speakers to play them. To quickly see if you like a transition, point to one in the Transition Quick Style gallery to display a live preview of it. When you add a transition effect to a slide, the effect takes place between the previous slide and the selected slide.

Apply a Transition to an Individual or All Slides

1 Click the slide(s) to which you want to add a transition effect.

2 Click the **Transitions** tab.

3 Click the scroll up or down arrow, or click the **More** list arrow in the Transition To This Slide group.

4 Point to a transition to view a live preview, and then click the transition effect you want.

◆ To remove a slide transition, click **None**.

5 Click the **Effects Options** button, and then an option for the selected effect, such as direction or color.

6 To apply the current transition to all slides in the presentation, click the **Apply To All** button.

Did You Know?

You can show animation and transition effects while viewing your presentation in a browser. Click the File tab, click Options, click Advanced, click Web Options, click the Show Slide Animation While Browsing check box, and then click OK. Click OK again to close the Options dialog box.

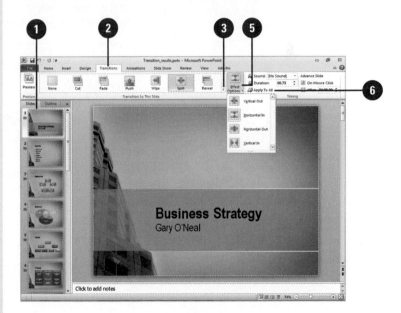

Inserting Videos and Audio

You can insert videos or audio into a presentation by inserting them from the Clip Art task pane, a file, or a social media Web site (**New!**), such as YouTube or hulu, using an embed code. Videos can be either animated pictures—also known as animated GIFs, such as cartoons—or they can be digital videos. Videos and audio are inserted as objects. When you insert a video, it becomes part of the presentation (**New!**), and not a linked file. When you insert an audio, a small icon appears representing the sound. PowerPoint supports the following audio file formats—ADTS (**New!**), AIFF, AU, MP3, MP4 (**New!**), WAV, WMA, QuickTime Audio (**New!**)—and video file formats—ASF, AVI, MP4 (**New!**), MPEG-2 TS (**New!**), MPG or MPEG, WMV, MOV or QT (QuickTime movie or video) (**New!**), SWF (Flash) (**New!**). After you insert a video or audio, you can play it back using the playback bar (**New!**) or the Playback tab under Video or Audio Tools.

Insert a Video or Audio from a File

1 Click the **Insert** tab.

2 Click the **Video** or **Audio** button arrow, and then click **Video from File** or **Audio from File**.

3 Locate and select a video or audio file.

4 Click **Insert**.

◆ To link a video to a presentation, click the **Insert** button arrow, and then click **Link to File**.

Play a Video or Audio

1 Select the video or audio icon.

2 Click the **Play/Pause** button on the playback bar or on the Playback tab under Video Tools.

◆ To move 0.25 seconds, click the **Move Forward** or **Move Backwards** button on the playback bar.

3 To change the volume, click the **Mute/Unmute** button or point to it, and then adjust the volume slider.

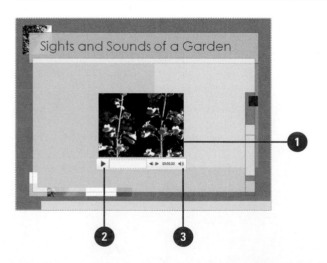

Insert a Clip Organizer Video or Audio

1. Click the **Insert** tab.

2. Click the **Video** or **Audio** button arrow, and then click **Clip Art Video** or **Clip Art Audio**.

3. Search for and click the media clip you want to insert.

4. Select the clip, and then click the **Playback** tab under Video or Audio Tools.

5. Click the **Start** list arrow, and then select an option:

   ◆ **Automatically.** Plays the media clip automatically when you go to the slide.

   ◆ **On Clicked.** Play the media clip only when you click it.

   ◆ **Play Across Slides.** Play the media clip across slides.

6. When you're done, click the **Close** button on the task pane.

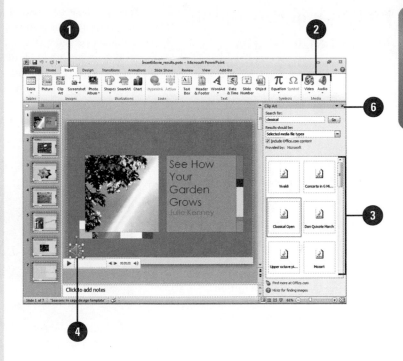

Insert a Video from a Web Site

1. Open your browser, and go to the social Web site with the embed code you want to use.

2. Go to the page with the video you want to use, select the embed code, and then press Ctrl+C to copy it.

3. In PowerPoint, click the **Insert** tab.

4. Click the **Video** button arrow, and then click **Video from Web Site**.

5. Press Ctrl+V to paste the embed code.

6. Click **Insert**.

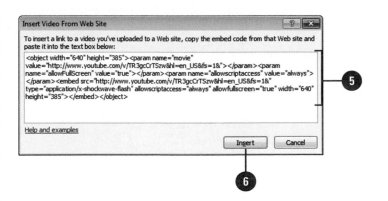

Editing and Formatting Videos and Audio

After you insert a video or audio, you can trim (**New!**) the start or end to remove the parts you don't want and make it shorter. You can also add text to a video or add bookmarks (**New!**) to indicate time points in a video or audio clip. Bookmarks are useful as a way to trigger animations or jump to a specific location in a video. In addition to editing videos, you can also use the Format tab under Video Tools to apply formatting (**New!**)—such as image correction, video styles, effects, and borders—to the video, which are similar to Picture Tools.

Trim a Video or Audio

1. Click the video or audio object you want to change.

2. Click the **Playback** tab under Video or Audio Tools.

3. Click the **Trim** button.

4. Point to the start point (green marker), and then drag it to a new starting point, or specify an exact Start Time.

5. Point to the end point (red marker), and then drag it to a new end point, or specify an exact End Time.

6. Click **OK**.

Add Text to a Video

1. Click the video object you want to change.

2. Click the **Insert** tab.

3. Click the **Text Box** button.

4. Point to where you want the text box, drag to draw a text box, and then enter text.

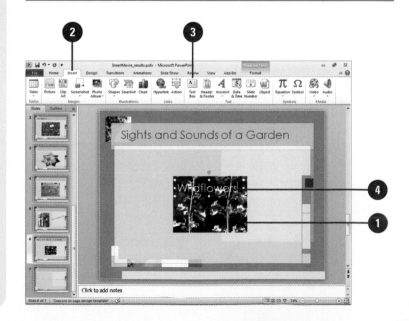

Add or Remove Video or Audio Bookmarks

1. Click the video or audio object you want to change.

2. Click the **Playback** tab under Video or Audio Tools.

3. Play and pause the video or audio where you want to insert a bookmark.

4. Click the **Add Bookmark** button.

   A dot appears on the timeline.

5. To remove a bookmark, click the bookmark (dot), and then click the **Remove Bookmark** button.

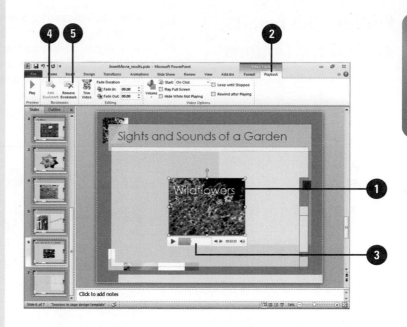

Format a Video

1. Click the video object you want to format; options are limited for a Flash object.

2. Click the **Format** tab under Video or Audio Tools.

3. Select from the available buttons:

   ◆ **Corrections.** Select a brightness and contrast option.

   ◆ **Color.** Select a recolor variation.

   ◆ **Poster Frame.** Creates a preview image for the video. Display a frame, and then select Current Frame, or Image from File to use a existing image.

   ◆ **Reset Design.** Resets the video back to the original.

   ◆ **Video Styles**, **Video Shape**, **Video Border**, or **Video Effects.** Click to apply a pre-defined style, change the video to a shape, add a border, or apply an effect, such as shadow, glow, reflection, or 3-D rotation.

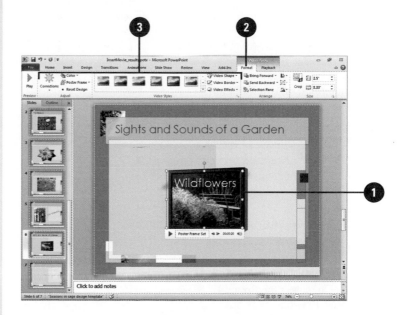

Setting Video and Audio Play Options

After you insert video, audio, or CD audio objects, you can set play options to determine how they will play back. You can change settings so they play continuously or just one time. Videos and audio can play in either Normal view or Slide Show view. You can also view and play movies using the full screen. To play sound and movies, you need to have Microsoft DirectShow or Microsoft Windows Media Player installed on your computer, which you can download from the Microsoft Web site.

Change Video or Audio Play Options

1. Click the video or audio object you want to change options.

2. Click the **Playback** tab under Video or Audio Tools.

3. To adjust slide show volume, click the **Volume** button, and then click an option: **Low**, **Medium**, **High**, or **Mute** (no audio).

4. Change the available video or audio settings.

   ◆ To change the way a movie plays, click the **Start** list arrow, and then select an option: **Automatically**, **On Clicked**, or **Play across slides**.

   ◆ To hide movie or sound, select the **Hide While Not Playing** check box.

   ◆ To play continuously, select the **Loop Until Stopped** check box.

   ◆ To resize the movie to fit the screen, select the **Play Full Screen** check box.

   ◆ To automatically rewind the movie, select the **Rewind After Playing** check box.

5. To add a fade in or out to a video or audio, specify the number of seconds you want to play a fade effect in the **Fade In** or **Fade Out** box.

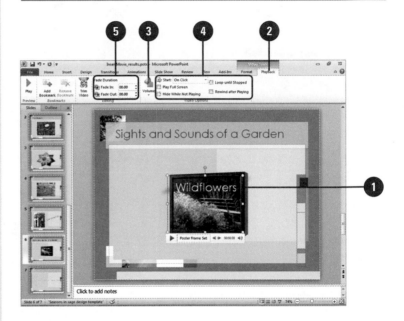

Recording a Narration

If you are creating a self-running presentation, you might want to add a narration to emphasize the points you make. PowerPoint lets you record your own narration as you rehearse your slide show (**New!**). You can record a narration before you run a slide show, or you can record it during the presentation and include audience comments. As you record the narration, you can pause or stop the narration at any time. When you play back a narration, the recording is synchronized with the presentation, including all slide transitions and animations. You can also delete a voice narration, as with any other PowerPoint object. You will need to set up a microphone and a sound card before recording a slide show.

Record a Narration and Slide Show

1. Click the **Slide Show** tab.

2. Click the **Record Slide Show** button arrow, and then click **Start Recording from Beginning** or **Start Recording from Current Slide**.

3. Select the **Narrations and laser pointer** check box, and then select or clear the **Slide and animation timings** check box.

4. Click **Start Recording**.

5. Speak clearly into the microphone and record your narration for each slide.

   ◆ To pause or resume the narration, right-click anywhere on the screen, and then click **Pause Narration**, or **Resume Narration**.

   ◆ To end the narration, right-click anywhere on the screen, and then click **End Show**.

   The recorded slide show timings are automatically saved and the slide show appears in Slide Show view.

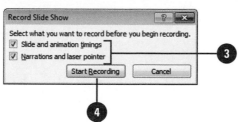

Setting Up a Slide Show

PowerPoint offers several types of slide shows appropriate for a variety of presentation situations, from a traditional big-screen slide show to a show that runs automatically on a computer screen at a conference kiosk. When you don't want to show all of the slides in a PowerPoint presentation to a particular audience, you can specify only a range of slides to show, or you can hide individual slides. You can also save a presentation to open directly into Slide Show view or run continuously.

Set Up a Show

1. Click the **Slide Show** tab.

2. Click the **Set Up Slide Show** button.

3. Choose the show type you want.

   - Click the **Presented by a speaker** option to run a full screen slide show.

   - Click the **Browsed by an individual** option to run a slide show in a window and allow access to some PowerPoint commands.

   - Click the **Browsed at a kiosk** option to create a self-running, unattended slide show for a booth or kiosk.

4. Select or clear the following show options check boxes:

   - **Loop continuously until 'Esc'.** Select to replay the slide show again until you stop it.

   - **Show without narration.** Select to not play narration.

   - **Show without animation.** Select to not play animation.

5. Select the **Manually** or **Using timings, if present** option.

6. Click **OK**.

7. Click the **Resolution** list arrow, and then click **Use Current Resolution**, or select a resolution.

8. If you have multiple monitors, click the **Show Presentation On** list arrow, and then select a monitor.

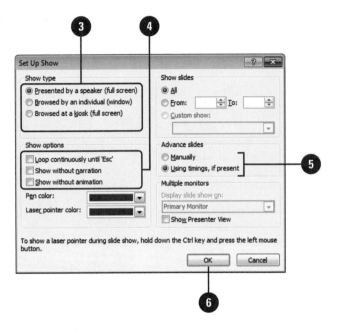

For Your Information

How Do You Choose a Screen Resolution?

The quality of a display system depends on its screen resolution, how many pixels it can display, and how many bits are used to represent each pixel. The screen resolution signifies the number of dots (pixels) on the entire screen. A higher screen resolution, such as 1024 by 768, makes items appear smaller, while a lower screen resolution, such as 640 by 480, makes items appear larger, which can help make a slide show easier to view.

Show a Range of Slides

1. Click the **Slide Show** tab.

2. Click the **Set Up Show** button.

3. Click the **From** option.

4. Enter the first and last slide numbers of the range you want to show.

5. Click **OK**.

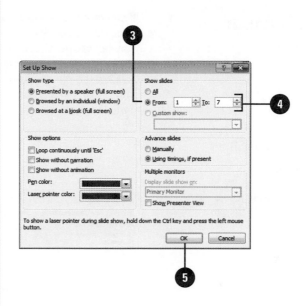

Hide Slides

1. In Slide Sorter view or Normal view, select or display the slide you want to hide.

2. Click the **Slide Show** tab.

3. Click the **Hide Slide** button.

   The slide number in the Slide pane or Slide Sorter view appears with a circle and a line through it.

4. To show a hidden slide, click it, and then click the **Hide Slide** button again.

Did You Know?

You can run a slide show continuously. Open the presentation you want to run, click the Slide Show tab, click the Set Up Show button, select the Loop Continuously Until 'Esc' check box, and then click OK.

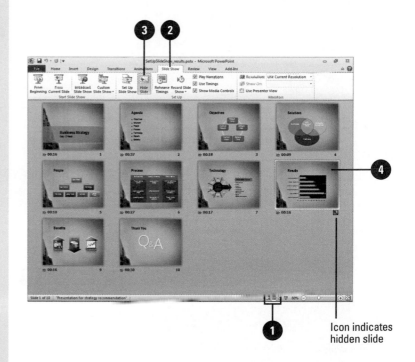

Icon indicates hidden slide

Creating a Custom Slide Show

If you plan to present a slide show to more than one audience, you don't have to create a separate slide show for each audience. Instead, you can create a custom slide show that allows you to specify which slides from the presentation you will use and the order in which they will appear. You can also edit a custom show which you've already created. Add, remove, and rearrange slides in a custom show to fit your various needs.

Create a Custom Slide Show

1. Click the **Slide Show** tab.

2. Click the **Custom Slide Show** button, and then click **Custom Shows**.

3. Click **New**.

4. Type a name for the show.

5. Click the slide(s) you want, and then click **Add**. To remove a slide, select it in the Slides In Custom Show list, and then click **Remove**.

6. Click **OK**.

7. Click **Close**.

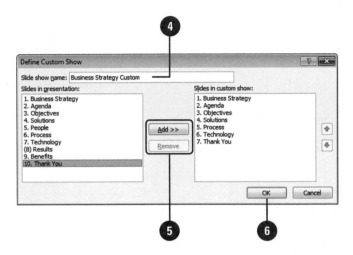

Show a Custom Slide Show

1. Click the **Slide Show** tab.

2. Click the **Custom Slide Show** button, and then click **Custom Shows**.

3. Click the custom slide show you want to run.

4. Click **Show**.

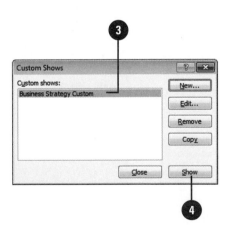

Did You Know?

You can print a custom show. Click the File tab, click Print, click the Print Range list arrow, select a custom show, and then click Print.

Starting a Slide Show

Once you have set up your slide show, you can start the show at any time. As you run your slide show, you can use the Slide Show toolbar, or Pop-up toolbar, to access certain PowerPoint commands without leaving Slide Show view. If your show is running at a kiosk, you might want to disable this feature.

Start a Slide Show and Display the Slide Show Toolbar

1. Click the **Slide Show** tab.

    TIMESAVER *Click the Slide Show View button on the Status bar to start a slide show quickly from the current slide.*

2. Click the **From Beginning** or **From Current Slide** button.

3. Move the mouse pointer to display the Slide Show toolbar.

4. Click a button on the Slide Show toolbar to move to the next or previous slide, or navigate the slide show, or end the show.

    TIMESAVER *Press Esc to stop a slide show.*

Did You Know?

You can set Slide Show options. Click the File tab, click Options, click Advanced, select the slide show and pop-up toolbar check box options you want (Show Menu On Right Click, Show Popup Toolbar, Prompt To Keep Ink Annotations When Exiting, or End With Black Slide), and then click OK.

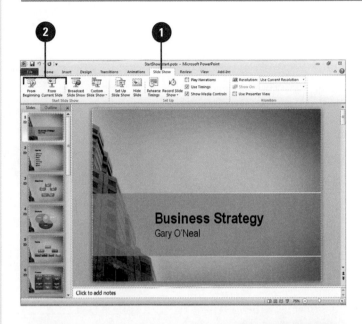

Navigating a Slide Show

In Slide Show view, you advance to the next slide by clicking the mouse button, pressing the Spacebar, or pressing Enter. In addition to those basic navigational techniques, PowerPoint provides keyboard shortcuts that can take you to the beginning, the end, or any particular slide in your presentation. You can also use the navigation commands on the shortcut menu to access slides in custom slide shows. After a period of inactivity during a normal full-screen slide show, PowerPoint hides the pointer and Slide Show toolbar.

Go to a Specific Slide

1. In Slide Show view, move the mouse to display the Slide Show toolbar, and then click the **Slide** button.

   TIMESAVER *Right-click a slide to display a shortcut menu.*

2. Point to **Go to Slide**, and then click the title of the slide to which you want to go.

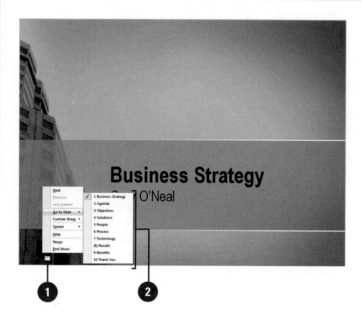

Did You Know?

You can turn your mouse into a laser pointer. In Slide Show view, hold down Ctrl, click the left mouse button, and the begin pointing (**New!**). To change the laser pointer color, click the Slide Show tab, click the Set Up Show button, click the Laser Pointer Color list arrow, select a color, and then click OK (**New!**).

You can add speaker notes in Slide Show. In Slide Show view, right-click a blank area on the slide, point to Screen, click Speaker Notes, type your notes, and then click Close.

You can switch to another program in Slide Show. In Slide Show view, right-click a blank area on the slide, point to Screen, and then click Switch Programs. Use the taskbar to switch between programs.

Slide Show View Shortcuts

Action	Result
Mouse click	Moves to the next slide
Right-mouse click	Moves to the previous slide (only if the Shortcut Menu On Right-Click option is disabled)
Press Enter	Moves to the next slide
Press Home or End	Moves to the first or last slide in the show
Press Page Up or Down	Moves to the previous or next slide
Enter a slide number and press Enter	Moves to the slide number you specified when you press Enter
Press B	Displays a black screen; press again to return
Press W	Displays a white screen; press again to return
Press Esc	Exits Slide Show view

Annotating a Slide Show

When you are presenting your slide show, you can turn your mouse pointer into a pen tool to highlight and circle your key points. If you decide to use a pen tool, you might want to set its color to match the colors in your presentation. When you are finished, you can turn the pen back to the normal mouse pointer. Mark ups you make on a slide with the pen tool during a slide show can be saved with the presentation, and then turned on or off when you re-open the presentation for editing.

Change Pointer Options

1. In Slide Show view, move the mouse to display the Slide Show toolbar.

2. Click the **Pen** button, point to **Arrow Options**, and then click a pointer option.

   ◆ **Automatic** hides the pointer until you move the mouse.

   ◆ **Visible** makes the pointer visible.

   ◆ **Hidden** makes the pointer invisible throughout the presentation.

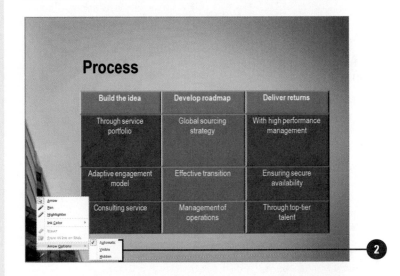

Use a Pen During the Slide Show

1. In Slide Show view, move the mouse to display the Slide Show toolbar.

2. Click the **Pen** button, and then click or point to an option.

   ◆ A writing tool (**Pen** or **Highlighter**).

   ◆ **Ink Color** to select an ink color.

3. Drag the mouse pointer to draw on your slide presentation with the pen or highlighter.

4. To remove ink, click the **Pen** button, and then click **Eraser** for individual ink, or click **Erase All Ink on Slide** for all ink.

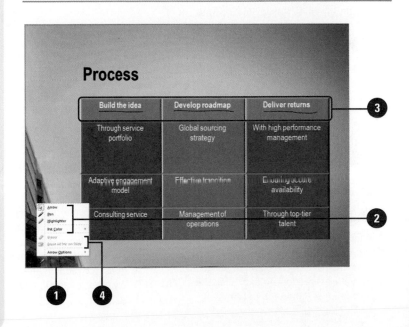

Saving a Presentation as a Slide Show

When you're giving a professional slide show presentation, you might not want your audience to see you start it from PowerPoint. Instead, you can save a presentation as a PowerPoint Show to open directly into Slide Show view. You can use the Save As dialog box to save a presentation as a PowerPoint Show (.ppsx) or PowerPoint Macro-Enabled (.ppsm). After you save a presentation as a PowerPoint Show file, you can create a shortcut to it on your desktop and then simply double-click the PowerPoint Show file to start it directly in Slide Show view. You need the Microsoft PowerPoint Viewer—available free online at *www.microsoft.com*—or PowerPoint software installed on your computer to display the slide show.

Save a Presentation as a PowerPoint Show

1 Click the **File** tab, and then click **Save As**.

   ◆ You can also click the **File** tab, click **Save & Send**, click **Change File Type**, and then click **PowerPoint Show**.

2 Click the **Save in** list arrow, and then click the drive or folder where you want to save the file.

3 Type a file name.

4 Click the **Save as type** list arrow, and then click **PowerPoint Show** or **PowerPoint Macro-Enabled Show**.

5 Click **Save**.

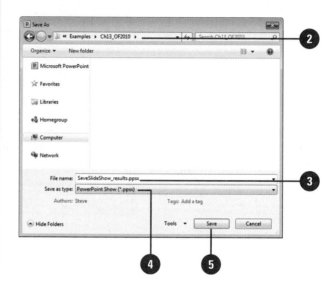

Did You Know?

You can broadcast a presentation over the Internet. You will need a Windows Live ID. Click the File tab, click Save & Send, click Broadcast Slide Show, click the Broadcast Slide Show button, click Start Broadcast, enter your Windows Live ID, and then click Copy Link or Send In Email to share the broadcast link. Click Start Slide Show and give presentation. To exit, click the End Broadcast button twice (**New!**).

For Your Information

Embedding Fonts

PowerPoint offers an assortment of tools for working with the fonts in your presentation. If you are using nonstandard fonts, you can embed the fonts you use so they "travel" with your presentation. Then, if the computer you use to show your presentation does not have all your fonts installed, the presentation quality will not suffer. To embed fonts, click the File tab, click Options, click Save in the left pane, select the Embed Fonts In The File check box, click the embed option you want (Embed only the characters used in the presentation (best for reducing file size) or Embed all characters (best for editing by other people)), and then click OK.

Saving a Presentation as a Video

Sometimes sharing a presentation as a video is the best approach. In PowerPoint, you can save a complete presentation, including slide timings and narration, as a Windows Media Video (.wmv). After you save a presentation as a video file, you can share it with others on a Web site, DVD, or network. It's a single file that you can run on most computers. If you need the video in a different video format, you need to use a third-party conversation software to convert the Windows Media Video file into another video format, such as MP4 or QuickTime.

Save a Presentation as a Video

1 Click the **File** tab, and then click **Save & Send**.

2 Click **Create a Video**.

3 Click the **Resolution** list arrow, and then select any of the following:

 ◆ **Computer & HD Displays.** Creates for large screen (960 x 720).

 ◆ **Internet & DVD.** Creates for medium screen (640 x 480).

 ◆ **Portable Devices.** Creates for small screen (320 x 240).

4 Click the **Timing** list arrow, and then click **Don't Use Recorded Timings and Narrations** or **Use Recorded Timings and Narrations**, and then specify a time.

5 Click the **Create Video** button.

6 Specify a name and location for the video.

7 Click **Save**.

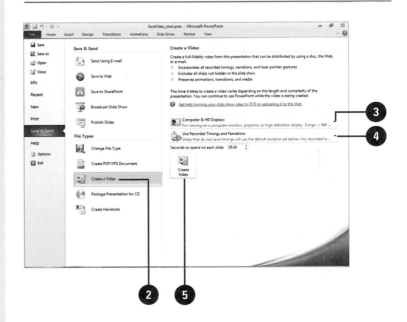

Did You Know?

You can compress a presentation with media to reduce the file size. Click the File tab, click Info, click Compress Media (**New!**), click Presentation Quality, Internet Quality, or Low Quality, and then click Close.

For Your Information

Creating a PDF or XPS Document

A PDF (Portable Document Format) developed by Adobe and XPS (XML Paper Specification) developed by Microsoft are documents you can share and read with Adobe Reader or XPS Viewer. You can publish your presentation as a PDF or XPS document. Click the File tab, click Save & Send, click Create PDF/XPS document, and then click Create a PDF/XPS. Specify a name and location. Click the Save As Type list arrow, and then click PDF or XPS Document. Select or clear the Open File After Publishing check box. Click the Standard or Minimum Size option. To specify a slide range and publishing options, click Options. When you're done, click Publish.

Packaging a Presentation on CD

The Package for CD feature allows you to copy one or more presentations and all of the supporting files, including linked files, on CD. You can choose packaging options to automatically or manually run your presentations. The PowerPoint Viewer is a program included on the packaged CD used to run presentations on computers that don't have PowerPoint installed. If you are packaging your presentation for use on your laptop, a DVD, or a network, you can use Package for CD to package your presentation to a folder or a network. PowerPoint doesn't support direct burning to DVDs, so you need to use DVD burning software to import the presentation files and create a DVD.

Package a Presentation on CD

1 Click the **File** tab, click **Save & Send**, and then click **Package Presentation for CD**.

2 Click the **Package for CD** button.

3 Type a name for the CD.

4 To add additional files to the CD, click **Add Files**, select the files you want, and then click **Add**.

   ◆ To reorder presentations, click **Move Up** or **Move Down**.

5 Click **Options**.

6 To link any external files, select the **Linked files** check box.

7 To ensure fonts are available on the play back computer, select the **Embedded TrueType fonts** check box.

8 If you want, type a password to open or modify the presentation.

9 To remove data, select the **Inspect presentations for inappropriate or private information** check box.

10 Click **OK**.

11 Click **Copy to CD**, and then follow the CD writer instructions, or click **Copy to Folder**, specify a folder location, and then click **OK**.

If a message alert appears, click the buttons you want to complete the process.

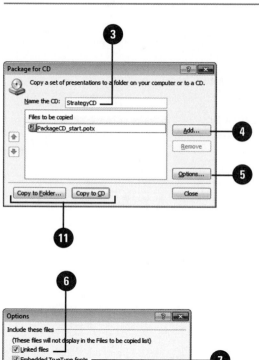

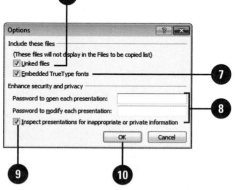

Copy to Folder options

Preparing Handouts

Prepare your handouts in the Print dialog box, where you can specify what to print. You can customize your handouts by formatting them in the handout master first, using the formatting and drawing tools. You can also add a header and footer to include the date, slide number, and page number, for example. In the Print dialog box, you can choose to print one, two, three, four, six, or nine slides per page.

Format the Handout Master

1. Click the **View** tab.

2. Click the **Handout Master** button.

3. Click the **Slides per page** button, and then select an option with how many slides you want per page.

4. Select or clear the **Header**, **Date**, **Footer**, or **Page Number** check boxes to show or hide handout master placeholders.

5. To add a background style, click the **Background Styles** button, and then click a style.

6. Use the formatting tools on the Home tab or drawing tools on the Format tab to format the handout master placeholders.

7. Click the **Close Master View** button.

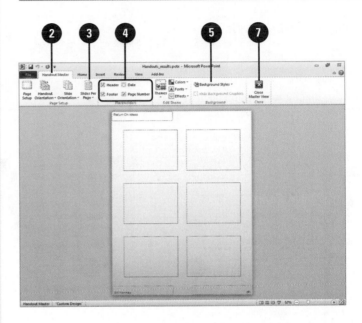

Did You Know?

What are the dotted rectangles in the handout master? The dotted rectangles are placeholders for slides and for header and footer information.

You can add headers and footers to create consistent handouts. Headers and footers you add to the handout master are also added to notes pages and the printed outline.

Preparing Speaker Notes

You can add speaker notes to a slide in Normal view using the Notes pane. Also, every slide has a corresponding **notes page** that displays a reduced image of the slide and a text placeholder where you can enter speaker's notes. Once you have created speaker's notes, you can reference them as you give your presentation, either from a printed copy or from your computer. You can enhance your notes by including objects on the notes master.

Enter Notes in Normal View

1. Click on the slide for which you want to enter notes.

2. Click to place the insertion point in the Notes pane, and then type your notes.

Did You Know?

You can view more of the Notes pane. To see more of the Notes pane in Normal view, point to the top border of the Notes pane until the pointer changes to a double-headed arrow, and then drag the border until the pane is the size you want.

Enter Notes in Notes Page View

1. Switch to the slide for which you want to enter notes.

2. Click the **View** tab.

3. Click the **Notes Pages** button.

4. If necessary, click the **Zoom** list arrow, and then increase the zoom percentage to better see the text you type.

5. Click the text placeholder.

6. Type your notes.

Reduced image of slide

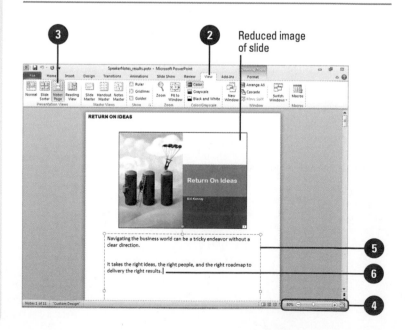

Format the Notes Master

1. Click the **View** tab.

2. Click the **Notes Master** button.

3. Select or clear the **Header**, **Slide Image**, **Footer**, **Date**, **Body** or **Page Number** check boxes to show or hide notes master placeholders.

4. To add a background style, click the **Background Styles** button, and then click a style.

5. If you want, add objects to the notes master that you want to appear on every page, such as a picture or a text object.

6. Use the formatting tools on the **Home** tab or drawing tools on the **Format** tab to format the handout master text placeholders.

7. To add a header and footer, click the **Insert** tab, and then click the **Header & Footer** button.

8. Click the **Close Master View** button.

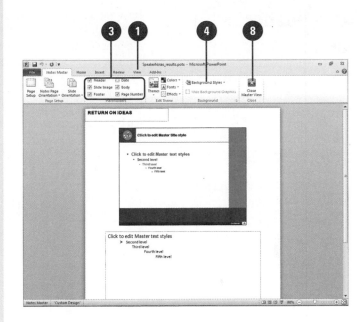

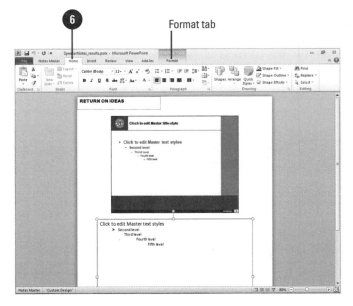

Format tab

Did You Know?

Why don't the objects on the Notes master appear in the Notes pane in Normal view? The objects that you add to the Notes master will appear when you print the notes pages. They do not appear in the Notes pane of Normal view or when you save your presentation as a Web page.

You can export notes and slides to Microsoft Office Word. Click the Send To Microsoft Word button on the Quick Access Toolbar (add it if necessary), click the page layout option you want for handouts, click the Paste Link option if you want to create a link, and then click OK.

Adding a Header and Footer

Headers and footers appear on every slide. You can choose to not have them appear on the title slide. They often include information such as the presentation title, slide number, date, and name of the presenter. Use the masters to place header and footer information on your slides, handouts, or notes pages. Make sure your header and footer don't make your presentation look cluttered. The default font size is usually small enough to minimize distraction, but you can experiment by changing their font size and placement to make sure.

Add a Header and Footer

1. Click the **Insert** tab, and then click the **Header & Footer** button.

2. Click the **Slide** or **Notes and Handouts** tab.

3. Enter or select the information you want to include on your slide or your notes and handouts.

4. To not include a header and footer on the title slide, select the **Don't show on title slide** check box.

5. Click **Apply** to apply your selections to the current slide (if available), or click **Apply to All** to apply the selections to all slides.

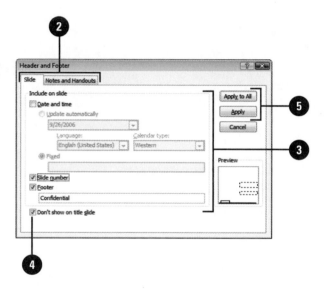

Change the Look of a Header or Footer

1. Click the **View** tab, and then click the master view (**Slide Master**, **Handout Master**, or **Notes Master** button with the master you want to change.

2. Make the necessary changes to the header and footer like any other text box. You can move or resize them or change their text attributes using the Home tab.

3. Click the **Close Master View** button on the Ribbon.

Make changes to the footer

Inserting the Date and Time

You can insert the date and time into your presentation. For example, you might want today's date to appear in a stock market quote. You can insert the date and time on every slide, notes page or handout, or only on a specific slide. To insert the date and time on every page, you place it in a placeholder on the slide master. To insert the date and time only on a specific page, you insert it in a text box on the slide you want. You can set the date and time to automatically update to your computer's clock or stay fixed until you change it.

Insert the Date and Time on a Specific Slide

1. Click to place the insertion point in the text object where you want to insert the date and time.

2. Click the **Insert** tab.

3. Click the **Date & Time** button.

4. Click the date or time format you want.

5. To have the date and time automatically update, select the **Update automatically** check box.

6. To change the default date and time format, click **Default**, and then click **Yes** to confirm.

7. Click **OK**.

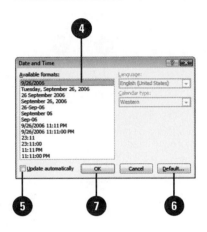

Insert the Date and Time on Slides, Notes, and Handouts

1. Click the **Insert** tab.

2. Click the **Date & Time** button.

3. Click the **Slide** or **Notes and Handouts** tab.

4. Click the **Date and time** check box.

5. Click the **Update automatically** or **Fixed** option, and then specify or select the format you want.

6. Click **Apply** to apply your selections to the current slide, or click **Apply to All** to apply the selections to all slides.

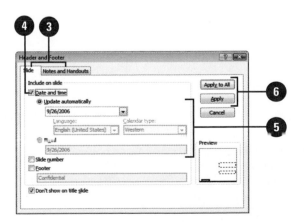

Inserting Slide Numbers

You can insert slide numbers into the text of your presentation. When you insert slide numbers, PowerPoint keeps track of your slide numbers for you. You can insert slide numbers on every slide or only on a specific slide. To insert a slide number on every page, you place it in a placeholder on the slide master. In the Slide Master view, PowerPoint inserts a code <#> for the slide number. When you view slides in other views, the slide number is shown. To insert a slide number only on a specific page, you insert it in a text box on the slide you want. You can even start numbering with a page number other than one.

Insert Slide Numbering

1. Select the slide in which you want to insert a slide number.

   ◆ **For a Master.** Click the **View** tab, and then click the **Slide Master**, **Handout Master**, or **Notes Master** button.

2. Click to place the insertion point in the text object where you want to insert the current slide number.

3. Click the **Insert** tab.

4. Click the **Insert Slide Number** button.

   The <#> symbol appears in the text.

5. To set a start number, click the master tab, click the **Page Setup** button, click the **Number slides from** up or down arrow to set the number, and then click **OK**.

6. To close the slide master, click the master tab, and then click **Close Master View** button.

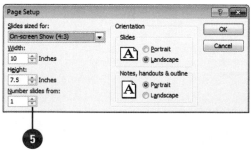

Did You Know?

Insert slide numbers on slides, notes, and handout using defaults placeholders. Click the Insert tab, click the Insert Slide Number button, click the Slide or Notes And Handouts tab, select the Slide Number check box, and then click Apply or Apply To All.

Previewing Slides

Slide preview allows you to see how your presentation will look before you print it. While in slide preview, you have the option of switching between various views. If you are using a black and white printer, you can preview your color slides in pure black and white or grayscale in print preview to verify that they will be legible when you print them.

Preview Slides in Pure Black and White or Grayscale

1. Click the **View** tab.

2. Click the **Pure Black and White** or **Grayscale** button.

3. On the Black and White or Grayscale tab, click the button with the specific color method you want to use.

4. When you're done, click the **Back To Color View** button.

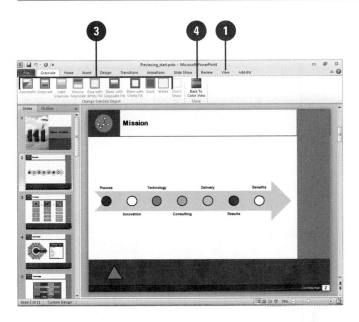

Print Preview a Presentation

1. To preview an outline, format your outline the way you want it to be in Outline pane.

2. Click the **File** tab, and then click **Print**.

3. Select the printer and print options you want.

   ◆ **Color/Grayscale.** Select **Color**, **Grayscale**, or **Pure Black and White**.

4. To preview slides, click the **Previous Slide** or **Next Slide** button.

5. To zoom slides, click the **Zoom In** or **Zoom Out** button, or drag the **Zoom** slider.

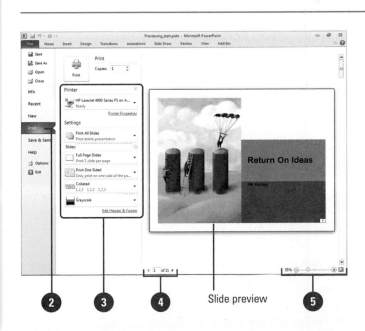

Slide preview

Printing a Presentation

You can print all the elements of your presentation—the slides, outline, notes, and handouts—in either color or black and white. PowerPoint makes it easy to print your presentation using the Print screen (**New!**); it detects the type of printer that you choose—either color or black and white—and then prints the appropriate version of the presentation. When you print an outline, PowerPoint prints the presentation outline as shown in Outline view. What you see in the Outline pane is what you get on the printout. PowerPoint prints an outline with formatting according to the current view setting. Set your formatting to display only slide titles or all of the text levels, and choose to display the outline with or without formatting.

Print a Presentation

1. To print an outline, format your outline the way you want it to be printed in Outline pane.

   ◆ Display with or without formatting. Right-click the outline, and then click **Show Text Formatting**.

2. Click the **File** tab, and then click **Print**.

3. Click the **Printer** list arrow, and then select a printer.

4. Click the list arrows to select the print options you want:

   ◆ Print Range. Select **Print All Slides**, **Print Current Slide**, or **Custom Range**. You can also select a custom show or **Print Hidden Slides**.

   ◆ Print What. Select **Full Page Slides**, **Notes Pages**, or **Outline**. You can also select **Frame Slides**, **Scale to Fit Paper**, **High Quality**, or **Print Comments and Ink Marks**.

   ◆ Print Side. Select **Print One Sided** or **Print on Both Sides**.

   ◆ Collated. Select **Collated** or **Uncollated**.

   ◆ Color/Grayscale. Select **Color**, **Grayscale**, or **Pure Black and White**.

5. Click **Print**.

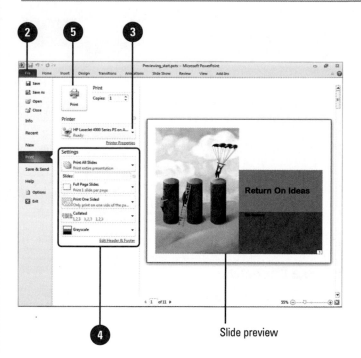

Slide preview

Creating a Database with Access

Introduction

Microsoft Office Access 2010 is a database program that allows you to:

- Store an almost limitless amount of information.
- Organize information in a way that makes sense for how you work.
- Retrieve information based on selection criteria you specify.
- Create forms that make it easier to enter information.
- Generate meaningful and insightful reports that can combine data, text, graphics, and other objects.

Microsoft Office Access helps you start working with databases right away by providing template database applications you can use to store your own personal or business data. Access also offers a few samples that aid you in creating common business databases. These sample databases may give you some ideas for designing your own database for storing types of data not covered by the existing databases.

When you are working with an existing database, however, you don't need to worry about the complexities of database design. You just need to know how to move around the database you are using. The tasks that you are likely to perform with an existing database include entering and viewing data or subsets of data, creating and printing reports, and working efficiently with all the windows in front of you.

What You'll Do

Understanding How Databases Store Data

Storing Data on a Computer

Some lists can serve a much more useful purpose when stored on a computer. For example, the names, addresses, and phone numbers you jot down on cards or in a paper address book are only used when you have the paper list in your hand. Suppose you currently store names and addresses on cards. All the information about a particular person is stored in one place.

If you store that list on a computer, however, you can do much more with it than just refer to it. For example, you can generate lists of your most important phone numbers to put next to every phone in the house, you can print mailing labels for greeting cards, you can create lists of this month's birthdays, and so on.

There are a number of ways to store lists on a computer. For example, you can store a list in a Microsoft Word table or on a Microsoft Excel spreadsheet.

If you place this information in a Word table or on an Excel spreadsheet, you are faced with a problem: you end up repeating some of the information. Consider what happens if a family moves or a last name is changed. You have to ensure that information is updated everywhere it's stored. For a small list that might not matter, but for a large list with information that requires constant updating (such as an address list), it is a huge task to keep data up-to-date in this way.

Storing Data in a Database

If, on the other hand, you save address information in an Access database, you can ensure that each piece of information is entered only once.

An Access database consists of objects, such as tables, forms, queries, reports, pages, macros, and modules.

- A **table** is a collection of related information about a topic, such as names and addresses. A table consists of fields and records. A field stores each piece of information in a table, such as first name, last name, or address. A record is a collection of all the fields for one person.

- A **form** provides an easy way to view and enter information into a database. Typically, forms display one record at a time.

- A **query** is a method to find information in a database. The information you find with a query is based on conditions you specify.

- **Reports** are documents that summarize information from the database.

- **Pages** enable you to access a database on the Internet using a Web browser; only backwards compatible for Access 2003 databases; not available in Access 2007-2010.

- A **macro** saves you time by automating a series of actions into one action.

- **Modules** are programs you create in a programming language called Visual Basic for Applications (VBA), which extend the functionality of a database.

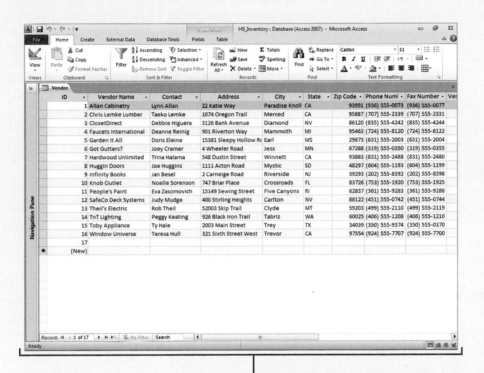

A database table with fields and records

Frequently Asked Questions

What is a Microsoft Access Project?

A Microsoft Office Access project is an Access data file (.adp) that provides access to a Microsoft SQL Server database through the OLE DB component architecture, which provides network and Internet access to many types of data sources. An Access project is called a project because it contains only code-based or HTML-based database objects: forms, reports, macros, and modules. Unlike an Access database, an Access project doesn't contain any data or data objects, such as tables, views, database diagrams, stored procedures, or user-defined functions. Working with an Access project is virtually the same as working with an Access database, except you need to connect to an SQL Server database, which stores the data.

Creating a Database

You can use a template to create a database, or you can create a custom database from scratch. The Access database templates (**New!**) help you create databases suited to your specific needs. Each template provides a complete out-of-the-box database with predefined fields, tables, queries, reports, and forms. If you can't find the template you want, additional templates are available online at Office.com (**New!**). If you need a custom database, you create a blank database or blank web database (**New!**), and then you can create the tables, forms, and reports that make up the inner parts of the database. When you create a database, you need to assign a name and location to your database. You can save an Access database in the .mdb format (for Access 2000 or 2002-2003) or .accdb format (for Access 2007-2010).

Create a Blank Database

1 Start Access, or click the **File** tab and then click **New**.

   The New screen opens, displaying templates and recently opened databases.

2 Click **Blank Database** or **Blank Web Database**.

3 Click the **Browse** button, click the **Save in** list arrow, select the location where you want to save the new database, select an Access database format, and then click **OK**.

4 Type in a name for the database.

5 Click **Create**.

6 To close the database, click the **Close** button in the database window or click the **File** tab, and then click **Close Database**.

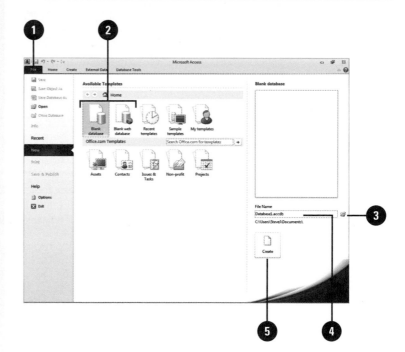

Did You Know?

You can open a sample database. Click the File tab, click New, click Sample Templates, click a sample database from the list, and then click Create or Download.

Create a Database Using a Template

1. Start Access, or click the **File** tab and then click **New**.

   The New screen opens, displaying templates and recently opened databases.

2. Click a template category (**New!**): Recent templates, Sample templates, My templates, or template folders on Office.com.

3. Click the template you want.

4. Click the **Browse** button, click the **Save in** list arrow, select the location where you want to save the new database, select an Access database format, and then click **OK**.

5. Type in a name for the database.

6. Click **Create** or **Download** for those on the Web.

7. If a security warning appears, click **Enable Content**.

8. To close the database, click the **Close** button in the database window or click the **File** tab, and then click **Close Database**.

Did You Know?

You can open Access with the last used database. Click the File tab, click Options, click Client Settings in the left pane, select the Open Last Used Database When Access Starts check box, and then click OK.

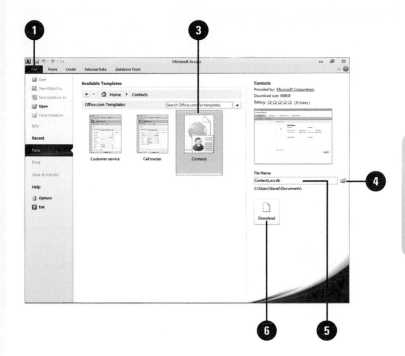

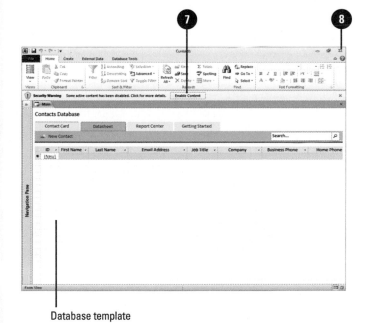

Database template

Viewing the Access Window

When you open a database, the Access program window opens and displays an improved tab-based user interface known as the Ribbon, the Navigation pane and one or more tabbed documents for the database. The Navigation pane displays objects—such as tables, queries, forms, reports, and macros—that make up the database. The tabbed documents are the open objects in the database. Typically, you have a main tab—previously known as a switchboard—that acts like a home page, where you perform tasks and get started with the database.

Parts of the Access Window

- The **database title bar** displays the name of the open database and the database version.

- The **Ribbon** contains tabs that represent groups of related commands.

- The **Quick Access Toolbar** displays the most needed buttons that you can click to carry out commands.

- The **Navigation pane** displays database objects, which replaces the Database window from earlier versions of Access.

- The **tabbed documents** displays tables, queries, forms, reports, and macros.

- The **View selector** displays view buttons.

- The **Status bar** displays information about the items you click or the actions you take.

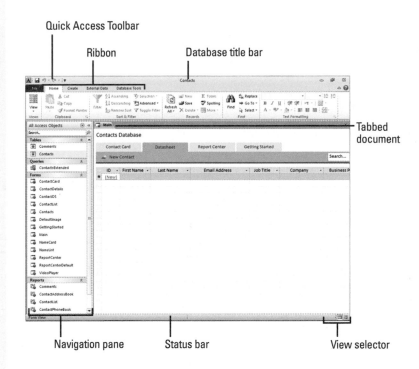

Quick Access Toolbar

Ribbon

Database title bar

Tabbed document

Navigation pane

Status bar

View selector

Did You Know?

You can customize Access startup.
Click the File tab, click Options, click Current Database in the left pane, set the options you want under Applications Options, and then click OK. Close and open the database to see the new startup.

Changing Database Display Options

Access Options allows you to personalize what appears in the Access window. You can customize the way Access appears when you work on the currently opened database. You can specify a title and select an icon to create a database application, and select the form—for a regular or web (**New!**) database—you want to display on startup. To customize the way you work with database objects, you can choose to display them as tabbed documents for easy access or overlapping windows for a custom interface. You can also display Layout view, which allows you to make design changes while you browse a form or report.

Change Current Database Display Options

1. Open the database you want to customize.

2. Click the **File** tab, and then click **Options**.

3. In the left pane, click **Current Database**.

4. Enter a database application title and then click **Browse** to select an application icon (optional).

5. Click the **Display Form** list arrow and **Web Display Form** list arrow, and then select the form object you want to display on startup.

6. Select or clear any of the check boxes to change the display options you want.

   ◆ **Display Status Bar.** Set to display the Status bar. (Default on).

   ◆ **Document Window Options**. Click the Overlapping windows or Tabbed documents option to hide or show tabs.

   ◆ **Enable Layout View for this database**. (Default on).

   ◆ **Enable design changes for tables in Datasheet view for this database.** (Default on).

7. Click **OK**.

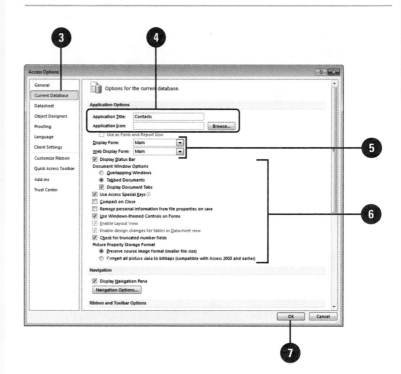

Viewing Database Objects

When you open an existing database, the first thing you usually see is the Database window. Access databases can contain seven database object types, which you use to build a database application. The table on the facing page identifies the database objects that you use when creating a database. To work with database objects, you need to open the Navigation pane, which replaces the Database window used in earlier versions of Access, and can also replace switchboards using custom categories. The Navigation pane divides database objects into categories and includes a file tab at the top, which you can use to set or change the object categories. The categories appear on the Navigation pane as bars, which you can expand or close.

View Database Objects in the Navigation Pane

1. Open the database you want to use.

   If no special startup options are specified, the Database window opens automatically.

2. To open or close the Navigation pane, click the **Shutter Bar Open/Close button**.

   TIMESAVER *Press F11 to open and close the Navigation pane.*

3. To expand or close a group, click the up or down arrows.

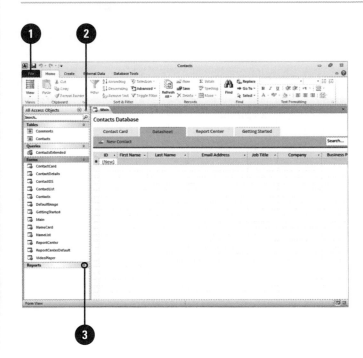

Did You Know?

You can switch between Datasheet and Design view. For many of the tasks you do in Access, you will switch back and forth between Design and Datasheet view. In Design view, you format and set controls for queries, reports, forms, or tables that you are creating from scratch or modifying from an original design. In Datasheet view, you observe the result of the modifications you have made in Design view. To switch between the two, click the View button on the Home tab, and then select the appropriate view.

View a List of Database Objects

① Open the database whose objects you want to view.

② Click the **Navigation pane file** tab.

The upper section of the file tab displays categories and the lower section displays groups.

◆ **Categories.** Displays the predefined and custom categories for the open database.

◆ **Groups.** Displays the predefined and custom groups for the selected category. Groups change as you select different categories.

The title of the file tab changes as you select categories and groups.

③ Click a category, and/or then click a group.

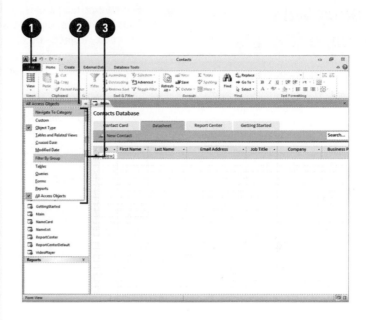

Did You Know?

You can display and use a Search box to find objects. Right-click a blank area in the Navigation pane at the bottom, and then click Search Box to display it. Type part or all of the object name. As you type, the Navigation pane hides any groups that do not contain objects with a match. When you're done, click the Search button. Delete the text or click the Clear Search String button to restore any hidden groups.

You can prevent the Navigation pane from appearing by default. Click the File tab, click Options, click Current Database in the left pane, clear the Display Navigation Pane check box, and then click OK.

Database Objects

Database Object	Description
Tables	Grids that store related information, such as a list of customer addresses.
Queries	A question you ask a database to help locate specific information.
Forms	A window that is designed to help you enter information easily and accurately.
Reports	Summaries of information that are designed to be readable and accessible.
Pages	Separate files outside the Access data base in HTML format that can be placed on the Web to facilitate data sharing with the world-wide Internet community; backwards compatible for Access 2003, not available in Access 2007-2010.
Macros	Stored series of commands that carry out an action.
Modules	Programs you can write using Microsoft Visual Basic.

Working with Database Objects

The Navigation pane is the container for all the objects in a database. These database objects work together to help you store and manage your data. Objects are organized into categories by object type in the Navigation pane. You can open, create, hide, group, rename, and delete database objects. If the predefined categories and groups don't meet your needs, you can create custom groups. You can create a simple object or a combination one based on the currently active object. For example, if a table is active and you click the Form button, Access creates a new form based on the active table.

Manage Database Objects

◆ **Open.** Double-click the object to open it for use, or right-click the object, and then click Design View to work with the object's design.

◆ **Create.** Click the Create tab, click the button (Application Parts (**New!**), Table, Form, Report, Query, or Macro) with the type of object you want. To create an object based on another, select the object before you click a button on the Create tab.

◆ **Delete.** Right-click the object, and then click Delete.

◆ **Rename.** Right-click the object, click Rename, type a new name, and then press Enter.

◆ **Group.** Right-click the group header, and then select an option, such as Rename or Delete.

◆ **Hide** or **Unhide.** Right-click the object, and then click Hide in this Group or click Unhide this Group.

◆ **Import.** Right-click a table, point to Import, select the object type (a database table, text file, or Excel workbook), and then complete the wizard.

◆ **Close.** Click the Close button in the upper-right corner of the object.

Create tab

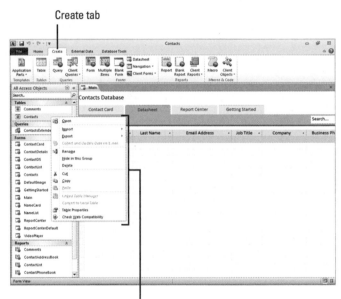

Right-click an object to perform management operations

Customize the Navigation Pane

1. Right-click a blank area of the Navigation pane, and then click **Navigation Options**.

2. Click a category, and then select or clear the item check boxes in Groups you want to show or hide.

3. To add, delete or rename a custom category, click **Add Item** and type a name, or select a custom category, and click **Rename Item** or **Delete Item**, or use **Up** or **Down** buttons to change order.

4. To create or change a group, click **Add Group** and type a name, or select a group and click **Rename Group** or **Delete Group**, or use **Up** or **Down** buttons to change order.

5. Select or clear check boxes to change the options you want.

   ◆ **Show Hidden Objects.** Select to show hidden objects as semi-transparent. (Default off).

   ◆ **Show System Objects**. Select to show system objects, such as system tables. (Default off).

   ◆ **Show Search Bar**. (Default off).

6. Click the **Single-click** or **Double-click** option to open objects.

7. Click **OK**.

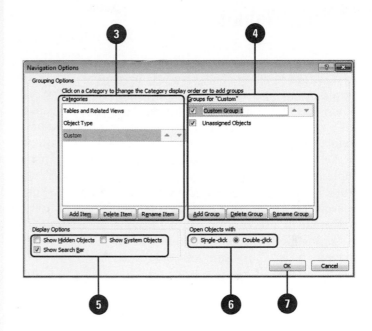

Did You Know?

You can use AutoCorrect to rename objects. When you rename an object, the Name AutoCorrect feature automatically fixes other Access objects that use the object you just renamed. Click the File tab, click Options, click Current Database in the left pane, and then select the Name AutoCorrect options you want.

Planning Tables

Although you can always make changes to your database when necessary, a little planning before you begin can save time later on. When you plan a database, consider how you will use the data. What kind of data are you collecting? What kind of data are you entering? How are data values related to one another? Can your data be organized into separate, smaller groups? What kinds of safeguards can you create to ensure that errors do not creep into your data? As you consider these questions, you should apply the answers as you structure your database.

Plan Tables

Tables are one of the fundamental building blocks of a database. Database planning begins with deciding how many and what kinds of tables your database will contain. Consider organizing your database information into several tables—each one containing fields related to a specific topic—rather than one large table containing fields for a large variety of topics. For example, you could create a Customers table that contains only customer information and an Orders table that contains only order information. By focusing each table on a single task, you greatly simplify the structure of those tables and make them easier to modify later on.

Choose Data Types

When you create a table, you must decide what fields to include and the appropriate format for those fields. Access allows you to assign a data type to a field, a format that defines the kind of data the field can accept. Access provides a wide variety of data types, ranging from text and number formats to object-based formats for images, sound, video clips, and embedded macros. Choosing the correct data type helps you manage your data and reduces the possibility of data-entry errors. To make it easier to create fields, Access provides the Add New Field column in Datasheet view so you can quickly enter a field name. If you already have a defined field in the database that you want to use again, you can drag the existing field from the Field List pane on to the datasheet and Access automatically creates a relationship or steps you through the process. You can also use field templates for creating new fields. A **field template** is a design for a field, complete with a name, data type, length, and predefined properties. You can drag field templates on to the datasheet. Field templates are XSD based so that you can set up standard definitions for shared use. If you create a field for numbers, you can use the Totals row to calculate values using functions such as sum, count, average, maximum, minimum, standard deviation, or variance.

Specify a Primary Key

You should also identify which field or fields are the table's primary keys. Primary keys are those fields whose values uniquely identify each record in the table. A social security number field in a personnel table could be used as a primary key, since each employee has a unique social security number. A table with time-ordered data might have two primary keys—a date field and a time field (hours and minutes), which together uniquely identify an exact moment in time. Although primary keys are not required, using them is one way of removing the possibility of duplicate records existing within your tables.

Creating a Table by Entering Data

Access allows you to display many of its objects in multiple viewing modes. Datasheet view displays the data in your tables, queries, forms, and reports. Design view displays options for designing your Access objects. You can create a new table in both views. When you create a table in Datasheet view, you enter data and Access creates the table as you type. Access determines the data type of each field based on the data you enter (**New!**). The Click to Add column shows you where to add a new field. You can also paste data from Microsoft Excel tables into a new database and Access recognizes the data types (**New!**).

Enter Data to Create a Table

1. Click the **Create** tab.

2. Click the **Table** button.

3. Enter the data.

   Press Tab to move from field to field or click in a cell.

4. To change a field name, click the *Click to Add* field name, type the new name, and then press Enter.

5. Click the **Save** button on the Quick Access Toolbar.

6. Type a table name.

7. Click **OK**.

8. To have Access set the primary key, click **Yes**.

9. Click the **Close** button in the Table window.

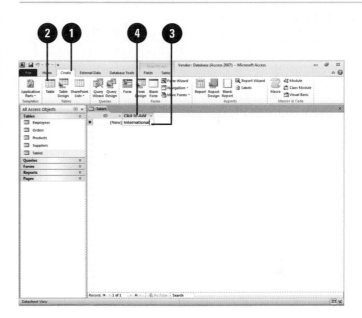

Did You Know?

You can select or resize a column or row like in Excel. To select a column or row in a table, click the Column or Row selector. To resize a column or row, drag the border between the Column or Row selector. You can also click the Home tab, and then click the More button to access commands to resize columns and rows.

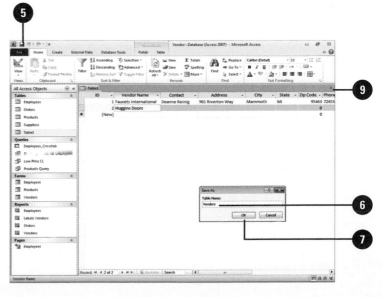

Creating an Application Part Using a Template

An application part template (**New!**) is a predefined portion of a database, such as a table or form, or an entire database application that you can quickly insert and use in a database. Access provides several templates including: Comments, Contacts, Issues, Tasks, Users, and Blank Forms. You can use the Create tab to quickly insert an application part template. When you insert an application part, such as Contacts, you get a table, form, and report, and the option to create a relationship. After you insert an application part, you can add and change fields to meet your own needs, and then name and save it in the database.

Create an Application Part Using a Template

1. Click the **Create** tab.

2. Click the **Application Parts** button.

3. Click a template (**Blank Forms and Quick Starts: Comments**, **Contacts**, **Issues**, **Tasks**, or **Users**) you want.

4. Follow the Create Relationship wizard as prompted to create a simple relationship.

5. Add information and data to the template.

6. When you're done, click the **Close** button in the window.

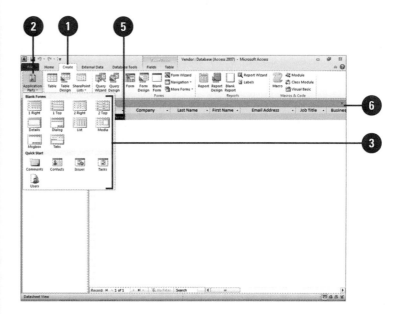

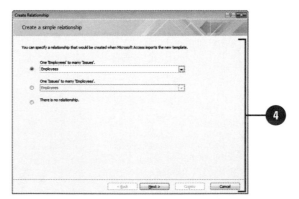

Did You Know?

You can insert a subdatasheet in a table. In the Datasheet view of a table, click the Home tab, click the More button, point to Subdatasheet, and then click Subdatasheet. Click the Tables tab, click the table, specify the foreign key in the Link Child Fields box and the primary key in the Link Master Fields box, and then click OK.

You can view a subdatasheet. In the Datasheet view of a table, click the plus box next to the record to display the subdatasheet. Click the minus box to hide the subdatasheet.

Creating a Table Using SharePoint

If you have access to a Microsoft Office SharePoint Services site, you can import a SharePoint list into an Access database as a table. A SharePoint Services site is a server application that uses Web site templates to create, organize, and share information. To access a SharePoint Services site, you might need access privileges. See your network administrator for a user name and password. Access provides several SharePoint list table templates including: Contacts, Tasks, Issues, Events, Custom, and Existing SharePoint List.

Create a Table Using a SharePoint List

1. Click the **Create** tab.

2. Click the **SharePoint Lists** button.

3. Click the SharePoint list template (**Contacts**, **Tasks**, **Issues**, **Events**, **Custom**, or **Existing SharePoint List**) you want.

4. Enter a SharePoint site address or select an existing one.

5. Type a name and description.

6. To open the list, select the **Open the list when finished** check box.

7. Click **OK**.

8. When you're done, click the **Close** button in the Table window.

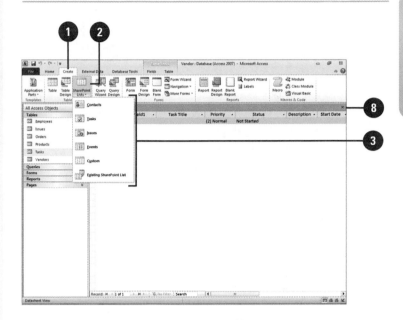

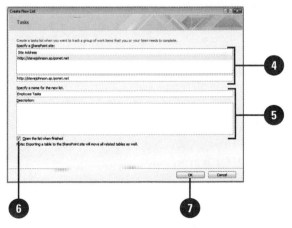

Did You Know?

You can create a field with multiple values. Access supports multivalue fields. For example, you can assign a field, such as a task assignment field, to more than one person. This can be helpful when you work with multivalue field types used in a SharePoint site.

Working with a Table

A **database** is made up of groups of fields organized into tables. A **field** is a specific category of information, such as a name or a product. Related fields are grouped in tables. You usually enter data into fields one entity at a time (one customer at a time, one product at a time, and so on). Access stores all the data for a single entity in a record. You can view a table in Datasheet or Design view. Design view allows you to work with your table's fields. Datasheet view shows a grid of fields and records. The fields appear as columns and the records as rows. The first field in a table is often an **AutoNumber** field, which Access uses to assign a unique number to each record. You can't select or change this value.

Enter a New Record and Move Around in a Table

1. In the Navigation pane, double-click the table you want to open.

2. Click the **New Record** button.

3. Press Tab to accept the AutoNumber entry.

4. Enter the data. If you make a typing mistake, press Backspace.

5. Press Tab to move to the next field or Shift+Tab to move to the previous field.

6. When you reach the end of the record, click one of the Record buttons:

   ◆ **First Record** button.

   ◆ **Previous Record** button.

   ◆ **Specific Record** box. Enter a record number in the box, and then press Enter.

   ◆ **Next Record** button.

   ◆ **Last Record** button.

   TIMESAVER *You can also use buttons in the Records group on the Home tab to perform the same commands.*

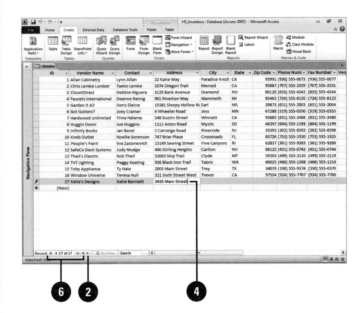

Find Records

1. In the Navigation pane, double-click the table you want to open.

2. If you want, click in the table field in which you want to search.

3. Click the **Home** tab, and then click the **Find** button.

4. Type the text you want to find.

5. Click the **Look In** list arrow, and then select a search location.

6. Click the **Match** list arrow, and then select an option.

7. Click the **Search** list arrow, and then select a search direction.

8. To match upper and lower case, select the **Match Case** check box.

9. Click **Find Next**.

10. When you're done, click **Cancel**.

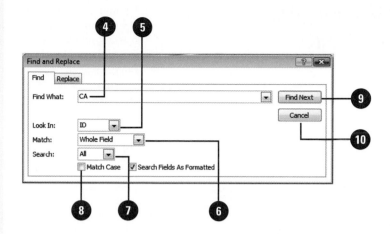

Delete a Record from a Table

1. In the Navigation pane, double-click the table you want to open.

2. Click the row selectors you want.

3. Click the **Home** tab.

4. Click the **Delete** button, and then click **Yes** to confirm.

> **TIMESAVER** *Right-click a row selector, and then click Delete Record.*

Did You Know?

You might want to delete related data. When you delete a record, such as a supplier, you might want to also delete the products the supplier supplies.

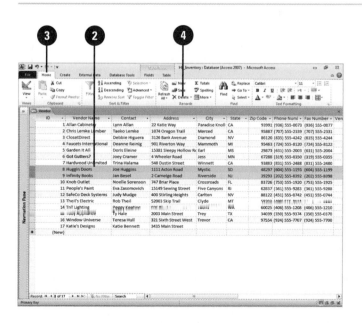

Importing Data into Tables

You can create new tables from other Access databases by importing and linking tables. When you import a table, you copy data from a table in one Access database and place it in a new table in your database. When you link a table, the data stays in its original location, but you can display and access that data from within your database. If data in the original database changes, the changes will appear in your linked database, too. You can also import data from other programs.

Import a Table from a Database

1. Click the **External Data** tab.

2. Click the **Import Access Database** button.

3. Click **Browse**, locate and select the database file that contains the data you want to import, and then click **Open**.

4. Click the import option you want.

5. Click **OK**.

6. Click the tables you want to import. To deselect a table, click the table again.

7. Click **OK**.

8. To save import steps, select the **Save import steps** check box, enter a name and description, and then click **Save Import**.

   Otherwise, click **Close**.

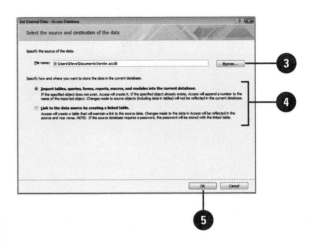

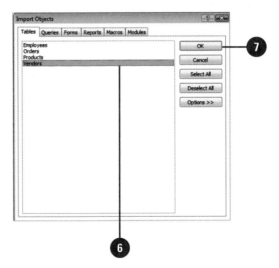

Working with a Table in Design View

Most Access objects are displayed in Design view, which allows you to work with the underlying structure of your tables, queries, forms, and reports. To create a new table in Design view, you define the fields that will comprise the table before you enter any data. In Design view for tables, each row corresponds to a field. You can edit, insert, and delete fields in your database tables in Design view. You insert a field by adding a row, while you delete a field by removing a row. You can also change field order by dragging a row selector to a new position.

Create or Modify a Table in Design View

1. Click the **Create** tab, and then click the **Table Design** button, or select the table you want to modify in the Navigation pane, and then click the **Design View** button.

2. Click in a **Field Name** cell, and then type a modified field name.

3. Click in a **Data Type** cell, click the Data Type list arrow, and then click a data type.

4. Click in a **Description** cell, and then type a description. If the **Property Update Options** button appears, select an option, if necessary.

5. To insert a field, click the row selector below where you want the field, and then click the **Insert Rows** button on the Ribbon.

6. To delete a field, click the row selector for the field you want to delete, and then click the **Delete Rows** button on the Ribbon.

7. Click the **Save** button on the Quick Access Toolbar, and then if necessary, enter a table name and click **OK**.

8. When you're done, click the **Close** button in the Table window.

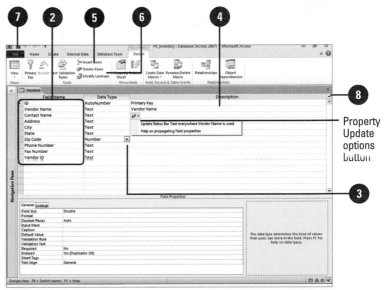

Property Update options button

Working with Fields

To make it easier to create fields, Access provides the Add New Field column in Datasheet view so you can quickly enter a field name. If you already have a defined field in the database that you want to use again, you can drag the existing field from the Field List pane on to the datasheet and Access automatically creates a relationship or steps you through the process. You can also use buttons on the Fields tab under Table Tools for creating new fields. If you create a field for numbers, you can use the Totals row to calculate values using functions such as sum, count, average, maximum, minimum, standard deviation, or variance. To help you find and choose a date, the Date/Time field automatically displays a calendar button.

Add and Delete Fields

1. In the Navigation pane, double-click the table you want to open.

2. Click the **Fields** tab under Table Tools.

3. Select the field next to where you want to insert a field.

4. To insert fields, use either of the following methods.

   ◆ **Add Common Fields.** In the Add & Delete group, use the field related buttons to insert the type of field you want.

   ◆ **Add Other Fields.** Click the **More Fields** button, and then select the type of field you want to insert.

   ◆ **Use the Field List pane.** Open the Field List pane, and then drag the field you want on to the datasheet between the headers of existing fields.

   ◆ **Delete Fields.** Select the field you want to delete, and then click the **Delete** button.

   ◆ **Hide and Unhide Fields.** Right-click a field, and then click **Hide Fields**. To unhide, right-click a field, and then click **Unhide Fields**.

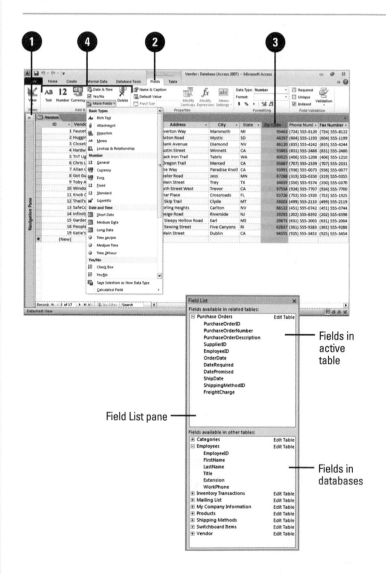

Fields in active table

Field List pane

Fields in databases

Use the Total Row to Perform a Calculation

1. In the Navigation pane, double-click the table you want to open.

2. Click the field with the numbers you want to use in a calculation.

3. Click the **Home** tab.

4. Click the **Totals** button to insert the Totals row at the bottom of the table.

5. Click the Total row field in the column with the numbers you want to use in a calculation.

6. Click the list arrow, and then select the function you want to use.

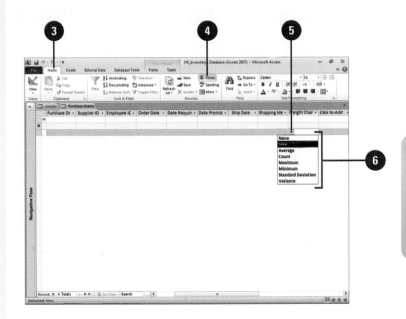

Find and Choose a Date

1. In the Navigation pane, double-click the table you want to open.

2. Select a date field.

   TROUBLE? *If the date field contains an input mask, the date picker doesn't appear.*

3. Click the calendar button.

4. Click the **Next** and **Previous** button to find the month you want, and then click the date you want.

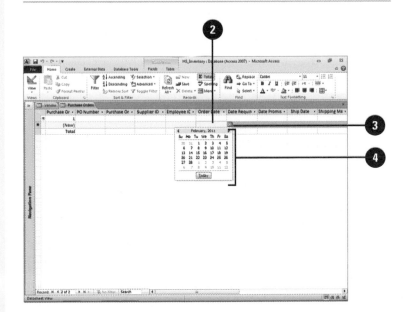

Did You Know?

You can use rich text in memo fields. Access supports rich text in the memo field. You can format text with formatting options. The rich text is stored in a compatible HTML-based format. In the field property, set the Text Format property to Rich Text.

Specifying Data Types and Field Properties

Access provides different **data types**— field formats that define the kind of data the field can accept—which cover a wide variety of data. When you choose a data type for a field, Access will accept data entered only in the format specified by the data type. Selecting the appropriate data type makes it easier for users to enter and retrieve information in the database tables. It also acts as a check against incorrect data being entered. For example, a field formatted to accept only numbers removes the possibility that a user will erroneously enter text into the field.

You can change the data type for a field even after you have entered data in it. However, you might need to perform a potentially lengthy process of converting or retyping the field's data when you save the table. If the data type in a field conflicts with a new data type setting, you may lose some or all of the data in the field.

Once you've selected a data type, you can begin to work with field properties. A **field property** is an attribute that defines the field's appearance or behavior in the database. The number of decimal places displayed in a numeric field is an example of a property that defines the field's appearance. A property that forces the user to enter data into a field rather than leave it blank controls that field's behavior. For the Date/Time field, a calendar button automatically appears next to the field to make it easy to find and choose a date. In Design view for tables, Access provides a list of field properties, called the **properties list**, for each data type.

Data Types

Data Type	Description
Text (default)	Text or combinations of text and numbers, as well as numbers that don't require calculations, such as phone numbers. Limited to 255 characters.
Memo	Text with rich text formatting options (in an HTML-based format).
Number	Numeric data used in mathematical calculations.
Date/Time	Date and time values for the years 100 through 9999. An automatic calendar for data picking appears next to a date field.
Currency	Currency values and numeric data used in mathematical calculations involving data with one to four decimal places. Values are accurate to 15 digits on the left side of the decimal separator.
AutoNumber	A unique sequential number (incremented by 1) or a random number. Access assigns whenever you add a new record to a table. AutoNumber fields can't be altered.
Yes/No	A field containing only one of two values (for example, Yes/No, True/False, On/Off).
OLE Object	An object linked to or embedded in an Access table.
Hyperlink	A link that, when clicked, takes the user to another file, a location in a file, or a site on the Web.
Attachment	A file stored in an Access table.
Calculated	A value calculated from data in the same table (**New!**).
Lookup Wizard	A wizard that helps you to create a field whose values are chosen from the values in another table, query, or list of values.

Changing Field Properties

After you create fields in a table, you can specify properties that define the field's appearance or behavior in the database. In Design view for tables, Access provides a list of field properties for each data type. The properties list changes depending on the data type. Some of the field text properties include Field Size, Format, Input Mask, Caption, Default Value, Validation Rule, Validation Text, Required, Allow Zero Length, and Smart Tags.

Change Field Properties

1. Display the table in Design view.

2. Click the field you want to change.

3. Click the field property box you want to change.

4. Type or change the value, or click the list arrow, and then select a value or option.

   TIMESAVER *You can also use buttons in the Data & Formatting group on the Datasheet tab under Table Tools to quickly change field properties.*

5. Click the **Save** button on the Quick Access Toolbar.

6. When you're done, click the **Close** button in the Table window.

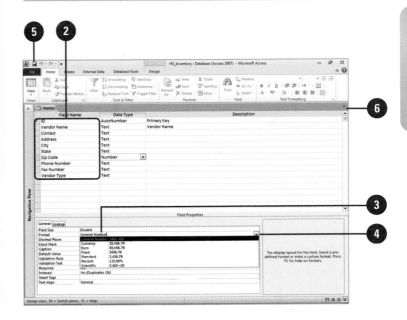

Did You Know?

You can set the number of decimal places. Another way to set the number of decimal places for numeric fields is to specify the number of decimal places in the Decimal Places box in the list of field properties.

You can use different formats for different values. Access allows you to specify different formats for positive, negative, zero, and null values within a single field. Use online Help for more information.

Creating Input Masks

An **input mask** allows you to control what values a database user can enter into a field. Input masks consist of literal characters, such as spaces, dots, parentheses, and placeholders. A **placeholder** is a text character, such as the underline symbol (_), that indicates where the user should insert values. An input mask for a phone number field might appear as follows: (_ _ _) _ _ _ - _ _ _ _. The parenthesis and dash characters act as literal characters, and the underscore character acts as a placeholder for the phone number values. Access provides several predefined input masks, which cover most situations, but you can create your own customized masks, if necessary. The **Input Mask Wizard** is available only for text and date fields. If you want to create an input mask for numeric fields, you must enter the formatting symbols yourself.

Specify an Input Mask

1. Display the table in Design view, and then click a field for which you want to specify an input mask.

2. Click the **Input Mask** box.

3. Click the **Build** button to start the **Input Mask Wizard**.

4. Scroll thru the predefined list to find an input mask form.

5. Type some sample values to see how the input mask affects your sample values, and then click **Next**.

6. If you change the input mask, type new formatting codes.

7. If you want to display a different placeholder, click the Placeholder list arrow, and select the placeholder you want to use.

8. Enter values to test the final version of your input mask, and then click **Next**.

9. Indicate whether you want to store the input mask symbols along with the data values.

10. Click **Next**, and then click **Finish**.

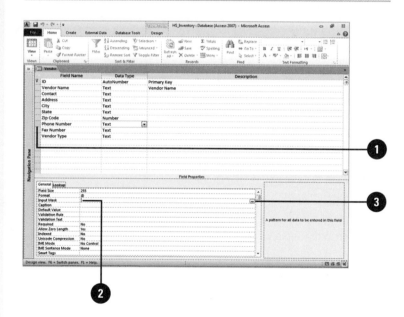

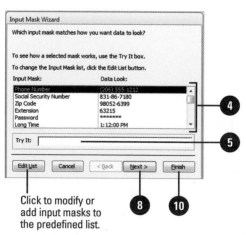

Click to modify or
add input masks to
the predefined list.

Creating a Lookup Field

The **Lookup Wizard** helps you create a field that displays either of two kinds of lists during data entry: a **Lookup** list that displays values looked up from an existing table or query, or a **Value** list that displays a fixed set of values you enter when you create the field. Because values are limited to a predefined list, using Lookup fields helps you avoid data entry errors in situations where only a limited number of possible values are allowed. The lists are not limited to a single column. You can include additional columns that could include descriptive information for the various choices in the list. However, only a single column, called the **bound column**, contains the data that is extracted from the list and placed into the Lookup field.

Create a Field Based on a Lookup List

1. Display the table in Design view, enter a new field, click the **Data Type** list arrow, and then click **Lookup Wizard**.

   You can also open a table in Datasheet view, select a field, click the **Datasheet** tab under Table Tools, and then click the **Lookup Column** button.

2. Click the **I will type in the values that I want** option button. Click **Next** to continue.

3. Specify the number of columns you want in the Value list.

4. Enter the values in the list. Resize the column widths, if necessary. Click **Next** to continue.

5. Choose which column will act as the bound column. Click **Next** to continue.

6. Enter a label for the Lookup column.

7. Click **Finish**.

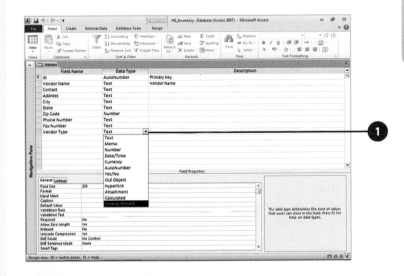

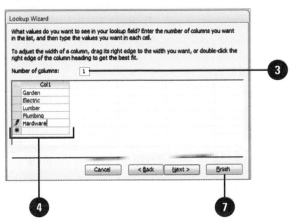

Planning Table Relationships

When you place data into separate tables, you need some way of merging this data together for forms and reports. You can do this by establishing table relationships that indicate how data in one table relates to data in another.

Specifying Common Fields

Data from several different tables is related through the use of common fields. A common field is a field existing in two or more tables, allowing you to match records from one table with records in the other tables. For example, the Customers table and the Orders table might both contain a Customer ID field, which functions as a primary key that identifies a specific customer. Using Customer ID as a common field allows you to generate reports containing information on both the customer and the orders the customer made. When you use a primary key as a common field, it is called a **foreign** key in the second table.

Building Table Relationships

Once you have a way of relating two tables with a common field, your next task is to express the nature of that relationship. There are three types of relationships: one-to-one, one-to-many, and many-to-many.

A table containing customer names and a second table containing customer addresses exist in a one-to-one relationship if each customer is limited to only one address. Similarly, a one-to-many relationship exists between the Customers table and the Orders table because a single customer could place several orders. In a one-to-many relationship like this, the "one" table is called the **primary table**, and the "many" table is called the **related table**.

Table Relationships

Choice	Description
One-to-one	Each record in one table is matched to only one record in a second table, and visa versa.
One-to-many	Each record in one table is matched to one or more records in a second table, but each record in the second table is matched to only one record in the first table.
Many-to-many	Each record in one table is matched to multiple records in a second table, and visa versa.

Finally, if you allow several customers to be recorded on a single order (as in the case of group purchases), a many-to-many relationship exists between the Customers and Orders tables.

Maintaining Referential Integrity

Table relationships must obey standards of **referential integrity**, a set of rules that control how you can delete or modify data between related tables. Referential integrity protects you from erroneously changing data in a primary table required by a related table. You can apply referential integrity when:

- The common field is the primary table's primary key.

- The related fields have the same format.

- Both tables belong to the same database.

Referential integrity places some limitations on you.

◆ Before adding a record to a related table, a matching record must already exist in the primary table.

◆ The value of the primary key in the primary table cannot be changed if matching records exist in a related table.

◆ A record in the primary table cannot be deleted if matching records exist in a related table.

Access can enforce these rules by cascading any changes across the related tables. For example, Access can automatically copy any changes to the common field across the related tables. Similarly, if a record is deleted in the primary table, Access can automatically delete related records in all other tables.

As you work through these issues of tables, fields, and table relationships, you will create a structure for your database that will be easier to manage and less prone to data-entry error.

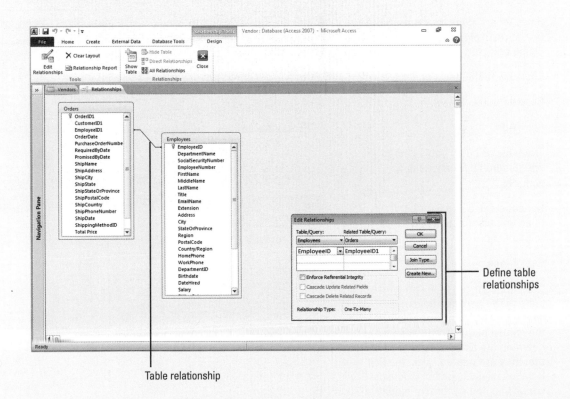

Table relationship

Define table relationships

Defining Table Relationships

You can define table relationships in several ways. After you create tables in your database, you can define table relationships between them. You can define and manage relationships using buttons on the Database Tools tab. This gives you control over your table relationships and also gives you a quick snapshot of all the relationships in your database. After you define a relationship, you can double-click the connection line to modify or add to the relationship.

Define Table Relationships

1. Click the **Database Tools** tab.

2. Click the **Relationships** button.

   If relationships are already established in your database, they appear in the Relationships window. In this window you can create additional table relationships.

3. If necessary, click the **Show Table** button to display the Show Table dialog box.

4. Click the **Tables** tab.

5. Click the table you want.

6. Click **Add**.

   The table or query you selected appears in the Relationships window.

   Repeat steps 5 and 6 for each table you want to use in a relationship.

7. Click **Close**.

8. Drag the common field in the first table to the common field in the second table. When you release the mouse button, a line appears between the two tables, signifying that they are related. Also, the Edit Relationships dialog box opens, in which you can confirm or modify the relationship.

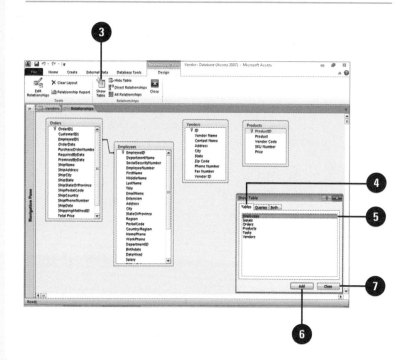

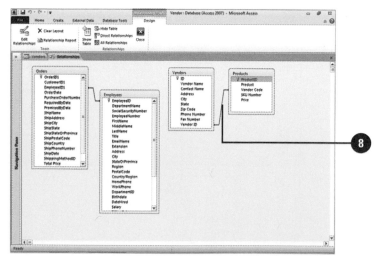

9 Click the **Join Type** button if you want to specify the join type. Click **OK** to return to the Edit Relationships dialog box.

10 Click **Create** to create the relationship.

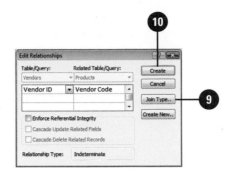

Did You Know?

You can view the relationships you want to see. Click the Design tab under Relationship Tools, click the Show Direct Relationships button to see tables that are directly related to each other. Click the All Relationships button to see all the relationships between all the tables and queries in your database.

You can print the Relationships window. Click the Design tab under Relationship Tools, click the Relationships Report button in the Relationships window you want to print, click the Print button, select the print settings you want, and then click OK.

You can delete a table relationship. In the Relationships window, right-click the line that joins the tables that you no longer want related to one another, and then click Delete. In the message box, click Yes to confirm that you want to permanently delete this relationship. You will not be able to undo this change.

Join Types

Join Types	Description
Include rows only where the joined fields from both tables are equal	Choose this option if you want to see one record in the second table for every record that appears in the first table. The number of records you see in the two tables will be the same.
Include ALL records from "xxx" (the first table) and only those records from "yyy" (the second table) where the joined fields are equal	Choose this option if you want to see all the records in the first table (even if there is no corresponding record in the second table) as well as the records from the second table in which the joined fields are the same in both tables. The number of records you see in the first table might be greater than the number of records in the second table.
Include ALL records from "yyy" (the second table) and only those records from the "xxx" (the first table) where the joined fields are equal	Choose this option if you want to see all the records in the second table (even if there is no corresponding record in the first table) as well as the records from the first table in which the joined fields are the same in both tables. The number of records you see in the second table might be greater than the number of records in the first table.

Ensuring Referential Integrity

Referential integrity in table relationships keeps users from accidentally deleting or changing related data. If a primary table contains a list of employees and related tables contain additional information about those employees, and an employee quits, his record is removed from the primary table. His records should also be removed in all related tables. Access allows you to change or delete related data, but only if these changes are cascaded through the series of related tables. You can do this by selecting the Cascade Update Related Fields and Cascade Delete Related Records check boxes in the Edit Relationships dialog box.

Ensure Referential Integrity

1 Click the **Database Tools** tab.

2 Click the **Relationships** button.

3 Click the join line for the relationship you want to work with.

4 Click the **Edit Relationships** button.

5 Click to select the **Enforce Referential Integrity** check box to ensure that referential integrity always exists between related tables in the database.

6 If you want changes to the primary field of the primary table automatically copied to the related field of the related table, click to select the **Cascade Update Related Fields** check box.

7 If you want Access to delete records in the related tables whenever records in the primary table are deleted, click to select the **Cascade Delete Related Records** check box.

8 Click **OK**.

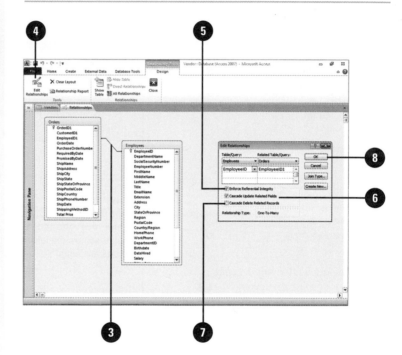

Locating and Managing Data with Access

Introduction

Once you've created a database, you'll want to be able to manage the records and information within that database. Microsoft Office Access 2010 gives you numerous ways to manage the records and information stored within the database.

Some of the techniques you might utilize to manage your databases could include sorting records in either ascending or descending order based on the contents of a specific field, and filtering certain records out of a database for a special mailing to certain clients.

Other techniques include creating queries to help you retrieve specific information about particular customers. A **query** is a description of the records you want to retrieve from a database. As the name implies, a query helps answer specific questions about the information in your database, for example, "Which customers have placed orders in the last six months?" or "Who sent us greeting cards over the holidays in the last two years?" The description of the records you want to retrieve identifies the names of the fields and the values they should contain; this description is called the selection criteria. With a query you can do the following:

◆ Focus on only the information you need by displaying only a few fields from a large table.

◆ Apply functions and other expressions to fields to arrive at calculated results.

◆ Summarize and group values from one table and display the result in another table.

◆ Retrieve information stored in multiple tables, even if the tables are not open.

Sorting Records

You can change the order in which records appear in a table, query results, forms, or reports by sorting the records. You can select a field and then sort the records by the values in that field in either ascending or descending order. Ascending order means that records appear in alphabetical order (for text fields), from most recent to later, (for date fields), or from smallest to largest (for numeric fields). In Descending order, the order is reversed. You might also want to sort records by more than one field; this is referred to as a **secondary sort**. For example, in a table containing information about products, you might need to view information about specific prices for each product. You can sort the records first by product and then, in records with the same product, sort the records by price.

Sort Records

① In the Datasheet view, display the table, query results, form, or report in which you want to sort records.

② To sort multiple columns, drag the column headers to rearrange them to be adjacent.

③ Click the column selector of the column you want to sort. To select another column, press and hold Shift, and then click the column selector.

④ Click the **Home** tab.

⑤ Click the **Sort Ascending** button (A to Z), or click the **Sort Descending** button (Z to A).

The list arrow displays an arrow icon indicating the field is sorted. The direction of the arrow indicates the sort direction.

⑥ To clear all sorts in the current table, click the **Remove Sort** button.

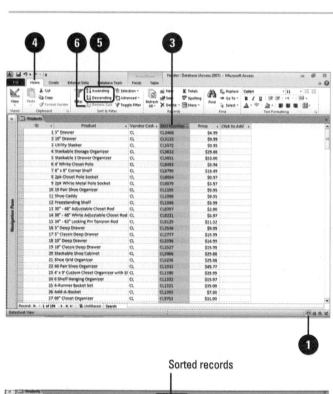

Sorted records

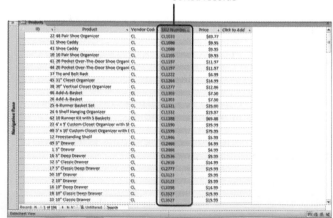

Filtering Out Records

Instead of displaying all the records in a table, you can use a **filter** to display only those records that you want to see. You can display records based on a specific value in one field or on multiple values in multiple fields. You can filter by selecting common filter options (**New!**) or Quick filter options (**New!**) for the field values on which to base the filter in Datasheet view or by using Filter By Form to help you create more complex filters involving multiple field values. After you apply a filter, Access displays only those records that match your specifications. You can remove a filter to return the datasheet to its original display.

Filter a Table

1. Display the table in Datasheet view.

2. Click the list arrow for the field you want to filter.

3. Select the most common filter options or any check boxes with the items that records must match in order to be included in the table.

4. To use built-in filters, point to **<Column Name> Filters**, and then select a filter option, such as Equals, Begins With, or Contains.

5. Repeat steps 2 through 4, as necessary, to filter out more records using additional fields, and then click **OK**, if necessary.

   The list arrow displays an icon indicating the field is filtered. Also, *Filter* appears in the Status bar.

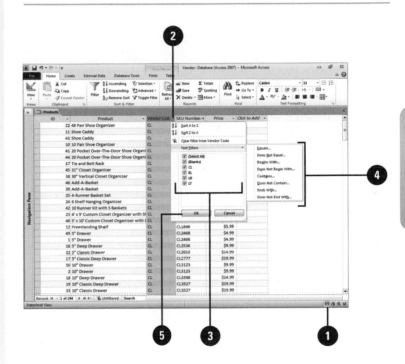

Did You Know?

You can quickly clear a filter from a table. Display the filtered table in Datasheet view, click the Toggle Filter button.

You can save a filter as a query. Display the filtered table in Datasheet view, click the Home tab, click the Advanced button, and then click Advanced Filter/Sort. Click the Save button on the Quick Access Toolbar, type a name, and then click OK.

Creating Complex Filters Using Forms

The Filter By Form feature allows you to create a more complex filter. Adding criteria on a particular tab in the form restricts the filter so that records must match all the criteria on the form for the records to be displayed; this is called an AND filter. To expand the filter to include more records, you can create an OR filter by specifying criteria on the subsequent Or tab in the Filter By Form grid. To be displayed, a record needs to match only the criteria specified on the Look For tab or the criteria specified on any one of the Or tabs.

Create an AND or OR Filter

1. Click the **Home** tab.

2. In Datasheet view, click the **Advanced** button, and then click the **Filter By Form**.

3. Click in the empty text box below the field you want to filter.

4. Click the list arrow, and then click the field value by which you want to filter the records.

5. For each field by which you want to filter, click the list arrow, and select the entry for your filter. Each new field in which you make a selection adds additional criteria that a record must match to be included.

6. If you want to establish Or criteria, click the **Or** tab at the bottom of the form to specify the additional criteria for the filter. If not, proceed to step 7.

7. Click the **Toggle Filter** button to turn the filter on or off.

Did You Know?

You can clear previous filters. If necessary, click the Home tab, click the Advanced button, and then click Clear All Filters to clear the previous filter.

Filter value

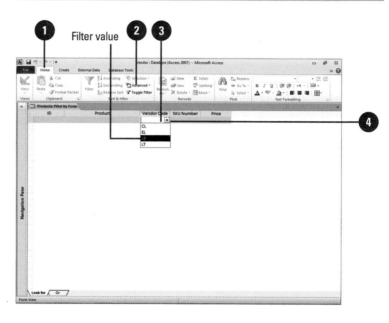

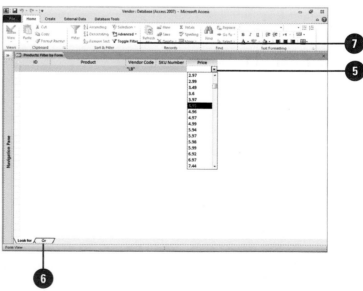

Understanding the Different Types of Queries

Access offers several types of queries that help you retrieve the information you need—select queries, crosstab queries, action queries, and parameter queries.

- A select query retrieves and displays records in the Table window in Datasheet view.

- A crosstab query displays summarized values (sums, counts, and averages) from one field in a table, and groups them by one set of fields listed down the left side of the datasheet and by another set of fields listed across the top of the datasheet.

- An action query performs operations on the records that match your criteria. There are four kinds of action queries that you can perform on one or more tables: delete queries delete matching records; update queries make changes to matching records; append queries add new records to the end of a table; and make-table queries create new tables based on matching records.

- A parameter query allows you to prompt for a single piece of information to use as selection criteria in the query. For example, instead of creating separate queries to retrieve customer information for each state in which you do business, you could create a parameter query that prompts the user to enter the name of a state, and then continues to retrieve those specific records from that state.

Creating Queries in Access

As with most database objects you create in Access, there are several ways to create a query. You can create a query from scratch or use a wizard to guide you through the process of creating a query.

With the Query Wizard, Access helps you create a simple query to retrieve the records you want. All queries you create and save are listed under the Queries bar in the Navigation pane. You can then double-click a query to run it and display the results. When you run a select query, the query results show only the selected fields for each record in the table that matches your selection criteria. Of course, once you have completed a query, you can further customize it in Design view. As always, you can begin creating your query in Design view without using the wizard at all. Queries are not limited to a single table. Your queries can encompass multiple tables as long as the database includes a field or fields that relate the tables to each other.

Query Wizard

Creating a Query Using a Wizard

A query is a simple question you ask a database to help you locate specific information within the database. When you create a query with the **Query Wizard**, you can specify the kind of query you want to create and type of records from a table or existing query you want to retrieve. The Query Wizard guides you through each step; all you do is answer a series of questions, and Access creates a query based on your responses. All queries you create are listed under the Queries bar in the Navigation pane.

Create a Simple Query Using the Query Wizard

1. Click the **Create** tab.

2. Click the **Query Wizard** button.

3. Click **Simple Query Wizard**, and then click **OK**.

4. Select a table or existing query.

5. Click to select the fields that you want included in the query.

6. Click **Next** to continue.

7. If you selected numeric or date fields in step 5, indicate whether you want to see detail or summary information.

8. If you choose Summary, click **Summary Options** to specify the calculation for each field, and then click **OK**.

9. Click **Next** to continue.

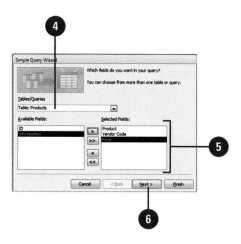

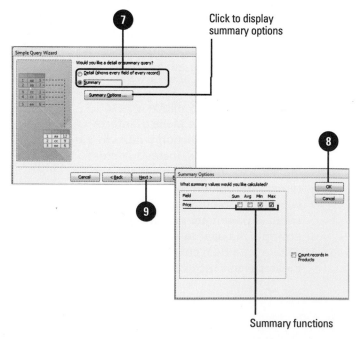

Click to display summary options

Summary functions

10 In the final wizard dialog box, type the name of the query.

11 Choose whether you want to view the results of the query or modify the query design in Design view.

12 Click **Finish**.

Did You Know?

You can include fields from another source. Click the Tables/Queries list arrow if you want to include a field from another source.

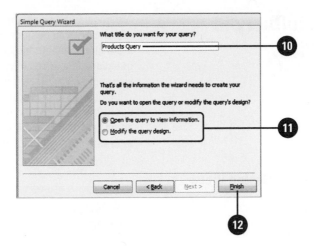

Name of query   Results of query

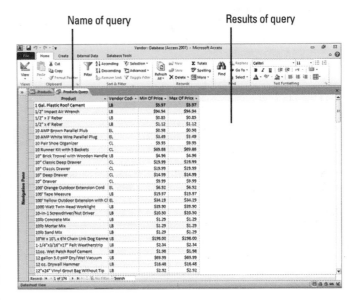

Creating a Query in Design View

Although a wizard can be a big help when you are first learning to create a query, you do not need to use a wizard. If you prefer, you can create a query without the help of a wizard. Instead of answering questions in a series of dialog boxes, you can start working in Design view right away. As you create a query, you can include more than one table or even another query in Design view. You can use comparison operators, such as >, <, or =, to compare field values to constants and other field values in the Criteria box. You can also use logical operators to create criteria combining several expressions, such as >1 AND <5.

Create a Query in Design View

1. Click the **Create** tab.

2. Click the **Query Design** button.

3. Select the table or query you want to use.

4. Click **Add**.

5. Repeat steps 3 and 4 for additional tables or queries, and then click **Close**.

6. Double-click each field you want to include in the query from the field list.

7. In the Design grid, enter any desired search criteria in the Criteria box.

8. Click the list arrow in the Sort box, and then specify a sort order.

9. Click the **Save** button, type a name for the query, and then click **OK**.

See Also

See "Performing Calculations in Queries" on page 415 for information on using the expression builder to add search criteria.

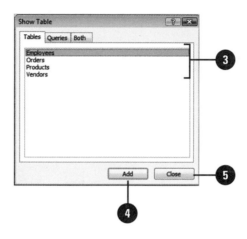

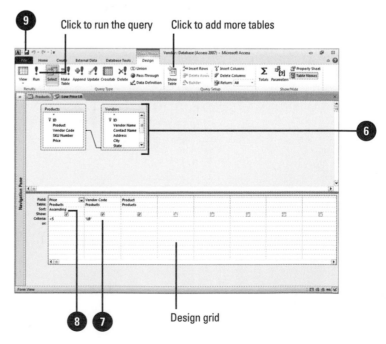

Click to run the query   Click to add more tables

Design grid

Getting Information with a Query

Access saves and lists the queries you create on the Queries bar in the Navigation pane. You can double-click a query to run it and display the results. When you run a query, the query results show only the selected fields for each record in the table that matches your selection criteria. After you run a query, you can close it for use again later.

Run a Query

1. In the Navigation pane, click the Queries bar to display the available queries in the database.

2. Double-click the query you want to run.

   TIMESAVER *You can also drag the object or objects onto the Access work area.*

   The query opens in a table called a dynaset. The dynaset displays the records that meet the specifications set forth in the query.

3. To close the query, click the **Close** button.

Results of query

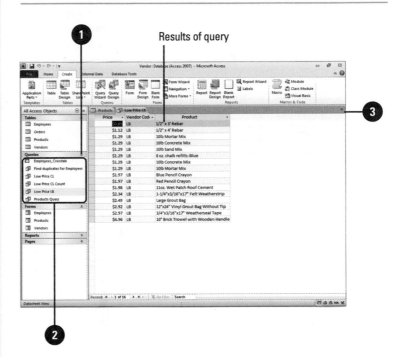

Modifying a Query in Design View

Once you have completed a query, you can further customize it in Design view. However, you can also create a query in Design view without using the wizard. Queries are not limited to a single table. Your queries can encompass multiple tables as long as the database includes a field or fields that relate the tables to each other. You can create a query using specific criteria and sort the results. If you no longer want to include a table or field, you can remove it from the query. In some cases you might want to hide a field from the query results while keeping it part of the query design for selection design purposes.

Modify a Query in Design View

1. In the Navigation pane, click the Queries bar to display the available queries in the database.

2. Click the query you want to modify.

3. Click the **Design View** button.

4. Double-click or drag each field you want to include in the query from the field list.

5. In the Design grid, enter any search criteria in the Criteria box.

6. Click the list arrow in the Sort box, and then specify a sort order.

7. To hide a field, clear the **Show** check box.

8. To delete a field, select the field, and then press Delete.

9. Click the **Save** button on the Quick Access Toolbar.

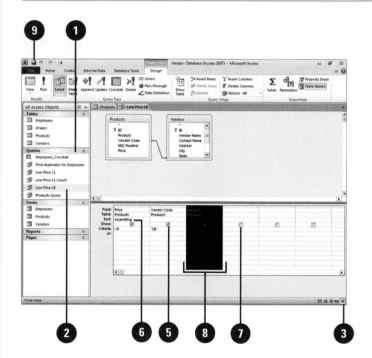

Did You Know?

You can remove a table. In the query, right-click the table, and then click Remove Table.

Performing Calculations in Queries

In addition to the built-in functions you can use to compare values in a query, you can use the **Expression Builder** to create your own calculations using arithmetic operators. By clicking the operator buttons you want to use and entering constant values as needed, you can use the Expression Builder to include expressions in a query. For example, to determine fees based on a contract amount, you can create an arithmetic expression in your query to compute the results. When you run the query, Access performs the calculations and displays the results. You can also insert functions, such as AVG and Count, to perform other operations. When you insert a function, <<expression>> appears in parentheses, which represents an expression. Select <<expression>> and replace it with a field name, which you can select in Expression Builder. When you type an expression, Expression Builder uses IntelliSense to display your options and help link to complete it (**New!**).

Create a Calculated Field

1. Within Query Design view, position the insertion point in the Field row of a blank column in the Design grid.

2. Click the **Builder** button.

3. Double-click the field (or fields) you want to use in the calculation, and then build an expression using the operator buttons and elements area.

   ◆ Click the button corresponding to the calculation you want.

   ◆ Click the Operators folder, click the Arithmetic folder, and then click the operator you want to use.

   ◆ Click the Functions folder, click Built-In Functions, and then click the function you want to use.

4. Type any other values (constants) you want to include in the expression.

5. Click **OK**.

6. Click the **Run** button.

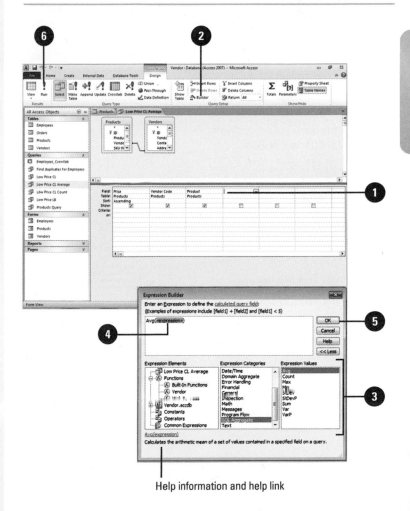

Help information and help link

Summarizing Values with a Crosstab Query

A **crosstab query** allows you to summarize the contents of fields that contain numeric values, such as Date fields or Number fields. In this type of query, the results of the summary calculations are shown at the intersection of rows and columns. For example, you can use a crosstab query to calculate the total number of toy products on sale, broken down by toy type. Crosstab queries can also involve other functions such as the average, sum, maximum, minimum, and count. You cannot update crosstab queries. The value in a crosstab query cannot be changed in order to change the source data.

Create a Crosstab Query

1. Click the **Create** tab.

2. Click the **Query Wizard** button.

3. Click **Crosstab Query Wizard**, and then click **OK**.

4. From the list at the top of the dialog box, select the table or query that contains the records you want to retrieve.

5. Click the view option you want: **Tables**, **Queries**, or **Both**.

6. Click **Next** to continue.

7. Double-click the field(s) you want to use in the crosstab query.

8. Click **Next** to continue.

Did You Know?

You can change column headings in a crosstab query. If you want to change the column headings, open the query in Design view, and then open the Property Sheet for the query. Enter the column headings you want to display in the Column Headings property box, separated by commas.

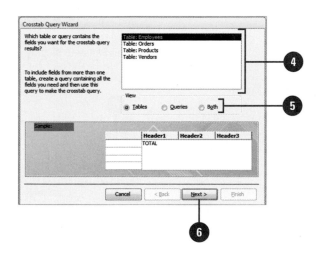

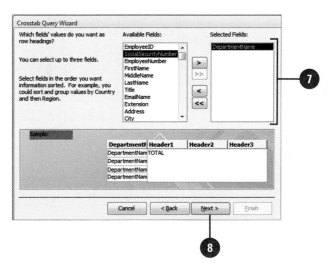

9 Select the field for the columns in the crosstab query.

10 Click **Next** to continue.

11 Click the field whose values you want to be calculated and displayed for each row and column intersection.

12 Click the function you want for the calculation to be performed.

13 Select the **Yes, include row sums** check box if you want to see a total for each row, or clear the check box if you do not want to see a total for each row.

14 Click **Next** to continue.

15 Enter a name for your query.

16 Indicate whether you want to immediately view the query or modify the design.

17 Click **Finish**.

Did You Know?

You can use a PivotTable instead of a crosstab query. Display crosstab data without creating a separate query in your database by creating a PivotTable in a form. Click the Create tab, click the More Forms button, and then click PivotTable. Click the Field List button to display the PivotTable Field List, and then drag the fields where you want on the PivotTable.

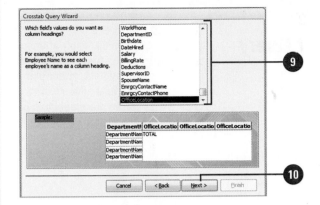

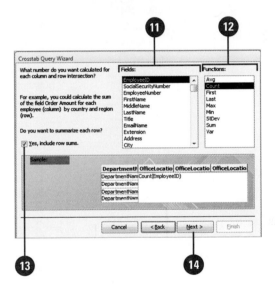

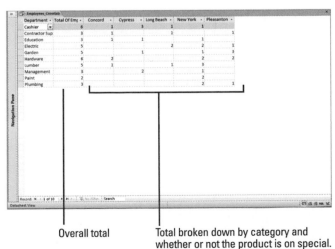

Overall total

Total broken down by category and whether or not the product is on special.

Creating a Parameter Query

When you need to change the criterion value for a query, you either must edit the old query or create a new one. However, if the change involves simply altering a value, you might consider using a parameter query. A **parameter query** prompts the user for the value of a particular query field, rather than having the value built into the query itself. For example, if you want to display the records for particular toy types, a parameter query can prompt you for the type, saving you from creating a separate query for each type.

Create a Parameter Query

1. In Query Design view, click the Criteria box.

2. Enter the text of the prompt surrounded by square brackets.

3. Click the **Run** button.

4. Enter a criteria value in response to the prompt.

5. Click **OK**.

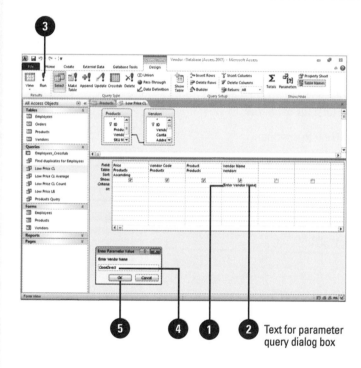

Text for parameter query dialog box

Access retrieves records with ClosetDirect Vendor

Finding Duplicate Fields

In some tables, you need to find records that have duplicate values in particular fields. For example, in a table of employees, you might want to discover which employees work at the same location. You can create a query that retrieves all the records from the Employees table that have duplicate values for the Office Location field. Access provides the Find Duplicate Query Wizard to guide you through each step to help you create the query.

Find Duplicate Records

1. Click the **Create** tab.

2. Click the **Query Wizard** button.

3. Click **Find Duplicates Query Wizard**, and then click **OK**.

4. Choose the table or query that you want to search for duplicate records.

5. Click **Next** to continue.

6. Select the field or fields that might contain duplicate information.

7. Click **Next** to continue.

8. Select any other fields that you want displayed in the query.

9. Click **Next** to continue.

10. Enter a name for the new query.

11. Specify whether you want to view the query results or further modify the query design.

12. Click **Finish**.

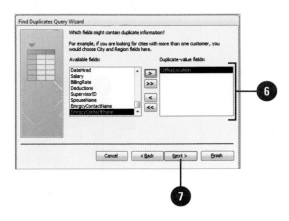

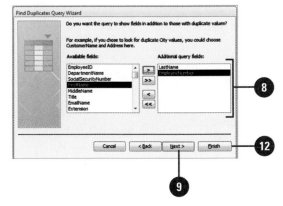

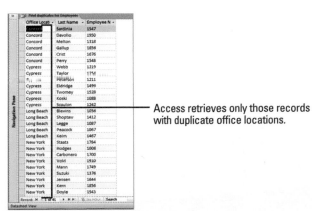

Access retrieves only those records with duplicate office locations.

Identifying Object Dependencies

As you develop a database, you create a relationship between objects to share data and provide the information in forms and reports. When you make changes to one object, it might affect another object. For example, if you no longer need a field in a table, instead of deleting it right away and possibly creating problems, you can check object dependencies to make sure that the field you want to delete is not used in another table. Checking for object dependencies helps you save time and avoid mistakes. Access generates dependency information by searching name maps maintained by the Name AutoCorrect feature. If Track Name AutoCorrect Info is turned off on the Advanced pane in the Access Options, you cannot view dependency information.

View Dependency Information

1. In the Navigation pane, click the object in which you want to view dependencies.

2. Click the **Database Tools** tab.

3. Click the **Object Dependencies** button, and then click **OK**, if necessary to update.

4. Click the **Objects that depend on me** option or the **Objects that I depend on** option.

   The Dependency pane shows the list of objects that use the selected object.

5. To view dependency information for an object listed in the pane, click on the **Expand** icon (+) next to it.

6. To open an object in Design view, click the object on the task pane.

7. When you're done, click the **Close** button on the task pane.

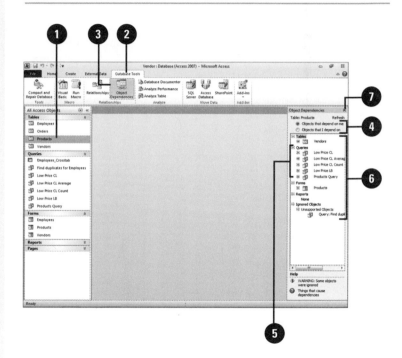

Did You Know?

You can view a list of database objects. Click the File tab, click Info, click the View And Edit Database Properties link, and then click the Contents tab. When you're done, click OK.

Backing Up and Repairing a Database

It is vital that you make back up copies of your database on a regular basis so you don't lose valuable data if your computer encounters problems. When you make a back up copy of your database, save the file to a removable disk or network drive to make sure it's safe if problems occur. If you need the back up copy of the database, you can use the Open button to restore and view your data. If you encounter corruption problems with a database, you can use the Compact & Repair Database command to compress the database, which rearranges data and fills in the space left behind by the deleted objects, and repairs any problems.

Back up an Access Database

1. Save and close all objects in a database.

2. Click the **File** tab, and then click **Save & Publish**.

3. Click **Save Database As**.

4. Click **Back Up Database**.

5. Click the **Save As** button.

6. Click the **Save in** list arrow to select a location for the back up copy.

7. Specify a different backup name.

8. Click **Save**.

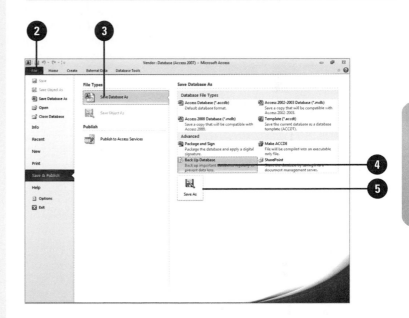

Compact and Repair a Database

1. Save and close all objects in a database.

2. Click the **Database Tools** tab.

3. Click the **Compact & Repair Database** button.

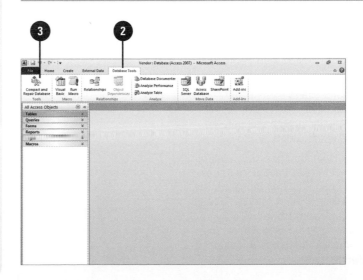

Sharing a Database

If you want to share your database with others, you have several options: Package and Sign, Make ACCDE, SharePoint, and Access Services. Package and Sign allows you to package, digitally sign, and distribute a database in the Access Deployment file format (.accdc). Other users can extract the database from the package and work directly in the database. If you share your modules with others, you may want to convert the database file to ACCDE format. In an ACCDE file, Access removes the editable source code and then compacts it into a smaller, faster more optimized database. Your VBA programs will continue to run, but others cannot view or edit them. If you have access to a SharePoint Server, (workspace collaboration using a network or Web server), you can synchronize file content with SharePoint libraries. If the SharePoint Server is running Access Services (**New!**), you can publish the database to the server and use the database in a Web browser.

Share a Database

1. Save and close all objects in a database.

2. Click the **File** tab, and then click **Save & Publish**.

3. Click **Save Database As**, click the type of database you want, and then click the **Save As** button:

   ◆ **Package and Sign.** Packages the database and applies a digital signature. Select a digital certificate, click **OK**, and specify a name and location, and then click **Create**.

   ◆ **Make ACCDE.** Compiles the database into an executable only file. Specify a name and location, and then click **Save**.

   ◆ **SharePoint.** Saves the database to a document managed SharePoint Server. Specify a name and network location, and then click **Save**.

4. To publish to Access Services on the Web, click **Publish to Access Services**, click **Run Compatibility Checker** to check for Web related issues, specify a SharePoint Server URL and Site Name, and then click **Publish to Access Services**.

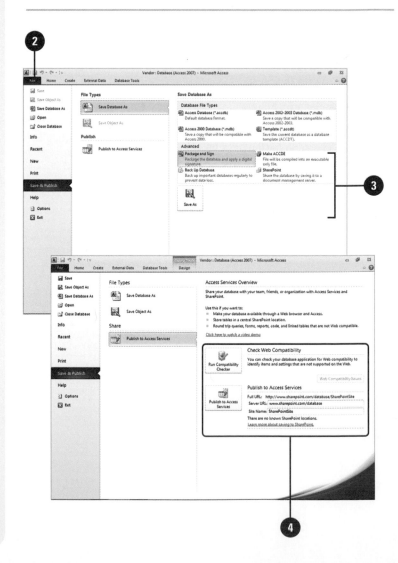

Presenting Data with Access

Introduction

Microsoft Office Access 2010 makes it easy to use your data in a form to enter data, report, in a report to print for review, or on the Web using a data access page, which allows you to create dynamic Web pages.

Forms allow a database designer to create a user-friendly method of data entry. Instead of entering records in the grid of rows and columns in Datasheet view, you can use a form that can represent a paper form. Such a form can minimize data-entry errors because it closely resembles the paper-based form containing the information you want to enter in your table. A form can include fields from multiple tables, so you don't have to switch from one table to another when entering data. You can add borders and graphics to the form to enhance its appearance.

To print a simple list of the records in your table, you can use the Print command on the File tab. But if you want to include calculations, graphics, or a customized header or footer, you can create a report. A report is a summary of information in one or more tables. Reports allow you to include enhancements that a simple printout of records in a table does not provide. In many cases a report answers important questions about the contents of your database.

You can open and work with a form or report in Form or Report view, Design view, or Layout view. Form or Report view allows you to view all the information associated with a record; Design view allows you to modify the design; and Layout view allows you to view information associated with the record and make changes to the form or report.

What You'll Do

Create a Form

Work with a Form in Design View

Enter and Edit Data in a Form

Modify a Form

Create a Report

Modify a Report in Design View

Perform Calculations in Reports

Format a Form or Report

Align and Size Controls

Group and Sort in Reports

Format a Datasheet

Change the Page Setup

Preview and Print Information

Create Mailing Labels

Creating a Form

To create a simple form in Access, you can use one of the form buttons available on the Create tab. You can create a basic form, blank form, split form, navigation form (**New!**), tabular form using multiple items, datasheet form, and PivotChart or PivotTable form. If you're not sure how to create a form, you can use the Form Wizard to step you through the process. These buttons quickly arrange the fields from the selected table or query into an attractive form. The new form is based on the active object. For example, if a table is active and you click the Form button, Access creates a new form based on the active table. After you create a form, you can save and name it so that you can use it again. If you need a more custom form, you can use the Form wizard to select the information you want to include from a variety of places.

Create a Custom Form Using the Form Wizard

1. Click the **Create** tab.

2. Click the **Form Wizard** button.

3. Click the list arrow for choosing a table or query on which to base the form, and then click the name of the table or query you want.

4. Specify the fields that you want included in the form by double-clicking the fields.

5. Click **Next** to continue.

6. Determine the arrangement and position of the information on the form (Columnar, Tabular, Datasheet, or Justified). Click **Next** to continue.

7. Specify the style of the form, which affects its formatting and final appearance. In the preview area of the dialog box, you can see a preview of the selected style.

8. Click **Next** to continue.

9. Enter a name for your form.

10. Indicate whether you want to open the form or display it in Design view.

11. Click **Finish**.

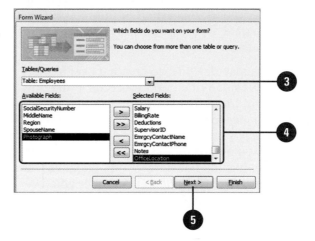

Custom form

Create a Form

① In the Navigation pane, click the **Tables** bar, and then click the table you want to use in the form.

② Click the **Create** tab.

③ Click any of the following form buttons:

- **Form.** Creates a columnar form.

- **Blank Form.** Creates a blank form.

- **Form Wizard.** Creates a form using a step-by-step approach.

- **Navigation.** Creates a form to browse different forms and reports (**New!**).

- **More Forms.** Displays a menu with additional options:

  - **Multiple Items.** Creates a tabular form.

  - **Datasheet.** Creates a form from a table datasheet.

  - **Split Form.** Creates a columnar form and includes the table datasheet; not available in web databases (**New!**).

  - **Modal Dialog.** Creates a dialog based custom form.

  - **PivotChart.** Creates a form with a PivotChart based on the table datasheet.

  - **PivotTable.** Creates a form with a PivotTable based on the table datasheet.

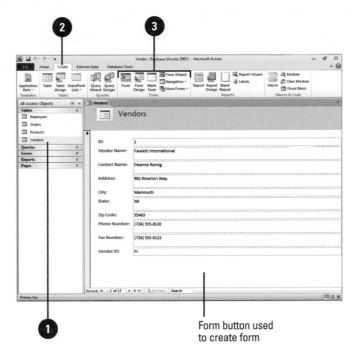

Form button used to create form

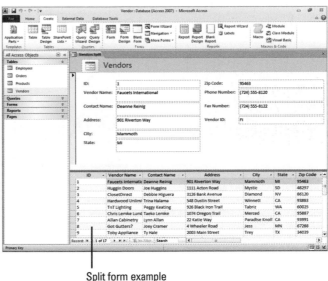

Split form example

Did You Know?

You can save a new form. While the new form is displayed, click the Save button on the Quick Access Toolbar. Type the name of your form in the Save As dialog box, and then click OK.

Working with a Form in Design View

Although a wizard can be a big help when you are first learning to create a form, you can create a form without the help of a wizard if you have a good idea of how you want the form to look. Instead of answering questions in a wizard, you can start working in Design view right away. You can create, modify, move, and format controls using tabs (**New!**) under Form Design Tools to create the exact form you want.

Create or Modify a Form in Design View

1. Click the **Create** tab.

2. Do either of the following to create or modify a form:

   ◆ **Create.** Click the **Form Design** button, and then click the **Design View** button.

   ◆ **Modify.** Double-click the form you want to change in the Navigation pane, and then click the **Design View** button.

3. If necessary, click the **Add Existing Fields** button on the Design tab under Form Design Tools to add a bound control.

4. Select the field you want to add to the form, drag the field to the location in the form where you want the field to appear.

5. Add new controls; use any of the control buttons on the Design tab under Form Design Tools, drag to create the control and then follow the wizard as needed (**New!**).

6. To apply a theme, click the **Themes** button, and then select one. You can also use the **Theme Colors** or **Theme Fonts** button (**New!**).

7. To format the text, click the **Format** tab, and then use the buttons on the Ribbon to format selected elements (**New!**).

8. Click the **Save** button on the Quick Access Toolbar to name the form, and then save it in the database.

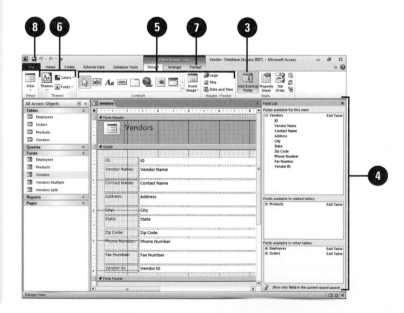

Entering and Editing Data in a Form

Database designers often display data in forms that mimic the paper forms used to record data. Forms facilitate data entry and record viewing. They can also contain buttons that allow you to perform other actions, such as running macros, printing reports, or creating labels. The options that appear on a form depend on what features the database designer included. A form directs you to enter the correct information and can automatically check your entries for errors. Access places the data you've entered in the form into the proper table. You can open a form in Form, Design, or Layout view. Form view allows you to view all the information associated with a record; Design view allows you to modify the form's design; and Layout view allows you to view information associated with the record and make changes to the form.

Enter a New Record in a Form

1. In the Navigation pane, click the Forms bar, and then double-click the form you want to open.

2. Click the **Form View** or **Layout View** button.

3. Click the **New Record** button.

4. Enter the data for the first field.

5. Press Tab to move to the next field or Shift+Tab to move to the previous field.

   When you have finished entering the data, you can close the form, click the New Record button to enter another record, or view a different record.

New Record button on Home tab

Did You Know?

You can delete a record from a form. In Form view, display the record you want to delete, click the Home tab, click the Delete Record button, and then click Yes.

Modifying a Form

Controls can make a form easier to use and improve its appearance. Controls also allow you to display additional information on your forms. To create a control on a form, you click the appropriate control button on the Design tab under Form Design Tools. With the control pointer, drag in the form where you want the control to appear. When you release the mouse for some controls, such as the Combo box or List box, the Control Wizard starts, which steps you through the creation process. You can also edit and format controls to change text using themes (**New!**) and the Format tab (**New!**) under Form Design Tools and delete controls that you no longer want.

Add Fields and Controls to a Form

1. In the Navigation pane, click the Forms bar, and then double-click the form you want to open.

2. Click the **Design View** button.

3. Click the button on the Design tab under Form Design Tools for the type of control you want to create.

4. In the Form window, drag the pointer to draw a box in the location where you want the control to appear.

5. If you want to switch to Layout view, click the **Layout View** button.

6. Click the **Add Existing Fields** button to display the Field List.

7. Select the field you want to add to the form, drag the field to the location in the form where you want the field to appear.

8. To apply a theme, click the **Themes** button, and then select one. You can also use the **Theme Colors** or **Theme Fonts** button (**New!**).

9. To format the control, click the **Format** tab, and then use the buttons on the Ribbon to format selected elements (**New!**).

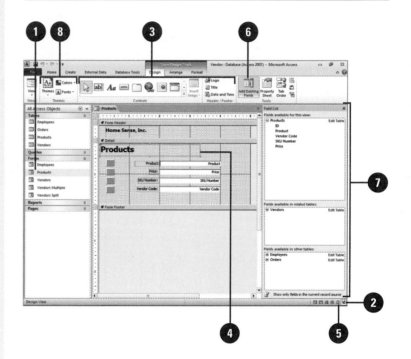

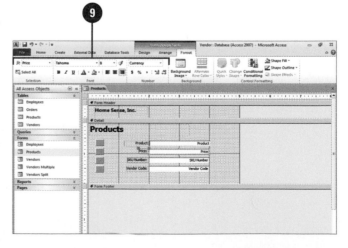

Edit Controls and Modify Properties in a Form

1. Open the form in which you want to edit controls in Design view or Layout view.

2. Click the **Design** tab in Design view or **Layout** tab in Layout view.

3. Click the control you want to edit.

   Small boxes, called handles, appear around the control to indicate it is selected. You can use them to resize the control.

4. To remove the control, press Delete.

5. To edit the control, click the control to place the insertion point, and then use the Backspace or Delete key to remove text or type to insert text.

6. To change control properties, click the **Property Sheet** button, enter the property information you want to add or change, and then click the **Close** button.

See Also

See "Modifying a Report in Design View" on page 432 for information on the different types of controls.

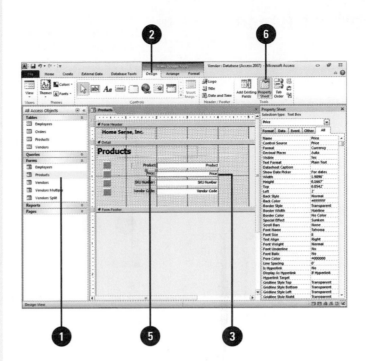

Creating a Report

To quickly create a simple report in Access, you can use one of the form buttons available on the Create tab. You can create a basic report, blank report, and labels. These buttons quickly arrange the fields from the selected table or query into an attractive report. The new report is based on the active object. For example, if a table is active and you click the Report button, Access creates a new report based on the active table. After you create a report, you can save and name it so that you can use it again. You can also create a report using the Report Wizard, which allows you to select the fields and information you want presented and to choose from available formatting options that determine how the report will look.

Create a Report

1. In the Navigation pane, click the **Tables** bar, and then click the table you want to use in the report.

2. Click the **Create** tab.

3. Click any of the following form buttons:

   - **Report.** Creates a columnar report.

   - **Labels.** Creates a columnar report of labels.

   - **Blank Report.** Creates a blank report.

   Access displays the form in Print Preview, but you can switch to Design view, save, print, or close the report.

4. Click the **Save** button, type a name for your report, and then click **OK**.

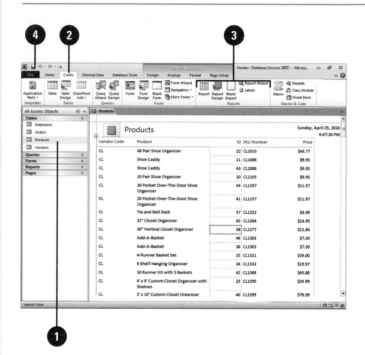

Did You Know?

You can create an unbound report.
Create a report without choosing a table or query on which it is based. Such reports are called unbound reports. A dialog box is an example of an unbound report.

Create a Report Using the Report Wizard

1. Click the **Create** tab.

2. Click the **Report Wizard** button.

3. Click the list arrow for choosing a table or query on which to base the form, and then click the name of the table or query you want.

4. Select the fields you want to include, indicating the source of any fields you want to include from other tables or queries. Click **Next** to continue.

5. If necessary, specify any groupings of the records, choosing any or all of the selected fields (up to ten). Click **Next** to continue.

6. Specify the order of records within each group, sorting by up to four fields at a time, and then specify ascending or descending order. Click **Next** to continue.

7. Determine the layout and orientation of your report. Click **Next** to continue.

8. In the final wizard dialog box, name your report, and then indicate whether you want to preview the report or display it in Design view. Click **Finish**.

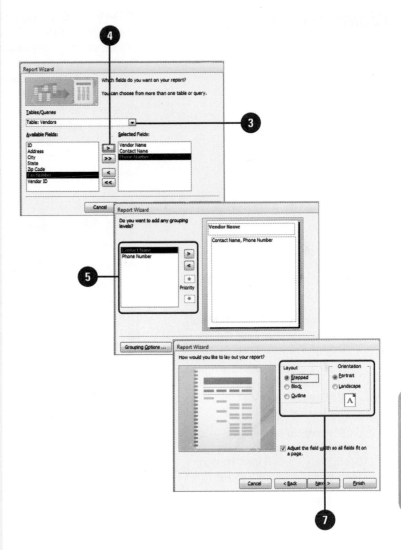

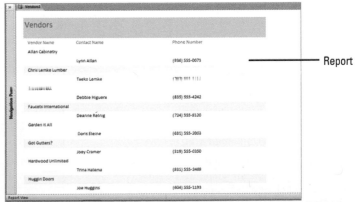

Report

Modifying a Report in Design View

When you create a report from scratch in Design view, three sections appear: Page Header, Detail, and Page Footer. Once you create the report, you need to populate it with data. You can add **bound controls**—fields of data from a table or query—directly from the Field List, or you can add other types of **unbound controls**—text boxes, labels, pictures, buttons, and so on—from the Ribbon. In Design view, you see two parts for every control: the control itself and its corresponding label. When you select a control, sizing handles appear around the control, which you can drag to size it. You can also drag inside a selected control to move it, which moves a corresponding label with it. If you don't want to use the header and footer sections, you can hide them.

Create or Modify a Report in Design View

1. Click the **Create** tab.

2. Do either of the following to create or modify a form:

    ◆ **Create.** Click the **Report Design** button, and then click the **Design View** button.

    ◆ **Modify.** Double-click the report you want to change in the Navigation pane, and then click the **Design View** button.

3. If necessary, click the **Add Existing Fields** button on the Design tab under Report Design Tools to add a bound control.

4. Use the Ribbon commands and Field List to create or modify a report in Design view.

5. Use the following to resize or move a control and label:

    ◆ **Resize.** Position the pointer over a sizing handle, and then drag it.

    ◆ **Move.** Position the pointer over an edge of a control until the pointer changes to a four-headed arrow, and then drag it.

6. To hide or view headers and footers, right-click a heading bar, and then click **Report Header/Footer** or **Page Header/Footer**.

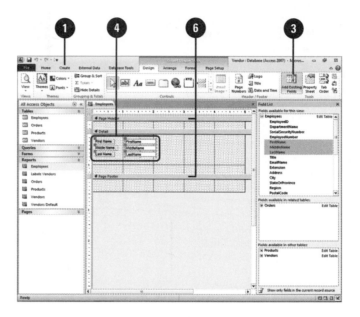

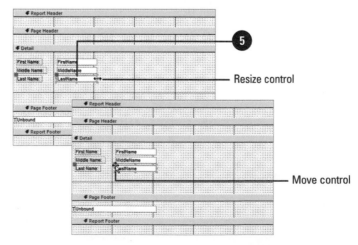

Resize control

Move control

Add a Bound or Unbound Control

1. Display the report in Design view.

2. Click the **Design** tab under Report Design Tools.

3. To add a bounded control, click the control button you want to add, such as a text box, and then drag to draw a box in the location where you want the control.

4. To add an unbounded control, select the fields you want to include from the Field List; press Shift or Ctrl while you click to select multiple fields. Drag the selected field or fields to the section in which you want the field to appear. Two boxes appear for each field: one containing the label and one for the field values.

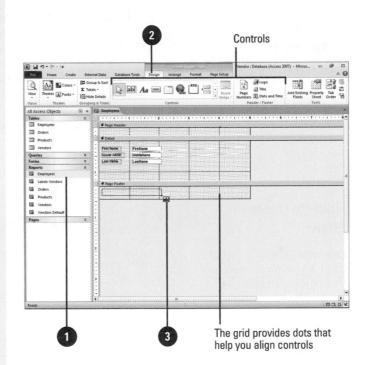

Controls

The grid provides dots that help you align controls

Adjust Page or Section Spacing

1. Display the report or form in Design view whose page or section size you want to change.

2. Position the mouse pointer over the edge of the page or section.

3. Drag the resize pointer to a new location.

Did You Know?

You can display or hide the ruler and grid. The ruler and grid provide guides to help you arrange your controls. Click the Arrange tab under Report Design Tools, click the Size/Space button, and then click Ruler or Grid.

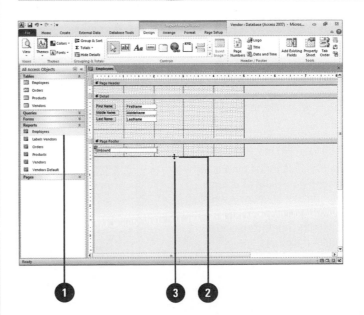

Performing Calculations in Reports

When you create a report, you might want to include summary information or other calculations. The wizards often include built-in functions, but you can use the **Expression Builder** to create your own by clicking buttons for the arithmetic operators you want to use and including constant values as needed. For example, if you want to determine bonuses based on a percentage of sales, you can create an arithmetic expression to compute the results. When you generate the report, Access will perform the required calculations and display the results in the report. To display the calculations in the appropriate format, you can also use the Properties feature to specify formats for dates, currency, and other numeric data.

Choose Fields to Use in a Calculation

1. In Design view, create a text box control and position it where you want the calculated field to appear, or select an existing unbound control.

2. Click the **Design** tab under Report Design Tools.

3. Click the **Property Sheet** button.

4. Click the **Control Source** property box, which specifies what data appears in a control, and then click the **Expression Builder** button.

5. Click the equal sign (=) button, and then enter the values and operators you want to use.

   ◆ Click operator buttons to supply the most common operations.

   ◆ Double-click folders in the left pane to open lists of objects you can use in your expression, including existing fields, constants, operators, and common expressions.

   ◆ Manually type an expression.

6. Click **OK** to insert the calculation.

7. Click the **Close** button.

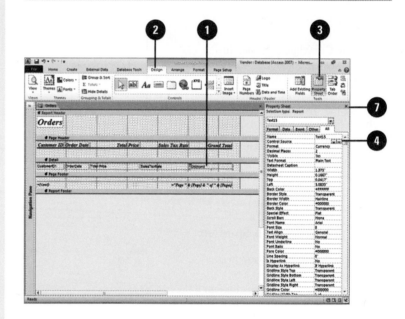

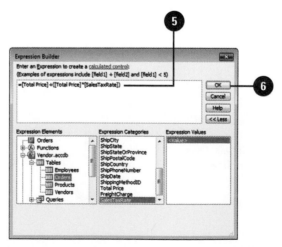

Format Values in a Report

① In Design view, position the insertion point in the field whose format you want to change.

② Click the **Design** tab under Report Design Tools.

③ Click the **Property Sheet** button.

④ On either the **All** tab or the **Format** tab of the property sheet, click the Format property box, click the list arrow that appears, and then click the format you want to use.

The names of the formats appear on the left side of the drop-down list, and examples of the corresponding formats appear on the right side.

⑤ If you are formatting a number (rather than a date), and you do not want to accept the default, "Auto," click the Decimal Places property box, click the list arrow, and then click the number of decimal places you want.

⑥ Click the **Close** button.

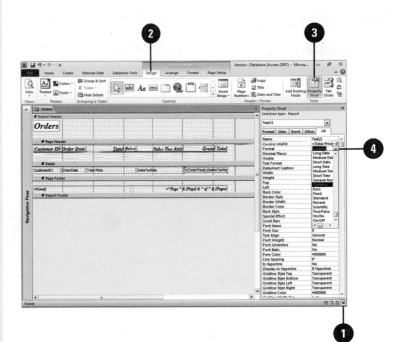

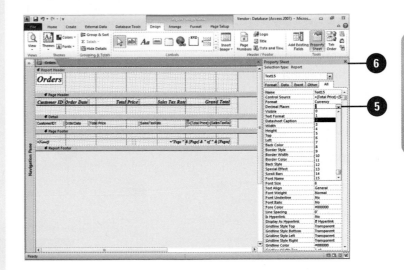

Did You Know?

You can use a builder. Access makes it easy to change many types of settings by providing builders, or tools that simplify tasks. The Expression Builder is just one of many builders in Access. You know a builder is available for a task when you click a property box and a Build button appears.

Formatting a Form or Report

A fast way to format a form or report is with the Theme button, available in Design or Layout view. When you click this button, you can select from a variety of themes. After you make your selection, Access formats the selected portion of a report or form consistently for you. After using theme, you can always make additional formatting changes to individual elements. For example, you can change control shapes, and apply Quick Styles, Shape Effects, and fill and outline colors just like you can in other Office programs (**New!**). You can also add formatting—including data bars when comparing records (**New!**)—based on conditions just like you can in Microsoft Excel. For example, if a value exceeded a certain amount, Access bolds or highlights it to make it easier to see.

Format a Form or Report with a Theme

1. Display the form or report you want to format in Design or Layout view, and then click the **Design** tab.

2. Select all or part of the form or report you want to format.

3. Click the **Theme** button, and then click the theme style you want.

   ◆ To change theme colors or fonts, click the **Theme Colors** or **Theme Fonts** button.

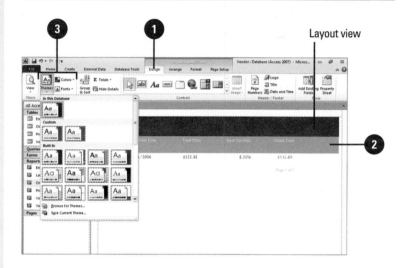

Layout view

Format a Form or Report Using Formatting Tools

1. Display the form or report you want to format in Design or Layout view.

2. Click the **Format** tab.

3. Select the item you want to format.

4. Use formatting buttons to apply the following:

   ◆ Text style, color, and alignment.

   ◆ Box fill and line/border color, line/border width, and special effects, such as shadowed, etched, and raised.

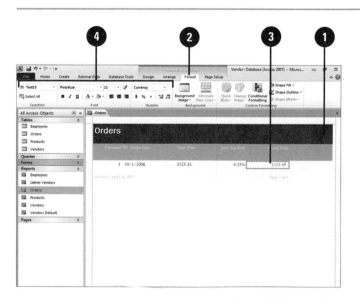

Apply Conditional Formatting

1. Display the form or report in Design view.

2. Click the **Format** tab.

3. Select the item you want to format.

4. Click the **Conditional Formatting** button.

5. Click **New Rule**, or select an existing conditional format, and then click **Edit Rule**.

6. Select a rule type.

7. Specify a rule description using a conditional statement and formatting.

8. Click **OK**.

9. Click **OK**.

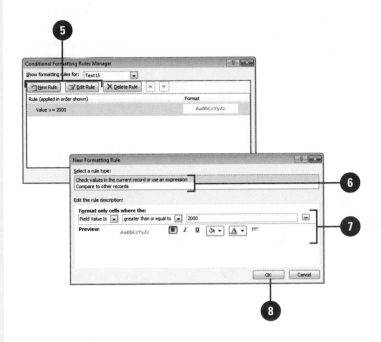

Format Controls

1. Display the form or report in Design view.

2. Click the **Format** tab.

3. Select the item you want to format.

4. Select any of the following:

   ◆ **Quick Style.** Select a quick style for a shape type control.

   ◆ **Change Shape.** Select a shape for a shape type control.

   ◆ **Shape Fill.** Select a fill color.

   ◆ **Shape Outline.** Select a border color.

   ◆ **Shape Effects.** Select an effect (shadow, glow, soft edge, or bevel) for a shape type control.

   ◆ **Alternate Row Color.** Select the rows, click the button, and then select a color.

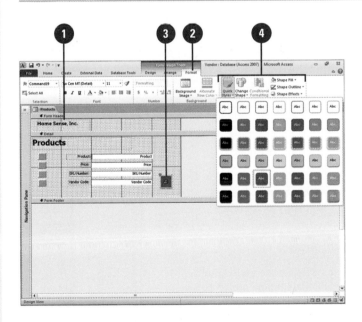

Aligning and Sizing Controls

Often when you work with multiple controls and objects, they look best when aligned with each other. You can quickly create a predefined tabular and stacked layout, or you can manually align and group controls and objects to create your own layout. Access provides tools to change the horizontal and vertical spacing between controls and objects and resize controls and objects relative to each other and group them together.

Align Controls and Objects to Each Other

1. Display the form or report in Design view.

2. Select the controls and objects you want to align.

3. Click the **Arrange** tab.

4. To align controls to each other using the grid, click the **Align** button, and then click the **To Grid** to select it. To disable it, click the **To Grid** command to deselect it.

5. Click the **Align** button, and then click **Left**, **Right**, **Top**, or **Bottom**.

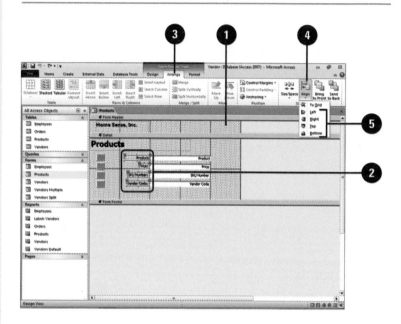

Change Horizontal or Vertical Spacing

1. Display the form or report in Design view.

2. Select the controls and objects whose spacing you want to change.

3. Click the **Arrange** tab.

4. Click the **Size/Space** button, and then click the spacing option you want. You can increase or decrease horizontal or vertical spacing or make horizontal or vertical spacing equal.

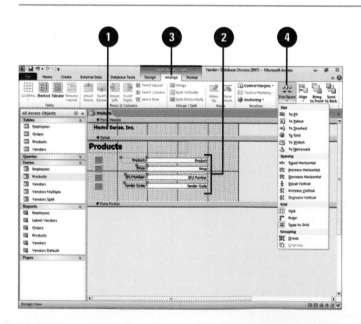

Change the Size of Controls and Objects

1. Display the form or report in Design view.

2. Select the controls and objects you want to resize.

3. Click the **Arrange** tab.

4. Click the **Size/Space** button, and then click the sizing option you want: **To Fit, To Grid, To Tallest, To Shortest, To Widest,** or **To Narrowest**.

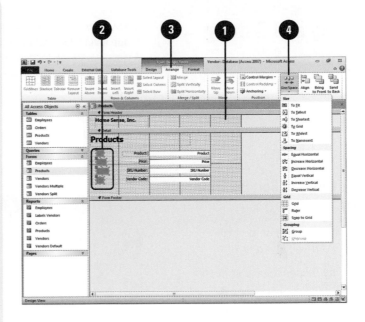

Change Layout Controls to Tabular or Stacked

1. Display the form or report in Design view.

2. Select the fields you want to change.

3. Click the **Arrange** tab.

4. Click the **Tabular** or **Stacked** button.

   ◆ To remove a layout, click the **Remove Layout** button.

Did You Know?

You can turn off the Snap To Grid to align controls and lines. In Design view, the objects you create align themselves along an invisible grid as you move them. You can turn on and off the Snap To Grid option. Click the Arrange tab under Form or Report Design Tools, click the Size/Space button, and then click Snap To Grid.

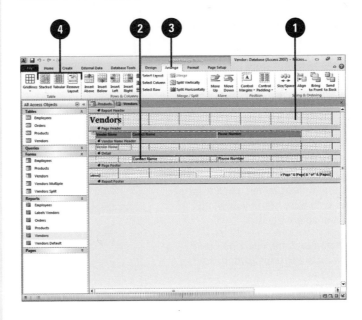

Grouping and Sorting in Reports

In Layout view, you can use the Group, Sort, and Total pane to create group levels and add totals. The Group, Sort, and Totals pane provides a visual interface to make it easy to understand, use, and navigate. In Layout view, you see group, sort, and total changes right when you make them, so you can quickly decide if you need to make any changes. You can quickly add simple grouping and sorting, or take a little more time to create complex ones. The Totals drop-down list makes it quick and easy to add a sum, average, count, maximum or minimum to report headers or footers.

Create a Group or Sort in a Report

1. Display the report or form you want to format in Layout view.

2. Click the **Design** tab under Report Layout Tools.

3. Click the **Group & Sort** button.

4. Click **Add a group** or **Add a sort**.

5. Click the **select field** list arrow on the Group on or Sort by bar.

6. Click the field you want to group or sort by.

   The grouping or sorting is applied to the report.

7. To create a more complex grouping or sorting, click the **More** arrow (toggles to Less) on the Group on or Sort by bar, click a list arrow with the criteria you want, and then select options.

8. When you're done, click the **Close** button on the Group, Sorting, and Totals pane.

See Also

See "Working with Fields" on page 394 for more information on creating a Totals row.

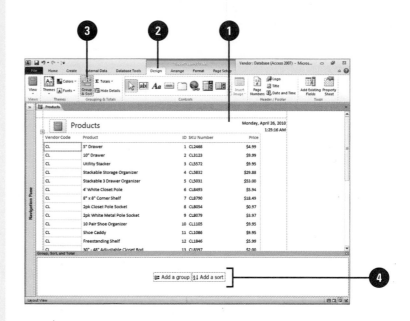

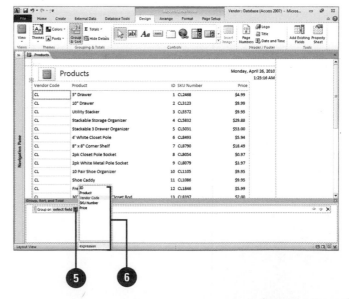

Change or Delete a Group or Sort in a Report

1. Display the report or form you want to format in Layout view.

2. Click the **Design** tab under Report Layout Tools.

3. Click the **Group & Sort** button.

4. To change the order of grouping and sorting, click the **Move Up** or **Move Down** button at the end of the Group on or Sort by bar.

5. To delete a grouping or sorting, click the **Delete** button at the end of the Group on or Sort by bar.

6. When you're done, click the **Close** button on the Group, Sorting, and Totals pane.

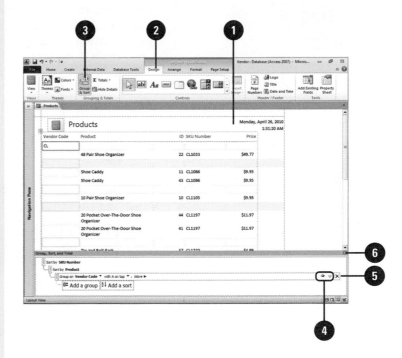

Add a Totals Function to a Report

1. Display the report or form you want to format in Layout view.

2. Click the **Design** tab under Report Layout Tools.

3. Click the field you want to use with a Totals function.

4. Click the **Totals** button, and then select the function you want.

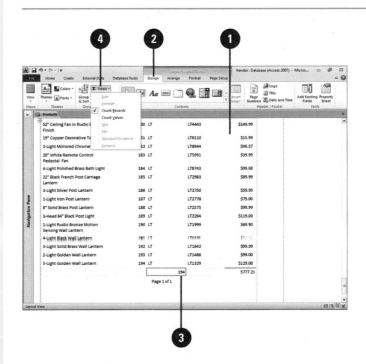

Formatting a Datasheet

If you want to print a datasheet, you can use formatting tools to make it look better than the standard display. You can apply special effects to cells, change the background and gridline color, and modify border and line styles. If you don't want to show the gridlines, you can hide either the horizontal or vertical gridlines, or both. The default display for a datasheet is to display the columns from left to right. If you prefer, you can change the column display to appear from right to left.

Format a Datasheet

1. Open the datasheet you want to format.

2. Click the **Home** tab.

3. Click the **Select** button, and then click **Select All**, or select part of the datasheet.

4. Use other formatting buttons in the Font group to format the datasheet.

   ◆ To change the fill/background color, click the **Alternate Fill/Back Color** button arrow, and then select a color.

   ◆ To change the gridline format, click the **Gridlines** button arrow, and then select an option.

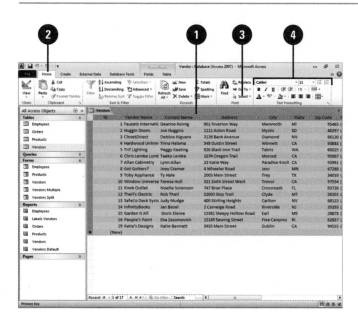

Change Datasheet Default Formatting Options

1. Click the **File** tab, and then click **Options**.

2. In the left pane, click **Datasheet**.

3. Change the datasheet default formatting options you want.

4. Click **OK**.

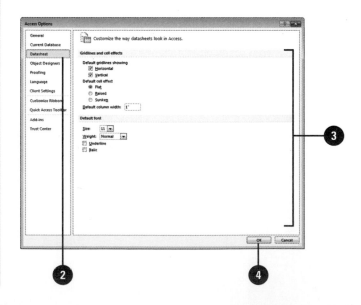

Changing the Page Setup

Once you have created a report or form, you can change the page setup, which includes the margin, paper size and orientation, and grid and column settings. Margins are the blank space between the edge of a page and the text. You can also select the page orientation (portrait or landscape) that best fits the entire document or any section. Portrait orients the page vertically (taller than it is wide), and landscape orients the page horizontally (wider than it is tall). When you shift between the two, the margin settings automatically change.

Change Page Setup Options

1. In the Navigation pane, click the report, form, table, query, or any data you want to preview.

2. Click the **File** tab, click **Print**, and then click **Print Preview**.

3. To change margin settings, click the **Margins** button, and then click **Normal**, **Wide**, or **Narrow**.

4. To change paper settings, click the **Size** button, and then select the size you want.

5. To change paper orientation, click the **Portrait** or **Landscape** button.

6. To change column settings, click the **Columns** button, change or select the column and row grid settings, column size, and column layout (Down, Then Across or Across, Then Down) you want, and then click **OK**.

7. When you're done, click the **Close Print Preview** button.

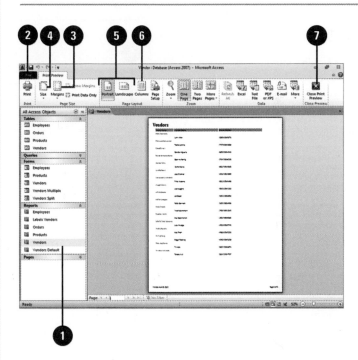

Previewing and Printing Information

Before printing, you should verify that the data you want to print looks the way you want. You save time, money, and paper by avoiding duplicate printing. Print Preview shows you exactly how your data will look on each printed page. The Print Preview tab provides the tools you need to display the look of each page. You can print a report, a table, a query, or any data in a single step using the Print button, in which case Access prints a single copy of all pages in the report. If you want to print only selected pages or if you want to specify other printing options, use the Print command on the File tab.

Preview Data

1. In the Navigation pane, click the report, form, table, query, or any data you want to preview.

2. Click the **File** tab, click **Print**, and then click **Print Preview**.

3. Use the **One Page**, **Two Pages**, or **More Pages** buttons to view the data pages the way you want.

4. Use the record navigation buttons (First, Previous, Record Selection box, Next, and Last) to display pages.

5. To print from the Print Preview window, click the **Print** button, specify the options you want, and then click **OK**.

6. When you're done, click the **Close Print Preview** button.

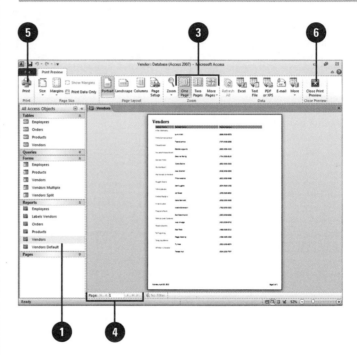

Did You Know?

You can create a report snapshot. Open the report you want to use in Print Preview, click the More button, click Snapshot Viewer, and then follow the wizard instructions to create and save a snapshot report.

Print Data

① Display the report, form, table, query, or any data you want to format in Design View.

② Click the **File** tab, and then click **Print**.

In Print Preview, click the **Print** button.

③ If necessary, click the **Name** list arrow, and then select the printer you want to use.

④ Select the print range you want.

◆ To print all pages, click the **All** option.

◆ To print selected pages, click the **Pages** option, and then type the first page in the From box and the ending page in the To box.

◆ To print selected record, click the **Selected Record(s)** option.

⑤ Click **OK**.

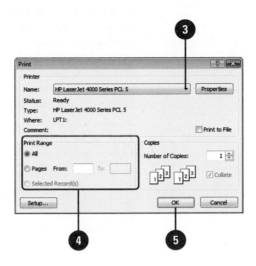

Did You Know?

You can check spelling in tables.
Before you print, it's a good idea to check spelling. Display the table in Datasheet view, select the rows or columns you want to check, click the Spelling button on the Home tab, and then use the Ignore and Change buttons to correct spelling mistakes. You can also use the Add button to add words to the dictionary.

Creating Mailing Labels

Access provides a **Label Wizard** to help you create mailing labels quickly. The wizard supports a large variety of label brands and sizes. You can also create customized labels for brands and sizes not listed by the wizard, provided you know the dimensions of your labels and label sheets. You can create labels by drawing data from any of your tables or queries. In addition to data values, labels can also include customized text that you specify.

Create Mailing Labels

1. In the Navigation pane, click the **Tables** bar, and then click the table you want to use.

2. Click the **Create** tab.

3. Click the **Labels** button.

4. Select the type of mailing label you're using. Click **Next** to continue.

5. Specify the font style and color for the label text. Click **Next** to continue.

6. Double-click the field names in the Available Fields list to place them on your mailing labels. Type any text that you want to accompany the field values. Click **Next** to continue.

7. If necessary, select a field to sort your labels by. Click **Next** to continue.

8. Enter a name for your mailing labels report, and then choose whether to preview the printout or modify the label design.

9. Click **Finish**.

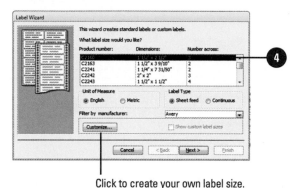

Click to create your own label size.

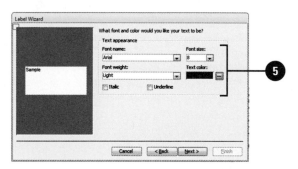

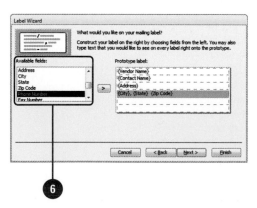

Communicating with Outlook

17

Introduction

Microsoft Office Outlook 2010 takes managing and organizing your daily routine to a new level. Its updated look gives you a larger viewing area and easier access to the tools that you want to use. You can customize its features so that they are seamlessly interwoven as you move from your electronic mail to your calendar to your notes to your journal.

Managing your personal communications and information has become an intricate and important aspect of every-day life at the workplace and at home. With Outlook, you can store, track, and manage all your information and communications in one place. You can track your appointments, meetings, and tasks on your Calendar and store information, including phone numbers, addresses, e-mail addresses, about all your business associates, family, and friends in your Contacts list. Use Notes to write reminders to yourself and Tasks to record your daily or weekly to-do list, checking them off as you complete them. Of course, one of the most important parts of your day is communicating, and Outlook provides the tools that help you address all your electronic communications needs.

Preparing for Outlook

Outlook is Microsoft's personal information manager and electronic mail (e-mail) software for handling incoming and outgoing e-mail messages.

To use Outlook as your personal information management (PIM) and e-mail tool, you need to be connected to the Internet or a network. Through this connection, you can take full advantage of the e-mail, scheduling, and contact capabilities of Outlook. Before you start Outlook for the first time, you need to know about the different types of connections and e-mail servers you can use with Outlook.

You can use Outlook on a standalone computer or one that is part of a network of computers, also called a **local area network (LAN)**. When you connect your standalone or networked computer to the Internet so you can communicate electronically, your computer becomes part of a worldwide network. You need two things to establish a connection to the Internet: a physical connection and an **Internet service provider (ISP)**.

Options for physical connections include a modem via a phone line (also called a dial-up network connection), a cable broadband modem, or a **digital subscriber line (DSL)** connected directly to your computer or through a LAN. Your options for an ISP, however, are numerous and vary greatly, both in cost and features, and depend upon the type of physical connection you choose. ISPs can include your local telephone or cable company, or a company, such as MSN or AOL (American Online), that provides only Internet access service.

The ISP provides the names of your incoming and outgoing **e-mail servers**, which collect and store your e-mail until you are ready to retrieve or send it. If you are using a modem, your ISP provides the phone number and modem settings needed to establish an Internet connection.

If you are working on a LAN that uses its own mail server, such as Microsoft Exchange Server, to send and receive e-mail, your network administrator provides all the information that you need for establishing a connection. However, you still need to set up your Outlook Profile with the Exchange mail connector. You will need the Exchange Server name from your system administrator.

Once you establish your connection, you can send and receive e-mail, or you can communicate using instant messaging, participating in a chat room, or subscribing to a newsgroup.

There are several different types of e-mail accounts that you can use with Outlook: POP3, IMAP, and HTTP.

- **Post Office Protocol 3 (POP3)** is a common e-mail account type provided by ISPs. Messages are downloaded from the e-mail server and stored on your local computer.

- **Internet Message Access Protocol (IMAP)** is similar to POP3 except that messages are stored on the e-mail server.

- **Hypertext Transfer Protocol (HTTP)** is a common type of Web e-mail account. Messages are stored, retrieved, and displayed as individual Web pages. Hotmail is an example of an HTTP e-mail account.

Using Outlook for the First Time

When you start Outlook for the first time, what you see depends on whether you installed Outlook as a new program or as an upgrade. In either case, a setup wizard appears to step you through the process of setting up a profile and an e-mail service. A **profile** is a collection of all the data necessary to access one or more e-mail accounts and address books. A **service** is a connection to an e-mail server where you store and receive e-mail messages. Before you use Outlook, the Auto Account Setup tries to configure the account for you. All you need to do is specify your e-mail account name and password. If Outlook is unable to complete the account set up, you can manually enter account information, including the names of the incoming and outgoing e-mail servers, which you need to get from your ISP. If you installed Outlook as an upgrade, Outlook 2010 uses existing settings.

Use Outlook for the First Time

1. Click the **Start** button on the taskbar, point to **All Programs**, click **Microsoft Office**, and then click **Microsoft Office Outlook 2010**.

2. Click **Next**, click **Yes** or **No** to let Outline configure an E-mail account, and then click **Next**.

   Follow the Add New Account wizard instructions.

3. Click the **E-mail Account** option and enter account information, or click the **Manually configure server settings or additional server types** option, and then click **Next**.

4. Enter required information to complete it, and then click **Finish**.

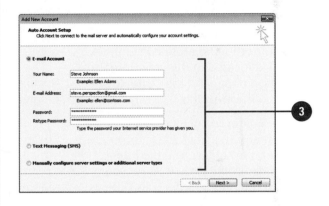

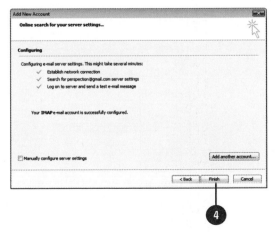

Did You Know?

You can have more than one e-mail account. Click the File tab, click Info, click the Account Settings button, click Account Settings, click the E-mail tab, click Add to add a new e-mail account (or click Change to modify an existing account), read and follow the setup wizard instructions, and then click Finish.

Viewing the Outlook Window

Title bar. The title bar displays the name of the current folder followed by the account name and Outlook program name.

Ribbon. The ribbon (**New!**) provides commands and tools grouped by category on different tabs you use to accomplish your tasks in Outlook.

Quick Access toolbar. The Quick Access toolbar (**New!**) provides a place to add frequently used buttons you click to quickly execute commands.

Navigation pane. The Navigation pane is your central station for moving around in Outlook. The Folder list is located in the upper portion of the Navigation pane, and the Outlook view bars occupy the lower portion.

Folder list. The Folder list displays the contents of the folder you select. In Outlook, you store information in folders and the folder you use depends on the Outlook item you are using. Some of the default folders in Outlook

include Inbox, Calendar, Contacts, Tasks, Notes, Journal, Deleted Items folder, and so on.

Outlook view bars. Click one of the four major Outlook view bars—Mail, Calendar, Contacts, or Tasks—to work in that view. You can use the other Outlook views—Notes, Folder List, or Shortcuts—by clicking one of the icons located below the view bars.

Folder pane. In Mail view, the middle pane of the Outlook windows displays the contents of the folder you select. You can control how the contents are displayed (e.g., by date, order of importance, sender, and so on).

Reading pane. The Reading pane gives you a greater area for reading your e-mail messages without having to scroll to view them.

To-Do Bar. The To-Do Bar displays your tasks, e-mail messages flagged for follow up, upcoming appointments, and calendar information in a central place.

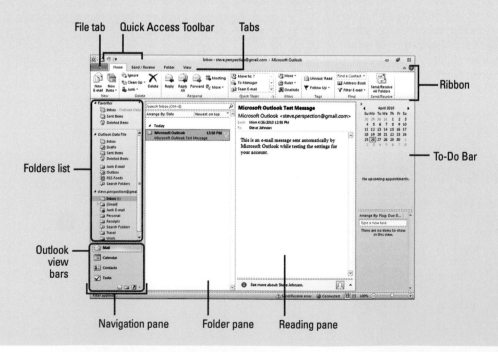

Using the To-Do Bar

The To-Do Bar can display a calendar and your meetings, appointments and tasks so you can see what you have in store for the day. You can customize the Outlook To-Do Bar to display what you need to see most. You can specify the number of days displayed in your calendar and show or hide appointments and tasks in the To-Do Bar. You can view the To-Do Bar by using the To-Do Bar button on the View tab or the Expand arrow on the To-Do Bar itself.

View the To-Do Bar

① Click the **View** tab.

② Click the **To-Do Bar** button, and then click **Normal**.

TIMESAVER *To hide or show the To-Do Bar, click the Minimize/Maximize arrow.*

③ To minimize the To-Do Bar, click the **To-Do Bar** button, and then click **Minimize**.

④ To turn the To-Do Bar off, click the **To-Do Bar** button, and then click **Off**. To turn it back on, use the Normal command.

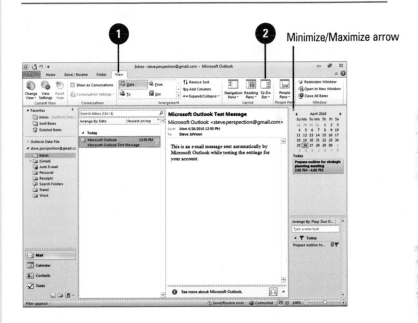

Minimize/Maximize arrow

Customize the To-Do Bar

① Click the **View** tab.

② Click the **To-Do Bar** button.

③ Set the options you want.

◆ **Date Navigator.** Show or hide the Date Navigator.

◆ **Appointments.** Show or hide all appointments.

◆ **Task List.** Show or hide the Task list.

◆ **Options.** Select or clear the check boxes to show or hide options, and then click OK.

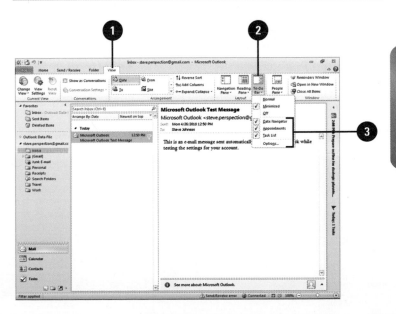

Using the Navigation Pane

The Navigation pane is designed to display more of what you need to see in a simple and straightforward layout. When you click an Outlook view bar in the Navigation pane, the entire Outlook window transforms to provide a clear, uncluttered view of your Mail, Calendar, Contacts, and Tasks. The Notes, Folder list, and Shortcuts views do not appear by default, but you can access each view by clicking its icon at the bottom of the Navigation pane. You can reorder the view bars and determine whether a view appears as a view bar or an icon. If you need more space, you can also minimize it.

Use the Navigation Pane to Move Around

1. Click a button (such as Calendar) on the Navigation pane.

   TIMESAVER *To hide or show the Navigation pane, click the Minimize/Maximize arrow.*

Did You Know?

You can minimize, turn off, or set options for the Navigation pane. Click the View tab, click the Navigation Pane button, and then select an option: Normal (on and maximized), Minimized (hide), Off, Favorites, or Options.

Minimize/Maximize arrow

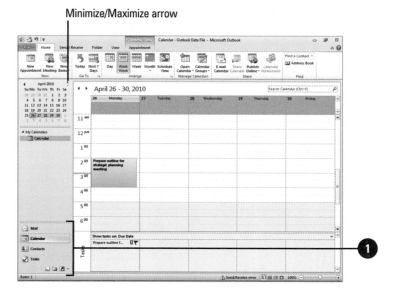

Change the Look of the Navigation Pane

1. Click the **Configure Buttons** button on the Navigation pane.

2. Click **Navigation Pane Options**.

3. To remove a view from the Navigation pane, clear the check box for the view button.

4. To change Navigation pane order, click the view button, and then click the **Move Up** or **Move Down** button.

5. Click **OK**.

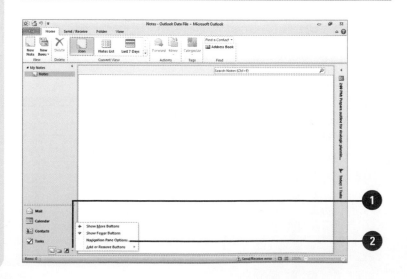

Viewing Items and Folders

When you use Outlook, you work with views. The main views in Outlook are Mail, Calendar, Tasks, Contacts, Notes, and Shortcuts. Within those views, Outlook stores related items in folders. For each of these views, you can choose how to display the items and folders in which you stored the items.

View an Item

1. Click a view bar or icon on the Navigation pane to switch to that Outlook view.

2. Click the **View** tab.

3. Click the **Change View** button to display the available options.

4. Click the view you want to apply.

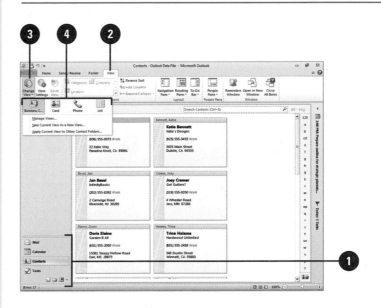

View a Folder

1. Click the **Folder List** icon on the Navigation pane.

2. Click a folder in the Folder list.

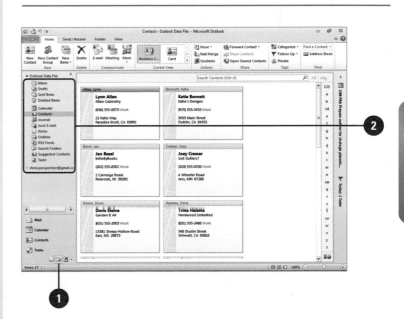

> ### Did You Know?
>
> ***You can customize a view.*** Click the View tab, click the Change View button, and then click Manage Views. Use the dialog box to create a new view or modify existing view options to better suit your working environment or needs.

Creating a Contact

A contact is a person or company with whom you want to communicate. One contact can have several mailing addresses, various phone and fax numbers, e-mail addresses, and Web sites. You can store all this data in the Contacts folder along with more detailed information, such as job titles, and birthdays. When you create a contact you also create an **Electronic Business Card (EBC)**, which you can customize and share with others as an attachment or as part of your signature. When you double-click a contact, you open a dialog box in which you can edit the detailed contact information. You can also directly edit the contact information from within the Contacts folder. If you send the same e-mail message to more than one person, you can group contacts together into a distribution list.

Create or Modify a Contact

1. Click the **Contacts** button in the Navigation pane.

2. Click the **New Contact** button to create, or double-click an existing contact to edit a contact.

   ◆ In Mail view, you can also right-click a message header or an EBC, and then click **Add to Outlook Contacts.**

3. Click the **General** button.

4. Type the contact's first and last name in the Full Name box.

5. Type as much information as you know about the contact.

6. Click the **Details** button, and then type as much information as you know in the appropriate boxes.

7. Click the **Save & Close** button.

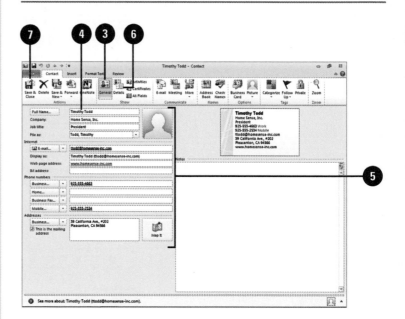

Did You Know?

You can delete a contact. Click Contacts on the Navigation pane, click the contact you want to delete, and then click the Delete button on the Home tab. Any journal entries that refer to that contact remain intact.

Change Contacts Views

1. Click the **Contacts** button on the Navigation pane.

2. Click the **More** button in the Current View group.

3. Click a view option.

   ◆ Business Cards

   ◆ Card

   ◆ Phone

   ◆ List

4. To customize the current view, click the **View** tab, and then click **View Settings** button.

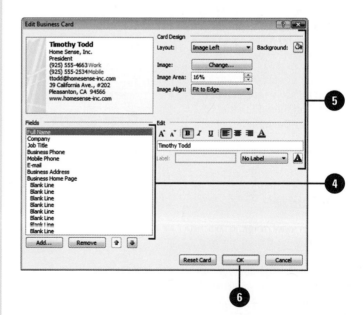

Show a Business Card

1. Click the **Contacts** button in the Navigation pane.

2. Double-click the contact with the Business Card you want to view.

3. Click the **Business Card** button.

4. Select the EBC line you want to change.

5. Make the formatting changes you want.

6. Click **OK**.

7. Click the **Close** button in the Contact window.

Sorting Contacts

Outlook allows you to sort contacts in any view and by any field, either in ascending order (A to Z) or descending order (Z to A). You can sort contacts by a specific field or by a column header appearing at the top of the view's table (Company, Job Title, Personal Home Page, and so on). When sorted in a view, the contacts maintain the same view, but their order has changed. It's also possible to generate multi-layered sorts within a sort by adding more fields to the sort. For example, you might want to sort contacts by their company names first and then alphabetically by their last names.

Sort Contacts

1. Click the **Contacts** button on the Navigation pane.

2. Click the **View** tab, and then click the **View Settings** button.

3. Click the **Sort** button.

4. Click the **Sort items by** list arrow, and then click a sort field.

5. Click the **Ascending** or **Descending** option.

   TIMESAVER *Click a column head in a table format view to sort in ascending order by that column; click the column head again to re-sort in descending order.*

6. To add another sort field, click the first **Then by** list arrow, select a sort field, and then click the **Ascending** or **Descending** option.

7. Click **OK**, and then click **OK** again.

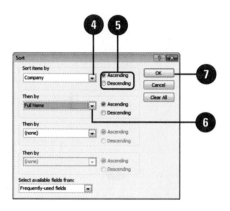

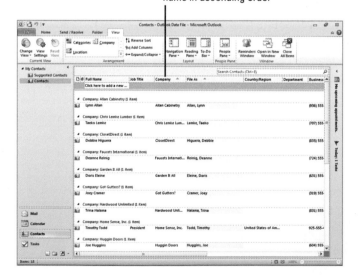

Indicates contacts sorted by company name in ascending order

Did You Know?

You can find a contact quickly. Click Contacts on the Navigation pane, and then start typing the name of the contact you want to find. The contact that best matches the text is displayed.

You can sort a distribution list by category. If you associate a distribution list with a category, you can then sort and view the names in the list.

Creating a Contact Group

A **contact group** is a collection of contacts usually grouped together because of a specific task or association and then identified by one name. You can use a contact group, also known as a distribution list, in your e-mail messages, task requests, and other contact groups. When you address an e-mail message using a contact group, you are sending the message to everyone whose address is included in the list. Because a contact group often contains many names, it provides a faster, more efficient way to address an e-mail message to multiple recipients.

Create a Contact Group

1. Click the **Contacts** button on the Navigation pane.

2. Click the **New Contact Group** button.

3. Type the name for the contact group.

4. To add members to the group, click the **Add Members** button, click **From Outlook Contacts**, **From Address Book**, or **New E-mail Contact**, and then select the members you want.

5. To remove a member, select the contact, and then click the **Remove Member** button.

6. Click the **Categorize** button, and then select the category you want, or click **All Categories** to create your own, and then click **OK**.

7. Click the **Save & Close** button.

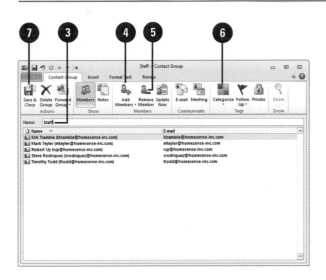

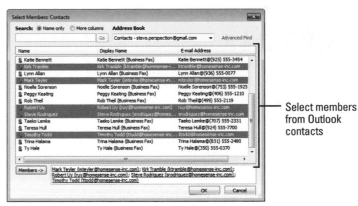

Select members from Outlook contacts

Did You Know?

You can change the name format of contacts. Change the name format of contacts in the Contact dialog box. Edit the entry in the Full Name box, and then select a different choice in the File As list, or edit the entry in the Display As box.

Creating and Addressing an E-Mail Message

When you create an e-mail message, the Untitled Message window opens with all the tools you need to communicate electronically. Your first step is addressing the message. You must identify who will receive the message or a copy of the message. For each recipient, you enter an e-mail address. You can enter the address manually by typing it in the To or Cc box, or you can select an address from your list of contacts. If you enter multiple addresses, you must separate the addresses with a semicolon (;). You can type a semicolon after each recipient's e-mail address, or you can just press Enter after a recipient's address. Addressing a new message also means indicating the purpose of the message by entering a subject. Try to indicate the intent of the message as briefly and clearly as possible.

Create and Address an E-Mail Message

1. Click the **Mail** button on the Navigation pane to display the Inbox folder.

2. Click the **New E-mail** button on the Home tab.

3. Enter the e-mail address of each recipient, or click the **To** button.

4. Enter the e-mail addresses for those recipients who should receive a copy of the message, or click the **Cc** button.

5. To check addresses for sendability, click the **Check Names** button.

6. Type a subject that indicates the purpose of the message.

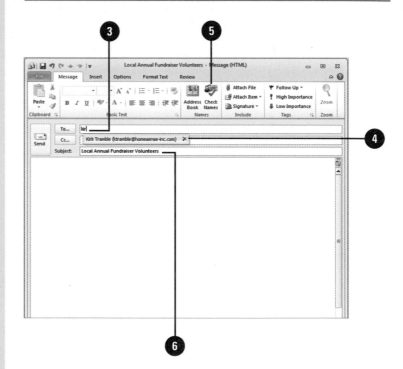

Did You Know?

You can save time with AutoComplete Addressing. If you begin to enter the e-mail address of a recipient to which you have previously sent a message, Outlook recognizes the address and completes it using AutoComplete Addressing.

Write a Message

1. In the message window, click in the message area.

2. Type the content of your message.

3. Right-click any word that appears with a green or red wavy underline to display a list of suggested corrections, and then correct the error, if necessary.

4. Click a suggested word to replace the error, or click one of the other options.

5. To check spelling, insert research, use Thesaurus, translate text, set a language, click the **Review** tab, and then click the appropriate button on the Ribbon.

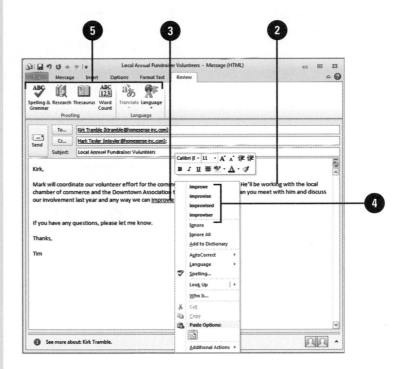

Select Addresses for an E-Mail Message

1. In the message window, click the **To** or **Cc** button.

2. If necessary, click the **Address Book** list arrow, and then select an Address Book.

3. Click the name of a recipient.

4. Click the **To** button or the **Cc** button. To select multiple recipients in the list, click the first name, and then press and hold Shift (to select adjacent names) or Ctrl (to select nonadjacent names) as you click the other recipients.

5. To send a blind copy (address not included in recipients' list) of your message, select the recipient, and then click **Bcc**.

6. Click **OK**.

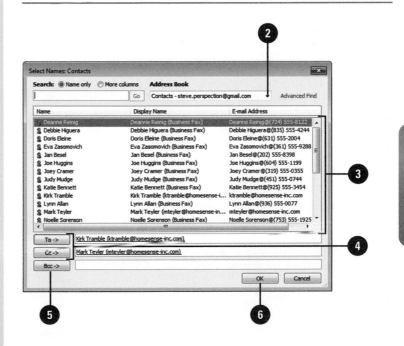

Formatting Message Text

You can specify a file format for message text. The Plain Text format is one that all e-mail programs recognize, but it doesn't support text formatting. The Rich Text and HTML formats allow text formatting, but are not always supported. However, most programs that don't recognize Rich Text or HTML, convert the message to plain text. When you use Rich Text or HTML, you can use tools, such as bold, italicize, and underline text, on the Ribbon and Mini-Toolbar to help draw the reader's attention to key words and emphasize the meaning of your message. With Word as the Outlook e-mail editor, you can take advantage of Word's formatting features, including Quick Styles and Themes, when you write the text of your e-mail messages.

Format the Message Text

1. Compose a new message, or open an existing message you want to format.

2. Click the **Options** tab.

3. Use the Themes and Page Color buttons to format the message text and background.

4. Click the **Format Text** tab.

5. Click the **Rich Text**, **HTML**, or **Plain Text**.

6. Select the text you want to format.

7. If you selected Rich Text or HTML, use the tools on the Ribbon and Mini-Toolbar to format the message text, including Quick Styles.

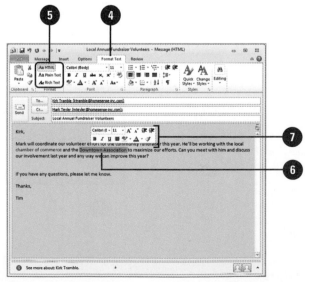

Did You Know?

You can specify the file format for all messages. Click the File tab, click Options, click Mail in the left pane, click the Compose Text In This Format list arrow, and then select HTML, Rich Text, or Plain Text.

Attaching a File or Item to a Message

You can also add an attachment to your e-mail messages. An attachment can be a file, such as a document or a picture. The attachment can also be an Outlook item, such as a contact, task, or note. When you add an attachment to a message, an attachment icon appears under the Subject box, identifying the name and size of the attachment. Although you can add multiple attachments to a message, you should limit the number and size of the attachments. The size of the attachment affects the time it takes to send the message. The larger the attached file, the longer it takes to send. If an attached file is too large, the message might not be sent. After you send the message with the attachment, which appears with a paper clip icon, message recipients can double-click the attachment icon to open and view the file or item.

Attach a File to a Message

1. Compose a new message, or open an existing message.

2. Click the **Insert** or **Message** tab.

3. Click the **Attach File** button.

4. Navigate to the folder that contains the file.

5. Click the file you want to attach.

6. Click **Insert**.

Attached file

Attach an Item to a Message

1. Compose a new message, or open an existing message.

2. Click the **Insert** or **Message** tab.

3. Click the **Attach Item** button.

4. Navigate to the folder that contains the item.

5. Click the item you want to attach.

6. Click **OK**.

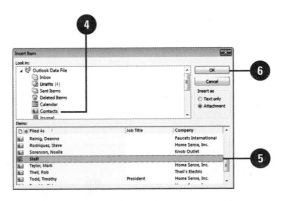

Using Stationery

Your e-mail messages can be as expressive as you are or want to be. Outlook provides stationery and themes that you can apply to your e-mail messages to give them a personalized look. The stationery in Outlook comes in a wide variety of patterns, colors, and designs. A theme helps you create professional-looking e-mail that use an appropriate balance of color for your document content. Themes are made up of a palette of twelve coordinated colors, which are used consistently in all Office 2010 programs.

Apply Stationery to a Message

1. Click the **Mail** button on the Navigation pane.

2. Click the **New Items** button on the Home tab.

3. Point to **E-mail Message Using**.

4. Click **More Stationery**.

5. Click the stationery or theme you want to use.

6. Click **OK**.

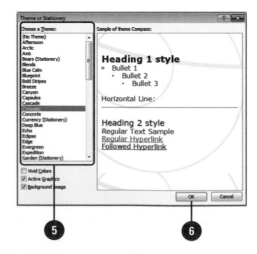

Did You Know?

You can create your own stationery. Click the File tab, click Options, click Mail in the left pane, click Stationery And Fonts, specify the theme or stationery you want for a new HTML e-mail message, click OK, and then click OK.

Stationery applies only to HTML formatted messages. You can use stationery only if you use HTML as your message format. If you are using the Plain Text or Rich Text format message setting, you can't apply stationery to your message.

Creating a Signature

If you type the same information at the end of each e-mail message that you create, then you can automate that task by creating a signature. A signature can consist of both text and pictures. You can customize your signature with a variety of formatting styles, such as font type, size and color. For example, for your personal correspondence you can create a signature that includes a closing, such as Best Regards and your name; for business correspondence, you can create a signature that includes your name, address, job title, and phone and fax numbers. You can even include a logo image, hyperlink, or Electronic Business Card (EBC). You can create as many signatures as you want.

Create and Use a Signature

1. Click the **File** tab, click **Options**, and then click **Mail** in the left pane.

2. Click **Signatures**.

3. Click **New** or select an existing signature.

4. Type a name for the new signature, and then click **OK**.

5. Type your signature text, and then select the signature.

6. Use formatting buttons to customize the text.

7. Select an e-mail account, and a signature for new messages and for your replies and forwarded messages.

8. Click **Save**.

9. Click **OK**.

10. Click **OK**.

11. To insert a signature, click the **Signature** button in a message window, and then select a signature.

    ◆ To switch between two signatures, right-click the default signature in your new message, and then click the signature you want to use.

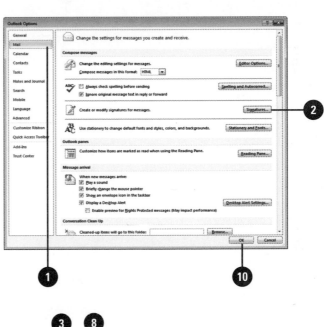

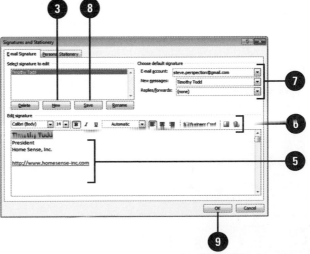

Inserting Message Content

In addition to message text, you can also insert other content, including business cards, calendars, signatures, tables, pictures, and other illustrations. This content allows you to add a visual aspect to your e-mail communication. When you insert an Electronic Business Card into a message, the recipient can quickly insert your contact information into an Address Book without having to retype the information. In the message window, you can use the Insert tab to insert additional content into a message with the HTML and Rich Text format.

Insert Message Content

1. In the message window, click the **Insert** tab.

2. Click the button with the message content you want to insert.

   ◆ **Attach File**.

   ◆ **Outlook Item**.

   ◆ **Business Cards**.

   ◆ **Calendar**.

   ◆ **Signature**.

   ◆ **Table**.

   ◆ **Picture**.

   ◆ **Clip Art**.

   ◆ **Shapes**.

   ◆ **SmartArt**.

   ◆ **Chart**.

   ◆ **Screenshot (New!)**.

   ◆ **WordArt**.

   ◆ **Quick Parts**.

   ◆ **Equation**.

   ◆ **Symbol**.

3. When you're done, you can send the message.

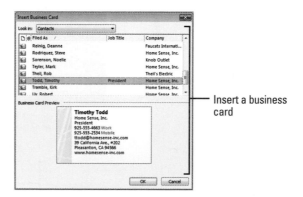

Business card

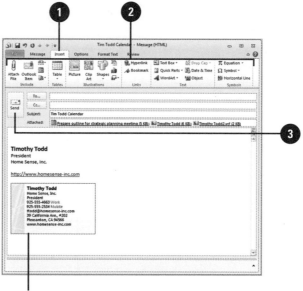

Insert a business card

Did You Know?

You can insert a snapshot of your calendar in an e-mail message. In the message window, click the Insert tab, and then click the Calendar button.

Sending Messages

When you click the Send button, Outlook connects to the e-mail server, and moves the message to the Outbox folder, which sends your message to its recipient and checks the server for incoming mail. You can also send and check for messages from one or more accounts by clicking the Send/Receive Groups button on the Send / Receive tab. If you need customization, you can set send and receive options. If you just want to send messages without receiving new ones, you can use the Send All button on the Send / Receive tab.

Send a Message

1. Create a new message, or open an existing message saved in the Drafts folder.

2. Click the **Send** button, or click the **Send All** button or the **Send/Receive Groups** button on the Send / Receive tab, and then select the send option you want.

Did You Know?

You can resend a message. In Mail view, click Send Items, open the message to resend, click the File tab, click Info, click the Resend or Recall button, and then click Send This Message.

Set Send/Receive Options

1. Click the **Send / Receive** tab.

2. Click the **Send/Receive Groups** button, and then click **Define Send/Receive Groups**.

3. Use the **New**, **Edit**, **Copy**, **Remove**, and **Rename** buttons to work with account groups.

4. Select or clear the check box for send and receive options.

5. Click **Close**.

6. Click **OK**.

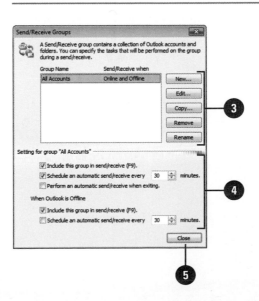

Setting Message Delivery Options

When you send a message, you can set message delivery options to help you track, manage, and secure it. You can specify the level of importance, high, low, and normal (the default). If you need a recipient to follow up on an e-mail, you can set a follow up flag or reminder. If you need delivery confirmation, you can set options to make sure an e-mail arrives and is read. You can also set options to deliver messages on specific dates or have replies sent to another address. If security is an issue, you can set access permissions, encrypt contents, or add a digital signature. You can even use e-mail to track voting.

Set Importance, Follow Up, and Permission Options

1. In the message window, click the **Message** tab.

2. To set a follow up option, click the **Follow Up** button, and then select the option you want, or click **Custom** and create your own.

3. To set an importance level, click the **High Importance** or **Low Importance** button.

4. To set access permissions, click the **Options** tab, click the **Permission** button (if available), and then click **Do Not Forward** or **Manage Credentials**, and then follow the instructions.

5. When you're done, you can send the message.

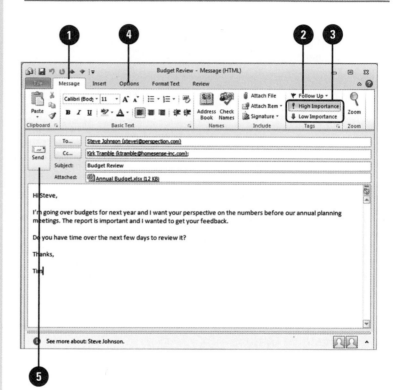

Did You Know?

You can specify where sent items are stored. In the message window, click the Options tab, click the Save Sent Items button, and then click Use Default Folder, Do Not Save, or click Other Folder and select your own.

You can change the e-mail format. In the message window, click the Format Text tab, and then click HTML, Plain Text, or Rich Text.

Set Tracking and Voting Options

1. In the message window, click the **Options** tab.

2. Select or clear the **Request a Delivery Receipt** check box.

3. Select or clear the **Request a Read Receipt** check box.

4. To send a voting opinion, click the **Use Voting Buttons** button, and then select the option you want, or click **Custom** to create your own.

5. When you're done, you can send the message.

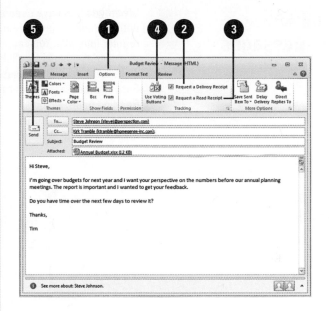

Set Message Delivery and Security Options

1. In the message window, click the **Options** tab.

2. Click the **Delay Delivery** button.

3. Specify the level of Importance and the level of Sensitivity.

4. Select the check boxes with the delivery options you want, and then specify additional settings:

   ◆ **Have replies sent to.**

   ◆ **Save copy of sent message.**

   ◆ **Do not deliver before.**

   ◆ **Expires after.**

5. To set message security options, click **Security Settings**, select or clear the **Encrypt message contents and attachments** or **Add digital signature to this message** check boxes.

6. Click **Close**.

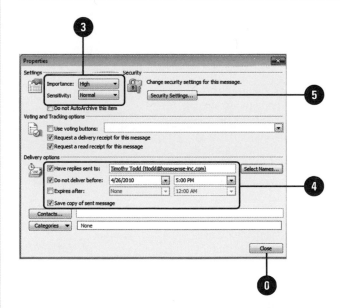

Receiving and Reading Messages

Messages that have been sent to you are stored on your e-mail server until Outlook retrieves them. By default, Outlook retrieves your mail at regular intervals. You can also retrieve your messages between scheduled retrieval times by clicking the Send/Receive button. When a message is retrieved, its message header appears in the Outlook Inbox. Click the message header to display the contents of the message in the Reading pane, which increases the area for reading your e-mail. If you receive a message that contains an attachment, you can preview (using Office 2010 installed viewers), open, or save it.

Receive and Read Messages

1. Click the **Send/Receive All Folders** button on the Home or Send / Receive tab. If a message arrives when you're online, a mail alert appears above the taskbar. Click the alert to open it.

2. To display a message in the Inbox, click the message header.

3. Read the contents of the message in the Reading pane.

4. If the message contains an attachment, do any of the following:

   ◆ **Preview.** Click the attachment file in the Reading pane, and then click Preview File, if necessary. To return to the message body, click the Show Message button.

   ◆ **Open.** Double-click the attachment file.

   ◆ **Save.** Right-click the attachment file, and then click Save As, specify a location, and then click Save.

Did You Know?

You can close, open, or move the Reading pane. Click the View tab, click the Reading Pane button, and then click Right, Bottom, Off, or Options.

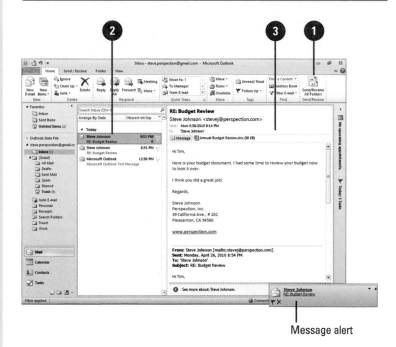

Message alert

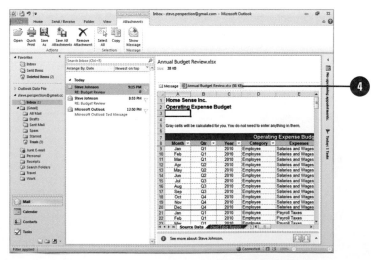

Flagging Messages

As you look through the list of messages that you have received, you might find messages that require your attention, though you don't have the time to respond when you are reading the message. To make sure you don't overlook an important message, you can click the flag icon next to the message to mark it with a Quick Flag. The Quick Flag icon will help jog your memory so you can respond promptly to the message. The To-Do Bar provides an up-to-date list of messages marked with Quick Flags in your mailbox.

Flag and Follow Up a Message

1. Click the **Mail** button on the Navigation pane.

2. Click the **Inbox** folder.

3. Select the messages you want to flag and follow up.

4. To set a follow up flag, click the **Quick Flag** icon located on the right side of the message header.

5. To remove a follow-up flag, right-click the **Quick Flag** icon on a message, and then click **Clear Flag**.

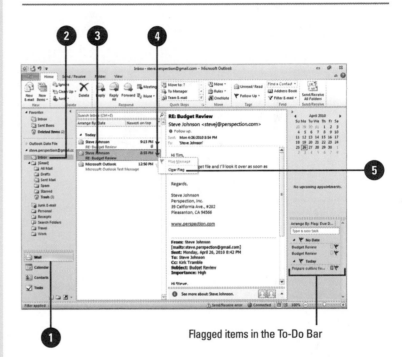

Flagged items in the To-Do Bar

Did You Know?

You can sort messages according to flag color. To sort messages by flag color, click the View tab, click the Arrangement More button, and then click a Flag option.

You can send e-mail with tracking and delivery options. Create a new mail message, click the Options tab, and then select the delivery options or the tracking options you want.

You can change the e-mail format. Create a new mail message, click the Format Text tab, and then click HTML, Plain Text, or Rich Text.

Categorizing Messages By Color

When a folder is full of messages, sometimes it's hard to distinguish between them. To help you locate and manage related messages and other items in Outlook, you can assign a color category to e-mail, calendar, and task items. When you're working on a project, you can quickly see all related items at a glance. You can customize the color categories by name. For example, you can name the green category Finance and assign it the money related items.

Color Categorize Messages

1. Click the **Mail** button on the Navigation pane.

2. Select a folder.

3. Click the **Color Category** icon to apply the Quick Click option, or right-click the Color Category icon in the message header, and then click the color you want.

4. To set the quick click, right-click the Color Category icon, click **Set Quick Click**, select a color category, and then click **OK**.

5. To customize a color category, right-click the Color Category icon, click **All Categories**, use any of the following, and then click **OK**.

   ◆ **New.** Click to create a new color category.

   ◆ **Rename.** Click to rename a color category.

   ◆ **Color.** Select a color category, and then select a color.

   ◆ **Shortcut Key.** Select a color category, and then select a shortcut key.

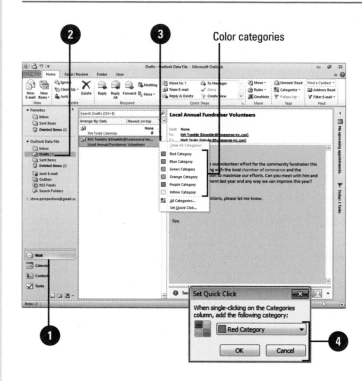

Color categories

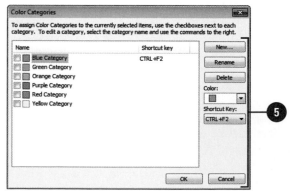

Deleting Messages

As your Inbox or other folders get full and harder to manage, you can quickly delete messages you no longer need. When you delete a message, it's not permanently deleted from your computer. The message is placed in the Deleted Items folder, where it stays until you empty it. If you have a back and forth conversation of e-mails, you can delete them or just the redundant ones (**New!**). If you delete a message by mistake, you can move it out of the Deleted Items folder to restore it. If you don't want to delete your messages just in case you might need to reference them later, you can archive them or move them to another folder.

Delete Messages

1. Click the **Mail** button on the Navigation pane.

2. Select a folder.

3. Select the message you want to delete.

4. Use any of the following options:

   - **Delete Message.** Click the **Delete** button or press Delete.

   - **Delete Conversation.** Click the **Ignore** button; deletes current and all future messages (**New!**).

   - **Delete Redundant Conversation.** Click the **Clean Up** button, and then select an option (**New!**).

5. To restore a deleted message, click the **Deleted Items** folder, and then drag the message to another folder, or click the **Recover Deleted Items** button on the Folder tab.

6. To permanently delete all messages, right-click the **Deleted Items** folder, and then click **Empty Folder** or click the **Empty Folder** button on the Folder tab.

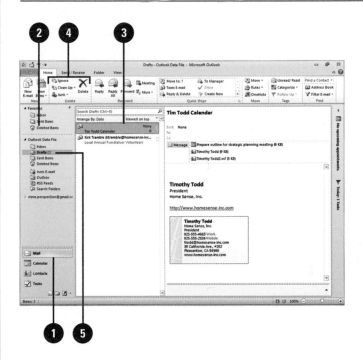

For Your Information

Managing Deleted Items

If your mailbox is getting hard to manage, you can use other clean up tools to help you get it under control. Click the File tab, click Info, and then click the Cleanup Tools button. Click Empty Deleted Items Folder to permanently delete all messages or click Mailbox Cleanup (**New!**) to view the size of the Deleted Items folder or empty (permanently delete) all messages in the Deleted Items folder. You can also automatically empty the Delete Items folder. Click the File tab, click Options, click Advanced, select the Empty Deleted Items Folders Upon Exiting Outlook check box, and then click OK.

Replying To and Forwarding a Message

You can respond to messages in your Inbox in two ways: you can reply to the person who sent you the message, or you can forward the message to others. Replying to a message sends a copy of the original message and new text that you type to the sender, or to both the sender and all the other original recipients. You can reply by returning a message to only the sender or to the sender and all other original recipients. The reply message recipient sees RE: and the original subject in the message header. Forwarding a message sends a message to someone who was not on the original recipient list. You can also type additional information at the start of the forwarded message before sending the message. To forward a message, you click the Forward button. The recipient sees FW: and the original subject in the message header.

Reply To a Message

1. Select the message to which you want to reply.

2. Click the **Reply** button to reply to the sender only, or click the **Reply To All** button to send a message to the sender and all the recipients of the original message.

3. Type any new message text.

4. Click the **Send** button.

Did You Know?

Outlook does not resend the attachment in the reply message. When you reply to a message, Outlook doesn't include a copy of the attachment; however, it does lists the file name(s).

Outlook sends a copy of the attachment in a forwarded message. When you forward a message, Outlook includes a copy of any attachments received with the original message.

You can customize reply and forwarded messages. Click the File tab, click Options, click Mail in the left pane, select an option under Replies and Forwards to specify how to handle the text of messages that you reply to or forward, and then click OK.

Subject automatically inserted with RE: added to indicate you are replying to a message

Message to go to the sender of the original message

Message header and text from original message

Forward a Message

1. Select the message that you want to forward.

2. Click the **Forward** button on the Home tab.

3. Enter the name(s) of the recipient(s) in the To and Cc boxes.

4. Type any new message text.

5. Click the **Send** button.

Did You Know?

You can forward a message as an attachment. In Mail view, open the message you want to forward, click the More Respond Actions button, click Forward As Attachment, and then click Send.

Add an e-mail address to your contact list. Open the e-mail message, right-click the e-mail address you want, click Add To Outlook Contacts on the shortcut menu, enter any additional information, and then click the Save & Close button.

You can turn a message into a meeting request (**New!**). In Mail view, select the message you want to create a meeting request, click the Home tab, click the Meeting button, specify a location, time, and message, and then click Send.

You can get new e-mail quickly. The moment you receive new e-mail messages, the New Mail icon appears next to the clock on the taskbar. You can double-click the icon to switch to your Inbox. Depending on your e-mail service, you might have to log on to a network or dial in to an Internet service provider (ISP) to receive your new e-mail messages.

Subject automatically inserted with FW: added to indicate this is a forwarded message

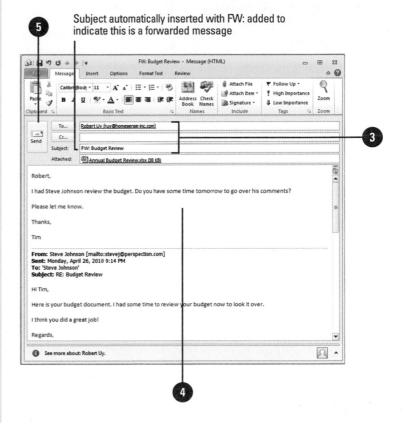

For Your Information

Creating an Out of Office Message

If you're out of the office and you want to automatically let people know, you can create an Out Of Office message. If you have a Microsoft Exchange account, use the Out of Office Assistant command, and then follow the instructions. If you have a POP3 or IMAP account, click the Mail button in the Navigation pane, click the New Items button, point to E-mail Message Using, click Plain Text, create a message template, click the File tab, click Save As, enter a name, and then set the file format to Outlook Template (.oft). Create a rule using the Rules button on the Home tab to automatically send the Outlook template to anyone who sends you an e-mail message. See "Managing Messages with Rules" on page 478 for more information.

Finding and Filtering Messages

By using the Instant Search bar and Search tab, you can easily and quickly locate one particular piece of e-mail among what may be hundreds of stored messages. If you know that the message contains a specific word or phrase in its title, contents, or properties, you can conduct a search using that word or phrase as the criteria. If you assign categories to your messages, you can locate them searching by category. You can use a filter to view only the items that meet the conditions you have defined. For example, you can filter your messages so the only ones that appear are those that you flagged as high priority or have categorized as business items. To quickly filter messages, you can use the Filter E-mail button on the Home tab (**New!**) or the Arrangement options on the View tab (**New!**), which also allows you to show the messages in a group.

Find a Message Using Instant Search

1. Click the **Mail** button on the Navigation pane.

2. Click in the Instant Search bar or press Ctrl+E.

   The Search tab under Search Tools opens.

3. To perform an recent search, click the **Recent Searches** button, and then select the search.

4. To define the scope of the search, use buttons in the Scope group, such as Current Folder.

5. To refine the Instant Search pane, use the buttons in the Refine group, such as From, Subject, or click More.

   As you enter criteria, Outlook displays and highlights the results.

6. To change the way Outlook searches, click the **Search Tools** button, click **Search Options**, select the options you want, and then click **OK**.

7. To redisplay all your messages, click the **Close Search** button on the Search tab or Instant Search bar.

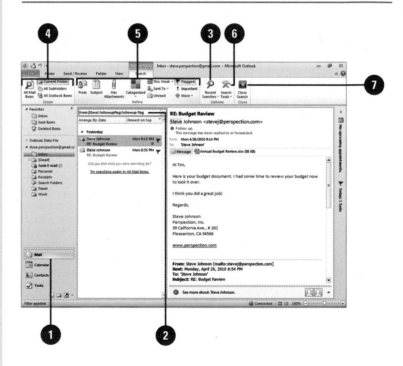

Filter Your Messages Quickly

1. Click the **Mail** button on the Navigation pane, and then display the folder you want to filter.

2. Click the **View** tab.

3. Click the **More** button, and then select the filter option you want.

   ◆ You can also click the Filter E-mail button on the Home tab, and then select a filter option.

4. To show the folder in a group, click **Show in Groups** on the More menu to select it. To not show the folder in a group, click Show in Groups to deselect it.

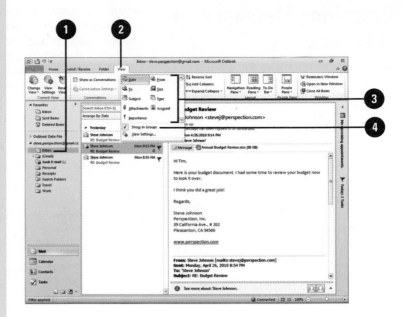

Filter Your Messages Based on Content

1. Click the **Mail** button on the Navigation pane, and then display the folder you want to filter.

2. Click the **View** tab, and then click the **View Settings** button.

3. Click **Filter**.

4. Click the **Messages** tab.

5. To filter your messages, enter the word or phrase, and then select one of the options provided.

6. To filter your messages using preset conditions, click the **Search for the word(s)** list arrow, and then select the option that you want to use as a filter.

7. Click **OK**.

8. Click **OK**.

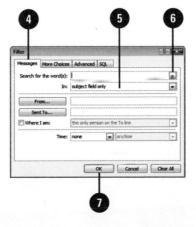

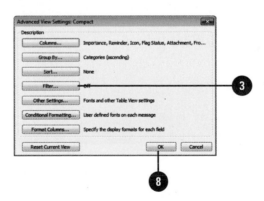

Organizing Messages in Folders

To help you organize your messages using folders, you can use the buttons on the Folder tab. Although Outlook provides the Inbox folder, this folder will become cluttered with messages unless you decide how you want to handle the messages that you have read. Some messages will be deleted immediately; others you will reply to or forward. With the exception of the deleted messages, all messages will remain in the Inbox until you move them elsewhere. To organize the messages you want to keep, you can create folders and move messages between the folders. You can also rename folders, copy or move folders, or delete ones you no longer want. If you have a message that is part of a conversation, you can have Outlook move it to a specified folder (**New!**).

Create a New Folder

1. Click the **Mail** button on the Navigation pane, and then select the folder in which where you want to create a new folder.

2. Click the **Folder** tab.

3. Click the **New Folder** button.

4. Type a new name for the folder.

5. Click the **Folder contains** list arrow, and then click **Mail And Post Items**.

6. Select where you want to store the new folder.

7. Click **OK**.

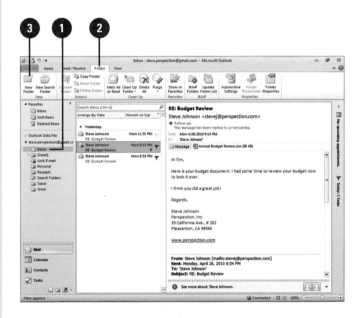

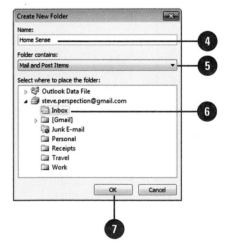

Did You Know?

You can save a mail message as a file. Click the mail message you want to save, click the File tab, click Save As, click the Save As Type list arrow, click a file type, type a new file name, and then click Save.

Sort items within a folder. If available, click a column button to sort items in the folder by that column in either ascending or descending order. You can also use the Reverse Sort button on the View tab to change the sort.

Work with Folders

1. Click the **Mail** button on the Navigation pane, and then select the folder you want to work with.

2. Click the **Folder** tab.

3. Use any of the following buttons:

   ◆ **Delete Folder.** Click Yes to confirm the deletion.

   ◆ **Rename Folder.** Type a new folder name, and then press Enter.

   ◆ **Copy Folder.** Select the folder where you want to copy the folder, and then click OK.

   ◆ **Move Folder.** Select the folder where you want to move the folder, and then click OK.

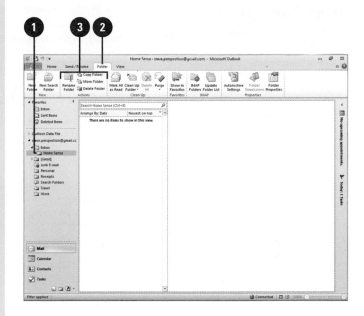

Move or Copy a Message to a Folder

1. Click the **Mail** button on the Navigation pane, and then select the folder that contains the message you want to move.

2. Click the **Home** tab.

3. Select the messages you want to move or copy.

4. Drag the message to a folder in the Folders list or click the **Move** button, and then select the folder, **Other Folder**, or **Copy to Folder**.

   ◆ To move the current and all future messages in a conversation to a folder, click **Always Move Messages in This Conversation**, select a folder, and then click **OK**.

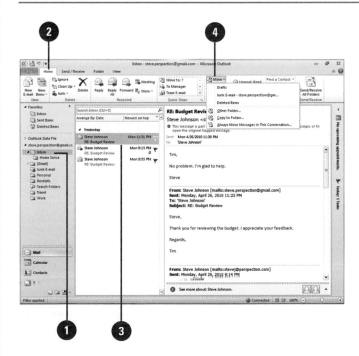

Managing Messages with Rules

Outlook provides a way to organize messages in folders using specific criteria, known as **rules**, that you set. For example, you can create a rule to automatically move, color-code, categorize, forward, and delete messages. The rule conditions can be based on a recipient, subject, sender, keywords, category, priority, or action flag to name a few. You can use the basic options to create rules for common tasks or the advanced options to create more complex rules with the Rules Wizard.

Create and Manage Messages Using Rules

① Click the **Home** tab.

② Click the **Rules** button, and then click **Manage Rules and Alerts**.

③ Click the **E-Mail Rules** tab, and then click a button option:

  ◆ **New Rule.** Creates a new rule.

  ◆ **Change Rule.** Edits the selected rule.

  ◆ **Delete.** Deletes the selected rule.

  ◆ **Run Rules Now.** Runs the selected rule.

④ Click a template.

⑤ Edit the rule description, and then follow the wizard instructions.

⑥ Click **Next** to continue each step of the wizard.

⑦ When you're done with the wizard, click **Finish**.

⑧ Click **OK**.

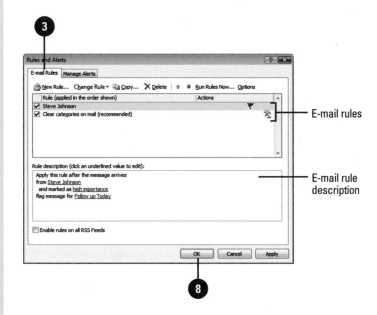

E-mail rules

E-mail rule description

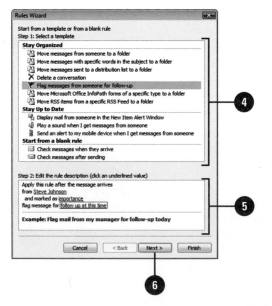

Managing Messages with Quick Steps

Quick Steps (**New!**) make it easier to perform multiple actions with one click on the Home tab. Outlook comes with several default Quick Steps—such as Move to:?, To Manager, Team E-mail, Reply & Delete, and Create New—that you can use right away, or you can create your own. You can even customize the default Quick Steps. When you create a new Quick Step, you can specify a type, such as Move to Folder, Flag & Move, New E-mail To, Forward To, New Meeting, or Custom.

Use, Create, and Manage Messages Using Quick Steps

1. Click the **Mail** button on the Navigation pane, and then select the folder you want to use.

2. Click the **Home** tab.

3. To use a Quick Step, select the message you want to use, click the Quick Steps **More** button, and then click a Quick Step.

4. To create a new Quick Step, click the Quick Steps **More** button, point to **New Quick Step**, click an option, and then follow the wizard.

   - ◆ **Move to Forward.**
   - ◆ **Flag & Move.**
   - ◆ **New E-mail To.**
   - ◆ **Forward To.**
   - ◆ **New Meeting.**
   - ◆ **Custom.**

5. To manage and edit Quick Steps, click the Quick Steps **More** button, click **Manage Quick Step**, make changes, and then click **OK**.

   - ◆ **Move.**
   - ◆ **New.**
   - ◆ **Edit.**
   - ◆ **Duplicate.**
   - ◆ **Delete.**

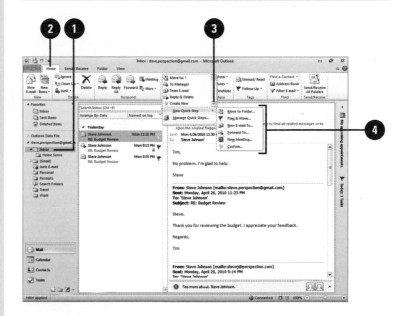

New Quick Step

Using Search Folders

Outlook's search folders are another way that Outlook makes managing mail easier. Search folders are not like the folders that you create or even like the Outlook default folders. Search folders store information about your messages, without having to move the messages to a specific folder. In the New Search dialog box, you can use a defined search folder—such as Mail sent directly to me, Old mail, Large mail, Mail with attachments, and Mail with specific words—or create a custom search folder for the messages that meet your specific criteria.

Create or Change a Search Folder

1. In Mail view, use either of the following:

   ◆ **Create.** Click the **Folder** tab, click the **New Search Folder** button, scroll down the list, select a search folder or click **Create a custom Search Folder**, and then click **Choose**.

   ◆ **Change.** Right-click the search folder in the Folder list you want to change, and then click **Customize this Search Folder**.

2. Type or edit the name of the folder.

3. Click **Criteria**.

4. Specify the criteria for the messages for this search folder.

5. Click **OK**.

6. Click **Browse**, select the folders you want searched, and then click OK.

7. Click **OK**.

8. Click **OK** again.

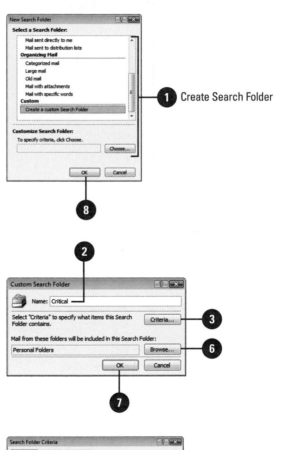

Create Search Folder

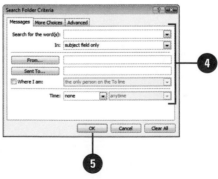

Working with a Message Conversation

When you send and reply messages back and forth between another recipient, Outlook keeps track of them—including sent messages and messages in other folders—in a conversation (**New!**). Conversation view groups related messages together to make is easier to work with. You can see the entire conversation, including a visual relationship between messages, so you can determine which ones are important for you to keep. After you finish with a conversation, you can delete the current and all future messages or remove all redundant messages to clean up the clutter of the conversation.

Work with a Message Conversation

1. Click the **View** tab.

2. To turn conversations on or off, click **Conversations** in the Arrangement group, select or clear the **Show as Conversations** check box, and then click **All folders** or **This folder**.

3. To set conversation settings, click the **Conversation Settings** button, and then select an option.

   - **Show Messages from Other Folders.**

   - **Show Senders Above the Subject.**

   - **Always Expand Conversations.**

   - **Use Classic Indented View.**

4. To expand or open the conversation, click the arrow on the message header.

5. To delete conversation messages, click the **Home** tab, and then use any of the following options:

   - **Delete Conversation.** Click the **Ignore** button; deletes current and all future messages.

   - **Delete Redundant Conversation.** Click the **Clean Up** button, and then select an option.

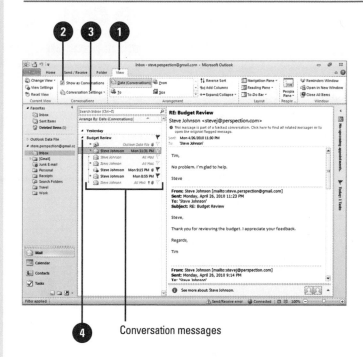

Conversation messages

Reducing Junk Messages

You can have Outlook handle junk e-mail for you. You can specify what should be considered junk e-mail and how Outlook should handle that e-mail. You can ensure that e-mail from certain addresses or domains, which might seem to be junk e-mail, but is actually from a person or site you want using Outlook E-mail Postmark. You can also make sure that the mail you send isn't treated as junk e-mail. Outlook also tracks suspicious e-mail (potential phishing), and automatically disables message links until you approve it.

Reduce Junk E-Mail and Spam

1 Click the **Mail** button on the Navigation pane, and then click the **Inbox** folder.

2 Click the **Junk** button, and then click **Junk E-mail Options**.

3 Click the **Options** tab, and then select the options you want.

4 Click the **Safe Senders** tab, and then specify the messages from the addresses or domains that should not be junk e-mail.

5 Click the **Safe Recipients** tab, and then specify the messages sent to the e-mail addresses or domains that should never be treated as junk mail.

6 Click the **Blocked Senders** tab, and then specify the messages from addresses or domains that should not be junk e-mail.

7 Click **OK**, and then click **OK** again.

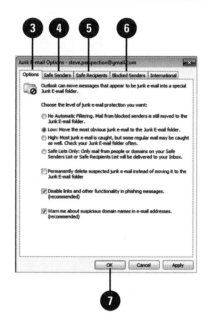

Did You Know?

You can deal with junk mail as it arrives. If you receive a message that is junk mail, click the Home tab, click the Junk button, and then select the option for dealing with the message.

Set mail to junk as it arrives

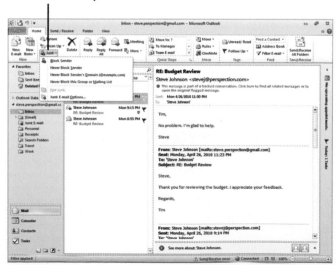

Archiving Messages

Archiving compresses messages into files that are stored on your hard drive. You can archive messages manually or automatically using AutoArchive. This Outlook tool automates the task of archiving your messages (as well as files and folders) based on a period of time you set. For example, you could archive all the messages you sent in the last six months. Archived items are saved in the personal store (.pst) file format. This format compresses the message so it takes up less space. It also stores the file on your computer and not on the e-mail server.

Set Archive Options for a Folder

1 Click the **File** tab, and then click **Info**.

2 Click the **Cleanup Tools** button, and then click **Archive**.

3 Click a folder, such as the Inbox, and then specify the other options you want for the archive.

4 Click **OK**.

5 To set or apply AutoArchive settings, click the **Folder** tab, click the **AutoArchive Settings** button, select an option, and then click **OK** or **Apply**.

◆ **Do not archive items in this folder.**

◆ **Archive items in this folder using the default settings.**

◆ **Archive this folder using these settings.**

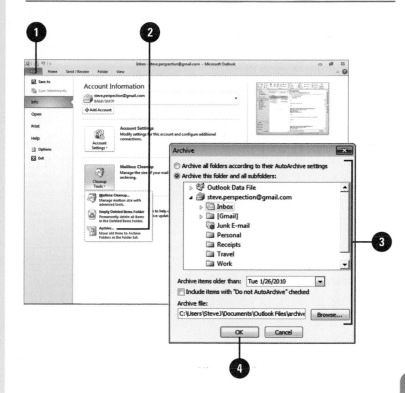

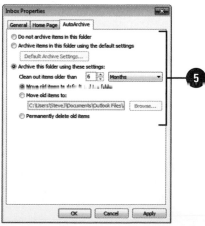

Did You Know?

You can retrieve an archived file. Click the File tab, click Open, click Import to start the Import and Export Wizard. Select the Import from another program or file option, click Next, scroll down and click Personal Folder File (.pst), click Next, click Browse, navigate to the folder where the archive is stored, double-click the archive, click Next, and then click Finish. The file is restored to the Inbox.

Cleaning Up Messages

If your mailbox is getting hard to manage, you can use clean up tools to help you get it under control. The cleanup tools are available on the Info screen on the File tab. In the Mailbox Cleanup dialog box (**New!**), you can view the mailbox size, find old or large messages, AutoArchive old items, view the size of the Deleted Items folder, permanently empty (delete) all messages in the Deleted Items folder, and delete all alternate version of items in your mailbox. When you delete a message, it gets automatically moved to the Deleted Items Folder. If you don't want a message to be moved, you can set Purge options to have it marked and remain in its current location. If you want to delete it later, you can use one of the Purge Marked Items commands.

Set Mailbox Cleanup Options

1. Click the **Mail** button on the Navigation pane, and then click the **Inbox** folder.

2. Click the **File** tab, and then click **Info**.

3. Click the **Cleanup Tools** button, and then click **Mailbox Cleanup**.

4. Select the cleanup options you want:

   ◆ **View Mailbox Size.** Displays the size of mailbox folders.

   ◆ **Find Items.** Select options to find older or larger items.

   ◆ **AutoArchive.** Moves old items to the archive file on this computer. You can access it in the Archive folders in the Folder list.

   ◆ **Empty Deleted Items Folder.** Empties the Deleted Items Folder.

   ◆ **View Deleted Items Size.** Displays the size of items in the Deleted Items folder.

   ◆ **Delete Alternate Items.** Deletes alternate versions of items.

   ◆ **View Alternate Items Size.** Displays the size of alternate items.

5. Click **Close**.

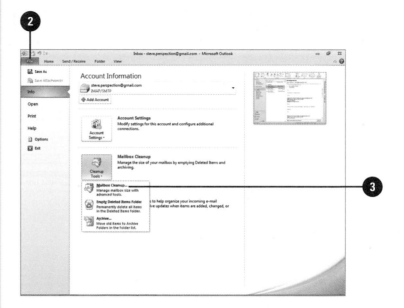

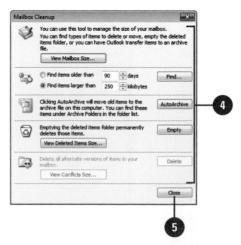

Purge Marked Items

1. Click the **Mail** button on the Navigation pane, and then click the **Inbox** folder.

2. Click the **Folder** tab.

3. Click the **Purge** button, and then click **Purge Options**.

4. Click the **Mark items for deletion but do not move them automatically** option.

   ◆ To reset message deletion back to the Deleted Items Folder, click the **Move deleted items to the following folder on the server** option, and then select the folder.

5. Click **OK**.

6. Select and delete the messages you want to mark for purging.

7. Click the **Purge** button, and then click one of the Purge Marked Items commands.

See Also

See "Deleting Messages" on page 471 for more information on deleting messages and managing the Deleted Items Folder.

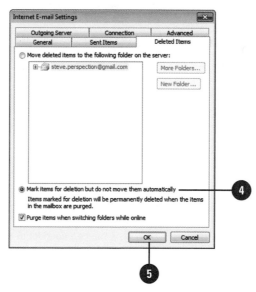

Working with Outlook Data

The Account Settings dialog box provides a central place to work with different types of data in Outlook. You can work with e-mail, data folders, RSS feeds, SharePoint lists, Internet Calendars, published calendars, and Address Books. Outlook stores all your data in folders, which you can archive or save in the personal store (.pst) file format for use on other computers. You can add, remove, and change settings—such as default location or name—for each of the data types. If you already have data, such as address book information or a personal store file, you can use the Import and Export wizard to help you import the data.

Add and Remove Outlook Data

1 Click the **File** tab, and then click **Info**.

2 Click the **Account Settings** button, and then click **Account Settings**.

3 Click the **Data Files** tab.

4 Click **Add**.

5 To open a data file, select it. To create a data file, type a name and select a save as type.

6 To specify a password (optional), select the **Add Optional Password** check box.

7 Click **OK**.

8 Specify a password, and then click **OK**.

9 To remove an address book, select the address book, and then click **Remove**.

10 Click **Close**.

For Your Information

Connecting to an Exchange Server

You can connect to an Exchange server over the Internet using RPC. Click the File tab, click Info, click the Account Settings button, and then click Account Settings. In the Account Setting dialog box, click the E-mail tab, select the Exchange account, and then click Change. Click More Settings, select the Connect to Microsoft Exchange using HTTP check box, click Exchange Proxy Settings, specify the options provided by your Exchange administrator, and then click OK twice.

Add an Address Book

① Click the **File** tab, and then click **Info**.

② Click the **Account Settings** button, and then click **Account Settings**.

③ Click the **Address Books** tab.

④ Click **New**.

⑤ Click the **Additional address books** option, and then click **Next**.

⑥ Click the address book you want to add, and then click **Next**.

⑦ Click **Finish**, and then exit and restart Outlook to use the address book.

⑧ To remove an address book, select the address book, click **Remove**, and then click **Yes**.

⑨ Click **Close**.

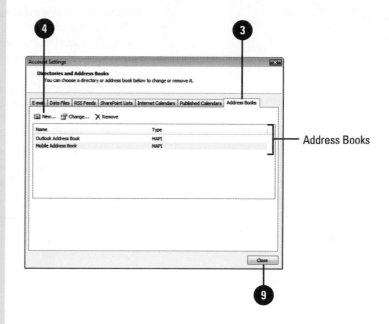

Address Books

Import Data in Outlook

① Click the **File** tab, click **Open**, and then click **Import**.

② Select an import option, and then click **Next**.

③ Select a file type, and then click **Next**.

④ Follow the wizard instructions. Direction vary depending on the import option you selected.

⑤ When you're done, click **Finish**.

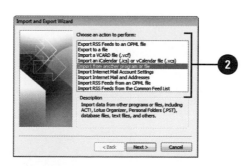

Sending and Receiving Instant Messages

When you display a message in the Reading pane, or open a message in Outlook, the online status indicator appears next to the sender's name. You can click the online status indicator to display a menu with options to reply with an instant message. The online status icon provides a visual indicator of online availability. When you select a send option in Outlook, a Conversation window from Windows Live Messenger opens, where you can type your message and send and receive instant messages. While you are communicating in Windows Live Messenger, you can click a link to view your Inbox or send an e-mail message to a Windows Live Messenger contact. Outlook needs to be your default e-mail program. After you start a conversation with someone, you can add others to the conversation, so that up to five people are communicating in the same session.

Start an Instant Message from Outlook

1. Open a message from a contact signed into Instant Messenger.

2. Point to the online status indicator or the e-mail address.

3. Click the **Send an instant message t:o:** icon.

4. In the Conversation window, type the message, and then press Enter or click **Send**.

Did You Know?

You can change your online status anytime. Click the My Status button, and then click the status you want: Available, Busy, Away, or Appear Offline.

You can send an e-mail from Windows Live Messenger. In Windows Live Messenger, click Show Menu button, point to Actions, point to Send Other, and then click Send An E-mail Message.

You can close Windows Messenger while you are signed in. Click the Close button. Windows Messenger continues to run in the background as long as you are signed in.

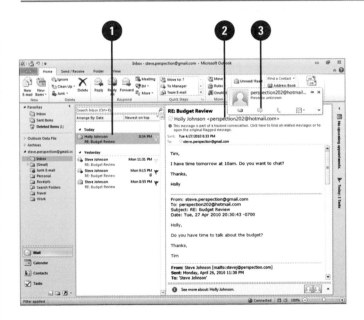

Managing Information with Outlook

Introduction

Microsoft Office Outlook 2010 provides an easy and efficient way to track and organize all the information that lands on your desk. You can use Outlook tools for your personal information management needs. With Outlook, you can organize and manage your day-to-day information, from e-mail and calendars to contacts and tasks. It's easy to share information with others, and organize and view your schedule and communications in one place.

Using the Calendar feature, you can manage your time by doing much more than circling dates. Among its many features, the Outlook Calendar lets you schedule **Appointments** (dates that are noted with data referring to that day's activity and do not require attendance by other individuals) and **Events** (an appointment that lasts 24 hours or more). Outlook also allows you to share your calendar with others. In Outlook, you view the schedules of your coworkers before you schedule meetings or appointments so that you can determine when all the people in your group are free at the same time.

You can use Outlook to create a to-do list and assign the items on the list to others as needed from Tasks. Rather then cluttering your desk or obscuring your computer with sticky pad notes, use Notes to jot down your immediate thoughts, ideas, and other observations. With everything related to your work in one place, you can always locate what you nood files, notes for a project, or even the time of a phone call with a certain contact. Just check the Journal timeline to find it. To help organize and locate information, Outlook allows you to group, sort, and filter items.

What You'll Do

View and Customize the Calendar

Schedule an Appointment and Event

Schedule Meetings

Respond to Meeting Requests

Update and Cancel Meeting Requests

Work with Calendars

Create and Update Tasks

Assign and Monitor Tasks

Organize and Manage Tasks

Track Activities with Contacts

Record Items in the Journal

Open and Modify Journal Entries

Organize Items by Categories

Customize How You View Items

Create and Modify Notes

Preview and Print Items from Outlook

Connect to a Social Network

Share Calendars Over the Internet

Viewing the Calendar

The **Calendar** is an electronic version of the familiar paper daily planner. You can schedule time for completing specific tasks, meetings, vacations, holidays, or for any other activity with the Calendar. You can change the Calendar to show activities for the Day, Work Week (five business days), Week (all seven days), Month, or Schedule view (horizontal layout for multiple calendars) (**New!**). You can also quickly go to today or the next 7 days (**New!**). The Calendar is split into two sections: the Appointment area and the Date Navigator. The Appointment area serves as a daily planner where you can schedule activities by the day, work week, full week, or month. Appointments are scheduled activities such as a doctor's visit, and occupy a block of time in the Appointment area. Events are activities that last 24 hours or longer, such as a seminar, and do not occupy blocks of time in your calendar. Instead, they appear in a banner at the beginning of a day. At the bottom of Calendar view, Outlook displays the tasks associated with the days displayed in the calendar.

Open and Change the Calendar View

1. Click the **Calendar** button on the Navigation pane.

2. You can change the Calendar view in several ways.

   - Click one of the Calendar view buttons (**Day**, **Work Week**, **Week**, **Month**, or **Schedule View** (**New!**)) on the Home tab. The Month button provides additional view options.

   - Click one of the Go To buttons (**Today** or **Next 7 Days**) (**New!**) on the Home tab.

   - Click the left arrow or right arrow on the Date Navigator to change the current month.

   - Click a date on the Date Navigator to view that day's schedule. The date highlighted in red is today's date.

   - Click the **View** tab, and then click the view option you want.

3. View and work with tasks associated with the current Calendar view.

Date Navigator   Calendar view button and options

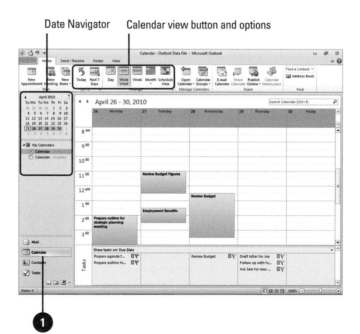

Customizing the Calendar

As with other folders in Outlook, you can customize Calendar to suit your needs. For example, you can change the background color or the text font if you like. You can also set Calendar to display week numbers (from 1 to 52) to the left of each week in the Date Navigator. If you change the background color of the Calendar, it only applies to Day and Work Week views. The Week and Month views use system colors. Another way to customize the Outlook Calendar is to change the work week settings. For example, if you are in the medical field and you work three twelve-hour shifts a week, Wednesday through Friday, you might want to change the work week in your Calendar to reflect this. You can change the days included in the work week, the start day of the work week, the start and end times of the work day, and the first week of the work year.

Customize the Calendar View

① Click the **File** tab, and then click **Options**.

② Click **Calendar** in the left pane.

③ Select the Work time options you want to customize.

④ Select the Calendar options check boxes you want, including default reminder times, add holidays, and free/busy options.

⑤ Select the Display options you want to use, including calendar color, and when to switch layouts.

⑥ Select the Time zones and Resource scheduling options.

⑦ Click **OK**.

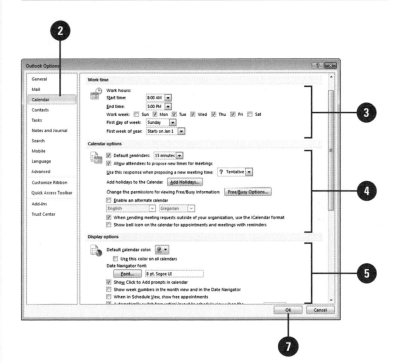

Did You Know?

You can open or create a new calendar. Switch to Calendar view, click the Home tab, click the Open Calendar button, and then click an option to open a calendar from a source or Create New Blank Calendar (**New!**).

Scheduling an Appointment and Event

In Outlook, an **appointment** is any activity you schedule that doesn't include other people or resources. An **event** is any appointment that lasts one or more full days (24-hour increments), such as a seminar, a conference, or a vacation. You can mark yourself available (free or tentative) or unavailable (busy or out of the office) to others during a scheduled appointment or an event. You enter appointment or event information in the same box; however, when you schedule an event, the All Day Event check box is selected; the check box is cleared when you schedule an appointment.

Schedule an Appointment

1 Click the **Calendar** button on the Navigation pane.

◆ In Outlook, you can also right-click an e-mail address, and then click **Schedule a Meeting**.

2 Click the start time of the appointment in the Appointment area.

3 Type a short description of the appointment, and then press Enter.

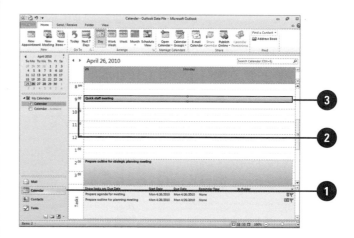

Include Appointment Details

1 In Calendar view, double-click a block of time or an appointment.

2 Add or change the subject, location, start and end times, as necessary.

3 Type any information needed for the appointment, or insert a file.

4 To set a reminder, click the **Reminder** list arrow, and then specify a reminder time.

5 Click the **Show as** list arrow, and then select an availability option.

6 Click the **Save & Close** button.

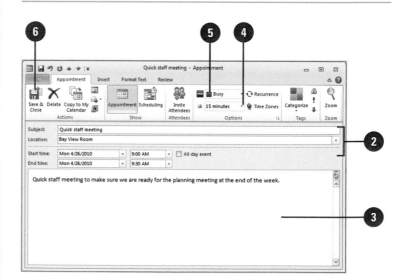

Schedule an Event and Include Details

1. Click the **Calendar** button on the Navigation pane.

2. Click the top of the day in the Appointment area.

3. Type a description of the event, and then press Enter.

4. Double-click the event.

5. Add or change the subject, location, start and end times, as necessary.

6. Type any information needed for the event, or insert a file.

7. To set a reminder, click the **Reminder** list arrow, and then specify a reminder time.

8. Click the **Show as** list arrow, and then select an availability option: **Free**, **Tentative**, **Busy**, or **Out of Office**.

9. To add a color category, click the **Categorize** button, and then click a color category.

10. To create a private meeting, click the **Private** button. A lock icon appears in the calendar (**New!**).

11. Click the **Save & Close** button.

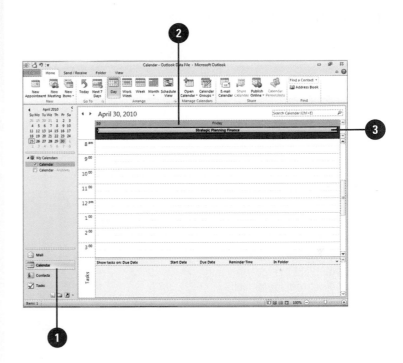

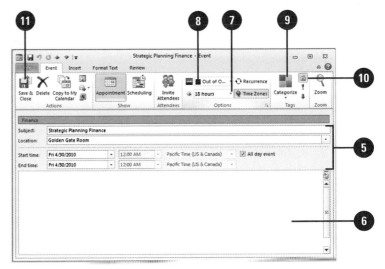

Did You Know?

You can schedule a new recurring appointment. In Calendar view, select a block of time, click the New Items button, point to More Items, click Recurring Appointment, fill in the appointment times and recurrence information, click OK, and then click the Save & Close button.

Scheduling Meetings

Scheduling a meeting can mean inviting people outside your organization, locating a place to have the meeting, making sure you have the right equipment for the meeting. Outlook can help you do all this. When you schedule a meeting using Outlook you are sending a special kind of e-mail message—a message request. Each invited attendee and the person responsible for the resource that you may have requested receive a message request. It is to this message that the invitee must respond. If you're using Outlook with a Microsoft Exchange Server, you can also reserve resources, such as a conference room. Resources are added to the Global Address List by the system administrator.

Schedule a New Meeting

1. Click the **Calendar** button on the Navigation pane.

2. In the Navigation pane, display the date you want the meeting, and then select the people and resources you want, if available.

3. Select a calendar view button, and then select a time slot.

4. Click the **New Meeting** button, and then (if needed) click **New Meeting** or **New Meeting with All** (**New!**).

5. Click the **Scheduling** button on the Meeting tab.

6. To add others, click **Add Others**, and then click **Add from Address Book**.

7. Click the **Address Book** list arrow, and then click **Contacts** or **Global Address Book**.

8. Click a name, and then click **Required** and **Optional** for each person you want to invite them.

9. To schedule a resource, click a resource, and then click **Resources**.

10. Click **OK**.

11. Click the **Appointment** button on the Meeting tab.

12. Enter meeting related information, and then click the **Send** button.

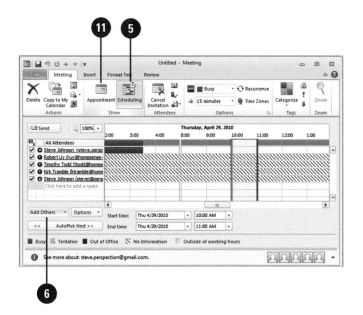

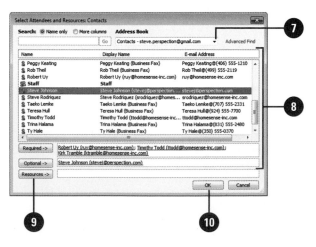

Add People to a Meeting

1. Click the **Calendar** button on the Navigation pane.

2. Scroll the Date Navigator to display the date you want to schedule the meeting.

3. Double-click the meeting to which you want to add people.

4. Click the **Scheduling** button.

5. Click **Add Others**, click **Add from Address Book**, and then display the names you want.

6. Select the required and optional attendees.

7. Select the resource you need, and then click **Required** or **Optional**.

8. Click **OK**.

9. To track who has responded to the meeting, click the **Tracking** button.

10. To send a message to attendees, click the **Contact Attendees** button, and then click the option you want.

11. Click the **Appointment** button, enter meeting related information, and then click the **Send** or **Send Update** button.

12. Click the response option you want, and then click **OK**.

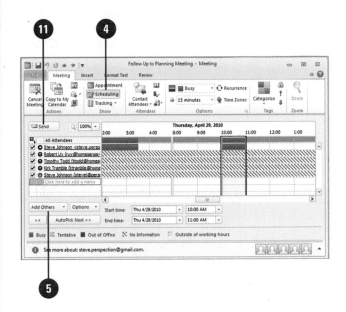

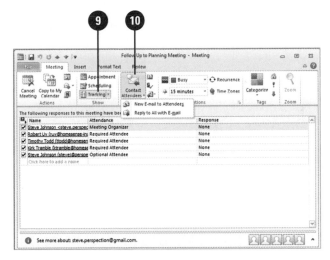

Did You Know?

You can schedule a resource for an existing meeting. In Calendar view, double-click the scheduled meeting, click the Scheduling button, click Add Others, click Add From Address Book, display the resources you want, click Resources, click OK, and then click the Send button.

Responding to Meeting Requests

When you receive a meeting request it appears in your Inbox such as any message would. The difference is when you view the message you can also view your calendar to see where the meeting is scheduled. Once you are sure whether or not you can attend a meeting, then you use the Accept button or the Decline button at the top of the meeting request e-mail. If you want to propose a different time, you can use the Propose Time button. A message is sent to the sender of the meeting request with your response. If you need to view your calendar while viewing the meeting request e-mail, you can use the Calendar button.

Accept a Meeting Request

1. Display your Inbox, and then click the e-mail with the meeting request.

2. To view the meeting in your Calendar, click the **Calendar** button, review, and then close the Calendar.

3. Click **Accept**, and then select an option (**New!**). To tentatively accept, click **Tentative**, and then select an option (**New!**).

4. Click the **Send the response now** option.

5. Click **OK**.

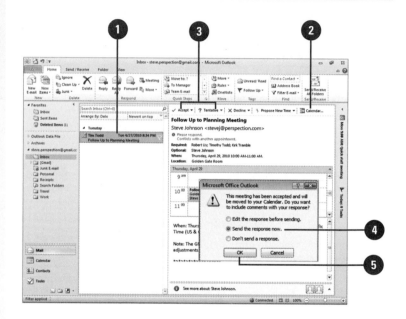

Propose a New Meeting Time

1. Display your Inbox, and then click the e-mail with the meeting request.

2. Click **Propose New Time**, and then click **Tentative and Propose New Time** or **Decline and Propose New Time** (**New!**).

3. Specify a new meeting time.

4. Click **Propose Time**.

5. Enter information in the e-mail regarding the meeting, and then click the **Send** button.

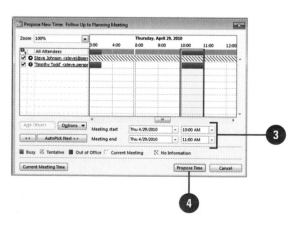

Decline a Meeting Request

1. Display your Inbox, and then click the e-mail with the meeting request.

2. To view the meeting in your Calendar, click the **Calendar** button, and then close the Calendar.

3. Click **Decline**, and then select an option: **Edit the Response before Sending**, **Send the Response Now**, or **Do Not Send a Response** (**New!**).

4. Click the **Edit the response before sending** option.

5. Click **OK**.

6. Type a message that explains why you are unable to attend the meeting.

7. Click the **Send** button.

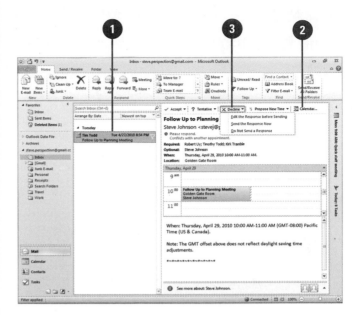

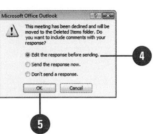

Did You Know?

You can automate and track meeting resources. If you are responsible for resources made available for meetings, click the File tab, click Options, click Calendar in the left pane, click Resource Scheduling, select the options for dealing with requests for resources, and then click OK.

Updating and Canceling Meeting Requests

Planning meetings can be a difficult task when you have to coordinate multiple schedules, schedules that often change with little or no notice. You can spend endless hours on the phone trying to keep all the meeting attendees up-to-date. However, there is an easier way. You can use the Outlook Calendar to reschedule or cancel meetings. You can send a meeting update request, or cancel the meeting, if necessary via e-mail to let everyone who should be at the meeting know about the change without having to spend hours on the phone. When you send attendees an updated meeting request, the attendee receives an e-mail message, the original meeting is deleted, and the new meeting time is added to his/her Calendar. If you send a cancellation notice about the meeting, the meeting is deleted from the attendees' Calendars.

Update a Meeting Request

1. Display your Calendar, and then double-click the scheduled meeting.

2. Click the **Scheduling** button.

3. Click a new slot, and then drag the length of the meeting.

4. If necessary, click **Add Others** to invite others or add more resources, and then click **OK**.

5. Click the **Send** button, select an update option, and then click **OK**.

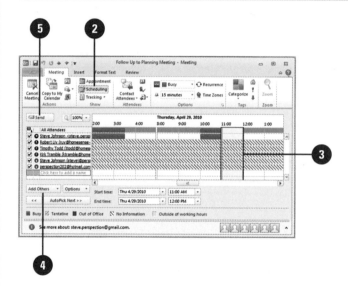

Cancel a Meeting Request

1. Display your Calendar, and then double-click the scheduled meeting.

2. Click the **Cancel Meeting** button, and then click **Yes** to confirm.

3. Click the **Send Cancellation** button.

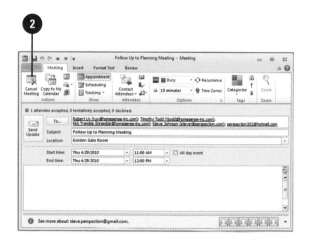

Working with Calendars

Instead of putting all your appointments on a single calendar, you can spread them out based on content. For example, you can have a calendar for work and another one for home. You can view multiple calendars at the same time in any of the views. If you want a horizontal view, you can use the Schedule view (**New!**). If you need to manage calendars for a group, you can create a calendar group (**New!**). You can create a new calendar from scratch or open one from different sources (**New!**).

Open and Work with Calendars

① Click the **Calendar** button on the Navigation pane.

② Click the **Home** tab.

③ To open or create a calendar, click the **Open Calendar** button, and then click one of the following options:

- ◆ **From Address Book.** Select contacts from the Address Book.

- ◆ **From Room List.** Select rooms from the resources list.

- ◆ **From Internet.** Specify a URL to an ICS calendar.

- ◆ **Create New Blank Calendar.** Specify a name to create a blank calendar.

- ◆ **Open Shared Calendar.** Opens another person's shared calendar.

④ To create a calendar group, click the **Calendar Group** button, click **Create New Calendar Group** or **Save as New Calendar Group**, type a group name, click **OK**, select your group members, and then click **OK**.

⑤ In the Navigation pane, select a calendar check box to display a calendar.

⑥ To view multiple calendars in a layout view, click the **Schedule View** button.

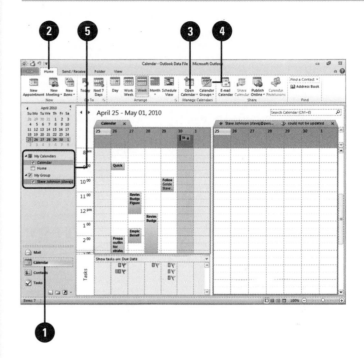

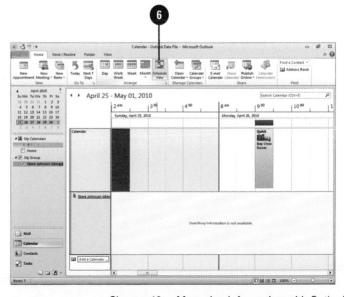

Creating and Updating Tasks

You can quickly create a task by name only using the create a task box on the To-Do Bar or Tasks view, or a more detailed task using the New Task button on the Home tab. The New Task window allows you to set a Due Date (the date by which the task must be completed), Start Date, the Priority, and select the Reminder check box to have a reminder window open the morning of the due date. To keep track of the task, you can set the Status (Not Started, In Progress, Completed, Waiting On Someone Else, or Deferred) and the Percentage Complete (0 to 100%). You can type additional information about the task in the Notes area at the bottom of the window.

Create or Update a Task

1. To quickly create a task, click the create a task box at the top of the Task pane, or in the To-Do List Bar, type a name and then press Enter.

   To create a detailed task, click the **Tasks** button on the Navigation pane, and then click the **New Task** button on the Home tab.

2. In the Tasks folder, double-click the task.

3. Type a short description of the task in the Subject box.

4. Click the **Start Date** list arrow, select the start date, click the **Due Date** list arrow, and then select the due date.

5. Click the **Status** list arrow, and then click an option.

6. Select the percentage in the % Complete box, and then type a new percentage.

7. Click in the Notes area, and then type additional information about the task.

8. To set a reminder, select the **Reminder** check box, and then select a date and time.

9. Click the **Save & Close** button.

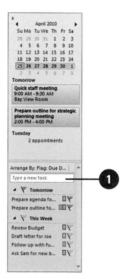

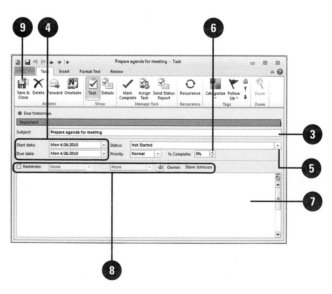

Organizing Tasks

You can display tasks in a variety of views. The default Simple List view displays the task's description, the due date, and a check box to indicate that the task is completed. To see more information about each task, you can switch to Detailed view, which includes columns for the task's priority, whether a file is attached, the status of the task, the percentage complete, and the category of each task. Detailed view does not include the column with the check box to indicate that a task is completed (although in both views, completed tasks are indicated with strikethrough text). To show all your tasks that are over due, you can switch to Overdue view to see a horizontal timeline with tasks noted on their due dates. You can also display views by the To-Do List, Prioritized, Active, Complete, and Server Tasks with SharePoint.

Change Tasks Views

① Click the **Tasks** button on the Navigation pane.

② Click the **Change View** button on the Home tab, and then select an option:

◆ **View.** Click Detailed, Simple List, To-Do List, Prioritized, Active, Complete, Today, Next 7 Days, Overdue, Assigned, or Server Tasks.

◆ **Manage Views.** Select to create, copy, and modify task views.

◆ **Save Current View As a New View.** Select to create a new view based on the current view.

◆ **Apply Current View to Other Task Folders.** Select to apply the current view settings to another task folder.

③ To collapse or expand a task group, click the arrow next to the left of the group name.

For Your Information

Using Outlook Today

Outlook Today can display your Calendar, Tasks, and Inbox so you can see what you have in store for the day. You can customize the look of Outlook Today by specifying which folders you want to display in your calendar, the number of tasks, and the layout of the Outlook Today pane. To view Outlook Today, click the Outlook Data File in the Mail view in the Navigator pane. Click the Custom Outlook Today link to change the display.

Assigning Tasks to Others

Because most projects involve the efforts and input of several people, it will often be necessary to delegate responsibilities for a task to other members on your team of contacts. In Outlook, you can assign or forward and send a task assignment to a co-worker. To assign or forward a task, you use the Assign Task or Forward button, and then assign the task to someone in your Contacts list. If a task is assigned to you, you will receive an e-mail that contains the task request. You can accept or decline the task, and send your reply back to the sender.

Assign or Forward a Task

1. Double-click the task or create a task.

2. Click the **Assign Task** or **Forward** button.

3. Click the **To** button, select a recipient, click the **To** button, and then click **OK**.

4. Click the **Send** button.

Assign Task button toggles to Cancel Assignment button

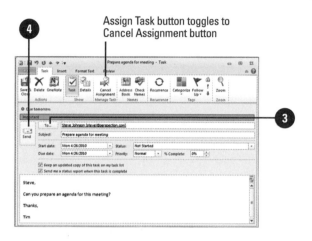

Accept or Decline a Task

1. Open the task request.

2. Click the **Accept** or **Decline** button.

3. To reply to the sender with a comment, click the **Edit the response before sending** option, click **OK**, type a comment, and then click the **Send** button.

   To send a response, click the **Send the response now** option, and then click **OK**.

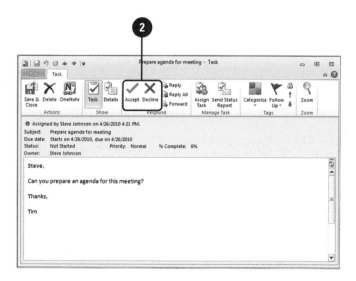

Did You Know?

You can reclaim a rejected task. Open the message with the task request (Sent Items folder), and then click the Return To List button.

Monitoring Task Progress

After you've passed along ownership of a task, you will want to keep track of it. Outlook enables you to automatically keep track of assigned tasks and receive regular updates on their progress. When you create a task, you are designated as the owner of that task. As its owner, you are the only person who can edit the task, unless you assign it to someone else and they accept the assignment. In that case, however, you can still opt to maintain an updated copy in your Tasks folder and obtain status updates whenever the task is edited or completed.

Receive Updates for an Assigned Task

1. Double-click the assigned task.

2. Click the **To** button, select a recipient, click **To**, and then click **OK**.

3. If it is not already selected, select the **Keep an updated copy of this task on my task list** check box.

4. If it is not already selected, select the **Send me a status report when this task is complete** check box.

5. Click the **Send** button.

6. To view the tasks by assignment, click the **Home** tab, click the **Change View** button, and then click **Assigned**.

Click to make private

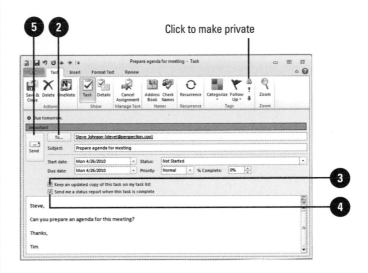

Did You Know?

You can cancel a task assignment. In Tasks view, double-click the task, and then click the Cancel Assignment button on the Task tab.

You can make a task private. In Tasks view, double-click the task, and then click the Private button on the Task tab.

You can get a status report. In Tasks view, double-click the task, and then click the Send Status Report button on the Task tab, and then address and send the message.

Owner of task

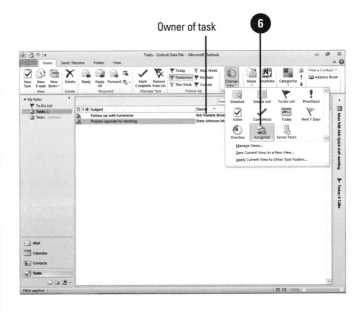

Managing Tasks

As you work with tasks, you'll want to keep your Tasks folder updated to reflect the status of each task. One obvious tactic is to mark each task as completed once you've finished the task. To do this, you select or open the task, and then click the Mark Complete button on the Ribbon. Once you've marked a task as complete, it appears in the Tasks folder with a line through it. Some tasks are jobs that you need to complete on a regular basis. In this case, you can make a task recurring. Recurring tasks have a small icon with two circling arrows in the Tasks folder. If you no longer need a task, you can remove it from the list.

Mark a Task as Completed or Remove a Task

1. Select the task in the Tasks folder, or double-click the task to open it.

2. Click the **Mark Complete** button on the Task or Home tab.

3. Click the **Save & Close** button, if needed, on the Task tab.

4. Select the task you want remove, and then click the **Remove from List** button on the Home tab.

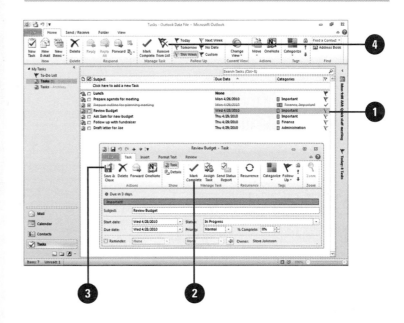

Change a Task to Recurring

1. In the Tasks folder, double-click the task.

2. Click the **Recurrence** button on the Task tab.

3. Click the recurrence pattern option you want.

4. Select the check boxes with the recurrence pattern you want.

5. Click the end date option you want.

6. Click **OK**.

7. Click the **Save & Close** button.

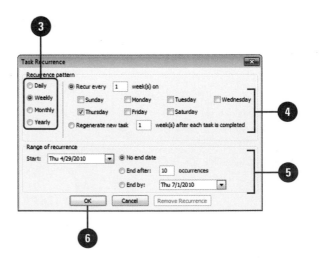

Tracking Activities with Contacts

A powerful feature in Outlook is the ability to track your activities associated with each contact. You can create a journal entry to track the length of time you spend dealing with a contact, and you can take notes during this entry. You can also schedule meetings with a contact and assign tasks to a contact. All journal entries, meetings, and tasks associated with a contact appear on the Activities view in the Contact window. Journal entries are handy for tracking the amount of time you spend dealing with a contact, and for taking notes about that contact. To associate a journal entry with a contact, you select the contact, and then click Journal Entry from the More button on the Home tab.

Create a Journal Entry for a Contact

1. In the Contacts folder, click a contact to select it.

2. Click the **More** button on the Home tab, and then click **Journal Entry**.

   TIMESAVER *Right-click the contact, point to Create, and then click Journal Entry on the shortcut menu.*

3. Click the **Entry Type** list arrow, and then select a category type.

4. Click the **Start Timer** button to start the timer.

5. Click in the message box, and then type notes about the contact.

6. Click the **Pause Timer** button to stop the timer.

7. Click the **Save & Close** button.

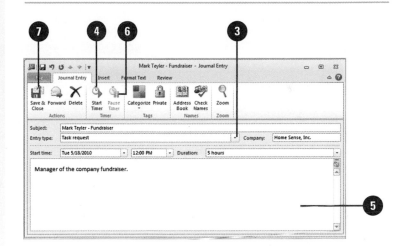

Did You Know?

You can display all tasks for a contact. In Contacts view, double-click the contact you want to view, and then click the Activities button.

Recording Items in the Journal

The Outlook **Journal** is a diary of all the activities and interactions from your day. With everything organized on a timeline, you can see an overview of what you accomplished and when and how long certain activities took. The Journal also provides an alternate way to locate a particular item or a file. You can have the Journal automatically record entries of your phone calls, e-mail messages, meeting requests and responses, tasks, faxes, and documents on which you've worked. You must record tasks, appointments, personal conversations, and existing documents manually.

Automatically Record New Items and Documents

1. Click the **File** tab, and then click **Options**.

2. Click **Notes and Journal** in the left pane.

3. Click **Journal Options**.

4. Select the check boxes for the items you want to record in the Journal automatically.

5. Select the check boxes of the contacts for whom you want to record the selected items.

6. Select the check boxes of the programs that you want recorded.

7. Click **OK**.

8. Click **OK**.

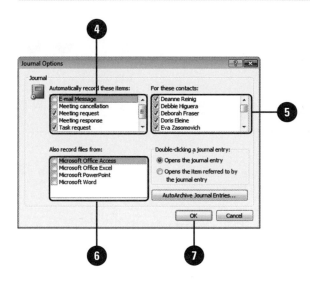

Record a Journal Entry Manually

1. Click the **Folder List** icon on the Navigation pane.

2. Click **Journal** in the Folders list.

3. Click the **Journal Entry** button on the Home tab.

    TIMESAVER *Press Ctrl+N in Journal view to create a new journal entry.*

4. Enter text in the Subject box that describes the journal entry.

5. Click the **Entry Type** list arrow, and then select the type of activity you want to record.

6. Specify the date, time, and duration of the activity.

7. Type a description of the activity.

8. Click the **Save & Close** button.

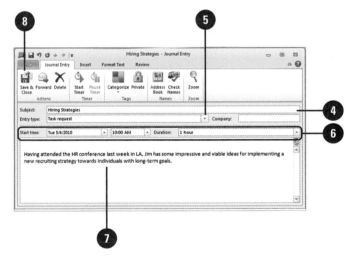

Did You Know?

You can time how long an activity takes. Open the Journal, click the Journal Entry button, enter a subject, select the type of entry, and then click the Start Timer to begin timing how long the activity takes. Take notes as you continue the activity. Click the Pause Timer button if necessary, and then click the Start Timer button to resume. Click the Pause Timer button when you have completed the activity.

You can display the Journal icon on the Navigation pane. Click the Configure Buttons button, point to Add or Remove Buttons, and then click Journal.

Opening and Modifying Journal Entries

Journal entries and their related items, documents, and contacts are easy to open, move, and even delete. When you modify a journal entry, its associated item, document, or contact is not affected. Likewise, when you modify an item, document, or contact, any existing related journal entries remain unchanged. If you no longer need a journal entry, you can select the entry and press Delete or click the Delete button to remove it.

Open the Journal

1. Click the **Folder List** icon on the Navigation pane.

2. Click **Journal** in the Folders list.

   TIMESAVER *Press Ctrl+8 to open the Journal.*

3. Click the Current View **More** button, and then select the view in which you want to display your journal entries.

   ◆ Select the view that displays the journal entry in a way that best meets your needs.

Modify a Journal Entry

1. Open the Journal.

2. Double-click the journal entry to open it in its own window.

3. Modify the journal entry by selecting the options you want to change.

4. Click the **Save & Close** button.

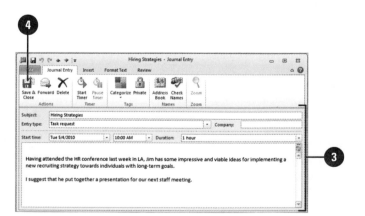

Organizing Items by Categories

A category is one or more keywords and a color you assign to items so you can find, group, sort, or filter them. Color categories provide additional flexibility in how you organize and store items and files. By using color categories you can coordinate related items in different folders or unrelated items. You can add the same color category to e-mail, calendar, and tasks items so that you can quickly locate them at a glance. Outlook starts you off with a basic list of color categories, but you can add, remove, and change to fit your purposes. Color categories are saved with an Outlook data file, so you can transfer them.

Set the Quick Click Category

1. Click the **Categorize** button on the Home tab, and then click **Set Quick Click**.

2. Click the list arrow, and then click the color you want.

3. Click **OK**.

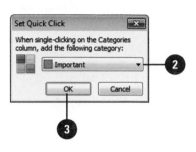

Add or Remove a Color Category

1. Click the **Categorize** button on the Home tab, and then click **All Categories**.

2. To show or hide a category on the Categorize button menu, select or clear a category check box.

3. To add a category, click **New**, type a name, select a color, and then click **OK**.

4. To rename or delete a category, select a category, and then click **Rename** or **Delete**.

5. To change a category color, select a category, click the **Color** list arrow, and then select a color.

6. Click **OK**.

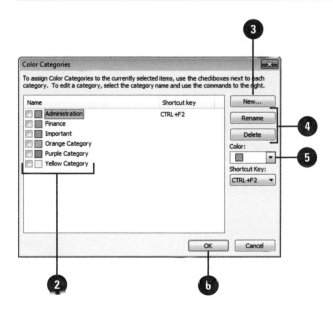

Customizing How You View Items

You can look at items, such as messages, in a variety of ways, or views. By default, the messages in your Inbox are listed by the date you received them. You can quickly reorder your messages by clicking one of the column headings so your messages appear in alphabetical order by the name of the sender. To control what and how much information you see, you can choose a default view or customize a view in Outlook so your items always appear in an order or format that works best for you. Outlook allows you to group, sort, and filter items. Group organizes items base on a particular column (an element for storing a particular type of information). Sort arranges items in ascending or descending order according to a specified column. Filter shows items that match specific criteria, such as "High Priority."

Customize the View of Your Messages

1. In Mail view, display the folder you want to customize.

2. Click the **View** tab, and then click the **View Settings** button.

3. Click **Columns**.

4. Double-click the columns that you want to appear in the Folder view, or select a column and use the **Add** button.

5. Double-click the columns that you don't want to appear in the Folder view, or select a column and use the **Remove** button.

6. To change the order of the columns, click the column in the **Show these columns in this order** list box, and then click the **Move Up** or **Move Down** button until the column is in the position you want.

7. Click **OK**.

8. To reset the current view, click the **Reset Current View** button.

   ◆ You can also click the **Reset View** button on the View tab to reset all views to defaults.

9. Click **OK**.

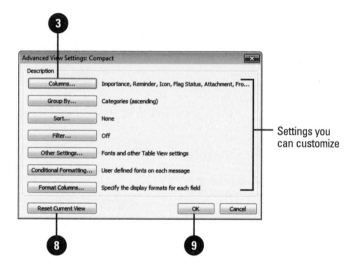

Settings you can customize

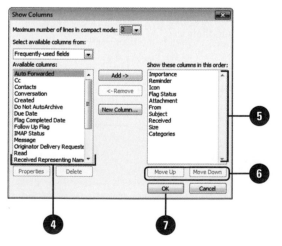

Set a Filter to Show Certain Items and Files

1 Click the **View** tab, and then click the **View Settings** button.

2 Click **Filter**.

3 Type a word to search for.

4 Click the **In** list arrow, and then click a column.

5 Enter the sender, recipient, and time frame as necessary.

6 Click **OK**.

7 Click **OK**.

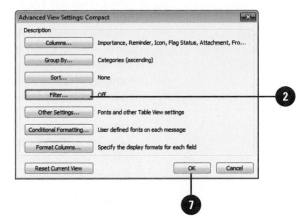

> ### Did You Know?
>
> *You can change the color scheme of Outlook.* Click the File tab, click Options, click General in the left pane, click the Color Scheme list arrow, and then select Blue, Black, or Silver (**New!**).

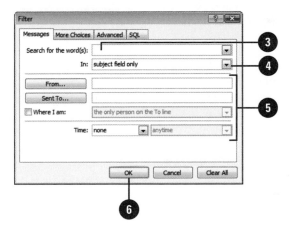

Remove a Filter

1 Click the **View** tab, and then click the **View Settings** button.

2 Click **Filter**.

3 Click **Clear All**.

4 Click **OK**.

5 Click **OK**.

Creating and Modifying Notes

Notes in Outlook are electronic versions of paper sticky notes. Notes replace the random scraps of paper on which you might jot down reminders, questions, thoughts, ideas, or directions. Like the popular sticky notes, you can move an Outlook note anywhere on your screen and leave it displayed as you work. Any edits you make to a note are saved automatically. The ability to color-code, size, categorize, sort, or filter notes makes these notes even handier than their paper counterparts. When you open a new Note window in Outlook, you simply type text to create a note. The first paragraph becomes the note name in the Notes folder. Outlook inserts the date and time that you created the note for your reference.

Create a Note

1. Click the **Notes** button on the Navigation pane, and then click the **New Note** button on the Home tab.

   TIMESAVER *Press Ctrl+N in Notes view, or press Ctrl+Shift+N in any another view to create a note.*

2. Type your note.

3. Click the **Close** button.

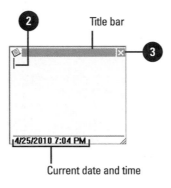

Title bar

Current date and time

Modify a Note

1. Click the **Notes** button on the Navigation pane

2. Double-click a note icon.

3. Type new text or edit the existing text.

4. Click the **Close** button.

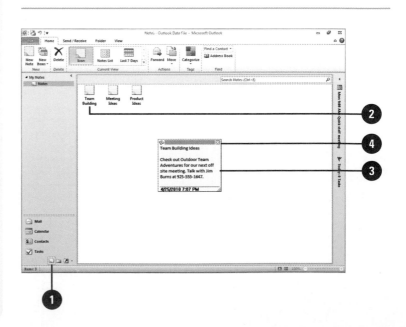

Previewing and Printing Items from Outlook

Just as you might preview a document in Word before printing it, you can preview items, such as a message, task list or calendar, in Outlook. In Print screen (**New!**), you can change print and page set up for the current printing style. For example, the calendar print styles include the Daily Style, Weekly (Agenda or Calendar) Style, Monthly Style, Tri-Fold Style, and Calendar Details Style. The default or preset printing style is different for each view depending on what type of information you are printing. From the Print screen, you can print any item in Outlook. Printing options change depending on the item and view.

Preview and Print an Item or View

1. Click the item you want to print.

2. Click the **File** tab, and then click **Print**.

3. Click the **Printer** list arrow, and then select a printer.

4. Select the print settings you want (settings differ depending on the item you choose).

5. Click **Print Options**, click a print style (styles differ depending on the item you choose), specify a page and print range, and number of pages, and then click **Preview**.

   ◆ To change page setup format (layout and fonts), paper, and header/footer options, click **Page Setup**.

   ◆ To change a print style, click **Define Styles**.

6. Use the **Previous Page** and **Next Page** buttons to display pages.

7. Use the **Actual**, **One Page**, and **Multiple Pages** buttons to view pages.

8. To print from the Print Preview window, click the **Print** button.

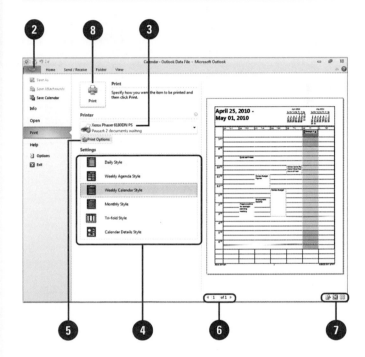

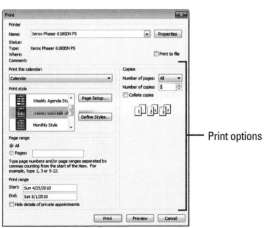

Print options

Connecting to a Social Network

Outlook bridges the gap between your Inbox and your social network, such as Linkedin, MySpace, and Facebook. Each social network provides a Outlook Social Connector add-in (**New!**)—available for download and install from the social network site—that allows you to connect and synchronize your information between them. You can view activities in the People pane, synchronize your contact list to your Outlook contacts, and get one-click access to the social network site. After you install the add-in, you can use the Social Network Accounts dialog box to setup your account, and then use the People pane to view your social network information.

Setup a Social Network

1. Before first use, download and install the Outlook Social Connector add-in for a specific social network.

2. Click the **View** tab.

3. Click the **People Pane** button, and then click **Account Settings**.

4. Select the check box next to the social network, and then type your user name and password.

5. Click **Connect**.

6. To change access and data management settings, click **Settings**.

7. Click **Finish**.

Did You Know?

You can show, hide, or minimize the People pane. Click the View tab, click the People Pane button, and then click Normal (On), Minimized, or Off.

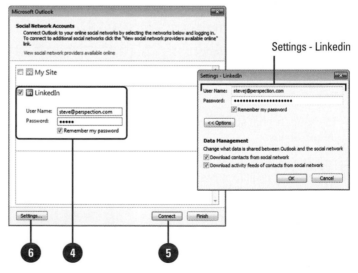

Settings - Linkedin

Use the People Pane to a View Social Network

1. In Mail view, select the folder, and then select the message associated with a person you know from your social network.

2. Click the **Expand arrow**, if necessary, to display the People pane.

3. Click the icon tabs to display information relating to the person.

4. To access contact information for the person, double-click the contact picture.

5. To access the user profile of the social network, click the icon for the social network.

6. To add this person to one of your social networks, click the **Add** button.

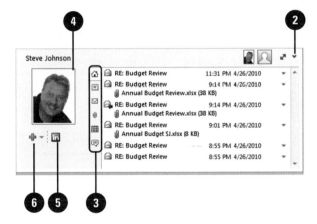

Sharing Calendars Over the Internet

If you're not using Outlook with a Microsoft Exchange, you can still share your calendar with others over the Internet. Outlook allows you to share Internet Calendars and publish calendars to Microsoft Office Online. Internet Calendars are downloaded from calendar publishing services or special Web sites on a subscription basis. Internet Calendars use the iCalendar format and the .ics file extension. You can also send a snapshot of your calendar in an e-mail message, which recipient's can open in Outlook or a Web browser for Web mail. When you have multiple calendars in Outlook, you can view them side by side or overlaid. In overlay mode, you can navigate multiple calendars to make it easier to compare one calendar with another and check for free time. You can also drag appointments from one calendar to another.

Publish a Calendar to Office.com

1. Click the **Calendar** button on the Navigation pane.

2. Click the **Publish Online** button on the Home tab, and then click **Publish to Office.com**.

   If necessary, complete sign-in and registration for Office Online.com.

3. Specify the time span you want to publish.

4. Click the **Detail** list arrow, and then select the type of calendar information you want to share.

5. Specify the permission and upload method you want to use.

6. Click **OK**.

7. Click **Yes** to send an invitation to access the calendar, and then address and send the message.

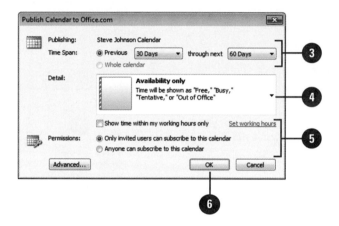

Did You Know?

You can send a calendar in e-mail. In the Message window, click the Insert Calendar button on the Insert tab. In Calendar view, select a calendar, and then click the E-mail Calendar button on the Home tab.

Add an Internet Calendar to Outlook

1. In the Inbox, double-click the message with the link for the Internet Calendar Subscription.

2. Click the **Subscribe to this Calendar** button.

3. Click **Yes** to add this calendar to Outlook and subscribe to updates.

4. To show or hide calendars, select or clear the calendar check box on the Navigation pane.

5. To switch between side by side and overlay calendars, use the calendar tab arrow buttons.

6. If you want, drag an appointment between calendars.

7. To change publishing options, click the **Publish Online** button, and then select an option:

   ◆ **Change Publishing Options.** Change options for the published calendar.

   ◆ **Share Published Calendar.** Invite people in a message to view and share your published calendar.

   ◆ **Change Sharing Permissions.** Change options to specify who can view your published calendar.

   ◆ **Publish to WebDAV Server.** Published your calendar to a Web server that supports WebDAV.

   ◆ **Remove from Server.** Deletes the published calendar from the online server.

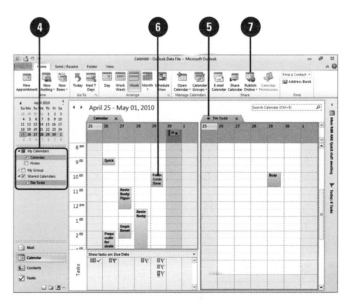

Adding and Viewing an RSS Feed

An RSS (Really Simple Syndication) provides a way for Internet content publishers to make news, blogs, and other content available to subscribers in an standardized XML format. You can quickly add a featured RSS feed from the RSS Feeds folder on the Navigation pane or add other feeds from the Account Settings dialog box. Once you add a feed, you can also use the Account Settings dialog box to modify settings. To view an RSS feed, click the RSS Feeds folder on the Navigation pane, and then click the subfolder with the RSS feed. Click the individual items to display it in the Reading pane, where you can click a link to the original information source.

View an RSS Feed

1. Click the **RSS Feeds** folder on the Navigation pane in Mail view.

2. To add a features RSS feed, click the feed, and then click **Yes**.

3. Click the RSS feed subfolder (under the RSS Feeds folder) you want.

4. Click an individual feed article.

5. To view the original source, click the link on the Reading pane.

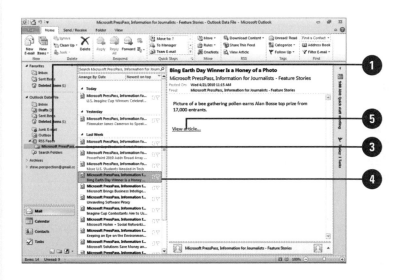

Add or Change an RSS Feed

1. Click the **File** tab, click **Info**, click the **Account Settings** button, and then click **Account Settings**.

2. Click the **RSS Feeds** tab.

3. Do any of the following:

   ◆ **New.** Click New, enter a URL address for the feed and then click Add.

   ◆ **Change.** Select an existing feed, and then click Change.

   ◆ **Remove.** Select an existing feed, and then click Remove.

4. Click **Close**.

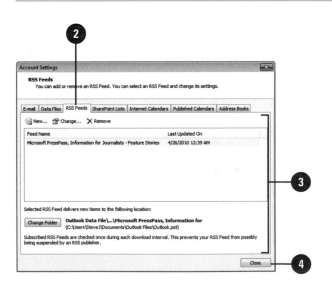

Creating a Publication with Publisher

Introduction

When you need to create a great looking publication, such as a business card, letterhead, newsletter, Web page, or brochure, use Microsoft Office Publisher 2010 to get the job done quickly and easily.

Publisher is a **desktop publishing program**—software you can use to combine text, graphics, and original drawings with sophisticated formatting, all in one easy-to-use package. With Publisher you can use creative layout and design techniques that were once in the exclusive realm of high-priced publishers or graphic designers.

Publisher combines the fundamental power of a word processor and the creativity of a graphics package into a program that is flexible and easy to use. This combination lets you create unique and exciting documents that you could not easily create in any other single application.

After you create a publication, you can enter and edit text. Text objects are enclosed in a frame, which serves as a container to hold a block of text. If you created a publication with a task pane, you see placeholder text, which you replace with your own text in the frame. You can add more text by adding new text frames or by inserting text into an existing text frame. For example, to add a new heading (or some other text) to a brochure, you create a text frame. You create new frames using the corresponding frame tool located on the Ribbon at the left side of the window.

Once you have created the publication you want, you can print it on your own printer, package it (electronically) to submit it to a commercial printer, or even publish it on the Web. In fact, you can do all of these things to the same publication.

What You'll Do

View the Publisher Window

Create a New Publication

Download a New Publication

Create a Blank Publication

Change Your View

Work with Pages

Insert and Edit Text

Insert Content

Control Pages Appearance with Masters

Apply Color

Check Your Design

Set Up the Page

Use Commercial Printing Tools

Print a Publication

Viewing the Publisher Window

File tab
Click to access Office Publisher file commands.

Quick Access Toolbar
Click to access command comments on this customizable toolbar.

Tabs
Click to access tools and commands.

Dialog Box Launcher
Click to open dialog boxes or task panes.

Ribbon
Commands and tools grouped by category onto different tabs.

Lists and Galleries
Click the down arrow to access lists and galleries.

Publication
Enter text and graphics here.

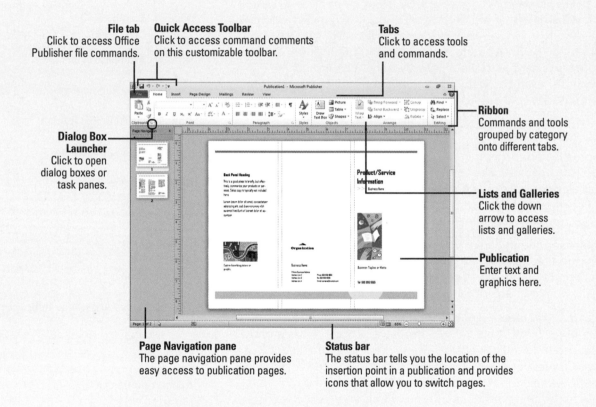

Page Navigation pane
The page navigation pane provides easy access to publication pages.

Status bar
The status bar tells you the location of the insertion point in a publication and provides icons that allow you to switch pages.

Creating a New Publication

When you first start Publisher, you see the New window, which you can use to create a new publication or open an existing publication. Publisher provides hundreds of templates organized in different categories, which include quick publications, advertisements, flyers, brochures, and newsletters. A template is a document with predefined formatting and placeholder text that specifies what information you should enter. After you select a template, you can modify the layout and select options in the right pane to help you customize the page.

Create a New Publication

1. Start Publisher.

   If you have already started Publisher, click the **File** tab, and then click **New**.

2. Click the publication type you want to use.

3. To return to the Home page, click the **Home** button or **Back** button.

4. Click the thumbnail that displays the design for the publication you want to create.

5. Click the **Color Scheme** or **Font Scheme** list arrow, and then select what you want to customize the layout.

6. Select other options, such as page size. The options vary depending on the publication type.

7. Click **Create**.

8. Click a text box placeholder, and then replace it with your text.

9. Click the **Save** button on the Quick Access Toolbar, select a location, name the file, and then click **Save**.

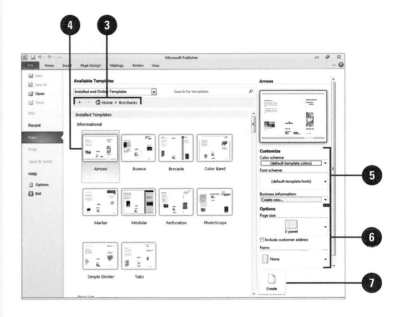

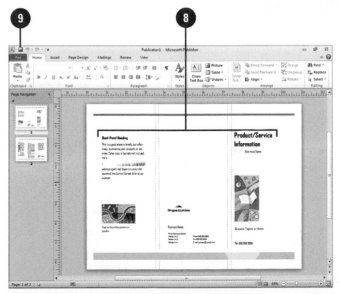

Downloading a New Publication

When you want to create a publication, you can use one of the templates provided by Publisher. Some of the templates are installed on your computer while others are not. However, you can quickly download them from Office.com using the Download button on the New window. You can choose a publication design for newsletters, calendars, resumes, gift certificates, labels, and business forms. You can create a publication based on the job you want to get done, or on design sets for special events, personal stationery, or fundraisers to name a few. You can also create publications for print, Web site, or e-mail.

Download a New Publication

1. Start Publisher.

   If you have already started Publisher, click the **File** tab, and then click **New**.

2. Click the publication type you want to use.

3. To return to the Home page, click the **Home** button or **Back** button.

4. Click the thumbnail that displays the design for the publication you want to create under the Office.com Templates heading.

5. Click **Download**.

6. Click a text box placeholder, and then replace it with your text.

7. Click the **Save** button on the Quick Access Toolbar, select a location, name the file, and then click **Save**.

Did You Know?

You don't have to display the New window at startup. Click the File tab, click Options, click General, clear the Show The New Template Gallery When Starting Publisher check box, and then click OK.

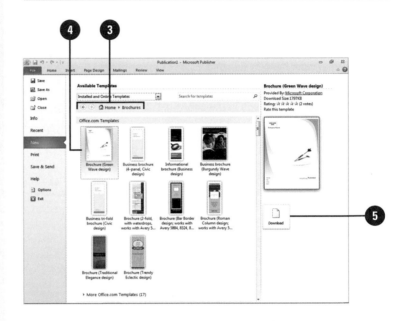

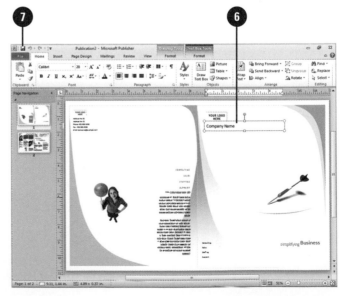

Creating a Blank Publication

Publisher's preset designs can be a big help in getting you started when you create a new publication. Every so often, however, you want to create a unique publication, and none of the preset designs will do the job. In that case, you can start a blank publication. If you know how to create and use frames, you can create a publication from scratch. If you have a name tag, label, business card, or stationery page based on a specific manufacturer, you can use a blank template provided by Publisher. If none of the sample blank publications meet your needs, you can also create a custom page.

Create a Blank Publication

1. Start Publisher.

   If you have already started Publisher, click the **File** tab, and then click **New**.

2. To quickly create a standard 8.5 by 11 inch blank publication, click **Blank 8.5 x 11"** or **Blank 11 x 8.5"**; skip to Step 8.

3. Click **More Blank Page Sizes**.

4. Click the thumbnail that displays the design for the publication you want to create.

5. Click the **Color Scheme** or **Font Scheme** list arrow, and then select what you want to customize the layout.

6. Select other options, such as page size. The options vary depending on the publication type.

7. Click **Create**.

8. Click the **Save** button on the Quick Access Toolbar, select a location, name the file, and then click **Save**.

Did You Know?

You can open an existing publication. Click the File tab, click Open, select the publication you want to open, and then click Open.

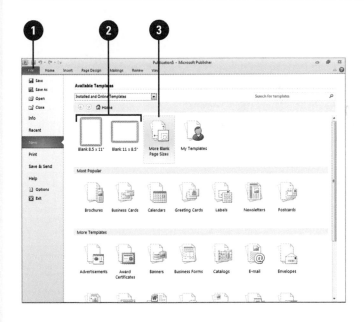

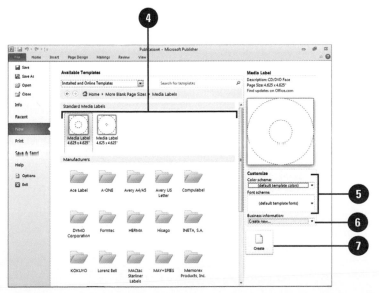

Changing Your View

You can view the pages in your publication in a one-page or a two-page spread. A two-page spread mimics the layout of a book or magazine that is lying open in front of you, where two pages face each other. You can also switch among various magnification levels. Viewing the page at a reduced size allows you to see an overview of your design. Zooming in on the pages makes type legible and provides a higher degree of accuracy when creating or positioning frames.

View a Publication in One or Two-Page View

1. Click the **View** tab.

2. Click the **Two-Page Spread** button or the **Single Page** button.

   The button is selected which indicates the current view.

   TIMESAVER *Click the Single Page or Two Page button on the Status bar.*

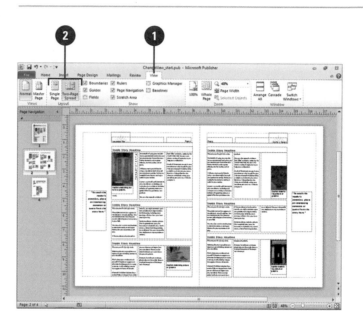

Change the View Size of a Page

1. Click the **View** tab.

2. To select standard view sizes, click any of the following buttons: **100%**, **Whole Page**, **Page Width**, or **Selected Objects**.

   TIMESAVER *Press F9 to toggle between current and 100% views.*

3. To specify a custom view size, click the **Zoom** list arrow, and then select a view percentage.

   TIMESAVER *Click the Zoom In or Zoom Out button or drag the Zoom slider on the Status bar.*

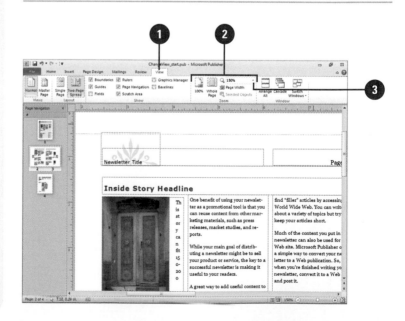

Working with Pages

As you layout your publication, you may find it necessary to add a page or two in order to include more information or graphics. You can do this anytime during the design process. After viewing your publication, you may need to delete a page. If so, you can only delete one page or one spread at a time. You can see information on the other pages of a publication by clicking the page thumbnail in the status bar at the bottom of the window. Each thumbnail corresponds to a page on your publication.

Insert One or More Pages

1. Display the page before or after the one you want to insert.

2. Click the **Insert** tab, and then click the **Page button arrow**, and then click **Insert Page**.

   ◆ To insert a blank page, click **Insert Blank Page**.

   ◆ To insert a duplicate page, click **Insert Duplicate Page**.

3. Select a page (left or right) type to insert, and then click **More**.

4. Specify the number of pages to add.

5. Click the option to indicate the location of the new pages.

6. Click **OK**.

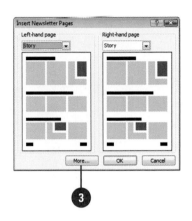

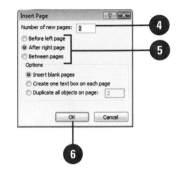

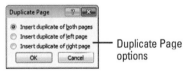

Duplicate Page options

Delete, Rename, or Move a Page

1. Select the page you want to use in the Page Navigation pane.

2. Click the **Page Design** tab.

3. Click a button in the Pages group.

   ◆ **Delete.** In two-page view, select a delete option.

   ◆ **Rename.** Type page titles.

   ◆ **Move.** Select page and location options; you can also drag a page icon in the Page Navigation pane.

4. Click **OK**.

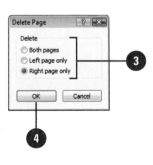

Move Page options

Rename Page options

Inserting and Editing Text

When you create a publication, Publisher places generic text in a text frame, which is called a **text object**. The frame serves as a container in which you can easily format, move, and resize an area of text. The generic text acts as a placeholder. Replace the placeholder text with your own text. The insertion point indicates where text appears when you type. You can insert and update information, such as your name and address. If you change the information, Publisher updates it throughout the publication.

Insert and Edit Text in a Frame

1 Click the text in a frame if it isn't already selected.

The small boxes on the frame indicate that it is selected.

2 Click to place the insertion point where you want to enter or edit text.

3 To delete text, press Delete or Backspace.

4 Type the text you want to enter.

5 Click outside the text frame to deselect it.

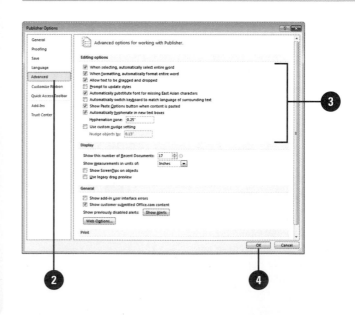

Change Edit Options

1 Click the **Tools** tab, and then click **Options**.

2 Click **Advanced** in the left pane.

3 Select the editing check boxes you want, including:

◆ Drag-and-drop text editing

◆ Automatic selecting or formatting entire word

◆ Automatic hyphenating in new text frame

4 Click **OK**.

Enter or Update Business Information

1. Click the **Insert** tab, click the **Business Information** button, and then click **Edit Business Information**.

   On first use, skip step 2.

2. Click **New**, or select the Business Information Set you want to edit, and then click **Edit**.

3. Enter the information you want, and then enter a set name.

4. Click **Save**.

5. Click **Update Publication**.

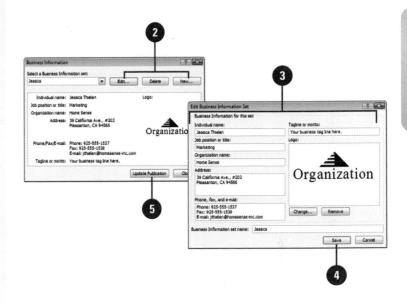

Insert Business Information

1. Select the text box or place the insertion point where you want to insert information.

2. Click the **Insert** tab.

3. Click the **Business Information** button, and then click the information set you want.

   A new text frame is created or the text is inserted.

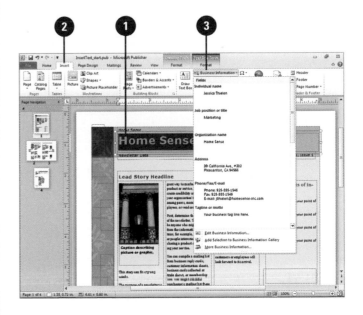

Did You Know?

Insert page numbers. Click in the text or table frame where you want to insert a page number, click the Insert tab, and then click Page Numbers.

You can check spelling in a publication. Click the Spelling button on the Review tab, click Ignore, or click the correct spelling, and then click Change. When you're done, click OK.

Inserting Content

Publisher makes adding content to your publication quick and easy. With the Insert tab, you have everything you need to add the type of content you want for your publication. You can insert tables, illustrations (such as pictures, clip art, and shapes), building blocks, symbols, date & time, text, hyperlinks, and bookmarks. Building blocks (**New!**) are pre-built content (such as headings, pull quotes, sidebars, stories, calendars, borders & accents and advertisements), style galleries, and font and color themes that make inserting content quick and easy. You can also insert a header, footer, and page number manually.

Insert Content

1. Display the page where you want to insert content.

2. Click the **Insert** tab.

3. Click the button with the content you want to insert.

   - **Tables.** Click the **Table** button, and then drag to select the table size you want.

   - **Illustrations.** Click the **Picture** or **Clip Art** button to insert a picture. Click the **Shapes** button, select a shape, and then drag to draw it. Click the **Picture Placeholder** button to drag a box for a picture.

   - **Building Blocks.** Click the **Page Part** button to insert headings, pull quotes, sidebars, or stories. Click the **Calendars**, **Borders & Accents**, or **Advertisements** button to insert the content (**New!**).

   - **Text.** Click buttons to draw a text box, insert WordArt, a file, symbol, date & time, or an object.

   - **Links.** Click the **Hyperlink** or **Bookmark** button to insert a link to a Web page or bookmark to a publication page.

   - **Header & Footer.** Click the **Header**, **Footer**, or **Page Number** button to insert the content.

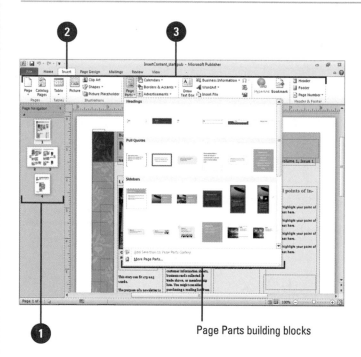

Page Parts building blocks

Modify and Format Content

1. Display the page where you want to change or format content.

2. Select the object you want to change or format.

   For the selected object, such as a shape, text, or picture, a Format tab appears, displaying a Ribbon of button options for the specific object type.

3. Click the **Format** tab.

4. Click the button with the content you want to insert.

   - ◆ **Drawing Tools.** Click buttons to insert or edit a shape, apply a shape style, add shadow effects, or add 3-D effects.

   - ◆ **Text Box Tools.** Click buttons to make text fit, change text direction, change hyphenation, format text, align text, adjust margins, create columns, add text effects, and change typography, such as drop cap, number style, swash, or stylistic alternates.

   - ◆ **Picture Tools.** Click buttons to insert a picture, adjust the picture color, swap pictures, apply a picture style, or add shadow effects.

See Also

See "Creating a Hyperlink" on page 560 for information on creating text hyperlinks to other pages.

Format tab for a picture

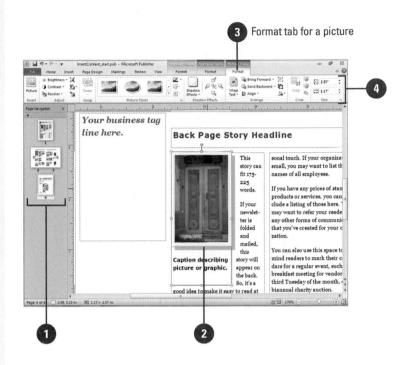

Format tab for a text box

Controlling Pages Appearance with Masters

If you want an object, such as a company logo or clip art, to appear on every slide in your publication, place it on the **Slide Master**. All of the characteristics of the Slide Master (background color, text color, font, and font size) appear on every page. The Master Page tab contains several buttons to add, delete, rename, duplicate, and apply masters. When you add a master, you can add a single page or two-page (for a two-page spread). You can also show headers and footers, and insert a page number, date, or time.

Work with Master Pages

1. Click the **View** tab.

2. Click the **Master Page** button.

   Every publication contains at least one master page, even if it is blank.

3. To create a new master page, click the **Add Master Page** or **Two Page Master** button.

4. To show a header and footer, click the **Show Header/Footer** button.

5. To insert a page number, date, or time, click to place the insertion point in a text box, and then click the **Insert Page Number**, **Insert Date**, or **Insert Time** button.

6. To apply the master page changes to the publication, click the **Apply To** button, and then click an option: **Apply to All Pages**, **Apply to Current Page**, or **Apply Master Page** (for a page range).

7. To duplicate, rename or delete a master, select the master page in the Page Navigation pane, and then click a button: **Duplicate**, **Rename**, or **Delete**.

   You can't delete the last master.

8. Click the **Close Master Page** button.

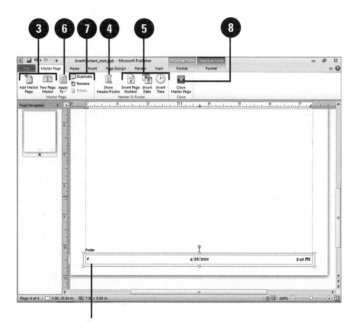

Footer with page number, date, and time

Applying Color

You can change the look of your publication by selecting a **color scheme**—a predesigned layout containing a variety of colors for bullets, backgrounds, color, and lines to create specific moods. You can use the default color scheme or apply a custom one that you develop. Apply color schemes at any time—not just when you create the pages. You can also modify any color in a color scheme, and you can create and save your own custom color schemes.

Apply Page Background Colors

1. Select the pages you want to apply a page background in the Page Navigation pane.

2. Click the **Page Design** tab.

3. Click the **Background** button, point to a background to preview it on current page, and then click a background color.

   ◆ **Custom Backgrounds.** Click **More Backgrounds** on the menu, select options for a custom fill effect (Gradient, Texture, Pattern, Picture, or Tint), and then click **OK**.

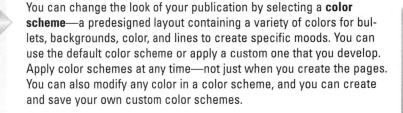

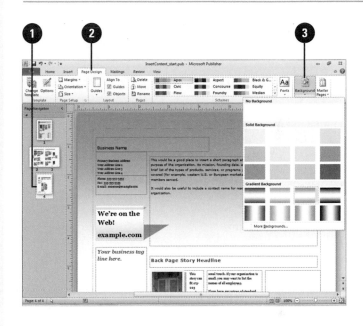

Change a Color Scheme

1. Click the **Page Design** tab.

2. Click the Schemes **More** button, and then select a color scheme.

   ◆ **Custom Color Scheme.** Click **Create new color scheme** on the More menu, click any **New** list arrow(s), select the colors you want, type a name for your scheme, and then click **Save**.

   All pages with scheme colors are changed.

3. To apply a scheme color to an object, select the object, and then select a scheme color from a color button menu, such as Font Color.

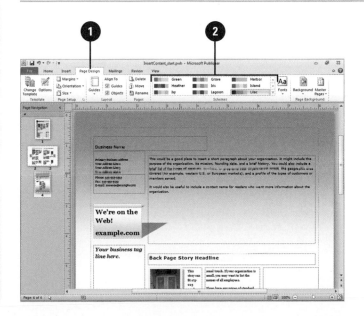

Checking Your Design

You can check the design of your publication for errors. The **Design Checker** looks over your publication for problems, such as empty frames, text in overflow areas off the page, covered objects, objects in nonprinting regions, disproportional pictures, and poor spacing between sentences. Once the Design Checker identifies problems, it suggests solutions, which you can accept or ignore. You determine Design Checker's settings in its Options box.

Check Your Design

1. Click the **File** tab, and then click **Info**.

2. Click the **Run Design Checker** button.

3. Point to the design suggestions in the Design Checker task pane.

4. Click the list arrow, and then click an option to view, fix, or ignore the item.

5. When you're done, click the **Close** button on the task pane.

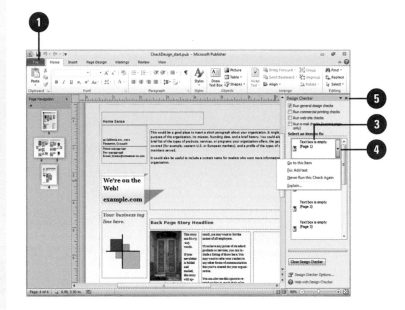

Change Design Checker Options

1. Click the **File** tab, and then click **Info**.

2. Click the **Run Design Checker** button.

3. Click **Design Checker Options** on the task pane.

4. Click the **Checks** tab.

5. Select the check boxes for the types of errors you want to find.

6. Click **OK**.

7. When you're done, click the **Close** button on the task pane.

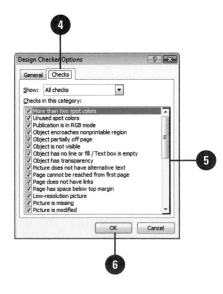

Setting Up the Page

When you set up a publication, you can determine how you want it to print by using the Page Setup buttons and Page Setup dialog box. You can visually select the page size and layout you want. Page layout determines the general size and orientation of your publication and affects how the pages will be arranged when you print. Paper size refers to the physical dimensions of the paper in your printer. Publisher's page size refers to the dimensions of your publication, which can be the same, smaller, or larger than the paper size.

Set Up the Page and Printer

1. Click the **Page Design** tab.

2. Click any of the following buttons:

   ◆ **Margins.** Click the **Margins** button, and then select a preset margin or click **Custom Margins**.

   ◆ **Orientation.** Click the **Orientation** button, and then click **Portrait** or **Landscape**.

   ◆ **Size.** Click the **Size** button, and then select a preset size or click **Page Setup** to change any page, margin, and layout options.

3. To create a new page size, click the **Size** button, and then select an option:

   ◆ **New Page Size.** Click **Create New Page Size**, type a name, change any page, margin, and layout options, and then click **OK**.

   ◆ **New Preset Page Size.** Click **More Preset Page Sizes**, click a folder with the page size you want, select a page size, and then click **OK**.

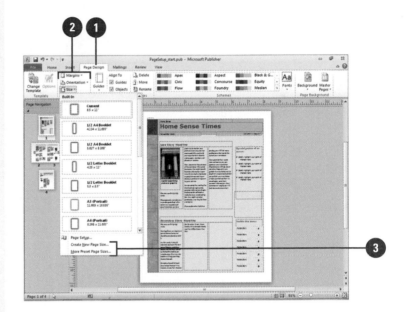

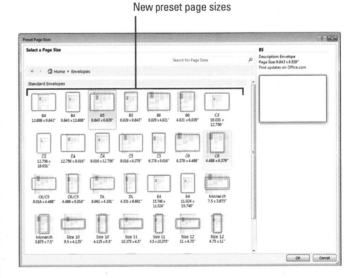

New preset page sizes

Using Commercial Printing Tools

Publisher provides full support for commercial printing, including automatic conversion to spot or process color with automatic color separation. In addition, advanced tools such as **trapping** (overlapping the edges of different colors), graphic link management, and font lists provide commercial printers with the features they need to print high-quality publications. Check with your commercial printer for the specific settings and options you need to complete your print job. If you have special printing needs, you might want to use a commercial printing service which can deliver high-quality color documents. The **Pack and Go Wizard** compacts all the information a printer needs across multiple disks, embedded fonts, includes linked graphics, and prints composite and separation proofs. If needed, you can double-click the Unpack.exe file to unpack and open the Pack and Go file.

Change Color Print Settings

1. Click the **File** tab, and then click **Info**.

2. Click the **Commercial Printing Settings** button, and then click **Choose Color Model**.

3. Click the color define option you want.

4. Specify the inks or colors you want.

5. Click **OK**.

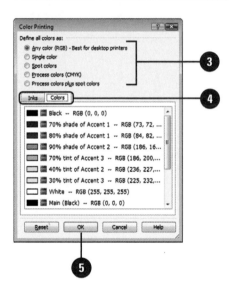

Change Trapping Preferences

1. Click the **File** tab, and then click **Info**.

2. Click the **Commercial Printing Settings** button, and then click **Registration Settings**.

3. Select the trapping and over-printing check boxes you want.

4. If necessary, click **Reset All** to restore settings.

5. Click **OK**.

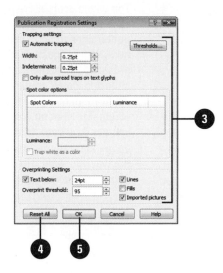

Create a File for Commercial Printing

1. Click the **File** tab, and then click **Save & Send**.

2. Click **Save for a Commercial Printer**.

3. Click the **Type** list arrow, and then select an option: Commercial Press, High quality printing, Standard, Minimum size, or Custom.

4. Click the **File** list arrow, and then select an option: Both PDF and Publisher .pub files, or PDF file, or Publisher .pub file.

5. Click the **Pack and Go Wizard** button.

6. Complete the wizard instructions to specify a location, and other options, and then click **Finish**.

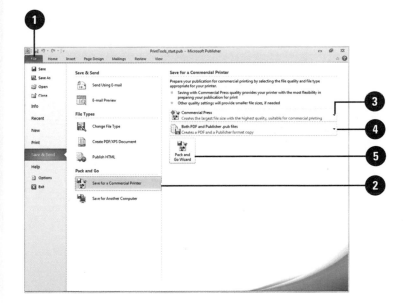

Printing a Publication

The whole point of creating publications is to publish them, which—except for Web pages—means printing the publications. If you have a printer connected to your computer you can print publications right away. When you're ready to print your publication, you can choose several printing options on the Print screen (**New!**) on the File tab, such as choosing a new printer, selecting the number of pages in the publication you want printed and the number of copies, specifying the page size, whether to print on one side or two, and selecting a color mode. If you want to save your print settings with the publication, you can select an option to do so. Before printing, you should verify that the page looks the way you want. The Print screen (**New!**) makes it easy to switch pages and zoom in and out to view pages more comfortably.

Preview and Print a Publication on Your Printer

1. Click the **File** tab, and then click **Print**.

2. Click the **Printer** list arrow, and then click the printer you want to use.

3. To change printer properties, click the **Printer Properties** link, select the options you want, and then click **OK**.

4. Select whether you want to print the entire document or only the pages you specify.

5. Select the other print options you want.

6. Use the zoom page options to preview the publication on the Print screen.

7. To save print settings, select the **Save settings with publication** check box.

8. Click **Print**.

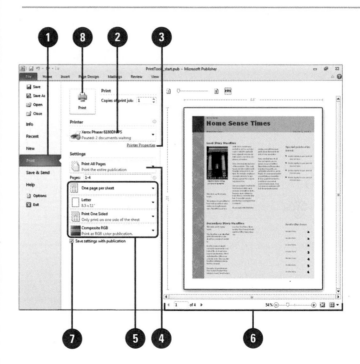

Designing a Publication with Publisher

Introduction

After you create a publication in Microsoft Office Publisher 2010, you can modify any design element you see. Each element in a publication is enclosed in a **frame**. The frame serves as a container to hold objects, such as a block of text, a picture, or a graphic element you've created yourself. If you created a publication using the task pane, you see placeholder text, which you replace with your own text in the frame. You can add more elements by adding new frames. For example, to add a new heading (or some other text) to a brochure, you create a text frame. To add a graphic, you insert a picture into a frame. You create new frames using the corresponding tools, such as the Draw Text box button, on the Insert tab. After you create a frame, you can move it or change its size to allow for more text (in the case of a text frame) or a larger or smaller image (as in a picture frame). You can rotate frames or change their order when you want to place different pictures or text on top of, or behind each other. And with the building blocks you can add ready-made elements such as banners, business cards, calendars, newsletters, and signs.

If you already know how to use Microsoft Word's text and picture frames, you'll be on familiar ground with Microsoft Publisher's frames. If using frames is new to you, you will find working with frames a snap to learn.

What You'll Do

Set Up Layout Guides

View Elements and Tools

Work with Text

Connect Text Frames

Create a Consistent Look

Create Tables

Work with Pictures and Shapes

Wrap Text Around an Object

Layer Objects

Group Objects Together

Align with Precision

Rotate and Flip Objects

Setting Up Layout Guides

Each page of a publication—like any business letter—should have uniform margins. This gives your publication a consistent, professional look. Since a publication is composed of many elements (which may have their own margins), each page is controlled using layout guides. Since they are automatically included in each page of a publication, layout guides are located on background pages. In publications with mirrored pages, any adjustment made to one page is automatically reflected on its companion page.

Set Up Layout Guides

1. Click the **Page Design** tab.

2. To select a preset layout guide, click the **Guides** button, and then select a preset.

3. To add a horizontal or vertical ruler guide, click the **Guides** button, and then click **Add Horizontal Ruler Guide** or **Add Vertical Ruler Guide**.

   TIMESAVER *Click a ruler and drag to create a ruler guide.*

   ◆ To create exact ruler guides, click the **Guides** button, click **Ruler Guides**, specify the guide values, and then click **OK**.

4. To adjust margin, grid, and baseline guides to exact positions, click the **Guides** button, click **Grid and Baseline Guides**, specify the following, and then click **OK**.

   ◆ Click the **Margin Guides** tab, and then specify the measurement for each of the margin guides (Left, Right, Top, and Bottom) you want to adjust.

   ◆ Click the **Grid Guides** tab, and then select the value for the column and row guides you want to adjust.

   ◆ Click the **Baseline Guides** tab, and then select the value for the horizontal guides you want to adjust.

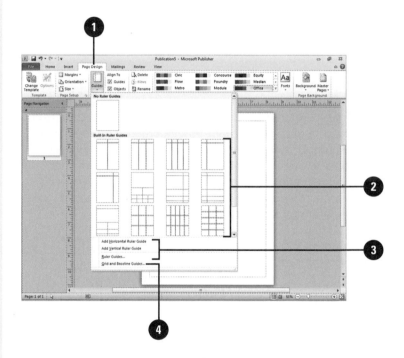

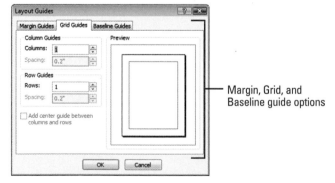

Margin, Grid, and Baseline guide options

Viewing Elements and Tools

As you work with objects in a publication, Publisher provides tools to help you identify and work with objects, pages and graphics. With the View tab, you can show and hide object elements and tools. These include frame boundaries, guides, fields, rulers, baseline grid, scratch area, Page Navigation pane, and Graphics Manager pane. Simply, select the check box to show the item or clear the check box to hide it.

Show and Hide Elements and Tools

1 Click the **View** tab.

2 In the Show group, select a check box to show or clear a check box to hide the element or tool.

- **Boundaries.** Shows or hides the boundaries for shapes, text boxes and pictures.

- **Guides.** Shows or hides guides.

- **Fields.** Shows or hides fields.

- **Rulers.** Shows or hides the vertical and horizontal rulers.

- **Page Navigation.** Shows or hides the Page Navigation pane, where you can work with pages.

- **Scratch Area.** Shows or hides the objects that are located outside the page boundaries.

- **Graphics Manager.** Shows or hides the Graphics Manager pane, where you can work with pictures in a publication.

- **Baselines.** Shows or hides a baseline grid to help you align objects.

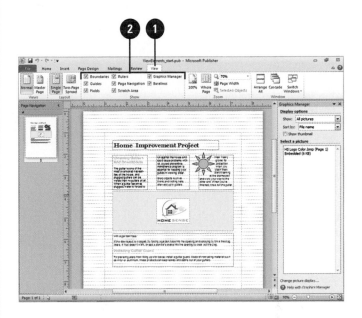

Working with Text

When you want to add new text to your publication, you need to create a text frame. Using the Text Frame tool, you drag a rectangle that will contain your text. When you release the mouse, the insertion point blinks inside the frame, indicating that you can start typing. After entering text, you can resize and move the text box, or format the text to change its font, size, and color. Similarly, you can also change the color of the background of the frame (behind the text) and add interesting borders to the frame.

Create a Text Frame

1 Click the **Insert** tab.

2 Click the **Draw Text Box** button.

3 Position the mouse pointer where you want the frame to start.

4 Drag to create a rectangle the size you want.

5 Type the text you want in the frame.

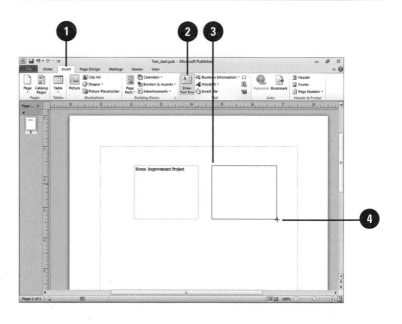

Resize or Move a Text Frame

1 Click the text frame to select it.

2 To resize a text frame, drag a handle.

3 To move a text frame, position the pointer over the dotted edge of the frame, and then drag the text frame to a new location.

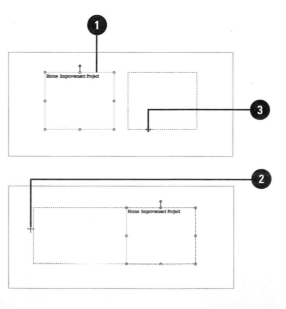

Format Text in a Frame

1. Select the text that you want to format.

2. Click the **Format** tab under Text Box Tools.

3. Use the buttons on the Ribbon to format the text.

   ◆ **Font.** Click buttons to change the font type, size, style, color, and spacing.

   ◆ **Alignment.** Click buttons to align text, create columns, and adjust margins.

   ◆ **Effects.** Click buttons to add a shadow, outline, engrave, or emboss effect to text.

   ◆ **Typography.** Click buttons to fine-tune the look of characters.

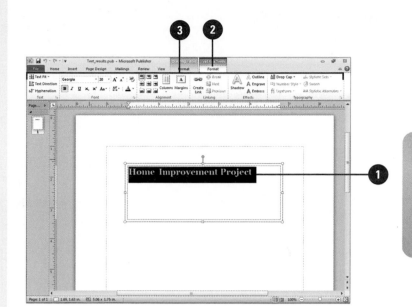

Format a Text Frame

1. Select the text frame you want to format.

2. Click the **Format** tab under Drawing Tools.

3. Use the buttons on the Ribbon to format the text.

   ◆ **Shape Styles.** Click buttons to change the text frame style with presets, fill, outline, and shape.

   ◆ **Shape Effects.** Click buttons to add shadow effects, adjust the shadow, and add 3-D effects.

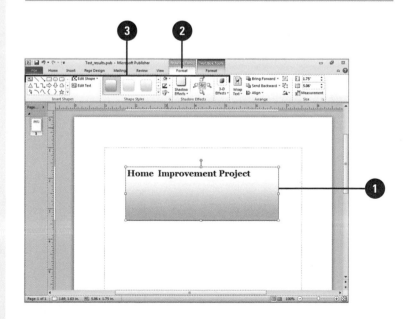

Connecting Text Frames

You can control the way the text flows in your publications. You can link and unlink frames that are adjacent to each other on the same page or different pages. Special text frame buttons appear when text is in the overflow area or when two or more text frames are linked in a chain. You can insert continued notices to help readers follow text from page to page. In addition, you can use **AutoFit Text** to resize text to fit the size of the text frame. When you insert a text file, you can have Publisher use AutoFlow to insert the text in frames and connect them together.

Connect Text Frames

1. Select the first text frame you want to connect; this frame can be empty or it can contain text.

2. Click the **Format** tab under Text Box Tools.

3. Click the **Create Link** button.

4. Position the pitcher pointer over the empty text frame you want to connect.

5. Click the empty text frame to connect the two frames.

   Any overflow text will flow into the newly connected text frame.

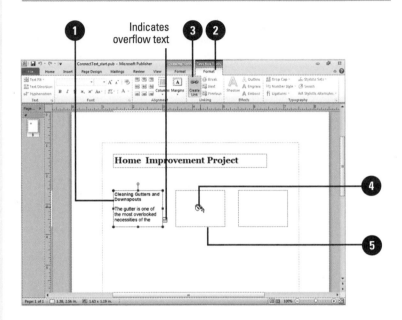

Disconnect a Text Frame

1. Select the text frame you want to disconnect.

2. Click the **Format** tab under Text Box Tools.

3. Click the **Break** button.

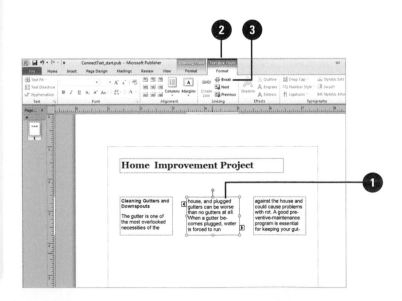

Insert a Continued Notice

1. Select the text frame in which you want to add a notice.

2. Click the **Format** tab under Text Box Tools.

3. Click the **Text Dialog Box Launcher**.

4. Click the **Text Box** tab.

5. Select one or both of the **Include Continued on page** and **Include Continued from page** check boxes.

6. Click **OK**.

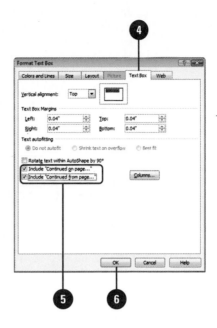

AutoFit Text

1. Select the text frame you want to format.

2. Click the **Format** tab under Text Box Tools.

3. Click the **AutoFit Text** button.

4. Click **Best Fit**, **Shrink Text On Overflow**, or **Grow Text Box to Fit**.

   ◆ To turn off AutoFit Text, click **Do Not AutoFit**.

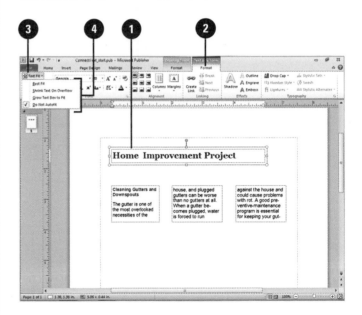

Did You Know?

You can delete a text frame from a chain. Select the text frame you want to delete, and then press Delete.

Creating a Consistent Look

When you create a collection of related publications, such as those for a specific event or organization, make sure that all the publications look similar. By using consistent choices of colors, design elements, and text formatting, your readers will instantly recognize all your publications are related to the same effort or company. Publisher's Catalog and color schemes can help you achieve consistent designs. Use **text styles**, which store text formatting settings, to ensure your text formatting is consistent in all your publications. After creating a text style in a publication, you can import the style to other publications.

Create a New Style by Example

1. Select the text with the style you want to use as the base.

2. Click the **Home** tab.

3. Click the **Styles** button, and then click **New Style**.

4. Enter a name for the new style.

5. Click each of the formatting options, and then change the formatting settings for the new style.

6. Click **OK**.

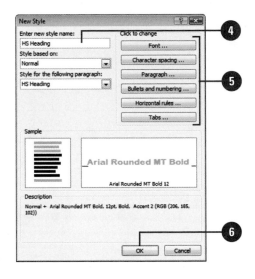

Apply a Style

1. Select the text or text frame to which you want to apply a style.

2. Click the **Home** tab.

3. Click the **Styles** button, and then select a style.

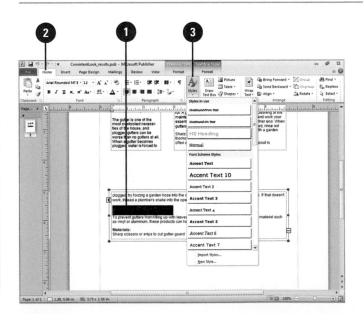

Delete a Style

1 Select text or text frame.

2 Click the **Home** tab.

3 Click the **Styles** button, and then point to the style you want to remove.

4 Right-click the style, and then click **Delete**.

5 Click **Yes** to confirm that you want to delete the style.

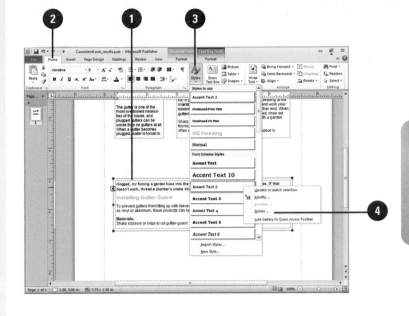

Import a Style

1 Click the **Home** tab.

2 Click the **Styles** button, and then click **Import Styles**.

3 Double-click the publication that contains the styles you want to import.

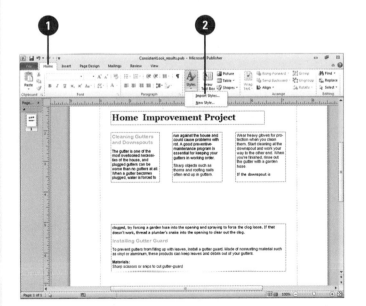

Creating Tables

A **table** is an arrangement of text in a grid of rows and columns. Within a table, the intersection of a row and a column is called a cell. You can use tables to align text. Tables are a convenient way to create schedules, calendars, and forms. You create a table with the Table button on the Insert tab. After you create a table, you can format the color, line and border style, or shadow of individual cells or the entire table with the Design tab under Table Tools. If you need to add rows or columns, merge or split cells, or align text, you can use the Layout tab under Table Tools.

Create and Modify a Table

1. Click the **Insert** tab.

2. Click the **Table** button.

3. Drag the number of rows and columns you want in the table, and then release the mouse.

4. To insert a row or column, click to place the insertion point next to where you want a row or column, click the **Layout** tab, and then click one of the following:

   ◆ **Insert Above.** Inserts a row above the current one.

   ◆ **Insert Below.** Inserts a row below the current one.

   ◆ **Insert Left.** Inserts a column to the left of the current one.

   ◆ **Insert Right.** Inserts a column to the right of the current one.

5. To merge or split cells, select one or more cells, click the **Layout** tab, and then click one of the following:

   ◆ **Merge Cells.** Merges selected cells into one cell.

   ◆ **Split Cells.** Splits a selected cell into two cells.

6. To enter text in the table, click to place the insertion point in a cell, and then type text.

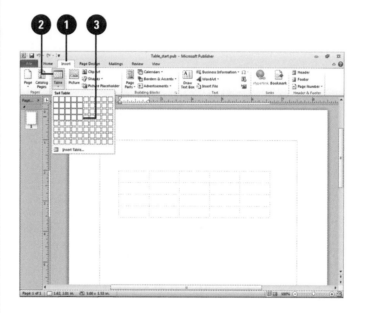

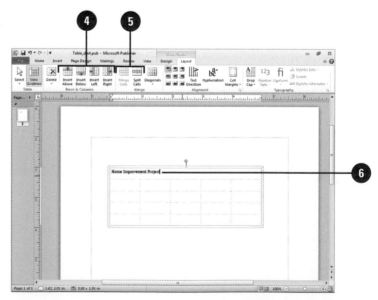

Format a Table

1. Select the table, rows, columns, or cells you want to format.

   ◆ Click in the cell, column, or row, click the **Layout** tab, click the **Select** button, and then click **Select Cell**, **Select Column**, **Select Row**, or **Select Table**.

2. Click the **Design** tab under Table Tools.

3. Click the Table Formats **More** button, and then select a table format.

4. To change a color fill or border, click an option:

   ◆ **Fill.** Select cell, row, or column, click the **Fill** button, and then select a color.

   ◆ **Border.** Select the cell, row, or column, click the **Line Weight**, **Line Color**, or **Border** button arrow, and then select an option.

5. Click the **Layout** tab under Table Tools.

6. Use the buttons on the Ribbon to adjust the table text.

   ◆ **Alignment.** Click buttons to align text, change text direction and hyphenation, and adjust cell margins.

   ◆ **Typography.** Click buttons to fine-tune the look of characters.

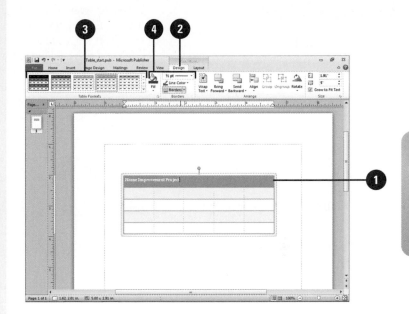

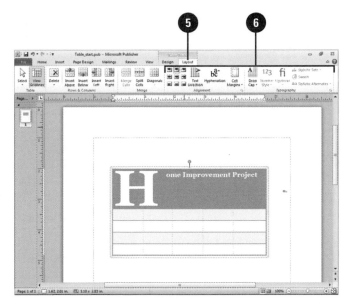

Did You Know?

You can delete a row, column, or table Click in a cell, row, or column, click the Layout tab, click the Delete button, and then click Delete Columns, Delete rows, or Delete Table.

Working with Pictures and Shapes

When you want to insert a picture from a file or a clip art picture from the Clip Gallery, you need to create a picture frame. Using buttons on the Insert tab, you can insert a picture, picture placeholder, or clip art. Then you can modify the picture with picture styles, shadow effects, and captions (**New!**). You can also create your own original drawing. Using the drawing tools, you can create lines and basic shapes, as well as custom shapes that include stars, cartoon balloons, arrows, and many more elements that are sure to add interest to your publication.

Insert a Picture

1 Click the **Insert** tab.

2 Click the **Insert Picture From File** button.

- ◆ To insert a picture placeholder where you can insert a picture later, click the **Picture Placeholder** button. To insert a picture, click the Picture icon.

- ◆ To insert clip art, click the **Clip Art** button, and then double-click the image you want in the task pane.

3 Locate and then double-click the file you want to insert.

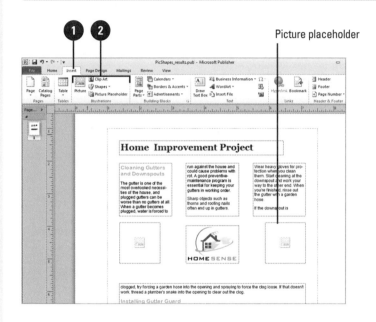

Picture placeholder

Change the Picture

1 Select the picture you want to change.

2 Click the **Format** tab under Picture Tools.

3 Use the buttons on the Ribbon to change the picture.

- ◆ **Adjust.** Click buttons to adjust brightness, contrast, and color.

- ◆ **Picture Styles.** Click buttons to apply a preset picture style, and add a caption (**New!**).

- ◆ **Shadow Effects.** Click buttons to apply apply shadow effects.

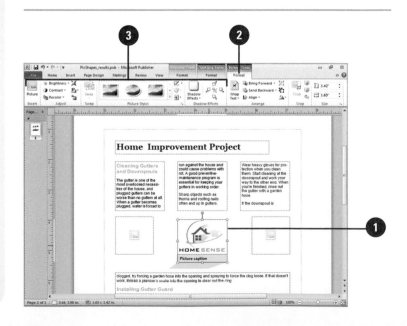

Create a Line, Arrow, Oval, Rectangle, or Custom Shape

1. Click the **Insert** tab.

2. Click the **Shapes** button.

3. Click a **Line**, **Arrow**, **Oval**, or **Rectangle**, or custom shape.

4. Position the mouse pointer where you want the object to start.

5. Click and drag to create an object the size you want.

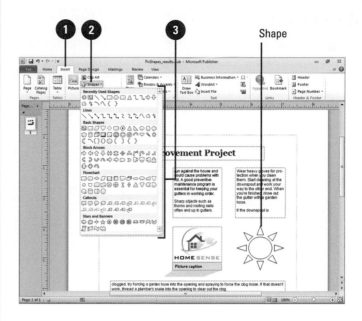

Change the Shape

1. Select the shape you want to change.

2. Click the **Format** tab under Drawing Tools.

3. Use the buttons on the Ribbon to change the shape.

   ◆ **Insert Shapes.** Click buttons to insert or edit shapes.

   ◆ **Shape Styles.** Click buttons to apply a preset shape style, fill, outline, or shape change.

   ◆ **Shadow Effects.** Click buttons to apply shadow effects and 3-D effects.

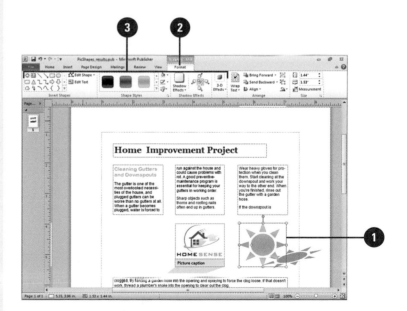

Wrapping Text Around an Object

You can wrap text around a filled object, such as a graphic, to attractively integrate text and objects. By default, Publisher flows text around an object's rectangular frame. So that there are no unsightly gaps between text and nearby graphics, you can wrap the text to flow tightly around irregularly shaped or round objects. Use the Text Wrap option to have text follow the outlines of the object itself. Brochures and newsletters often use this technique to combine text and graphics.

Wrap Text Around an Object

1. Select the text frame that you want to wrap.

2. Click the **Format** tab under Drawing Tools.

3. To wrap text, click the **Wrap Text** button, and then select a wrap option: **Square**, **Tight**, **Top and Bottom**, **Through**, or **In Line with Text**.

4. Drag the object to overlap the text frame.

   The text object must be under the graphic object.

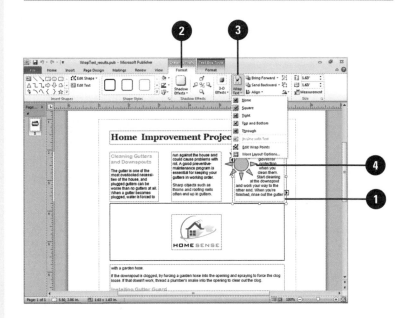

Use Wrap Text Options

1. Select the text frame that you want to wrap.

2. Click the **Format** tab under Drawing Tools.

3. Click the **Wrap Text** button, and then click **More Layout Options**.

4. Click the **Layout** tab.

5. Click a wrapping style option.

6. Click **OK**.

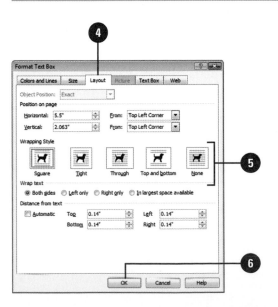

Fine-tune Text Flow Around an Object

1. Click the object which you want the text to flow around.

2. Click the **Format** tab under Drawing Tools.

3. Click the **Wrap Text** button, and then click **Edit Wrap Points**.

4. Position the pointer over an adjust handle until you see the adjust pointer, and then drag the handle to change the shape of the boundary.

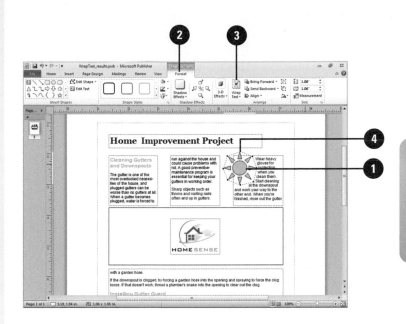

Add or Remove an Adjust Handle

1. Click the object which you want the text to flow around.

2. Click the **Format** tab under Drawing Tools.

3. Click the **Wrap Text** button, and then click **Edit Wrap Points**.

4. Press and hold Ctrl as you click the dotted-line boundary (add) or an adjust handle (remove).

Did You Know?

You can precisely control the shape of an object's boundary. Adjust handles appear at corners or other significant changes in direction of the shape. The more complex the shape, the more adjust handles you see. You can delete extra adjust handles.

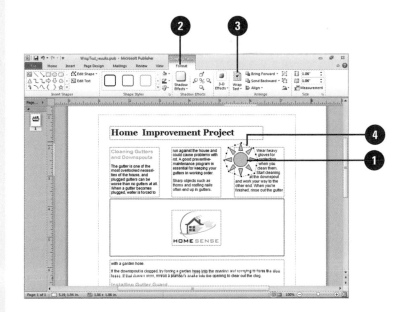

Layering Objects

Like pieces of paper arranged on your work surface, you can arrange objects in a publication on top of each other. The object you created or edited last appears on top of the stack of other objects. Layering objects allows you to achieve effects like shadows and complex designs that include many shapes. You can rearrange the order of the objects in the stack by sending individual objects behind one another, or to the back of the stack, or by bringing other objects in front of one another, or to the front of the stack.

Change Object Stacking Order

1 Select the object you want to change.

2 Click the **Format** tab under Drawing Tools.

3 To send objects forward in a stack, click the **Bring Forward** button arrow, and then click **Bring Forward** or **Bring to Front**.

4 To send objects backward in a stack, click the **Bring Backward** button arrow, and then click **Bring Backward** or **Bring to Back**.

Did You Know?

You need to ungroup objects before changing the order. If you see no change in the order of the objects in the stack, click the Ungroup button on the Format tab under Drawing Tools, and then select the object you want to move. Be sure to regroup the objects after you are satisfied with the layers.

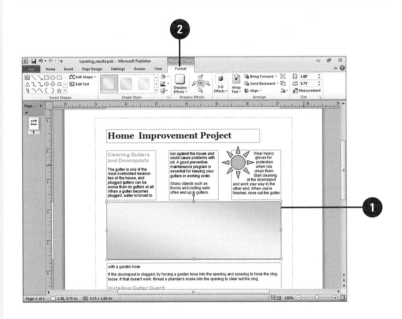

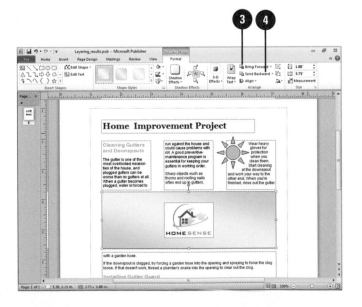

Grouping Objects Together

Often you want Publisher to treat several objects as a single one. That way, if you decide to move one object, you can also move other objects. In Publisher, you can accomplish this with the grouping feature. Group objects when you want to move, resize, or format a set of objects as a single object. If you decide that you want to work with each object independently, you can ungroup them.

Group Objects

1. Select the first object you want to group.

2. Press and hold Shift while you click the other objects that you want to group together.

3. Click the **Format** tab under Drawing Tools.

4. Click the **Group** button.

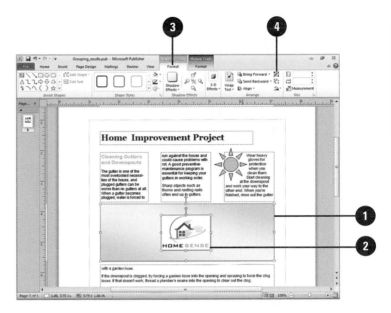

Ungroup Objects

1. Select the object you want to ungroup.

2. Click the **Format** tab under Drawing Tools.

3. Click the **Ungroup** button.

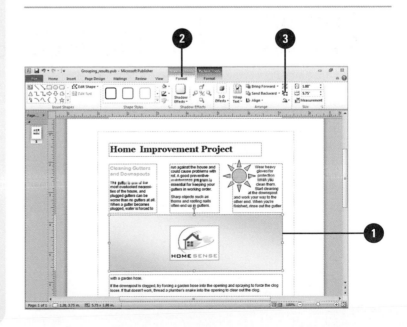

Did You Know?

Sizing handles help identify grouped objects. When you click an object and you see multiple highlighted frames but only one set of sizing handles, it means that the object is part of a group.

Aligning with Precision

Not only can you align objects with each other, you can create controls within a publication that help you align objects. You can create an unlimited number of **ruler guides**—green vertical and horizontal lines you place on a page—to help you line up any objects you choose. Ruler guides can be moved and deleted as you see fit, can be placed on foreground and background pages, and can vary from page to page. Once in place, an object appears to have a magnetic attraction to a ruler guide due to the Snap To feature.

Create a Ruler Guide

1. Point to the vertical or horizontal ruler.

2. Drag from the ruler to create a vertical or horizontal guide.

3. Release the mouse button when the guide is in position.

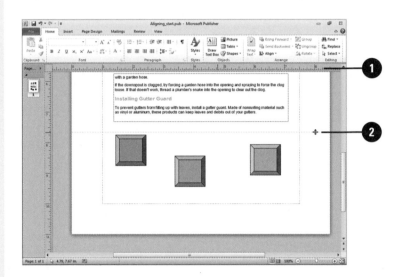

Snap an Object to a Guide

1. Click the **Page Design** tab.

2. Select the **Guides** check box to enable the snap to guide option.

   ◆ **Snap to Object**. To enable the snap to object option, select the **Objects** check box.

3. Drag the object you want to snap to a ruler guide.

4. Release the mouse button once the object snaps to the guide.

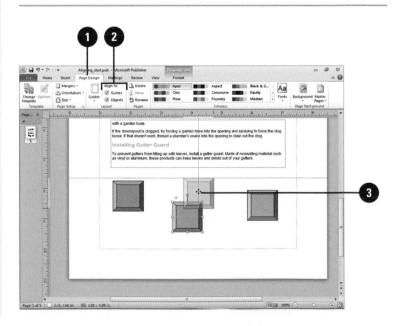

Align Objects

1. Press and hold Shift while clicking each object you want to align.

2. Click the **Home** tab or the **Format** tab under Drawing Tools.

3. Click the **Align** button.

4. Click the align or distribute option you want.

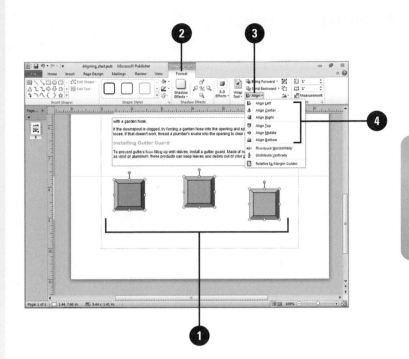

Did You Know?

You can clear all ruler guides quickly. Click the Page Design tab, click the Guides button, click Ruler Guides, click Clear All, and then click OK.

See Also

See "Setting Up Layout Guides" on page 538 for information on aligning objects to the layout guides.

Rotating and Flipping Objects

To fit objects together in a specific way or to achieve a dramatic effect, consider rotating an object. Flipping objects, either vertically or horizontally, is a fast way to change their position. You can flip an object horizontally or vertically to create a mirror image of it along its vertical or horizontal axis.

Free Rotate an Object

① Select the object you want to rotate.

② Position the pointer over the rotate handle (green handle that points up from the object).

③ Drag to free rotate the object.

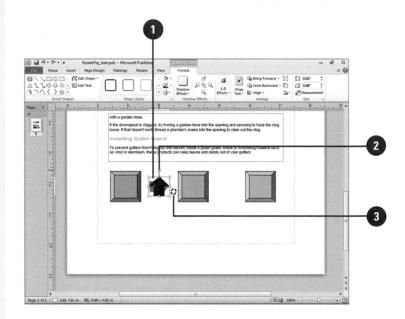

Rotate and Flip an Object

① Select the object you want to flip.

② Click the **Home** tab or the **Format** tab under Drawing Tools.

③ Click the **Rotate** button, and then click an option:

◆ **Flip.** Click **Flip Vertical** or **Flip Horizontal**.

◆ **Rotate.** Click **Rotate Right 90** or **Rotate Left 90**.

◆ **More Options.** Click **More Rotation Options**, specify options, and then click **OK**.

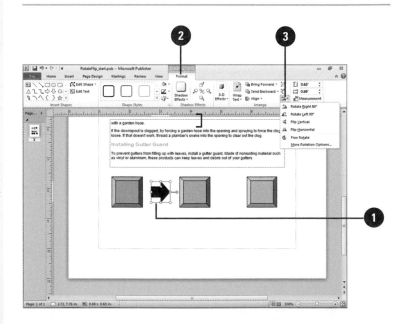

Publishing Office Documents on the Web

Introduction

Web pages are multimedia documents that provide information and contain links to other documents on the Internet, an intranet, a local network, or a hard disk. These links—also called hyperlinks—are highlighted text or graphics that you click to follow a pathway from one Web page to another. Incorporating hyperlinks within your Office documents adds an element of connectivity to your work. Web pages are based on **Hypertext Markup Language (HTML)**—a simple coding system used to format Web pages. A browser program, such as Microsoft Internet Explorer, interprets these special codes to determine how a certain Web page should be displayed. Different codes mark the size, color, style, and placement of text and graphics as well as which words and graphics should be marked as hyperlinks and to what files they link.

Web technology is available for all your Microsoft Office programs. Office provides you with the tools you need to create and save your documents as a Web page and to publish it on the Web. Office makes it easy to create a Web page without learning HTML. Saving your Office documents in HTML format means you can use most Web browsers to view them. By saving your Office documents as Web pages, you can share your data with others via the Internet. You can also preview how your document will look as a Web page in your Office program or in your browser. Office uses HTML as a companion file format; it recognizes the .html filename extension as accurately as it does those for its own Office programs (.docx, .xlsx, .accdb, .pptx, and .pub).

What You'll Do

Open a Web Page

Preview a Web Page

Create a Hyperlink

Add Hyperlinks to Slide Objects

Format a Cell Hyperlink

Change Web Page Options

Save a Web Page

Publish a Web Page

Save Slides as Web Graphics

Create Refreshable Web Queries

Get Data from Web Queries

Save Web Queries

Access Office Information on the Web

Get Documents from the Web

Opening a Web Page

After saving an Office document as a Web page, you can open the Web page, an HTML file. This allows you to quickly and easily switch from HTML to the standard Office program format and back again without losing any formatting or functionality. For example, if you create a formatted chart in an Excel workbook, save the workbook file as a Web page, and then reopen the Web page in Excel, the chart will look the same as the original chart in Excel. Excel preserves the original formatting and functionality of the workbook.

Open an Office Document as a Web Page

1. Click the **File** tab, and then click **Open**.

2. Click the **Files of type** list arrow, and then click **All Web Pages**.

3. Click the **Look in** list arrow, and then select the folder where the file is located.

4. Click the Web file.

5. Click **Open**.

♦ To open the Web page in your browser, click the **Open** button arrow, and then click **Open in Browser**.

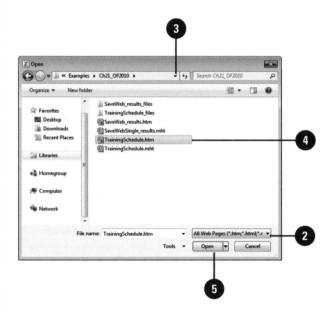

Previewing a Web Page

You can view any Office document as if it were already on the Web by previewing the Web page. By previewing a file you want to post to the Web, you can see if there are any errors that need to be corrected, formatting that needs to be added, or additions that need to be made. Just as you should always preview a document before you print it, you should preview a Web page before you post it. Previewing the Web page in your browser shows you what the page will look like once it's posted on the Internet. You do not have to be connected to the Internet to preview a document as a Web page.

View an Office Document as a Web Page

1. Open the Web file you want to view as a Web page.

2. Click the **Web Page Preview** button on the Quick Access Toolbar.

   ◆ To add the button to the toolbar, click the **Customize Quick Access Toolbar** list arrow on the Quick Access Toolbar, click **More Commands**, add the Web Page Preview button, and then click **OK**.

   Your default Web browser starts and displays the Web page.

3. Click the **Close** button to quit your Web browser.

Customize Quick Access Toolbar list arrow

Workbook Web Page

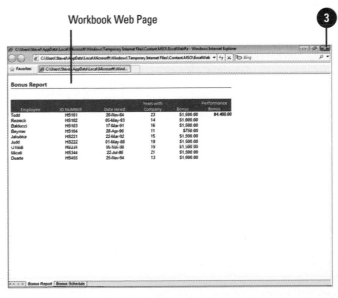

Did You Know?

Web addresses and URLs mean the same thing. Every Web page has a Uniform Resource Locator (URL), or Web address. Each URL contains specific parts that identify where a Web page is located. For example, the URL for Perspection's Web page is: *http://www.perspection.com/index.htm* where "http://" shows the address is on the Web, "www.perspection.com" shows the computer that stores the Web site, and "index.htm" is a Web page on the Web site.

Creating a Hyperlink

With instant access to the Internet, your documents can contain links to specific sites so you and anyone else using your documents can access Web information. You can create a **hyperlink**—a graphic object or colored, underlined text that you click to move (or jump) to a new location (or destination). The destination can be in the same document, another file on your computer or network, or a Web page on your intranet or the Internet. When you point to hyperlinked text or an object, the cursor changes to a pointing hand to indicate it's a hyperlink. To connect to the linked location, just click the hyperlink.

Create or Edit a Hyperlink

1. Select the text, cell, or object, such as a picture, where you want to create or edit a hyperlink.

2. Click the **Insert** tab.

3. Click the **Hyperlink** button.

   TIMESAVER *Press Ctrl+K.*

4. Click one of the icons on the Link To bar for quick access to frequently used files, Web pages, and links.

   ◆ **Existing File or Web Page.** Click to link to a document or other file.

   ◆ **Place in This Document.** Click to link to another location in the current document. Select or type a cell reference, or select a defined name.

   ◆ **Create New Document.** Click to link to a new document.

   ◆ **E-mail Address.** Click to create a link to an e-mail address. When you click the e-mail address, your e-mail program automatically opens with the address.

5. Type or select the name and location of the file or Web page you want to link to.

6. Click **OK**.

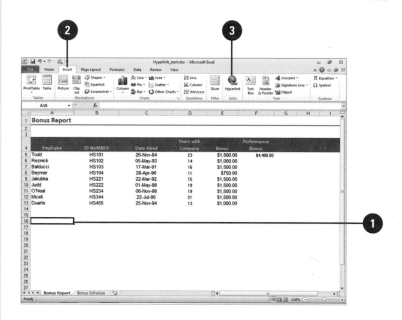

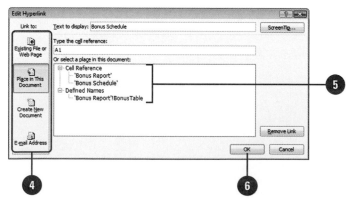

Jump to a Hyperlink

① Click the hyperlink on your document.

Office opens the linked location. For Web addresses, Office opens your Web browser, displaying the Web page associated with the hyperlink.

Did You Know?

You can create a custom ScreenTip for a hyperlink. Select the hyperlink you want to customize, click the Insert tab, click the Hyperlink button, click ScreenTip, type the ScreenTip text you want, and then click OK twice.

Remove a Hyperlink

① Right-click the cell containing the hyperlink you want to remove.

② Do one of the following:

◆ **Clear Contents** to delete a hyperlink and the text.

◆ **Remove Hyperlink** to remove the hyperlink and keep the text.

Did You Know?

You can select a hyperlink without activating the link. To select a hyperlink without activating the link, click the cell that contains the hyperlink, hold down the mouse button until the pointer becomes a cross, and then release the mouse. If the hyperlink is a graphic, hold down Ctrl, and then click the graphic.

Adding Hyperlinks to Slide Objects

In PowerPoint, you can turn one of the objects on your slide into an action button so that when you click or move over it, you activate a hyperlink and jump to the new location. You can point hyperlinks to almost any destination, including slides in a presentation and Web pages on the Web. Use the Action Settings dialog box to add sound to a hyperlink. You can add a default sound such as Chime, Click, or Drum Roll, or select a custom sound from a file.

Add a Hyperlink to a Slide Object

1. In PowerPoint, click the object (not within a SmartArt graphic) you want to modify.

2. Click the **Insert** tab.

3. Click the **Action** button.

4. Click the **Mouse Click** or **Mouse Over** tab.

5. Click the **Hyperlink to** option.

6. Click the **Hyperlink to** list arrow.

7. Click a destination for the hyperlink.

8. Click **OK**.

9. Run the slide show and test the hyperlink by pointing to or clicking the object in the slide show.

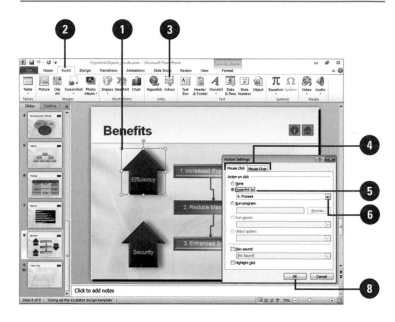

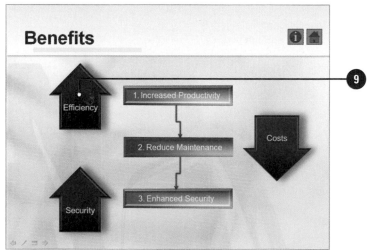

Did You Know?

You can edit a hyperlink quickly.
Right-click the object with the hyperlink, and then click Edit Hyperlink.

You can highlight a click or mouse over. When you click or move over a hyperlink, you can highlight the object. In the Action Settings dialog box, select the Highlight Click or Highlight When Mouse Over check box.

Add a Sound to a Hyperlink

1. In PowerPoint, click the object (not within a SmartArt graphic) you want to modify.

2. Click the **Insert** tab.

3. Click the **Action** button.

4. Click the **Mouse Click** or **Mouse Over** tab.

5. Select the **Play sound** check box.

6. Click the **Play sound** list arrow, and then click the sound you want to play when the object is clicked during the show.

   ◆ **Custom Sound.** Or scroll to the bottom of the Play Sound list, and then click Other Sound, locate and select the sound you want to use, and then click OK.

7. Click **OK**.

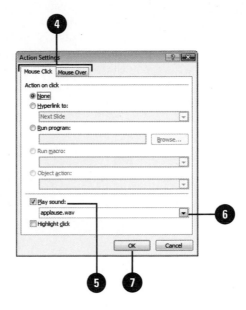

Create a Hyperlink to a Program

1. In PowerPoint, click the object (not within a SmartArt graphic) you want to modify.

2. Click the **Insert** tab, and then click the **Action** button.

3. On the Mouse Click tab, click the **Run program** option.

4. Click **Browse**, and then locate and select the program you want.

5. Click **OK**.

6. Click **OK** again.

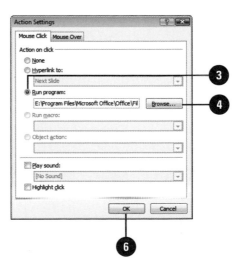

Formatting a Cell Hyperlink

Excel comes with a set of predefined cell styles for various data types, including hyperlinks, in a worksheet. When you create a hyperlink, the default cell style is used to format the text. If you want to change the appearance of hyperlinks in your workbook, you need to change the cell style for hyperlinks.

Change the Hyperlink Cell Style

1. In Excel, click the **Home** tab.

2. Click the **Cell Styles** button.

3. Right-click the **Hyperlink** or **Followed Hyperlink**, and then click **Modify**.

4. Click **Format**.

5. Select the formatting options you want on the Font and Fill tabs, and then click **OK**.

6. Select the check boxes with the formatting style you want to include in the modified cell style.

7. Click **OK**.

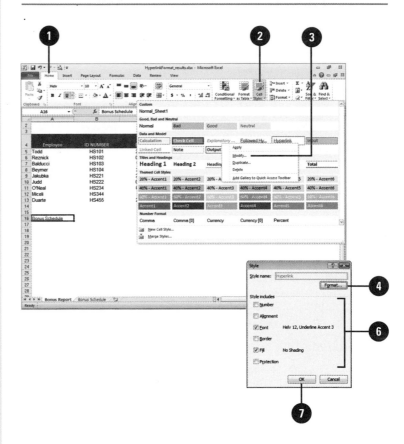

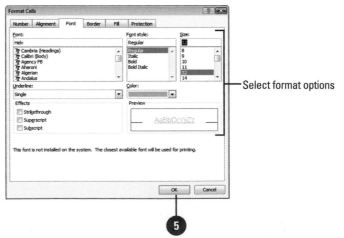

Select format options

Did You Know?

You can change the text or graphic for a hyperlink. Select the cell with the hyperlink, click in the formula bar, and then edit the text. Right-click the graphic, and then click the option you need to change in the hyperlink.

You can copy or move a hyperlink. Right-click the hyperlink you want to copy or move, and then click Copy or Cut. Right-click the cell you want to copy or move the hyperlink to, and then click Paste.

Changing Web Page Options

When you save or publish a document as a Web page, you can change the appearance of the Web page by changing Office's Web options. You can set Web options to save any additional hidden data necessary to maintain formulas, allow PNG as a graphic format, rely on CSS for font formatting, reply on VML for displaying graphics in browser, and save new Web pages as Single File Web Pages. Web pages are saved using the appropriate international text encoding so users on any language system are able to view the correct characters.

Change Web Page Options

1. Click the **File** tab, and then click **Options**.

2. In the left pane, click **Advanced**.

3. Click **Web Options**.

4. Click the **General** tab, and then select or clear the Web pages options:

   ◆ **Save any additional hidden data necessary to maintain formulas.**

   ◆ **Load pictures from Web pages not created in <Program>.**

5. Click the **Browsers** tab.

6. Click the **Target Browsers** list arrow, and then select the version you want to support.

7. Select or clear the Web page options:

   ◆ **Allow PNG as a graphics format.**

   ◆ **Rely on CSS for font formatting.** Cascading Style Sheets for Web page formatting.

   ◆ **Reply on VML for displaying graphics in browsers.** VML is Vector Markup Language, XML based graphics.

   ◆ **Save new Web pages as Single File Web Pages.**

8. Click **OK**.

9. Click **OK**.

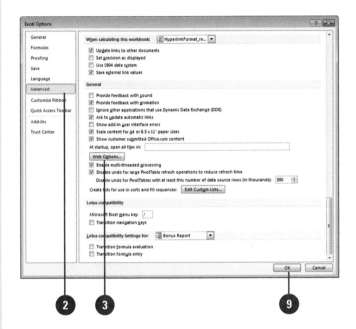

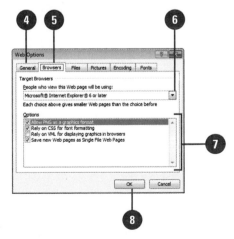

Saving a Web Page

You can place an existing Office document on the Internet for others to use. In order for any document to be placed on the Web, it must be in HTML (Hypertext Markup Language) format—a simple coding system that specifies the formats a Web browser uses to display the document. This format enables you to post, or submit information and data on a Web site for others. You don't need any HTML knowledge to save an Office document as a Web page. When you save an Office document as a Web page, you can save it using the Web Page or Single File Web Page format. The Web Page format saves the document as an HTML file and a folder that stores supporting files, such as a file for each graphic, document, and so on. Office selects the appropriate graphic format for you based on the image's content. A single file Web page saves all the elements of a Web site, including text and graphics, into a single file in the MHTML format, which is supported by Internet Explorer 4.0.1 or later.

Save an Office Document as a Web Page

1. Click the **File** tab, and then click **Save As**.

2. Click the **Save as type** list arrow, and then click **Web Page.**

3. Click the **Save in** list arrow, and then select a location for your Web page.

4. Type the name for the Web page.

5. In Excel, click the **Entire Workbook** or **Selection: Sheet** option.

6. To change the title of your Web page, click **Change Title**, type the new title in the Set Page Title box, and then click **OK**.

7. To save a thumbnail preview of the Web page, select the **Save Thumbnail** check box.

8. Click **Save**.

9. If necessary, click **Yes** to keep formatting.

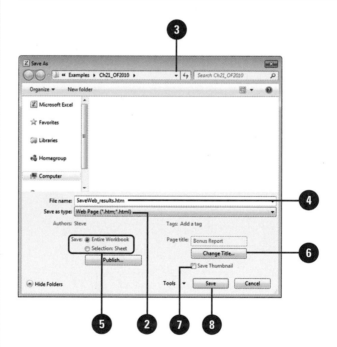

Save an Office Document as a Single File Web Page

1. Click the **File** tab, and then click **Save As**.

2. Click the **Save as type** list arrow, and then click **Single File Web Page.**

3. Click the **Save in** list arrow, and then select a location for your Web page.

4. Type the name for the Web page.

5. In Excel, click the **Entire Workbook** or **Selection: Sheet** option.

6. To change the title of your Web page, click **Change Title**, type the new title in the Set Page Title box, and then click **OK**.

7. To save a thumbnail preview of the Web page, select the **Save Thumbnail** check box.

8. Click **Save**.

9. If necessary, click **Yes** to keep formatting.

   The Web page is saved as a single file.

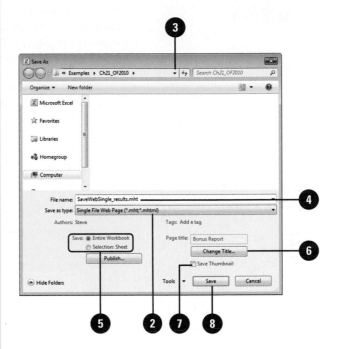

Publishing a Web Page

At times, you'll want to publish a copy of your current workbook or presentation in HTML format directly to a **Web server** (a computer on the Internet or intranet that stores Web pages) so others can view and manipulate your data. Publishing to a Web server is as simple as saving a file. You can publish a complete document, or part of a document. A document saved as a Web page retains all its spreadsheet, charting, or PivotTable functionality and formatting properties. This interactivity means that while your document is on the Web, others can manipulate your data. You can elect to let anyone using Internet Explorer 4.01 or later interact with your data from Office.

Save and Publish an Office Document as a Web Page

1. To publish part of a worksheet in Excel, select the range you want saved as a Web page.

2. In Excel or PowerPoint, click the **File** tab, and then click **Save As.**

3. Click the **Save as type** list arrow, and then click **Web Page.**

4. Click the **Save in** list arrow, and then select a publish location.

5. In Excel, click the **Selection: Sheet** or **Entire Worksheet** option.

6. Type the name for the Web page or Web address.

7. To change the title of your Web page, click **Change Title**, type the new title in the Set Page Title box, and then click **OK.**

8. Click **Publish.**

9. Click the **Choose** list arrow, and then select the items you want to publish in the Web page.

10. Select or clear the **AutoRepublish everytime this <document> is saved** check box.

11. Select or clear the **Open published web page in browser** check box.

12. Click **Publish.**

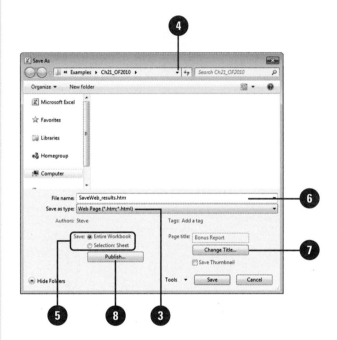

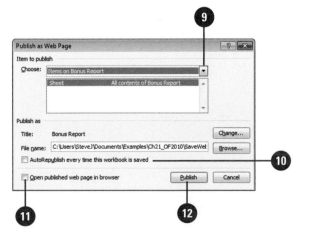

Saving Slides as Web Graphics

As you develop a Web site, you can incorporate slides from any of your PowerPoint presentations. You can save any slide in a presentation in the GIF, JPEG, or PNG Web graphic format. **Graphics Interchange Format (GIF)** is a form of compression for line drawings or other artwork. Office converts to GIF such images as logos, graphs, line drawings, and specific colored objects. **Joint Photographic Experts Group (JPEG)** is a high-quality form of compression for continuous tone images, such as photographs. Office converts to JPEG such images as photographs or other images that have many shades of colors. **Portable Network Graphics Format** is a new bit-mapped graphics format similar to GIF.

Save a PowerPoint Slide as a Web Graphic

1. In PowerPoint, open the presentation with the slide you want to save as a Web graphic, and then display the slide.

2. Click the **File** tab, and then click **Save As**.

3. Click the **Save as type** list arrow, and then click **GIF Graphics Interchange Format, JPEG File Interchange Format**, or **PNG Portable Network Graphics Format**.

4. Click the **Save in** list arrow, and then select a location for the file.

5. Type a name for the file.

6. Click **Save**.

7. Click **Every Slide** or **Current Slide Only**.

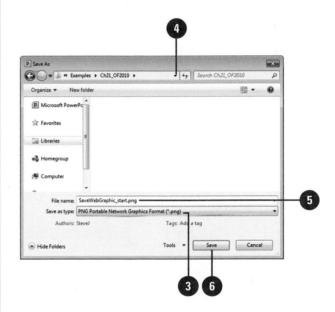

See Also

See "Saving an Office Document with Different Formats" on page 24 for information on saving files with different file formats.

Creating Refreshable Web Queries

If you need to analyze Web data in a worksheet, you can use the copy and paste commands to bring the data from a Web page into the worksheet. The Paste Options button allows you to specify whether you want the information to keep the data as it is right now or make it refreshable to the current data on the Web. As the data changes on the Web, you can use the Refresh button to quickly update the data in your worksheet. You don't need to copy the information again.

Copy and Paste Refreshable Data from the Web

1. Open the Web page with the information you want to copy into an Excel worksheet, and then select the data.

2. Copy the data.

3. Switch to Excel, and then click the active cell where you want the data.

4. Click the **Paste** button on the Home tab.

5. Click the **Paste Options** button, and then click **Refreshable Web Query**.

6. Click the arrow buttons to select the information you want.

7. Click **Import**.

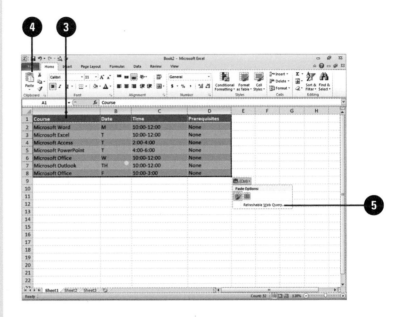

Did You Know?

You can quickly refresh a Web query. Click a cell in the worksheet with the query data, click the Data tab, and then click the Refresh button. A spinning refresh icon appears in the status bar to indicate that the query is running. You can double-click the icon to check the status of the query.

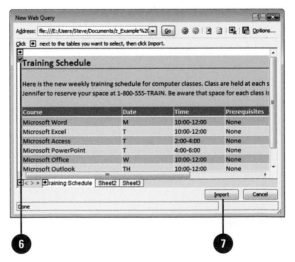

Getting Data from Web Queries

You can import data into Excel through database and Web queries and analyze data with formulas and formatting. You can insert columns within query tables and apply formulas and formatting. When data is refreshed, the formatting and analysis are retained. Excel helps you through the process of bringing data from a Web page to your worksheet. You can create a new Web query as you choose the URL and parameters for how you want to import the Web data. Once you save the query, you can run it again at any time.

Get Data from a New Web Query

1. In Excel, click the **Data** tab.

2. Click the **From Web** button.

3. Type the address for the Web page that contains the data you want.

4. Click the arrow buttons to select the information you want.

5. Click **Options** to select the formatting you want your data to keep.

6. Click **Import**.

7. Click the **Existing worksheet** option and specify a starting cell, or click the **New worksheet** option.

8. Click **OK**.

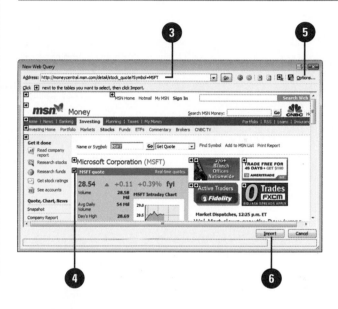

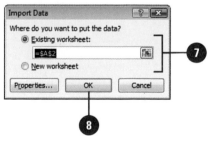

Saving Web Queries

When you create a Web query in Excel, it is automatically saved for use in the current workbook. If you need the same query in another workbook, you can save the Web query in a separate file. When you save a query, the file uses the .iqy extension, which you can import into another workbook. After you save a Web query, you can use the Existing Connections button to import the query data into a worksheet.

Save a Web Query

1. In Excel, click the **Data** tab.

2. Click the **From Web** button.

3. Display the Web page that contains the data you want.

4. Click the **Save Query** button.

5. Select the drive and folder in which you want to save the query.

6. Type a name for the query.

7. Click **Save**.

8. Click **Cancel**.

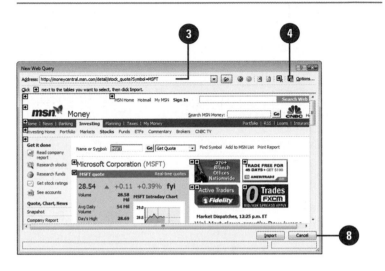

Import a Query

1. In Excel, click the **Data** tab.

2. Click the **Existing Connections** button.

3. Click the Web query you want to import.

4. Click **Open**.

5. Click the **Existing worksheet** option and specify a cell location, or click the **New worksheet** option, and then click **OK** to insert the query data.

6. To refresh the query data, click the **Refresh All** button arrow, and then click **Refresh**.

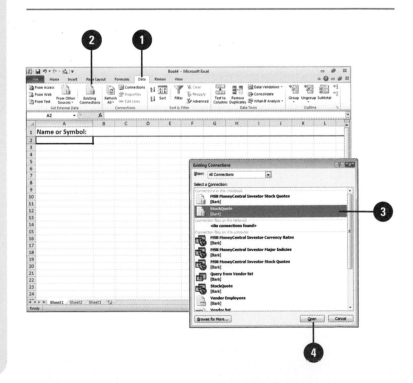

Accessing Office Information on the Web

New information about programs comes out with great frequency. You have access to an abundance of information about Office programs and other programs in the Office Suite from Microsoft. This information is constantly being updated. Answers to frequently asked questions, user forums, and update offers are some of the types of information you can find about Microsoft Office. You can also find out about conferences, books, and other products that help you learn just how much you can do with your Microsoft Office software.

Find Online Office Information

1. Click the **File** tab, and then click **Help**.

2. Click any of the following option to display online information:

   ◆ **Getting Started.** Accesses information to help you get started with the product.

   ◆ **Contact Us.** Accesses the Microsoft Support web site, where you can get assistance.

   ◆ **Check for Updates.** Accesses Windows Update to check for the latest Office updates.

   Your Web browser opens, displaying a Microsoft Office Online Web page.

3. Click a hyperlink of interest.

4. Click the **Close** button to quit the browser and return to the Office program.

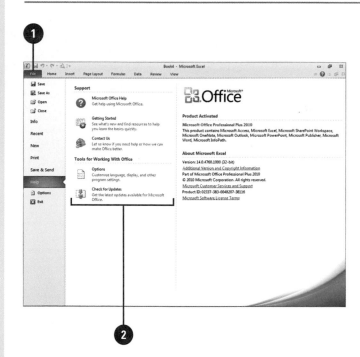

Getting Documents from the Web

File Transfer Protocol (FTP) is an inexpensive and efficient way to transfer files between your computer and others on the Internet. You can download or receive, from another computer, any kind of file, including text, graphics, sound, and video files. To download a file, you need an ID and password to identify who you are. Anonymous FTP sites are open to anyone; they usually use *anonymous* as an ID and your *e-mail address* as a password. You can also save the FTP site address to revisit the site later.

Add FTP Locations

1 Click the **File** tab, and then click **Open**.

2 Click **Computer** in the left pane.

3 Right-click a blank area, and then click **Add a network location**.

4 Follow the Add Network Location wizard to create a link to an FTP site or other network, and then click **Finish** to complete it.

◆ To complete the process, you need the complete address for an FTP site, and a username and password.

Access an FTP Site

1 Click the **File** tab, and then click **Open**.

2 Click **Computer** in the left pane.

3 Double-click the FTP site to which you want to log in.

4 Enter a password (your E-mail address or personal password), and then select a log on option.

5 Click **Log On**.

6 Select a folder location, and then select a file.

7 Click **Open**.

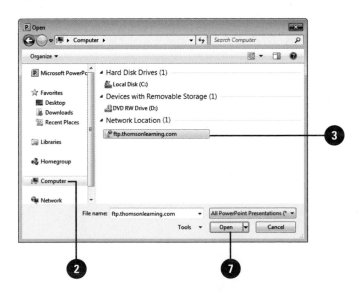

Protecting and Securing Office Documents

Introduction

When you've developed content in your document and want feedback, you can electronically send an Office document to reviewers so that they can read, revise, and comment on the document without having to print it. Instead of reading hand-written text or sticky notes on your printout, you can get clear and concise feedback.

Adding a password to protect your document is not only a good idea for security purposes, it's an added feature to make sure that changes to your document aren't made by unauthorized people. You can protect all or part of a work-sheet or an entire document. In each case, you'll be asked to supply a password, and then enter it again when you want to work on the file. Not only can you guard who sees your doc-ument, you can set rights on who can add changes and com-ments to your document. If you need to validate the authenticity of a document, you can add an invisible digital signature, an electronic secure stamp of authentication on a document, or a visible signature line. A signature line allows you to create a paperless signature process for documents, such as contracts.

The Trust Center is a place where you set security options and find the latest technology information as it relates to doc-ument privacy, safety, and security from Microsoft. The Trust Center allows you to set security and privacy settings and provides links to Microsoft privacy statements, a customer Improvement program, and trustworthy computing practices.

What You'll Do

Inspect Documents

Protect a Worksheet

Lock or Unlock Worksheet Cells

Add Security Encryption to a Document

Add Password Protection to a Document

Add a Digital Signature

Add a Signature Line

Avoid Harmful Attacks

Use the Trust Center

Select Trusted Publishers and Locations

Set File Related Security Options

Set Add-In, ActiveX and Macro Security Options

Change Message Bar Security Options

Set Privacy Options

Set External Content Security Options

Work with Office Safe Modes

Mark a Document as Read-Only

Inspecting Documents

While you work on your document, Office automatically saves and manages personal information and hidden data to enable you to create and develop a document with other people. The personal information and hidden data includes comments, revision marks, versions, ink annotations, document properties, invisible content, header and footer information, rows and columns, document server properties, and custom XML data. The **Document Inspector** uses inspector modules to find and remove any hidden data and personal information specific to each of these modules that you might not want to share with others. If you remove hidden content from your document, you might not be able to restore it by using the Undo command, so it's important to make a copy of your document before you remove any information.

Inspect an Office Document

1. Click the **File** tab, click **Save As**, type a name to save a copy of the original, specify a folder location, and then click **Save**.

2. Click the **File** tab, and then click **Info**.

3. Click the **Check for Issues** button, and then click **Inspect Document**.

4. Select the check boxes with the content you want to find and remove:

   ◆ **Comments and Annotations.** Includes comments and ink annotations.

   ◆ **Document Properties and Personal Information.** Includes metadata document properties (Summary, Statistics, and Custom tabs), the file path for publishing Web pages, document server properties, and content type information.

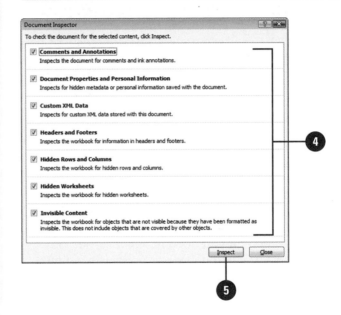

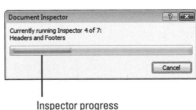

Inspector progress

Did You Know?

What is metadata? Metadata is data that describes other data. For example, text in a document is data, while the number of worksheets is metadata.

- **Custom XML Data.** Includes any custom XML data.

- **Headers and Footers.** Includes information in headers and footers.

- **Hidden Rows and Columns.** Includes information in hidden rows and columns.

- **Hidden Worksheets.** Includes information in hidden worksheets.

- **Invisible Content.** Includes objects formatted as invisible. Doesn't include objects covered by other objects.

5 Click **Inspect**.

6 Review the results of the inspection.

7 Click **Remove All** for each inspector module in which you want to remove hidden data and personal information.

TROUBLE? *Before you click Remove All, be sure you want to remove the information. You might not be able to restore it.*

8 Click **Close**.

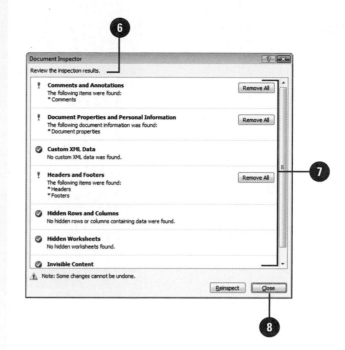

Protecting a Worksheet

To preserve all your hard work—particularly if others use your files—protect it with a password. You can protect a sheet or an entire document. In each case, you'll be asked to supply a password, and then enter it again when you want to work on the file. Passwords are case sensitive, so be sure to supply your password as it was first entered. If you forget a password, there is no way to open the file, so it's very important to remember or write down your password(s). Keep your password in a safe place. Avoid obvious passwords such as your name, your company, or your favorite pet.

Apply a Password to a Worksheet

1. In Excel, click the **Review** tab.

2. Click the **Protect Sheet** button.

3. Select the check boxes for the options you want protected in the worksheet.

4. Type a password.

5. Click **OK**.

6. Retype the password.

7. Click **OK**.

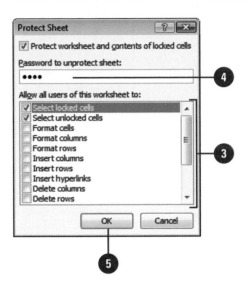

Did You Know?

You can protect document elements.
Click the Review tab, click the Protect Document button, and then select or clear the Structure or Windows check boxes. Select the Structure check box to prevent users from viewing, copying, moving, or inserting worksheets. It also prevents users from recording new macros, displaying data from PivotTable reports, using analysis tools, or creating scenario summary reports. Select the Windows check box to prevent users from moving, resizing, or closing windows.

Apply a Password to Edit Parts of a Worksheet

1. In Excel, select the range in which you want to apply a password.

2. Click the **Review** tab.

3. Click the **Allow Users to Edit Ranges** button.

4. Click **New**.

5. If you want, type a range title.

6. Type a range password.

7. Click **OK**.

8. Retype the password.

9. Click **OK**.

10. To modify or delete a range, click a range, and then click **Modify** or **Delete**.

11. Click **OK**.

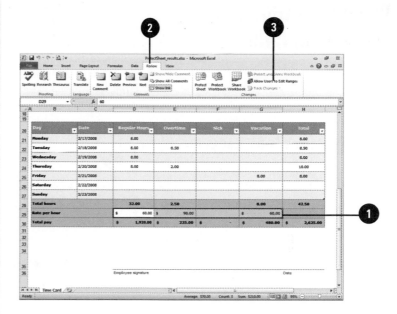

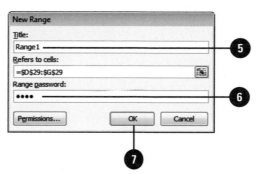

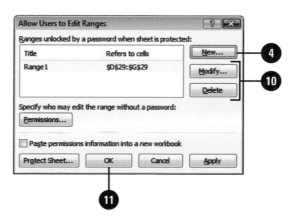

Locking or Unlocking Worksheet Cells

To prevent accidental changes to your data, you can lock worksheet cells. When you lock selected cells, you cannot make changes to them until you unlock them. When you lock cells, users can unlock the data and make changes unless you add password protection to the worksheet. For security or confidentiality reasons, you might want to hide formulas from view. If so, you can hide or unhide them using the Protection tab in the Format Cells dialog box.

Lock or Unlock Worksheet Cells

1. In Excel, select the cell or range you want to lock or unlock.

2. Click the **Home** tab.

3. Click the **Format** button, and then click **Lock Cell** to lock or unlock the current selection.

   This toggle command turns on or off the Locked check box on the Protection tab in the Format Cells dialog box.

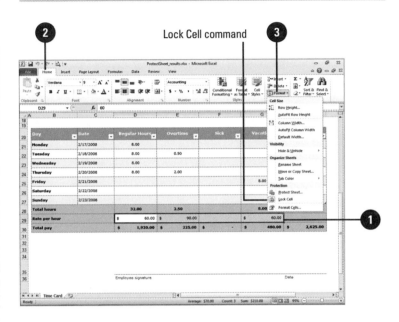

Lock Cell command

Hide or Show Formulas

1. In Excel, select the cell or range with the formulas you want to hide or show.

2. Click the **Home** tab.

3. Click the **Format** button, and then click **Format Cells**.

4. Click the **Protection** tab.

5. Select the **Hidden** check box to hide formulas or clear it to show formulas.

6. Click **OK**.

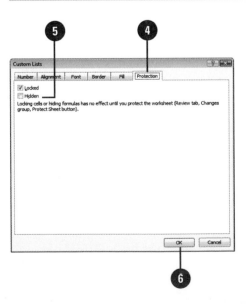

Adding Security Encryption to a Document

File encryption is additional security you can apply to a document. File encryption scrambles your password to protect your document from unauthorized people from breaking into the file. You don't have to worry about the encryption, Office handles everything. All you need to do is remember the password. If you forget it, you can't open the file. Password protection takes effect the next time you open the document. To set password protection using file encryption, use the Encrypt with Password command on the Info screen, enter a password, write it down for safekeeping, and then reenter the password again.

Apply File Encryption

1. Click the **File** tab, and then click **Info**.

2. Click the **Protect <Document>** button, and then click **Encrypt with Password**.

3. Type a password.

4. Click **OK**.

5. Retype the password.

6. Click **OK**.

Did You Know?

You can remove file encryption. Click the File tab, click Info, click the Protect <Document> button, click Encrypt With Password, delete the file encryption password, and then click OK.

Adding Password Protection to a Document

You can assign a password and other security options so that only those who know the password can open the document, or to protect the integrity of your document as it moves from person to person. At times, you will want the information to be used but not changed; at other times, you will want only specific people to be able to view the document. Setting a document as read-only is useful when you want a document, such as a company-wide bulletin, to be distributed and read, but not changed. Password protection takes effect the next time you open the document.

Add Password Protection to an Office Document

1. Open the document you want to protect.

2. Click the **File** tab, and then click **Save As**.

3. Click **Tools**, and then click **General Options**.

4. Type a password in the Password to open box or the Password to modify box.

   IMPORTANT *It's critical that you remember your password. If you forget your password, Microsoft can't retrieve it.*

5. Select or clear the **Remove automatically created personal information from this file on save** check box.

6. To set macro security options in the Trust center, click **Macro Security**.

7. Click **OK**.

8. Type your password again.

9. Click **OK**.

10. If you entered passwords for Open and Modify, type your password again, and then click **OK**.

11. Click **Save**, and then click **Yes** to replace existing document.

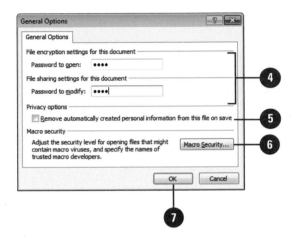

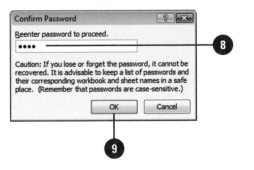

Open a Document with Password Protection

1. Click the **File** tab, click **Open**, navigate to a document with password protection, and then click **Open**.

2. Click **Read Only** if you do not wish to modify the document, or type the password in the Password dialog box.

3. Click **OK**.

Change or Remove the Password Protection

1. Click the **File** tab, click **Open**, navigate to a document with password protection, and then click **Open**.

2. Type the password in the Password dialog box.

3. Click **OK**.

4. Click the **File** tab, click **Save As**, click **Tools**, and then click **General Options**.

5. Select the contents in the Password to modify box or the Password to open box, and then choose the option you want:

   ◆ **Change password.** Type a new password, click **OK**, and then retype your password.

   ◆ **Delete password.** Press Delete.

6. Click **OK**.

7. Click **Save**, and then click **Yes** to replace existing document.

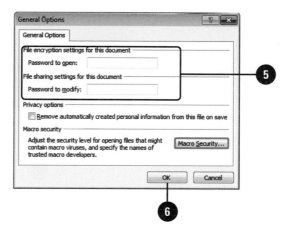

Adding a Digital Signature

After you've finished a document, you might consider adding an invisible digital signature—an electronic, secure stamp of authentication on a document. Before you can add a digital signature, you need to get a **digital ID**, or **digital certificate**, which provides an electronic way to prove your identity. A digital certificate checks a public key to validate a private key associated with a digital signature. To assure a digital signature is authentic, it must have a valid (non expired or revoked) certificate issued by a reputable certification authority (CA), and the signing person must be from a trusted publisher. If you need a verified authenticate digital certificate, you can obtain one from a trusted Microsoft partner CA. If you don't need a verified digital certificate, you can create one of your own. If someone modifies the file, the digital signature is removed and revoked. If you're not sure if a document is digitally signed, you can use the Signatures task pane to view or remove valid signatures.

Create an Digital ID

1. Click the **File** tab, click **Info**, click the **Protect <Document>** button, and then click **Add a Digital Signature**.

2. If an alert message appears, click **Signature Services from the Office Marketplace** to open an informational Web site where you can sign up for a digital certificate, or click **OK** to create your own.

   If you don't want to see this dialog box again, select the **Don't show this message again** check box.

3. If necessary, click **OK** and verify your Rights Management account credentials using your .NET password.

4. If you don't have a digital ID, click the option to get an ID from a Microsoft Partner or create your own, and then click **OK**.

5. Enter your name, e-mail address, organization name, and location.

6. Click **Create**.

   You can sign a document, or click **Cancel**.

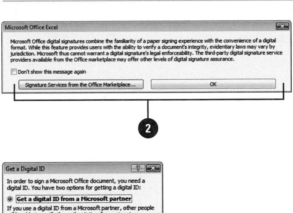

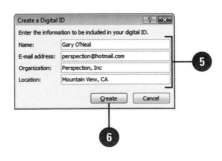

Add a Digital Signature to a Document

1. Click the **File** tab, point to **Prepare**, and then click **Add a Digital Signature**.

2. To change the digital signature, click **Change**, select the one you want, and then click **OK**.

3. Enter the purpose for signing this document.

4. Click **Sign**.

5. If necessary, click **OK**.

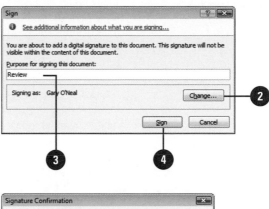

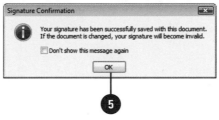

View or Remove Signatures

1. Click the **Signature** icon on the Status bar, or click the **File** tab, click **Info**, and then click the **View Signatures** button.

   The Signatures task pane appears, displaying valid signatures in the document. Invalid signatures are no longer automatically removed.

2. Point to a signature, and then click the list arrow.

3. To see signature details, click **Signature Details**, select a signature, click **View**, click **OK** when you're done, and then click **Close**.

4. To remove a signature, point to a signature, click the list arrow, click **Remove Signature**, click **Yes**, and then if necessary click **OK**.

5. Click the **Close** button on the task pane.

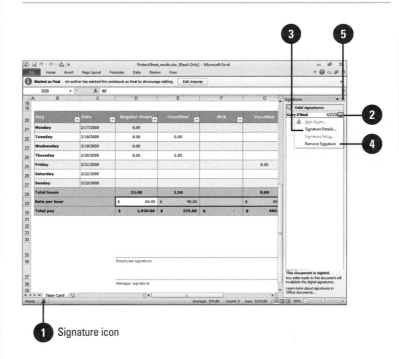

Signature icon

Adding a Signature Line

If you prefer a visible signature line instead of an invisible digital signature, you can insert a visible signature line along with a digital certificate of authenticity. Signature lines allow you to create a paperless signature process for documents, such as contracts. A visible signature line looks like a typical signature line with a name, a date and a line for a signature. When you send a document out with a signature request, the signer sees a signature line and a notification request with instructions. The signer can type—or ink with a Tablet PC—a signature next to the *X*, or select a signature image. To add a signature line and digital signature at the same time, first you insert a signature line into your document, and then you sign it.

Add a Signature Line

1. In Word and Excel, click the **Insert** tab.

2. Click the **Signature Line** button arrow, and then click **Microsoft Office Signature Line**.

3. If an alert message appears, click **Signature Services from the Office Marketplace** to open an informational Web site where you can sign up for a digital certificate, or click **OK** to create your own.

4. Type information about the person who will be signing on this signature line.

5. If you want, type any instructions for the signer.

6. To show the signature date, select the **Allow the signer to add comments in the Sign dialog** check box.

7. To show the signature date, select the **Show sign data in signature line** check box.

8. Click **OK**.

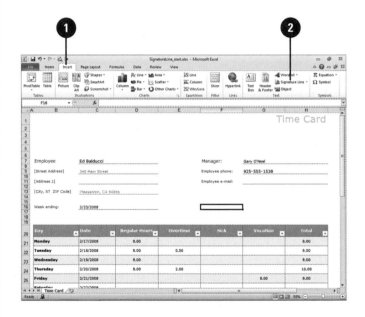

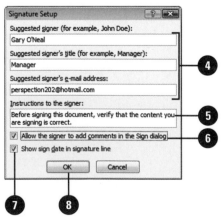

Sign the Signature Line

1. In Word and Excel, double-click the signature line that needs a signature.

2. To add a printed version of your signature, type your name.

   If you have a Tablet PC, you can sign your name.

3. To select an image of your written signature, click **Select Image**, navigate to the signature image, and then click **Select**.

4. Click **Sign**.

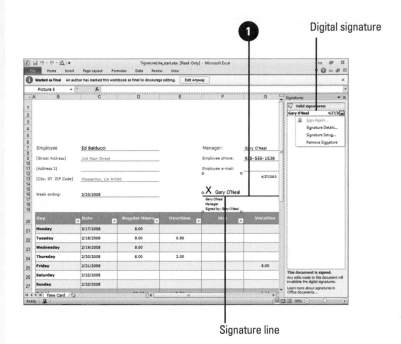

Digital signature

Signature line

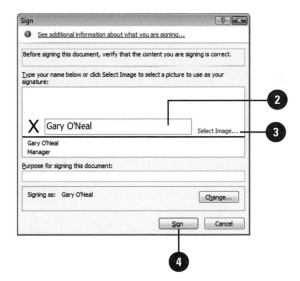

Avoiding Harmful Attacks

Spreading Harmful Infections

Many viruses and other harmful attacks spread through file downloads, attachments in e-mail messages, and data files that have macros, ActiveX controls, add-ins, or Visual Basic for Applications (VBA) code attached to them. Virus writers capitalize on people's curiosity and willingness to accept files from people they know or work with, in order to transmit malicious files disguised as or attached to benign files. When you start downloading files to your computer, you must be aware of the potential for catching a computer virus, worm, or Trojan Horse. Typically, you can't catch one from just reading a mail message or downloading a file, but you can catch one from installing, opening, or running an infected program or attached code.

Understanding Harmful Attacks

Phishing is a scam that tries to steal your identity by sending deceptive e-mail asking you for bank and credit card information online. Phishers spoof the domain names of banks and other companies in order to deceive consumers into thinking that they are visiting a familiar Web site.

Phishers create a Web address that looks like a familiar Web address but is actually altered. This is known as a **homograph**. The domain name is created using alphabet characters from different languages, not just English. For example, the Web site address "www.microsoft.com" looks legitimate, but what you can't see is that the "i" is a Cyrillic character from the Russian alphabet.

Don't be fooled by spoofed Web sites that looks like the official site. Never respond to requests for personal information via e-mail; most companies have policies that do not ask for your personal information through e-mail. If you get a suspicious e-mail, call the institution to investigate and report it.

Spam is unsolicited e-mail, which is often annoying and time-consuming to get rid of. Spammers harvest e-mail addresses from Web pages and unsolicited e-mail. To avoid spam, use multiple e-mail addresses (one for Web forms and another for private e-mail), opt-out and remove yourself from e-mail lists. See the Microsoft Windows and Microsoft Outlook Help system for specific details.

Spyware is software that collects personal information without your knowledge or permission. Typically, spyware is downloaded and installed on your computer along with free software, such as freeware, games, or music file-sharing programs. Spyware is often associated with **Adware** software that displays advertisements, such as a pop-up ad. Examples of spyware and unauthorized adware include programs that change your home page or search page without your permission. To avoid spyware and adware, read the fine print in license agreements when you install software, scan your computer for spyware and adware with detection and removal software (such as Ad-aware from Lavasoft), and turn on Pop-up Blocker. See the Microsoft Windows Help system for specific details.

Avoiding Harmful Attacks Using Office

There are a few things you can do within any Office 2010 program to keep your system safe from the infiltration of harmful attacks.

1) Make sure you activate macro, ActiveX, add-in, and VBA code detection and notification. You can use the Trust Center to help protect you from attached code attacks. The Trust Center checks for trusted publisher and code locations on your computer and provides security options for add-ins, ActiveX controls, and macros to ensure the best possible protection. The Trust Center displays a security alert in the Message Bar when it detects a potentially harmful attack.

2) Make sure you activate Web site spoofing detection and notification. You can use the Trust Center to help protect you from homograph attacks. The *Check Office documents that are from or link to suspicious Web sites* check box under Privacy Options in the Trust Center is on by default and continually checks for potentially spoofed domain names. The Trust Center displays a security alert in the Message Bar when you have a document open and click a link to a Web site with an address that has a potentially spoofed domain name, or you open a file from a Web site with an address that has a potentially spoofed domain name.

3) Be very careful of file attachments in e-mail you open. As you receive e-mail, don't open or run an attached file unless you know who sent it and what it contains. If you're not sure, you should delete it. The Attachment Manager provides security information to help you understand more about the file you're opening. See the Microsoft Outlook Help system for specific details.

Avoiding Harmful Attacks Using Windows

There are a few things you can do within Microsoft Windows to keep your system safe from the infiltration of harmful attacks.

1) Make sure Windows Firewall is turned on. Windows Firewall helps block viruses and worms from reaching your computer, but it doesn't detect or disable them if they are already on your computer or come through e-mail. Windows Firewall doesn't block unsolicited e-mail or stop you from opening e-mail with harmful attachments.

2) Make sure Automatic Updates is turned on. Windows Automatic Updates regularly checks the Windows Update Web site for important updates that your computer needs, such as security updates, critical updates, and service packs. Each file that you download using Automatic Update has a digital signature from Microsoft to ensure its authenticity and security.

3) Make sure you are using the most up-to-date antivirus software. New viruses and more virulent strains of existing viruses are discovered every day. Unless you update your virus-checking software, new viruses can easily bypass outdated virus checking software. Companies such as McAfee and Symantec offer shareware virus checking programs available for download directly from their Web sites. These programs monitor your system, checking each time a file is added to your computer to make sure it's not in some way trying to change or damage valuable system files.

4) Be very careful of the sites from which you download files. Major file repository sites, such as FileZ, Download.com, or TuCows, regularly check the files they receive for viruses before posting them to their Web sites. Don't download files from Web sites unless you are certain that the sites check their files for viruses. Internet Explorer monitors downloads and warns you about potentially harmful files and gives you the option to block them.

Using the Trust Center

The **Trust Center** is a place where you set security options and find the latest technology information as it relates to document privacy, safety, and security from Microsoft. The Trust Center allows you to set security and privacy settings—Trusted Publishers, Trusted Locations, Trusted Documents (**New!**), Add-ins, ActiveX Settings, Macro Settings, Protected view (**New!**), Message Bar, External Content, File Block Settings (**New!**) ,and Privacy Options—and provides links to Microsoft privacy statements, a customer improvement program, and trustworthy computing practices.

View the Trust Center

1. Click the **File** tab, and then click **Options**.

2. In the left pane, click **Trust Center**.

3. Click the links in which you want online information at the Microsoft Online Web site.

   ◆ **Show the Microsoft Office privacy statement.** Opens a Microsoft Web site detailing privacy practices.

   ◆ **Office.com privacy statement.** Opens a Microsoft Office Web site detailing privacy practices.

   ◆ **Customer Experience Improvement Program.** Opens the Microsoft Customer Experience Improvement Program (CEIP) Web site.

   ◆ **Microsoft Trustworthy Computing.** Opens a Microsoft Web site detailing security and reliability practices.

4. When you're done, close your Web browser or dialog box, and return to Office.

5. Click **OK**.

Selecting Trusted Publishers and Locations

The Trust Center security system continually checks for external potentially unsafe content in your documents. Hackers can hide Web beacons in external content—images, linked media, data connections and templates—to gather information about you or cause problems. When the Trust Center detects potentially harmful external content, the Message Bar appears with a security alert and options to enable or block the content. Trusted publishers are reputable developers who create application extensions, such as a macro, ActiveX control, or add-in. The Trust Center uses a set of criteria—valid and current digital signature, and reputable certificate—to make sure publishers' code and source locations are safe and secure. If you are sure that the external content is trustworthy, you can add the content publisher and location to your trusted lists, which allows it to run without being checked by the Trust Center.

Modify Trusted Publishers and Locations

1. Click the **File** tab, and then click **Options**.

2. In the left pane, click **Trust Center**.

3. Click **Trust Center Settings**.

4. In the left pane, click **Trusted Publishers**.

5. Select a publisher, and then use the **View** and **Remove** buttons to make the changes you want.

6. In the left pane, click **Trusted Locations**.

7. Select a location, and then use the **Add new location**, **Remove**, and **Modify** buttons to make the changes you want.

8. Select or clear the **Allow Trusted Locations on my network (not recommended)** check box.

9. Select or clear the **Disable all Trusted Locations** check box.

10. Click **OK**.

11. Click **OK**.

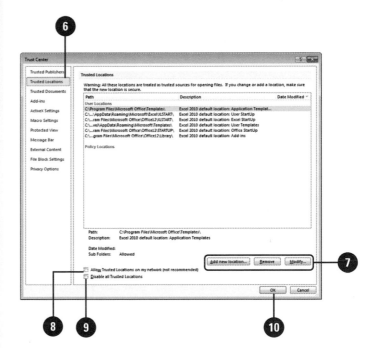

Setting Document Related Security Options

The Trust Center security system allows you to set file-related options to check for potentially unsafe content in your documents (**New!**). In Trusted Documents (**New!**), you can set options to open trusted documents without any security prompts for macros, ActiveX controls and other types of active content in the document. For a trusted document, you won't be prompted the next time you open the document even if new active content was added to the document or changes where made to existing active content. You should only trust documents if you trust the source. Protected view (**New!**) provides a place to open potentially dangerous files, without any security prompts, in a restricted mode to help minimize harm to your computer. If you disable Protected view, you could expose your computer to possible harmful threats. In File Block Settings (**New!**), you can select the Open and Save check boxes to prevent each file type from opening, or just opening in Protected view, and from saving.

Set Options for Trusted Documents

1. Click the **File** tab, and then click **Options**.

2. In the left pane, click **Trust Center**.

3. Click **Trust Center Settings**.

4. In the left pane, click **Trusted Documents**.

5. Select or clear the check boxes you do or don't want.

   ◆ **Allow documents on a network to be trusted.**

   ◆ **Disable Trusted Documents.**

6. To clear all trusted documents so they are no longer trusted, click **Clear**.

7. Click **OK**.

8. Click **OK**.

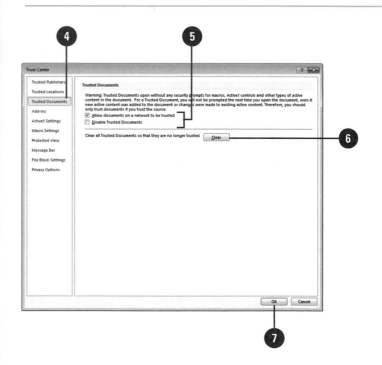

Set Options for Protected View

1. Click the **File** tab, and then click **Options**.

2. In the left pane, click **Trust Center**.

3. Click **Trust Center Settings**.

4. In the left pane, click **Protected View**.

5. Select or clear the check boxes you do or don't want.

   ◆ **Enable Protected View for files originating from the Internet.**

   ◆ **Enable Protected View for files located in potentially unsafe locations.**

   ◆ **Enable Protected View for Outlook attachments.**

6. Click **OK**.

7. Click **OK**.

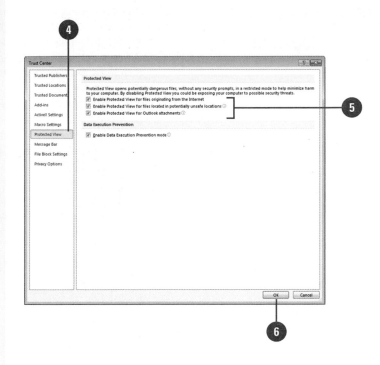

Set Options for File Block Settings

1. Click the **File** tab, and then click **Options**.

2. In the left pane, click **Trust Center**.

3. Click **Trust Center Settings**.

4. In the left pane, click **File Block Settings**.

5. Select the **Open** and **Save** check boxes you want to block for the different file types from opening or saving or clear the ones you don't want.

6. Select the open behavior option you want.

7. Click **OK**.

8. Click **OK**.

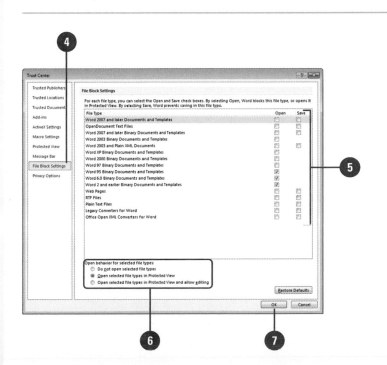

Setting Add-in Security Options

An add-in, such as smart tags, extends functionality to Microsoft Office programs. An add-in can add buttons and custom commands to the Ribbon. When an add-in is installed, it appears on the Add-Ins tab of an Office program and includes a special ScreenTip that identifies the developer. Since add-ins are software code added to Microsoft Office programs, hackers can use them to do malicious harm, such as spreading a virus. The Trust Center uses a set of criteria—valid and current digital signature, reputable certificate and a trusted publisher—to make sure add-ins are safe and secure. If it discovers a potentially unsafe add-in, it disables the code and notifies you in the Message Bar. If the add-in security options are not set to the level you need, you can change them in the Trust Center.

Set Add-in Security Options

1. Click the **File** tab, and then click **Options**.

2. In the left pane, click **Trust Center**.

3. Click **Trust Center Settings**.

4. In the left pane, click **Add-ins**.

5. Select or clear the check boxes you do or don't want.

   ◆ **Require Application Add-ins to be signed by Trusted Publisher.** Select to check for a digital signature on the .dll file.

   ◆ **Disable notification for unsigned add-ins (code will remain disabled).** Only available if the above check box is selected. Select to disable unsigned add-ins without notification.

   ◆ **Disable all Application Add-ins (may impair functionality).** Select to disable all add-ins without any notifications.

6. Click **OK**.

7. Click **OK**.

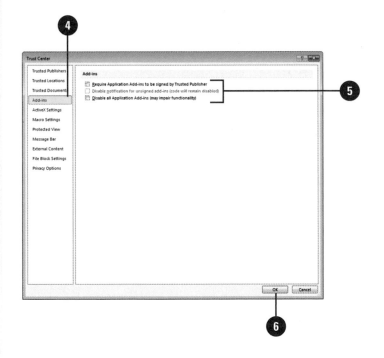

For Your Information

Setting Outlook Security for Messages

If you want to send all your messages securely, click the File tab, click Options, click Trust Center in the left pane, click Trust Center Settings, and then click E-mail Security in the left pane. Select or clear the Encrypt Contents And Attachments For Outgoing Messages, Add Digital Signature To Outgoing Messages, or Send Clear Text Signed Message When Sending Signed Messages check boxes, click OK, and then click OK.

Setting ActiveX
Security Options

An ActiveX control provides additional functionality, such as a text box, button, dialog box, or small utility program. ActiveX controls are software code, so hackers can use them to do malicious harm, such as spreading a virus. You can use the Trust Center to prevent ActiveX controls from harming your computer. If the ActiveX security options are not set to the level you want, you can change them in the Trust Center. If you change ActiveX control settings in one Office program, it effects all Microsoft Office programs. The Trust Center uses a set of criteria—checks the kill bit and Safe for Initialization (SFI) settings—to make sure ActiveX controls run safely.

Change ActiveX Security Settings

1. Click the **File** tab, and then click **Options**.
   - ◆ Not available in Access.
2. In the left pane, click **Trust Center**.
3. Click **Trust Center Settings**.
4. In the left pane, click **ActiveX Settings**.
5. Click the option you want for ActiveX in documents not in a trusted location.
   - ◆ Disable all controls without notification.
   - ◆ Prompt me before enabling Unsafe for Initialization (UFI) controls with additional restrictions and Save for Initialization (SFI) controls with minimal restrictions (default).
   - ◆ Prompt me before enabling all controls with minimal restrictions.
   - ◆ Enable all controls with restrictions and without prompting (not recommended, potentially dangerous controls can run).
6. Click **OK**.
7. Click **OK**.

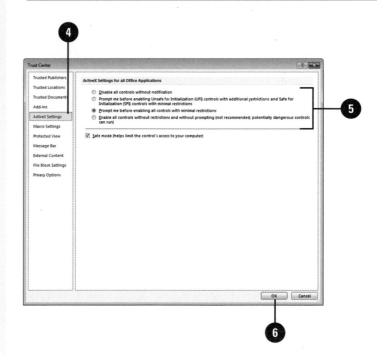

Setting Macro Security Options

A macro allows you to automate frequently used steps or tasks to save time and work more efficiently. Macros are written using VBA (Visual Basic for Applications) code, which opens the door to hackers to do malicious harm, such as spreading a virus. The Trust Center uses a set of criteria—valid and current digital signature, reputable certificate and a trusted publisher—to make sure macros are safe and secure. If the Trust Center discovers a potentially unsafe macro, it disables the code and notifies you in the Message Bar. You can click Options on the Message Bar to enable it or set other security options. If the macro security options are not set to the level you need, you can change them in the Trust Center.

Change Macro Security Settings

1. Click the **File** tab, and then click **Options**.

2. In the left pane, click **Trust Center**.

3. Click **Trust Center Settings**.

4. In the left pane, click **Macro Settings**.

5. Click the option you want for macros in documents not in a trusted location.

   ◆ Disable all macros without notification.

   ◆ Disable all macros with notification (default).

   ◆ Disable all macros except digitally signed macros.

   ◆ Enable all macros (not recommended, potentially dangerous code can run).

6. If you're a developer, select the **Trust access to the VBA project object model** check box.

7. Click **OK**.

8. Click **OK**.

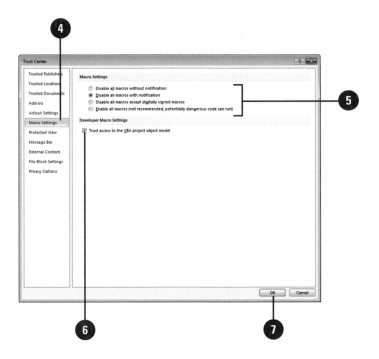

Changing Message Bar Security Options

The Message Bar displays security alerts when Office detects potentially unsafe content in an open document. The Message Bar appears below the Ribbon when a potential problem arises. The Message Bar provides a security warning and options to enable external content or leave it blocked. If you don't want to receive alerts about security issues, you can disable the Message Bar.

Modify Message Bar Security Options

1. Click the **File** tab, and then click **Options**.

2. In the left pane, click **Trust Center**.

3. Click **Trust Center Settings**.

4. In the left pane, click **Message Bar**.

5. Click the option you want for showing the Message bar.

   ◆ Show the Message Bar in all applications when active content, such as ActiveX and macros, has been blocked (default).

   This option is not selected if you selected the Disable all macros without notification check box in the Macros pane of the Trust Center.

   ◆ Never show information about blocked content.

6. Click **OK**.

7. Click **OK**.

Setting Privacy Options

Privacy options in the Trust Center allow you to set security settings that protect your personal privacy online. For example, the *Check Office documents that are from or link to suspicious Web sites* option checks for spoofed Web sites and protects you from phishing schemes. If your kids are doing research online using the Research task pane, you can set Privacy Options to enable parental controls and a password to block sites with offensive content.

Set Privacy Options

1. Click the **File** tab, and then click **Options**.

2. In the left pane, click **Trust Center**.

3. Click **Trust Center Settings**.

4. In the left pane, click **Privacy Options**.

5. Select or clear the check boxes you do or don't want.

   ◆ **Connect to Office.com for updated content when I'm connected to the Internet.**

   ◆ **Download a file periodically that helps determine system problems.** Select to have Microsoft request error reports, update help, and accept downloads from Office.com.

   ◆ **Automatically detect installed Office applications to improve Office.com search results.** Select to automatically detect applications.

   ◆ **Check Microsoft Office documents that are from or link to suspicious Web sites.** Select to check for spoofed Web sites.

   ◆ **Allow the Research task pane to check for and install new services.**

   ◆ **Allow sending files to improve file validation.**

6. Click **OK**.

7. Click **OK**.

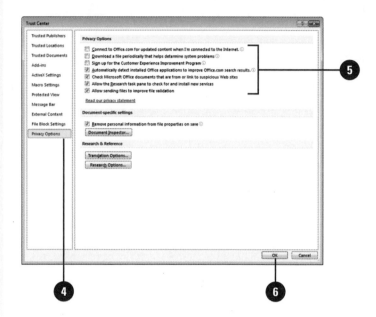

Set Parental Controls for Online Research

1. Click the **File** tab, and then click **Options**.

   ◆ Not available in Access.

2. In the left pane, click **Trust Center**.

3. Click **Trust Center Settings**.

4. In the left pane, click **Privacy Options**.

5. Click **Research Options**.

6. Click **Parental Control**.

7. Select the **Turn on content filtering to make services block offensive results** check box.

8. Select the **Allow users to search only the services that can block offensive results** check box, if necessary.

9. Enter a password, so users cannot change these settings.

10. Click **OK**, retype the password, and then click **OK**.

11. Click **OK**.

12. Click **OK**.

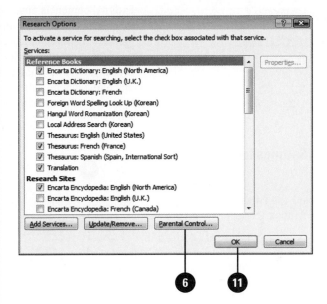

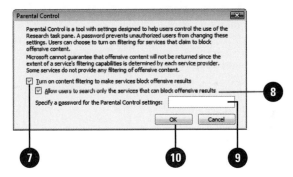

Setting External Content Security Options

External content is any content that is connected or linked to a document from a potentially unsafe external source, such as images, linked media, hyperlinks, data connections, or templates. Excel allows you to connect to external data from databases and other documents. Blocking external content prevents hackers from hiding malicious code in it that might do harm to your files and computer. You can set security options for data connections and document links to enable or disable the external content or display a security warning.

Set Security Settings for Data Connections

1. In Excel, click the **File** tab, and then click **Options**.

2. In the left pane, click **Trust Center**.

3. Click **Trust Center Settings**.

4. In the left pane, click **External Content**.

5. Click the option you want for data connections security.

   ◆ **Enable all Data Connections (not recommended).** Select to open documents with external data connections or to create external data connections without security warnings.

   ◆ **Prompt user about Data Connections.** Select to receive a security warning when you open or create documents with external data connections.

   ◆ **Disable all Data Connections.** Select to not allow any external data connections.

6. Click **OK**.

7. Click **OK**.

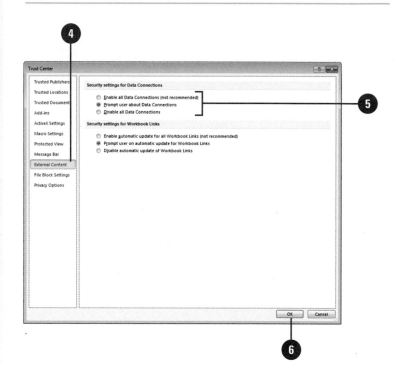

Set Security Settings for Document Links

1. In Excel, click the **File** tab, and then click **Options**.

2. In the left pane, click **Trust Center**.

3. Click **Trust Center Settings**.

4. In the left pane, click **External Content**.

5. Click the option you want for document links security.

   ◆ **Enable automatic update for all <Document> Links (not recommended).** Select to automatically update links to data in another document without security warnings.

   ◆ **Prompt user on automatic update for <Document> Links.** Select to receive a security warning when you run automatic updates for links to data in another document.

   ◆ **Disable automatic update of <Document> Links.** Select to not allow any automatic updates for links to data in another document.

6. Click **OK**.

7. Click **OK**.

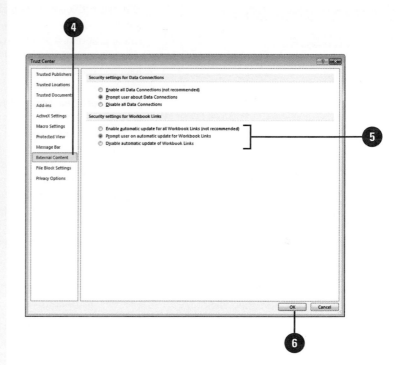

Working with Office Safe Modes

Microsoft Office uses two types of safe modes—Automated and User-Initiated—when it encounters a program problem. When you start an Office program, it automatically checks for problems, such as an extension not properly loading. If the program is not able to start the next time you try, the programs starts in **Automated Safe mode**, which disables extensions—macros, ActiveX controls, and add-ins—and other possible problem areas. If you're having problems and the Office program doesn't start in Automated Safe mode, you can start the program in **User-Initiated Safe mode**. When you start an Office program in Office Safe mode, not all features are available. For instance, templates can't be saved, AutoCorrect list is not loaded, Smart tags are not loaded, preferences cannot be saved, and all command-line options are ignored except /a and /n. Before you can use Office Safe mode, you need to enable it in the Trust Center. When you're in safe mode, you can use the Trust Center to find out the disabled items and enable them one at a time to help you pin point the problem.

Enable Safe Mode

1. Click the **File** tab, and then click **Options**.

   ◆ Not available in Access.

2. In the left pane, click **Trust Center**.

3. Click **Trust Center Settings**.

4. In the left pane, click **ActiveX Settings**.

5. Select the **Safe Mode (helps limit the control's access to your computer)** check box.

6. Click **OK**.

7. Click **OK**.

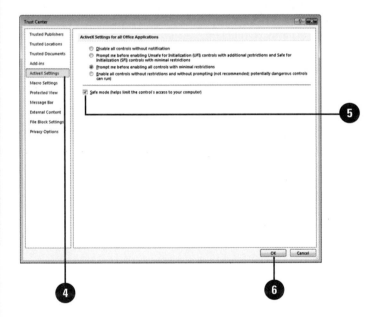

See Also

See "Diagnosing and Repairing Office" on page 30 for information on fixing problems with a Microsoft Office 2010 program.

Start User-Initiated Safe Mode

1. Click the **Start** button on the taskbar, point to **All Programs**, and then click **Microsoft Office**.

2. Press and hold Ctrl, and then click **Microsoft Office <Program> 2010**.

Did You Know?

You can use the Run dialog box to work in Safe mode. At the command prompt, you can use the */safe* parameter at the end of the command-line to start the program.

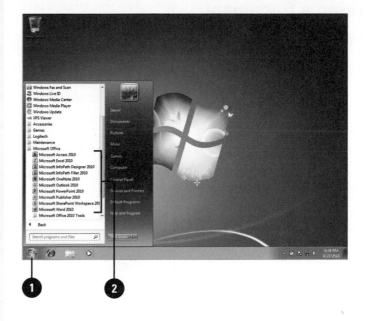

View Disabled Items

1. Click the **File** tab, and then click **Options**.

2. In the left pane, click **Add-Ins**.

3. Click the **Manage** list arrow, and then click **Disabled Items**.

4. Click **Go**.

5. In the dialog box, you can select an item, click **Enable** to activate and reload the add-in, and then click **Close**.

6. Click **OK**.

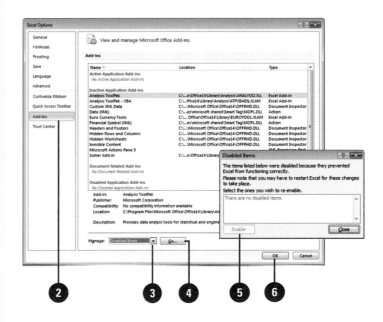

Marking a Document as Read-Only

As a precaution to prevent readers and reviews from making accidental changes, you can use the Mark as Final command to make a Office document read-only. The Mark as Final command disables or turns off typing, editing commands, and proofing marks, and sets the *Status property* field in the Document Information Panel to Final. The Mark as Final command is not a security option; it only prevents changes to the document while it's turned on and it can be turned off by anyone at any time.

Mark an Office Document as Final

1 Click the **File** tab, click **Info**, click the **Protect <Document>** button, and then click **Mark as Final**.

2 Click **OK**.

The document is marked as final and then saved.

3 If necessary, click **OK**.

The Mark as Final icon appears in the Status bar to indicate the document is currently marked as final.

IMPORTANT *An Office 2010 document marked as final is not read-only when opened in an earlier version of Microsoft Office.*

Did You Know?

You can enable editing for a document marked as final. Click the Edit Anyway button in the Message Bar or click the File tab, click Info, click the Protect <Document>, and then click Mark As Final again to toggle off the Mark As Final feature.

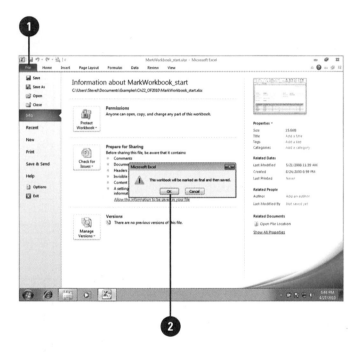

Reviewing and Sharing Office Documents

23

Introduction

Creating successful documents is not always a solitary venture; you may need to share a document with others or get data from other programs before a project is complete. In Microsoft Office 2010, you have several methods that you can use to create a joint effort. In many offices, your co-workers (and their computers) are located across the country or the world. They are joined through networks that permit users to share information by opening each other's files and to simultaneously modify data.

Microsoft Office makes it easy for you to communicate with your teammates. Instead of writing on yellow sticky notes and attaching them to a printout, you can insert electronic comments within worksheet cells. You can also track changes within a document made by you and others. After you finish making changes to your document, you can quickly send it to another person for review using e-mail or an Internet Fax service.

XML (Extensible Markup Language) is a universal language that enables you to create documents in which data is stored independently of the format so you can use the data more seamlessly in other forms. When you work with XML, you can attach an XML Schema—a set of rules that defines the elements and content used in an XML document. XML schemas are created by developers who understand XML.

By using a variety of techniques, you can link, embed, hyperlink, export, or convert data to create one seamless document that is a group effort by many co-workers. You can also use Office to create and edit connections to external data sources, such as Microsoft Access, to create more permanent links to data.

Sharing Workbooks

When you're working with others in a networked environment, you may want to share workbooks you have created. You may also want to share the responsibilities of entering and maintaining data. Sharing means users can add columns and rows, enter data, and change formatting, while allowing you to review their changes. When sharing is enabled, "[Shared]" appears in the title bar of the shared workbook. This type of work arrangement is particularly effective in team situations where multiple users have joint responsibility for data within a single workbook. In cases where multiple users modify the same cells, Office can keep track of changes, and you can accept or reject them at a later date.

Enable Workbook Sharing

1. In Excel, open the workbook you want to share.

2. Click the **Review** tab.

3. Click the **Share Workbook** button.

4. Click the **Editing** tab.

5. Select the **Allow changes by more than one user at the same time** check box.

6. Click **OK**.

7. Click **OK** again to save your workbook.

Did You Know?

You can set file options to prompt to open as read-only. To prevent accidental changes to a document, you can display an alert requesting (not requiring) the user open the file as read-only. A read-only file can be read or copied. If the user makes changes to the file, the modifications can only be saved with a new name.

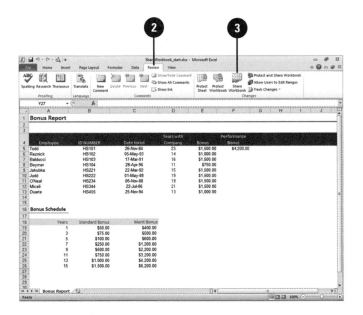

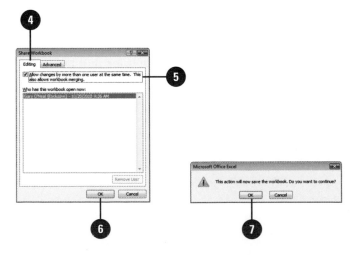

Change Sharing Options

1. In Excel, open the workbook you want to share.

2. Click the **Review** tab.

3. Click the **Share Workbook** button.

4. Click the **Advanced** tab.

5. To indicate how long to keep changes, select one of the Track changes options, and then set the number of days, if necessary.

6. To indicate when changes should be saved, select one of the Update changes options, and then set a time internal, if necessary.

7. To resolve conflicting changes, select one of the Conflicting changes between users options.

8. Select one or both of the Include in personal view check boxes.

9. Click **OK**.

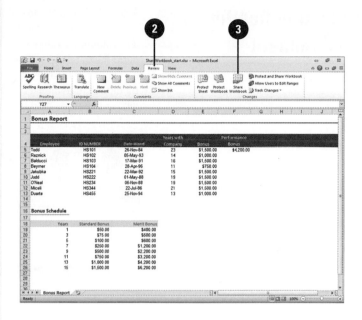

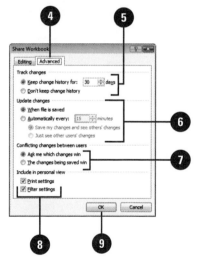

Creating and Reading a Cell Comment

Any cell on a worksheet can contain a **comment**—information you might want to share with co-workers or include as a reminder to yourself without making it a part of the worksheet. (Think of a comment as a nonprinting sticky note attached to an individual cell.) A cell containing a comment displays a red triangle in the upper-right corner of the cell. By default, comments are hidden and are displayed only when the mouse pointer is held over a cell with a red triangle.

Add a Comment

1. In Excel, click the cell to which you want to add a comment.

2. Click the **Review** tab.

3. Click the **New Comment** button.

4. Type the comment in the comment box.

5. Click outside the comment box when you are finished, or press Esc twice to close the comment box.

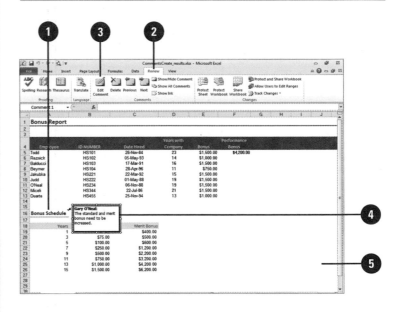

Read a Comment

1. In Excel, position the mouse pointer over a cell with a red triangle to read its comment.

2. Move the mouse pointer off the cell to hide the comment.

3. Click the **Review** tab.

4. Do any of the following navigation buttons:

   ◆ Click the **Previous Comment** or **Next Comment** button to move from comment to comment.

   ◆ Select a cell, and then click the **Show/Hide Comment** button to show or hide comments.

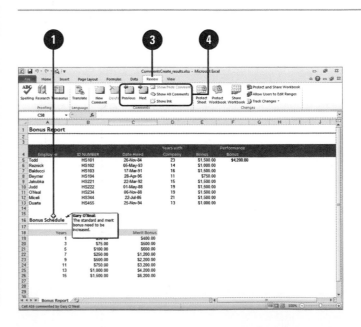

Editing and Deleting a Cell Comment

You can edit, delete, and even format cell comments just as you do other text on a worksheet. If you are working with others online, they may want to delete a comment after reading it. You might want to format certain comments to add emphasis. You can use formatting buttons—such as Bold, Italic, Underline, Font Style, Font Color, or Font Size—on the Home tab. When you no longer need a comment, you can quickly delete it.

Edit a Comment

1. In Excel, click the cell with the comment you want to edit.

2. Click the **Review** tab.

3. Click the **Edit Comment** button.

4. Make your changes using common editing tools, such as the Backspace and Delete keys, as well as the Format tab buttons.

5. Press Esc twice to close the comment box.

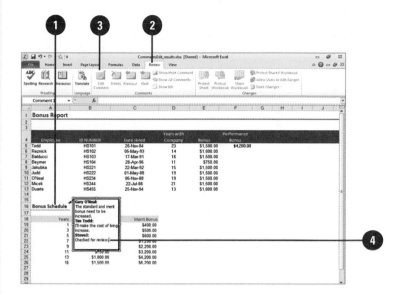

Delete a Comment

1. In Excel, click the cell with the comment you want to delete.

2. Click the **Review** tab.

3. Click the **Delete Comment** button.

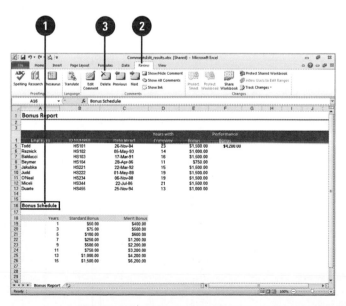

Adding Comments to a Presentation

When you review a presentation, you can insert comments to the author or other reviewers. **Comments** are like electronic adhesive notes tagged with your name. They typically appear in yellow boxes in PowerPoint. You can use comments to get feedback from others or to remind yourself of revisions you plan to make. A comment is visible only when you show comments using the Show Markup button and place the mouse pointer over the comment indicator. You can attach one or more comments to a letter or word on a slide, or to an entire slide. When you insert a comment, PowerPoint create a comment thumbnail with your initials and a number, starting at 1, and a comment box with your user name and date. When you're reviewing a presentation, you can use the Show Markup button on the Review tab to show and hide comments and saved annotations during a slide show.

Insert a Comment

1. In PowerPoint, click the slide where you want to insert a comment or select an object.

2. Click the **Review** tab.

3. Click the **New Comment** button.

4. Type your comment in the comment box or pane.

5. Click outside the comment box.

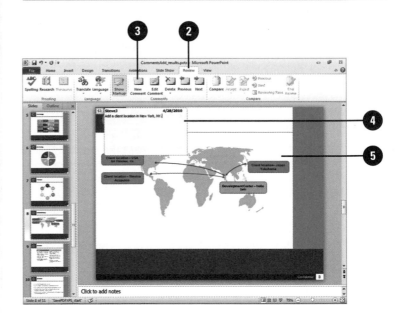

Did You Know?

You can move a comment. Drag it to a new location on the same slide.

You can show annotations. During a slide show you can add annotations to a slide, which you can save. When you show markups in PowerPoint, annotations are included. You can select, move, and delete them.

My reviewer initials and name are incorrect. You can change them in PowerPoint Options. Click the File tab, click Options, click General, enter your User name and Initials in the boxes provided, and then click OK.

Read a Comment

① In PowerPoint, click the **Review** tab.

② Click the **Show Markup** button to show all comments.

The Show Markup button toggles to show (button highlighted) or hide (button not highlighted) comments and annotations.

③ Point to the comment box.

④ Read the comment.

⑤ Click the **Previous** or **Next** button to read another comment.

⑥ When you reach the end of the presentation, click **Continue** to start at the beginning again or **Cancel**.

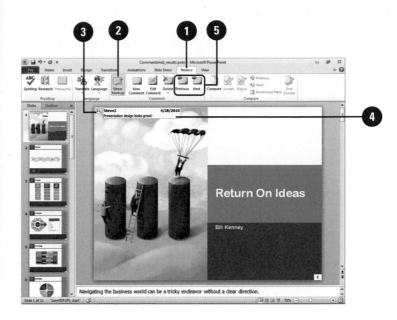

Did You Know?

You cannot merge PowerPoint 2010 comments back into a PowerPoint 2003 presentation. If you use PowerPoint 2003 or earlier to send your presentation for review, reviewers who use Office PowerPoint 2010 can view and add commands to your presentation, but you cannot merge their comments into your presentation.

Next comment

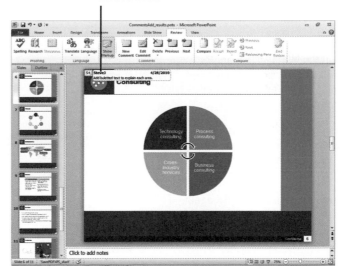

Tracking Workbook Changes

As you build and fine-tune a workbook—particularly if you are sharing workbooks with co-workers—you can keep track of all the changes that are made at each stage in the process. The Track Changes feature makes it easy to see who made what changes and when, and to accept or reject each change, even if you are the only user of a worksheet. When you or another user applies the Track Changes command to a workbook, the message "[Shared]" appears in the title bar of the workbook to alert you that this feature is active. To take full advantage of this feature, turn it on the first time you or a co-worker edits a workbook. Then, when it's time to review the workbook, all the changes will be recorded. You can review tracked changes in a workbook at any point. Cells containing changes are surrounded by a blue border, and the changes made can be viewed instantly by moving your mouse pointer over any outlined cell. When you're ready to finalize the workbook, you can review each change and either accept or reject it.

Turn On Track Changes

1. In Excel, click the **Review** tab.

2. Click the **Track Changes** button, and then click **Highlight Changes.**

3. Select the **Track changes while editing** check box.

4. Select the **When**, **Who**, and/or **Where** check box. Click an associated list arrow, and then select the option you want.

5. Select or clear the **Highlight changes on screen** or **List changes on a new sheet** check boxes.

6. Click **OK**, and then click **OK** again, if necessary.

7. Make changes in worksheet cells.

   Column and row indicators for changed cells appear in red. The cell containing the changes has a blue outline.

8. To view tracked changes, position the mouse pointer over an edited cell.

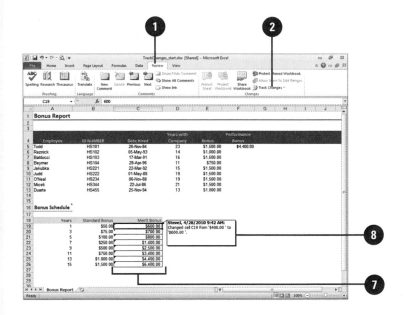

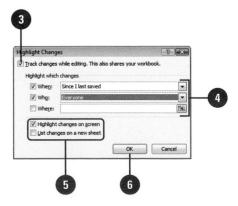

Accept or Reject Tracked Changes

1. In Excel, click the **Review** tab.

2. Click the **Track Changes** button, and then click **Accept/Reject Changes**. If necessary, click **OK** in the message box.

3. If you want, change tracking, and then click **OK** to begin reviewing changes.

4. If necessary, scroll to review all the changes, and then click one of the following buttons:

   ◆ Click **Accept** to make the selected change to the worksheet.

   ◆ Click **Reject** to remove the selected change from the worksheet.

   ◆ Click **Accept All** to make all of the changes to the worksheet after you have reviewed them.

   ◆ Click **Reject All** to remove all of the changes to the worksheet after you have reviewed them.

5. Click **Close**.

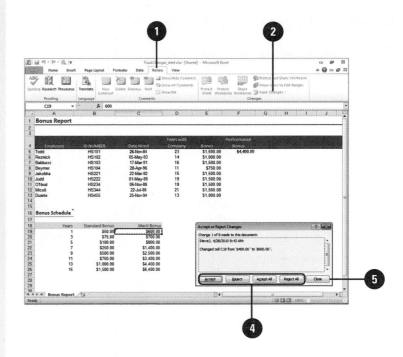

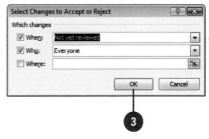

Did You Know?

You can protect a shared workbook. Open the shared workbook you want to protect. Click the Review tab, click the Protect Shared Workbook button, select the Shared With Track Changes check box, type a password if you want, and then click OK. You can only add a password if the workbook is unshared.

Comparing and Merging Presentations

If you want to compare an earlier version of a presentation with the current version, or if you receive multiple edited versions of the original presentation back from the recipients, you can compare the presentations and merge the changes into one presentation (**New!**). The changes can be merged into one presentation or viewed for comparison. When you compare or merge presentations, the text that differs between the two versions will be identified by a Change icon and list, and displayed by slide or details in the Reviewing pane.

Compare and Merge Presentations

1. In PowerPoint, open the original presentation in which you want to compare and merge.

2. Click the **Review** tab.

3. Click the **Compare** button.

4. Select the presentation to which you want to compare and merge, and then click **Open**.

   The Reviewing pane opens, displaying the Slides or Details tab with information about the differences between the presentations. A Change icon appears displaying a list of the individual changes.

5. To move between the slide changes, click the **Previous** or **Next** button.

6. To accept or reject a change, select or clear a Change icon check box, or click the **Accept** or **Reject** button arrow, and then click an option to accept or reject an individual change, all changes to the current slide, or all changes to the presentation.

7. To close or open the Reviewing pane the review, click the **Reviewing Pane** button.

8. To end the review, click the **End Review** button.

Reviewing pane

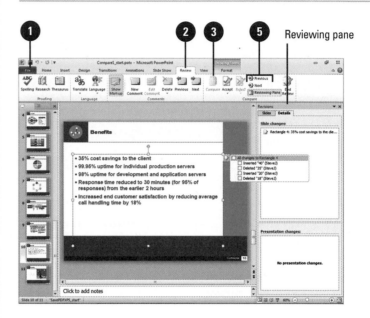

Change icon with changes

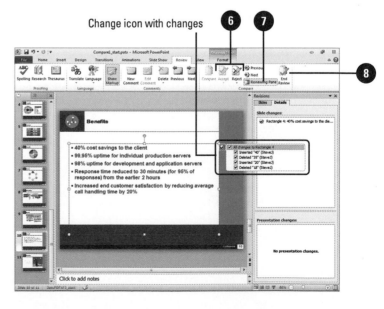

Creating and Opening OneNotes

Microsoft Office OneNote is a digital notebook program you can use to gather, manage, and share notes and information. In PowerPoint and Word, you can create and open notes directly from the Review tab (**New!**) by using the Linked Notes button. OneNote auto-links notes to the Office document you're viewing, which you can disable or change in the Advanced section of OneNote Options. You can open a OneNote note by clicking the Linked Notes button. The Linked Notes button is not available on the Review tab until you start the program and create an initial account, which is quick and easy.

Create and Open OneNotes

① In PowerPoint or Word, open a document.

② Click the **Review** tab.

③ Click the **Linked Notes** button.

④ On first document use, select a section or page in which to put the notes, and then click **OK**.

⑤ In OneNote, enter the notes you want for the page.

⑥ To work with notes in OneNote, click the **Linked Note** icon, and then click an option:

- ◆ **Linked File(s).** Use to select a linked Office document to view.

- ◆ **Delete Link(s) on This Page.** Use to delete links on the current page.

- ◆ **Linked Notes Options.** Select to open OneNote Options.

⑦ When you're done, click the **Linked Note** icon in OneNote, and then click **Stop Taking Linked Notes**. To restart it, click **Start Taking Linked Notes** on the file tab.

⑧ To view linked notes, click the **Linked Notes** button to open OneNotes if needed, point to a note, and then click the Office program icon.

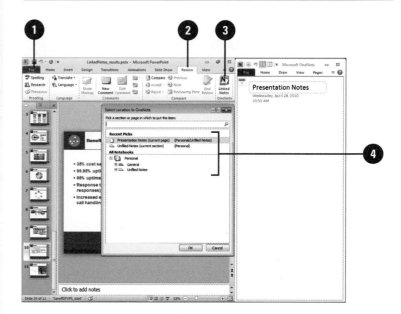

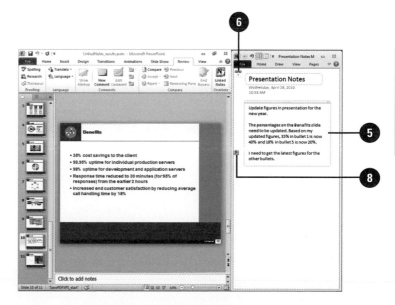

Sending a Document for Review Using E-Mail

After you finish making changes to a document, you can quickly send it to another person for review using e-mail. Office allows you to send documents out for review as an attachment, either a document, PDF, or XPS document, using e-mail from within the program so that you do not have to open your e-mail program. An e-mail program, such as Microsoft Outlook, needs to be installed on your computer before you begin. When you send your document out for review, reviewers can add comments and then send it back to you.

Send an Office Document for Review Using E-Mail

① Click the **File** tab, click **Save & Send**, and then click **Send Using E-mail**.

② Click the **Send as Attachment**, **Send a Link**, **Send as PDF**, or **Send as XPS**.

③ If the Compatibility Checker appears, click **Continue** or **Cancel** to stop the operation.

> **IMPORTANT** *To complete the following steps, you need to have an e-mail program installed on your computer and an e-mail account set-up.*

An e-mail message opens in Microsoft Outlook with your document attached. The subject line contains the file name of the document that you are sending.

④ Enter your recipients and subject (appears with document name by default).

◆ To add recipients from your address book or contacts list, click **To**, click the recipient names, click **To**, **Cc**, or **Bcc** until you're done, and then click **OK**.

⑤ Enter a message for your reviewer with instructions.

⑥ Click the **Send** button.

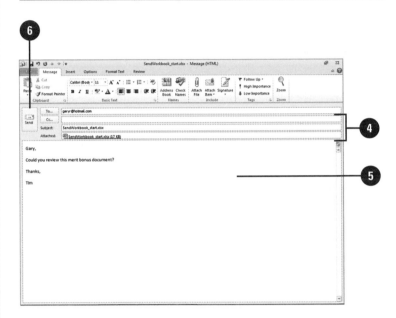

Sending a Document by Internet Fax

If you are a member of an online fax service—such as eFax, InterFAX, MyFax, or Send2Fax—you can use Office to send and receive faxes over the Internet directly from within your Microsoft Office program. If you're not a member, a Web site can help you sign up. You also need to have Microsoft Outlook and Word installed to use the fax service and Outlook must be open to send your fax. If Outlook is not open and you send the fax, it will be stored in your Outbox and not sent until you open Outlook again.

Send an Office Document by Internet Fax

1. Click the **File** tab, click **Save & Send**, and then click **Send Using E-mail**.

2. Click the **Send as Internet Fax** button.

3. If you're not signed up with an Internet Fax service, click **OK** to open a Web page and sign up for one. When you're done, return to Office, and then repeat Step 1.

4. If the Compatibility Checker appears, click **Continue** or **Cancel** to stop the operation.

   An e-mail message opens in Microsoft Outlook with your document attached as a .tif (image) file.

5. Enter a Fax Recipient, Fax Number and Subject (appears with workbook name by default).

   ◆ You can enter a fax number from your address book. Country codes must begin with a plus sign (+).

   ◆ To send your fax to multiple recipients, click Add More, and then enter fax information.

6. In the Fax Service pane, choose the options you want.

7. Complete the cover sheet in the body of the e-mail message.

8. Click the **Send** button.

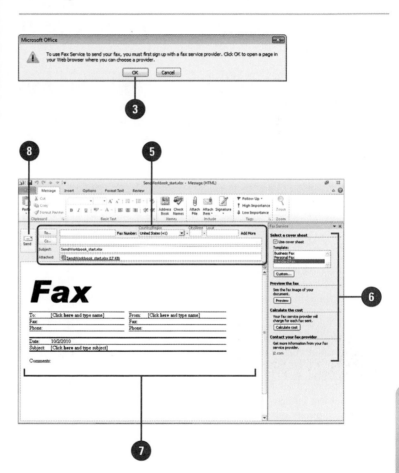

Creating a PDF Document

Portable Document Format (PDF) is a fixed-layout format developed by Adobe Systems that retains the form you intended on a computer monitor or printer. A PDF is useful when you want to create a document primarily intended to be read and printed, not modified. Office allows you to save a document as a PDF file, which you can send to others for review in an e-mail. To view a PDF file, you need to have Acrobat Reader—free downloadable software from Adobe Systems—installed on your computer.

Save an Office Document as a PDF Document

1. Click the **File** tab, click **Save & Send**, and then click **Create PDF/XPS Document**.

2. Click the **Create PDF/XPS** button.

3. Click the **Save as type** list arrow, and then click **PDF**.

4. Click the **Save in** list arrow, and then click the drive or folder where you want to save the file.

5. Type a PDF file name.

6. To open the file in Adobe Reader after saving, select the **Open file after publishing** check box.

7. Click the **Standard** or **Minimum size** option to specify how you want to optimize the file.

8. Click **Options**.

9. Select the publishing options you want, such as what to publish, range to publish, whether to include non-printing information, or PDF options.

10. Click **OK**.

11. Click **Publish**.

12. If necessary, install Adobe Acrobat Reader and related software as directed.

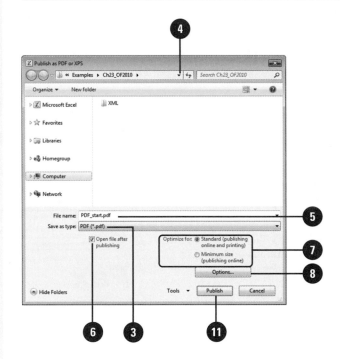

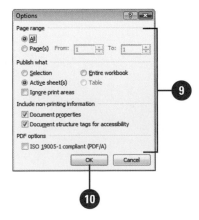

Creating an XPS Document

XML Paper Specification (XPS) is a secure fixed-layout format developed by Microsoft that retains the form you intended on a monitor or printer. An XPS is useful when you want to create a document primarily intended to be read and printed, not modified. Office allows you to save a document as an XPS file, which you can send to others for review in an e-mail. XPS includes support for digital signatures and is compatible with Windows Rights Management for additional protection. The XPS format also preserves live links with documents, making files fully functional. To view an XPS file, you need to have a viewer—free downloadable software from Microsoft Office Online—installed on your computer.

Save an Office Document as an XPS Document

1. Click the **File** tab, click **Save & Send**, and then click **Create PDF/XPS Document**.

2. Click the **Create PDF/XPS** button.

3. Click the **Save as type** list arrow, and then click **XPS Document.**

4. Click the **Save in** list arrow, and then click the drive or folder where you want to save the file.

5. Type an XPS file name.

6. To open the file in viewer after saving, select the **Open file after publishing** check box.

7. Click the **Standard** or **Minimum size** option to specify how you want to optimize the file.

8. Click **Options**.

9. Select the publishing options you want, such as what to publish, range to publish, whether to include non-printing information, or XPS options.

10. Click **OK**.

11. Click **Publish**.

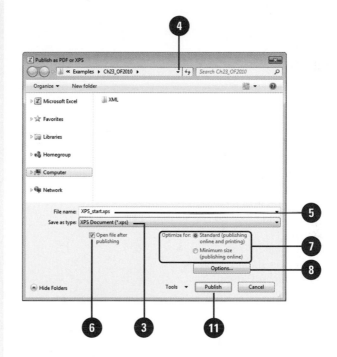

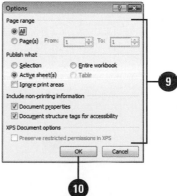

Working with XML

XML (Extensible Markup Language) is a universal language that enables you to create documents in which data is stored independently of the format so you can use the data more seamlessly in other forms. XML is supported in Office 2010 through Word, Excel, and Access. XML allows you to work with the familiar Office interface and create and save documents as XML, without ever knowing the XML language. When you work with XML, you can attach an XML Schema—a set of rules that defines the elements and content used in an XML document. XML schemas are created by developers who understand XML. After you attach a schema, you should change XML map properties before you map schema elements to cells in your worksheet.

Attach a Schema

① In Excel, click the **Developer** tab.

② Click the **Source** button.

③ In the task pane, click **XML Maps**.

④ Click **Add**.

⑤ Locate and select the XML schema file you want to attach, and then click **Open**.

⑥ If necessary, click **OK** to create a schema based on the XML source data.

⑦ To rename or delete an XML schema, select the schema, and then click **Rename** or **Delete**.

⑧ Click **OK**.

⑨ When you're done, click the **Close** button on the task pane.

Did You Know?

You can change XML view options. In the XML Source task pane, click Options to turn on or off options to preview data in the task pane, hide help text in the task pane, automatically merge elements when mapping, include data heading, and hide border of inactive lists.

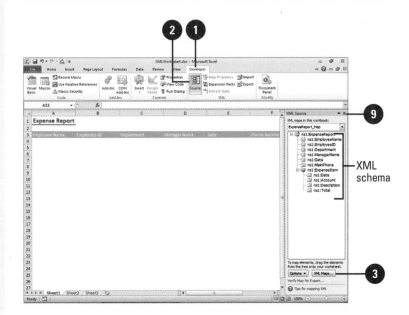

XML schema

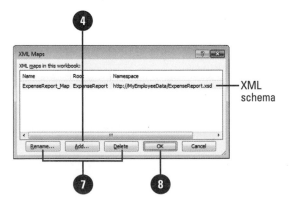

XML schema

Change XML Data Map Properties

1. In Excel, open the worksheet in which you want to map the XML data.

2. Click the **Developer** tab.

3. Click the **Source** button.

4. Click the **Map Properties** button.

5. If you want, change the name of the XML Map.

6. Select or clear the following options:

   ◆ **Validate data against schema for import and export.**

   ◆ **Save data source definition in workbook.**

   ◆ **Adjust column width.**

   ◆ **Preserve column filter.**

   ◆ **Preserve number formatting.**

7. Select the refreshing or importing data option you want.

8. Click **OK**.

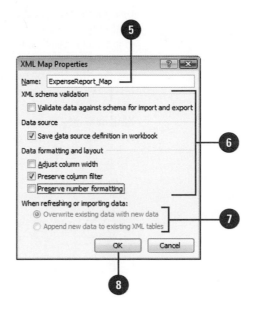

Did You Know?

You can attach a schema in Word.
Click the Developer tab, click the Schema button, click Add Schema, locate and select the XML schema file, click Open, and then click OK.

You can set XML options in Word.
Click the Developer tab, click the Schema button, click XML Options Schema, select the options you want, and then click OK.

For Your Information

Showing and Hiding the Developer Tab

If the Developer tab doesn't appear on the Ribbon, you can use the Customize Ribbon option (**New!**) in the Options dialog box to show it. Click the File tab, click Options, and then click Customize Ribbon in the left pane. In the right column, select the Developer check box to show the Developer tab, or clear the check box to hide it. When you're done, click OK.

Creating an XML Data Map

Using XML data in Office follows the same basic process: (1) Add an XML schema file (.xsd) to a workbook, (2) map XML schema elements to individual cells, (3) Import an XML data file (.xml), (4) enter data, and (5) export revised data from mapped cells to an XML data file. You can use the XML Source task pane to create and manage XML maps. The task pane displays a hierarchical list of XML elements in the current XML map that you use to map to worksheet cells. After you create an XML data map, you can import XML data to fill in the information you want from a data source.

Create an XML Data Map

1. In Excel, open the worksheet in which you want to map the XML data.

2. Click the **Developer** tab.

3. Click the **Source** button.

4. Click the **Map name** list arrow, and then click the XML schema you want to use.

5. Drag the named elements from the XML Source task pane to the corresponding cells in the worksheet.

6. Click the **Header Options** button, and then click the header option you want.

7. When you're done, click the **Close** button on the task pane.

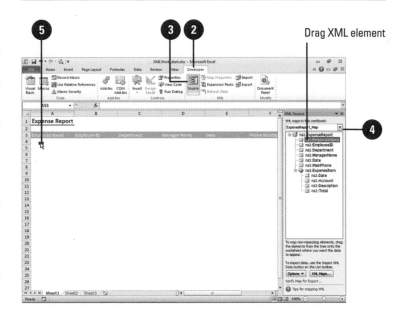

Drag XML element

Did You Know?

You can change the list of XML elements in the XML Source task pane. In the XML Source task pane, click the Options button, and then click the display option you want.

An XML data map is a potential security risk. From a security perspective, Office saves an XML map and its data source with a document, which any user can view using VBA.

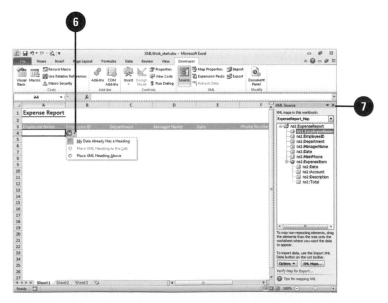

Import XML Data

1. In Excel, open the worksheet in which you want to map the XML data.

2. Click the **Developer** tab.

3. Click the **Import** button.

4. Click the **Files of type** list arrow, and then click **XML Files**.

5. Locate, and then select the XML data file you want to import.

6. Click **Import**.

Did You Know?

You can add XML expansion packs. In Excel and Word, click the Developer tab, click the Expansion Packs button, click Add, locate and select an expansion pack, and then click Open. You can also attach, update, or delete XML expansion packs.

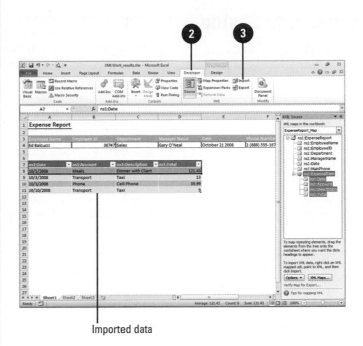

Imported data

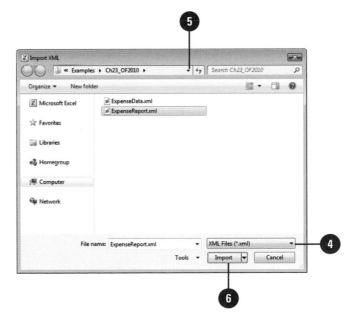

Exporting and Saving Data in XML

After you finish working with your XML document, you can export or save the data for use in other XML compatible documents and applications. You can save the contents of a mapped range with the XML Data format or XML Spreadsheet format. The XML Data format is an independent XML industry standard that uses a separate XML schema, while the XML Spreadsheet format is a specialized Excel XML file that uses its own XML schema to store information, such as file properties.

Export XML Data

① In Excel, open the worksheet with the XML data.

② Click the **Developer** tab.

③ Click the **Export** button.

④ If necessary, click the XML map you want to use, and then click **OK**.

⑤ Select a location where you want to export the XML data.

⑥ Type a name for the XML file.

⑦ Click **Export**.

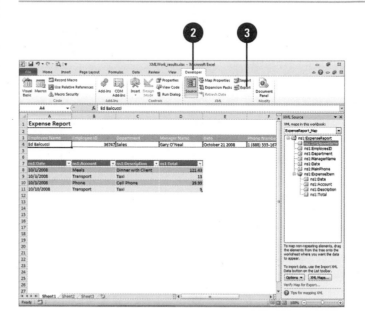

Did You Know?

You can quickly verify a data map before you export the data. Click the Developer tab, click the Source button, click the Verify Map For Export link at the bottom of the task pane, and then click OK when it's done.

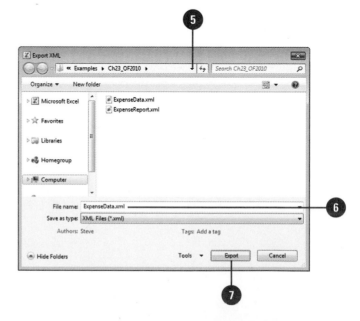

Save XML Data

① In Excel, open the worksheet with the XML data.

② Click the **File** tab, and then click **Save As**.

③ Click the **Save as type** list arrow, and then click **XML Data** or **XML Spreadsheet 2003**.

④ Select a location where you want to save the XML data.

⑤ Type a name for the XML file.

⑥ Click **Save**.

⑦ If necessary, click **Continue**, click the XML map you want to use, and then click **OK**.

IMPORTANT *When you save with the XML Data format, the active worksheet is now the XML data. To work with the original worksheet, you need to re-open it.*

Did You Know?

You can also open an XML data file. Click the File tab, click Open, click the Files of type list arrow, click XML Files, select the XML data file, click Open, click the As An XML Table, As A Read-only Workbook, or Use The XML Source task pane option, and then click OK.

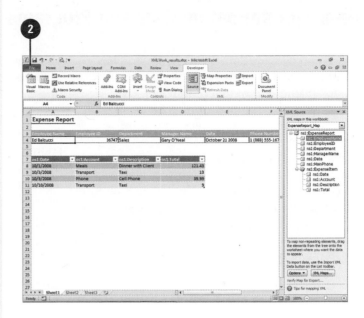

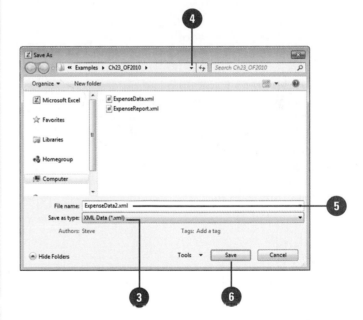

Sharing Information Between Programs

Office can convert data or text from one format to another using a technology known as **object linking and embedding (OLE)**. OLE allows you to move text or data between programs in much the same way as you move them within a program. The familiar cut and paste or drag and drop methods work between programs and documents just as they do within a document. In addition, all Office programs have special ways to move information from one program to another, including importing, exporting, embedding, linking, and hyperlinking.

Importing and Exporting

Importing and exporting information are two sides of the same coin. **Importing** copies a file created with the same or another program into your open file. The information becomes part of your open file, just as if you created it in that format. Some formatting and program-specific information such as formulas may be lost. **Exporting** converts a copy of your open file into the file type of another program. In other words, importing brings information into your open document, while exporting moves information from your open document into another program file.

Embedding

Embedding inserts a copy of a file created in one program into a file created in another program. Unlike imported files, you can edit the information in embedded files with the same commands and buttons used to create the original file. The original file is called the **source file**, while the file in which it is embedded is called the **destination file**. Any changes you make to an embedded object appear only in the destination file; the source file remains unchanged.

For example, if you place an Excel chart into a PowerPoint presentation, Excel is the source program, and PowerPoint is the destination program. The chart is the source file; the document is the destination file.

Linking

Linking displays information from one file (the source file) in a file created in another program (the destination file). You can view and edit the linked object from either the source file or the destination file. The changes are stored in the source file but also appear in the destination file. As you work, Office updates the linked object to ensure you always have the most current information. Office keeps track of all the drive, folder, and file name information for a source file. However, if you move or rename the source file, the link between files will break.

Embedding and Linking	
Term	**Definition**
Source program	The program that created the original object
Source file	The file that contains the original object
Destination program	The program that created the document into which you are inserting the object
Destination file	The file into which you are inserting the object

Once the link is broken, the information in the destination file becomes embedded rather than linked. In other words, changes to one copy of the file will no longer affect the other.

Hyperlinking

The newest way to share information between programs is hyperlinks—a term borrowed from World Wide Web technology. A **hyperlink** is an object (either colored, underlined text or a graphic) that you can click to jump to a different location in the same document or a different document.

Deciding Which Method to Use

With all these different methods for sharing information between programs to choose from, sometimes it is hard to decide which method to use. To decide which method is best for your situation, answer the following questions:

1 Do you want the contents of another file displayed in the open document?

◆ **No**. Create a hyperlink. See "Creating a Hyperlink" on page 560.

◆ **Yes**. Go to question 2.

2 Do you want to edit the content of the file from within the open document?

◆ **No**. Embed the file as a picture. See "Linking and Embedding Files" on page 630.

◆ **Yes**. Go to question 3.

3 Is the source program (the program used to create the file) available on your computer?

◆ **No**. Import the file. See "Exporting and Importing Data" on page 628.

◆ **Yes**. Go to question 4.

4 Do you want to use the source program commands to edit the file?

◆ **No**. Import the file. See "Exporting and Importing Data" on page 628.

◆ **Yes**. Go to question 5.

5 Do you want changes you make to the file to appear in the source file (the original copy of the file)?

◆ **No**. Embed the file. See "Exporting and Importing Data" on page 628.

◆ **Yes**. Link the file. See "Linking and Embedding Files" on page 630.

Exporting and Importing Data

In cases where you don't need the data you are using from another source to be automatically updated if the source data changes, the most expedient way to get the data is to copy and paste it. In cases where you want to copy data from one program to another, you can convert the data to a format that the other program accepts. If you have text you want to include in an Office document, you can **import**, or open, a text file in a document.

Export Data Using Copy and Paste

1. Select the cell or range that you want to copy.

2. Click the **Home** tab.

3. Click the **Copy** button.

4. Open the destination file, or click the program's taskbar button if the program is already open.

5. Select the cell where you want the data to be copied.

6. Click the **Paste** button.

7. Click the **Paste Options** button, and then click the option icon you want.

   ◆ You can point to a paste option icon to display a ScreenTip with the function name, and display a preview of the data (**New!**).

Did You Know?

Office can save a file to a format only with an installed converter. If the format you want to save a file in does not appear in the Save As Type list, you'll need to install it by running Setup from the Microsoft Office 2010 disc.

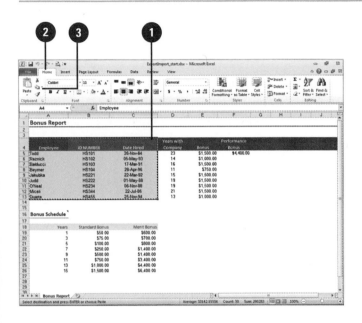

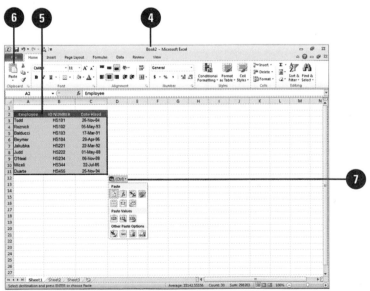

Export a File to Another Program Format

1. Open the file from which you want to export data.

2. Click the **File** tab, and then click **Save As**.

3. Click the **Save in** list arrow, and then click the drive or folder where you want to save the file.

4. Click the **Save as type** list arrow, and then click the format you want.

5. If you want, change the file name.

6. Click **Save**.

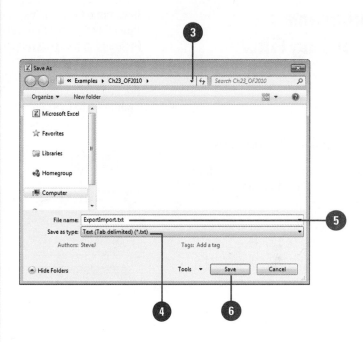

Import a Text File

1. Click the **File** tab, and then click **Open**.

2. Click the **Files of type** list arrow, and then click **Text Files**.

3. Click the **Look in** list arrow, and then select the folder where the text file is located.

4. Click the text file you want to import.

5. Click **Open**.

6. If a wizard starts, follow the instructions to import the text the way you want.

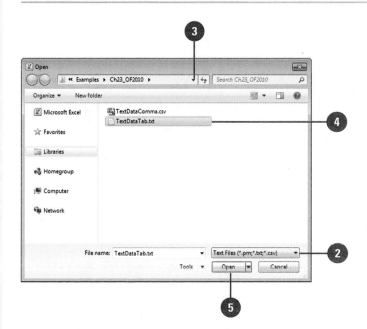

Linking and Embedding Files

Information created using other Office programs can be shared among them. This means that data created in an Office document, can be included in a Excel worksheet without being retyped. This makes projects such as annual or departmental reports simple to create. Information can be either **linked** or **embedded**. Data that is linked has the advantage of always being accurate because it is automatically updated when the linked document is modified.

Create a Link to Another File

1. Open the source file and any files containing information you want to link.

2. Select the information in the source file.

3. Click the **Home** tab.

4. Click the **Copy** button.

5. Click the insertion point in the file containing the link.

6. Click the **Paste** button arrow, and then click **Paste Link**.

   ◆ You can point to a paste option icon to display a ScreenTip with the function name, and display a preview of the data (**New!**).

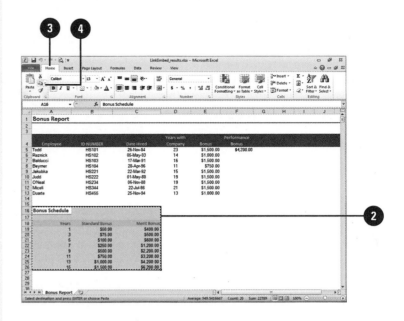

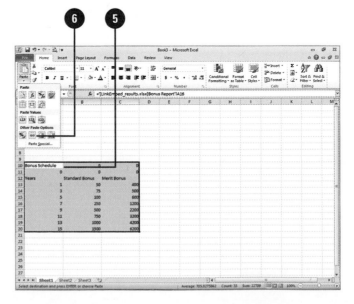

Did You Know?

You can edit an embedded object. Edit an embedded object only if the program that created it is installed on your computer.

Embed a New Object

1. Click the **Insert** tab.

2. Click the **Insert Object** button.

3. Click the **Create New** tab.

4. Click the object type you want to insert.

5. Click **OK**.

6. Follow the necessary steps to insert the object.

   The steps will vary depending on the object type.

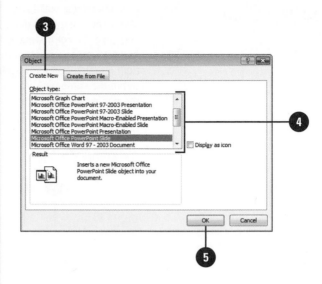

Embed or Link to an Existing Object

1. Click the **Insert** tab.

2. Click the **Insert Object** button.

3. Click the **Create from File** tab.

4. Click **Browse**, locate and select the file that you want to link, and then click **Open**.

5. To create a link to the object, select the **Link to file** check box.

6. Click **OK**.

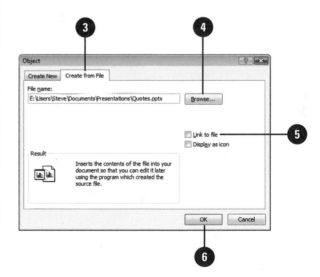

Did You Know?

You can update links each time you open a linked document. When you open a document that contains links, a warning dialog box opens asking you if you want to update all linked information (click Yes) or to keep the existing information (click No).

Consolidating Data in Excel

In some cases, you'll want to consolidate data from different worksheets or workbooks into one workbook, rather than simply linking the source data. For instance, if each division in your company creates a budget, you can pull together, or **consolidate**, the totals for each line item into one company-wide budget. If each divisional budget is laid out in the same way, with the budgeted amounts for each line item in the same cell addresses, then you can very easily consolidate the information without any retyping. If data in individual workbooks change, the consolidated worksheet or workbook will always be correct.

Consolidate Data from Other Worksheets or Workbooks

1. In Excel, open all the workbooks that contain the data you want to consolidate.

2. Open or create the workbook that will contain the consolidated data.

3. Select the destination range.

4. Click the **Data** tab.

5. Click the **Consolidate** button.

6. Click the **Function** list arrow, and then select the function you want to use to consolidate the data.

7. Type the location of the data to be consolidated, or click the **Collapse Dialog** button, and then select the cells to be consolidated.

Did You Know?

You can include all labels. Make sure you select enough cells to accommodate any labels that might be included in the data you are consolidating.

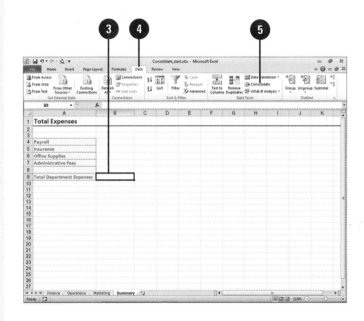

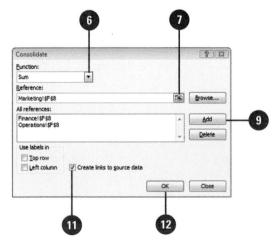

8 Click the **Expand Dialog** button.

9 Click **Add** to add the reference to the list of consolidated ranges.

10 Repeat steps 7 through 9 until you have listed all references to consolidate.

11 Select the **Create links to source data** check box.

12 Click **OK**.

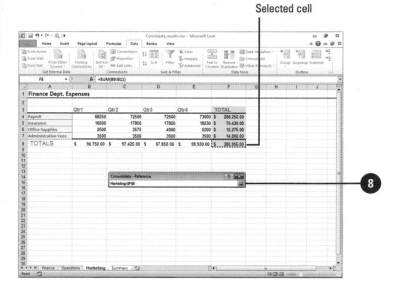

8

Did You Know?

You can consolidate worksheets even if they are not laid out identically. If the worksheets you want to consolidate aren't laid out with exactly the same cell addresses, but they do contain identical types of information, select the Top Row and Left Column check boxes in the Consolidate dialog box so that Excel uses labels to match up the correct data.

You can arrange multiple documents. Use the Window group on the View tab to move between documents or to arrange them so they are visible at the same time.

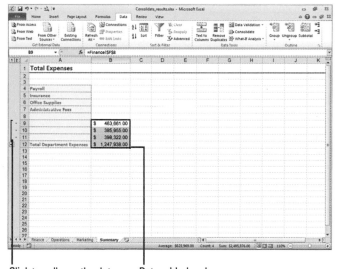

Click to collapse the data   Data added up here

Linking Data in Excel

A link can be as simple as a reference to a cell on another worksheet, or it can be part of a formula. You can link cells between sheets within one workbook or between different workbooks. Cell data to be linked is called the source data. The cell or range linked to the source data is called the destination cell or destination range. If you no longer want linked data to be updated, you can easily break a link. Create links instead of making multiple identical entries; it saves time and ensures your entries are correct.

Create a Link Between Worksheets or Workbooks

1. In Excel, select the cell or range that contains the source data.

2. Click the **Home** tab.

3. Click the **Copy** button.

4. Click the sheet tab where you want to link the data.

5. Select the destination cell or destination range.

6. Click the **Paste** button.

7. Click the **Paste Options** button, and then click **Paste Link**.

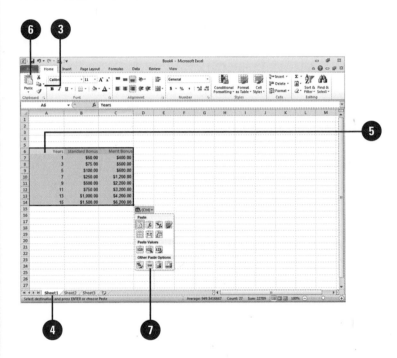

Did You Know?

You can include a link in a formula and treat the linked cell as one argument in a larger calculation. Enter the formula on the formula bar, and then select a cell in the worksheet or workbook you want to link. A cell address reference to a worksheet is =tab name!cell address (=Orders!A6). A cell reference to a workbook is ='[workbook name.xls]tab name'!cell address (='[Product Orders.xls]Orders'!A6).

You can arrange worksheet windows to make linking easier. To arrange open windows, click the View tab, and then click the Arrange All button.

Getting External Data in Excel

Introduction

If you need to temporarily exchange data between programs, copying and pasting or linking works the best. However, if you need to permanently exchange data, creating a connection to the data source is the best solution. A **data source** is a stored set of information that allows Excel to connect to an external database. A cell range, table, PivotTable report, or PivotChart report in Excel can be connected to an external data source.

External Data Sources

Microsoft allows you to retrieve data from several types of databases, including Microsoft Office Access, Microsoft Office Excel, Microsoft SQL Server, Microsoft SQL Server OLAP services, dBASE, Microsoft FoxPro, Oracle, Paradox, and text file databases. You can also use ODBC (Open Database Connectivity) drivers or data source drivers from other manufactures to retrieve information from other data sources. You can use the Data Connection Wizard to connect to an external data source that has already been

established. To open the Data Connection Wizard, click the Data tab, click the From Other Sources button, and then click From Data Connection Wizard. The Data tab also includes buttons to access Microsoft Access, Web, and Text data.

You retrieve data from a database by creating a query, which is data selection criteria to retrieve the data you want. Microsoft Query makes connections to external data sources and shows you what data is available. The **Query Wizard** helps you select data from different tables and fields in the data source, such as a database. During the wizard process you can sort and filter the data to retrieve only the information you want. After you create a query and import the data in a workbook, Microsoft Query provides Excel with query and data source information that you can use for other purposes.

After you connect to an external data source in an Excel workbook, all you need to do is refresh the data to update it from the source. You can refresh external data automatically when you open a workbook or at regular time intervals, or you can manually refresh external data using the Refresh button on the Data tab.

Security

When you open a workbook that connects to external data, the connection to the data source might be disabled if Excel detects a possible security risk. To connect to data when you open a workbook, you need to enable data connections by using the Trust Center, or by putting the workbook in a trusted location.

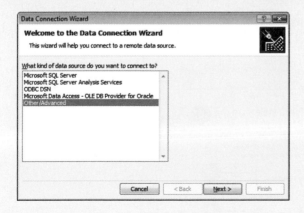

Connecting to Data in Excel

You can use Excel to create and edit connections to external data sources. When you create a connection, Excel stores the connection in the workbook or a connection file, such as Office Data Connection (ODC) file or a Universal Data Connection (UDC) file. A connection file is useful for sharing connections with other users. When you use a connection file, Excel copies the connection information into your Excel workbook. However, if you change connection information, the connection file is not updated. You can manage one or more connections to external data sources using the Workbook Connections dialog box. You can use the Connection Properties dialog to set options for connections to external data sources, and to use, reuse, or switch connection files.

Connect to External Data Using an Existing Connection

1. In Excel, click the **Data** tab.

2. Click the **Existing Connections** button.

   The Existing Connections dialog box opens.

3. Click the **Show** list arrow, and then click **All Connections** or the specific connection type you want to display.

4. Select the connection you want to use. If you don't see the connection you want, click **Browse for More**, and then click **New Source** to start the Data Connection Wizard.

5. Click **Open**.

6. If requested, click the table you want, and then click **OK**.

   The Import Data dialog box opens.

7. Click the **Table, PivotTable Report** or **PivotChart and PivotTable Report** option.

8. Click the **Existing worksheet** option, and then specify a cell location, or click the **New worksheet** option.

9. Click **OK**.

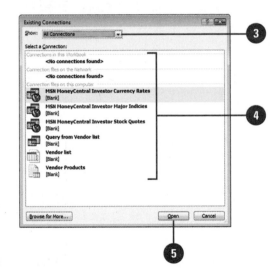

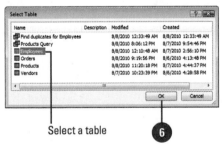

Select a table

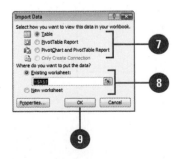

Change Connection Properties

① In Excel, click the **Data** tab.

② Click the **Connections** button.

③ To manage connections, do any of the following:

◆ **Add.** Click **Add**, click **OK** (if necessary for the security alert), and then connect to external data using the Existing Connections dialog box.

◆ **Remove.** Select the connection you want to remove, click **Remove**, and then click **OK**.

◆ **Properties.** Select the connection you want to change, click **Properties**, set refresh, formatting, and layout options, and then click **OK**.

◆ **Refresh.** Select a connection, click the **Refresh** button arrow, and then click a refresh option.

④ Click **Close**.

Data source definition information

Refresh options

OLAP options

Did You Know?

You can refresh data in Excel from the data source. Click the Data tab, and then click the Refresh button arrow, and then click Refresh All to refresh multiple external data ranges. To refresh imported text, click the Refresh button arrow, click Refresh, select the text file, and then click Import.

You can remove the data connection from the external data range. Click the Name box arrow, click the name of the external data range you want to remove the data connection, click the Tools tab, and then click the Unlink button.

Getting Query Data from a Database

If you have data in a database, you can use functions in Excel to retrieve data from a table in a database. To retrieve the data, you can select or create a data source, build a query to create a link to the data, and optionally, create a filter to limit the information. When you select or create a data source, you need to identify the database type and then connect to it. To build a query, you can use the Query wizard to step you through the process, or you can manually create a query the same way you do in Microsoft Access. You can also retrieve data from other sources. If you use the same table in a database for data, you can define and save the data source for use later.

Define a New Data Source

1. In Excel, click the **Data** tab.

2. Click the **From Other Sources** button, and then click **From Microsoft Query**.

3. Click the **Databases** tab.

4. Click **<New Data Source>**.

5. Click **OK**.

6. Type the name of the source.

7. Click the second box list arrow, and then select a driver for the type of database, such as Driver do Microsoft Access (*.mdb).

8. Click **Connect**.

9. Click **Select**.

10. Navigate to the folder with the database you want to use, and then click **OK**.

11. Click **OK** again.

12. Click the fourth box list arrow, and then click the default table for the data source.

13. Click **OK**.

Follow the steps to create a query on the next page, starting with step 6.

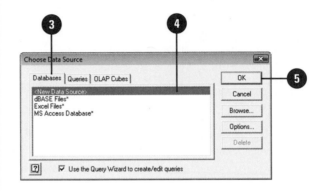

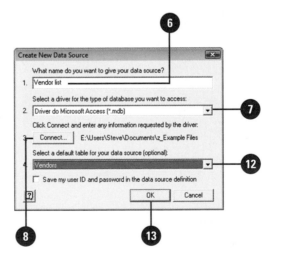

Create a Database Query

1. In Excel, click the **Data** tab.

2. Click the **From Other Sources** button, and then click **From Microsoft Query**.

3. Click the **Databases** tab.

4. Click the name of the data sources you want to use.

5. Click **OK**.

6. Click a table column name, and then click **Add** to add it to your query. Add the columns you want.

7. Click **Next** to continue.

8. Click the name of the column by which you want to filter the results.

9. Click the first comparison operator list arrow, and then click the operator you want to use.

10. Type the first value to use in the comparison.

11. If necessary, type a second value in the second value box.

12. Click **Next** to continue.

13. Click the **Sort by** list arrow, and then click the name of the column by which to sort the query results.

14. Click **Next** to continue.

15. Click **Save Query**, type a name for the query, and then click **Save**.

16. Click **Finish**.

17. Select the import options you want.

18. Click **OK**.

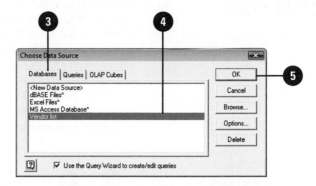

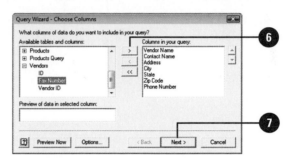

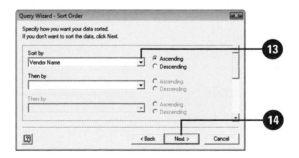

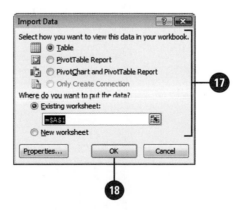

Getting Data from Access

Information you want to analyze may not always exist in an Excel workbook; you might have to retrieve it from another Office program, such as Access. Access table data can be easily converted into Excel worksheet data. Before you can analyze Access data in a workbook, you must convert it to an Excel file. You can either use the Excel command in Access to export data as an Excel table file, or use the PivotTable or PivotChart and PivotTable Report option in Excel to use the Access data as a PivotTable, a table you can use to perform calculations with or rearrange large amounts of data.

Export an Access Database Table into an Excel Workbook

1. In Access, open the database you want, and then display Tables in the task pane.

2. Click the table you want to analyze.

3. Click the **External Data** tab.

4. Click the **Excel** button in the Export group.

5. Specify the destination file name and format.

6. Specify the export options you want.

7. Click **OK**, and then click **Close**.

8. Use Excel tools to edit and analyze the data.

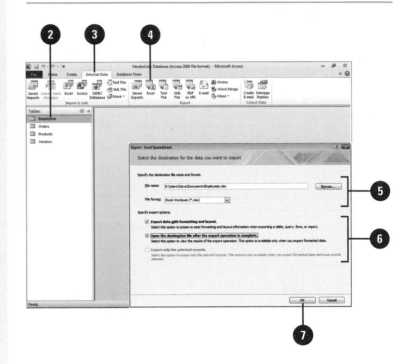

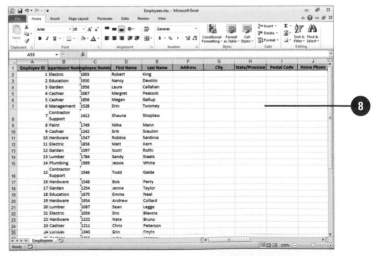

Create an Excel Workbook PivotTable from an Access Database

1. In Excel, click the **Data** tab.

2. Click the **From Access** button.

3. Select the Access database file, and then click **Open**.

4. Click the table from Access you want to use.

5. Click **OK**.

6. Click the **PivotTable Report** or **PivotChart and PivotTable Report** option.

7. Click the **Existing worksheet** option, and then specify a cell location, or click the **New worksheet** option.

8. To set refresh, formatting, and layout options for the imported data, click **Properties**, make the changes you want, and then click **OK**.

9. Click **OK**.

10. Use tabs under PivotChart Tools to create and format the PivotChart.

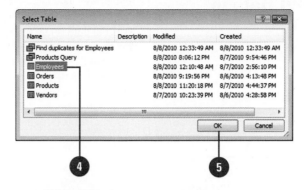

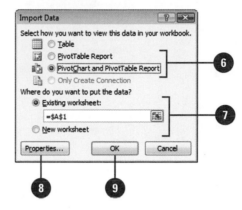

Getting Text Data in Excel

If you have data in a text file, you can either open the file using the Open command on the File tab, or you can import the text file as an external data range using the From Text button on the Data tab. There are two commonly used text file formats to store data that you can import in Excel: Tab delimited text (.txt) and Comma separated values text (.csv). When you open a .txt file, Excel starts the Import Text Wizard. When you open a .csv file, Excel opens the file using current default data format settings.

Import a Text File

1. In Excel, open the workbook in which you want to insert text data.

2. Click the **Data** tab.

3. Click the **From Text** button.

4. Click the **Files of type** list arrow, and then click **Text Files**.

5. Click the **Look in** list arrow, and then select the folder where the text file is located.

6. Click the text file you want to import.

7. Click **Import**.

8. If the file is a text file (.txt), Excel starts the Import Text Wizard. Step through the wizard (3 steps), and then click **Finish**.

9. Click the **Existing worksheet** option, and then specify a cell location, or click the **New worksheet** option.

10. Click **OK**.

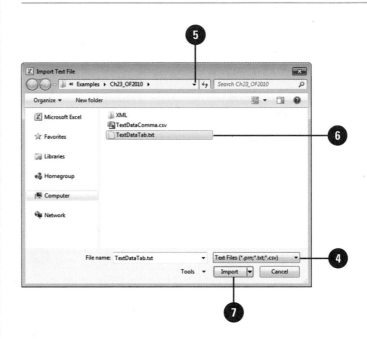

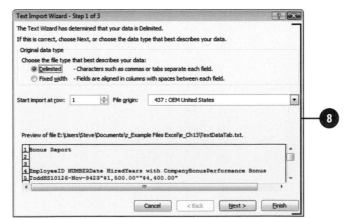

Saving a Document to a SharePoint Server

You can save documents to a Document Management Server, such as a Document Library on an Office SharePoint site, in a similar way that you save documents on your hard disk. After you save the document for the first time using the Save to SharePoint option, you can click the Save button on the Quick Access Toolbar as you do for any document to update the document on the site. If you save a file to a library that requires you to check documents in and out, the SharePoint site checks it out for you. However, you need to check the document in when you're done with it. If the site stores multiple content types, you might be asked to specify the content type.

Save an Office Document to a SharePoint Server

1. Open the Office document you want to save to a Document Management Server.

2. Click the **File** tab, click **Save & Send**, and then click **Save to SharePoint**.

3. Click the **Save As** button.

4. Navigate to the network folder location on the SharePoint server where you want to save the file.

5. Type a document file name.

6. If necessary, click the **Save as type** list arrow, and then click the file format you want.

7. Click **Save**.

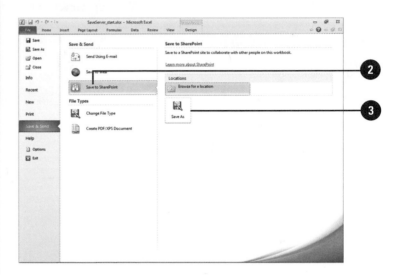

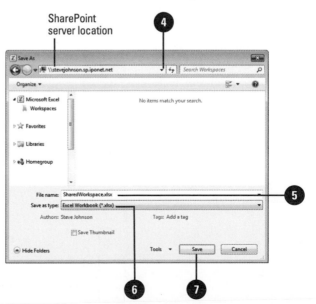

SharePoint server location

Did You Know?

You can access SharePoint resources.
After you save or publish an Office document to a SharePoint Server site, you can click the File tab, click Save & Send, and then click Save To SharePoint to access other server related commands.

Saving Documents to Windows Live

Windows Live is a Web site, where you can store and share information, such as contacts, e-mail (using hotmail), photos, and files. Windows Live is a free service provided by Microsoft. Windows Live provides drive space, called a SkyDrive, for you to store files and photos in a folder, just like your computer drive, where others with permission can access them using a browser. To make storing files on the SkyDrive quick and easy, Office 2010 programs provide a Save As command on the Save & Send screen for you to save Office documents directly to a SkyDrive folder (**New!**) using a Windows Live account. Once the Office documents are stored on the SkyDrive, or a Microsoft SharePoint server as another option, you can view or edit them in a browser using a Microsoft Office Web App (**New!**), which is installed and provided by Windows Live.

Save an Office Document to Windows Live

1. Open the document you want to save to the Web.

2. Click the **File** tab, click **Save & Send**, and then click **Save to Web**.

3. If necessary, click the **Sign In** button, enter your Windows Live ID e-mail address and password, and then click **OK**.

4. Select a folder on the Windows Live Web site, either a personal or shared folder.

   ◆ To create a new folder, click the **New Folder** button to open your browser to Windows Live, type a name, select a Share with location, click **Next**, and then complete the instructions.

5. Click the **Save As** button.

6. Use the default location, specify a name, and then click **Save**.

7. To open Windows Live Web site, click the **Windows Live** link.

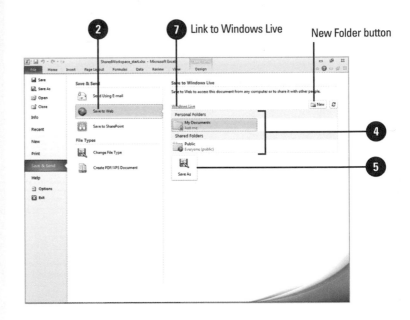

Link to Windows Live   New Folder button

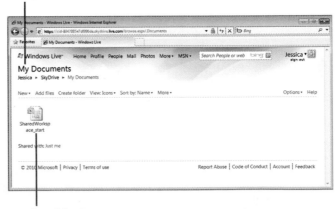

My Documents folder on the Windows Live Web site

Saved document

Open an Office Document Directly from Windows Live

① Click the **File** tab, and then click click **Open**.

◆ To access a recently used file stored on Windows Live, click the **File** tab, click **Recent**, and then click the recent file or recent folder to open it.

② Navigate to the Windows Live SkyDrive.

③ Select the file you want to open.

④ Click **Open**.

⑤ If necessary, enter your Windows Live ID e-mail address and password, and then click **OK**.

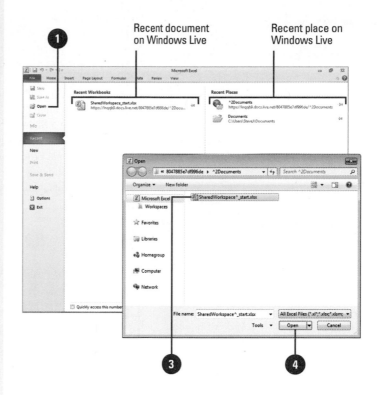

Recent document on Windows Live

Recent place on Windows Live

Open an Office Document in a Browser from Windows Live

① Open your browser, go to *www.live.com*, and then sign in to Windows Live.

② Navigate to the Windows Live SkyDrive, and then navigate to the folder with the Office document.

③ Double-click the Office document, the file you want to open, and then click the **View** or **Edit** link.

◆ You can click the **Open in Excel** link to work locally in Excel.

④ Use the Ribbon tabs to make changes to the Office document; any changes in an Office Web App are automatically saved.

Navigation links

Publishing Slides to a Library

You can publish one or more slides directly from PowerPoint Professional Plus 2010 to a Slide Library on a network running Office SharePoint Server or to a folder location on your computer or network to store, share, track, and reuse later. Before you can publish slides to a Slide Library, you need to create a Slide Library on the Office SharePoint Server (with at least Designer permissions), where you can also identify the online location for the publishing process. When you publish slides to a Slide Library to a SharePoint Server, team members can use the Reuse Slides task pane to quickly insert the ones they want into presentations. When you make changes to slides in a Slide Library, the next time you open your presentation locally with the reused slides, PowerPoint notifies you there is a change.

Publish Slides to a SharePoint Document Library

1. In PowerPoint Professional Plus 2010, click the **File** tab, click **Save & Send**, click **Publish Slides**, and then click the **Publish Slides** button.

2. Select the check boxes next to the slides you want to publish, or click **Select All** to select all the slides.

    PowerPoint automatically names each slide file by using the presentation name and a unique ID number in sequential order.

3. To show only selected slides, select the **Show Only Selected Slides** check box.

4. To rename a slide file name, click the existing file name, and then type a new name.

5. To include a description, click in the description area, and then type a description.

6. Click the **Publish To** list arrow, click a location, or click **Browse** to select a SharePoint Slide Library location; display the library on the SharePoint site, click Settings, and then click Slide Library Settings.

7. Click **Publish**.

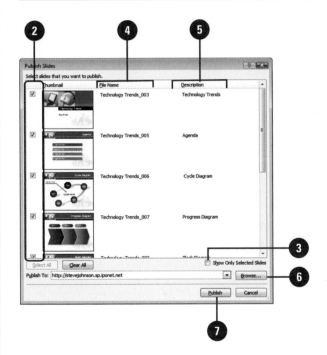

Reuse Published Slides

1. In PowerPoint, open the present-ation, and then click the **Home** tab.

2. Click the **New Slide** button arrow, and then click **Reuse Slides**.

3. If the presentation you want is not available, click **Browse**, click **Browse Slide Library**, locate and select the shortcut to the library you want, and then click **Select**.

4. Click a slide to insert it, or right-click a slide, and then click **Insert All Slides**.

5. To be notified when a slide change happens, select the slide, and then select the **Tell me when this slide changes** check box.

6. When you're done, click the **Close** button on the task pane.

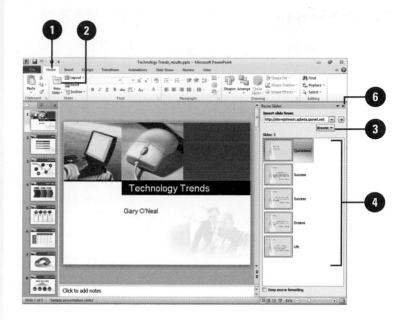

Check Reused Slides for Updates

1. In PowerPoint, open the present-ation that contains reused slides.

2. In the Alert dialog box, click **Get Updates**.

   If the dialog box doesn't appear, right-click the reused slide in the Slide pane (Normal view), point to **Check for Updates**, and then click **Check This Slide for Changes** or **Check All Slides for Changes**.

3. If no slides in the presentation need to be updated, a message alert appears. Click **OK**.

4. If the Confirm Slide Update dialog box appears, click **Replace** to replace the local slide with the changed slide from the Slide Library, or click **Append** to add the changed slide after the outdated one in your presentation.

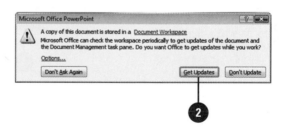

Broadcasting a Presentation

If you want to share your presentation with others at different locations, the Broadcast Slide Show command (**New!**) allows you to display a slide show over the Internet. Before you start the broadcast, you send a URL link to your remote audience via an e-mail or copied link that they can use to access and watch your slide show in their browser, which supports Internet Explorer, Firefox, and Safari for Mac. To use the Broadcast Slide Show command, you need to use the PowerPoint Broadcast Service provided by Microsoft at no charge along with a Windows Live ID or use a broadcast service provided by your organization on a server that has the Microsoft Office Web Apps installed. In the browser delivery of your slide show, some features are changed, including transitions shown as fades, no audio or video, no ink annotations, can't follow a hyperlink, and screensavers and e-mail popup can disrupt the view.

Broadcast a Presentation

1. In PowerPoint, open the presentation you want to broadcast.

2. Click the **Slide Show** tab.

3. Click the **Broadcast Slide Show** button.

4. Click **Start Broadcast**.

5. Enter your Windows Live ID e-mail address and password, and then click **OK**.

6. Click the **Copy Link** or **Send in Email** link to share the link to access the broadcast.

7. Click **Start Slide Show**.

   Your audience can open the link in their browser to follow along with your slide show as you display it in PowerPoint.

8. To invite more people to the slide show, switch to Normal view, and then click the **Send Invitations** button.

9. To end the broadcast, click the **End Broadcast** button on the Message bar or on the **Broadcast** tab, and then click **End Broadcast** to confirm it.

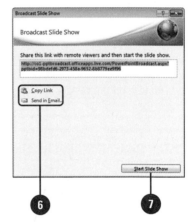

Broadcast slide show in a browser

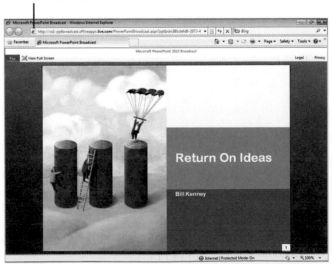

Expanding Office Functionality

24

Introduction

An add-in extends the functionality of Microsoft Office programs. For example, Excel includes a variety of add-ins—including Analysis ToolPak, Analysis ToolPak VBA, Euro Currency, and Solver—that are useful to almost anyone using Excel. Before you can use an add-in, you need to load it first. When you load an add-in, the feature may add a command to a Ribbon tab.

If you want to customize Microsoft Office and create advanced documents, you'll need to learn how to work with the Microsoft Office programming language, **Microsoft Visual Basic for Applications (VBA)**. VBA is powerful and flexible, and you can use it in all major Office programs. To create a VBA application, you have to learn VBA conventions and syntax. Office makes VBA more user-friendly by providing the Visual Basic Editor, an application that includes several tools to help you write error-free VBA applications. The Visual Basic Editor provides extensive online Help to assist you in this task.

A practical way to use VBA is to create macros. Macros can simplify common repetitive tasks that you regularly use. Macros can reside on the Quick Access Toolbar for easy access. If a macro has a problem executing a task, the Visual Basic Editor can help you debug, or fix the error in your macro.

An ActiveX control is a software component that adds functionality to an existing program. An ActiveX control supports a customizable, programmatic interface for you to create your own functionality, such as a form. Office includes several pre-built ActiveX controls—including a label, text box, command button, and check box—to help you create a user interface.

What You'll Do

View and Manage Add-ins

Load and Unload Add-ins

Enhance a Document with VBA

View the Visual Basic Editor

Set Developer Options

Understand How Macros Automate Your Work

Record or Create a Macro

Run and Control a Macro

Build a Macro

Add a Digital Signature to a Macro Project

Assign a Macro to a Toolbar

Save and Open a Workbook with Macros

Insert and Use ActiveX Controls

Set ActiveX Control Properties

Add VBA Code to an ActiveX Control

Play a Movie Using an ActiveX Control

Change the Document Information Panel

Viewing and Managing Add-ins

An add-in, such as smart tags, extends functionality to Microsoft Office programs. An add-in can add buttons and custom commands to the Ribbon. You can get add-ins for Office programs on the Microsoft Office Online Web site in the Downloads area, or on third-party vendor Web sites. When you download and install an add-in, it appears on the Add-Ins or other tabs in Office programs depending on functionality, and includes a special ScreenTip that identifies the developer. You can view and manage add-ins from the Add-Ins pane in Options.

View Installed Add-ins

① Click the **Add-Ins** tab.

Add-ins with buttons and controls appear on the Ribbon. To display a ScreenTip, point to a button or control.

② Click the **File** tab, and then click **Options**.

③ In the left pane, click **Add-Ins**.

The installed add-ins appear in the list by category.

◆ **Active Application Add-ins.** Lists the registered and running add-ins. A selected check box for a COM add-in appears here.

◆ **Inactive Application Add-ins.** Lists the installed add-ins, but not currently loaded. A cleared check box for a COM add-in appears here.

◆ **Document Related Add-ins.** Lists template files currently open in a document.

◆ **Disabled Application Add-ins.** Lists automatically disabled add-ins causing Office programs to crash.

④ Click an add-in to display information about it.

⑤ Click **OK**.

Add-in

Add-in

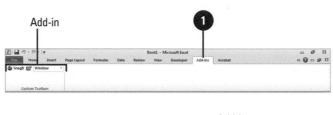

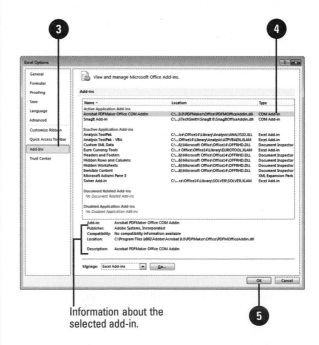

Information about the selected add-in.

Manage Installed Add-ins

1. Click the **File** tab, and then click **Options**.

2. In the left pane, click **Add-Ins**.

3. Click the **Manage** list arrow, and then click the add-in list you want to display:

   ◆ **COM Add-ins.** Opens the COM Add-Ins dialog box and lists the Component Object Model (COM) add-ins.

   ◆ **<Program> Add-ins.** Opens the Add-Ins dialog box and lists the currently installed add-ins.

   ◆ **Actions.** Opens the AutoCorrect dialog box with the Actions tab and list the installed actions (**New!**).

   ◆ **XML Expansion Pack.** Opens XML Expansion Packs that provide additional XML functionality.

   ◆ **Disabled Items.** Opens the Disabled Items dialog box and lists the disabled items that prevent Office from working properly. If you want to try and enable an item, select it, click Enable, click Close, and then restart Office.

4. Click **Go**.

5. Click **OK**.

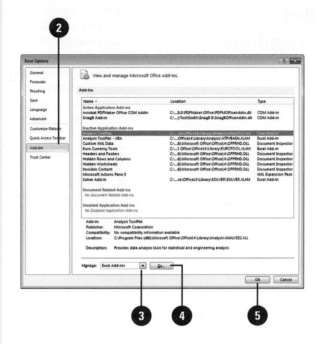

Add-ins Installed with Excel

Add-in	Descriptions
Analysis ToolPak	Provides data analysis tools for statistical and engineering analysis.
Analysis ToolPak VBA	VBA Functions for Analysis ToolPak.
Euro Currency Tools	Conversion and formatting for the euro currency.
Solver	Tool for optimization and equation solving.

Loading and Unloading Add-ins

Add-ins are additional programs, designed to run seamlessly within Office. There are two main types of add-ins: Program and **Component Object Model (COM)**. Program add-ins are custom controls designed specifically for the Office program, while COM add-ins are designed to run in one or more Office programs and use the file name extension .dll or .exe. Some add-ins are installed when you run the Setup program, while others can be downloaded from Microsoft Office Online or purchased from third-party vendors. To load or unload add-ins, Office provides commands you can access from an added button on the Developer tab (**New!**) or the Add-Ins pane in Options. When you load an add-in, the feature may add a command to a tab or toolbar. You can load one or more add-ins. If you no longer need an add-in, you should unload it to save memory and reduce the number of commands on a tab. When you unload an add-in, you also may need to restart the Office program to remove an add-in command from a tab.

Load or Unload an Add-in

1. Click the **Developer** tab.

   ◆ To display the Developer tab, use the Customize Ribbon pane in Options.

2. Click the **Add-Ins** button.

3. To add an add-in to the list, click **Browse**, locate and select the add-in you want, and then click **OK**.

4. Select a check box to load an add-in or clear a check box to unload an add-in.

5. Click **OK**.

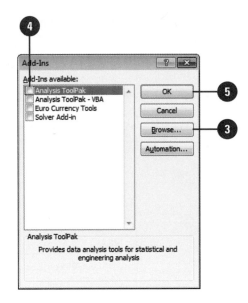

Did You Know?

You can open the Add-Ins dialog box from Options. Click the File tab, click Options, click Add-ins, click the Manage list arrow, click <Program> Add-ins, and then click Go.

Load or Unload a COM Add-in

1. Click the **Developer** tab.

   ◆ To display the Developer tab, use the Customize Ribbon pane in Options.

2. Click the **COM Add-Ins** button.

3. Select the check box next to the add-in you want to load, or clear the check box you want to unload.

   TROUBLE? *If the add-in is not available in the list, click Add, locate and select the add-in you want, and then click OK.*

4. To remove the selected add-in, click **Remove**.

5. Click **OK**.

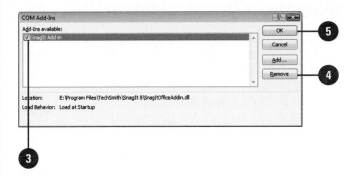

Did You Know?

You can open the COM Add-Ins dialog box from Options. Click the File tab, click Options, click Add-ins, click the Manage list arrow, click COM Add-ins, and then click Go.

You can can get more information about COM online. Visit *www.microsoft.com/com*.

See Also

See "Working with the Ribbon and Toolbars" on page 6 for information on adding a button to the Quick Access Toolbar.

For Your Information

Dealing with an Add-in Security Alert

When there is a problem with an add-in, Office disables it to protect the program and your data. When a problem does occur, a security alert dialog box appears, displaying information about the problem and options you can choose to fix or ignore it. You can choose an option to help protect you from unknown content (recommended), enable this add-in for this session only, or enable all code published by this publisher. See "Setting Add-in Security Options" on page 594 for more information about setting options that trigger the Add-in security alert.

Enhancing a Document with VBA

Office applications like Office, Access, Word, PowerPoint, and Visio share a common programming language: Visual Basic for Applications (VBA). With VBA, you can develop applications that combine tools from these Office products, as well as other programs that support VBA. Because of the language's power and flexibility, programmers often prefer to use VBA to customize their Office applications.

Introducing the Structure of VBA

VBA is an object-oriented programming language because, when you develop a VBA application, you manipulate objects. An object can be anything within your Office document, such as a shape, text box, picture, or table. Even the Office program itself is considered an object. Objects can have properties that describe the object's characteristics. Text boxes, for example, have the Font property, which describes the font Office uses to display the text. A text box also has properties that indicate whether the text is bold or italic.

Objects also have methods—actions that can be done to the object. Deleting and inserting are examples of methods available with a record object. Closely related to methods are events. An event is a specific action that occurs on or with an object. Clicking a button initiates the Click event for the button object. VBA also refers to an event associated with an object as an event property. The form button, for example, has the Click event property. You can use VBA to either respond to an event or to initiate an event.

Writing VBA Code

A VBA programmer types the statements, or **code**, that make up the VBA program. Those statements follow a set of rules, called **syntax**, that govern how commands are formulated. For example, to change the property of a particular object, the command follows the general form:

    Object.Property = Expression

Where **Object** is the name of a VBA object, **Property** is the name of a property that object has, and **Expression** is a value that will be assigned to the property. The following statement places text "Expense Report" in cells A1 and A5 on Sheet1 in Excel:

    Worksheets("Sheet1").Range("A1, A5") =
        "Expense Report"

You can use Office and VBA's online Help to learn about specific object and property names. If you want to apply a method to an object, the syntax is:

    Object.Method arg1, arg2, ...

Where **Object** is the name of a VBA object, **Method** is the name of method that can be applied to that object, and **arg1**, **arg2**, ... are optional **arguments** that provide additional information for the method operation. For example, to set columns A and B on Sheet2 in Excel to AutoFit cell contents, you could use the AutoFit method as follows:

    Worksheets("Sheet2").Column(A:B).AutoFit

Working with Procedures

You don't run VBA commands individually. Instead they are organized into groups of commands called **procedures**. A procedure either performs an action or calculates a value. Procedures that perform actions are called **Sub procedures.** You can run a Sub procedure directly, or Office can run it for you in response to an event, such as clicking a button or opening a form. A Sub procedure initiated by an event is also called an **event procedure**. Office provides event procedure templates to help you easily create procedures for common events. Event procedures are displayed in each object's event properties list.

A procedure that calculates a value is called a **function procedure.** By creating function procedures you can create your own function library, supplementing the Office collection of built-in functions. You can access these functions from within the Expression Builder, making it easy for them to be used over and over again.

Working with Modules

Procedures are collected and organized within **modules**. Modules generally belong to two types: class modules and standard modules. A **class module** is associated with a specific object. In more advanced VBA programs, the class module can be associated with an object created by the user. **Standard modules** are not associated with specific objects, and they can be run from anywhere within a database. This is usually not the case with class modules. Standard modules are listed in the Database window on the Modules Object list.

Building VBA Projects

A collection of modules is further organized into a **project**. Usually a project has the same name as a file. You can create projects that are not tied into any specific file, saving them as add-ins that provide extra functionality.

Using the Visual Basic Editor

You create VBA commands, procedures, and modules in Office's **Visual Basic Editor.** This is the same editor used by Excel, PowerPoint, Word, and other Office programs. Thus, you can apply what you learn about creating programs in one Office program to these other applications.

The Project Explorer

One of the fundamental tools in the Visual Basic Editor is the Project Explorer. The **Project Explorer** presents a hierarchical view of all of the projects and modules currently open, including standard and class modules.

The Modules Window

You write all of your VBA code in the **Modules** window. The Modules window acts as a basic text editor, but it includes several tools to help you write error-free codes. Office also provides hints as you write your code to help you avoid syntax errors.

The Object Browser

There are hundreds of objects available to you. Each object has a myriad of properties, methods, and events. Trying to keep track of all of them is daunting, but the Visual Basic Editor supplies the **Object Browser**, which helps you examine the complete collection of objects, properties, and methods available for a given object.

Viewing the Visual Basic Editor

The Project Explorer displays a hierarchical list of all open projects and modules.

The Modules window allows you to enter VBA commands.

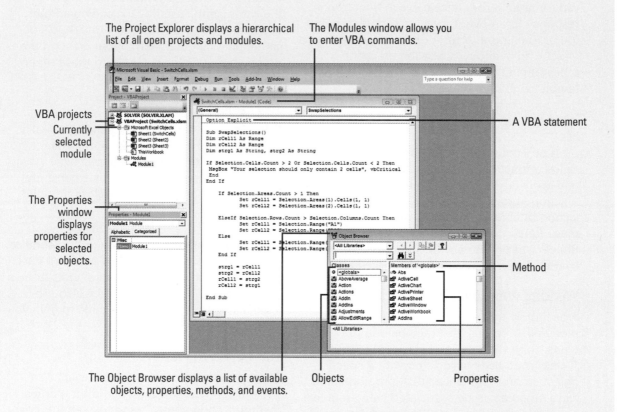

VBA projects
Currently selected module

A VBA statement

The Properties window displays properties for selected objects.

The Object Browser displays a list of available objects, properties, methods, and events.

Objects

Method

Properties

Setting Developer Options

The Developer tab is a specialized Ribbon that you can use to access developer controls, write code, or create macros. You can set an option in the Customize Ribbon pane in Options to show or hide the Developer tab. As a developer, you can also set an option to show errors in your user interface customization code.

Set Developer Options

1. Click the **File** tab, and then click **Options**.

2. In the left pane, click **Customize Ribbon**.

3. Select the **Developer** check box to display the Developer tab.

4. In the left pane, click **Advanced**.

5. Select the **Show add-in user interface errors** check box.

6. Click **OK**.

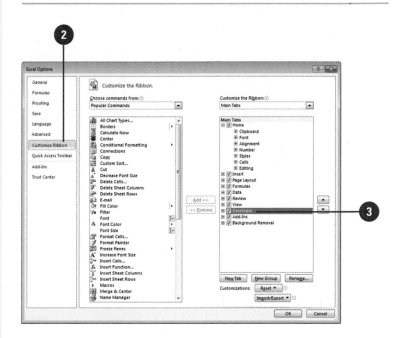

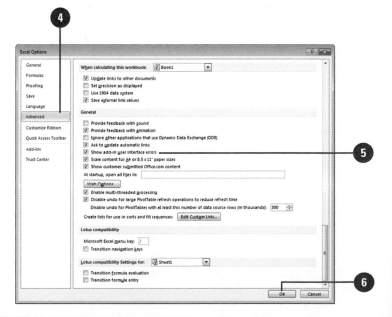

Understanding How Macros Automate Your Work

To complete many tasks, you need to execute a series of commands and actions. To print two copies of a selected range of Sheet2 of a worksheet, for example, you need to open the workbook, switch to Sheet2, select the print area, open the Print dialog box, and specify that you want to print two copies. If you often need to complete the same task, you'll find yourself repeatedly taking the same series of steps. It can be tiresome to continually repeat the same commands and actions when you can easily create a mini-program, or macro, that accomplishes all of them with a single command.

In Excel and Word, creating a **macro** is easy and requires no programming knowledge on your part. In PowerPoint, you need to know Visual Basic for Applications (VBA). Excel and Word simply record the steps you want included in the macro while you use the keyboard and mouse. When you record a macro, Excel and Word store the list of commands with any name you choose. You can store your macros in the current document, in a new document, or in Excel's Personal Macro workbook.

In Excel, you can store your macros in the Personal Macro workbook, which makes the macros available to you from any location in Excel, even when no document is open. When you select the Personal Macro Workbook option to store a macro, Excel create a hidden personal macro file (Personal.xlsb) and saves the macro in this file. The file is stored in the XLStart folder so it will load automatically when Excel starts. The XLSTART folder is typically located in the C:\Users\user name\App Data\Roaming\Microsoft\Excel folder for Windows 7 or Vista and C:\Documents and Settings\user name\Application\Data\ Microsoft\Excel folder for Windows XP.

Once a macro is created, you can make modifications to it, add comments so other users will understand its purpose, and test it to make sure it runs correctly.

You can run a macro by choosing the Macro command on the View or Developer tab, or by using a shortcut key or clicking a Quick Access Toolbar button you've assigned to it. From the Macro dialog box, you can run, edit, test, or delete any macro on your system, or create a new one.

If you have problems with a macro, you can step through the macro one command at a time, known as **debugging**. Once you identify any errors in the macro, you can edit it.

Indicates the workbook(s) from which you can access the selected macro.

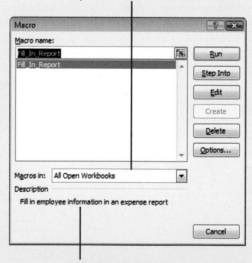

When you create a macro, you can add a description of what the macro does.

Recording a Macro

If you find yourself repeating the same set of steps over and over, you can record a macro. Macros can run several tasks for you at the click of a button. When you turn on the macro recorder, Excel and Word record every mouse click and keystroke action you execute until you turn off the recorder. Then you can "play," or run, the macro whenever you want to repeat that series of actions—but Excel or Word will execute them at a much faster rate. The macro recorder doesn't record in real time, so you can take your time to correctly complete each action.

Record a Macro

1. In Excel or Word, click the **Developer** or **View** tab.

2. To record a macro with actions relative to the initially selected cell, click the **Use Relative References** button.

3. Click the **Record Macro** button.

   ◆ If you use the View tab, click **View Macros** on the menu.

   TIMESAVER *To quickly start or stop a macro recording, click the Record icon or Stop Record icon on the Status bar (left side).*

4. Type a name for the macro.

5. Assign a shortcut key to use a keystroke to run the macro.

6. Click the **Store macro in** list arrow, and then select a location.

   ◆ **Personal Macro workbook**. The macro is available whenever you use Excel.

   ◆ **New <file type>**. The macro is available in new documents.

   ◆ **This <file type>**. The macro is available only in this document.

7. If you want, type a description.

8. Click **OK**.

9. Execute the commands or actions you want to complete the task.

10. Click the **Stop Recording** button.

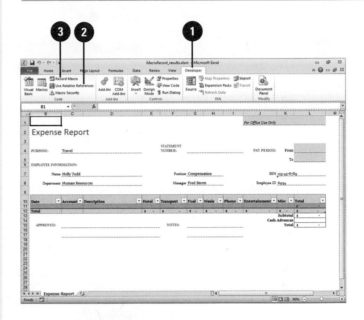

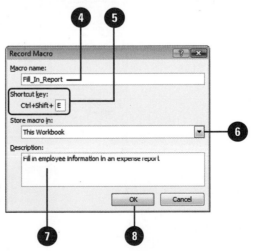

Creating a Macro

If you find yourself repeating the same set of steps over and over, or if you need to add new functionality, you could create a macro in Excel or Word. If you find it difficult to record a macro, you can create one using a programming language called Microsoft Visual Basic for Applications (VBA). With VBA, you create a macro by writing a script to replay the actions you want. The macros for a particular Office document are stored in a macro module, which is a collection of Visual Basic codes.

Create a Macro

1. In Excel or Word, click the **Developer** or **View** tab.

2. Click the **Macros** button.

    ◆ If you use the View tab, click **View Macros** on the menu.

3. Type a name for the macro.

4. Click the **Macros in** list arrow, and then click **All Open <Document type>** or the document to which you want the macro stored.

5. Click **Create**.

    The Microsoft Visual Basic window opens.

6. Click the Module window (if necessary), and then type new Visual Basic commands, or edit existing ones.

    To run the macro, press F5.

7. When you're done, click the **Save** button, and then click the program **Close** button.

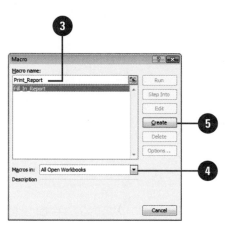

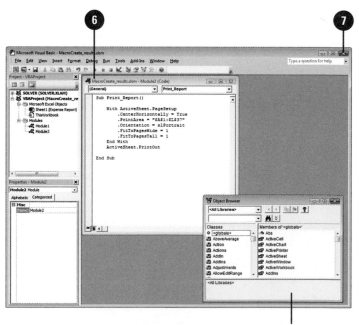

Object Browser helps you insert commands.

Running a Macro

Running a macro is similar to choosing a command. When you record or edit the macro in Excel or Word, you have the choice of making it available through a menu command, a keyboard combination, or even a toolbar button. As with other program options, your choice depends on your personal preferences—and you can choose to make more than one option available. Where you store a macro when you save it determines its availability later. Macros stored in the Personal Macro workbook or All Documents are always available, and macros stored in any other documents are only available when the document is open.

Run a Macro

① In Excel or Word, click the **Developer** or **View** tab.

② Click the **Macros** button.

◆ If you use the View tab, click **View Macros** on the menu.

TIMESAVER *Click the Macros button on the Status bar.*

③ Click the macro you want to run.

④ Click **Run**.

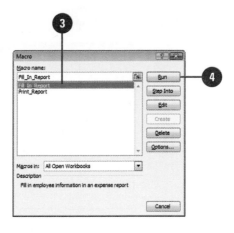

Delete a Macro

① In Excel or Word, click the **Developer** or **View** tab.

② Click the **Macros** button.

◆ If you use the View tab, click **View Macros** on the menu.

③ Click the macro you want to delete.

④ Click **Delete**, and then click **Delete** again to confirm the deletion.

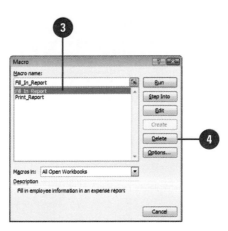

Did You Know?

You can stop a macro. Press Ctrl+Break to stop a macro before it completes its actions.

Controlling a Macro

If a macro doesn't work exactly the way you want it to in Excel or Word, you can fix the problem using Microsoft Visual Basic for Applications (VBA). VBA allows you to **debug**, or repair, an existing macro so that you change only the actions that aren't working correctly. All macros for a particular document are stored in a macro module, a collection of Visual Basic programming codes that you can copy to other files. You can view and edit your Visual Basic modules using the Visual Basic editor. By learning Visual Basic you can greatly increase the scope and power of your programs.

Debug a Macro Using Step Mode

① In Excel or Word, click the **Developer** or **View** tab.

② Click the **Macros** button.

   ◆ If you use the View tab, click **View Macros** on the menu.

③ Click the macro you want to debug.

④ Click **Step Into**.

   The Microsoft Visual Basic window opens.

⑤ Click the **Debug** menu, and then click **Step Into** (or press F8) to proceed through each action.

   ◆ You can also use other commands like **Step Over** and **Step Out** to debug the code.

⑥ When you're done, click the **Save** button, and then click the program **Close** button.

⑦ Click **OK** to stop the debugger.

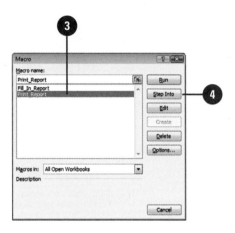

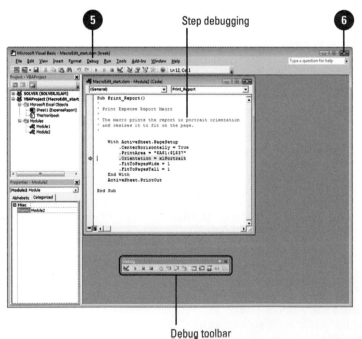

Step debugging

Debug toolbar

Did You Know?

You can display the Debug toolbar. In the Visual Basic editor, click the View menu, point to Toolbars, and then click Debug.

Edit a Macro

1. In Excel or Word, click the **Developer** or **View** tab.

2. Click the **Macros** button.

   ◆ If you use the View tab, click **View Macros** on the menu.

3. Click the macro you want to edit, and then click **Edit**.

4. Click the Module window containing the Visual Basic code for your macro.

5. Type new Visual Basic commands, or edit the commands already present.

6. Click the **Save** button, and then click the program **Close** button.

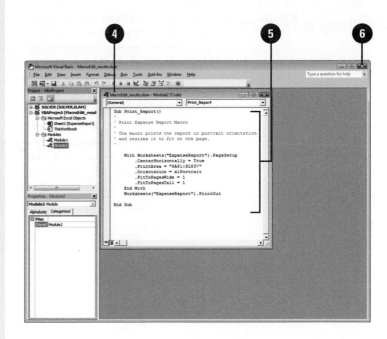

Copy a Macro Module to Another Document

1. In Excel or Word, open the files you want to copy the macro from and to.

2. Click the **Developer** tab.

3. Click the **Visual Basic** button.

4. Click the **View** menu, and then click **Project Explorer**.

5. Drag the module you want to copy from the source to the destination document.

6. Click the **Save** button, and then click the program **Close** button.

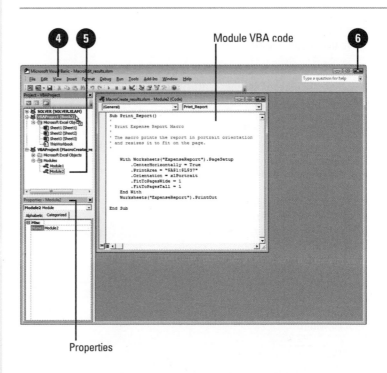

Module VBA code

Properties

Building a Macro

You can also use macros in Access. The process is a little different than in Excel or Word. You can build a macro to open tables, queries, forms, or reports in any view, export data to a file, execute commands on the Ribbon, display messages, play sounds, and start applications to name a few. You can also execute Visual Basic functions. You create a macro by specifying actions you want to execute and related settings for each of the actions in the macro builder (**New!**). After you create a macro, you need to save it before you can run it. You can run a macro from the Navigation pane or from the Macros window. All macros are stored in a macro module, a collection of Visual Basic programming codes that you can copy to other files. You can view and edit your Visual Basic modules using the Visual Basic editor.

Build a Macro

1. In Access, open the database you want to use to create a macro.

2. Click the **Create** tab.

3. Click the **Macros** button.

   The Design tab under Macro Tools opens.

4. To show or hide the Action Catalog pane with a catalog of actions, click the **Action Catalog** button.

5. Click the **Add New Action** list arrow, and then select an action.

   ◆ You can double-click an action from the Action Catalog pane.

6. Specify any parameters or conditions for the action; options vary depending on the action.

7. To another action to the macro, click the **Add New Action** list arrow, and then select an action.

8. Click the **Save** button on the Quick Access Toolbar, enter a name, and then click **OK**.

9. Click the **Close** button in the Macro window.

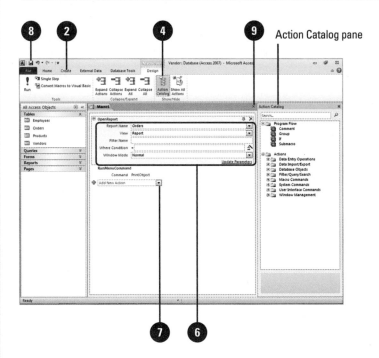
Action Catalog pane

Saving a macro

Edit a Macro

1. In Access, click the Macros bar in the Navigation pane to display the available macros in the database.

2. Right-click the macro you want to edit, and then click **Design View**.

3. Click an action you want to edit.

4. To delete an action, click the **Delete** button for the action.

5. To re-order an action, click the **Move** button for the action.

6. To add another action to the macro, click the **Add New Action** list arrow, and then select an action.

7. To step debug a macro, click the **Single Step** button, click the **Run** button, and then click **Step**.

8. Click the **Save** button on the Quick Access Toolbar, and then click the **Close** button in the Macro window.

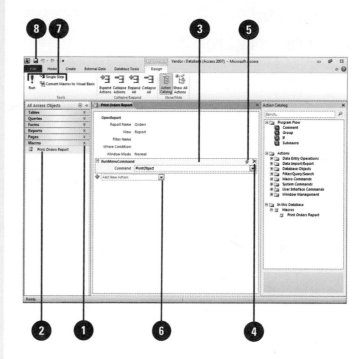

Run a Macro

1. In Access, click the Macros bar in the Navigation pane to display the available macros in the database.

2. Click the macro you want to run.

3. Click the **Database Tools** tab.

4. Click the **Run Macro** button.

5. Click the **Macro Name** list arrow, and then select the macro you want to run.

6. Click **OK**.

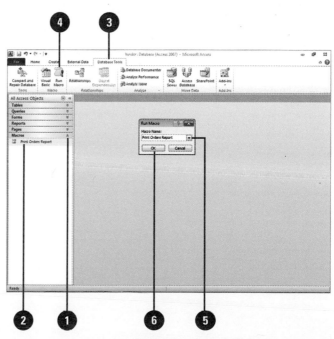

Adding a Digital Signature to a Macro Project

If you want to add a digital signature to a document with a macro, you need to add it using the Visual Basic editor. If you open a document that contains a signed macro project with a problem, the macro is disabled by default and the Message Bar appears to notify you of the potential problem. You can click Options in the Message Bar to view information about it. For more details, you can click Show Signature Details to view certificate and publisher information. If a digital signature has problems—it's expired, not issued by a trusted publisher, or the document has been altered—the certificate information image contains a red X. When there's a problem, contact the signer to have them fix it, or save the document to a trusted location, where you can run the macro without security checks.

Sign a Macro Project

① Open the document that contains the macro project, and then click the **Developer** tab.

② Click the **Visual Basic** button to open the Visual Basic window.

③ Click the **Tools** menu, and then click **Digital Signature**.

④ Click **Choose**.

⑤ Select a certificate in the list.

⑥ To view a certificate, click **View Certificate**, and then click **OK**.

⑦ Click **OK**.

⑧ Click **OK** again.

⑨ Click the **Save** button, and then click the program **Close** button.

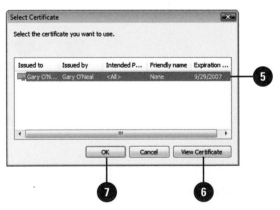

Did You Know?

You can create a self-signing certificate for a macro project. Click the Start button, point to All Programs, click Microsoft Office, click Microsoft Office Tools, click Digital Certificate For VBA Projects, enter a name, and then click OK. Office programs trust a self-signed certificate only on the computer that created it.

Assigning a Macro to a Toolbar

After you create a macro, you can add the macro to the Quick Access Toolbar for easy access. When you create a macro, the macro name appears in the list of available commands when you customize the Quick Access Toolbar in Options. When you point to a macro button on the Quick Access Toolbar, a ScreenTip appears, displaying Macro: *<Program> name!macro name*.

Assign a Macro to a Toolbar

1. Click the **Customize Quick Access Toolbar** list arrow, and then click **More Commands**.

2. Click the **Choose commands from** list arrow, and then click **Macros**.

3. Click the **Customize Quick Access Toolbar** list arrow, and then click **For all documents (default)**.

4. Click the macro you want to add (left column).

5. Click **Add**.

6. Click the **Move Up** and **Move Down** arrow buttons to arrange the toolbar commands in the order you want them to appear.

7. Click **Modify**.

8. Type a name for the button.

9. Click an icon in the symbol list.

10. Click **OK**.

11. Click **OK**.

See Also

See "Working with the Ribbon and Toolbars" on page 6 for information on using the Quick Access Toolbar.

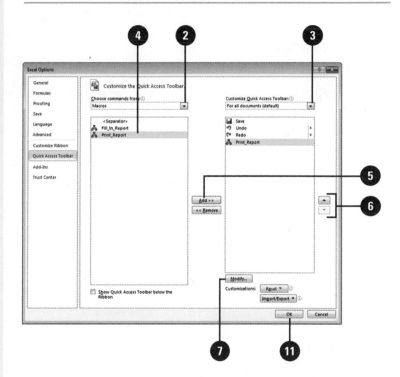

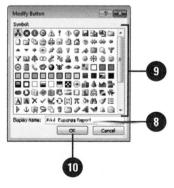

Macro button

Saving a Document with Macros

Macros are created using Visual Basic for Applications (VBA) code. If you add a macro to a document, you need to save it with a file name extension that ends with an "m", such as Excel Macro-Enabled Workbook (.xlsm), or Excel Macro-Enabled Template (.xltm). If you try to save a document containing a macro with a file name extension that ends with an "x" (such as .xlsx or .xltx), the Office program displays an alert message, restricting the operation. These file types are designated to be VBA code-free.

Save an Office Document with Macros

1. Click the **File** tab, and then click **Save As**.

2. Click the **Save in** list arrow, and then click the drive or folder where you want to save the file.

3. Type a file name.

4. If necessary, click the **Save as type** list arrow, and then select the macro format you want:

   ◆ **<Program> Macro-Enabled <File type>.** A document that contains VBA code.

   ◆ **<Program> Macro-Enabled Template.** A template that includes preapproved macros.

5. Click **Save**.

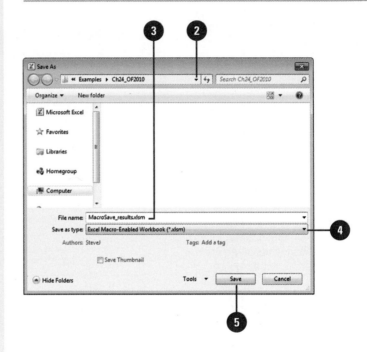

Opening a Document with Macros

When you open a document with a macro, VBA, or other software code, the Office program displays a security warning to let you know the document might contain potentially harmful code that may harm your computer. If you know and trust the author of the document, you can change security options to enable the macro content and use the document normally. If you don't trust the content, you can continue to block and disable the content and use the document with limited functionality. If you don't want a security alert to appear, you can change security settings in the Trust Center in Options.

Open an Office Document with Macros

1. Click the **File** tab, and then click **Open**.

2. If necessary, click the **File as type** list arrow, and then select the document type that contains a macro.

3. If the file is located in another folder, click the **Look in** list arrow, and then navigate to the file.

4. Click the document with macros you want to open, and then click **Open**.

5. Click **Options** in the Message Bar with the Security Warning.

   ◆ You can also click the **File** tab, click **Info**, click the **Enable Content** button, and then click **Advanced Options**. To enable all content, click **Enable All Content** on the menu.

6. If you trust the document content, click the **Enable this content** option (if available) or the **Trust all documents from this publisher** option (if available) to open it. If you don't trust it, click the **Help protect me from unknown content** option to block and disable the macros.

7. Click **OK**.

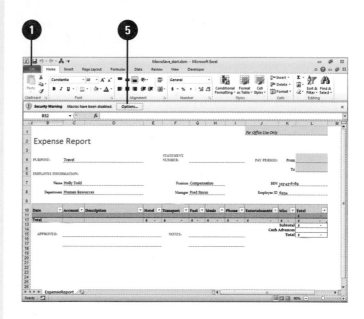

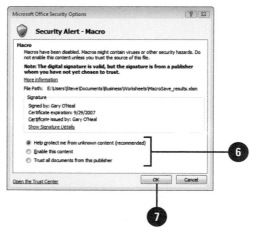

Inserting ActiveX Controls

An ActiveX control is a software component that adds functionality to an existing program. An ActiveX control is really just another term for an OLE (Object Linking and Embedding) object, known as a Component Object Model (COM) object. An ActiveX control supports a customizable, programmatic interface. Office includes several pre-built ActiveX controls on the Developer tab, including a label, text box, command button, image, scroll bar, check box, option button, combo box, list box, and toggle button. To create an ActiveX control, click the Insert button on the Developer tab, and then click the ActiveX control you want, and then drag to insert it with the size you want. If there is a problem with an ActiveX control, Office disables it to protect the program and your data. When a problem does occur, a security alert dialog box appears, displaying information about the problem and options you can choose to leave it disabled or enable it.

Insert ActiveX Controls

1. Click the **Developer** tab.

2. If necessary, click the **Design Mode** button (highlighted).

3. Click the **Insert** button arrow, and then click the button with the ActiveX control you want to use.

    See the next page for a list and description of each ActiveX control.

4. Display the document where you want to place the ActiveX control.

5. Drag (pointer changes to a plus sign) to draw the ActiveX control the size you want.

6. To resize the control, drag a resize handle (circles) to the size you want.

7. To add Visual Basic code to the ActiveX control, click the **View Code** button, or to change display properties, click the **Properties** button. To exit, click the **Save** and **Close** buttons.

8. If necessary, click the **Design Mode** button (not highlighted) to exit.

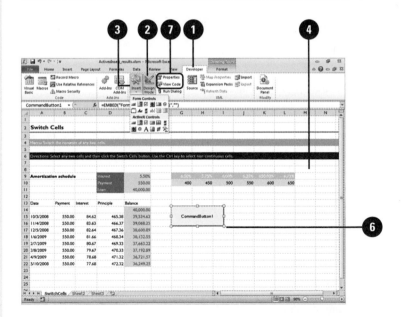

For Your Information

Using Form Controls

Form controls are objects that users can interact with to enter or manipulate data. For example, you can add a Check box control to your document so that users can turn an option on and off. You can select a control from the Developer tab and drag to create the control directly on your document just like an ActiveX control. For an example on using form controls, see project downloads for Office 2010 On Demand available on the Web at *www.perspection.com*.

Deal with an ActiveX Control Security Alert

1 Click the **File** tab, and then click **Open**.

2 Click the **File as type** list arrow, and then click the document type that contains the ActiveX control.

3 If the file is located in another folder, click the **Look in** list arrow, and then navigate to the file.

4 Click the document with the ActiveX control you want to open, and then click **Open**.

5 Click **Options** in the Security Warning.

6 If you trust the document content, click the **Enable this content** option (if available) to open it. If you don't trust it, click the **Help protect me from unknown content** option to block and disable the macros.

7 Click **OK**.

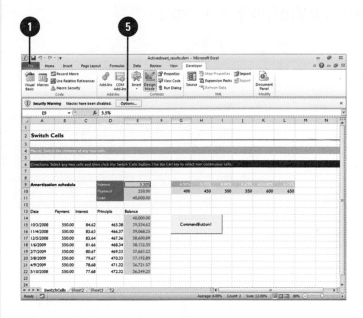

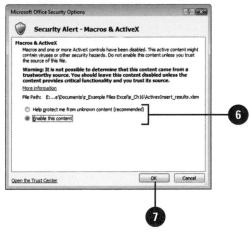

See Also

See "Setting ActiveX Security Options" on page 595 for more information about setting options that trigger the ActiveX security alert.

See "Setting ActiveX Control Properties" on page 673 for more information about setting ActiveX display properties.

Using ActiveX Controls

	ActiveX Controls	
Button	**Name**	**Description**
A	Label	This button creates a text label. Because the other controls already include a corresponding label, use this button to create labels that are independent of other controls.
abl	Text Box	This button creates a text box in which the user can enter text (or numbers). Use this control for objects assigned to a text or number data type.
⬍	Spin Button	This button creates a box in which the user can click arrows to increase or decrease numbers in a box. Use this control assigned to a number data type.
▬	Command Button	This button creates a button that runs a macro or Microsoft Visual Basic function when the user clicks the button in the form.
🖼	Image	This button inserts a frame, in which you can insert a graphic in your form. Use this control when you want to insert a graphic, such as clip art or a logo.
▤	Scroll Bar	This button creates a scroll bar pane in which the user can enter text (or numbers) in a scrollable text box. Use this control or objects assigned to a text or number data type.
☑	Check Box	This button creates a check box that allows a user to make multiple yes or no selections. Use this control for fields assigned to the yes/no data type.
◉	Option Button	This button creates an option button (also known as a radio button) that allows the user to make a single selection from at least two choices. Use this control for fields assigned to the yes/no data type.
▦	Combo Box	This button creates a combo box in which the user has the option to enter text or select from a list of options. You can enter your own options in the list, or you can display options stored in another table.
▤	List Box	This button creates a list box that allows a user to select from a list of options. You can enter your own options in the list, or can have another table provide a list of options.
◨	Toggle Button	This button creates a button that allows the user to make a yes or no selection by clicking the toggle button. Use this control for fields assigned to the yes/no data type.
🛠	More Controls	Click to display other controls, such as Adobe Acrobat Control for ActiveX, Microsoft Forms 2.0, Microsoft Office InfoPath controls, and Microsoft Web Browser.

Setting ActiveX Control Properties

Every ActiveX control has properties, or settings, that determine its appearance and function. You can open a property sheet that displays all the settings for that control in alphabetic or category order directly from Office. The ActiveX controls appear in the Properties window in two columns: the left column displays the name of the control, and the right column displays the current value or setting for the control. When you select either column, a list arrow appears in the right column, allowing you to select the setting you want. After you set properties, you can add VBA code to a module to make it perform.

Set ActiveX Control Properties

1. Click the **Developer** tab.

2. If necessary, click the **Design Mode** button (highlighted).

3. Select the control whose properties you want to modify.

4. Click the **Properties** button.

5. To switch controls, click the **Controls** list arrow (at the top), and then select the one you want.

6. Click the **Alphabetic** or **Categorized** tab to display the control properties so you can find the ones you want.

7. Click the property box for the property you want to modify, and then do one of the following.

   ◆ Type the value or information you want to use, such as the control name.

   ◆ If the property box contains a list arrow, click the arrow and then click a value in the list.

   ◆ If a property box contains a dialog button (...), click it to open a dialog box to select options or insert an object.

8. When you're done, click the **Close** button on the Properties window.

9. If necessary, click the **Design Mode** button (not highlighted) to exit.

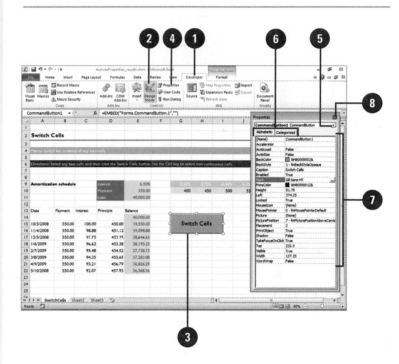

Adding VBA Code to an ActiveX Control

After you add controls and set properties, you can add VBA code to a module to determine how the controls respond to user actions. All controls have a predefined set of events. For example, a command button has a Click event that occurs when the user clicks the button. When you select a control in Design Mode and then click the View Code button, the Visual Basic Editor opens with a Code window, displaying the start of a procedure that runs when the event occurs. The top of the Code window displays the active object and event procedure. The Object list displays the ActiveX control, such as *CommandButton1*, and the Procedure list displays the trigger event, such as *Click*.

Add VBA Code to an ActiveX Control

1. Click the **Developer** tab.

2. If necessary, click the **Design Mode** button (highlighted).

3. Select the control to which you want to add VBA code.

4. Click the **View Code** button.

   The Visual Basic Editor window opens.

5. To show the Properties window, click the **Properties Window** button.

6. To help with scripting commands, click the **Object Browser** button on the toolbar.

7. Click in the Code window between the beginning and ending line of the procedure, and then type VBA code to perform the task you want.

   The Object list is set to *CommandButton1*, and the Procedure list is set to *Click*.

8. When you're done, click the **Save** button on the toolbar.

9. Click the **Close** button.

10. If necessary, click the **Design Mode** button (not highlighted) to exit.

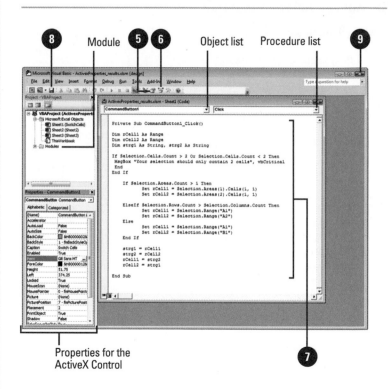

Properties for the ActiveX Control

Playing a Movie Using an ActiveX Control

Although you cannot insert a Flash movie into an Office document, you can play one using an ActiveX control and the Flash player. Before you can use the control, the ActiveX control and Flash player need to be installed on your computer. You can get the ActiveX control at *http://activex.microsoft.com/activex/activex/*. To play the Flash (.swf) movie, you add the Shockwave Flash Object ActiveX control to the document and create a link to the file. If a movie doesn't play, check ActiveX security options in the Trust Center in Options.

Play a Flash Movie

1. Save the Flash file to a Flash movie file (.swf) using the Flash software.

2. Click the **Developer** tab.

3. If necessary, click the **Design Mode** button (highlighted).

4. Click the **Insert** button arrow (if necessary), and then click the **More Controls** button.

5. Click **Shockwave Flash Object**.

6. Click **OK**.

7. Drag to draw the movie control.

8. Right-click the Shockwave Flash Object, and then click **Properties**.

9. Click the **Alphabetic** tab.

10. Click the **Movie** property, click in the value column next to Movie, type full path and file name (c:\MyFolder\Movie.swf), or the URL to the Flash movie you want.

11. To set specific options, choose any of the following:

   ◆ To play the file automatically when the document appears, set the Playing property to True.

   ◆ To embed the Flash file, set the EmbedMovie property to True.

12. Click the **Close** button.

13. If necessary, click the **Design Mode** button (not highlighted) to exit.

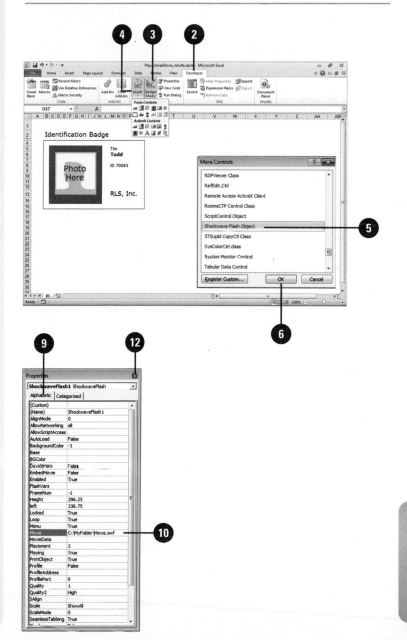

Changing the Document Information Panel

The Document Information Panel helps you manage and track document property information—also known as metadata—such as title, author, subject, keywords, category, and status. The Document Information Panel displays an XML-based mini-form using an InfoPath Form Template (.xsn) file developed in Microsoft InfoPath. By using an XML InfoPath form, you can create your own form templates to edit the document property data and perform data validation.

Select a Document Information Panel Template

1. Click the **Developer** tab.

2. Click the **Document Panel** button.

3. Click **Browse**, locate and select the custom template you want, and then click **Open**.

   ◆ **URL.** Short for Uniform Resource Locator. The address of resources on the Web.

   http://www.perspection.com/index.htm

   ◆ **UNC.** Short for Uniform or Universal Naming Convention. A format for specifying the location of resources on a local-area network (LAN).

   \\server-name\shared-resource-pathname

   ◆ **URN.** Short for Uniform Resource Name.

4. Click the **Display by default** list arrow, and then select the default properties you want.

5. Select the **Always show Document Information Panel on document open and initial save** check box.

6. Click **OK**.

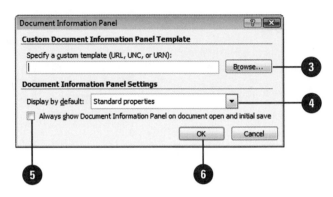

Working with Other Office Tools

Introduction

In addition to the main Office programs—Word, Excel, Power-Point, Access, Outlook, and Publisher—that most people know about, Microsoft Office 2010 also comes with other useful programs and tools, including OneNote, InfoPath (Designer and Filler), Clip Organizer, Picture Manager, SharePoint Workspace, and Upload Center. You can access these programs on the Start menu under the Microsoft Office folder or the Microsoft Office 2010 Tools subfolder.

Office **OneNote 2010** is a digital notebook program you can use to gather, manage, and share notes and information. Office **InfoPath 2010** (Designer and Filler) are information gathering programs you can use to design, collect, share, and reuse data in dynamic forms.

Microsoft **Clip Organizer** is a program that comes along with Office that allows you to add, remove, or organize clips for use in the Clip Art task pane. With Office **Picture Manager**, you can manage, edit, and share your pictures. If you need to edit a picture, you can use Picture Manager to change brightness, contrast, and color, and to remove red eye.

Office **SharePoint Workspace** is a program that allows you to create a personal copy of the SharePoint server, or selected lists and libraries you want to take offline and synchronize, so you can maintain access to a SharePoint server whether or not you are connected to a network. In addition to SharePoint, you can also connect to a Groove workspace, or create a shared folder in Windows.

As you upload files to a server, you can use Office Upload Center to get a progress on the file transfer. Office **Upload Center** is a program that allows you to keep track of the upload of one or more files and whether any of the files have a problem. If so, you can stop the process or remove the file.

What You'll Do

View the OneNote Window

Work with OneNote

View the InfoPath Designer Window

Work with InfoPath Designer

View the InfoPath Filler Window

Work with InfoPath Filler

Organize Clips

Manage Pictures

Work with SharePoint Workspaces

Work with Office Online

Viewing the OneNote Window

File tab
Click to access Office file commands.

Quick Access Toolbar
Click to access command comments on this customizable toolbar.

Tabs
Click to access tools and commands.

Sections
Tabs to switch between sections.

Navigation pane
Work with notebooks and sections

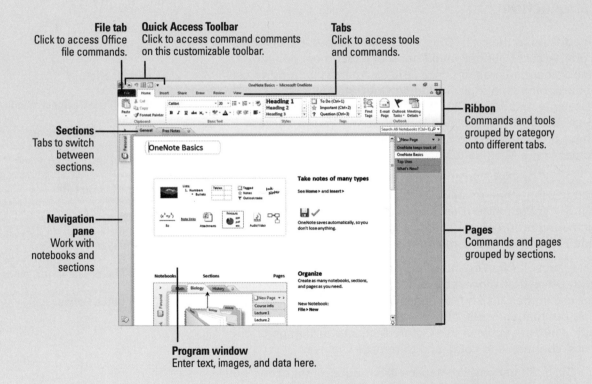

Ribbon
Commands and tools grouped by category onto different tabs.

Pages
Commands and pages grouped by sections.

Program window
Enter text, images, and data here.

Working with OneNote

Microsoft OneNote can function just like a yellow legal pad. You can take notes, draw pictures, highlight, and scratch out text. However, OneNote is much more. OneNote enables you to flag important items within your notes and search for them later. You can create detailed multilevel outlines, gather and paste research information from a variety of sources, insert images, move notes around between pages and sections, and create Outlook tasks directly from your notes. Notes are entered on pages. A page can store any piece or pieces of information. Pages are organized into sections. Sections help you organize notes on a particular subject and quickly access them by clicking a section tab. Use folders to group sections together. The notebook is where all your folders, sections, and note pages are stored.

Work with OneNote

1. Click the **Start** button, point to **All Programs**, click **Microsoft Office**, and then click **Microsoft Office OneNote 2010**.

2. To create a notebook, click the **File** tab, click **New**, click a store location (Web, Network, or My Computer), specify a name and location, and then click **Create Notebook**.

3. To create a section, click the **Create Section** tab, enter a name, and then press Enter.

4. To create a page, click the **New Page** button, and then enter a title.

5. To enter text, click and then start typing.

6. To insert other content, click the **Insert** tab, and then use the available buttons.

7. To draw on a page, click the **Draw** tab, and then use the available pens, erasers, and tools.

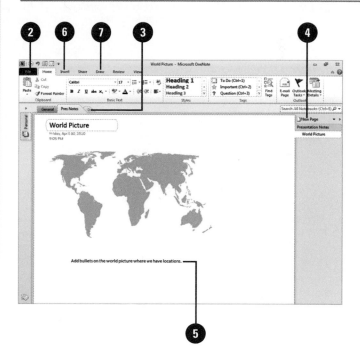

Viewing the InfoPath Designer Window

File tab
Click to access Office file commands.

Quick Access Toolbar
Click to access command comments on this customizable toolbar.

Tabs
Click to access tools and commands.

Dialog Box Launcher
Click to open dialog boxes or task panes.

Program window
Enter text and form controls here.

Ribbon
Commands and tools grouped by category onto different tabs.

Lists and Galleries
Click the down arrow to access lists and galleries.

Status bar
Displays information about the active document.

Fields pane
Drag to place fields on the form.

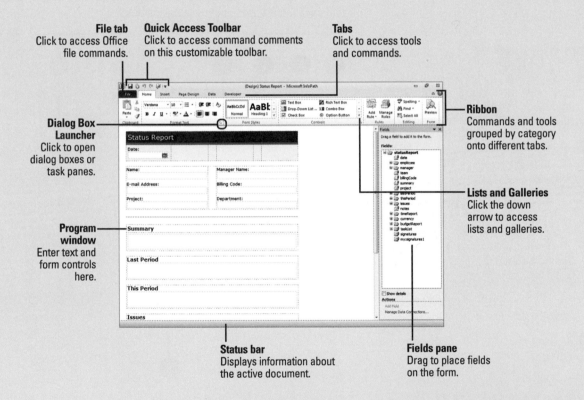

Working with InfoPath Designer

With Microsoft InfoPath Designer, you can create dynamic forms to gather and track information. If you're not sure where to start, you can use the New command on the File tab to create a form with predefined pages and section layout styles from a template, SharePoint list, and other data sources. You can quickly add content, such as tables and pictures, by using the Insert tab. You can use the Home tab to quickly add form controls, such as test boxes, check boxes, and buttons to the form as well as use the Fields pane to add data fields. You can use the Data tab to connect and store the data as well as use Quick Rules to validate the data. If you're not sure how to add color to your form, you can use one of the many themes available on the Page Design tab. When you're done, you can preview the form in Microsoft InfoPath Filler.

Work with InfoPath Designer

1. Click the **Start** button, point to **All Programs**, click **Microsoft Office**, and then click **Microsoft Office InfoPath Designer 2010**.

2. To create a new form, click the **File** tab, click **New**, select a template or **Blank Form**, and then click the **Design Form** button.

3. To insert tables and other content, click the **Insert** tab, and then use the available buttons.

4. To add text labels, form controls, and rules, click the **Home** tab, and then use the available buttons.

5. To add form fields, click the **Data** tab, click the **Show Fields** button, and then drag fields onto the form.

6. To apply a design theme to the form, click the **Page Design** tab, and then click a theme.

7. Click the **Save** button on the Quick Access Toolbar, enter a name, and then click **Save**.

8. To preview the form in InfoPath Filler, click the **Preview** button on the Quick Access Toolbar.

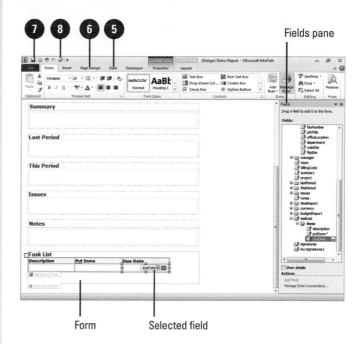

Fields pane

Form

Selected field

Viewing the InfoPath Filler Window

File tab
Click to access Office
file commands.

Quick Access Toolbar
Click to access command comments
on this customizable toolbar.

Tabs
Click to access tools
and commands.

Dialog Box Launcher
Click to open
dialog boxes or
task panes.

Ribbon
Commands and tools
grouped by category
onto different tabs.

Program window
Enter text and
data here.

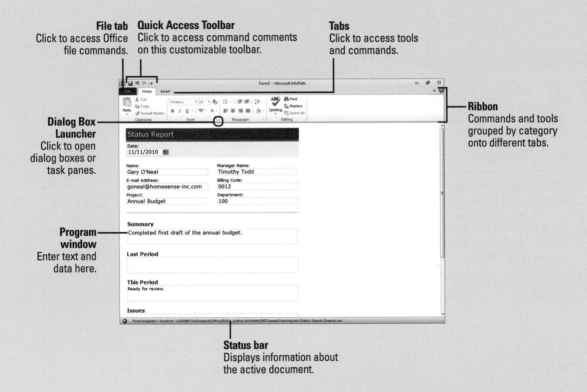

Status bar
Displays information about
the active document.

Working with InfoPath Filler

After you create a form in Microsoft InfoPath Designer, you can preview and enter data in Microsoft InfoPath Filler. InfoPath Filler makes it easy to quickly enter the data you want into a form. Filler also provides improved copy and paste functionality and improved Tablet PC compatibility. As you work with an offline form and a connect becomes available, the form automatically synchronizes to submit the data. If you're working in InfoPath Designer, you can use the Preview button on the Quick Access Toolbar to quickly and conveniently open and preview the form in InfoPath Filler.

Work with InfoPath Filler

1. Click the **Start** button, point to **All Programs**, click **Microsoft Office**, and then click **Microsoft Office InfoPath Filler 2010**.

2. Click the **File** tab, and then click **Open**.

3. Navigate to and select the form you want to use, and then click **Open**.

4. Enter data into the form.

5. To insert pictures, links, and other content, click the **Insert** tab, and then use the available buttons.

6. To spell check the form, click the **Spelling** button on the Home tab.

7. To export the data, click the **File** tab, click **Save & Send**, and then use the available commands to export or mail the data, or create a PDF/XPS document.

   ◆ You can also use the **Save As** command on the **File** tab to save the form and data as an XML document.

Organizing Clips

Microsoft Clip Organizer is a program that comes along with Office that allows you to add, remove, or organize clips for use in the Clip Art task pane. You can import and categorize your own clips (pictures, photographs, sounds, and videos) into the Clip Organizer for easy access in the future. For example, if you have a company logo that you plan to include in more than one document, add it to the Clip Organizer. To help you quickly locate a clip, you can place it in one or more categories. You can also assign one or more keywords to a clip and modify the description of a clip. If you no longer need a picture in the Clip Organizer, you can remove it, which also saves space on your computer.

Add and Remove a Clip

1 Click the **Start** button, point to **All Programs**, click **Microsoft Office**, click **Microsoft Office Tools**, and then click **Microsoft Clip Organizer**.

2 Click the **File** menu, point to **Add Clips to Organizer**, and then click **On My Own**.

3 Navigate to the folder that contain the clip you want to import.

   ◆ To narrow the list by a file type, click the **File as type** list arrow, and then select the file type.

4 Click the clips you want to import, and then click **Add**.

5 Point to the clip you want to remove, and then click the list arrow.

6 To delete the clip from all Clip Organizer categories, click **Delete from Clip Organizer**.

7 Click the **Close** button to close the Clip Organizer dialog box.

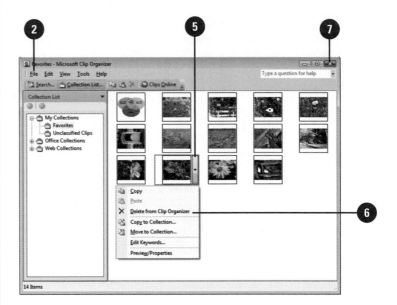

Change Clip Properties

1. Click the **Start** button, point to **All Programs**, click **Microsoft Office**, click **Microsoft Office Tools**, and then click **Microsoft Clip Organizer**.

2. To create a new collection folder, click the **File** menu, click **New Collection**, type a name, select a location, and then click **OK**.

3. In the Clip Organizer, find and point to the clip you want to categorize or change the properties of, click the list arrow, and then click one of the following:

   ◆ Click **Copy to Collection** to place a copy of the clip in another category.

   ◆ Click **Move to Collection** to move the clip to another category.

   ◆ Click **Edit Keywords** to edit the caption of the clip and to edit keywords used to find the clip.

4. Click the **Close** button to close the Clip Organizer dialog box.

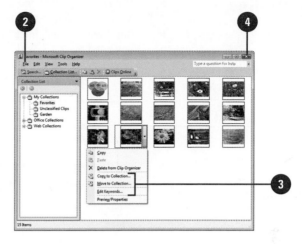

Create a new collection

Edit keywords

Managing Pictures

With Microsoft Office Picture Manager, you can manage, edit, and share your pictures. You can view all the pictures on your computer and specify which file type you want to open with Picture Manager. If you need to edit a picture, you can use Picture Manager to change brightness, contrast, and color, and to remove red eye. You can also crop, rotate and flip, resize, and compress a picture.

Open Picture Manager and Locate Pictures

1. Click the **Start** button, point to **All Programs**, click **Microsoft Office**, click **Microsoft Office Tools**, and then click **Microsoft Office Picture Manager**.

   The first time you start the program, it asks you to select the file types you want to open with Picture Manager. Select the check boxes with the formats you want, and then click **OK**.

2. If necessary, click **Add Picture Shortcut**.

3. Click **Locate Pictures**.

4. Click the **Look in** list arrow, and then click a drive location.

5. Click **OK**.

6. Use the **View** buttons to view your pictures.

7. Click the **Edit Pictures** button on the Standard toolbar.

8. Use the editing tools on the Edit Pictures task pane to modify the picture.

9. Use the sizing tools on the Edit Pictures task pane to change the picture size.

10. When you're done, click the **Close** button.

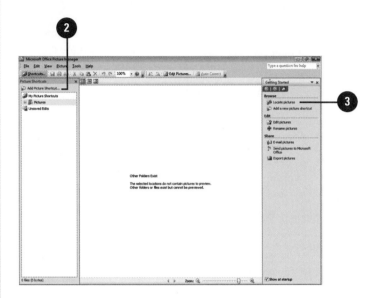

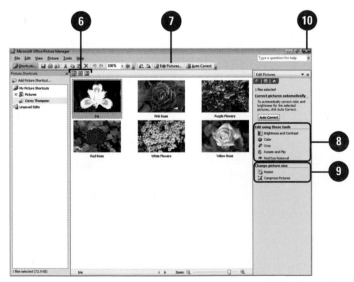

Working with SharePoint Workspaces

A SharePoint workspace is your own personal copy of the SharePoint server, or selected lists and libraries you want to take offline and synchronize. A SharePoint workspace is useful when you want access to a SharePoint server whether or not you are connected to your network. You are the only member of the workspace and share content updates with other SharePoint members. In addition to SharePoint, you can also connect to a Groove workspace, or create a shared folder in Windows. SharePoint is a centralized server based sharing solution, while Groove is a local computer based sharing solution. When you start Microsoft Office SharePoint Workspace 2010 (**New!**), the Launcher opens, where you can create and work with workspaces and contacts. SharePoint and Groove workspaces open in Workspace Explorer while shared folders open in a special layout in Windows Explorer.

Work with Workspaces

1. Click the **Start** button, point to **All Programs**, click **Microsoft Office**, click **Microsoft Office SharePoint Workspace 2010**.

   ◆ On first use, use the wizard to create an account or select an existing one.

2. To create a workspace, click the **New** button, and then select an option: **SharePoint Workspace**, **Groove Workspace**, or **Shared Folder**.

3. To work with a workspace in the Launcher, right-click it, and then select an option.

4. To open a workspace in the Launcher, double-click it.

5. In the Workspace or Windows Explorer, use the available options to work with people and files.

6. To add a contact in the Launcher, click the **Add Contact** button, and then select a contact from the server list. Click the Contacts bar to display and work with them.

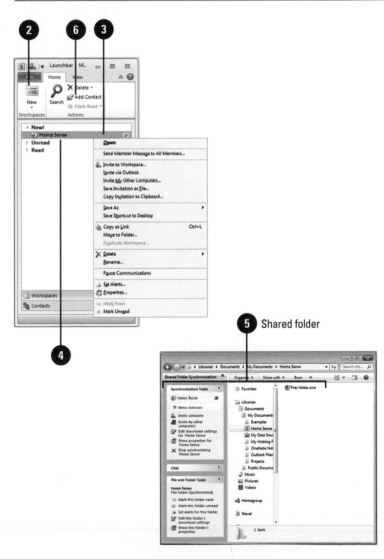

Shared folder

Working with Office Online

Using Office Co-authoring

If you have a Microsoft SharePoint server, you can have multiple authors work on the same Office document from the server at the same time (**New!**). When multiple authors are working on the same document, you can see who is editing the document and where they are working in the Status bar or on the File tab Info screen. Any changes made by other authors get merged into the main document where you can review and modify them.

Using Office Web Apps

An Office Web App (**New!**) allows you to work with an Office document in a browser. When you store an Office document on the Windows Live SkyDrive or on a Microsoft SharePoint server configured with Office Web Apps, you can view or edit the document in a browser using the same look and feel as an Office 2010 program. Windows Live is a Web site, where you can store and share information, such as contacts, e-mail (using hotmail), photos, and files. Windows Live is a free

service provided by Microsoft, which is available at *www.live.com* with a Windows Live ID. To make storing files on the SkyDrive quick and easy, Office 2010 programs provide a Save to Web command on the Save & Send screen on the File tab for you to save Office documents directly to a SkyDrive folder.

Using Office Mobile 2010

If you have a Windows Mobile 6.5 phone, you can use Office Mobile 2010 (**New!**) to work with your files from anywhere. If you have a touch screen device, you can intuitively scroll through menus and navigation documents.

You can use an Office Mobile 2010 program to view and edit Office documents stored on your phone, sent to you as e-mail attachments, or stored on a Microsoft SharePoint server through SharePoint Workspace Mobile 2010. When you use the SharePoint Workspace Mobile, you can save document changes to the SharePoint server or sync changes when you're offline. If you need a secondary monitor, you can connect your phone to your computer using Bluetooth, and use your phone as a secondary monitor to deliver a document or presentation slide show.

Excel Web App using Windows Live

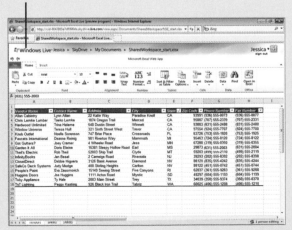

New! Features

Microsoft Office 2010

Microsoft Office 2010 provides you with the tools you need to manage your business and personal life. Each of its programs—Word, Excel, PowerPoint, Access, Outlook, Publisher, OneNote, and InfoPath (Designer and Filler)—has a special function, yet they all work together. With enhancements to the user interface, Backstage view, and the addition of advanced tools, page layout, SmartArt graphics, Office themes and Quick Styles for text, shapes, tables, and pictures, you can accomplish a variety of tasks more easily in Office 2010.

Only New Features

If you're already familiar with Microsoft Office 2007, you can access and download all the tasks in this book with Microsoft Office 2010 New Features to help make your transition to the new version simple and smooth. The Microsoft Office 2010 New Features as well as other 2007 to 2010 transition helpers are available on the Web at *www.perspection.com*.

What's New

If you're searching for what's new in Office 2010, just look for the icon: **New!**. The new icon appears in the table of contents and throughout this book so you can quickly and easily identify a new or improved feature in Office 2010. The following is a brief description of each new feature and it's location in this book.

Office 2010

- **64-bit Office programs (p. 2)**   The 64-bit version of an Office program is built specifically for 64-bit computers. For example, in the 64-bit version of Excel, you can break through the physical memory (RAM) limitation of 2 GB that exists with the 32-bit version, and crunch numbers with ease.

- **File tab (p. 4-5)**   The File tab replaces the Office button from Office 2007 and provides access to Backstage view, which lets you access common file management tasks, such as opening, saving, and sharing files.

- **Customize Ribbon (p. 6-7, 621)**   In the Options dialog box, you can customize the Ribbon by adding tabs, groups, and command buttons.

◆ **Recently Used Files (p. 13)**   For easy access, you can add recently used documents to the File tab. In addition to Recent Document, you can also access files on the Recent Places list.

◆ **Accessibility Checker (p. 27)**   The Accessibility Checker identifies potential difficulties that people with disabilities might have reading or interactive with an Office document.

◆ **Auto Recovered (p. 28-29)**   You can select the *Keep the last Auto Recovered file if I close without saving* check box in Options as a safe guard to protect your unsaved work. You can use the Manage Versions button on the Info screen under the File tab to open any available recovered unsaved files.

◆ **Live Preview of Paste Options (p. 36-37, 628, 630)**   When you point to an option on a Paste menu, a live preview of the paste contents appears in the document. When you point to a paste option, use the ScreenTip to determine the option.

◆ **Math AutoCorrect (p. 40)**   If you use math symbols in your work, you can use Math AutoCorrect to make it easier to insert them. It works just like AutoCorrect.

◆ **Mini-Translator (p. 50)**   In Word, Outlook, PowerPoint, or OneNote, you can enable the Mini Translator that translates words or phrases in a small window when you point to them.

◆ **Language Preferences (p. 51)**   You can set language preferences for editing, display, ScreenTip, and Help languages. If you don't have the keyboard layout or related software installed, you can click links to add or enable them.

◆ **Print and Preview Screen (p. 54-55, 374, 513, 536)**   Instead of a dialog box, you can preview a document and choose printing options together on the same Print screen on the File tab; it detects the type of printer that you choose—either color or black and white—and then prints the appropriate version.

◆ **Office.com (p. 58)**   In the Clip Art task pane, you can select the *Include Office.com content* check box to access clip content on the Web at Office.com.

◆ **Screenshot (p. 60, 464)**   With the Screenshot button, you can capture a screenshot of your computer and insert it into an Office document. As you capture screens, the Screenshot gallery stores them, so you can use them later.

◆ **Artistic Quick Style Gallery (p. 61, 337)**   With the Artistic Quick Style gallery, you can change the look of a picture to a sketch, drawing, or painting.

◆ **Crop to Shape Gallery (p. 63)**   The Crop to Shape gallery makes it easy to choose the shape you want to use.

◆ **Compress a Picture (p. 68)**   Office allows you to compress pictures in order to minimize the file size of the image. In doing so, however, you may lose some visual quality, depending on the compression setting.

◆ **Correct a Picture (p. 69)**   The brightness and contrast controls change a picture by an overall lightening or darkening of the image pixels. In addition, you can sharpen and soften pictures by a specified percentage.

n

◆ **Recolor a Picture (p. 70)** The Color Picture Quick Style gallery provides a variety of different recolor formatting combinations.

◆ **Crop a Picture (p. 72)** Use the Crop button to crop an image by hand. In addition, you can crop a picture while maintaining a selected resize aspect ratio or crop a picture based on a fill or fit.

◆ **Remove Picture Background (p. 74)** With the Remove Background command, you can specify the element you want in a picture, and then remove the background.

◆ **SmartArt Graphic Types (p. 80, 85)** Office provides more built-in SmartArt graphic types: picture and Office.com. With SmartArt graphic layouts, you can insert pictures in the SmartArt shapes.

◆ **Record Macros with Chart Elements (p. 88)** When you use the macro recorder with charts, it now records formatting changes to charts and other objects.

◆ **Unlimited Points in a Data Series (p. 91)** In previous Office versions, you were limited to 32,000 data points in a data series for 2-D charts. Now you can have as much as your memory to store.

◆ **More Themes and Styles (p. 123)** Office comes with more themes and styles.

◆ **Trust Center (p. 590, 592-593)** The Trust Center provides new security and privacy settings for Trusted Documents, Protected view, and File Block Settings. In Trusted Documents, you can set options to open trusted documents without any security prompts for macros. Protected view provides a place to open potentially dangerous files, without any security prompts, in a restricted mode to help minimize harm to your computer. In File Block Settings, you can select the Open and Save check boxes to prevent each file type from opening, or just opening in Protected view, and from saving.

◆ **Linked OneNotes (p. 615)** In PowerPoint and Word, you can create and open linked notes directly from OneNote by using the Linked Notes button on the Review tab.

◆ **Save to Web (p. 644)** Office programs provide a Save As command on the Save & Send screen to save Office documents directly to a Windows Live SkyDrive folder using a Windows Live account.

◆ **SharePoint Workspaces (p. 687)** An Office program that allows you to create and work with local versions of workspaces (SharePoint and Groove, or shared folders) and contacts.

◆ **Office Web App (p. 644-645, 688)** After you store Office documents on the Windows Live SkyDrive, or a Microsoft SharePoint server, you can view or edit them in a browser using a Microsoft Office Web App.

◆ **Office Mobile (p. 688)** You can use an Office Mobile 2010 program to view and edit Office documents stored on your phone, sent to you as e-mail attachments, or stored on a Microsoft SharePoint server through SharePoint Workspace Mobile 2010.

Word 2010

◆ **Full Screen Reading View (p. 136)** In the Full Screen Reading view, you can display the Navigation pane with the Browse Heading or Browse Pages tab to quickly jump to different parts of your document.

◆ **Navigation Pane (p. 138)** If you have a long document with headings or you're searching for keywords, you can use the Navigation pane to find your way around it.

◆ **Formatting (p. 154-155)** Word provides additional formatting effects to text, including Shadow, Outline, Reflection, Glow, and 3-D.

◆ **Character Spacing (p. 164)** You can set text formatting for OpenType/TrueType fonts that include a range of ligature settings (where two or three letters combine into a single character), number spacing and forms, and stylistic sets (added font sets in a given font).

◆ **Numbering List (p. 170)** You can insert a customize numbering list style— including fixed-digits, such as 001, 002, etc.

◆ **Watermarks (p. 175)** More Watermarks are available from Office.com.

◆ **Text Boxes (p. 182)** More Text Boxes are available from Office.com.

◆ **AutoText (p. 184)** You can insert AutoText with the Quick Parts button on the Insert tab.

◆ **Cover Pages (p. 210)** More Cover Pages are available from Office.com.

Excel 2010

◆ **Functions (p. 258)** Functions—such as beta and chi-squared distributions—for the academic, engineering, and scientific community have been improved for more accuracy. Some statistical functions have been renamed for consistency with the real world.

◆ **AutoFilter (p. 276)** The column headers in a table now remain visible in long lists for ease of use. In the AutoFilter menu, you can use the Search box to quickly find what you want in a long list.

◆ **Conditional Formatting (p. 286-290)** For data bars, you can set the bar direction, and specify custom formatting for negative values. With an expanded set of icons, you can mix and match icons for a custom look as well as hide them based on your criteria. You can apply multiple formatting to the same data in order to achieve the results you want. In addition, you can refer to values in other worksheets.

◆ **Sparkline (p. 292)** A sparkline is a tiny chart in the background of a cell that provides a visual representation of a data range. Sparklines are useful for showing trends in a series of data, which you can print in a worksheet.

◆ **Slicers** Slicers allow you a visible way to filter data in PivotTables. After you insert a slicer, you use buttons to quickly segment and filter the data.

PowerPoint 2010

◆ **Grid and Guides (p. 108)** In the Grid and Guides dialog box, you can select from a variety of options, such as snapping objects to the grid or to other objects and displaying drawing and smart guides on-screen.

◆ **Reading View (p. 308-309)** Reading view presents your slides one at a time in a slide show in a separate window. Use this view when you're ready to rehearse your presentation. This view is especially useful when you want to show two presentations in a slide show in separate windows at the same time.

◆ **Presentation Sections (p. 325)** When you're working on large presentations or collaborating on a presentation with others, you can create sections and arrange slides into a more organized workflow process.

◆ **Separate PowerPoint Windows (p. 328)** When you can drag slides between presentations, the presentations appear in separate windows. You can use commands in the Window group to display the presentations, drag slides between them, and then use the Paste Options button to apply a theme.

◆ **Animation Painter (p. 345)** After you create an animation, you can use the Animation Painter to quickly copy it to another object, just like the Format Painter.

◆ **Improved Animations (p. 345)** There are four types of animations: Entrance, Exit, Emphasis and Motion Path (animations along a line). Using specialized animations, you can quickly apply animations specific to certain objects using the Animations tab.

◆ **Control Animations (p. 348-349)** You can control the animation of each object, the order each object appears, the time between animation effects, when an animation takes place—on click or video bookmark trigger—and remove unwanted animations.

◆ **Slide Transitions (p. 351)** If you want a more excite or dynamic effect, you can use transitions with 3-D motion effects, such as 3D rotation or orbit.

◆ **Insert Video from Social Web Site (p. 352)** You can insert videos or audio into a presentation by inserting them from a social media Web site, such as YouTube or hulu, using an embed code.

◆ **Embedded Video (p. 352)** When you insert a video, it becomes part of the presentation, and not a linked file.

◆ **Audio and Video Supported Formats (p. 352)** PowerPoint supports the following new audio file formats—ADTS, MP4, and QuickTime Audio—and new video file formats—MP4, MPEG-2 TS, QT (QuickTime movie or video), and SWF (Flash).

◆ **Audio and Video Playback (p. 352)** After you insert a video or audio, you can play it back using the onscreen playback bar or the Playback tab under Video or Audio Tools.

◆ **Trim Video (p. 354)** After you insert a video or audio, you can trim the start or end to remove the parts you don't want and make it shorter.

- **Video Overlay Text (p. 354)** You can add overlay text to a video.

- **Video Bookmarks (p. 354)** You can add bookmarks to indicate time points in a video or audio clip. Bookmarks are useful as a way to trigger animations or jump to a specific location in a video.

- **Format Video (p. 354)** In addition to editing videos, you can use the Format tab under Video Tools to apply formatting—such as image correction, video styles, effects, and borders—to the video, which are similar to Picture Tools.

- **Record a Slide Show (p. 357)** You can record a narration before you run a slide show, or you can record it during the presentation and include audience comments.

- **Laser Pointer (p. 362)** You can turn your mouse into a laser pointer. In Slide Show view, hold down Ctrl, click the left mouse button, and the begin pointing.

- **Compress a Presentation (p. 365)** You can compress a presentation with media to reduce the file size.

- **Broadcast a Presentation (p. 364, 648)** The Broadcast Slide Show command allows you to display a slide show over the Internet. To use the Broadcast Slide Show command, you need to use the PowerPoint Broadcast Service provided by Microsoft at no charge along with a Windows Live ID or use a broadcast service provided by your organization on a server that has the Microsoft Office Web Apps installed.

- **Compare and merge two version of a presentation (p. 614)** Compares and combines the content in two presentations.

Access 2010

- **Database Templates (p. 378-379)** Access database templates help you create databases suited to your specific needs. Each template provides a complete out-of-the-box database with predefined fields, tables, queries, reports, and forms. If you can't find the template you want, additional templates are available online at Office.com.

- **Web Database (p. 378-379, 381)** In addition to a regular database, you can also create a Web database for use on the Internet. The functionality of the database is reduced for use on the Internet.

- **Application Parts (p. 384, 388)** An application part template is a predefined portion of a database, such as a table or form, or an entire database application that you can quickly insert and use in a database.

- **Enter Data in a Table (p. 387)** Access determines the data type of each field based on the data you enter. The Click to Add column shows you where to add a new field. You can also paste data from Microsoft Excel tables into a new database and Access recognizes the data types.

- **Calculate Field (p. 396)** Access includes a data type for calculating a value in a field from data in the same table.

◆ **Filter Records (p. 407)**   You can filter records by selecting common filter options or Quick filter options for the field values on which to base the filter in Datasheet view or by using Filter By Form to help you create more complex filters involving multiple field values.

◆ **Expression Builder (p. 415)**   When you type an expression, Expression Builder uses IntelliSense to display your options and help link to complete it.

◆ **Share a Database (p. 422)**   If a SharePoint Server is running Access Services, you can publish the database to the server and use the database in a Web browser.

◆ **Navigation and Split Forms (p. 424-425)**   You can create a navigation form to browse different forms and reports, and a split columnar form that includes a table datasheet; a split form is not available in Web databases.

◆ **Format a Form in Design View (p. 426, 428-429, 436)**   You can apply a theme to a form and format selected elements using buttons on the Format tab.

◆ **Build a Macro (p. 664)**   You create a macro by specifying actions you want to execute and related settings for each of the actions in the macro builder.

Outlook 2010

◆ **Ribbon (p. 450)**   The Ribbon is a new look for Outlook 2010. It replaces menus, toolbars, and most of the task panes found in Outlook 2007. The Ribbon is comprised of tabs with buttons and options that are organized by task.

◆ **Quick Access Toolbar and Mini-Toolbar (p. 450)**   Office includes its most common commands, such as Save and Undo, on the Quick Access Toolbar. The Mini-Toolbar appears above selected text and provides quick access to formatting tools.

◆ **Mailbox Cleanup (p. 471, 484)**   The cleanup tools are available on the Info screen on the File tab. In the Mailbox Cleanup dialog box, you can view the mailbox size, find old or large messages, AutoArchive old items, view the size of the Deleted Items folder, permanently empty (delete) all messages in the Deleted Items folder, and delete all alternate version of items in your mailbox.

◆ **Delete Conversation Messages (p. 471)**   If you have a back and forth conversation of e-mails, you can delete them or just the redundant ones.

◆ **Meeting From a Message (p. 473)**   You can turn a message into a meeting request. In Mail view, select the message you want to create a meeting request, and then click the Meeting button on the Home tab.

◆ **Filter Messages (p. 474)**   You can use the Filter E-mail button on the Home tab to quickly filter messages, or the Arrangement options on the View tab, which also allows you to show the messages in a group.

◆ **Conversation Messages (p. 476, 481)**   When you send and reply messages back and forth between another recipient, Outlook keeps track of them—including sent messages and messages in other folders—in a conversation. Conversation view groups related messages together to make is easier to work with.

◆ **Quick Steps (p. 479)**   Quick Steps make it easier to perform multiple actions with one click on the Home tab. Outlook comes with several default Quick Steps—such as Move to:?, To Manager, Team E-mail, Reply & Delete, and Create New—that you can use right away, or you can create your own.

◆ **Calendar View (p. 490, 499)**   You can change the Calendar display to show activities in Schedule view (horizontal layout for multiple calendars). You can also click buttons to quickly go to today or the next 7 days.

◆ **Private Icon (p. 493)**   When you click the Private button, a lock icon appears in the calendar.

◆ **More Meeting Options (p. 494, 496-497)**   When scheduling, accepting, declining, or canceling meeting, you now have more options. If you need to manage calendars for a group, you can create a calendar group.

◆ **Outlook Color Scheme (p. 511)**   You can change the color scheme of Outlook to Blue, Black, or Silver in the Options dialog box.

◆ **Connect to a Social Network (p. 514)**   Outlook bridges the gap between your Inbox and your social network, such as Linkedin, MySpace, and Facebook. Each social network provides a Outlook Social Connector add-in that allows you to connect and synchronize your information between them.

Publisher 2010

◆ **Ribbon (p. 520)**   The Ribbon is a new look for Publisher 2010. It replaces menus, toolbars, and most of the task panes found in Publisher 2007. The Ribbon is comprised of tabs with buttons and options that are organized by task.

◆ **Quick Access Toolbar and Mini-Toolbar (p. 520)**   Office includes its most common commands, such as Save and Undo, on the Quick Access Toolbar. The Mini-Toolbar appears above selected text and provides quick access to formatting tools.

◆ **Building Blocks (p. 528)**   Building blocks are pre-built content (such as headings, pull quotes, sidebars, stories, calendars, borders & accents and advertisements), style galleries, and font and color themes that make inserting content quick and easy.

◆ **Add a Caption to a Picture (p. 548)**   After you insert a picture, you can insert and modify a caption.

n

Microsoft Certified Applications Specialist

About the MCAS Program

The Microsoft Certified Applications Specialist (MCAS) certification is the globally recognized standard for validating expertise with the Microsoft Office suite of business productivity programs. Earning an MCAS certificate acknowledges you have the expertise to work with Microsoft Office programs. To earn the MCAS certification, you must pass a certification exam for the Microsoft Office desktop applications of Microsoft Office Word, Microsoft Office Excel, Microsoft Office PowerPoint, Microsoft Office Outlook, or Microsoft Office Access. (The availability of Microsoft Certified Applications Specialist certification exams varies by program, program version, and language. Visit *www.microsoft.com* and search on *Microsoft Certified Applications Specialist* for exam availability and more information about the program.) The Microsoft Certified Applications Specialist program is the only Microsoft-approved program in the world for certifying proficiency with Microsoft Office programs.

What Does This Logo Mean?

It means this book has been approved by the Microsoft Certified Applications Specialist program to be certified courseware for learning Microsoft Office Word 2010, Excel 2010, PowerPoint 2010 and Outlook 2010, and preparing for the certification exam. This book will prepare you for the Microsoft Certified Applications Specialist exam for Microsoft Office Excel 2010. Each certification level has a set of objectives, which are organized into broader skill sets. The Microsoft Certified Applications Specialist objectives and the specific pages throughout this book that cover the objectives are available on the Web at *www.perspection.com*.

Microsoft Certified Application Specialist

EX10S-1.1
PP10S-2.2

Preparing for a MCAS Exam

Every Microsoft Certified Applications Specialist certification exam is developed from a list of objectives based on how Microsoft Office programs are actually used in the workplace. The list of objectives determine the scope of each exam, so they provide you with the information you need to prepare for MCAS certification. Microsoft Certified Applications Specialist Approved Courseware, including the On Demand series, is reviewed and approved on the basis of its coverage of the objectives. To prepare for

the certification exam, you should review and perform each task identified with a MCAS objective to confirm that you can meet the requirements for the exam.

Taking a MCAS Exam

The Microsoft Certified Applications Specialist certification exams are not written exams. Instead, the exams are performance-based examinations that allow you to interact with a "live" Office program as you complete a series of objective-based tasks.

All the standard ribbons, tabs, toolbars, and keyboard shortcuts are available during the exam. Microsoft Certified Applications Specialist exams for Office 2010 programs consist of 25 to 35 questions, each of which requires you to complete one or more tasks using the Office program for which you are seeking certification. A typical exam takes from 45 to 60 minutes. Passing percentages range from 70 to 80 percent correct.

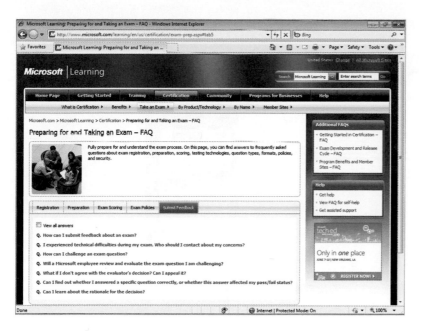

The Exam Experience

After you fill out a series of information screens, the testing software starts the exam and the Office program. The test questions appear in the exam dialog box in the lower right corner of the screen.

◆ The timer starts when the first question appears and displays the remaining exam time at the top of the exam dialog box. If the timer and the counter are distracting, you can click the timer to remove the display.

◆ The counter at the top of the exam dialog box tracks how many questions you have completed and how many remain.

◆ If you think you have made a mistake, you can click the Reset button to restart the question. The Reset button does not restart the entire exam or extend the exam time limit.

◆ When you complete a question, click the Next button to move to the next question. It is not possible to move back to a previous question on the exam.

◆ If the exam dialog box gets in your way, you can click the Minimize button in the upper right corner of the exam dialog box to hide it, or you can drag the title bar to another part of the screen to move it.

Tips for Taking an Exam

◆ Carefully read and follow all instructions provided in each question.

◆ Make sure all steps in a task are completed before proceeding to the next exam question.

◆ Enter requested information as it appears in the instructions without formatting unless you are explicitly requested otherwise.

- Close all dialog boxes before proceeding to the next exam question unless you are specifically instructed otherwise.

- Do not leave tables, boxes, or cells "active" unless instructed otherwise.

- Do not cut and paste information from the exam interface into the program.

- When you print a document from an Office program during the exam, nothing actually gets printed.

- Errant keystrokes or mouse clicks do not count against your score as long as you achieve the correct end result. You are scored based on the end result, not the method you use to achieve it. However, if a specific method is explicitly requested, you need to use it to get credit for the results.

- The overall exam is timed, so taking too long on individual questions may leave you without enough time to complete the entire exam.

- If you experience computer problems during the exam, immediately notify a testing center administrator to restart your exam where you were interrupted.

Exam Results

At the end of the exam, a score report appears indicating whether you passed or failed the exam. An official certificate is mailed to successful candidates in approximately two to three weeks.

Getting More Information

To learn more about the Microsoft Certified Applications Specialist program, read a list of frequently asked questions, and locate the nearest testing center, visit:

www.microsoft.com

For a more detailed list of Microsoft Certified Applications Specialist program objectives, visit:

www.perspection.com

Index